**Reading & Language**

# INSIDE

LANGUAGE · LITERACY · CONTENT

**PROGRAM AUTHORS**

David W. Moore

Deborah J. Short

Michael W. Smith

Alfred W. Tatum

Josefina Villamil Tinajero

NATIONAL GEOGRAPHIC LEARNING | CENGAGE Learning·

**Acknowledgments**

Grateful acknowledgment is given to the authors, artists, photographers, museums, publishers, and agents for permission to reprint copyrighted material. Every effort has been made to secure the appropriate permission. If any omissions have been made or if corrections are required, please contact the Publisher.

**Photographic Credits**

**Cover:** Arctic Fox, Prudhoe Bay, Alaska, Patrick Endres. Photograph © Patrick Endres/Visuals Unlimited/Corbis.

Acknowledgments continue on page 604.

Copyright © 2014 National Geographic Learning, Cengage Learning

ALL RIGHTS RESERVED. No part of this work covered by the copyright herein may be reproduced, transmitted, stored, or used in any form or by any means graphic, electronic, or mechanical, including but not limited to photocopying, recording, scanning, digitizing, taping, web distribution, information networks, or information storage and retrieval systems, except as permitted under Section 107 or 108 of the 1976 United States Copyright Act, without the prior written permission of the publisher.

National Geographic and the Yellow Border are registered trademarks of the National Geographic Society.

For product information and technology assistance, contact us at
**Cengage Learning Customer & Sales Support, 888-915-3276**

For permission to use material from this text or product, submit all requests online at **www.cengage.com/permissions**
Further permissions questions can be emailed to
**permissionrequest@cengage.com**

**National Geographic Learning | Cengage Learning**
1 Lower Ragsdale Drive
Building 1, Suite 200
Monterey, CA 93940

Cengage Learning is a leading provider of customized learning solutions with office locations around the globe, including Singapore, the United Kingdom, Australia, Mexico, Brazil, and Japan. Locate your local office at **www.cengage.com/global**.

Visit National Geographic Learning online at **ngl.cengage.com**
Visit our corporate website at **www.cengage.com**

Printer: Quad/Graphics, Versailles, KY

ISBN: 978-12854-37095

Printed in the United States of America
19 20 21 22
10 9

# Contents at a Glance

# Reviewers

We gratefully acknowledge the many contributions of the following dedicated educators in creating a research-based program that is appealing to and motivating for middle school students. In addition to the contributors listed below, we also thank the many teachers, students, and administrators whose feedback over the last several years helped shape the original program and this updated program.

## Dr. René Saldaña, Jr., Ph.D.
Texas Tech University

Dr. Saldaña teaches English and education and is a widely published trade book writer. His books include *The Jumping Tree* and *Finding Our Way: Stories.* His stories have also appeared in anthologies such as *Guys Write for GUYS Read, Face Relations, Every Man for Himself,* and in magazines like *Boy's Life* and *READ.*

## Teacher Reviewers

**Idalia Apodaca**
English Language Development Teacher
*Shaw Middle School*
*Spokane, WA*

**Pat E. Baggett-Hopkins**
Area Reading Coach
*Chicago Public Schools*
*Chicago, IL*

**Judy Chin**
ESOL Teacher
*Arvida Middle School*
*Miami, FL*

**Sonia Flores**
Teacher Supporter
*Los Angeles Unified School District*
*Los Angeles, CA*

**Brenda Garcia**
ESL Teacher
*Crockett Middle School*
*Irving, TX*

**Margaret Jan Graham**
*Montford Middle School*
*Tallahassee, FL*

**Susan Harris**
Department Head Language Arts
*Cobb Middle School*
*District - Leon*
*Tallahassee, FL*

**Kristine Hoffman**
Teacher on Special Assignment
*Newport-Mesa Unified School District*
*Costa Mesa, CA*

**Patricia James**
Reading Specialist
*Brevard County*
*Melbourne Beach, FL*

**Dr. Margaret R. Keefe**
ELL Contact and Secondary Advocate
*Martin County School District*
*Stuart, FL*

**Julianne Kosareff**
Curriculum Specialist
*Paramount Unified School District*
*Paramount, CA*

**Lore Levene**
Coordinator of Language Arts
*Community Consolidated School*
*District 59*
*Arlington Heights, IL*

**Kathleen Malloy**
9th Grade Coordinator and Reading Coach
*Godby High School*
*Tallahassee, FL*

**Natalie M. Mangini**
Teacher/ELD Coordinator
*Serrano Intermediate School*
*Lake Forest, CA*

**Laurie Manikowski**
Teacher/Trainer
*Lee Mathson Middle School*
*San Jose, CA*

**Patsy Mills**
Supervisor, Bilingual-ESL
*Houston Independent School District*
*Houston, TX*

**Juliane M. Prager-Nored**
High Point Expert
*Los Angeles Unified School District*
*Los Angeles, CA*

**Patricia Previdi**
ESOL Teacher
*Patapsco Middle School*
*Ellicott City, MD*

**Dr. Louisa Rogers**
Middle School Team Leader
*Broward County Public Schools*
*Fort Lauderdale, FL*

**Rebecca Varner**
ESL Teacher
*Copley-Fairlawn Middle School*
*Copley, OH*

**Hailey F. Wade**
ESL Teacher/Instructional Specialist
*Lake Highlands Junior High*
*Richardson, TX*

**Cassandra Yorke**
ESOL Coordinator
*Palm Beach School District*
*West Palm Beach, FL*

# Program Authors

## David W. Moore, Ph.D. Arizona State University

Dr. Moore taught high school in Arizona public schools before becoming a professor of education. He co-chaired the International Reading Association's Commission on Adolescent Literacy and has published research reports, articles, book chapters, and complete books including *Developing Readers and Writers in the Content Areas, Teaching Adolescents Who Struggle with Reading,* and *Principled Practices for Adolescent Literacy.*

## Deborah J. Short, Ph.D. Center for Applied Linguistics

Dr. Short is a co-developer of the research-validated SIOP Model for sheltered instruction. She has directed scores of studies on English Language Learners and published scholarly articles in *TESOL Quarterly, The Journal of Educational Research, Language Teaching Research,* and many others. Dr. Short also co-wrote a policy report: *Double the Work: Challenges and Solutions to Acquiring Language and Academic Literacy for Adolescent English Language Learners.*

## Michael W. Smith, Ph.D. Temple University

Dr. Michael Smith has won awards for his teaching both at the high school and college level. He contributed to the Common Core State Standards initiative by serving on the Aspects of Text Complexity working group. His books include *"Reading Don't Fix No Chevys": Literacy in the Lives of Young Men, Fresh Takes on Teaching Literary Elements: How to Teach What Really Matters About Character, Setting, Point of View, and Theme,* and *Oh, Yeah?! Putting Argument to Work Both in School and Out.*

## Alfred W. Tatum, Ph.D. University of Illinois at Chicago

Dr. Tatum began his career as an eighth-grade teacher and reading specialist. He conducts research on the power of texts and literacy to reshape the life outcomes of striving readers. Dr. Tatum's books include *Reading for Their Life: Re-Building the Textual Lineages of African American Adolescent Males* and *Teaching Reading to Black Adolescent Males: Closing the Achievement Gap.*

## Josefina Villamil Tinajero, Ph.D. University of Texas at El Paso

Dr. Tinajero consults with school districts to design ESL, bilingual, literacy, and biliteracy programs. She has served on state and national advisory committees for standards development, including English as a New Language Advisory Panel of the National Board of Professional Teaching Standards. Dr. Tinajero has served as president of the National Association of Bilingual Education and the Texas Association of Bilingual Education.

# Finding Your Own Place

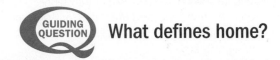 What defines home?

**Writing** ✐
▶ **Paragraph**
Topic and Details, Persuasive, Main Idea and Details

Pages 1W–31W

# WATER
## FOR LIFE

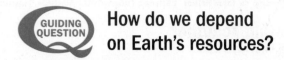

GUIDING QUESTION

**How do we depend on Earth's resources?**

**Writing** ✎
▶ **Sequence Paragraph**
▶ **Explanatory Paragraphs**

Pages 32W–93W

# NATURAL FORCES

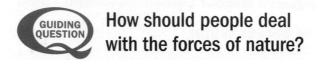

GUIDING QUESTION

How should people deal with the forces of nature?

**Writing** ✏

▶ **Friendly Letter**
▶ **Personal Narrative**

Pages 94W–137W

# Creepy Classics

 How can a powerful character inspire a range of reactions?

**Writing** ✏
▶ **Short Story**

Pages 138W–179W

# THE
## DRIVE
## TO
# Discover

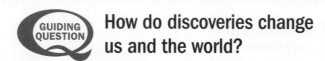

**GUIDING QUESTION** How do discoveries change us and the world?

# Unit 5

**Writing** ✏
▶ Information Report

Pages 180W–245W

# STRUGGLE FOR FREEDOM

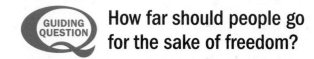
GUIDING QUESTION

How far should people go
for the sake of freedom?

**Writing** ✎
▶ **Summary Paragraph**
▶ **Cause-and-Effect Essay**

Pages 246W–281W

# Star Power

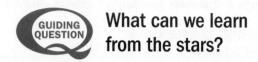

**GUIDING QUESTION**
What can we learn from the stars?

**Writing** ✎
► Speech
► Persuasive Business Letter

Pages 282W–321W

# ART AND SOUL

 GUIDING QUESTION Q What do we learn about people from their artful expressions?

**Writing** ✏
▶ **Editorial**
▶ **Literary Response**

Pages 322W–355W

# Genres at a Glance

# Finding Your Own Place

1

# What defines home?

**READ MORE!**

**Content Library**
**Communities Across America Today**
by Sarah Glasscock

**Leveled Library**
**Domitila**
by Jewell Reinhart Coburn
**Novio Boy**
by Gary Soto
**Pearl Harbor Is Burning!**
by Kathleen V. Kudlinski

**Web Links**
☐ **myNGconnect.com**

◀ A dwelling perches on a rock off the coast
of Tanzania.

# Focus on Reading

## Reading Strategies

Reading strategies are thinking tools that help you understand texts. Use reading strategies before, during, and after you read.

## Plan: How It Works

To plan, first preview what you will read. Look at headings, visuals, and boldface words to find out what the selection is about. Then set a **purpose**. Decide what you intend to gain from the text. Finally, predict what you will read in the text. Form an opinion about what will happen next, then check, or confirm, your predictions as you read.

▶ **Plan**
Preview, set a purpose, and predict what you will find in the text before reading it more carefully.

## Plan: Practice Together

Preview and set a **purpose** for reading "My New Neighborhood." Then, as you read, predict what will happen next. Confirm your predictions during and after reading.

### My New Neighborhood

I like my new neighborhood. I am beginning to feel at home. In my old neighborhood, we didn't have an outdoor basketball court. But my new school has one. I think I'll have to learn chess, though. Unlike the kids in my old neighborhood, the kids here really love it.

**Strategy in Action**

" The title and first sentence tell me the text is about moving to a new place. I predict he had good and bad experiences.... Yes, the text compares his experiences in his new neighborhood with his old one."

## Monitor: How It Works

To monitor means to keep track of or to check on. When you monitor your reading, stop when you don't understand something. Reread or read ahead to clarify ideas or vocabulary. Change your reading pace. Read slowly when something is confusing or difficult. Read more quickly if you understand things well.

## Monitor: Practice Together

Reread "My New Neighborhood." Tell a partner where you stopped and reread or read ahead. Explain how you changed your reading pace according to the difficulty of the text.

▶ **Monitor**
Notice confusing parts in the text then reread or read on to make them clear.

**Academic Vocabulary**
- **purpose** (**pur**-pus) *noun*
  A **purpose** is a reason for doing something.

## Make Connections: How It Works

When you make connections, you put together information from the text with information you know from outside the text to increase your understanding. As you read, you make connections to your past experiences. You also connect each text to other texts you have read. You can also connect the text to something that is happening or has happened in the world.

▶ **Make Connections**
Combine your knowledge and experiences with the author's ideas and information.

## Make Connections: Practice Together

Read "City and Country." Think about your own experiences and what you have read about the city and country in other texts or media. Make connections. Tell a partner about the connections you made and how they helped you understand the text.

### City and Country

Javier feels at home in the city, but Ana likes to live in the country. When Javier leaves his apartment, he hears noisy cars, buses, and taxis. Unlike Javier, Ana hears birds chirping in the trees and the soft hum of insects. Sometimes Javier and Ana have similar experiences. For example, they have both seen red-tailed hawks. Ana sees the hawks flying over her fields. Javier sees them land on buildings. However, Ana sees red-tailed hawks much more often than Javier does.

▲ A red-tailed hawk lands on a city building.

**Strategy in Action**

" The text is about living in the city. I read that Javier hears noisy cars, buses, and taxis. I just watched a documentary about New York City. I can imagine Javier's experiences."

**Strategy in Action**

" When I read these details I picture a big crowded city."

## Visualize: How It Works

When you visualize, you use your imagination to help you understand what you read. You can use the writer's words to create images in your mind. Look for words that tell you how things look, sound, smell, taste, and feel.

▶ **Visualize**
Imagine the sights, sounds, smells, tastes, and touch of what the author is describing.

## Visualize: Practice Together

Reread "City and Country." As you read, stop and create images in your mind. After reading, discuss what you visualized with a partner. Explain how your imagination helped you understand the text.

# Focus on Reading

## Ask Questions: How It Works

You ask questions to learn new information, to clarify, and to understand or figure out what's important. Use a question word such as *Who, What, When, Where, Why,* or *How.* Use the text and visuals to answer your questions.

You find answers in different places. Sometimes the answers are in one place. Sometimes you need to think and search different parts of the text for the answer. Some questions and answers are about big ideas based on the entire text. Sometimes you need to get inside the writer's head for a question and answer about the text's purpose or point of view.

## Ask Questions: Practice Together

Read "Feeling at Home." Pause when you read and ask a question. Answer the question clearly in your own words.

### Feeling at Home

My new best friend, Sophia, makes me feel at home in my neighborhood. We are both from Mexico and our families have a lot in common. We both have two brothers. My abuelita still lives in Mexico. Her abuelita lives in California. We like to make homemade tortillas together using my mom's famous recipe. Sophia's mom is a great cook, and I spend a lot of time at her house. Her mother makes the best mole and enchiladas. Enchiladas are my favorite meal. Her mole sauce has more than twenty ingredients and tastes like chocolate. Sophia's mother is going to teach us both how to cook, so I can make the rest of my family feel at home too.

## Determine Importance: How It Works

When you determine importance, you identify and focus on the most important points or the main ideas. A good way to tell what is most important in what you read is to summarize. When you **summarize**, you state the main idea in a sentence or two. Then you include details that back up the main idea.

> ▶ **Ask Questions**
> Think actively by asking and answering questions about the text.

**Strategy in Action**

" After reading I am wondering what mole is. What ingredients are in mole? What does it taste like? "

**Academic Vocabulary**
- **summarize** (**sum**-u-r z) *verb*
  When you **summarize** something, you cover the main points briefly.

## Determine Importance: Practice Together

Read "Feeling at Home" again. As you read look for the main idea and the details that support the main idea. Record the main idea. After reading, **summarize** the passage and share your summary with a partner.

▶ **Determine Importance**
Focus your attention on the author's most significant ideas and information.

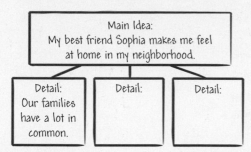

**Main Idea Chart**

Main Idea:
My best friend Sophia makes me feel at home in my neighborhood.

Detail:
Our families have a lot in common.

Detail:

Detail:

## Make Inferences: How It Works

When you make inferences, you figure out what the text is about based on what is in the text, what you already know, and what you have personally experienced.

▶ **Make Inferences**
When the author does not say something directly, use what you know to figure out what the author means.

**I read** _"We are both from Mexico"_ **+**

**I know** _sharing a background makes me feel comfortable_ **=**

**And so** _I think being from the same place is part of what makes the narrator feel at home._

## Make Inferences: Practice Together

Read "Feeling at Home" again. As you read, look for details in the text that are not fully explained. Use your own experience and knowledge to make inferences that help you figure out what the author means but does not directly tell.

# Focus on Reading

## Synthesize: How It Works

Reading is like putting a puzzle together. You put many different pieces together to form the whole of something. Synthesizing is the process of putting ideas and information together. When you synthesize, you draw conclusions, make generalizations, and compare. You form new ideas by putting together ideas and events.

- When you draw conclusions, you pay attention to everything you learn about a topic. Then you decide what you think is true about the topic.
- When you form generalizations, you take ideas from the text, together with your personal knowledge, and form an idea that applies to many situations.
- When you compare, you figure out how different texts are the same and how they are different.

## Synthesize: Practice Together

Read "Two Cities." Use text evidence from the selection and your own experience to draw conclusions, make generalizations, and compare as you read.

### Two Cities

Both New York City in New York and Mexico City in Mexico are home to millions of people. Both cities are important urban areas. Mexico City is the capital of Mexico, but New York City is not the capital of New York or of the United States. Both Mexico City and New York are made up of a collection of areas. Unlike Mexico City, the separate areas in New York City are called boroughs.

▲ Nearly nineteen million people live in and around Mexico City.

> ▶ **Synthesize**
> Bring together ideas gained from texts and blend them into a new understanding.

> **Strategy in Action**
> " I read that New York City and Mexico City are home to millions of people and have many different areas. I understand that these two cities are crowded."

Read "A New Home." Use the reading strategies you've been practicing before, during, and after reading. With a partner think of a statement or question for each strategy that you can use to help you understand the selection.

# A New Home

**Moving to a new place can be scary, especially for an immigrant who speaks a different language. What will the new place be like? Will it ever really feel like home? Hear the story of one young immigrant.**

Mami and Papi said it was a good opportunity. Lourdes wasn't so sure. Why did she have to leave Mexico? She did not want to immigrate to California to live with Tía, her aunt.

Lourdes had never met Tía Angela. She had seen photos of her. She looked like Mami—pretty and always smiling. *But*, Lourdes thought, *you never can tell what a person is like from a picture.*

Mami said Tía Angela had a small apartment. Lourdes would sleep on a couch.

How could a couch be a home? Lourdes was used to the ranch with the horses and chickens and goats. There was room to run and play—not that she played anymore. She was 13. But she liked the uncrowded space.

Mami promised that California would be wonderful. Papi was sick and could not work. Mami thought that Lourdes needed more attention than she could give her. Plus, Lourdes could study with the best teachers. Mami said she would email every day.

So, now Lourdes was walking off the bus to meet this woman she did not know.

She got her bags and watched as an unsmiling woman with rough hands stamped her passport. *I'm an* immigrant, Lourdes thought. She took a breath and walked through the doors to where hundreds of strangers stood.

A small woman was waving at her. Lourdes approached her slowly. Tía Angela gave Lourdes a giant hug, which Lourdes shyly returned.

Angela and Lourdes got into a car and drove through wide streets. They stopped in front of an ugly building and walked up broken concrete stairs to the second floor. Tía unlocked a dirty brown door and Lourdes followed her.

Inside, the apartment was an explosion of color and warmth. The walls were deep yellow, just like at the ranch. Lourdes looked around the kitchen. In the cupboard was a plate that Mami had painted and sent to Angela three years ago. Above the sink she saw little figures like the ones they sold in the market back home. On the wall there was a painting of Mami and Angela when they were young girls. Lourdes had heard Mami talk about that painting. Her *abuelo* had made it. Both girls looked so pretty and so happy.

Tía pulled out one of the red chairs and asked for Lourdes to sit down. She placed a dish of sopaipillas and a bowl of honey on the table. Lourdes noticed the glass cake plate. Mami had one just like it.

Tía brought a pot of tea and two mugs. She sat down in the other red chair and looked across the small table at her niece. They looked so much alike. Lourdes saw her mother's eyes and her mother's smile. Tía took one of Lourdes's hands and said, "Welcome home, mi'ja."

Lourdes felt Tía's soft, warm hand on hers. She glanced at the portrait of Mami and Tía. The sopaipillas smelled so good. They made her mouth water. Then she looked at Tía. Lourdes smiled. Yes, this is home.

# Focus on Vocabulary

## Use Context Clues for Multiple-Meaning Words

Some words are spelled the same but have different meanings. A dictionary lists the different definitions. If you aren't sure which meaning of a word fits in a sentence, try looking at the **context** .

Suppose you are reading a passage about dogs, and you see:

> Some dogs have a loud **bark** that can really scare you.

Since you're reading about dogs, you know that the word *bark* means the noise a dog makes. But suppose you read this sentence:

> The woodpecker tapped on the thick **bark** of a tall tree.

Here the word *bark* must mean something else. You can use the **context** to figure out its meaning. The words *woodpecker tapped* and *tall tree* help you know that *bark* means the outer covering of a tree.

### How the Strategy Works

When you read, you may come to a word that does not make sense to you. You may know one meaning of that word but not other meanings. Look for **context** clues to help you figure it out. Follow these steps:

1. Think about what the sentence is about.
2. Look at the other words in the sentence.
3. Read the sentences nearby to find more clues, or hints.
4. Use the clues to think of a meaning that makes sense.
5. Check the inferred meaning in a dictionary to make sure it is correct.

Use the strategy to figure out the meaning of each underlined word.

M y family <u>left</u> our homeland on a large boat. We all shared a tiny room. My brother and I had a bed in the <u>left</u> corner. Every day we ate one <u>can</u> of peas. I <u>can</u> still remember the awful taste!

☑ **REMEMBER** You can use **context** clues to figure out the meanings of multiple-meaning words.

**Academic Vocabulary**

● **context** (**kon**-tekst) *noun*
  **Context** refers to the parts nearby that help explain the meaning.

---

**bark** (**bark**) *noun* **1** the sound a dog makes **2** the outer covering of a tree

**can** (**kan**) *verb* **1** to be able to do something *noun* **2** a metal container in which food is sold

**left** (**left**) *adjective* **1** located on the left side, the side of the body where the heart is located *verb* **2** the past and past participle of *leave*

**Dictionary Entries**

---

**Strategy in Action**

" The paragraph is about moving to a new country. The word *homeland* gives me a clue that *left* means 'went away.' "

## Practice Together

Read this passage aloud. Look at each underlined word. Think about what the sentence is about. Use context clues to figure out the meaning of the underlined word. Check the inferred meaning in the Dictionary Entries.

# The Arrival

People are getting off the boat onto the dock. Nadia holds her bag tightly. Inside are the jars of berry <u>jam</u> she made for the <u>trip</u>. She moves with the line. The air is hot. A <u>fly</u> lands on her nose. People are anxious to get off the boat. They <u>jam</u> tightly together. Nadia is pushed around. Two little boys <u>trip</u> and knock over her bag. The jars <u>fly</u> from her bag and break. The sticky jam goes everywhere.

## Try It!

Read this passage aloud. What is the meaning of each underlined word? How do you know?

# A New Land

Antonio looks out the window of the airplane. The plane will <u>land</u> soon. The <u>light</u> shines in Antonio's eyes. His sister and the <u>rest</u> of his family talk excitedly. Antonio picks up his small, <u>light</u> bag. He is ready to go. But he is so tired. He hopes to <u>rest</u> soon. The journey is long, and he will be happy to be in his new <u>land</u>.

▲ An airplane prepares to land.

**fly (flī)** *verb* **1** to move in the air *noun* **2** a small flying insect

**jam (jam)** *verb* **1** to push tightly together *noun* **2** a sweet food made with fruit and sugar

**land (land)** *verb* **1** to arrive *noun* **2** a country or place

**light (līt)** *adjective* **1** not heavy *noun* **2** brightness

**rest (rest)** *verb* **1** to sleep or relax *noun* **2** the part that remains

**trip (trip)** *verb* **1** to fall over something *noun* **2** a journey

**Dictionary Entries**

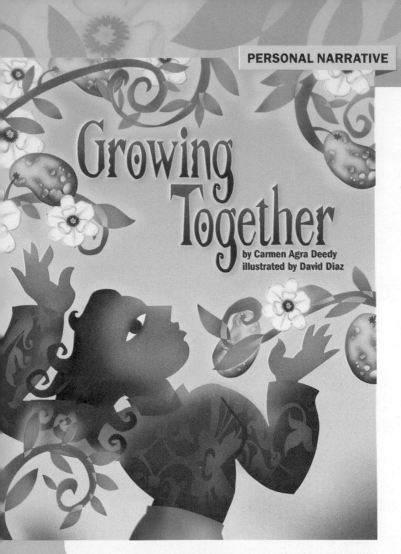

# Growing Together

by Carmen Agra Deedy
illustrated by David Diaz

## SELECTION 1 OVERVIEW

▶ **Build Background**

▶ **Language & Grammar**
Express Ideas and Feelings
Use Statements with *Am*, *Is*, and *Are*

▶ **Prepare to Read**
Learn Key Vocabulary
Plan, Monitor, Visualize

▶ **Read and Write**
Introduce the Genre
Personal Narrative
Focus on Reading
Plan, Monitor, Visualize
Critical Thinking
Reading Fluency
Read with Intonation
Vocabulary Review
Write About the Guiding Question

▶ **Connect Across the Curriculum**
Vocabulary Study
Use Context Clues
Literary Analysis
Analyze Narrator's Point of View
Language and Grammar
Express Ideas and Feelings
Writing and Grammar
Write About Someone You Know

# Build Background

## Meet the Author

Carmen Agra Deedy remembers how it felt to leave Cuba and call Georgia home.

## Connect

**Quickwrite** Read each proverb. Tell whether you agree or disagree with it. Explain why.

*Anywhere you live is your native land.*
*–Korean proverb*

*Go out from your village, but don't let your village go out from you.*
*–Afghan proverb*

**Digital Library** | **myNGconnect.com**
◉ View the video.

▲ Havana, Cuba, is Carmen Agra Deedy's birthplace.

## Express Ideas and Feelings  CD

Listen to the song and the poem.
Then sing along with the song, and read the poem.

SONG and POEM

# Who I Am

*I'll tell you who I am,*
*I'll tell you who I'm not.*
*What I feel is what I feel.*
*What I think are my own thoughts.*

## My New Home

This country is my new home.
There are things I must learn.
But I am not afraid.
I love my new home,
But Cuba is always in my heart.

# Use Statements with *Am, Is,* and *Are*

A **statement** is one kind of sentence. It tells something.

A statement begins with a **capital letter** and ends with a **period**.

> EXAMPLE    <u>T</u>hey are from Brazil ⊙

- Use **am** to tell about yourself.
  > EXAMPLE    I **am** American.

- Use **is** to tell about one other person, place, thing, or idea.
  > EXAMPLE    She **is** my sister.

| Am, Is, Are | |
|---|---|
| **One** | **More Than One** |
| I **am** | we **are** |
| you **are** | you **are** |
| he, she, it **is** | they **are** |

- Use **are** to tell about yourself and another person or persons.
  > EXAMPLE    We **are** in a new place.

- Use **are** when you talk to one or more people.
  > EXAMPLE    You **are** my neighbor.

- Use **are** to tell about other persons, places, things, or ideas.
  > EXAMPLE    My friends **are** at the airport.

## Practice Together

Say each sentence. Choose the correct form of the verb.

1. I (am/are) from Russia.
2. You (is/are) from Russia, too.
3. We (is/are) new students at this school.
4. The kids (am/are) nice.
5. The school (is/are) big, though.
6. Sometimes I (am/is) confused.

## Try It!

Read each sentence. Write the correct form of the verb on a card. Then hold up the card as you say the sentence.

7. My parents (am/are) teachers.
8. They (is/are) happy with their new jobs here.
9. My brother (am/is) still in grammar school.
10. I (am/are) older than my brother.
11. You (am/are) the same age as me.
12. We (is/are) in middle school.

▲ **Russia is a beautiful country.**

# Make a Self-Portrait

## EXPRESS IDEAS AND FEELINGS

You are an artist! Draw a portrait of yourself. Write statements to describe your portrait.

Look at yourself in the mirror. Think about these questions. Then draw a picture of yourself that shows who you are.

- What kind of person are you?
- How do you feel about yourself?
- What things are important to you?

Exchange portraits with a partner. Look at your partner's portrait and read the statements. Express your ideas and feelings about them. Remember:

> You are happy in this portrait. I like this drawing. It shows what you are really like.

## HOW TO EXPRESS IDEAS AND FEELINGS

1. Tell what you see.
2. Tell how you feel.
3. Explain your thoughts about what you see and feel.

## USE STATEMENTS WITH *AM, IS,* AND *ARE*

When you tell what you see and feel and explain your thoughts, you will use statements. When you make statements with **am**, **is**, and **are**, be sure to use the verb forms correctly.

EXAMPLES    You **are** a happy person.
I **am** able to see that in your eyes.
Your family **is** important to you.

# Prepare to Read

## Learn Key Vocabulary

**Study the Words** Use the steps below.

1. Pronounce the word. Say it aloud several times. Spell it.
2. Rate your word knowledge.
3. Study the example. Tell more about the word.
4. Practice it. Make the word your own.

**Rating Scale**

**1** = I have never seen this word before.

**2** = I am not sure of the word's meaning.

**3** = I know this word and can teach the word's meaning to someone else.

### Key Words

**angry** (an-grē) *adjective*
▶ page 19

When you are **angry**, you are mad at someone or something. An **angry** leopard hisses a warning.

**change** (chānj) *noun*
▶ page 18

A **change** is something new and different. A sudden **change** in weather can surprise people!

**curious** (kyoor-ē-us)
*adjective* ▶ page 20

If you are **curious**, you want to know more about something. A **curious** person shows interest in things.

**immigrant** (i-mu-grunt)
*noun* ▶ page 19

An **immigrant** is a person who comes to live in a new country. **Immigrants** say a pledge, or promise, when they become citizens.

**learn** (lurn) *verb*
▶ page 18

To **learn** means to know about a subject by studying or practicing it. You can **learn** many things by reading.

**leave** (lēv) *verb*
▶ page 19

When you **leave** a place, you go away from it. The bird **leaves** its nest to find food.
*Past tense:* **left**
*Present participle:* **leaving**

**ordinary** (or-du-nair-ē)
*adjective* ▶ page 18

An **ordinary** thing is plain. The brown box looks **ordinary**.

**strange** (strānj) *adjective*
▶ page 19

Something that is **strange** is not familiar. The reflection in this mirror is **strange**.

**Practice the Words** Make a Study Card for each Key Word. Then compare your cards with a partner's.

> **angry**
>
> **What it means:** mad
>
> **Example:** how Mom felt after I ripped my new shirt
>
> **Not an example:** how I felt when I wore my new shirt

**Study Card**

# Plan, Monitor, and Visualize

**Plan** Look over the text before you start to read. Set a purpose for what you want to learn from the text. Predict what might happen or what you might learn about.

**Monitor** When you don't understand something, reread the text or read on to clarify ideas.

**Visualize** Form mental images, or pictures in your mind, by using the details in the text.

**Look Into the Text**

**Plan:** I think this story will be about a tree. I want to learn why this tree is so special.

There is only one tree in my yard—a magnolia tree. It has no fruit, but it does bear flowers.

It is no ordinary tree. It has a story.

When my family came to this small town in Georgia, it was a big change from our tropical island. In time, though, I started to like my new home. Soon I learned enough English to make a best friend. An American friend.

" I was confused when I read that the tree wasn't ordinary, so I read on to clarify. I see that the tree has a story, so it must be special. "

| What I Read | What It Makes Me Think |
|---|---|
| Only one tree in the yard. | A big climbing tree with nothing around it. |

**Visualize Chart**

## Practice Together

**Begin a Reading Strategies Log** Use the Reading Strategies Log to show how the strategies help you understand the text. The first row shows how one strategy helped one reader. Reread the passage and add to the Log.

| Text I Read | Strategy I Used | How I Used the Strategy |
|---|---|---|
| **Page:** 18 <br> **Text:** There is only one tree in my backyard. | ☒ **Plan** <br> ❑ **Monitor** <br> ❑ **Visualize** <br> ❑ _____ | Planning helped me predict that the story would be about the tree. |

## Personal Narrative

A personal narrative is nonfiction. It tells about a certain event in the life of a real person. The writer is also the **narrator**, or the person who tells the story.

As you read, notice how the narrator gives **details** that help you visualize her life. Look for words that help you imagine the sights, sounds, smells, taste, and touch of what the narrator describes.

Not everything will be familiar to you as you read. If you don't know what the narrator is trying to explain, you can go back and reread or read on to help you understand the text.

**Look Into the Text**

Some days I still get homesick for Cuba, with its warm sea breezes and its mango trees. I live in Georgia now, far from the sea. There is winter here, when the days are short and cold. There is only one tree in my yard—a magnolia tree.

Before you read a personal narrative or any other text, it is important to preview, set a purpose, and predict. Planning before you read will help you read the text more carefully.

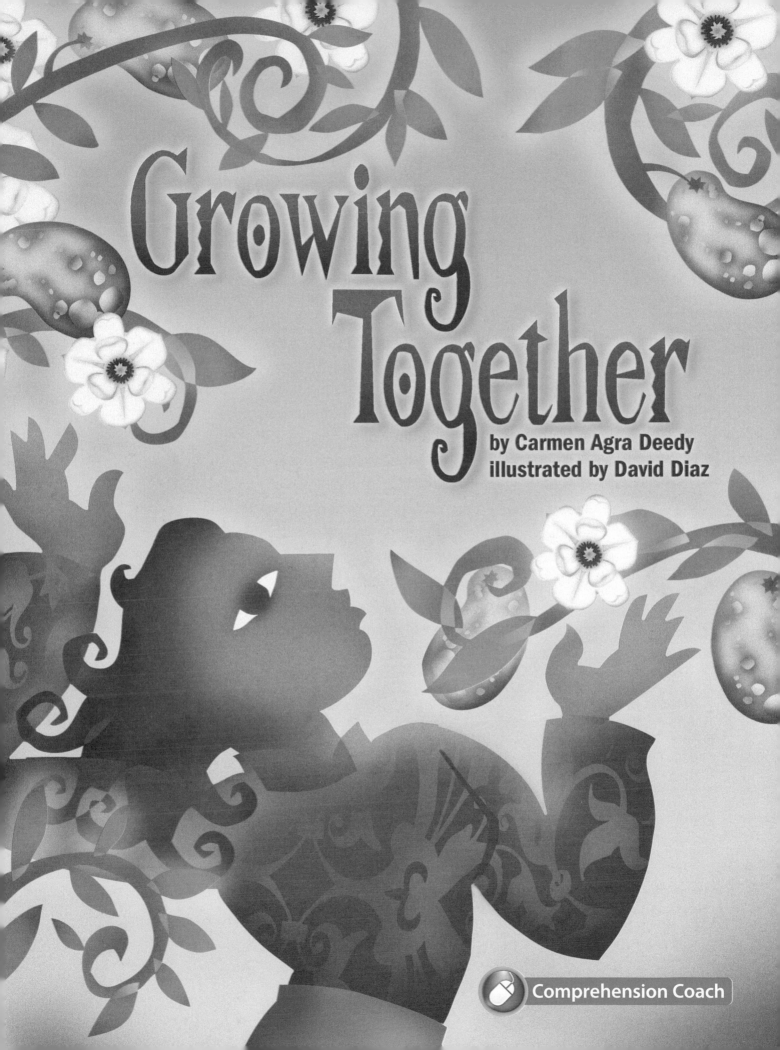

# Growing Together

by Carmen Agra Deedy

illustrated by David Diaz

Comprehension Coach

Some days I still **get homesick for** Cuba, with its warm sea **breezes** and its mango trees. I live in Georgia now, far from the sea. There is winter here, when the days are short and cold. There is only one tree in my **yard**—a magnolia tree. It has no fruit, but it does **bear** flowers.

It is no **ordinary** tree. It has a story.

When my family came to this small town in Georgia, it was a big **change** from our tropical island. In time, though, I started to like my new home. Soon I **learned** enough English to make a best friend. An American friend.

One day, we had a silly fight over a bike, and my friend called me **an ugly** name. I remember that Saturday as if it were today . . .

**Key Vocabulary**

**ordinary** *adj.*, plain; not special in any way

**change** *n.*, something new and different

**learn** *v.*, to know about a subject by studying it

**In Other Words**

**get homesick for** feel sad about moving away from

**breezes** winds

**yard** garden

**bear** make

**an ugly** a mean

My face is hot and red. I drop the bike in the driveway and run to find my father. I see him in the garden under the big magnolia. He is digging in the red **Georgia clay**. He stands up as I run to him. I cry **angry** tears.

A **moment** like this comes for every **immigrant** child.

It is hard to **leave** a home you know. It is even harder to make another place

home. Everything is new. Everything is **strange**. Everything is different.

I tell Papi how I feel.

"I hate it here! I am not like them, and they are not like me!" I say to him.

**Key Vocabulary**
**angry** *adj.*, mad
**immigrant** *n.*, someone who comes to live in a new country
**leave** *v.*, to go away
**strange** *adj.*, not familiar

**In Other Words**
**Georgia clay** sticky dirt found in Georgia
**moment** time

**Look Into the Text**

1. **Narrator's Point of View** On that Saturday, how did Carmen feel about her new home? Why?
2. **Main Idea and Details** Give two details from the text that show how Carmen's life in Georgia is different from her life in Cuba.

Papi pulls out a **handkerchief** and **hands** it to me.

My father, the gardener, looks at me **intently** for a few moments. Then he asks, "Carmita, do you remember our mango tree in Cuba?"

"Yes," I **sniff**. I am **curious** now.

"Do you know what it means to graft a tree?"

I nod. "You take a branch from one tree and **attach** it to another tree. The branch and the tree grow together. Right?"

**Key Vocabulary**

**curious** *adj.*, wanting to know more about something

**In Other Words**

**handkerchief** cloth to dry my eyes
**hands** gives
**intently** right in the eyes
**sniff** say as I try not to cry anymore
**attach** join

"*Sí*, that is right," Papi says.

My father tells me that I am like a branch from that Cuban mango tree. He says Georgia is like the magnolia tree. I must wait. **Eventually**, the mango and magnolia will grow together.

I **lean** over and smell a sweet magnolia flower from the tree in our yard.

I smile. I will wait.

I am a tree that **gives forth** both mangoes and magnolias.

I am an American. ❖

## About the Author

Carmen Agra Deedy

**Carmen Agra Deedy** (1960– ) based this story on events from her childhood. She was born in Havana, Cuba, and came to the United States with her family in 1963. Deedy grew up in two cultures. She was always trying to find her own place. Her father's words were helpful.

"Sometimes I still feel like I don't fit in," Deedy says. "Then I remember Papi's story, and I know that I don't have to stop eating the fruit to smell the flowers."

**In Other Words**
*Sí* Yes (in Spanish)
**Eventually** After a while
**lean** bend
**gives forth** makes

**Look Into the Text**

1. **Confirm Prediction** What does Papi tell Carmen that makes her feel better?
2. **Metaphor** In what way is Carmen like a tree that gives mangoes and magnolias?

# When I Grow Up
### by Janet S. Wong

I want to be an artist, Grandpa—
write and paint, dance and sing.

Be accountant.
Be lawyer.
5  Make good living,
buy good food.
Back in China,
in the old days,
everybody
10  so, so poor.
Eat one chicken,
work all year.

Grandpa, things are different
here.

**In Other Words**

**accountant** someone who keeps track of the money a business makes and spends
**lawyer** someone who knows about laws
**Make good living** Earn a lot of money

## Look Into the Text

1. **Author's Style** How many speakers are in this poem? How does the author show this?
2. **Compare and Contrast** How are the speakers' ideas different?

# Connect Reading and Writing

**Vocabulary**

angry

change

curious

immigrants

learn

leave

ordinary

strange

## CRITICAL THINKING

1. **SUM IT UP** Review the visualizations you wrote about on the Reading Strategies Log. Describe the story to a partner.

| Text I Read | Strategy I Used | How I Used the Strategy |
|---|---|---|
| Page: 18<br><br>Text: There is only one tree in my backyard. | ☑ Plan<br>❑ Monitor<br>❑ Visualize<br>❑ _____ | Planning helped me predict that the story would be about the tree.<br><br>_____ |

**Reading Strategies Log**

2. **Interpret** What does the author mean when she says "A moment like this comes for every **immigrant** child"? Do you agree? Explain your answer.

3. **Compare** Compare the messages of "Growing Together" and "When I Grow Up." What does each one say about how people **learn** to fit in after **leaving** their home country?

4. **Interpret** Carmen Agra Deedy says, "I don't have to stop eating the fruit to smell the flowers." What does she mean by this? Do you agree? Explain.

## READING FLUENCY

**Intonation** Read the passage on page 558 to a partner. Assess your fluency.

1. My tone never/sometimes/always matched what I read.

2. What I did best in my reading was _____.

## READING STRATEGY

> What strategy helped you understand this selection? Tell a partner about it.

## VOCABULARY REVIEW

**Oral Review** Read the paragraph aloud. Add the vocabulary words.

> My parents and I are _____ from a small country. There, we lived in a quiet, _____ town like any other. Our new home is _____ and different to me. Living here is a big _____. Everyone is busy all the time. I am _____ about why people hurry so much. I would like to _____ the reasons. My parents _____ early every morning for work and come home late, too. It makes me _____ that they are always busy. It is hard to compare my old life to my new life.

**Written Review** Write a journal entry from Carmen's point of view as an **immigrant**. Explain how she defines home. Use four vocabulary words.

 **WRITE ABOUT THE** GUIDING QUESTION

**Explore Finding Your Own Place**
What do you think Papi means when he says the mango and the magnolia grow together? Reread the text to find support for your ideas.

# Connect Across the Curriculum

## Use Context Clues

**Academic Vocabulary**
- **explain** (ik-**splān**) *verb*
  When you **explain** an idea, you make it clear so people can understand it.

Some English words have the same spellings but different meanings. Use **context clues** to find the meaning. In the sentence below, *tree* is a clue to find the meaning of *branch*.

**branch** (**branch**) *noun* **1** a part of a tree that grows out from the trunk   **2** a store or an office away from the main building

**Dictionary Entry**

I am like a branch from that Cuban mango tree.

**Use Context Clues** With a partner, find these words. Take turns **explaining** which context clues you used. Confirm your ideas using a dictionary.

**1.** cold, p. 18    **2.** yard, p. 18    **3.** drop, p. 19    **4.** cry, p. 19

## Analyze Narrator's Point of View

**Academic Vocabulary**
- **analyze** (a-nu-līz) *verb*
  To **analyze** means to break down information into parts to understand it better.

In **first-person point of view**, the narrator is one of the characters and tells his or her view, or thoughts and feelings, of the events. In **third-person point of view**, the narrator is not one of the characters. You learn the thoughts and feelings of more than one character. **Analyze** the passage to find the narrator's point of view. Describe the clues you used.

I drop the bike in the driveway and run to find my father.
I see him in the garden under the big magnolia.

**Change Point of View** With a partner, find a passage from *Growing Together* and **analyze** the point of view. Retell the passage to change the narrator's point of view. Describe how the narrator's thoughts and feelings changed.

## Express Ideas and Feelings

**Act It Out** Work in a group. Take turns acting out a feeling (such as being sad, angry, happy, or curious). Use your face and body language. Group members ask questions to guess your feeling. If they guess correctly, answer with a statement. After three guesses, say the correct answer.

Are you jealous?

Yes, I am jealous.

**Writing and Grammar**

## Write About Someone You Know

**Study the Models** When you write about someone you know, include enough details to make your statements clear and interesting.

**JUST OK**

> My friend is Kimi. She is nice. I am usually at her house. Both our families are from another place. Kimi and I do things together.

This writer leaves out a lot of details. The reader thinks: **"This is boring."**

**BETTER**

> My best friend is Kimi. She is kind and nice. She makes me feel at home in my new neighborhood. I am usually at her house, or she is at my house. We are like sisters. Both our families are from Japan. Kimi and I cook Japanese food and sing Japanese songs together.

Details make the statements interesting and clear.

**Add Sentences** Add two statements to the BETTER model above. Make the statements interesting and clear by adding details.

**WRITE ON YOUR OWN** Write about someone you know who makes you feel at home. Include details. If you write statements with **am**, **is**, or **are**, be sure to use the verb forms correctly.

**REMEMBER**

There are different forms for the verb *be*.

| One | More Than One |
|---|---|
| I **am** | we **are** |
| you **are** | you **are** |
| he, she, it **is** | they **are** |

▲ Kimi and I like to be silly together.

# KIDS LIKE ME
## Voices of the Immigrant Experience

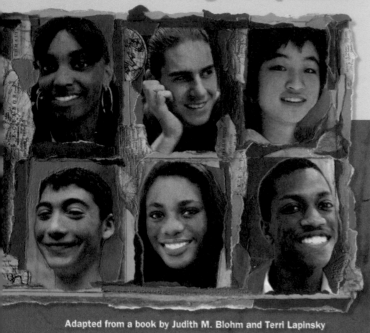

Adapted from a book by Judith M. Blohm and Terri Lapinsky

## SELECTION 2 OVERVIEW

▶ **Build Background**

▶ **Language & Grammar**
Ask and Answer Questions
Use Questions and Statements

▶ **Prepare to Read**
Learn Key Vocabulary
Make Connections, Ask Questions, Determine Importance

▶ **Read and Write**
Introduce the Genre
Interview
Focus on Reading
Make Connections, Ask Questions, Determine Importance
Critical Thinking
Reading Fluency
Read with Expression
Vocabulary Review
Write About the Guiding Question

▶ **Connect Across the Curriculum**
Vocabulary Study
Use Context Clues
Literary Analysis
Analyze Text Structure: Compare and Contrast
Language and Grammar
Ask and Answer Questions
Writing and Grammar
Write a Message

# Build Background

## Listen to Teens

People from all over the world move to the United States. Teens have a lot to share about their experience as immigrants.

**Digital Library**

**myNGconnect.com**
↻ View the video.

▲ It can be hard to make friends when you move to another country.

## Connect

**Anticipation Guide** Think about a time when you had to adapt to a new place. Read each statement. Tell whether you agree or disagree.

| | Agree | Disagree |
|---|---|---|
| **1.** A good way to adapt is to change the way you look. | _____ | _____ |
| **2.** You should keep your traditions no matter where you live. | _____ | _____ |
| **3.** Making friends is the first thing you should do in a new place. | _____ | _____ |

Anticipation Guide

# Language & Grammar

## Ask and Answer Questions

Look at the photos. Listen to the questions and answers.
Then ask your own questions about the photos.

**PICTURE PROMPT**

**What** is this place?

It is Pike Place Market.

**Where** is the market?

The market is in Seattle.

**When** is the market open?

The market is open every day.

**Who** is the man?

The man is a fish seller.

# Use Questions and Statements

You ask a **question** to find out something. Some questions start with *Am*, *Is*, or *Are*. The answer to these questions is a **statement** with *Yes* or *No*.

EXAMPLES    **Are** you from Miami?    **Yes**, I'm from Miami.
            **Is** he from Miami?      **No**, he is from Chicago.

Some questions start with *Who*, *What*, *When*, or *Where*. Ask these questions to get information.

EXAMPLES    **Who** is that boy? He is my cousin.

            **What** is that in his hand? That is his lunch.

            **When** is lunch time? It is at 12:00.

            **Where** is a good place to eat? That spot under the tree is a good place to eat.

| Question Word | Asks About |
|---|---|
| Who? | person |
| What? | thing |
| When? | time |
| Where? | place |

## Practice Together

Ask these questions. Answer questions 1–3 with a *Yes* or *No* statement.
Answer questions 4–6 with a statement that gives information.

1. Is this recipe from your home country?
2. Am I a good cook?
3. Are the potatoes ready?
4. Where is the sauce?
5. Who is here for dinner?
6. When is Asha coming?

## Try It!

Ask these questions. Write a *Yes* or *No* statement to answer questions 7–9.
Write a statement that gives information to answer questions 10–12.
Hold up each answer as you say it.

7. Is this Room 12?
8. Am I in the right place?
9. Are you in my class?
10. What is your name?
11. Who is the teacher?
12. When is class over?

▲ Where are the students? They are in class.

# Ask About Photos

## ASK AND ANSWER QUESTIONS

Find a photo you like. Choose a photo of your family or friends or a photo from a magazine. Trade photos with a partner.

Look at your partner's photo. Decide what questions to ask. Make a chart to record your ideas. Use the four question words as headings.

**Question Chart**

| Who? | What? | When? | Where? |
|---|---|---|---|
| Who is the woman in red? | What is in her hand? | | |
| | | | |

Now ask your partner the questions about the photo. Listen to the answers. Then change roles. Remember:

## HOW TO ASK AND ANSWER QUESTIONS

**1.** To find out something, ask a question. You can start a question with *Am, Is, Are, Who, What, When*, or *Where*.

**2.** To answer a question, give a *Yes* or *No* statement or give information.

*Who is the girl?*

*The girl is my friend Ayaka.*

## USE QUESTIONS AND STATEMENTS

When you answer a question about your photo, think about what the question word asks. Then form your statement.

EXAMPLES   **Is** this your mother?
No, that is my aunt.

**Who** is the man?
He is my uncle.

▲ **Where are they? They are in Morocco.**

# Prepare to Read

## Learn Key Vocabulary

**Study the Words** Use the steps below.

1. Pronounce the word. Say it aloud several times. Spell it.
2. Rate your word knowledge.
3. Study the example. Tell more about the word.
4. Practice it. Make the word your own.

### Key Words

**adjust** (u-just) *verb*
▶ page 38

To **adjust** means to change in order to become comfortable with something. I hope I can **adjust** to my new school.

**appreciate**
(u-**prē**-shē-āt) *verb* ▶ page 38

To **appreciate** means to care about something or someone. The boy shows he **appreciates** his mom by giving her flowers.
*Synonyms:* **enjoy, like**

**culture** (kul-chur) *noun*
▶ page 34

The ideas and way of life for a group of people make up their **culture**. Baseball and jazz are both part of American **culture**.

**different** (di-fu-runt)
*adjective* ▶ page 34

Something that is **different** is not the same. The red flower is **different** from the others.
*Antonym:* **alike**

**opportunity**
(ah-pur-**tü**-nu-tē) *noun* ▶ page 35

An **opportunity** is a good chance to do something. The sign tells about a job **opportunity** at the restaurant.

**relative** (re-lu-tiv) *noun*
▶ page 36

A family member is a **relative**. The mother and daughter are **relatives**.
*Synonym:* **family**

**understand** (un-dur-stand) *verb* ▶ page 38

To **understand** something is to know it well. This teacher **understands** the math problem and explains it to his students.
*Past tense:* **understood**

**value** (val-yū) *noun*
▶ page 37

A **value** is something that people care about. Respect is an important **value** in Japan.
*Synonym:* **ideal**

**Practice the Words** Work with a partner. Make a Word Web of Examples for each Key Word.

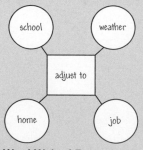

Word Web of Examples

# Make Connections, Ask Questions, and Determine Importance

**Make Connections** Connect the text to your past experiences, to other texts you have read, or to the world around you.

**Ask Questions** Stop and ask questions to check your understanding.

**Determine Importance** Use the main ideas and details that support the main ideas to summarize the text.

**Make Connections:**
I have a friend from South Korea.

**Look Into the Text**

Meet six teens who are from different parts of the world. Now they live in cities and towns across the United States. They have families and friends in the U.S. Yet they remember and still observe some of the customs of their culture from "home." This is true whether their native country is South Korea, Peru, French Guyana, Iraq, Somalia, or Ethiopia.

**Important Idea:**
I will read about six teens from different parts of the world.

" **I know that the first sentence often includes important ideas.** "

| What I Read | What It Makes Me Think |
|---|---|
| Where did the teens come from? | I should find these countries on a map. |

Question-Answer Chart

## Practice Together

**Begin a Reading Strategies Log** Use the Reading Strategies Log to show how the strategies help you understand the text. The first row shows how one strategy helped one reader. Reread the passage and add to the Log.

| Text I Read | Strategy I Used | How I Used the Strategy |
|---|---|---|
| **Page:** 34 <br><br> **Text:** their native country is South Korea | ☒ Make Connections <br> ☐ Ask Questions <br> ☐ Determine Importance <br> ☐ _____ | I know someone from South Korea. I can make connections between what I know about her culture and what I read. |

## Interview

An interview gives information and opinions. In an interview, one person asks **questions** and one or more people **answer**. Pay attention to the questions because they are important ideas.

When two **speakers** answer questions, you can see how the answers are different or alike. Make connections between the answers and your experiences or other texts you have read.

**Look Into the Text**

Q: **Why did you come to the United States?** < question

**Eunji**: My dad is in business school. We followed my dad. < answer

**Hewan**: Education is a top priority in my family. < answer

As you read, ask questions to make sure you understand what you are reading. Make connections between what you read and your own experiences.

# KIDS LIKE ME
## Voices of the Immigrant Experience

Adapted from a book by Judith M. Blohm and Terri Lapinsky

Comprehension Coach

**M**eet six teens who are from **different** parts of the world. Now they live in cities and towns across the United States. They have families and friends in the U.S. Yet they remember and still **observe** some of the **customs of** their **culture** from "home." This is true whether **their native country is** South Korea, Peru, French Guyana, Iraq, Somalia, or Ethiopia.

## Where the Teens Come From

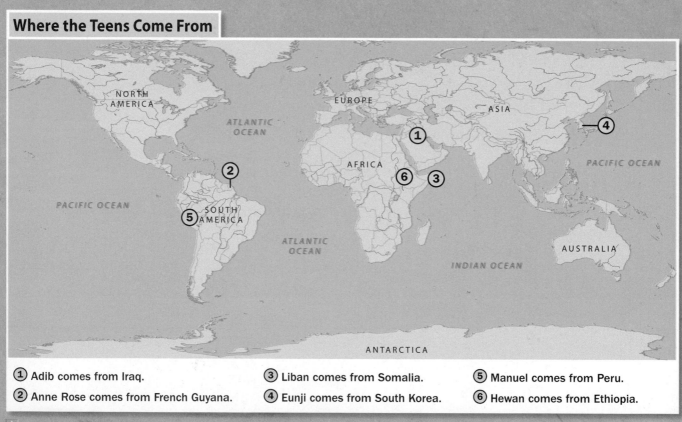

① Adib comes from Iraq.
② Anne Rose comes from French Guyana.
③ Liban comes from Somalia.
④ Eunji comes from South Korea.
⑤ Manuel comes from Peru.
⑥ Hewan comes from Ethiopia.

▲ **Interpret the Map** Find where Hewan's home country is. Whose home country is near hers?

**Key Vocabulary**
**different** *adj.*, not the same
**culture** *n.*, the ideas and way of life for a group of people

**In Other Words**
**observe** follow
**customs of** ways of doing things from
**their native country is** they were born in

# Q: Why did you come to the United States?

**Eunji:** My dad is in business school. We **followed** my dad.

**Hewan:** Education is **a top priority** in my family. My mother, older brother, and I are here for my education. Getting into medical school is my goal. My family **supports** this.

**Liban:** We are in the U.S. to have a better life. We are now away from the wars. We can get a good education for me and my sister. We are also free to be ourselves.

**Adib:** We are here because of war in our home country.

**Anne Rose:** My parents are from Haiti. They moved to French Guyana where I was born. Now we are in the U.S. We moved because my parents want a better and safer life for our family.

**Manuel:** I want a better education. I also want more **opportunities** to **succeed** in life. Unfortunately, my parents are still in Peru. They are working and taking care of my eight-year-old brother. I live with my aunt.

---

**Key Vocabulary**
**opportunity** *n.*, a chance to do something

**In Other Words**
**followed** came with
**a top priority** one of the most important things
**supports** wants to help me with
**succeed** do well

**Look Into the Text**
1. **Categorize** List four reasons that these teens' families came to the United States.
2. **Viewing** Look at the map. Which teens are from countries in South America? Which ones are from African countries?

# Q: What is different about living in the United States?

**Eunji:** School rules in Korea are a lot **stricter** than here. In Korea, we cannot have pierced ears or noses. We cannot have long hair or even colored hair clips.

**Hewan:** American families do not seem **that close-knit**. However, Ethiopian families are. Unlike American families, we share our food from one big plate. The entire family sits around the table. Then we all eat out of one dish.

**Liban:** In Somalia, there is no bus transportation. Everyone walks. People have cars, but everyone is close by. The store is next door. Your uncle is next door.

**Adib:** My mom says she noticed that in the U.S. you do not have as many **relatives** living with you as we do in Iraq and Lebanon.

Another thing that is different is school. There are more classes in school in Iraq and Lebanon.

Also, children and teens have to be **more polite** than American kids are to adults. When you talk to your teacher or when you are called on in class, students must first stand. Then you can ask or **respond to** a question.

---

**Key Vocabulary**
**relative** *n.*, a family member

**In Other Words**
**stricter** more difficult
**that close-knit** very close to each other
**more polite** nicer, more respectful
**respond to** answer

**Anne Rose:** There are many **similarities** between French Guyana and America.

**Manuel:** In Peru, family is the main **value**. Families always get together on weekends or at any holiday. The people in communities in Peru are closer to each other than in the neighborhoods in the U.S. The people in Peru don't have a lot of extra money to spend. So people are more helpful to each other. They try to find a way to help each other. They do things like selling food at **cheap** prices.

## Immigrants to the United States in 2006

More than 1.2 million people came to the United States in 2006. Most are from Asia or Latin America. This chart shows the top ten home countries.

| Home Country | Number |
|---|---|
| Mexico | 173,753 |
| People's Republic of China | 87,345 |
| Philippines | 74,607 |
| India | 61,369 |
| Cuba | 45,614 |
| Colombia | 43,151 |
| Dominican Republic | 38,069 |
| El Salvador | 31,783 |
| Vietnam | 30,695 |
| Jamaica | 24,976 |

Source: U.S. Department of Homeland Security, Computer Linked Application Information Management System, Legal Immigrant Data, 2006.

▲ **Interpret the Chart** Which country did most immigrants come from in 2006?

**Key Vocabulary**
**value** *n.*, something that people care about; a worthy idea

**In Other Words**
**similarities** things that are alike
**cheap** low

**Look Into the Text**

1. **Compare and Contrast** According to these teens, how are families in other countries closer than they are in the United States?
2. **Details** What details does Manuel use to support his claim that family is the main **value** in Peru?

# Q: What advice do you have for people who move to the United States?

**Eunji:** Ask many questions. That way, you learn about the person you are talking to. You can also learn about American culture.

**Hewan:** Quickly make friends in order to learn the language and culture. With their help, it is easier to settle into a new country. Friends can also make it easier to **adjust** to the different customs and ideas.

**Liban:** Be yourself. That is the main thing. Do not **put yourself down**. Do not let anybody put you down. Work hard. Talk to people. Ask for help if you need it. Say what you want to say (other than bad words).

**Adib:** Play sports to meet new people. **Make an effort** to be social and talk with people in your classes. This is hard at first.

**Anne Rose:** **Get involved** in everything you can. The more things you **get into**, the more opportunities you have to learn, **understand**, and **appreciate** life.

**Manuel:** I have one **piece of advice**. Don't be lazy! ❖

---

**Key Vocabulary**
**adjust** *v.*, to become comfortable with
**understand** *v.*, to know
**appreciate** *v.*, to care about; to see the worth of something

**In Other Words**
**put yourself down** think badly of yourself
**Make an effort** Try hard
**Get involved** Be active; Take part
**get into** do
**piece of advice** helpful idea

**Look Into the Text**
1. **Compare and Contrast** How is the advice of these teens alike? How are their ideas different?
2. **Inference** Based on the advice that Liban gives, what kind of a person is she? How does she feel about herself?

# Connect Reading and Writing

## Vocabulary

adjust

appreciate

cultures

different

opportunity

relatives

understands

values

## CRITICAL THINKING

1. **SUM IT UP** Look back at your Reading Strategies Log. Use the important ideas you found and connections you made to summarize "Kids Like Me."

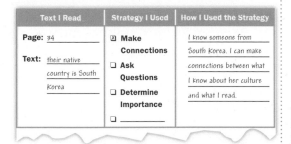

| Text I Read | Strategy I Used | How I Used the Strategy |
|---|---|---|
| Page: 34<br><br>Text: their native country is South Korea | ☑ Make Connections<br><br>☐ Ask Questions<br><br>☐ Determine Importance<br><br>☐ _____ | I know someone from South Korea. I can make connections between what I know about her culture and what I read. |

Reading Strategies Log

2. **Evaluate** What do you think is the most important idea to **understand** in "Kids Like Me"?

3. **Analyze** Look at the Anticipation Guide on page 26. Do you want to **adjust** any of your answers? Discuss with a partner.

4. **Compare** Name **values** that the six different teens share.

## READING FLUENCY

**Expression** Read the passage on page 559 to a partner. Assess your fluency.

1. My voice never/sometimes/always matched what I read.

2. What I did best in my reading was _____.

## READING STRATEGY

What strategy helped you understand this selection? Tell a partner about it.

## VOCABULARY REVIEW

**Oral Review** Read the paragraph aloud. Add the vocabulary words.

Many immigrants come to the United States for the _____ to have a better life. Sometimes they bring their parents and other _____ to live with them. It can be difficult for immigrants to _____ to living in a country that is new and _____. It can be easier if someone speaks and _____ the language. People soon learn that most Americans enjoy, or _____, differences among people. The country has many ways of life, or _____. However, people share many of the same _____, such as freedom.

**Written Review** Why do so many people come to the United States from **different** countries? Write your opinion. Use four vocabulary words.

**WRITE ABOUT THE** GUIDING QUESTION

### Explore Finding Your Own Place

Do you think it is easier for teens or for adults to **adjust** to living in a new country? Use examples from the text to state your opinion.

# Connect Across the Curriculum

## Use Context Clues

**Academic Vocabulary**
- **context** (kon-tekst) *noun*
  **Context** refers to the parts nearby that help explain the meaning.

**Use a Dictionary** If a word has more than one meaning, the meanings are numbered in a dictionary. Determine the correct meaning of a word using **context**.

**kid** (kid) *noun* **1** a young person **2** a young goat
*verb* **1** to tease someone or make jokes

**Dictionary Entry**

Think about the title "Kids Like Me." You can figure out the meaning of *kids* using *me* as a clue.

**Define Words** Find each of these words on page 35. Write the **context** clues you use to figure it out. Then check the meaning using a dictionary.

**1.** top    **2.** goal    **3.** support    **4.** free    **5.** country

## Analyze Text Structure: Compare and Contrast

**Academic Vocabulary**
- **compare** (kum-**pair**) *verb*
  When you **compare** two things, you think about how they are alike and different.

Sometimes writers organize nonfiction text by **comparing** and contrasting ideas. **Signal words** communicate this structure.

| Comparison | Contrast |
|---|---|
| also | but |
| and | however |
| just like | unlike |
| too | yet |

**Signal Words**

**Find Signal Words** Read this passage. Find **signal words** from the chart in the passage.

> **Hewan:** American families do not seem that close-knit. However, Ethiopian families are. Unlike American families, we share our food from one big plate. The entire family sits around the table. Then we all eat out of one dish.

**Make a Venn Diagram** Work with a partner. Make a Venn Diagram for the above passage. Then make another Venn Diagram with another passage from "Kids Like Me" to show **comparisons.**

## Ask and Answer Questions

**Play Twenty Questions** Imagine you are an animal, place, or thing. Your classmates will ask you questions with *Is* or *Are* to guess what you are. Answer only with *Yes* or *No* statements. If they can't guess in twenty questions, tell them the answer.

> Is your home in the forest?

> No, my home is in the jungle.

## Write a Message

**Study the Models** When you write a message to someone you don't know well, you can make your writing more interesting by including both statements and questions. Readers are more likely to enjoy and understand what you write if it has variety.

**JUST OK**

> Dear Ankur,
>
> My name is Jay Resnik. What are your hobbies? Where is your favorite place to go on the weekends? Who are your best friends?
>
> Jay

The writer mostly asks questions. The reader thinks: **"I wish Jay would tell me something about himself."**

**BETTER**

> Dear Ankur,
>
> My name is Jay Resnik. I am a student in Los Angeles, California. My teacher gave me your name to be my pen pal. What are your hobbies? I swim and play the guitar. Where is your favorite place to go on the weekends? I usually go to the movies with my friends. Who are your best friends?
>
> Jay

Now the writer uses questions and statements. This is more interesting for the reader.

**Add Sentences** Pretend that you are Jay. Add one statement and one question to the BETTER model above.

**WRITE ON YOUR OWN** Imagine that you have a new pen pal. Write an e-mail message to your pen pal. Include statements and questions.

**REMEMBER**
- To tell something, make a **statement**.
- To find out something, ask a **question**.

# Familiar Places
by Elizabeth Boylan

# Build Background

## See How Places Change

Communities change over the years. Take a tour of a city with a longtime resident. Explore the community's history.

## Connect

**TV Commercial** Imagine you and some friends are in charge of encouraging visitors to come to your city. Think about special events, customs, and places in your community. Then plan and present a short TV ad for your town.

**Digital Library**

myNGconnect.com
◉ View the video.

▲ Every town has its own history.

# Language & Grammar

## Give Commands

Listen to the rap. Then listen again and chime in.

**RAP**

### COME TO THE MARKET!

Come to the marketplace!
See the choices. Look!
Come to the marketplace!
Taste the samples. Yum!
See it! Try it!
Taste it! Buy it—
If it doesn't cost too much.

# Use Statements and Commands

A **statement** tells something. It begins with a capital letter and ends with a period.

> EXAMPLE    **W**e are hungry⊙

A **command** tells someone to do something. A command begins with a capital letter. It often ends with a period.

> EXAMPLE    **T**ry the Italian restaurant⊙

A strong command ends with an exclamation point.

> EXAMPLE    Be careful⓵

To make a polite command, use the word *please*.

> EXAMPLE    **Please** get in the taxi.

## Practice Together

Say each sentence. Tell whether it is a statement or a command. Then tell why.

1. This neighborhood is interesting.
2. Look at the signs.
3. They are in English and Vietnamese.
4. I see a newspaper stand.
5. Please buy me a paper.
6. The restaurant across the street is good.
7. There are a lot of cars.
8. Stay away from the curb!

▲ **This neighborhood in Westminster, California, is called Little Saigon.**

## Try It!

Read each sentence. Write *statement* or *command* on a card. Hold up the card as you say the sentence. Then tell why the sentence is a statement or a command.

9. I like this festival.
10. The bright lights are pretty.
11. Listen to the music.
12. It has a great beat.
13. Smell that chili!
14. Get two plates for us, please.

# Act Out a Market Scene

## GIVE COMMANDS

Imagine you are at a market. Work with a partner to act out a scene.

One of you plays the customer, or the person who is buying. The other plays the vendor, or the person who is selling. Include commands in your conversation.

First, decide who will be the customer and who will be the vendor. Then decide what kind of market you are going to. Is it a fruit or vegetable market? A fish market? A food stand? A clothing market?

Draw or list things you can find at the market. Add the prices.

Now role-play the scene. Use as many commands as you can. Remember:

## HOW TO GIVE COMMANDS

1. When you want to tell someone to do something, use a command.
2. Use *please* to make a polite command.

Please give me an apple.

## USE STATEMENTS AND COMMANDS

When you want to tell something, make a **statement**. When you want somebody to do something, give a **command**.

EXAMPLES

**Customer:** I want a pumpkin.
Please give me an orange one.

**Vendor:** Look at the white ones!
They are very nice. They are $4.00 each.

▲ The farmer sells produce at an outdoor market.

# Prepare to Read

## Learn Key Vocabulary

**Study the Words** Use the steps below.

1. Pronounce the word. Say it aloud several times. Spell it.
2. Rate your word knowledge.
3. Study the example. Tell more about the word.
4. Practice it. Make the word your own.

### Key Words

**agree** (u-grē) *verb*
▶ page 50

When you **agree** with someone, you have the same ideas. A handshake shows that people **agree** to something.
*Antonym:* **disagree**

**community** (ku-**myū**-nu-tē) *noun* ▶ page 50

A **community** is a place where people live, work, and carry out their daily lives. This **community** has an outdoor market.
*Synonyms:* **neighborhood**, **town**

**familiar** (fu-**mil**-yur) *adjective* ▶ page 51

Something that is **familiar** is already known. The man was happy to see a **familiar** face at the party.
*Antonym:* **unfamiliar**

**festival** (**fes**-tu-vul) *noun*
▶ page 54

A **festival** is a special event or party. Dancers perform at the **festival**.
*Synonyms:* **celebration**, **fiesta**

**native** (**nā**-tiv) *adjective*
▶ page 53

Something that belongs to you because of where you were born is **native** to you. People wave flags from their **native** countries.

**neighborhood** (**nā**-bur-hood) *noun* ▶ page 52

A **neighborhood** is a place where people live and work together. This **neighborhood** is in Boston.
*Synonym:* **community**

**population** (pah-pyu-**lā**-shun) *noun* ▶ page 50

**Population** means the number of people who live somewhere. Many people live in New York City. It has a large **population**.

**tradition** (tru-**di**-shun) *noun*
▶ page 50

A **tradition** is an activity or belief that people share for many years. It is a **tradition** for this family to celebrate Kwanzaa every December.
*Synonym:* **custom**

**Practice the Words** Work with a partner. Write a question using one or two Key Words. Answer your partner's question. Use at least one Key Word in your answer. Take turns until you have used all the Key Words twice.

| Questions | Answers |
|---|---|
| Do you have any traditions in your community? | Yes, we have a festival every spring. |

# Make Inferences and Synthesize

**Make Inferences** Put ideas together from what you read and what you know to make inferences.

**Synthesize** Put together events and ideas to form new understandings.

**Look Into the Text**

## Familiar Food

In any city, you can find all different kinds of food. Some foods feel more like home, though.

Ethiopian people who move to Little Ethiopia agree. The community has many restaurants that serve delicious Ethiopian foods.

**What I read:**
Food can make you feel at home.

" I know I like to eat foods that I am used to eating. So I think people who move from another country like to eat foods that remind them of their home country."

| Detail | My Experience | My Conclusion |
|---|---|---|
| There is a community called Little Ethiopia. | One time, I visited a neighborhood called Little Italy. Many people who came from Italy lived there. | People who moved from Ethiopia to the United States felt comfortable living near each other in Little Ethiopia. |

**Conclusion Chart**

## Practice Together

**Begin a Reading Strategies Log** A Reading Strategies Log can show how the strategies help you understand the text. The first row shows how one strategy helped one reader. Reread the passage and add to the log.

| Text I Read | Strategy I Used | How I Used the Strategy |
|---|---|---|
| Page: 50<br><br>Text: Some foods feel more like home, though. | ☒ Make Inferences<br>☐ Synthesize<br>☐ _____ | Making Inferences helped me understand how food can make people feel closer to home. |

## Expository Nonfiction

Expository nonfiction gives information and facts. Usually, the text is divided into sections. A heading tells the topic, or what the section is about. The text that follows includes a main idea that tells more about the topic.

As you read, synthesize by putting **ideas** and **information** together from different sections of the text to form new ideas. You can make inferences by combining information you learn in each section with what you already know.

### Look Into the Text

Walk into a restaurant. Order some food. Tear some of the *injera* to scoop up the hot stews. Taste the seasoned vegetables and spicy sauces.

The right food makes a new place feel like home.

Remember that you can synthesize by drawing conclusions, forming generalizations, and comparing.

▼ Chinatown in New York City is home to many people who moved to the United States from China.

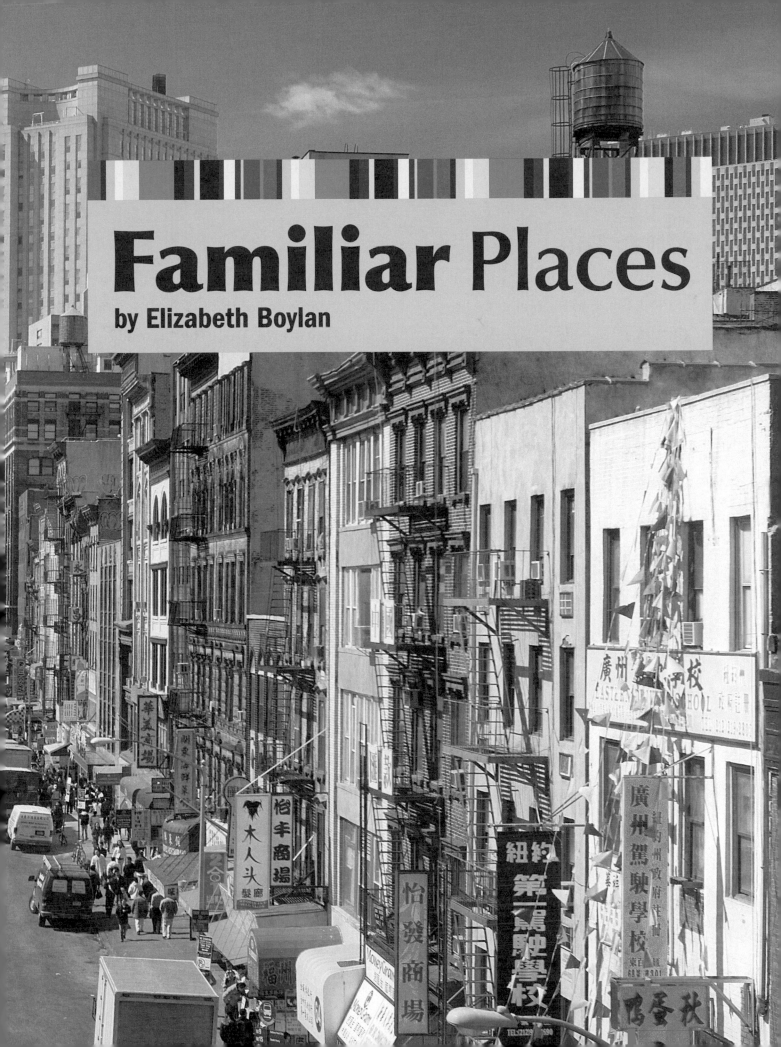

# Familiar Places

by Elizabeth Boylan

People are the heart of any **community**. When the **population** changes, so does the community. People bring their clothes, their furniture, and, of course, their **traditions**. Over time, the new community starts to feel a little like home.

# Familiar Food

In any city, you can find all different kinds of food. Some foods feel more like home, though.

Ethiopian people who move to Little Ethiopia **agree**. The community has many restaurants that serve **delicious** Ethiopian foods.

Walk into a restaurant. Order some food. **Tear** some of the *injera* to scoop up the hot **stews**. Taste the seasoned vegetables and spicy sauces.

The right food makes a new place feel like home.

◄ Washington, DC, has a community known as Little Ethiopia. There are many Ethiopian restaurants there. The first Ethiopian restaurants in Washington, DC, opened in the 1970s.

**Key Vocabulary**
**community** *n.*, where people live
**population** *n.*, the number of people in a place
**tradition** *n.*, an activity or belief that people share
**agree** *v.*, to have the same idea

**In Other Words**
**delicious** very good
**Tear** Pull off
*injera* Ethiopian flat bread ►
**stews** thick soups

# Familiar Clothes

In a community, shops sell many different kinds of clothes. Some clothes look more **familiar**, though.

Indian people who go to Little India agree. There are many clothing and jewelry shops there.

Walk into a shop and feel the soft **fabrics**. Look at the colorful *saris*. Try on a *kameez*.

Familiar clothes can make a new place feel like home.

▲ Many people from India moved to Chicago, Illinois, in the 1960s. They opened shops that sell Indian clothes, food, and jewelry. The community is called Little India.

**Key Vocabulary**
**familiar** *adj.*, already known

**In Other Words**
**fabrics** cloth
*saris* long, flowing dresses
*kameez* long shirt

## Look Into the Text

1. **Explain** How do the people of Little Fthiopia makc their **community** feel like home?
2. **Main Idea and Details** What is each section mainly about? What details tell about the main idea?

# Familiar Sounds

There are sounds all around a **neighborhood**. Some sounds are more familiar, though.

Haitian people who move to Little Haiti agree. The sounds you hear in Little Haiti are like the sounds you hear in Haiti. Walk into a shop and hear people speak Haitian Creole and French. Listen to the *compas music*. **Sway** to the strong beat.

Familiar sounds can make a new place feel like home.

▲ Thousands of Haitians moved to Miami, Florida, in the 1980s. They formed a neighborhood called Little Haiti. Dancers move to the music at a street market.

**Key Vocabulary**

**neighborhood** *n.*, a place where people live and work together

**In Other Words**

*compas* **music** Haitian music
**Sway** Move your body back and forth

# Familiar Language

When a language is new to you, the words can look so different. Sometimes it is nice to see your **native** language.

Korean people who move to Koreatown agree. In Koreatown, you can find words in English and Korean. Read the ***hangul signs***. Buy a book in Korean. Find a Korean newspaper.

Familiar words can make a new place feel like home.

▲ Many Koreans moved to Los Angeles, California, in the 1960s. Now many businesses have signs in Korean and English.

---

**Key Vocabulary**

**native** *adj.*, belonging to the place someone was born

**In Other Words**

***hangul* signs** signs that use Korean writing

**Look Into the Text**

1. **Interpret** What are some of the sounds you might hear if you go to Little Haiti?
2. **Main Idea and Details** According to the text, what **familiar** things can Korean immigrants find in Koreatown?

# Familiar Celebrations

Everyone likes to **celebrate**! There are always many reasons to have fun. Some celebrations are more familiar, though.

Every September, the people of Little Italy hold a **festival**. Look at the **decorations** and watch the parade. Then eat *cannoli* while you dance and sing Italian songs.

Familiar celebrations can make a new place feel like home.

Familiar foods, sounds, and celebrations can make you feel at home in a new neighborhood. As new people move in, the neighborhood will continue to change and become their home, too. ❖

▲ New York City, New York, has a neighborhood called Little Italy. Many Italians moved there in the late 1800s. Not many Italians move there now, though. People in Little Italy still celebrate Italian traditions.

**Key Vocabulary**
**festival** *n.*, a special event or party

**In Other Words**
**celebrate** have a party
**decorations** special lights and other things that people put up for the party
*cannoli* an Italian dessert

## Look Into the Text

1. **Evidence and Conclusion** Which words explain why **communities** often change over time?
2. **Explain** How do familiar celebrations and **festivals** make a new place feel like home?

# Connect Reading and Writing

Vocabulary

agrees

community

familiar

festival

native

neighborhoods

population

traditions

## CRITICAL THINKING

1. **SUM IT UP** Use your Reading Strategies Log to synthesize the information you learned in each section. Use your log to give a summary to a partner.

| Text I Read | Strategy I Used | How I Used the Strategy |
|---|---|---|
| Page: 50<br><br>Text: Some foods feel more like home, though. | ☒ Make Inferences<br>☐ Synthesize<br>☐ _____ | Making Inferences helped me understand how food can make people feel closer to home. |

Reading Strategies Log

2. **Paraphrase** Look back at the first paragraph of the selection. Use your own words to tell how **communities** change.

3. **Make Judgments** What do you think makes a new place feel comfortable? Do you **agree** with the author, or do you have different ideas? Explain.

4. **Analyze** Why do you think **familiar** things are important to immigrants? Explain.

## READING FLUENCY

**Phrasing** Read the passage on page 560 to a partner. Assess your fluency.

1. I did not pause/sometimes paused/ always paused for punctuation.

2. What I did best in my reading was _____.

## READING STRATEGY

> What strategy helped you understand this selection? Tell a partner about it.

## VOCABULARY REVIEW

**Oral Review** Read the paragraph aloud. Add the vocabulary words.

> In the 1880s, a _____ in Vancouver, Canada, was known as Chinatown. Today many Chinese people also live in other _____. Nearly one third of the city's _____ speaks a main Chinese language. Many people are _____ Chinese speakers even though they were born in Canada. Everyone _____ that art, music, and celebrations keep _____ alive. The Dragon Boat Festival is well-known, or _____, to nearly everyone in Vancouver. This _____ takes place on the water.

**Written Review** What **festivals** or special **traditions** does your **community** have? Write a TV ad for one of them. Use four vocabulary words.

**WRITE ABOUT THE** GUIDING QUESTION

**Explore Finding Your Own Place**

Look back at the photos in the selection. How might these **neighborhoods** change in the future? Write your opinion, and support it with reasons.

# Connect Across the Curriculum

## Use Context Clues

**Academic Vocabulary**

- **context** (kon-tekst) *noun*
  Context refers to the parts nearby that help explain the meaning.

When you find a word that has multiple meanings, use **context** to try to figure out the correct meaning. Then check a dictionary.

**Read a Dictionary Entry** In a dictionary, **entry words** are listed in alphabetical order. The entry tells what the word means and gives other information.

> pronunciation
>
> **stew (stū)** *noun* ← part of speech
> 1 meat, fish, or vegetables cooked for a long time on the stove ← meaning 1
> 2 a state of worry: *He is really in a stew.* ← meaning 2
>
> example sentence

**Find the Meaning** Read this sentence from "Familiar Places." Use nearby words to figure out the meaning of *stew*. Which dictionary meaning matches your meaning?

   Tear some of the *injera* to scoop up the hot stews.

**Look Up Words** Work with a partner. Find each word in the selection. Use **context** to figure out the meaning. Then check the word in a dictionary, and copy the correct definition.

   **1.** heart, p. 50    **2.** serve, p. 50    **3.** beat, p. 52    **4.** watch, p. 54

## Analyze Text Structure: Main Idea

**Academic Vocabulary**

- **topic** (tah-pik) *noun*
  A **topic** is the subject of a piece of writing or of a discussion.

Writers of nonfiction usually organize their text into sections. Each section has a **main idea**—what the writer is mostly telling about the **topic**. The section heading often gives a clue to the **topic** of the section.

**Read for the Main Idea** Read page 51 in "Familiar Places." Use the heading to figure out the **topic**. Then look for a sentence in the first paragraph that gives the main idea about the **topic**.

**Share with a Partner** Compare your thoughts with a partner's. Tell how the main idea relates to the **topic**.

## Give Commands

**Pair Talk** Imagine your partner is a visitor to your neighborhood. Describe some interesting places to visit. Tell your partner how to get to the places and what to do. Use commands. Switch roles.

> Try the Thai Garden. Go to 8th Street and turn right. Get there early!

## Write About a Special Event

**Study the Models** When you write about a special event, use a variety of sentence types. Include **statements**, **questions**, **exclamations**, and **commands** to communicate your ideas and engage your readers.

**JUST OK**

The International Parade in our neighborhood is a lot of fun. I like to go and see the costumes. Some of my friends are always in the parade. Ahmet wears traditional Turkish clothing. Nestor and Cande are in the Caribbean band. Shivaani dresses as an Indian dancer.

> This writer only uses statements. The reader thinks: "The topic is interesting, but the writer presents it in a boring way."

**BETTER**

Have you ever been to a Cinco de Mayo celebration? It's really fun. Dancers wear colorful Mexican costumes. They swirl to the beat of lively folk music. There are games and good things to eat. There's even a jalapeño-eating contest! So mark next May 5 on your calendar. Come and join the fun!

> This writer uses a variety of sentences. The text is more interesting.

**Revise It** Look back at the JUST OK passage. Work with a partner to improve it. Use a variety of sentences.

✎ **WRITE ON YOUR OWN** Imagine you are at a special event or celebration in your community. Write a description of it. Be sure to include different kinds of sentences.

**REMEMBER**
- A statement ends with a period (**.**).
- A question ends with a question mark (**?**).
- An exclamation ends with an exclamation point(**!**).
- A command ends with a period (**.**) or an exclamation point (**!**).

# from Call Me María

## by Judith Ortiz Cofer

1    My grandmother comes into the kitchen where I am sitting down at the table reading a magazine. It is a dark winter day. Rain and sleet have been predicted. **Abuela** shakes her head as she looks out the window of our basement apartment. All the feet that pass by are wearing boots. She pours herself a cup of coffee and sits down across from me. She sighs as if her heart is breaking. She shivers and pulls her sweater around her shoulders. Papi comes in whistling. It is his day off. He will spend it with friends he knew from when he was a boy in the **barrio**. They will go to the park, even if it's raining or cold, and talk about the good times they had as children.

2    Abuela says, shivering, "María, let me tell you about my Island in the sun. The place where I was born. A **paradise**."

**In Other Words**
**Abuela** Grandmother
**barrio** Spanish neighborhood
**paradise** perfect place

3     Papi, frowning as he struggles to put on his boots, says, "I know, I know your paradise. I lived there once, remember? In San Juan, I couldn't see the sun behind the buildings. I'll take **the island of Manhattan** anytime, if what I want is a paradise made of concrete."

4     Abuela, ignoring him, tapping my hand as she speaks.

5     I am trying to stay out of it, hiding behind my magazine: "*Ay, **bendita hija.***

When I was growing up on my Island, everyone treated each other nicely, like family. We shared what we had, and if you were poor, your neighbors helped you. ***La familia, los amigos, el amor***, that's what mattered. People were not always angry; people were not cold like they are here in this cold place, these are cold people . . . the sun shines every day on my Island."

6     Papi, sounding angry: "The familia on your Island made fun of me, called me *el gringo* because my Spanish sounded funny to their ears. They laughed when I complained that the mosquitoes were eating me alive. Fresh American blood, they joked, to fatten up our hungry bugs. I couldn't wait to come home to my country where people **understand** what I say, and the mosquitoes treat everyone the same."

7     Abuela, paying no attention to Papi, moving her chair closer to mine: "When I was your age on my Island there was no crime, no violence, no drugs. The children respected the adults. We obeyed the teachers, the priests, the Pope, the governor, and our parents. The sun shines every day. On my Island . . ."

8     Papi: "I once had my wallet stolen in the **plaza of your pueblo**, Señora. I used to watch the news in the bedroom, while everyone else sat hypnotized by the romantic **telenovelas** in the living room. On my screen was the same world I see on our TV here: drugs, guns, angry people, and violence. Only difference—the bad news was in Spanish."

9     Abuela, not listening. Looking into her cup as if she were watching a movie: "The sun shines every day. On my Island . . ."

10     Papi, in a mocking tone of voice: "The sun shines every day, that's true. While I was unhappy, missing my friends here, while I was lonely, the sun shone every day and it was 110 degrees in the shade."

> ❝ **The sun shines every day. On my Island...** ❞

11     Abuela: "On my Island . . ."

12     Before she can finish her sentence, the lights flash on and off, and then we hear the gasping sounds of electrical things shutting down and darkness. A roll of thunder shakes the glass window. We hear the sound of feet running on the sidewalk above our heads. Abuela gets a candle from a kitchen drawer, places it on the table, and lights it. There is another roll of thunder and the sound of pouring rain. I hear Papi opening the pantry door to get his flashlight. The telephone begins to ring. I run to get it, grateful that it has interrupted a **culture** clash I have been hearing all of my life. It is the old battle between Island Puerto Rican and mainland Puerto Rican. It is what finally drove my parents apart.

13     On the telephone, I hear Doña Segura's shaky voice asking me in Spanish if Papi can come see about a smell like gas in her apartment. Everyone else is away for the day. She is blind. She does not even know that it is dark. Abuela nods. I know she will go stay with Doña Segura.

14     Papi, already dressed for his day of freedom, listens to me tell Doña Segura that she will be right up. I look at my father by the light of the candle. Both of us sigh **in unison**, a big, deep, melodramatic, Puerto Rican sigh. Abuela's candle is blown out by our breath. Then there is the sound of three people laughing together in the dark.

---

**Key Vocabulary**
- **understand** *v.*, to know
- **culture** *n.*, the ideas and way of life for a group of people

**In Other Words**
*el gringo* American
**plaza of your pueblo** area in front of your house
**telenovelas** soap operas; TV shows
**in unison** at the same time

Oscar Ortiz

# Compare Across Texts

## Compare Points of View

"Growing Together," "Kids Like Me," "Familiar Places," and "*from* Call Me Maria" tell about **immigrants** coming to the United States from different points of view. **Compare** points of view in these texts.

## How It Works

**Collect and Organize Ideas** Use a chart to organize what you know.

| Selection | Point of View | Thoughts and Feelings |
|-----------|---------------|----------------------|
| "Growing Together" | first person | homesick for Cuba |
| "Kids Like Me" | first person | |
| "Familiar Places" | third person | |
| "Call Me Maria" | first person | |

Comparison Chart

## Practice Together

**Study and Compare Ideas** Look at the notes in the second column of the Comparison Chart. Write two sentences that **compare** points of view.

> "Growing Together," "Kids Like Me," and "*from* Call Me Maria" are told from first-person point of view. "Familiar Places" is told from third-person point of view.

## Try It!

Copy and complete the chart above. Write sentences to **compare** points of view by describing the thoughts and feelings of the characters or people in the texts. You may want to use frames like these to help you express your comparison.

_____ feels _____, but _____ feels _____. Both people feel _____.

_____ thinks _____, but _____ thinks _____. Both people think _____.

**Academic Vocabulary**

- **immigrant** (i-mu-grunt) *noun*
  An **immigrant** is someone who comes to live in a new country.
- **compare** (kum-**pair**) *verb*
  When you **compare** two things, you think about how they are alike and different.

# Finding Your Own Place

**What defines home?**

## Content Library

## Leveled Library

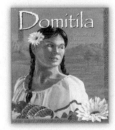  

## Reflect on Your Reading

Think back on your reading of the unit selections. Discuss what you did to understand what you read.

**Strategies**

In this unit, you were introduced to eight different reading strategies and how they can be applied to text to make you a better reader. Choose a selection from this unit. Explain to a partner how you applied reading strategies to better understand the text. Tell about at least four different strategies. Then explain how you will plan to use each of the eight reading strategies in the future.

## Explore the

Throughout this unit, you have been thinking about what defines home. Choose one of these ways to explore the Guiding Question:

- **Discuss** With a group, discuss what immigrants do to make a new place feel like home. Give details from the selections that support your ideas.
- **Ask Questions** Ask someone who has moved to the United States how his or her home country and the U.S. are alike and different. Share with the class.
- **Draw** Create a map of your neighborhood. Label places or areas that are important to you. Share your map with a classmate, and explain how your neighborhood is a home for you and your neighbors.

## Book Talk

Which Unit Library book did you choose? Explain to a partner what it taught you about the meaning of home.

# WATER
## FOR LIFE

2

GUIDING
QUESTION

# How do we depend on Earth's Resources?

**READ MORE!**

**Content Library**
**Deserts**
by Mary Tull

**Leveled Library**
**20,000 Leagues Under the Sea**
by Jules Verne,
adapted by Judith Conaway
**Knights of the Round Table**
adapted by Gwen Gross
**The Dragon Prince**
by Laurence Yep

**Web Links**
☐ myNGconnect.com

◀ This body of water is a source of food
for fishermen and their families.

# Focus on Reading

## Analyze Events and Ideas

There are two major kinds of text: **fiction** and **nonfiction**. Fiction is a made-up story with a series of episodes or events that form a plot. Nonfiction usually includes facts and ideas about something that really happened or someone who really existed.

## How It Works

Before you read, preview the text to determine if it is fiction or nonfiction. This will tell you whether the text tells a story or explains ideas.

**Analyze Events** The events in fiction are the **plot**. The characters are the people or animals that create the action. As the plot unfolds, characters **respond or change**. Think carefully about the characters and plot to analyze what is happening in the story.

### An Exciting Day

It is a lazy day at the lake. Even the fish are too lazy to swim. Josephina sighs. "Nothing exciting ever happens," she says.

Just then, a huge wind roars. Josephina has to tie her shoelaces to a tree to stay put. The wind blows until the entire lake is gone.

Then a thick, black cloud moves overhead. Like a sponge being squeezed out, the cloud dumps rain and fills the lake again.

"Well," Josephina exclaims. "That was exciting," she says.

**Characters** respond or change because of events in the story. Josephina was bored and because of the events in the story she grew excited.

**Analyze Ideas** Nonfiction writing introduces a **topic** and then gives more information to explain it. A writer states the **main idea** about the **topic**, and gives details, **examples**, and **anecdotes** that elaborate, or tell more about the main idea. Photographs or charts also illustrate the details.

### Forms of Water

Water has different forms. Pour water into any container and it fits right in. Freeze water and it becomes a solid like an ice cube. Heat water and it turns to steam, disappearing as water vapor. When the vapor cools, it returns to its liquid form. Rain is cooled vapor falling down to Earth.

**Topic**

**Main idea**

**Details**

**Academic Vocabulary**
- **topic** (tah-pik) *noun*
  A **topic** is the subject of a piece of writing or of a discussion.

## Practice Together

Read these passages aloud. As you read, listen for clues that tell you if the passage is fiction or nonfiction. Then determine what topic or series of events is introduced.

### Water Cycle

Water moves in a cycle that never ends. Above Earth, water is in the form of clouds. Clouds are made of tiny water drops or ice crystals. At some point, they fall to Earth as rain or snow. The water soaks into the ground or returns to rivers and oceans. Heat from the sun evaporates water from the surface of Earth, and water returns to the sky as clouds.

### Calling the Wind

Sage had an idea for bringing rain to the dry fields. She climbed the highest hill and called to Wind. "Wind, you are weak!"

That angered Wind. "You dare to call me weak!"

Sage shrugged and said, "You are not strong enough to blow a cloud this way." Wind began to howl. It blew until the sky filled with clouds and rain fell.

## Try It!

Read these passages aloud. Analyze each passage. Does something happen or is something explained? Does a character react to the plot events? How does he or she react? What topic is introduced? What details or examples does the author give to elaborate on the topic?

### A Mystery

Chang discovers all kinds of interesting things at the beach.

Today no one else is there. Even the birds are gone. Chang sees something purple rolling in the waves on the shore. He goes closer. It is a bottle, and it has something in it!

Chang reaches down to pick it up. Then he hears a voice. "Help me! I'm trapped in this bottle."

Chang knows a lot of folk tales. He knows that a voice in a bottle could be big trouble. So he turns around and walks away.

### Bodies of Water

Earth has very large bodies of water on its surface. The largest is the Pacific Ocean. It is about 15 times bigger than the United States.

The largest body of fresh water is Lake Superior. The lake is almost 2,800 miles around. You could fit Rhode Island in the middle of it.

The Missouri River is one of the longest rivers in the world. It stretches 2,341 miles in length. People use these bodies of water for food, transportation, and recreation.

# Focus on Vocabulary

## Relate Words

**Synonyms** are words that have nearly the same meaning. Synonyms can have different connotations, or connotative meanings. A connotative meaning is what a word implies or suggests as a particular meaning. Word choice can impact a sentence's meaning and tone.

EXAMPLE    The Great Lakes are all **big**, but Lake Superior is **enormous**.

## How the Strategy Works

The more words you know about an idea, the better you'll understand what people say and the better you will be able to express yourself.

1. Whenever you read, take time to learn new words.

2. Put words into groups, or **categories** , to help you understand their exact meanings and what they imply. This web shows four **categories** of words related to water.

3. Then use a Synonym Scale to rank words in the same **category** in order of their strength. Think about the impact these words have on meaning and tone.

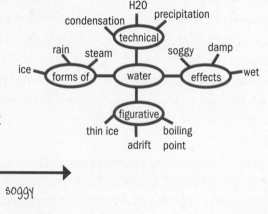

damp          wet          soggy

**Synonym Scale**

Use the strategy to analyze the impact word choice has on meaning and tone. Which words imply very wet? Which words imply somewhat wet?

### Rain in Washington

Washington State is known for its <u>damp</u> climate. Every year, it rains an average of 38 inches. In 1996, however, the state was <u>drenched</u>. That year, Seattle had almost 51 inches of rain. The ground was <u>soaked</u>.

**Strategy in Action**

" *Damp* and *drenched* both describe a shade of *wet*, but *drenched* has a much stronger connotation. "

☑ **REMEMBER** Knowing the exact and connotative meanings of synonyms will help you understand what you read.

**Academic Vocabulary**

- **category** (ka-tu-gor-ē) *noun*
  A **category** is a group of items that are related in some way.

## Practice Together

Read this passage aloud. Work with your class to categorize the underlined words and then make a Synonym Scale for them. Discuss what each word implies.

How would the tone change if the author replaced all the underlined words with *moved*? How would the meaning change if the author switched all the underlined words?

### River Fish

Last summer, my family went camping near a river. We had a great time watching as all the different fish <u>swam</u> around. Big fish <u>drifted</u> from one dark spot to another. Tiny fish <u>zoomed</u> around the rocks. A river eel <u>glided</u> through the water. We all laughed as my dog <u>paddled</u> around, chasing them all.

▲ Fish swim in the river.

## Try It!

Read this passage aloud. Notice the underlined synonyms. How are the meanings of these words similar? What does each word imply?

What are the fastest and slowest ways that river water moves, according to this writer? How does the writer's word choice allow you to better understand the meaning of the passage?

### Moving Water

Have you ever thought about how river water moves at different speeds all the time? In deep, wide areas, the water <u>flows</u> gently. It <u>splashes</u> through rocky, shallower areas. Then it <u>speeds</u> down a hill and <u>rushes</u> over a waterfall. When it comes to a flat area, it <u>crawls</u>. It even <u>stands still</u> in pools at the edge of the river.

▲ River water moves quickly over the rocks.

# THE SECRET WATER

by Daphne Liu
Illustrated by Jean and Mou-sien Tseng

## SELECTION 1 OVERVIEW

▶ **Build Background**

▶ **Language & Grammar**
Express Needs and Wants
Use Nouns

▶ **Prepare to Read**
Learn Key Vocabulary
Analyze Plot

▶ **Read and Write**
**Introduce the Genre**
Legend
**Focus on Reading**
Analyze Plot
**Apply the Focus Strategy**
Monitor: Clarify Ideas
**Critical Thinking**
**Reading Fluency**
Read with Expression
**Vocabulary Review**
**Write About the Guiding Question**

▶ **Connect Across the Curriculum**
**Vocabulary Study**
Create Word Categories
**Listening/Speaking**
Compare Tales Across Cultures
**Language and Grammar**
Express Needs and Wants
**Writing and Grammar**
Write About a Situation

# Build Background

## Visit a Village

"The Secret Water" takes place in a village in China. Often, people in villages have to walk to a stream or a river to get water.

## Connect

**Quickwrite** Imagine that you live in a mountain village in China long ago. Every day you walk to a river a mile away and return with two buckets of water that weigh 20 pounds each. Describe what it is like to carry the water each day. Share your writing with a partner.

**Digital Library**
myNGconnect.com
◎ View the video.

▲ Villagers collect water from a river.

# Language & Grammar

## Express Needs and Wants

Listen to the song. Then sing along with it.

**SONG**

# We Need Water!

I carry two buckets.
You carry one.
We need water.
We work in the sun.

I carry one bucket.
You carry two.
We cannot rest.
We have work to do!

1 TRY OUT LANGUAGE
2 LEARN GRAMMAR
3 APPLY ON YOUR OWN

# Use Nouns

A **noun** names a person, place, thing, or idea.

• A singular noun names one person, place, thing, or idea.

> EXAMPLE   The **farmer** carries a **bucket**.

• A plural noun names more than one person, place, thing, or idea.

> EXAMPLE   All the **farmers** carry **buckets**.

## Spelling Rules

**1.** To make most nouns plural, just add **-s**.

> EXAMPLE   **vegetable + -s = vegetables**
> They grow many **vegetables**.

**2.** If the noun ends in *s*, *z*, *sh*, *ch*, or *x*, add **-es**.

> EXAMPLE   **lunch + -es = lunches**
> He prepares all the **lunches**.

**3.** If the noun ends in *y* after the consonant, change the *y* to *i* and add **-es**.

> EXAMPLE   **famil*y* + -es = families**
> Twenty **families** live in the village.

**4.** Some nouns have special forms.

> EXAMPLE   **mouse = mice**
> The **mice** ate the seeds.

## Practice Together

Change the noun in the box to the plural form. Say it. Then say the sentence and add the plural form of the noun.

**1.** | person | There are many _____ in the village.

**2.** | box | Their houses look like small _____.

**3.** | field | Almost everyone works in the _____.

**4.** | baby | The grandparents take care of the _____.

▲ The villagers work outside.

## Try It!

Change the noun in the box to the plural form. Write the plural form on a card. Then say the sentence and add the plural form.

**5.** | stream | Two _____ flow by the village.

**6.** | bush | Some _____ grow near the water.

**7.** | Child | _____ bring their baskets every morning.

**8.** | berry | They pick the ripe _____.

# Make and Play a Memory Game

## EXPRESS NEEDS AND WANTS

What's the difference between *need* and *want*? Form a group and explore this topic. Think about different situations when you need or want something. Make a chart. Write the situations and your responses. If you're not sure about a vocabulary word, try to act it out or use other words to describe it.

**Response Chart**

| Situation | I need . . . | I want . . . |
|---|---|---|
| I am thirsty. | water | lemonade |
| I am hungry. | a sandwich | |
| I am cold. | | |
| I am hot. | | |
| My homework is hard. | | |
| I'm in a new country. | | |

Now play a memory game on the topic. Write each response on two cards. Turn the cards face down and mix them up. Spread them on a table.

Take turns with a partner or in a group. Turn over one card. Read the response. Explain how it might be something you need or want. Then turn over another card. If the response is the same, keep the pair and go again. If it is different, place the cards face down and let another person take a turn. Remember:

## HOW TO EXPRESS NEEDS AND WANTS

I need to do my homework.

I want to see a movie.

1. Use words like *must* and *need* to tell about important things. If you need something and do not get it, you could have problems.

2. Use *want* to talk about things you like or do not like. If you do not get what you want, you may be unhappy. But it does not cause a problem.

## USE NOUNS

You will often use **nouns** to express needs and wants. When you do, use singular nouns to talk about one thing you need or want. Use plural nouns to talk about more than one thing.

**Singular Noun:** pen

**Plural Noun:** pens

# Prepare to Read

## Learn Key Vocabulary

**Study the Words** Use the steps below.

1. Pronounce the word. Say it aloud several times. Spell it.
2. Rate your word knowledge.
3. Study the example.
4. Practice it. Make the word your own.

### Key Words

**available** (u-vā-lu-bul) *adjective* ▶ page 78

When something is **available**, it is here and ready for use. Fresh fruit is **available** in the summer.
*Antonym:* **unavailable**

**perfect** (pur-fikt) *adjective* ▶ page 78

Something that is **perfect** is just right. This girl makes a **perfect** dive into the water.
*Antonyms:* **wrong, bad**

**plan** (plan) *noun* ▶ page 82

A **plan** is an idea about how to do something. Drawings show the **plans** for building a new house.
*Synonym:* **blueprint**

**problem** (prah-blum) *noun* ▶ page 82

A **problem** is something that is wrong. A **problem** needs to be solved or fixed. This driver has a **problem**. His truck is stuck in the mud.
*Antonym:* **solution**

**secret** (sē-krut) *adjective, noun* ▶ page 80

**1** *adjective* Something that is **secret** is hidden from others. **2** *noun* A **secret** is something you hide from others. Can you keep a **secret**?
*Synonym:* **private** (*adjective*)

**statue** (sta-chü) *noun* ▶ page 82

A **statue** is a model of a person or thing. This **statue** shows Abraham Lincoln.

**village** (vi-lij) *noun* ▶ page 78

A **village** is a very small town. Not many people live in this farming **village**.

**worry** (wur-ē) *verb* ▶ page 80

To **worry** about something means to feel unhappy and afraid about what may happen. People often **worry** when they are late.
*Antonym:* **relax**

**Practice the Words** Make a Vocabulary Example Chart for each Key Word. Then compare your charts with a partner's.

| Word | Definition | Example from My Life |
|---|---|---|
| perfect | just right | 100% on my math test |

**Vocabulary Example Chart**

# Analyze Plot

**What Is Plot?** A plot is the **series** of events that make up a story. A plot usually has a problem and a solution. Most stories tell the problem at the beginning. Then a series of events, or the plot, happens that leads to a solution. The stories usually end soon after the solution is found and the problem is fixed. This passage shows the **problem** in "The Secret Water."

**Reading Strategies**

- Plan
- **Monitor** Notice confusing parts in the text then reread or read on to make them clear.
- Make Connections
- Visualize
- Ask Questions
- Determine Importance
- Make Inferences
- Synthesize

**Look Into the Text**

Every day, people must walk over the steep mountain to get the precious water. They fill their buckets with the water and carry it home.

One day, Shu Fa goes up the mountain. Near the path, she discovers a turnip. It is perfect for lunch. She pulls it out of the ground.

Snap! Water pours from the hole left by the turnip.

## Practice Together

**Begin a Problem-and-Solution Chart** A Problem-and-Solution Chart can help you keep track of events that happen in a story. This chart shows the problem from the passage above. The events show how the problem is solved. Reread the passage above, and add an event to the chart.

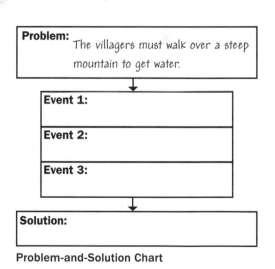

**Problem:** The villagers must walk over a steep mountain to get water.

**Event 1:**

**Event 2:**

**Event 3:**

**Solution:**

Problem-and-Solution Chart

**Academic Vocabulary**

- **series** (**sear**-ēz) *noun*
  A **series** is a group of related things that are put in a certain order.

# Legend

A legend is a very old story, usually about a hero, or person who acts with courage to solve a problem.

The **problem** is often introduced early in the legend. As the story continues the characters respond or change as the plot leads to a solution.

The setting is where and when a story happens. In a legend, the problem may be connected to the setting.

**Look Into the Text**

Shu Fa lives with Uncle and Auntie in a village by the mountain. The land is dry and dusty. There is no water available for the villagers.

Every day, people must walk over the steep mountain to get the precious water. They fill their buckets with the water and carry it home.

If you do not understand the problem, monitor your reading by clarifying ideas. As you read, stop and reread or read on. This may help the problem become clear to you.

# THE SECRET WATER

by Daphne Liu

Illustrated by Jean and Mou-sien Tseng

 Comprehension Coach

Shu Fa lives with Uncle and Auntie in a village by the mountain. The land is dry and dusty. There is no water **available** for the villagers.

Every day, people must walk over the steep mountain to get the **precious** water. They fill their buckets with the water and carry it home.

One day, Shu Fa goes up the mountain. Near the path, she discovers a **turnip**. It is **perfect** for lunch. She pulls it out of the ground.

Snap! Water pours from the hole left by the turnip. Shu Fa is **amazed**! Now the villagers will not have to walk so far for water.

**Key Vocabulary**
**village** *n.*, a small town
**available** *adj.*, here and ready for use
**perfect** *adj.*, just the right thing

**In Other Words**
**precious** valuable and important
**turnip** vegetable ▶
**amazed** very surprised

**Cultural Background**
This story takes place in China, where most people still live in the country. Many people in China, and in the world, have too little water. They dig wells or carry water using buckets.

Suddenly, a strong wind blows in from the mountain. It pushes the turnip back into the hole. A loud voice **roars**, "You cannot take my water!"

Shu Fa asks, "Who are you?"

"I am the Voice of the Mountain. This is MY water. You cannot take it."

"But my village needs water! Can you share it with us?" Shu Fa asks.

"No, I do not share!" the Voice says. Then it **warns her**: "If you tell anyone about the water, you will be punished!"

**In Other Words**
**roars** says with force
**warns her** tells her in a strong way

**Look Into the Text**

1. **Character** What kind of person is Shu Fa? How can you tell?
2. **Cause and Effect** What happens when Shu Fa pulls the turnip?

Shu Fa runs home. She wants to tell everyone about the **secret** water. But she is afraid.

Many days pass. Shu Fa sees how hard the villagers work to get water. She **worries** so much that her long, black hair turns white.

One day, Uncle walks over the mountain to get water. But he **trips** and hurts his head. *"Aiya!"* he cries.

Shu Fa cries, too. She knows now that she must help. She must bring the water to her village.

Shu Fa runs up the mountain and **smashes** the turnip. Water pours out of the hole. It becomes a river that goes into the village. The villagers dance with joy!

Then the Voice of the Mountain shouts, "Shu Fa, you told my **secret**! Now you must live in my river forever."

Shu Fa cries. She **begs** the Voice to let her say goodbye to her family. The Voice **grumbles**, "Go, but you must return here tonight."

**Key Vocabulary**
> **secret** *adj.*, hidden;
> *n.*, something that is hidden
> **worry** *v.*, to feel unhappy and afraid about what might happen

**In Other Words**
**trips** falls down
*Aiya!* Oh no! (in Chinese)
**smashes** breaks
**begs** asks
**grumbles** says unhappily

**Look Into the Text**

1.  **Inference** Why does Shu Fa's hair turn white?
2.  **Confirm Prediction** Was your prediction correct? What happened that you did not expect?

The Secret Water  **81**

*Predict*
*How will Shu Fa solve her problem?*

Shu Fa runs back to the village. "What can I do?" she asks herself. "I do not want to live in the river!" She decides to tell Uncle about the problem.

Uncle thinks for a few minutes. Then he says, "I have a **plan**."

Uncle works all day to **carve** a **statue** out of stone. The statue looks just like Shu Fa. He thinks the statue will trick the Voice of the Mountain.

"I just need one thing," Uncle tells Shu Fa. He cuts Shu Fa's long, white hair and attaches it to the statue. Then he places the statue in the river. Water flows over the statue. It carries the white hair over the mountain like a waterfall.

The Voice of the Mountain sees the statue. It says, "Hello, Shu Fa!"

The trick worked!

Today, the waterfall still flows to the village. The land is green, and the people are happy.

Once again, Shu Fa has long, black hair. ❖

**Key Vocabulary**
**problem** *n.*, something that is wrong
**plan** *n.*, an idea about how to do something
**statue** *n.*, a model of a person or thing

In Other Words
**carve** make, cut

**Look Into the Text**

1. **Character's Motive** Why does Shu Fa tell Uncle the **problem**?
2. **Paraphrase** How does Uncle's **plan** save Shu Fa?
3. **Viewing** What clue in the picture tells you if the trick worked?

**82 Unit 2** Water for Life

# Connect Reading and Writing

**Vocabulary**

available

perfect

plan

problem

secret

statue

village

worries

## CRITICAL THINKING

1. **SUM IT UP** Use your Problem-and-Solution Chart. Discuss how Shu Fa solves the **problem**. What do her actions say about her? Discuss your ideas with a partner.

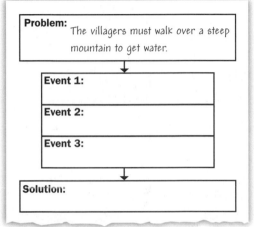

| Problem: The villagers must walk over a steep mountain to get water. |
| --- |
| Event 1: |
| Event 2: |
| Event 3: |
| Solution: |

Problem-and-Solution Chart

2. **Infer** Most legends are set in the past. How can you tell that what happens in Shu Fa's **village** takes place long ago? Find details in the story.

3. **Interpret** Explain the title. What is **secret** about water in this story?

4. **Analyze** What is the Voice of the Mountain like? Describe this character, based on the dialogue.

## READING FLUENCY

**Expression** Read the passage on page 561 to a partner. Assess your fluency.

1. My voice never/sometimes/always matched what I read.

2. What I did best in my reading was _____.

## READING STRATEGY

What strategy helped you understand this selection? Tell a partner about it.

## VOCABULARY REVIEW

**Oral Review** Read the paragraph aloud. Add the vocabulary words.

I live in a _____ where we eat a lot of fish. Fish are always _____ from the lake. No one ever _____ about hunger! To honor the fish, artists carved a large _____. They wanted to keep it a _____, so they didn't tell anyone. Then the artists had a _____ to solve: Where should they put the statue? They thought about it and decided on a _____. They found a _____ setting! The statue will sit in the lake!

**Written Review** Write a sentence to describe in detail each illustration in "The Secret Water." Assemble these into a narrative about the characters and the **village**. Use five vocabulary words.

**WRITE ABOUT THE** **GUIDING QUESTION**

### Explore Earth's Resources

Reread the selection. When is it OK to take an **available** resource from somebody to help others? Support your idea with examples from the text.

# Connect Across the Curriculum

## Create Word Categories

**Academic Vocabulary**
- **category** (ka-tu-gor-ē) *noun*
  A **category** is a group of items that are related in some way.

Words that relate to the same topic form a **category**. *Turnip* and *carrot* form a **category** because they are both related to the topic *vegetables*. Words within a **category** may be more specific than the topic of that **category**. *Turnip* and *carrot* are more specific than *vegetable*.

**Name a Category** Work with a partner. Think of a **category**, which can be a word or a phrase, for these words:

village          town          neighborhood          city

Explain how each word fits in the **category**. Then discuss what each word implies.

**Related Word Swap** With a partner, play a word game. One person writes a sentence using a word from the previous activity. The partner swaps that word with a related word. Discuss how the choice of word affects the meaning and tone of the sentence. Change roles.

## Compare Tales Across Cultures

SOCIAL SCIENCE

**Academic Vocabulary**
- **compare** (kum-**pair**) *verb*
  When you **compare** two things, you think about how they are alike and different.

Shu Fa helps save her village. You can find stories of strong women like her in many cultures.

1 **Read Another Story** Read the story of She-Who-Is-Alone, from the Comanche people. Think about the problem in the story and what She-Who-Is-Alone does to solve it.

2 **Analyze and Compare Characters** Work with a group to **compare** Shu Fa and She-Who-Is-Alone. Identify the problem in each story and explain how the character responds to each event. Pay attention to the similarities between the characters. How do Shu Fa and She-Who-Is-Alone change throughout their stories? What makes each woman a hero? Use examples from the story. Discuss your ideas with a group.

## Express Needs and Wants

**Act It Out** Work with a group, and imagine you are the characters in "The Secret Water." Use your own words to act out the story events and to tell what the characters need and want. Use precise, or exact, nouns.

> I want to get a bucket of water from the river.

## Write About a Situation

**Study the Models** When you write about a situation, like the need for water, choose **nouns** that let readers picture exactly what you are saying. Be sure to spell plural nouns correctly.

**NOT OK**

> The sun beats down on the **plants** in the **fieldes**. The farmers worry because there is no rain. **Ladys** watch the **flowers** in their gardens turn brown. **Pets** just lie in the shade. It is even too hot for **childrens** to play.

The writer spells some plural **nouns** incorrectly. The reader is confused: **"These words look wrong."**

**OK**

> The water pipe on our street is broken. It is hard for all the **families**. At my house, dirty **glasses** and **plates** sit by the kitchen sink. The stack must be two **feet** high! Dirty **socks** fill the laundry basket. We can't even take **baths**.

The writer spells plural **nouns** correctly. The nouns also add details. The reader thinks: **"I can really picture the writer's house."**

**Revise It** Look back at the NOT OK passage. Work with a partner to revise it. Change *plants*, *flowers*, and *pets* to precise nouns. Fix the incorrect plural forms.

**WRITE ON YOUR OWN** Imagine a time when you did not have enough water. Use nouns that will help your reader picture what you are saying. Pay attention to the spelling of plural forms.

**Spelling Rules**

**1.** To make most nouns plural, just add **-s**.

**street + -s = streets**

**2.** If the noun ends in *s*, *z*, *sh*, *ch*, or *x*, add **-es**.

**dish + -es = dishes**

**3.** If the noun ends in *y* after the consonant, change the *y* to *i* and add **-es**.

**stor~~y~~ⁱ + -es = stories**

**4.** Some nouns, such as *woman* (*women*), have special plural forms.

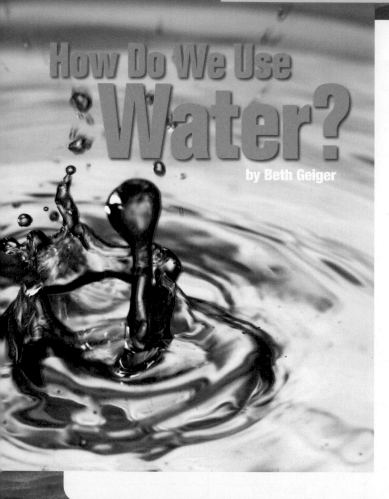

# How Do We Use Water?

by Beth Geiger

# Build Background

## Discuss How We Use Water

People use water every day. Look at each photo and talk about how many ways water was used in the scene.

**Digital Library**

myNGconnect.com
◆ View the images.

◀ Water covers much of Earth's surface.

## Connect

**Class Survey** Find out how your class used water today. Use a chart like this to record information. What do the results tell you about the importance of available water?

| Daily Uses of Water | Times in One Day | Total Uses |
|---|---|---|
| to drink | ⫽⫽⫽ ⫽⫽⫽ ⫽⫽⫽ | 15 |
| to prepare food | | |
| to wash hands or face | | |
| to brush teeth | | |

Survey Chart

## Give Information

Listen to the rap and the facts. Then repeat the lines of the rap after the rapper, and chime in with the facts.

**RAP and FACTS**

# Some Watery Facts

Earth is a watery planet.
Twenty-five percent is land.
The rest is oceans, ice, rivers, and lakes.
So learn to swim if you can.

Ocean water tastes salty.
Fresh water has salts in it, too,
But not enough to make you sick.
So that's a good thing for you.

Earth is a watery planet.
But there is no water to waste.
Only 3 percent of our water is fresh.
So don't use too much,
Unless you love the taste . . .

of salt.

**Fact 1:**
If the salt in the oceans could be spread out on land, it would cover all the continents. The salt would rise 500 feet!

**Fact 2:**
Seventy-five percent of Earth's fresh water is frozen. It makes the polar ice caps and all the world's glaciers.

**Fact 3:**
If you leave the water on when you brush your teeth, you use two gallons of water.

**Fact 4:**
A person can live without water for about one week.

OK, it's been a week!

# Use Complete Sentences

A complete sentence has a **subject** and a **predicate**.

All people drink water.

subject        predicate

To find the subject in a sentence, ask yourself: Whom or what is the sentence about? The sentence above is about people.

The **complete subject** includes all the words that tell about the subject. The most important word in the complete subject is usually a **noun**.

> EXAMPLE    **All people** drink water.
>                subject

The **complete predicate** often tells what the subject does. The **verb** shows the action.

> EXAMPLE    All people **drink water**.
>                        predicate

## Practice Together

Say each group of words. Add a subject with a noun, or add a predicate that tells what the subject does. Then say the complete sentence.

1. washes the dishes.
2. My sister
3. saves the dirty water in the sink.
4. My father
5. carries buckets of water to the garden.
6. Beautiful flowers

## Try It!

Read each group of words. Think about how to make a complete sentence. On a sheet of paper, write a subject with a noun, or write a predicate that tells what the subject does. Then say the complete sentence.

7. All animals
8. drink water.
9. live in water.
10. A bird
11. Bugs
12. wash pets in water.

▲ The elephants drink water.

# Make a Chant

## GIVE INFORMATION

What information about water can you give? Work with a group to write a chant with water facts.

Record facts about water. Use the water facts on page 87. Add other water facts. Make sure the information is correct.

> You can waste two gallons of water when you leave the water on while you brush your teeth.

Now choose some of the facts for your chant. Put fact sentences together. Use rhyming words, like *sea* and *me* or *fish* and *wish*.

Practice your chant. Then perform it for the other groups. After listening to other groups, tell each group what you learned from their chants.

Remember:

## HOW TO GIVE INFORMATION

1. When you give information, give facts about the topic.
2. Be sure the facts are correct.

> You brush your teeth. You leave the water on.

> Two gallons of water now are gone.

## USE COMPLETE SENTENCES

When you give information, speak in complete sentences. This will help you present the facts clearly. Remember, a complete sentence has a **subject** and a **predicate**.

EXAMPLE     **Earth** **has a lot of water.**

# Prepare to Read

## Learn Key Vocabulary

**Study the Words** Use the steps below.

1. Pronounce the word. Say it aloud several times. Spell it.
2. Rate your word knowledge.
3. Study the example.
4. Practice it. Make the word your own.

### Key Words

**alive** (u-līv) *adjective*
▶ page 96

Something that is living is **alive**. This girl looks happy to be **alive**.
*Antonym:* **dead**

**amount** (u-mount) *noun*
▶ page 94

An **amount** is the total number or quantity. What **amount** of wood is in this pile?
*Synonym:* **quantity**

**crop** (krop) *noun*
▶ page 96

**Crops** are plants that farmers grow. Corn, beans, and peaches are different **crops**.
*Synonym:* **produce**

**depend** (di-pend) *verb*
▶ page 98

When you **depend** on something, you need it. Babies **depend** on their parents for everything.
*Synonym:* **require**

**globe** (glōb) *noun*
▶ page 94

A **globe** is a model of Earth. The **globe** shows the shape of the land. The blue represents oceans.
*Synonym:* **world**

**material** (mu-tear-ē-ul) *noun* ▶ page 97

**Materials** are things you need to make a product or to do a project. Paint and brushes are **materials** you need for painting.
*Synonym:* **supplies**

**rainfall** (rān-fawl) *noun*
▶ page 96

**Rainfall** is the total rain, snow, or sleet that falls in a period of time. There has been a lot of **rainfall** this year.
*Synonym:* **rain**

**resource** (rē-sors) *noun*
▶ page 94

A **resource** is something that people need and use. Air, soil, and water are natural **resources**.

**Practice the Words** Work with a partner. Write four sentences. Use at least two Key Words in each sentence.

> The amount of rainfall this year will affect the crops.

# Analyze Main Idea and Details

**What's the Main Idea?** No matter what topic writers choose, they want you to get the **main idea**, or what they are mostly saying about the topic. How do you know if you are getting the main idea when you read the text? Sometimes writers tell you directly by including a main-idea statement in the text. Other sentences add details to **support** the main idea. As you read this passage, notice that the first sentence states the **main idea** .

### Reading Strategies

- Plan
- **Monitor:** Notice confusing parts in the text then reread or read on to make them clear.
- Make Connections
- Visualize
- Ask Questions
- Determine Importance
- Make Inferences
- Synthesize

**Look Into the Text**

People also use water as a resource to build things. They use water to mix concrete for floors and walls. They use water to make the paint that adds color to buildings.

People use water to make metal and glass, too. They need these materials to make most buildings.

## Practice Together

**Chart the Main Idea** Make a Main-Idea Chart to show how the main idea in the passage is connected to the details. Write the main idea in the top box. In the boxes below, write details that **support** the main idea. Reread the passage above and add to the Main-Idea Chart.

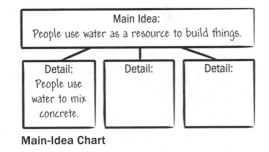

Main Idea:
People use water as a resource to build things.

| Detail: People use water to mix concrete. | Detail: | Detail: |

**Main-Idea Chart**

**Academic Vocabulary**

- **support** (su-**port**) *verb*
  When you **support** an idea, you give reasons or examples for it.

## Social Science Article

A social science article explains facts and ideas. In many social science articles, writers present one **main idea** at a time and add **details** to support it. **Photos** and **captions** illustrate and elaborate on ideas.

Look Into the Text

Farmers use fresh water to grow crops. Much of the fresh water in the United States is used for farming.

Many farms are in areas without much rainfall. Farmers irrigate to keep their crops alive. This means that they bring in water for their crops.

photo

◄ Farmers use fresh water to irrigate their crops.

caption

Clarifying vocabulary can help you better understand the main idea and details. Relate words and look for context clues to clarify vocabulary.

# How Do We Use Water?

by Beth Geiger

 Comprehension Coach

# All the World's Water

An incredible **amount** of water covers Earth. Look at a **globe**. The blue area **represents** the water. There are about 200 billion liters (53 billion gallons) of water for each person on Earth!

There is not always enough water to drink, however.

Most of Earth's water is salty ocean water. Salt water is fine for **sea creatures**. But it is not fine for humans and most other animals.

Only 3 percent of Earth's water is fresh water. Fresh water is an important **resource** that we need every day.

Water in the ocean is salt water.

Water in rivers, lakes, and streams is fresh water.

---

**Key Vocabulary**

**amount** *n.*, the total number, the quantity

**globe** *n.*, a model of Earth

**resource** *n.*, something found in nature and used by people

**In Other Words**

**represents** shows

**sea creatures** animals that live in the sea

# Water for Everyday Living

We need to drink fresh water to live. All day, we lose water from our bodies. We lose it when **we sweat** and when we **get rid of waste**. We drink water to **replace** the water we lose.

We use fresh water in other ways, too. Think about the water you use to wash dishes and to cook. You use water to brush your teeth. You also use water when you take a shower or bath.

People drink fresh water.

▲ Oceans cover most of Earth's surface.

**In Other Words**

**we sweat** our bodies work hard and give off water
**get rid of waste** use the toilet
**replace** put back

**Look Into the Text**

1. **Explain** Why is there not always enough water for people to drink?
2. **Details** What are some ways people use water every day? Cite three examples given in the article.

# Water for Farming

Farmers use fresh water to grow **crops**. Much of the fresh water in the United States is used for farming.

Many farms are in **areas without** much **rainfall**. Farmers irrigate to keep their crops **alive**. This means that they bring in water for their crops.

Farmers use fresh water to irrigate their crops.

Some crops, like cotton, need a lot of water.

**Key Vocabulary**

**crop** *n.*, plants that farmers grow

**rainfall** *n.*, the total rain that comes down

**alive** *adj.*, living, not dead

**In Other Words**

**areas without** places that do not have

# Water for Building

People also use water as a resource to build things. They use water to mix **concrete** for floors and walls. They use water to make the paint that adds color to buildings.

People use water to make metal and glass, too. They need these **materials** to make most buildings.

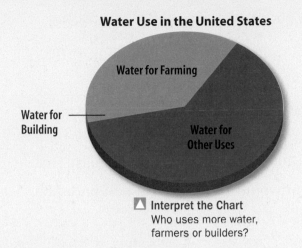

**Water Use in the United States**

Water for Farming

Water for Building

Water for Other Uses

△ **Interpret the Chart**
Who uses more water, farmers or builders?

People use water when they mix concrete.

---

**Key Vocabulary**
**material** *n.*, something that is needed to make a product

**In Other Words**
**concrete** a blend of sand, small rocks, and cement

**Look Into the Text**
1. **Cause and Effect** Why do farmers have to irrigate their **crops**?
2. **Main Idea and Details** How do people use water for building?

# It All Adds Up!

People **depend** on fresh water every day. They use it for drinking, for growing food, and for building.

People in the United States use a lot of fresh water. Each person uses about 378 liters (100 gallons) of water each day. That amount would fill two and a half bathtubs. That is a lot of water! ❖

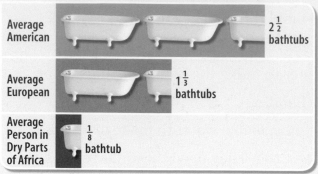

**Water Used by One Person Each Day**

| | | |
|---|---|---|
| Average American | | $2\frac{1}{2}$ bathtubs |
| Average European | | $1\frac{1}{3}$ bathtubs |
| Average Person in Dry Parts of Africa | | $\frac{1}{8}$ bathtub |

🔺 **Interpret the Graph** Who uses the most water each day? Who uses the least?

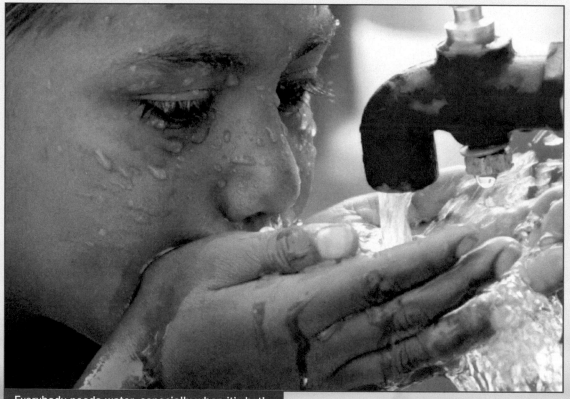

Everybody needs water, especially when it's hot! This boy drinks water on a hot summer day.

**Key Vocabulary**
**depend** v., to need, to require

**Look Into the Text**

1. **Evidence and Conclusion** What details show that Americans use a lot of water?
2. **Fact and Opinion** Facts can be proved. Opinions are people's ideas about something. Name one fact and one opinion on this page.

# Connect Reading and Writing

Vocabulary

alive

amount

crops

depend

globe

materials

rainfall

resource

## CRITICAL THINKING

1. **SUM IT UP** Use your Main-Idea Chart. Discuss ways we **depend** on water.

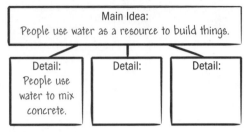

Main-Idea Chart

2. **Conclusion** Some farmers do not rely on **rainfall**. What other sources of water could they use to grow **crops**?

3. **Evaluate** We need water to stay **alive**. List the many uses of water in order of their importance. Explain the order.

4. **Infer** Look at the chart on page 98. Why do you think people in the United States use a greater **amount** of water than people in other parts of the world?

## READING FLUENCY

**Phrasing** Read the passage on page 562 to a partner. Assess your fluency.

1. I did not pause/sometimes paused/always paused for punctuation.

2. What I did best in my reading was _____.

## READING STRATEGY

What strategy helped you understand this selection? Tell a partner about it.

## VOCABULARY REVIEW

**Oral Review** Read the paragraph aloud. Add the vocabulary words.

A _____, or model of Earth, shows surface water. Some water, like _____, comes from clouds. Water is underground, too. We can reach this natural _____ with pipes made of sturdy _____. Some farmers live where there isn't enough rain to water their plants, or _____. They _____ on a large _____ of ground water. They irrigate to keep the plants _____.

**Written Review** Pick a photo in the article. Explain how people **depend** on water in that scene. Use four vocabulary words.

## WRITE ABOUT THE GUIDING QUESTION

**Explore Earth's Resources**
Reread the selection. How would your life change if you had a smaller **amount** of water to use? Support your ideas with examples from the text.

# Connect Across the Curriculum

## Vocabulary Study

## Use Synonyms

> **Academic Vocabulary**
> * **specific** (spi-**si**-fik) *adjective*
>   Something that is **specific** is detailed.

Synonyms are words that have almost the same meaning. Think about a word's connotative, or implied, meaning when selecting a synonym. The more **specific** a word is, the easier it is for readers to picture the meaning.

EXAMPLES  I <u>drink</u> the water.

I <u>gulp</u> the water. (Implies you are extremely thirsty.)

**Revise Sentences** Use a thesaurus to find a synonym for each underlined word. Then rewrite the paragraph below and using the synonyms. Discuss your sentences. How does the meaning change when the words are more **specific**?

The worker is <u>making</u> concrete. First, she <u>pours</u> the mix. Then she <u>gets</u> water. The dry mix <u>goes</u> everywhere! Making concrete can be <u>messy</u>.

## Research/Writing

## Research Water Use

**HEALTH & SCIENCE**

> **Academic Vocabulary**
> * **topic** (**tah**-pik) *noun*
>   A **topic** is the subject of a piece of writing or of a discussion.

How can people use less water at home? Research the **topic** of water use. Search for answers using library books or the Internet. Choose one way to save water to narrow your **topic** .

**Internet** <u>myNGconnect.com</u>
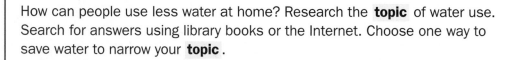 Find out what you can do to save water.

**Take Notes** Research your **topic** . Find statements from experts. Record the information you find and note where you find the information.

**Write a Paragraph** Write how people can use less water. Then support your main idea with details you found. Remember to put quotation marks around exact statements. Write who you quoted. Discuss your ideas with a group.

**Present Your Ideas** Read your paragraph to a group. Then listen to other people's ideas about water use.

## Give Information

**Share Information** Tell a classmate three ways people in your community use water. Use action verbs. Then listen as your classmate names three ways. Use complete sentences to report the information to the class.

> Big trucks clean the streets with water.

## Write About Water

**Study the Models** When you share what you know about a topic like water, it is important to express your thoughts completely. If you leave out the subject or the predicate in a sentence, the reader will get confused.

**NOT OK**

The biggest ocean on Earth. The Pacific Ocean covers more space than all the land on Earth. Has the deepest areas on Earth. Has powerful storms, too. You would not guess this because the word pacific means "peaceful."

> The writer leaves out important parts of sentences. The reader is confused: "The thoughts are not complete."

**OK**

The biggest ocean on Earth **is the Pacific**. The Pacific Ocean covers more space than all the land on Earth. **It** has the deepest areas on Earth. **The Pacific** has powerful storms, too. You would not guess this because the word pacific means "peaceful."

> The writer adds a missing **predicate** and two missing **subjects**. Now the writer's sentences are complete.

**Revise It** Read the passage below. Work with a partner to revise it. Add one subject and one predicate.

Water covers nearly three-fourths of the surface of Earth. A tiny amount of this water is fresh water. All the rest of the water. Earth's salt water is divided into five oceans. Are the Atlantic, Pacific, Indian, Arctic, and Southern Oceans.

**WRITE ON YOUR OWN** Choose an ocean, river, lake, or stream you know about. Write a paragraph about it. Make sure every sentence expresses a complete thought.

**REMEMBER**

A complete sentence has a <u>subject</u> and a <u>predicate</u>.

<u>The lake</u> <u>is huge</u>.

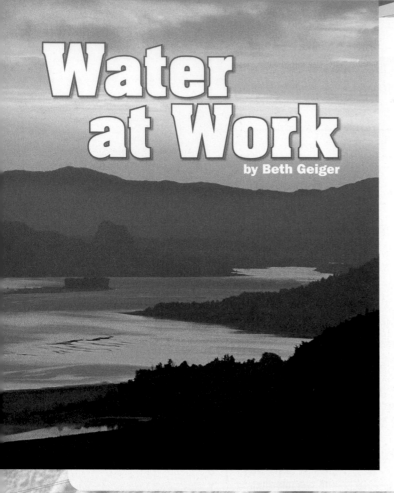

# Water at Work

### by Beth Geiger

# Build Background

## See How We Use Water

People can use a body of water such as a lake or river in numerous ways. They use it to move things, to make things, and just to play in.

**Digital Library**

myNGconnect.com
◉ View the video.

◀ Some people love to sail on the water.

## Connect

**KWL Chart** Think about what you know about how people depend on rivers. Write your ideas in column 1 of a KWL Chart. In column 2, write what you want to know. Use column 3 to list what you learned after you read the article.

| WHAT I KNOW | WHAT I WANT TO KNOW | WHAT I LEARNED |
|---|---|---|
| Some rivers have dams. | What do the dams do? | |

KWL Chart

# Language & Grammar

## Elaborate

When you elaborate on a topic, you tell more details and give examples about it. Look at the photo and listen as one person tells about it. Then listen to the other people elaborate.

**PICTURE PROMPT**

1 TRY OUT LANGUAGE
2 LEARN GRAMMAR
3 APPLY ON YOUR OWN

# Make Subjects and Verbs Agree

A **verb** must always agree with its **subject**. Study the forms of the verbs *be*, *have*, and *do*. Use the form of the verb that matches the subject.

| Subject | Forms of *Be* | Forms of *Have* | Forms of *Do* |
| --- | --- | --- | --- |
| I | am | have | do |
| he, she, it | is | has | does |
| we, you, they | are | have | do |

The **subject** of a sentence usually comes before the **verb**.

EXAMPLE    **We are** at the river.
**The river has** a dam.

## Practice Together

Say each sentence. Choose the correct form of the verb.

1. We (am/are) at the lake.
2. The lake (have/has) pine trees around it.
3. It (am/is) really pretty.
4. We (do/does) many things.
5. My friends (have/has) fishing poles.
6. I (have/has) a ball.
7. Our picnic lunch (is/are) great, too.

## Try It!

Say each sentence. Write the correct form of the verb on a card. Then hold up the card as you say the sentence.

8. My cousins (have/has) exciting jobs.
9. They (am/are) tour guides on white-water rafting trips.
10. They (do/does) this every summer.
11. The river (have/has) wild waves and many turns.
12. I (am/is) amazed at what they do!

▲ **The people have fun on the river.**

# Describe a Photo

## ELABORATE

When you elaborate on something, you tell more about it. Work with a partner to elaborate about a photo of a river.

Find an interesting photo of a river. Look in magazines, books, and on the Internet. Think about the main idea you want to share about the photo. Then use an Idea Web to collect ideas about it.

**Idea Web**

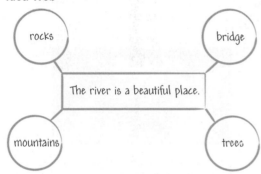

rocks

bridge

The river is a beautiful place.

mountains

trees

Show your photo to a group. One partner tells about the photo. The other elaborates, or tells more about it. Keep going until you have no more to say about the photo. Remember:

## HOW TO ELABORATE

1. Think about the main idea of your discussion.
2. Add details.
3. Tell more. Add examples.

*The river is a beautiful place.*

*The water is still and clear. Trees grow around the water.*

## MAKE SUBJECTS AND VERBS AGREE

When you elaborate, be sure to use the correct forms of *be*, *have*, and *do*. Also be sure to say the **subject** before the **verb**.

EXAMPLES  **The river has** a bridge.
**The trees are** tall.
**We do** sports in all seasons at the river.

▲ The river has a bridge.

# Prepare to Read

## Learn Key Vocabulary

**Study the Words** Use the steps below.

1. Pronounce the word. Say it aloud several times. Spell it.
2. Rate your word knowledge.
3. Study the example. Tell more about the word.
4. Practice it. Make the word your own.

### Key Words

**arrive** (u-rīv) *verb*
▶ page 113

To **arrive** means to reach a place. A plane **arrives** at an airport.
*Synonym:* **enter**
*Antonym:* **leave**

**electricity**
(i-lek-**tri**-su-tē) *noun* ▶ page 112

**Electricity** is a form of energy. Lamps and computers use **electricity** to work.

**flow** (flō) *verb*
▶ page 113

To **flow** means to move freely. A river **flows** without stopping.
*Synonyms:* **go, move**
*Antonym:* **stop**

**generate** (je-nu-rāt) *verb*
▶ page 112

To **generate** means to make something. Windmills **generate** energy that people can use.
*Synonyms:* **make, produce**

**goods** (goodz) *noun*
▶ page 114

**Goods** are things that people buy and sell. Stores sell **goods**. For this meaning, **goods** is always plural.

**power** (pow-ur) *noun*
▶ page 112

**Power** is energy that makes things work. A dam collects water to use as a source of **power**.
*Synonym:* **force**

**safely** (sāf-lē) *adverb*
▶ page 111

To do something **safely** is to do it without danger. The girl is working **safely** because her eyes are protected from the chemicals.
*Antonym:* **dangerously**

**treat** (trēt) *verb*
▶ page 111

When you **treat** something, you change it. You can **treat** a dirty shirt with soap to get stains off.

**Practice the Words** Work with a partner. Make an Expanded Meaning Map for each Key Word.

**What the Word Means**
a form of energy

**Example**
A radio uses electricity.

**Word**
electricity

**What It Is Like**
powerful

**Expanded Meaning Map**

# Analyze Main Idea and Details

**How Is Writing Organized?** The text in an article usually is organized into sections. All of the sections provide details for the whole article. Together, they **support** the main idea of the article.

The topic of the article "Water at Work" is the Columbia River. What is the writer mostly telling you about the river? She introduces the **main idea** directly.

### Reading Strategies

- Plan
- **Monitor:** Notice confusing parts in the text then reread or read on to make them clear.
- Make Connections
- Visualize
- Ask Questions
- Determine Importance
- Make Inferences
- Synthesize

**Look Into the Text**

The Columbia River runs through the states of Oregon and Washington. Millions of people depend on its water. How do they use it?

At 5 a.m. it is still dark outside. But Kevin Aiken has been awake for an hour. Kevin is a farmer. He grows cherries near Wenatchee, Washington. In the orchard, Kevin stops at an irrigation pipe. He turns a big wheel on the pipe. Water spouts from sprinklers under the cherry trees.

This area does not have enough rainfall to grow fruit trees. Instead, Kevin uses water from the Columbia River to water the trees. Pumps move the river water to the cherry trees.

## Practice Together

**Begin a Main-Idea Diagram** A Main-Idea Diagram is used to show how the sections **support** the main idea of the article. This diagram shows the main idea from the passage above. Reread the passage. Look for information that illustrates or elaborates the main idea. Then add the detail to the diagram.

Main Idea: Millions of people depend on water from the Columbia River.

Detail:

**Main-Idea Diagram**

**Academic Vocabulary**

- **support** (su-**port**) *verb*
  When you **support** an idea, you give reasons or examples for it.

## Social Science Article

Social science articles are nonfiction. They give information about special topics, such as geography, history, and transportation.

Nonfiction writers often use **unfamiliar words** when explaining **specific information** to readers learning about a new topic. **Headings** in nonfiction signal the main idea the writer is telling about in that section.

Look Into the Text

### Making Boxes and Bags

heading

Down the river, the water arrives at the Longview paper plant. Alan Whitford watches as recycled paper falls into huge tanks. The recycled paper is mixed with water from the river. Machines turn this mixture into paper boxes and bags.

As you read, clarify vocabulary to understand the main idea of the text.

# Water at Work

## by Beth Geiger

The Columbia River runs through the states of Oregon and Washington. Millions of people depend on its water. How do they use it?

Columbia River

# Growing Cherries

At **5 a.m.** it is still dark outside. But Kevin Aiken has been awake for an hour. Kevin is a farmer. He grows cherries near Wenatchee, Washington. In the **orchard**, Kevin stops at **an irrigation pipe**. He turns a big wheel on the pipe. Water **spouts from sprinklers** under the cherry trees.

This area does not have enough rainfall to grow fruit trees. Instead, Kevin uses water from the Columbia River to water the trees. Pumps move the river water to the cherry trees.

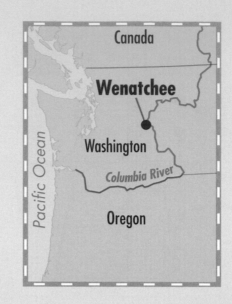

▼ Water from the Columbia River is used to grow cherry trees.

**In Other Words**
**5 a.m.** 5 o'clock in the morning
**orchard** field of fruit trees
**an irrigation pipe** a pipe that carries water to his trees
**spouts from sprinklers** sprays from tiny holes in the pipe

# Cleaning the Water

Farther down the Columbia River is the city of Pasco, Washington. Roberto López plays basketball at his school there. Roberto stops for a drink of water. The water in the water fountain comes from the Columbia River.

Before the water reaches Roberto's school, though, it has to be cleaned. People cannot **safely** drink water **directly from** rivers. The water is **treated** at a **water treatment plant** first.

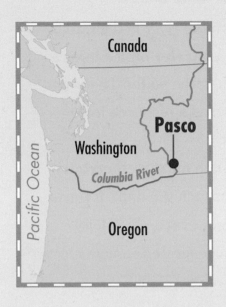

Water is cleaned in a water treatment plant. ▼

**Look Into the Text**

1. **Main Idea and Details** Why does Kevin Aiken use river water to grow cherry trees?

2. **Cause and Effect** Why does water need to be treated?

# Making Power

Farther down the river is the Dalles Dam. A dam is a **barrier** built across a river. It holds back the water. The water can then be used as a resource for different things.

The Dalles Dam makes **electricity**. Water rushes through the dam. It turns machines that **generate** electricity. The Dalles Dam generates enough electric **power** for two cities.

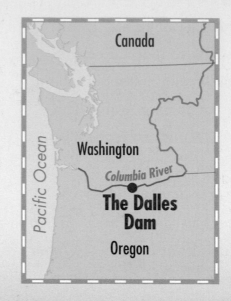

▼ The Dalles Dam makes electricity.

**Key Vocabulary**
**electricity** *n.*, a form of energy
**generate** *v.*, to make
**power** *n.*, energy that makes things work

**In Other Words**
**barrier** big wall

# Making Boxes and Bags

Down the river, the water **arrives** at the Longview **paper plant**. Alan Whitford watches as **recycled** paper falls into huge tanks. The recycled paper is mixed with water from the river. Machines **turn this mixture** into paper boxes and bags. Then most of the water from the plant **flows** back into the Columbia River.

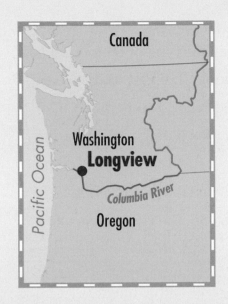

▲ This paper plant makes big rolls of paper. Then they use the paper to make boxes and bags.

**Key Vocabulary**
**arrive** v., to reach a place
**flow** v., to move freely

**In Other Words**
**paper plant** place that makes paper
**recycled** used
**turn this mixture** change the mix of paper and water

**Look Into the Text**

1. **Explain** How do dams use water to **generate electricity**?
2. **Steps In a Process** How are boxes and bags made from recycled paper? Tell the steps in order.

# Carrying Goods

Boats carry people and things along the Columbia River. One type of boat is called a barge. It is a long, flat boat. Barges carry wheat, **fuel**, and other **goods**. They take their goods to cities like Astoria, Oregon.

The Columbia River empties into the Pacific Ocean near Astoria. From its beginning to its end, the river helps many people in many ways. ❖

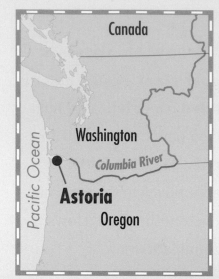

▲ This barge moves goods.

**Look Into the Text**

**Key Vocabulary**

**goods** *n.*, things that people buy and sell

**In Other Words**

**fuel** coal or tanks of gas

1. **Details** Describe where Astoria is along the Columbia River.
2. **Viewing** Look at the picture. Why do people use barges to move **goods**?

# Connect Reading and Writing

Vocabulary
arrives
electricity
flow
generate
goods
power
safely
treated

## CRITICAL THINKING

1. **SUM IT UP** Use your Main-Idea Diagram to explain the main idea and details from "Water at Work" and summarize the selection to a partner.

> Main Idea: Millions of people depend on water from the Columbia River.
>
> > Detail:

**Main-Idea Diagram**

2. **Infer** Dams make **electricity**, but they also create barriers. How can dams affect, or change, the lives of river wildlife?

3. **Predict** Millions of people use the Columbia River. What could happen if there is not enough water and the river stops **flowing**?

4. **Synthesize** Businesses depend on the Columbia River. They also depend on each other for **goods** and services. Give two examples of how.

## READING FLUENCY

**Intonation** Read the passage on page 563 to a partner. Assess your fluency.

1. My tone never/sometimes/always matched what I read.

2. What I did best in my reading was _____.

## READING STRATEGY

> What strategy helped you understand this selection? Tell a partner about it.

## VOCABULARY REVIEW

**Oral Review** Read the paragraph aloud. Add the vocabulary words.

> Rivers that _____ through a dam have force and _____. The force is used to _____, or create, _____. With power, towns light up and factories produce _____. With the help of pumps, water _____ at your home. Dirty water from sinks, tubs, and washing machines travels back out through pipes to plants where it is _____. After this process, water can be returned _____ to the environment.

**Written Review** Imagine that you **arrive** in one of the places in the selection. Write a paragraph about what you see and hear. Use four vocabulary words.

 **WRITE ABOUT THE** GUIDING QUESTION

### Explore Earth's Resources

Why do cities and towns often develop near rivers? Explain why people settle where a river **flows**. Include facts from the articles "How Do We Use Water?" and "Water at Work" as you write your paragraph.

# Connect Across the Curriculum

## Use Synonyms and Antonyms

**Academic Vocabulary**

• **relate** (ri-lāt) *verb*
  When you **relate** two things, you think about how they are connected.

Synonyms are words that have about the same meaning. Antonyms are words that have opposite meanings. You can use a scale to show how words **relate** to each other. Compare the words on each scale. Look at the order.

sprint

run

jog

**Synonym Scale**

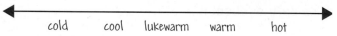

cold    cool    lukewarm    warm    hot

**Antonym Scale**

**Make a Scale** Make a scale for the antonyms *huge* and *tiny*. Think of other words that **relate**. Use a thesaurus for ideas. Write them in order on the scale.

**HEALTH & SCIENCE**

## Discuss Hydroelectric Power

**Academic Vocabulary**

• **resource** (rē-sors) *noun*
  A **resource** is something that people need and use.

We use different natural **resources** to produce electricity. Work with a partner to research hydroelectric power.

❶ **Gather Facts** Use different sources for your research. Take notes. Record your sources' claims and any reasons and evidence they give.

> **Internet** myNGconnect.com
> 🔄 Learn how hydroelectric power plants work.
> 🔄 Read about the costs to the environment.

❷ **Organize the Facts** Make a Comparison Chart to compare sources.

❸ **Make a Decision** Put the facts together and decide your position. Should we produce more hydroelectric power or use other **resources** instead? What reasons and evidence support your argument?

❹ **State Your Position** Tell your argument and claims. Explain your reasons and evidence. Listen to other people's ideas and reasons.

## Elaborate

**Pair Talk** Say one fact about how people use rivers. Your partner then gives more information about that fact. Then you tell something more. Keep going until you cannot elaborate anymore. Use precise action verbs as you elaborate. Then switch roles to tell a new fact.

> Farmers use river water.

> They irrigate the farm with the water.

## Write About a Day at a River

**Study the Models** When you write about things that happen, you use action verbs. Precise and interesting action verbs help bring your writing to life. They help readers get a clear picture of actions and events. Each verb must agree with the subject of the sentence.

**NOT OK**

Mr. Roja has a barge business on the Mississippi River. His barge **carry** passengers on trips down the river. The big barge **moves** down the Mississippi like a long, low box. It **passes** under bridges. It **travel** past towns. Passengers **walk** around the decks.

Some of the writer's **action verbs** are not precise. Other action verbs don't agree with their subjects.

**OK**

Mr. Roja has a barge business on the Mississippi River. His barge **carries** passengers on trips down the river. The big barge **floats** down the Mississippi like a long, low box. It **drifts** under bridges. It **travels** past towns. Passengers **stroll** around the decks.

The writer uses precise **action verbs**. All the verbs agree with their subjects.

**Add Sentences** Think of two sentences to add to the OK model above. Tell what one passenger does. Use precise action verbs. Be sure the verbs agree with their subjects.

**WRITE ON YOUR OWN** Imagine people spending the day at a river. Tell what happens. Be sure to use precise, interesting action verbs. Make sure each verb agrees with the subject of the sentence.

**REMEMBER**
- Add **-s** to the end of an action verb that tells what one other person or thing does.
  The barge float**s**.
- Do not add **-s** to an action verb when the subject names more than one.
  The barges float.

# Irrigation Pumps

April 18, 2012
by Sandra Postel

## CAN SAVE POOR FARMERS

1   One of the more useful tools ever developed for the world's poor farmers is a device called a treadle pump.

2   The treadle pump looks and operates much like an exercise machine that you'd find in a gym. But the farmers who use these devices are not trying to lose pounds; they're trying to gain them.

3   More than 850 million people in the world today are hungry most of the time. Oddly enough, many of these people live on farms. These farm families go hungry because they do not have the resources to make their land produce enough food to meet their needs.

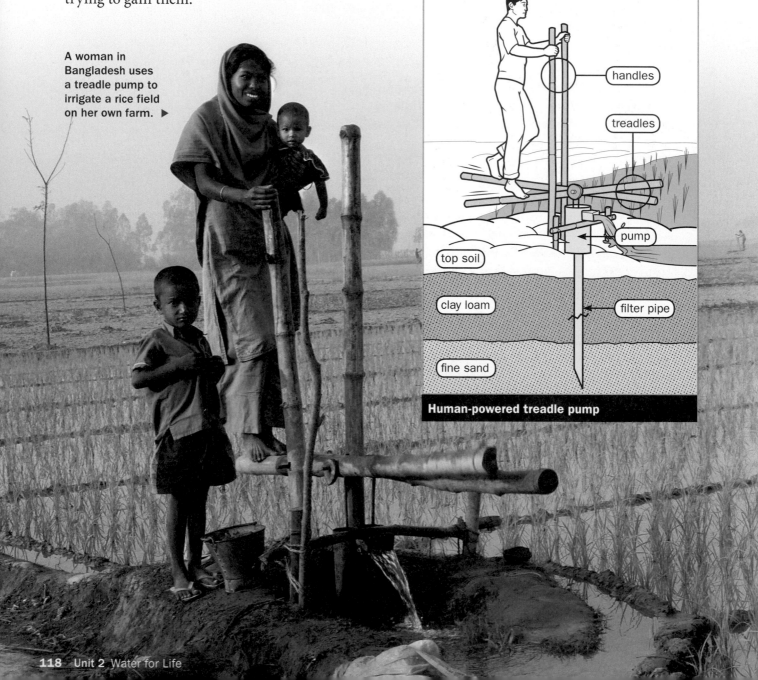

A woman in Bangladesh uses a treadle pump to irrigate a rice field on her own farm. ▶

handles

treadles

pump

top soil

clay loam

filter pipe

fine sand

**Human-powered treadle pump**

4　For many of them, the missing resource is water. And that's where the treadle pump **comes in.**

5　Traveling through Bangladesh some years ago, I saw vast areas of brown, **barren** land. It was January, which is the dry season in this country. The **amount** of **rainfall** is not enough for farmers to grow **crops**. Without access to irrigation water, small farmers leave their land unplanted, which in turn leaves them hungry and poor.

6　But northeast of Dhaka, the fields were green and filled with activity. Men and women, children and parents, were operating treadle pumps.

7　The operator of the treadle pump pedals up and down on two poles called treadles. This action sucks water up through a shallow well. The water then **flows** into an irrigation ditch that travels into the fields to water crops.

8　For a total investment of about $35, Bangladeshi farmers can irrigate half an acre (about 1.5 school gymnasiums) during the dry season. They can grow enough to support their families. They can also sell food at the market. The technology of a treadle pump is relatively simple and it does not cost very much money, making it "radically affordable" compared to other irrigation technologies.

9　Many small farms are owned by women.

> ～～～～～
> **"The treadle pump can radically change the lives of women . . ."**
> ～～～～～

So the treadle pump can radically change the lives of women by providing an opportunity for them to run their small farms. To help poor women buy their own pumps, a nonprofit organization called KickStart established a Mobile Layaway program. This program allows women farmers to pay for a pump by sending small payments through their mobile phones. Paying a little bit at a time, many women are able to pay for a pump within ten weeks.

10　In March, 2012 U.S. Secretary of State Hillary Clinton presented KickStart with the first-ever Innovation Award for the Empowerment of Women and Girls. Secretary Clinton said, "If you just stop and think that 60 to 70 percent of the small-holder farmers in the world are women, this [project] has **enormous potential.**"

11　People who use treadle pumps don't have to do the hard work of treadling forever. As they **move up the income ladder**, they can turn to a labor-saving irrigation system, perhaps powered by diesel or solar energy. With extra time, women may start a business. Girls will attend school. Unleashed from poverty and hunger, the entrepreneurial spirit will soar.

12　The power of a water pump—designed for its "radical affordability"—should not be underestimated.

---

**Key Vocabulary**
- **amount** *n.*, the total number, the quantity
- **rainfall** *n.*, the total rain that comes down
- **crops** *n.*, plants that farmers grow
- **flow** *v.*, to move freely

**In Other Words**
**comes in** is important
**barren** empty
**enormous potential** many possibilities
**move up the income ladder** make more money

# Compare Across Texts

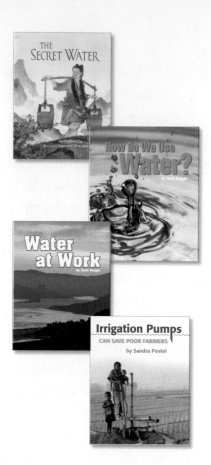

## Compare Ideas

"The Secret Water," "How Do We Use Water?," "Water at Work," and "Irrigation Pumps Can Save Poor Farmers" tell about the importance of water as a **resource**. **Compare** the ideas in these texts.

## How It Works

**Collect and Organize Ideas** Use a chart to organize what you know.

|  | The Secret Water | How Do We Use Water? | Water at Work | Irrigation Pumps Can Save Poor Farmers |
|---|---|---|---|---|
| Fiction | ✓ |  |  |  |
| Nonfiction |  | ✓ | ✓ | ✓ |
| Why Water Is Important: |  |  |  |  |

**Comparison Chart**

## Practice Together

**Analyze Events and Ideas** This comparison paragraph tells how two types of text express ideas about water.

> "The Secret Water" is fiction. "How Do We Use Water?," "Water at Work," and "Irrigation Pumps Can Save Poor Farmers" are nonfiction. "The Secret Water" uses imaginary characters and events to express ideas about water. The other three texts give facts about water.

## Try It!

Complete the chart to tell what each text says about the importance of water as a natural **resource**. Write a paragraph that **compares** the ideas across the texts. You may want to use this frame to help you write your paragraph.

"The Secret Water," "How Do We Use Water?," "Water at Work," and "Irrigation Pumps Can Save Poor Farmers" tell why people need water. In "The Secret Water," water is important because _____. "How Do We Use Water?" gives facts about _____. "Water at Work" explains how people in Oregon and Washington _____. "Irrigation Pumps Can Save Poor Farmers" explains how water helps _____.

**Academic Vocabulary**

- **resource** (rē-sors) *noun*
  A **resource** is something that people need and use.
- **compare** (kum-**pair**) *verb*
  When you **compare** two things, you think about how they are alike and different.

# WATER
## FOR LIFE

**How do we depend on Earth's resources?**

---

**Content Library**

**Leveled Library**

---

# Reflect on Your Reading

Think back on your reading of the unit selections. Discuss what you did to understand what you read.

**Focus on Reading** **Analyze Events and Ideas**

In this unit, you learned how to analyze events and ideas in fiction and nonfiction. Make a T Chart to compare "The Secret Water" with one of the other selections. List the event or topic and the supporting details of each selection. Use your chart to explain the texts to a partner.

**Focus Strategy** **Monitor**

As you read the selections, you learned to clarify ideas and vocabulary. Explain to a partner how you will use the strategy in the future.

# Explore the

Throughout this unit, you have been thinking about Earth's resources. Choose one of these ways to explore the Guiding Question:

- **Discuss** With a group, discuss the Guiding Question. Remember, there can be many answers. Give details from the selections that support your idea.

- **Report** With the class, brainstorm a list of Earth's resources. Write each resource on a slip of paper, and put the papers in a container. Then form groups. Each group draws a paper. The group researches and reports to the class about how people depend on that resource.

- **Write** Make a brochure that tells how to save Earth's resources.

# Book Talk

Which Unit Library book did you choose? Explain to a partner what it taught you about Earth's resources.

# NATURAL
# FORCES

# 3

# How should people deal with the forces of nature?

**READ MORE!**

**Content Library**
Introduction to Energy
by Glen Phelan

**Leveled Library**
Hercules
by Paul Storrie and Steve Kurth
Tornado
by Betsy Byars
Bearstone
by Will Hobbs

**Web Links**
myNGconnect.com

◀ As the Eyjafjallajökull volcano erupts in Iceland,
lightning crackles in its ash cloud.

# Focus on Reading

## Determine Viewpoints

A viewpoint is what a person thinks. Authors, narrators, and characters have viewpoints. Dialogue, quotes, word choice, and other details can tell you the author's or characters' viewpoint.

## How It Works

In **narrative** fiction, you can determine a narrator's or characters' viewpoint.

### A Dark Storm

At eight o'clock in the morning, it was already hot and dry. Uncle Roy walked into the kitchen. He had gone to work in the field just a few minutes before, so Aunt Doris was surprised to see him.

"What's wrong?" she asked.

"There's a storm coming," he replied. "But it's not like any storm I have ever seen."

The sky got darker and darker. They could hear the wind. It wasn't rain that was blowing, though. It was dust.

> **Characters' dialogue and thoughts can help readers determine viewpoint.**

In **narrative** nonfiction, you can determine an author's viewpoint. Authors will convey what they think through **phrases** like "I thought" or "I feel." You can also determine author's viewpoint through words, actions, or other details.

### The First Dust Storm

We were living in Oklahoma. I remember the first dust storm. We were walking home probably three or four miles and this huge, huge black cloud came. I thought it was going to be a thunderstorm or a rainstorm, but it was only dust. And it just blotted out the sun. It was just like night. People had to use their car lights. The town lights went on. Afterwards, dust piled up two feet high in front of the door. It went through windows and every place.

> **The author uses the phrase "I thought." This phrase conveys the author's viewpoint of the dust storm.**

**Academic Vocabulary**
- **narrative** (nair-u-tiv) *adjective*
  **Narrative** writing tells a story.

## Practice Together

Read the following text aloud. As you read, determine the character's viewpoint. Look at the character's dialogue, thoughts, and other details.

### An Oklahoma Farm

It was 1933. Karen was living on a tiny farm in Oklahoma. The first few years on the farm were wonderful, but this year was hard.

There had been no rain all year, and the winds blew the dusty ground. The dust came in through the cracks of the house.

Karen wiped her finger along the table in the living room. It left a clear line in the layer of dust. She sighed and looked out at the dry fields around the house.

Karen unfolded the bedsheet she was holding. She climbed onto a chair and carefully pinned the sheet over the big front window.

"Maybe this will keep out some of the dust," she said aloud.

## Try It!

Read aloud the following text about Ida Rockwell who lived in Kansas in the 1930s. Determine the author's viewpoint. What is conveyed through words, thoughts, and actions?

### Leaving Home

It seems like the entire state of Kansas is covered in dust. There is no rain. Not one stick of corn will grow, and without corn, we can't make money.

We had to leave. Albert sold the tractor. We said good-bye to our friends. Everything we own is in our little car, and we are on our way West. We hear there is no dust out there.

Around noon, we ran out of gas. We were just outside of Augusta. Albert walked into town, bought the gas, came back, and we went on.

Then, before we had gone a mile, a tire went flat. The man from the garage helped us again. This time when Albert asked for the bill, the man just said, "Best of luck on your journey, folks."

That turned our day around. The car acted great, and we were in great spirits. We found a wonderful campground where we'll sleep well tonight. And I'll dream of rain.

# Focus on Vocabulary

## Use Word Parts

Some English words are made up of meaningful parts, including **base words** and **suffixes**. A base word makes sense alone, with no other parts attached to it. A suffix is a word part that comes at the end of a word. It changes the meaning of a word or how the word is used.

Sometimes you can put two or more smaller words together to form a **compound word**.

**EXAMPLES**

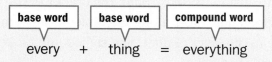

The suffix *-ly* means "in a certain way."

| base word | suffix |
| --- | --- |

slow   +   -ly   = slowly

*Slowly* means "in a way that is slow."

*Everything* is a compound word.

| base word | base word | compound word |
| --- | --- | --- |

every   +   thing   =   everything

*Everything* means "all things that exist."

## How the Strategy Works

When you read, you may come to a word that you don't know. Look for word part clues to help you **define** the word.

1. Look at words nearby for clues to the word's meaning.
2. Break down the word into meaningful parts.
3. Think about the meaning of each part.
4. Put the meanings together to **define** the whole word.
5. See if the meaning makes sense.

Follow the strategy to **define** each underlined word.

It rained all night, from <u>sunset</u> until <u>sunrise</u>. What a <u>downpour</u> it was! The streets <u>quickly</u> became flooded. When the <u>rainstorm</u> <u>finally</u> ended, we went <u>outside</u>. What a mess! There was water and mud <u>everywhere</u>.

### Strategy in Action

" I see meaningful parts in *sunset*. The *sun* is an object in the sky. *Set* means 'to go down.' A *sunset* is when the sun seems to go down. That meaning makes sense."

☑ **REMEMBER** Sometimes you can use word part clues to figure out the meaning of a whole word.

**Academic Vocabulary**
• **define** (di-fīn) *verb*
  When you **define** something, you tell what it means.

## Practice Together

Read this passage aloud. Figure out the meaning of each underlined word. Look for the word parts. Put their meanings together and **define** the underlined word.

| Suffix | Meaning | Example |
|--------|---------|---------|
| -ful | full of | hopeful |
| -ive | having qualities of | creative |
| -ly | in a certain way | quietly |
| -ment | action or process | payment |

## The Flood of 1993

When there is too much <u>rainfall</u>, rivers can <u>overflow</u>. Towns can get flooded. People who live near rivers may grow <u>fearful</u> when it rains for a long time.

A terrible flood happened in 1993. The Mississippi and Missouri Rivers both spilled over. About 50 people died.

Thousands more had to leave their homes. <u>Wildlife</u> suffered, too.

After days of rain, dirty water <u>quickly</u> covered roads and homes. Many <u>hardwood</u> trees fell down. Birds, turtles, and fish suffered, too. It was a difficult time for <u>everyone</u> in the Midwest.

## Try It!

Read this passage aloud. What is the meaning of each underlined word? How do you know?

## Storm Safety

If you prepare <u>properly</u>, you can survive a bad storm. Make a plan with your family. Have a radio, a <u>flashlight</u>, water, and a snack ready in a <u>backpack</u>. Go to your family's safe place. Stay there until an <u>announcement</u> tells you that you can <u>safely</u> leave. When you leave your safe place, be <u>careful</u> of <u>active</u> power lines and trees that are down.

Power lines that come down during a storm can be dangerous.

SCIENCE ARTICLE

# Volcano!

by Beth Geiger

# Build Background

## View Volcanoes

Volcanoes are powerful forces that begin deep inside the Earth. They create mountains and islands. They can also destroy life.

**Digital Library**

**myNGconnect.com**
▶ View the video.

▲ A huge crater was left after the volcano Mount St. Helens erupted.

## Connect

**Classify Senses** Imagine that you are near a volcano by the ocean. Lava is flowing into the water. What do you see, hear, and feel? How does the air smell? Write your ideas in a chart.

| I see . . . | I hear . . . |
|---|---|
| thick red rivers of lava | crackling lava |

| I feel . . . | I smell . . . |
|---|---|
| | |

Classification Chart

# Language & Grammar

## Engage in Conversation

Look at the picture as you listen to the conversation.
Then practice the conversation with a partner.

**CONVERSATION**

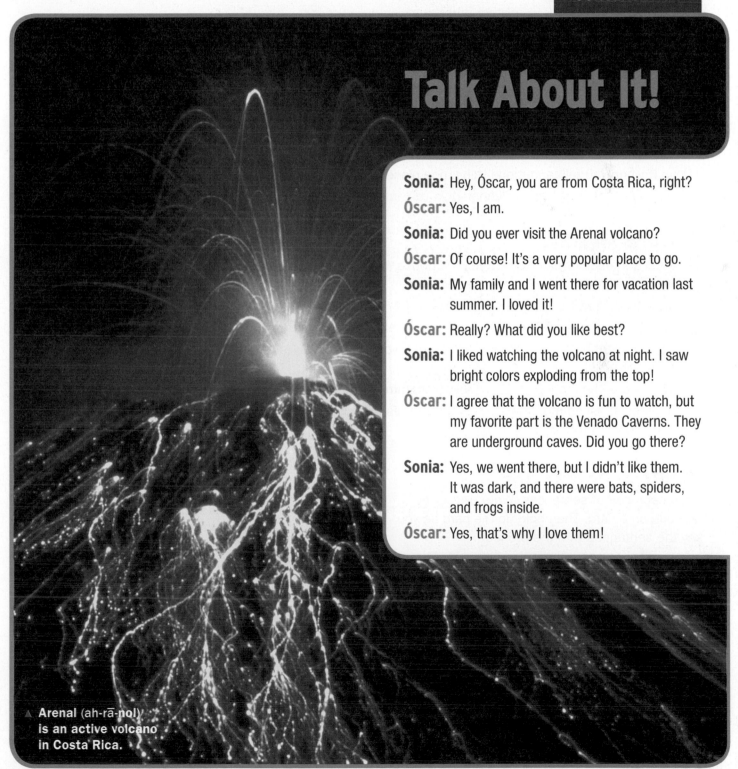

# Talk About It!

**Sonia:** Hey, Óscar, you are from Costa Rica, right?

**Óscar:** Yes, I am.

**Sonia:** Did you ever visit the Arenal volcano?

**Óscar:** Of course! It's a very popular place to go.

**Sonia:** My family and I went there for vacation last summer. I loved it!

**Óscar:** Really? What did you like best?

**Sonia:** I liked watching the volcano at night. I saw bright colors exploding from the top!

**Óscar:** I agree that the volcano is fun to watch, but my favorite part is the Venado Caverns. They are underground caves. Did you go there?

**Sonia:** Yes, we went there, but I didn't like them. It was dark, and there were bats, spiders, and frogs inside.

**Óscar:** Yes, that's why I love them!

▲ **Arenal** (ah-rā-nol) is an active volcano in Costa Rica.

# Use Subject Pronouns

Use a **subject pronoun** as the subject of a sentence.

- Use **I** when you talk about yourself.

    EXAMPLE    **I** visited a volcano.

- Use **you** when you talk to another person.

    EXAMPLE    **You** visited a volcano, too.

- Use **he** when you talk about one man or one boy.

    EXAMPLE    Juan has a camera. **He** takes photos of volcanoes.

- Use **she** when you talk about one woman or one girl.

    EXAMPLE    My aunt is a scientist. **She** studies volcanoes.

- Use **it** when you talk about one thing, one place, or one idea.

    EXAMPLE    Kilauea is a volcano. **It** is very interesting.

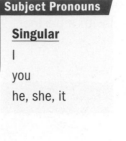

| Subject Pronouns |
| --- |
| **Singular** |
| I |
| you |
| he, she, it |

## Practice Together

Say each sentence or pair of sentences. Choose the correct pronoun from the chart above.

1. _____ am studying volcanoes in school.
2. My science teacher is Mr. Lin. _____ makes the subject exciting.
3. My sister helped me make a model of a volcano. _____ is a good artist.
4. Here is the model. _____ took a long time to make!
5. Mr. Lin asked me, "Do _____ want to display your model at the science fair?"

## Try It!

Read each pair of sentences. Write the correct pronoun on a card. Then hold up the card as you say the sentences with the pronoun.

6. My mother visited Pompeii. _____ liked it very much.
7. Pompeii is an ancient city. _____ was destroyed by a volcano.
8. Luis is writing a report about Pompeii. _____ knows a lot about it.
9. Luis gave me his report. I read it. _____ learned a lot from it.
10. "This is great," I told Luis. "_____ are a good writer."

▲ Pompeii is in Italy. It is near the active volcano Mt. Vesuvius.

# Discuss Vacations

## ENGAGE IN CONVERSATION

Think about a vacation you took or would like to take. Form a small group and have a conversation about your vacations.

Use a chart like this one to get started. Write notes about your vacation. Use subject pronouns in your chart. Then, write questions to ask others about their vacations. Be sure to use the correct subject pronouns.

**Question Chart**

| Topic | My Vacation | What I Can Ask My Partner |
|---|---|---|
| where? | Japan. It was beautiful. | Where did you go on vacation? |
| who went too? | Dad. He was born there. | Who went with you? |
| activities | I climbed Mt. Fuji. | What did you do? |
| favorite part | eating fresh fish | |

Take turns asking one another about your vacations. Remember:

## HOW TO ENGAGE IN CONVERSATION

**1.** When you have a conversation with someone, you ask and answer questions. You also give your ideas and opinions.

**2.** Sometimes you will agree with the person, and sometimes you will disagree. Be polite. Respect the other person's ideas.

> I climbed Mt. Fuji. It is a volcano in Japan.

> Really? I am afraid of volcanoes.

## USE SUBJECT PRONOUNS

Use the correct subject pronouns when you have a conversation. Use *I* to talk about yourself. Use *you* to talk to others. Choose the correct **subject pronoun** for the **noun**.

**Talk about yourself:**   **I** visited Japan.

**Talk to others:**   What did **you** like best?

**Talk about others:**   **Grandma** took us to Mt. Fuji. **She** is a great tour guide.

▲ Mt. Fuji is the highest mountain in Japan.

# Prepare to Read

## Learn Key Vocabulary

**Study the Words** Use the steps below.

1. Pronounce the word. Say it aloud several times. Spell it.
2. Rate your word knowledge.
3. Study the example. Tell more about the word.
4. Practice it. Make the word your own.

### Key Words

**active** (ak-tiv) *adjective*
▶ page 138

Something that is **active** is likely to move or to show action. Children are **active** when they run and play games outside.
*Base Word:* **act**

**dangerous** (dān-ju-rus)
*adjective* ▶ page 140

Something that is **dangerous** is not safe. It is **dangerous** to walk barefoot near broken glass. You could cut yourself.
*Base Word:* **danger**

**erupt** (i-rupt) *verb*
▶ page 137

To **erupt** means to break open or shoot out suddenly. When a volcano **erupts**, lava and ash shoot out.

**force** (fors)
*verb* ▶ page 136 *noun* ▶ page 142

**1** *verb* To **force** means to push. Too much weight **forces** the ice loose.
**2** *noun* A **force** is a great power in nature. The **force** sent ice flying.

**layer** (lā-ur) *noun*
▶ page 136

A **layer** is a section that is on top of or under another. The cake has many **layers**, with frosting in between.
*Base Word:* **lay**

**surface** (sur-fus) *noun*
▶ page 136

The **surface** is the outside part of something. The **surface** of the lake is calm.

**volcano** (vol-kā-nō) *noun*
▶ page 136

A **volcano** is an opening in Earth from which lava, ash, and steam escape.

**warning** (wor-ning) *noun*
▶ page 140

A **warning** is a sign that something bad may happen. The road sign gives us a **warning** that a railroad crossing is ahead.
*Base Word:* **warn**

**Practice the Words** Make a Frayer Model for each Key Word. Then compare your models with a partner's.

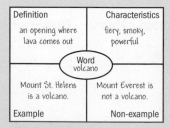

| Definition | Characteristics |
|---|---|
| an opening where lava comes out | fiery, smoky, powerful |
| Word volcano | |
| Mount St. Helens is a volcano. | Mount Everest is not a volcano. |
| Example | Non-example |

**Frayer Model**

# Analyze Text Structure: Cause and Effect

**How Is Text Organized?** Some nonfiction writers use **cause** and **effect** to organize their ideas. A cause is an event that leads to another event, called the effect. Authors use cause and effect to explain why something happens and how one thing leads to another.

**Reading Strategies**
- Plan
- Monitor
- **Make Connections**
  Combine your knowledge and experiences with the author's ideas and information.
- Visualize
- Ask Questions
- Determine Importance
- Make Inferences
- Synthesize

**Look Into the Text**

> The layer of rock below the Earth's crust is called the mantle. But the pressure and high temperature near the center of the Earth change the rock to liquid. The pressure can force the liquid rock upward. It moves up through cracks in the Earth's crust. This can form a volcano.

## Practice Together

**Make a Chain** A Cause-and-Effect Chain shows how one event leads to another. Read this passage from "Volcano!" Think about how the forces of Earth **create** volcanoes. The first box tells the first cause. The next box shows the effect of that cause. Reread the passage above and add to Cause-and-Effect Chain.

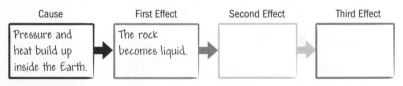

**Cause-and-Effect Chain**

| Cause | First Effect | Second Effect | Third Effect |
|-------|-------------|---------------|--------------|
| Pressure and heat build up inside the Earth. | The rock becomes liquid. | | |

**Academic Vocabulary**
- **create** (krē-āt) *verb*
  To **create** means to make something new.

# Science Article

Science articles give information about the natural world. They often have **diagrams** that explain information in the text. The **title** and **labels** in the diagram help you know what it is about.

Authors may organize information in science articles to show how events are related. One way they might be related is by **cause** and **effect**. Look for how the effect of one event can be the cause of something else.

**Look Into the Text**

How a Volcano Erupts

title

③ The melted rock, or lava, erupts from the volcano.

label

② Pressure forces the heated rock through cracks in the crust.

① Rock melts deep beneath Earth's surface, or crust.

Diagram

As you read, make connections to your own life, to what you have read, and to the world around you. Use these connections to understand cause and effect relationships in a text.

This volcano in Stromboli, Italy, erupts and shoots out melted rock, or lava. ▷

# Volcano!

## by Beth Geiger

◄ Some people study volcanoes. They wear special clothing to protect themselves from hot rocks.

# A Dangerous Job

Joanne Green walks by a glowing river. This river has no water, however. Instead, it is made of hot liquid rock, or lava.

The lava river is extremely hot, and so are the rocks surrounding it. "If you aren't careful," she says, "you'll melt your boots on the hot rock. Or worse!"

Green is used to these dangers. They are part of her job. She is a volcanologist, a scientist who studies **volcanoes**.

Green is studying Kilauea, a volcano in Hawaii. Green studies other volcanoes, too. Earth has thousands of them.

# Volcanoes on Earth

Most people think that volcanoes are simply large mountains that pour out lava. But a volcano actually starts deep beneath Earth's **surface**, or crust.

The **layer** of rock below the Earth's crust is called the mantle. But the **pressure** and high temperature near the center of the Earth change the rock to liquid. The pressure can **force** the liquid rock upward. It moves up through cracks in the Earth's crust. This can form a volcano.

**Key Vocabulary**
**volcano** *n.*, an opening in Earth from which lava pours
**surface** *n.*, the outside part
**layer** *n.*, a section that is on top of or under another
**force** *v.*, to push strongly

**In Other Words**
**pressure** push from inside Earth

**Language Background**
The ancient Romans believed in many gods. The word *volcano* comes from the name of their god Vulcan. Vulcan was the god of fire.

# How a Volcano Erupts

**3** The melted rock, or lava, **erupts** from the volcano.

**2** Pressure forces the heated rock through cracks in the crust.

**1** Rock melts deep beneath Earth's surface, or crust.

**Key Vocabulary**
**erupt** *v.*, to break open or shoot out suddenly

## Look Into the Text

1. **Explain** What dangers do scientists face when they study **volcanoes**?
2. **Cause and Effect** What happens to make a **volcano erupt**?

# It's About the Lava

About 1,500 of Earth's volcanoes are **active**. An active volcano is one that can erupt lava.

Some volcanoes make runny lava. The lava flows fast, like **pancake batter**. It piles up in thin layers. Over time, it forms low, wide mountains.

Other volcanoes erupt thick lava. It flows slowly, like toothpaste. It piles up in thick layers. Over time, it forms tall, steep mountains.

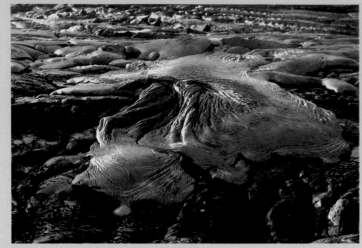

▲ Cooling lava forms rock. That is how the Hawaiian Islands developed.

# The Ring of Fire

Volcanoes are found all over Earth. Some form on land. Others rise up from the bottom of the ocean.

Most volcanoes are near the Pacific Ocean. They form a circle of volcanoes known as the Ring of Fire.

These volcanoes are found in areas where big pieces of Earth's surface, or plates, meet. Many volcanoes are formed along such **plate boundaries**.

THE RING OF FIRE

EURASIAN PLATE
JUAN DE FUCA PLATE
GORDA PLATE
PHILIPPINE PLATE
Ring of Fire
PACIFIC PLATE
NORTH AMERICAN PLATE
CARIBBEAN PLATE
COCOS PLATE
NAZCA PLATE
AUSTRALIAN PLATE
PACIFIC OCEAN
SOUTH AMERICAN PLATE
EURASIAN PLATE
ARABIAN PLATE
AFRICAN PLATE
SOMALI PLATE
INDIAN PLATE
SCOTIA PLATE
ANTARCTIC PLATE

△ **Interpret the Map** Name the largest plate within the Ring of Fire.

---

**Key Vocabulary**
**active** *adj.*, likely to show action

**In Other Words**
**pancake batter** a watery mixture
**plate boundaries** areas where Earth's plates meet

# Living with Volcanoes

Many people live near volcanoes. Some live close to the **base** of the mountains. Others farm nearby land. **Ash** from volcanoes is good for **soil**, so crops grow well.

▼ This farmer works near Mount Agung, a volcano in Bali.

**In Other Words**
**base** bottom, lowest level
**Ash** The dust that comes from burnt rocks
**soil** the dirt

**Look Into the Text**

1. **Summarize** What is the Ring of Fire?
2. **Evidence and Conclusion** Which details explain why people farm the land near **volcanoes**?

# A Dangerous Surprise

Living near a volcano can be **dangerous**, though. Volcanoes can erupt without **warning**.

That is just what happened in 1980 in Washington. On May 18, a volcano named Mount St. Helens erupted. Hot ash and steam blasted out of the volcano.

Few people were ready for it. Even scientists did not know it would happen that day. The volcano had not erupted since 1857.

The burning ash poured down the mountain, killing all the trees and **wildlife** in its path. The blast produced millions of tons of dust that covered 230 square miles.

## MT. ST. HELENS ERUPTS

**May 18, 1980 • 8:27:00 a.m.**
Mount St. Helens looked calm and peaceful. It wasn't. Scientists knew something would happen. But no one knew exactly when.

**May 18, 1980 • 8:32:37 a.m.**
The mountain exploded at 8:32 a.m. Ash soared 60,000 feet into the air.

**May 18, 1980 • 8:32:51 a.m.**
The blast produced 400 million tons of dust. It blanketed 230 square miles.

**Key Vocabulary**
**dangerous** *adj.*, not safe
**warning** *n.*, a sign that something bad may happen

**In Other Words**
**wildlife** animals

**Math Background**
In the United States, people often measure large areas of land in *square miles*. A square mile is one mile long and one mile wide.

# Life Returns

More than 20 years have passed since that day. Trees have now grown back. Animals live in the forests. Life has returned to Mount St. Helens. The people there will not forget what happened, though.

▲ Visitors compare an old photo of Mount St. Helens to the volcano today.

Trees now grow on Mount St. Helens.

**Look Into the Text**

1. **Sequence** Tell what happened to Mount St. Helens between 8:27 a.m. and 8:33 a.m.
2. **Compare and Contrast** How did Mount St. Helens look before it **erupted**? How does it look today?

# A Force on Earth

Volcanoes are all over the world. Some are active and some are not. Some, like Mount St. Helens, could erupt without much warning. Volcanoes are one of the **forces** on Earth that we live with but cannot control. ❖

People in this village in the Philippines used umbrellas to protect themselves from ash. Nearby, Mount Pinatubo was erupting. Ash from the volcano darkened the sky.

**Key Vocabulary**

**force** *n.*, a great power in nature

## Look Into the Text

1. **Determine Main Idea** Which sentence on this page best summarizes the central idea of the article?
2. **Viewing** Look at the picture. How can you tell that a **volcano** is **erupting**?

# Connect Reading and Writing

## Vocabulary
active
dangerous
erupt
forces
layers
surface
volcano
warnings

## CRITICAL THINKING

1. **SUM IT UP** Create a Fact Web using information from your Cause-and-Effect Chains and from the text. Write at least six facts about **volcanoes**. Then use your web to sum up the selection.

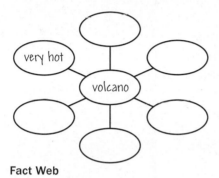

**Fact Web**

2. **Make Judgments** Why do people live near **active volcanoes**? Do you think they should? Explain your reasoning.

3. **Classify** Describe two different kinds of lava. Tell about the type of **layers** and mountains that each kind of lava forms.

4. **Infer** Many **volcanoes** form along the edges of big plates, or pieces of Earth's **surface**. Why do you think this is so? Use facts in the text to support your answer.

## READING FLUENCY

**Phrasing** Read the passage on page 564 to a partner. Assess your fluency.

1. I did not pause/sometimes paused/ always paused for punctuation.

2. What I did best in my reading was _____.

## READING STRATEGY

What strategy helped you understand this selection? Tell a partner about it.

## VOCABULARY REVIEW

**Oral Review** Read the paragraph aloud. Add the vocabulary words.

> A _____ is not just a mountain with hot lava. An _____ volcano is one that can _____, or explode. Pressure in the center of Earth _____ hot liquid rock through cracks in the crust. The hot rock, or lava, can be extremely _____! Scientists try to give _____ so people can escape. When lava from an explosion eventually cools, it adds new _____ to the _____ of Earth.

**Written Review** Pretend that you are a radio announcer. Write a **warning** about a **volcano** in your area that may **erupt**. Use five vocabulary words.

 **WRITE ABOUT THE** GUIDING QUESTION

**Explore Natural Forces**
Imagine that you are going to work with Joanne Green, the volcanologist in the selection. How do you prepare for this **dangerous** job? Reread the selection and look for details that support your answer.

# Connect Across the Curriculum

## Use Word Parts

> **Academic Vocabulary**
> • **define** (di-**fin**) *verb*
> When you **define** something, you tell what it means.

A compound word is made up of two or more smaller words. Sometimes you can **define** a compound word if you know the meanings of the smaller words, or you can use context clues to figure out the meaning. For example:

wild + life = wildlife    *Wildlife* is another word for plants and animals that live in their natural habitat.

**Define Compound Words** Work with a partner. Write the meaning of each underlined word. Explain how you **defined** it.

1. The earthquake shook the house.
2. Books were scattered everywhere.
3. We went to stay with my grandparents.
4. Every morning we ate pancakes for breakfast.
5. We brushed our teeth with mint toothpaste.

## Report on a Volcano

**MEDIA & TECHNOLOGY**

> **Academic Vocabulary**
> • **report** (ri-**port**) *verb*
> When you **report** on an event, you describe what happened.

Work with a partner to give a slide show that **reports** on a famous volcano.

❶ **Evaluate Information** Choose a volcano to research. Collect facts about the volcano, using reliable print and online sources.

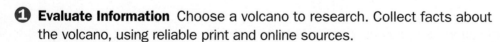

**Internet** myNGconnect.com
🌐 Gather information about a volcano.

❷ **Prepare Your Slide Show** Organize your ideas and write a script that **reports** the facts. Download photos and diagrams. Use only the visuals that you have the right to use. Put them together to make a slide show.

❸ **Give Your Slide Show** Speak clearly and loudly as you read your script. Answer your classmates' questions afterwards.

## Engage in Conversation

**Group Talk** With a group, look at the photos of Mount St. Helens on pages 140–141. Share your thoughts and ideas about the photos. Use subject pronouns.

> Animals probably ran away if they could.

> You're right. They were probably terrified.

## Write About an Interesting Place

**Study the Models** When you write about an interesting place, it's important not to repeat words too many times. Your writing will be choppy and hard to read if you keep using the same words. Using subject pronouns in place of the subject can help make sentences smooth.

**NOT OK**

**Paricutín** is a small volcano in Mexico. **Paricutín** started in a cornfield in 1943. **Paricutín** eventually destroyed the nearby town of San Juan. My **uncle** visited San Juan. My **uncle** took pictures of the town. My **uncle** told me that no one was killed by the lava and ash. The **town** is almost completely covered in lava rock, though. The **town** is a strange place.

> The writer repeats **nouns** in the subjects. The reader thinks: **"This is not very easy to read."**

**OK**

Paricutín is a small volcano in Mexico. **It** started in a cornfield in 1943. **It** eventually destroyed the nearby town of San Juan. My uncle visited San Juan. **He** took pictures of the town. **He** told me that no one was killed by the lava and ash. The town is almost completely covered in lava rock, though. **It** is a strange place.

> The writer replaces some nouns with **subject pronouns**.

✎ **WRITE ON YOUR OWN** Write about an interesting place that you or someone you know visited. When you can, use subject pronouns to make your sentences smooth.

**REMEMBER**

There are singular and plural subject pronouns.

| Singular | Plural |
|----------|--------|
| I | we |
| you | you |
| he, she, it | they |

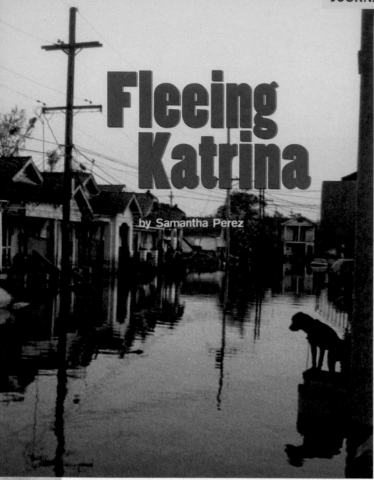

JOURNAL

# Fleeing Katrina

by Samantha Perez

# Build Background

## Explore Hurricanes

A hurricane is a storm that gathers power as winds blow over the warm ocean. Find out why hurricanes can be so destructive.

**Digital Library**
myNGconnect.com
🢒 View the video.

◀ **A hurricane hits the coast of Florida.**

## Connect

**Collaboration** In a group, share what you know about Hurricane Katrina. Record facts and details.

HURRICANE KATRINA
• When:
• Where:
• Damage:
• Health and Safety:

# Language & Grammar

## Ask and Answer Questions

Listen to the conversation. Then act out the dialogue with a partner.

**DIALOGUE**

## After the Hurricane

**Kate:** Does your family still have a house in New Orleans?

**Marcus:** Yes, we do, but it is completely destroyed.

**Kate:** Do you miss New Orleans?

**Marcus:** Yes, I miss it a lot.

**Kate:** Does your whole family live in Houston now?

**Marcus:** Yes, they all live here now.

**Kate:** Does your mother like living in Houston?

**Marcus:** No, she doesn't. She really misses our home.

**Kate:** Do you think you will go back to Louisiana soon?

**Marcus:** No, I don't think so.

**Kate:** Does your family plan to go back someday?

**Marcus:** Yes, we do!

# Use Correct Pronouns

Remember, the subject of a sentence can be a pronoun.

• Use **I** when you talk about yourself.

• Use **you** to talk to one or more persons.

• Use **we** to talk about another person or persons and yourself.

• Use **he**, **she**, or **it** to talk about one person, place, or thing.

• Use **they** to talk about more than one person, place, or thing.

A **subject pronoun** can refer to a **noun** in another sentence.

• Use the correct pronoun. Match the pronoun to the noun.

> ?
>
> UNCLEAR    **Dan** is from Louisiana. **It** lost his house in a hurricane.
>
> CLEAR    **Dan** is from Louisiana. **He** lost his house in a hurricane.

• Write clearly so it is easy to tell which noun your pronoun refers to.

> ?
>
> UNCLEAR    **Lalla** left before **Amelia**. **She** was looking for her dog.
>
> CLEAR    **Amelia** could not leave early. **She** had to find her dog.

## Practice Together

Say each pair of sentences. Replace the underlined subject with the correct subject pronoun.

1. The hurricane in 2005 was a big storm. The hurricane hit Cuba forcefully.

2. Winds pounded the island. Winds were very powerful.

3. Grandfather was in Cuba. Grandfather watched the storm.

4. Grandmother was in the United States. Grandmother felt worried.

## Try It!

Read each pair of sentences. Replace the underlined subject with the correct subject pronoun. Write it on a card. Hold up the card as you say the sentences with the pronoun.

5. Dave turns on the radio. Dave hears a weather report.

6. The storm is approaching. The storm is dangerous.

7. Waves hit the coast. Waves are huge.

8. Mom calls everyone. Mom gets the dog, too.

▲ A hurricane is dangerous. It brings strong winds.

# Discuss Natural Forces

## ASK AND ANSWER QUESTIONS

Many people experience the destructive forces of nature. Strong winds can knock down a tree, or heavy rains can flood a house. What powerful forces of nature do you know about? Write your ideas in a web.

**Idea Web**

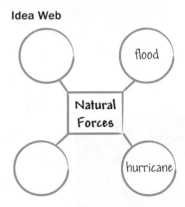

Work with a group to learn more about one of the forces in the Idea Web. Write questions to ask another group about the forces of nature they are studying. Take turns asking and answering questions with another group.

## HOW TO ASK AND ANSWER QUESTIONS

**1.** You can use the words *Do* or *Does* to start a question.

**2.** You can answer a *Do* or *Does* question with *Yes* or *No*.

**3.** You can also give a short or long answer to a *Do* or *Does* question.

## USE CORRECT PRONOUNS

When you ask and answer a question, use the correct pronoun. The **subject pronoun** in an answer often refers to a **noun** in the question.

**Question:** Does **California** have a lot of tornadoes?
**Answer:** No, **it** doesn't.

**Question:** Do your **parents** buy extra food before a blizzard?
**Answer:** Yes, **they** do.

# Prepare to Read

## Learn Key Vocabulary

**Study the Words** Use the steps below.

1. Pronounce the word. Say it aloud several times. Spell it.
2. Rate your word knowledge.
3. Study the example. Tell more about the word.
4. Practice it. Make the word your own.

### Key Words

**evacuate** (i-va-kyū-āt) *verb*
▶ page 154

To **evacuate** means to leave or to get out. The woman **evacuated** the building when the fire alarm rang.

**fortunate** (for-chu-nut)
*adjective* ▶ page 160

Someone who is **fortunate** is lucky. The family is **fortunate** that their house did not burn in the fire.
*Base Word:* **fortune**

**future** (fyū-chur) *noun*
▶ page 162

The **future** is what will happen in the time to come. I am going to a concert at some time in the near **future**.

**hurricane** (hur-u-kān) *noun*
▶ page 154

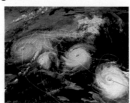

A **hurricane** is an ocean storm with strong winds. From space, a **hurricane** looks like a spiral of white clouds.

**levee** (le-vē) *noun*
▶ page 159

A **levee** is a structure that keeps a river from flooding. If rainfall is heavy for a long time, a river could rise and the water could spill over the **levee**.

**necessity** (ni-se-su-tē) *noun*
▶ page 156

A **necessity** is an item that someone needs. Food and water are the most basic **necessities** of life.

**severe** (su-vear) *adjective*
▶ page 154

Something that is **severe** is very serious or dangerous. Dad could not read because he had a **severe** headache.

**untouched** (un-tucht)
*adjective* ▶ page 162

Something that is **untouched** is not changed or hurt in any way. Few areas of the world have been **untouched** by humans.
*Base Word:* **touch**

**Practice the Words** Work with a partner. Write a question using a Key Word. Answer your partner's question using a different Key Word. Keep going until you have used all the words twice.

| Questions | Answers |
|---|---|
| What would you take if you evacuated your home in an earthquake? | I would take water, food, and other necessities. |

# Analyze Author's Viewpoint

**How Is Viewpoint Conveyed?** In **narrative** nonfiction, the author may use phrases like "I thought" or "I feel" to convey viewpoint. Words, actions, and other details also convey the author's viewpoint.

As you read, take note of the details the author includes and what the author says and does to help you analyze the author's viewpoint.

**Reading Strategies**

- Plan
- Monitor
- **Make Connections**
  Combine your knowledge and experiences with the author's ideas and information.
- Visualize
- Ask Questions
- Determine Importance
- Make Inferences
- Synthesize

### Look Into the Text

Monday, August 29, 2005

## Last Days in St. Bernard Parish

I lived in a place called St. Bernard Parish, Louisiana, a town just southeast of New Orleans. I say that I lived there, because I don't anymore. I don't live anywhere.

Friday night we heard that a hurricane in the Gulf of Mexico might be coming our way. Not a big deal, I thought.

## *Practice Together*

**Begin an Attribute Web** An Attribute Web can help you analyze the author's viewpoint. This web shows a detail that the author says in the passage above. On this web, you can also include details about how the author acts and feels and what other details the author includes. Reread the passage above, and add to the Attribute Web.

Acts:

Feels:

Author: Samantha Perez

Other details:

Says:
1. I don't live anywhere.

**Attribute Web**

## Academic Vocabulary

- **narrative** (nair-u-tiv) *noun*
  A **narrative** is writing that tells a story.

## Journal

A journal can be narrative nonfiction. People usually write journals to record their personal experiences, feelings, and thoughts. A journal often has **dates** that tell when events happen.

Analyzing author's viewpoint helps readers better understand what happens in a text and why. **Words, actions, and other details** from the journal can help you determine the author's viewpoint.

Look Into the Text

Saturday, September 3, 2005 ⟨ date

# Just Darkness and the Cry of a Million Crickets

I want to go home. I miss so many things about my home. We don't even know how long it'll be before they'll let us back into the parish, to save what we can and realize all that we lost.

As you read, make connections to what the author says and does to help you analyze the author's viewpoint.

New Orleans, Louisiana, on September 10, 2005, two weeks after Hurricane Katrina hit.

# Fleeing Katrina

by Samantha Perez

Monday, August 29, 2005

# Last Days in St. Bernard Parish

I lived in a place called St. Bernard Parish, Louisiana, a town just southeast of New Orleans. I say that I lived there, because I don't anymore. I don't live anywhere.

Friday night we heard that a hurricane in the Gulf of Mexico might be coming our way. Not a big deal, I thought.

Dad called from his work and suggested **evacuating**. Since **Hurricane Ivan** last year, he'd been fairly **paranoid** about hurricanes.

By Saturday morning, the hurricane's **projected** path showed New Orleans getting a direct hit. Dad doubled the efforts of his evacuation campaign.

By Saturday night, the decision had been made: we had to leave. Hurricane Katrina was now a **severe Category 4**, and it was coming straight for the city. We needed to get out of the parish.

**Hurricane Katrina's Path, August 23–30, 2005**

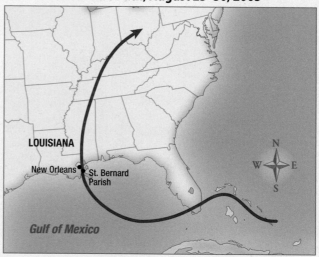

▲ **Interpret the Map** How many states did Hurricane Katrina pass through?

**Key Vocabulary**
  **hurricane** *n.*, an ocean storm with strong winds
  **evacuate** *v.*, to leave, to get out
  **severe** *adj.*, very serious

**In Other Words**
**Hurricane Ivan** a hurricane that hit Louisiana
**paranoid** worried, nervous
**projected** expected, likely
**Category 4** hurricane with winds of 131 to 155 miles per hour

▲ This business in St. Bernard Parish, Louisiana, was destroyed by Hurricane Katrina.

## Science Background

Hurricanes have winds of 119 kilometers (74 miles) or more per hour over a long period of time. When they occur in the Atlantic Ocean, they can affect the eastern United States. The winds turn around a central point, called the eye. The eye is the calmest part of a hurricane.

hurricane

eye

◄ Hurricane Rita passed over the Gulf of Mexico in 2005.

I filled a big plastic container with my clothes. I took my books off my shelves and stacked them high in my room so, just in case we did get water, they would be safe. I stacked everything **atop** my desk, bookshelf, and dresser, so it would all be safe.

## ... just in case we did get water, the books would be safe.

I looked at my pretty dress a lot that night. I was going to wear it to my senior **prom** this year. It was strapless, this beautiful shade of pastel pink. It was just hanging in my near-empty closet. I wanted to bring it so badly, but Mama said no. No room for dresses, only **necessities**.

**Key Vocabulary**
**necessity** *n.*, an item that someone needs

**In Other Words**
**atop** on top of
**prom** dance

Tuesday, August 30, 2005, part 1

# Fleeing Katrina

I grabbed the last of my things and turned off my light. Mom and I were in the car a minute later.

It took almost nine hours to get to the hotel in Bossier City. It didn't take any longer than it normally would, and we were lucky because there was very little traffic.

We spent the whole evening watching the news. Katrina's course had changed only slightly. **The track led it to make landfall** just east of New Orleans.

I looked at the projected path. The eye was going to pass over my parish. The storm was a Category 5 now, the highest possible.

▼ Samantha's family left quickly. Later, the roads were full of people leaving their homes before the hurricane arrived.

**Science Background**
There are five categories of hurricanes. For Category 5, the winds are greater than 155 miles per hour. Hurricane Katrina was a Category 5 over the Gulf of Mexico, before it reached land.

**In Other Words**
**The track led it to make landfall** It would cross from the ocean onto land

**Look Into the Text**

1. **Summarize** Tell how Samantha's family gets ready to **evacuate**.
2. **Problem and Solution** What problem does Samantha face as she packs **necessities** to take with her? Tell how she solves it.

▲ This home was damaged by the mud and water that covered
New Orleans after Hurricane Katrina.

*Predict*
*What will happen to Samantha's family and her home?*

Tuesday, August 30, 2005, part 2

# First News from Home

We lost our home. The **levees** broke and water spilled into the streets.

Our home is gone. St. Bernard is completely under the water, and we have nothing now.

Saturday, September 3, 2005

# Just Darkness and the Cry of a Million Crickets

I want to go home. I miss so many things about my home. We don't even know how long it'll be before they'll let us back into the parish, to save what we can and realize all that we lost.

Friday, September 16, 2005

# Guilt and Doubt

Now my family is in Ponchatoula, Louisiana.

We're living on a **lot** that used to belong to our friend's grandmother. The three of us are living in the **camper**, and it's tight.

Here, I have some friends from my old school, and even though I was never really close with any of them, it's comforting looking around and seeing something familiar.

**Key Vocabulary**
**levee** *n.*, a structure that keeps a river from flooding

**In Other Words**
**Crickets** Small insects
**lot** piece of land
**camper** trailer

## Look Into the Text

1. **Confirm Prediction** Was your prediction correct? What happened that you did not expect?
2. **Evidence and Conclusion** Does Samantha's family go back to their home? How do you know?

Saturday, September 17, 2005

## Going Home

I went home. But it wasn't home. Home isn't really there anymore.

Mud was **caked** everywhere on the ground. Things were brown and gray, not green as they used to be. It was like I stepped into some other **reality**. This wasn't the St. Bernard I remembered.

We **turned into** my neighborhood, and it was strange. Usually, I see green grass, green bushes, green shrubs, and trees. Now, the salt water had killed all of those things. It was brown now, an old, dry brown.

Dad stopped the truck in the middle of the street, and we spilled out.

When Mom walked onto the porch and looked through the front room door, I knew she wasn't expecting what she saw. And the smell was horrible. Mold and rotten food and mud scents mixing together.

**. . . the smell was horrible.**

I walked to the hall. There was mold growing everywhere on the walls. It was as if we had put up some **demented** circle-pattern wallpaper for fun.

My bedroom door was open, so I walked right in. Nothing was in its right place. My bed had flipped over. My bookshelf had fallen over. Papers were on my floor.

I climbed over my bed to get to the closet where my dresses had been hanging.

I was gasping for breath as I lifted a plastic bag and looked at my pink dress. It was fine, and I started yelling for my mom to come and see. My dress was fine!

As we drove away, I thought about walking around my house and seeing things that I had once treasured.

I realized that it didn't really matter anymore, any of it. I lost papers and stories and clothes, but I'm **fortunate** that I didn't lose the people that matter to me.

**Key Vocabulary**
**fortunate** *adj.*, lucky

**In Other Words**
**caked** stuck
**reality** place, world
**turned into** arrived in
**demented** crazy, wild

▲ After the flood, mold and mildew covered the walls, ceiling, and furniture of this home in New Orleans.

Sunday, May 14, 2006
## A Pink Dress at the Prom

Last night, my new school had its senior prom. My best friends from my old school and I decided to go together as a group. So this prom was a **reunion**, which in some ways was so much better than any dance normal kids can have.

And I had the chance to wear my pretty, pastel pink dress. The one that survived the hurricane. We had it cleaned a few weeks before, and it came out great. The smell of mold was gone, and it looked **immaculate** and **untouched**.

Tuesday, August 29, 2006
## One Year Since Katrina

It's been a year now, one year since Hurricane Katrina destroyed people's lives, dreams, and homes.

I am wiser than before. I have learned to adapt to whatever comes my way. And I've learned that if I work hard enough, I can make things better for the **future**. ❖

## About the Author

Samantha Perez

**Samantha Perez** (1988– ) was born in New Orleans, Louisiana. She is a proud resident of St. Bernard Parish, just southeast of New Orleans, where she has returned to rebuild in the wake of Hurricane Katrina. Her journalism for ReadTheTattoo.com brought attention to her hometown and won several awards, including the Scholastic Press Forum's Professor Mel Williams Award for Writing Excellence and a resolution praising her from the Louisiana State Senate in 2006.

**Key Vocabulary**
  **untouched** *adj.*, not hurt in any way
  **future** *n.*, what will happen in the time to come

**In Other Words**
  **reunion** time to be together again
  **immaculate** clean, perfect

**Look Into the Text**
1. **Details** What happened to Samantha's house and her belongings? How did she feel about it?
2. **Confirm Prediction** Was your prediction correct? How does the event change Samantha?

# Connect Reading and Writing

**Vocabulary**

evacuated

fortunate

future

hurricanes

levees

necessity

severe

untouched

## CRITICAL THINKING

1. **SUM IT UP** Use your Attribute Web to describe the author's viewpoint and summarize the selection to a partner.

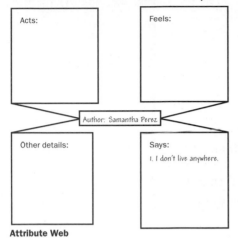

Acts:

Feels:

Author: Samantha Perez

Other details:

Says:
1. I don't live anywhere.

**Attribute Web**

2. **Paraphrase** In your own words, describe what Samantha secs in her home after the storm. How **severe** is the damage?

3. **Analyze** A special object is left **untouched** by the storm. What does it represent?

4. **Draw Conclusions** Samantha feels **fortunate** and thinks about the **future**. What do her thoughts tell you about her personality?

## READING FLUENCY

**Expression** Read the passage on page 565 to a partner. Assess your fluency.

1. My voice never/sometimes/always matched what I read.

2. What I did best in my reading was _____.

## READING STRATEGY

What strategy helped you understand this selection? Tell a partner about it.

## VOCABULARY REVIEW

**Oral Review** Read the paragraph aloud. Add the vocabulary words.

All _____ develop in the ocean. Cities on the coast are damaged by some of these storms but _____ by others. In 2005, New Orleans was hit by Hurricane Katrina. Many people left, or _____, but others were not so _____. New Orleans is in a low area of land, with water all around. The city has wall-like structures, or _____, to keep water out. These structures are a real _____! In 2005, flood water broke through and did _____ damage. Engineers will make the levees stronger in the _____.

**Written Review** Suppose you had to **evacuate**. Write a paragraph about one thing you would take that was not a **necessity**. Use four vocabulary words.

**WRITE ABOUT THE** GUIDING QUESTION

### Explore Natural Forces

Why was the impact of Hurricane Katrina more **severe** than other natural events in recent U.S. history? Write your opinion. Use examples from the text to support your ideas.

# Connect Across the Curriculum

## Vocabulary Study

### Use Word Parts

| Suffix | Meaning |
|--------|---------|
| **-hood** | quality of |
| **-less** | without |
| **-ly** | in a certain way |
| **-ness** | state of |

**Academic Vocabulary**
- **locate** (lō-kāt) *verb*
  To **locate** something is to find it.

A suffix changes the meaning of a word and how the word is used in a sentence.

fear + -less = fearless

The suffix *-less* means "without," so when you add it to the noun *fear*, you create the adjective *fearless*. Someone who is fearless is without fear.

**Define Words** Work with a partner. **Locate** the suffix in each word. Use the meaning of the suffix and the meaning of the base word to tell what the word means. Use the word in a sentence about "Fleeing Katrina."

1. fairly
2. strapless
3. badly
4. slightly
5. completely
6. darkness
7. hopeless
8. neighborhood

## Media/Speaking

### Compare Media Accounts

MEDIA & TECHNOLOGY

**Academic Vocabulary**
- **explanation** (ek-splu-**nā**-shun) *noun*
  An **explanation** is a statement that makes an idea clear.

What writers choose to tell or omit affects what ideas are expressed and how readers respond to those ideas. Think about the video you saw before you read this selection. Then find an article about Hurricane Katrina in a newspaper, magazine, or on the Internet.

> **Internet** myNGconnect.com
> Find an article about Hurricane Katrina.

❶ **Analyze Accounts** Review your notes from the video. What does the video show? What do you think the video wants you to understand about this event? Read the article carefully. Identify the words and images the writer uses. What does the writer choose to tell about? What do you think the writer wants you to understand about this event?

❷ **Compare Accounts** In a small group, compare the ideas in each account. Decide how each makes you think about the event. Which nonfiction piece gives a more effective **explanation** of what happened? Why?

## Ask and Answer Questions

**Interview a Classmate** Wind, rain, lightning, and thunder are forces of nature. List others. Ask a classmate questions about different forces of nature. For example: "Do you like snow? Does lightning scare you?" Switch roles. Use correct subject pronouns.

> Do you like thunder?

> Yes, thunder is exciting. It can be dangerous, though.

## Write About a Natural Disaster

**Study the Models** You may want to write about your experience with a storm or another natural force. Be sure to write sentences that are clear, so readers can follow what you write. One way to write clear sentences is to use the correct pronoun.

**NOT OK**

> Last **winter** was difficult. **He** was long and cold, and there were several snowstorms. My **sister** slipped on the ice during one storm. **They** broke her ankle. My **brother** fell off his bike on an icy road. **It** was OK, but the bike was damaged. My **parents** also had trouble. **She** had to cancel their vacation because the airport was closed.

The writer thinks: "**I'm confused. The nouns** and **pronouns** don't seem to go together."

**OK**

> **Danny Boy** is my dog. **He** survived Hurricane Katrina. My **family** had to leave in a hurry. **We** could not take Danny Boy. A **lady** rescued him after the storm. **She** found him all alone in front of our house. The **house** was empty. **It** was filled with water. I am so happy Danny Boy is back with us!

The reader can understand the text because the **pronouns** agree with their **nouns**.

**Revise It** Look back at the NOT OK passage. Work with a partner to revise it. Fix the pronouns so they agree with the nouns.

✏ **WRITE ON YOUR OWN** Write about your own experience in a storm or a natural disaster, or write about a natural disaster you have read about. Use the correct pronouns.

**REMEMBER**
- Use **he** to refer to a male.
- Use **she** to refer to a female.
- Use **it** to refer to a place or thing.
- Use **they** to refer to more than one person, place, or thing.

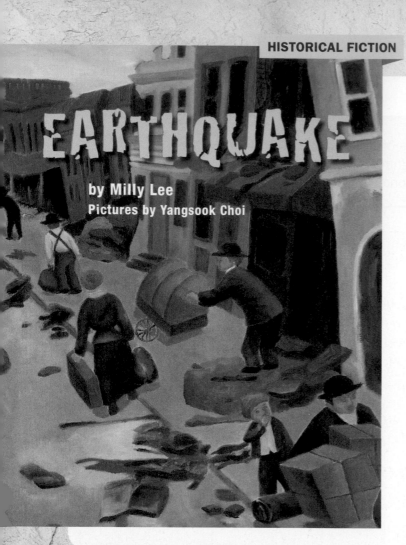

HISTORICAL FICTION

# EARTHQUAKE

by Milly Lee
Pictures by Yangsook Choi

# Build Background

## Connect

**Anticipation Guide** What do you know about the dangers of earthquakes? Tell whether you agree or disagree with each statement.

| | Agree | Disagree |
|---|---|---|
| 1. People should not live where earthquakes occur. | _____ | _____ |
| 2. No building is really earthquake safe. | _____ | _____ |
| 3. Earthquakes are scary but fun. | _____ | _____ |

Anticipation Guide

## Discuss the Great Quake

How did the 1906 earthquake affect people in San Francisco? How do earthquakes affect people today?

**Digital Library**

myNGconnect.com
◐ View the images.

▲ Buildings collapsed after the earthquake in 1906.

# Language & Grammar

1 TRY OUT LANGUAGE
2 LEARN GRAMMAR
3 APPLY ON YOUR OWN

## Give Advice

CD

Listen to the rap. Listen again and chime in.

RAP

# Earthquake

When an earthquake strikes,
When an earthquake strikes,
Things can tumble.
A wall could crumble.
Glass might crash
And fall on you.

So take my advice:
Stay calm, stay nice.
Get under your desk
And do your best
To protect yourself
When an earthquake strikes,
When an earthquake strikes.

# Use Helping Verbs

- A **helping verb** is a verb that works together with another verb. The **main verb** shows the action or state of being. The helping verb supports the main verb's meaning.

    EXAMPLE  Earthquakes are scary. They **can shake** buildings.

- The verbs *can, could, may, might,* and *should* are helping verbs. Use *can* to tell what someone or something is able to do. Use *could, may,* or *might* to tell what is possible. Use *should* to tell what is good for someone to do.

    EXAMPLES  I **can** read information about earthquakes on the Internet.
    An earthquake **might** happen. It **could** create panic.
    You **should** stay calm.

## Practice Together

Say each sentence. Add *can, could, may, might,* or *should.* More than one answer is possible.

1. An earthquake _____ strike our area soon.
2. Many people _____ be in danger.
3. They _____ get help from the government.
4. Other countries _____ help.
5. They _____ send food, supplies, and money.

## Try It!

Read each sentence. Write *can, could, may, might,* or *should* on a card. Then hold up the card as you say the sentence with the helping verb. More than one answer is possible.

6. We _____ need an earthquake kit.
7. We _____ make one this afternoon.
8. I _____ find a flashlight for the kit.
9. Ben _____ have some batteries.
10. He _____ give them to us.
11. You _____ fill those containers with water.
12. We _____ have candles and matches in the house.

▲ You might need these items during an earthquake.

# Share Safety Tips

## GIVE ADVICE

How can people stay safe during an earthquake or another dangerous situation? What advice could you give them?

With a group, brainstorm dangerous situations that people might face. In a chart like this one, write what might happen in the situation. Then write what people should do to stay safe.

**Idea Chart**

| Danger | What might happen? | What should you do? |
|---|---|---|
| earthquake | • Objects in the house might fall.<br>• Windows might break. | • Hide under sturdy furniture.<br>• Stay away from windows. |
| biking in traffic | • A car might hit you.<br>• You might hit something. | • Wear a helmet.<br>• Be careful when you ride. |

Then work with a partner. Take turns giving advice for different situations on the chart. Remember:

## HOW TO GIVE ADVICE

1. To give advice, tell what might happen.
2. Then give commands to tell people what to do.

> Heavy rains can flood your house. You should get sandbags. Put them at the bottom of your doors.

## USE HELPING VERBS

When you brainstorm what might happen, use the **helping verbs** *can*, *could*, *may*, or *might*. When you give advice, use the helping verb *should*.

EXAMPLES    In an earthquake, windows **might** break.

The glass **could** hurt you.

You **should** stay away from windows during an earthquake.

# Prepare to Read

## Learn Key Vocabulary

**Study the Words** Use the steps below.

1. Pronounce the word. Say it aloud several times. Spell it.
2. Rate your word knowledge.
3. Study the example. Tell more about the word.
4. Practice it. Make the word your own.

**Rating Scale**

**1** = I have never seen this word before.

**2** = I am not sure of the word's meaning.

**3** = I know this word and can teach the word's meaning to someone else.

### Key Words

**carefully** (kair-foo-lē)
*adverb* ▸ page 176

To act **carefully** means to act with care. You should carry an egg **carefully** so it does not break.
*Base Word:* **care**

**collapse** (ku-laps) *verb*
▸ page 174

To **collapse** means to fall down. The old building **collapsed**.
*Synonym:* **crumble**

**confused** (kun-fyūzd)
*adjective* ▸ page 177

To be **confused** means to be unsure or not clear. They are **confused** by the instructions of this recipe.
*Base Word:* **confuse**

**earthquake** (urth-kwāk)
*noun* ▸ page 174

An **earthquake** is a sudden shaking of the Earth. Strong **earthquakes** cause damage to roads and buildings.
*Word Parts:* **earth, quake**

**equipment** (i-kwip-munt)
*noun* ▸ page 174

Tools or machines for a certain use are **equipment**. Hospitals have **equipment** for treating people who are sick or hurt.

**frightened** (frī-tund)
*adjective* ▸ page 177

To be **frightened** is to be afraid or scared. When I'm **frightened** at the movies, I cover my face with my hands.
*Base Word:* **fright**

**prepare** (pri-pair) *verb*
▸ page 176

To **prepare** means to get ready. Dad is **preparing** vegetables for dinner tonight.

**shelter** (shel-tur) *noun*
▸ page 182

A **shelter** is a place where people can safely stay. An umbrella provides **shelter** from the rain.

**Practice the Words** Work with a partner to complete an Expanded Meaning Map for each Key Word.

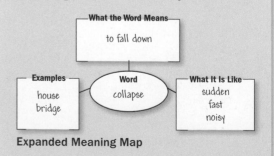

**Expanded Meaning Map**

# Analyze Characters' Viewpoints

**How Are Characters' Viewpoints Developed?** Character is an important **element** of fiction. Often, a character has a viewpoint about the events in the story. Characters' viewpoints are shown in dialogue, their thoughts, and other details.

### Reading Strategies
- Plan
- Monitor
- **Make Connections**
  Combine your knowledge and experiences with the author's ideas and information.
- Visualize
- Ask Questions
- Determine Importance
- Make Inferences
- Synthesize

### Look Into the Text

" I read the subject *we*. This tells me that the narrator is one of the characters. "

This morning the earth shook and threw us from our beds. We were not hurt, just stunned.

Drawers spilled, dishes crashed, pots and pans clanged as they fell. Ancestral portraits flew off the walls.

PoPo packed up all we could carry— bedding, clothing, food, utensils; Kwan Yin and ancestors, too.

" The highlighted text tells me what the characters were thinking when the earthquake happened. "

## Practice Together

**Begin a Chart** A Character Description Chart can help you organize information about the characters' viewpoints. This chart shows what the narrator and her family thought when the earthquake first hit. As you read, consider how the characters act and what they say and think. Reread the passage above, and add information to the chart.

| Character | What the Character Does | What the Character Says and Thinks |
|---|---|---|
| narrator and her family | | not hurt, just stunned |
| PoPo | | |
| MaMa | | |
| Policeman | | |

Character Description Chart

**Academic Vocabulary**
- **element** (e-lu-munt) *noun*
  An **element** is a basic part of a whole.

## Historical Fiction

Historical fiction is a type of narrative writing that is based on events from the past. The characters in the story are based on people who really lived. The setting and the events are based on facts of history.

Writers of historical fiction often include **dialogue** that they create. Dialogue, as well as characters' **thoughts** and other details, develop characters' viewpoints throughout a story. Readers should pay special attention to these details to determine characters' viewpoints.

**Look Into the Text**

In the early dawn, confused and frightened, we, gathered at Portsmouth Square. All of Chinatown must have been there.

"You must go to Golden Gate Park!" shouted the policeman.

As you read, make connections to help you analyze the characters' viewpoints.

# EARTHQUAKE

## by Milly Lee
## Pictures by Yangsook Choi

Comprehension Coach

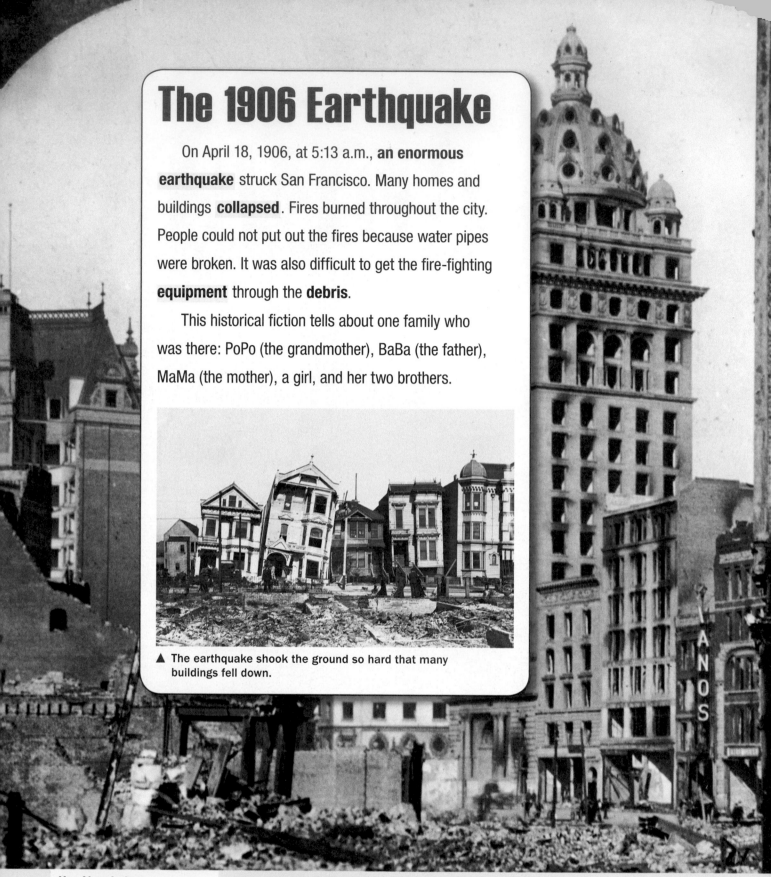

# The 1906 Earthquake

On April 18, 1906, at 5:13 a.m., **an enormous earthquake** struck San Francisco. Many homes and buildings **collapsed**. Fires burned throughout the city. People could not put out the fires because water pipes were broken. It was also difficult to get the fire-fighting **equipment** through the **debris**.

This historical fiction tells about one family who was there: PoPo (the grandmother), BaBa (the father), MaMa (the mother), a girl, and her two brothers.

▲ The earthquake shook the ground so hard that many buildings fell down.

**Key Vocabulary**
**earthquake** *n.*, a sudden shaking of the Earth
**collapse** *v.*, to fall down
**equipment** *n.*, tools, machines

**In Other Words**
**an enormous** a very big
**debris** bricks, wood, and other parts of broken buildings

This morning the earth shook and threw us from our beds. We were not hurt, just **stunned**.

Drawers spilled, dishes crashed, pots and pans clanged as they fell. **Ancestral portraits** flew off the walls.

PoPo packed up all we could carry— bedding, clothing, food, **utensils**; Kwan Yin and ancestors, too.

**In Other Words**
**stunned** surprised
**Ancestral portraits** Pictures of family members
**utensils** tools for cooking and eating

**Cultural Background**
Kwan Yin is a popular Chinese goddess of kindness and forgiveness. Many Chinese families keep a statue of Kwan Yin in their homes to honor her.

MaMa told us to hurry, wear extra layers of clothes, and **prepare** to leave for safety.

BaBa hurried out to **seek** help and returned with a cart and two **kinsmen**.

**Carefully** and slowly we made our way down the stairs to load the cart with **our belongings.**

**Key Vocabulary**
**prepare** *v.*, to get ready
**carefully** *adv.*, in a way that shows care

**In Other Words**
**seek** look for
**kinsmen** family members
**our belongings** all of the things we owned

In the early dawn, **confused** and **frightened**, we gathered at Portsmouth Square. All of Chinatown must have been there.

"You must go to Golden Gate Park!" shouted the policeman.

"The city is on fire. Go quickly now!" Dark smoke hurt our eyes. **Gritty** dust filled the air, our mouths and noses, too.

**Key Vocabulary**
**confused** *adj.*, not clear, unsure
**frightened** *adj.*, scared

**In Other Words**
**Gritty** Rough, Sandy

The earth shook again. We stopped, and watched in fear as buildings **crumbled** around us.

Elder Brother, Younger Brother, and I cleared a path for the cart carrying MaMa and PoPo and our belongings.

**In Other Words**
**crumbled** fell into pieces

We were hot and thirsty until we
**shed** the extra clothing and drank some
cold tea.

In the early-morning rush to leave, we
had not eaten anything.

PoPo gave us crackers and dried fruit.

Up the steep hills, across the city, we
pushed and pulled the heavy cart.

**In Other Words**
**shed** took off

**Look Into the Text**

1. **Paraphrase** Tell what the family did
   after the **earthquake**.
2. **Setting** What time of day is it
   now in the story? What clues give
   this information?
3. **Characters' Viewpoint** How
   does the family feel carrying their
   belongings through the city? What
   words or details help you know?

**A**ll around us, frightened people struggled with **loads too dear** to leave behind.

**Terrified** dogs, cats, and horses joined the people hurrying to safety.

Until, at last, we were away from the spreading fires. Away from falling buildings.

**In Other Words**
**loads too dear** things that were too important
**Terrified** Scared

In Golden Gate Park there was food,
water, and tents for **shelter**.
PoPo, BaBa, MaMa, Elder Brother,
Younger Brother, and I rested and ate.
    We were safe for now while the city still
burned and the earth still shook. ❖

## About the Author

**Milly Lee** grew up in San Francisco's Chinatown. Her parents, grandparents, uncles, aunts, cousins, and siblings all lived together in the same house. Lee speaks English and Cantonese, a language of China.

In her books, Lee tells about the part that Chinese Americans play in history. "I want my readers to know that 'we were there, too,'" she explains. "Earthquake" is the story of Lee's mother, who was 8 years old in 1906.

**Key Vocabulary**
**shelter** *n.*, a place where people can safely stay

**Look Into the Text**

1. **Confirm Prediction** What happens to the family at the end? What happened that you did not expect?
2. **Narrator's Viewpoint** How does the girl feel at the end of the story? How do you know?

# Connect Reading and Writing

**Vocabulary**
carefully
collapsed
confused
earthquake
equipment
frightened
prepare
shelter

## CRITICAL THINKING

**1. SUM IT UP** Use your Character Description Chart to describe the characters' viewpoints in "Earthquake" and summarize the story to a partner.

| Character | What the Character Does | What the Character Says and Thinks |
|---|---|---|
| narrator and her family | | not hurt, just stunned |
| PoPo | | |
| MaMa | | |
| Policeman | | |

Character Description Chart

**2. Evaluate** Review your Anticipation Guide on page 166. With a group, discuss how people deal with the dangers of **earthquakes**.

**3. Infer** When the family **prepares** to leave, PoPo packs pictures of ancestors. Later, BaBa asks family members to help. What do these clues tell you about the family?

**4. Compare** Imagine yourself in the pictures on pages 175–181. Would you be more **frightened** by the fires or by the falling buildings? Explain.

## READING FLUENCY

**Intonation** Read the passage on page 566 to a partner. Assess your fluency.

**1.** My tone never/sometimes/always matched what I read.

**2.** What I did best in my reading was _____.

## READING STRATEGY

What strategy helped you understand this selection? Tell a partner about it.

## VOCABULARY REVIEW

**Oral Review** Read the paragraph aloud. Add the vocabulary words.

In 1906, San Francisco had an awful _____. Buildings _____, fires burned, and water pipes broke. No one had been able to _____ for this unexpected disaster. People were scared, or _____. They did not know where to go, so they were _____. They walked quickly but _____ through the streets. The U.S. Army came to help. They brought supplies and special _____. They provided food, water, blankets, and tents for _____.

**Written Review** Imagine you are the mayor of San Francisco in 1906. Write a request to the army for more **equipment**. Use five vocabulary words.

 **WRITE ABOUT THE** GUIDING QUESTION

**Explore Natural Forces**
How should people **prepare** for, deal with, and recover from **earthquakes**? Give examples from the text.

# Connect Across the Curriculum

## Vocabulary Study

### Use Word Parts

**Academic Vocabulary**
- **discuss** (di-**skus**) *verb*
  When you **discuss** something, you talk about it.

| Suffix | Meaning | Changes . . . |
|--------|---------|---------------|
| **-ment** | act or process | a verb (*pay*) to a noun (*payment*) |
| **-ness** | state of | an adjective (*kind*) to a noun (*kindness*) |
| **-y** | having the quality of | a noun (*dirt*) into an adjective (*dirty*) |

A suffix changes the meaning of a base word and how the word is used in a sentence. For example, the word *grit* is a noun that means "a tiny piece of sand or stone." If you want to describe something that feels like sand, you could add the suffix *-y* and make the adjective *gritty*. Sometimes you need to change the spelling of the base word when you add a suffix.

| base word | suffix |
|-----------|--------|

grit    +    -y    =    gritty

**Define Words** Work with a partner. Cover the suffix in each word below. Tell the meanings of the base word and the suffix, using the chart above. **Discuss** how the suffix changes the base word. Use the word in a sentence to tell about the selection "Earthquake."

**1.** equipment    **2.** kindness    **3.** forgiveness    **4.** foggy    **5.** thirsty

## Research/Speaking

### Research Earthquakes

**Academic Vocabulary**
- **define** (di-**fin**) *verb*
  When you **define** something, you tell what it means.

**HEALTH & SCIENCE**

Nonfiction books often include tools to help readers.

- A **glossary** is a list of special terms used in the book and their meanings. It lists the terms in alphabetical order, near the end of the book.

- An **index** is a list of topics with page numbers. The topics are in alphabetical order. The numbers tell you the pages where you can find information about the topic. The index is usually at the end of the book.

**❶ Use Tools** Find a nonfiction book about earthquakes. Then:
  - Use the glossary to find and **define** terms about earthquakes.
  - Choose one term. Use the index to look up more information.

**❷ Share Your Research** **Define** the term for a group. Then tell what else you learned about it. Discuss how using a glossary and an index helped you with your research.

## Give Advice

**Role-Play** Work in pairs. Choose roles from "Earthquake." Each partner gives advice about what to do after the earthquake. Use helping verbs like *can*, *could*, *may*, *might*, and *should*.

> People at Golden Gate Park can help you. You should go there quickly. Only take what you need.

## Write Advice

**Study the Models** When you give people advice, give them ideas of what they should do. Include enough details to explain why they should do it, too.

**NOT OK**

An earthquake **can** be dangerous. You **should** be prepared. You **should** secure your belongings.

> The writer uses some **helping verbs** to give advice, but there are not many details.

**OK**

An earthquake **can** be dangerous. Vases **could** tumble off shelves and hit you. Bookshelves and other furniture **may** fall over on you.

You **should** be prepared. You **should** secure your belongings. You **can** use special wax to attach vases to the shelves. You **should** fasten bookshelves and furniture to the walls.

> Now the reader has more information. The writer uses more **helping verbs** to add details.

**Add Sentences** Think of two sentences to add to the OK model above. Use *can*, *could*, *may*, *might*, or *should*.

✎ **WRITE ON YOUR OWN** Imagine that a friend has moved to an area that has earthquakes. Write a letter with advice about what your friend should do and why.

**REMEMBER**
- Use **can** to tell what someone or something is able to do.
- Use **could**, **may**, or **might** to tell what is possible.
- Use **should** to tell what is good for someone to do.

◀ The people should stay away from the hole in the road.

# How Crisis Mapping Saved Lives in Haiti

BY PATRICK MEIER

1    The National Geographic Society has a long history of **crisis mapping** disasters. But what happened in Haiti on January 12, 2010 would forever change the very concept of a crisis map. A devastating **earthquake** struck the country's capital that Tuesday afternoon. I was overwhelmed with emotions when I heard the news just an hour later. Over 100,000 people were feared dead. Some very close friends of mine were doing research in Port-au-Prince at the time and I had no idea whether they had survived the earthquake. So I launched **a live** crisis map of Haiti. But this was an emotional reaction rather than a calculated plan with a detailed strategy. I was in shock and felt the need to do something, anything. It was only after midnight that I finally got an **SMS** reply from my friends. They had narrowly escaped a **collapsing** building. But many, many others were not near as lucky. I continued mapping.

**Key Vocabulary**
- **earthquake** *n.*, a sudden shaking of the Earth
- **collapse** *v.*, to fall down

**In Other Words**
**crisis mapping** making maps of places that need help during
**a live** an online
**SMS** short message service; text message

2   This is what the map looked like after midnight on January 13th. What was I mapping exactly? Tweets. I had found a dozen Haitians tweeting live from Port-au-Prince shortly after the earthquake. They were describing scenes of devastation but also hope.

**Crisis map**
Each dot shows where tweets came from and how many there were.

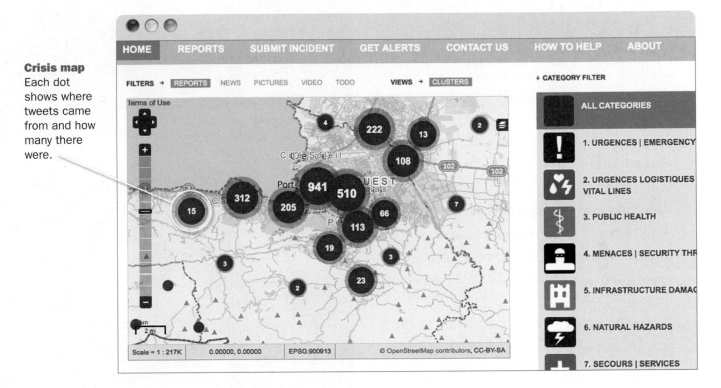

3   I added these Twitter users to my inbox and began mapping the most urgent Tweets (those that had enough geographic information to be mapped). The following night, several friends joined me in the living room of my dorm to help map Haiti's needs.

4   But within a couple days, we couldn't keep up with the vast amount of information being reported via both social media and mainstream media. So I reached out to friends at The Fletcher School (Tufts University) where I was **doing my PhD**. By the end of the week, we had trained over 100 graduate students on how to monitor social and mainstream media for relevant, mappable content. These **"digital humanitarians"** began to manually monitor hundreds and hundreds of online sources for information on Haiti almost **24/7**. The Ushahidi Haiti Crisis Map became a live map with some 2,000 individual reports added during the entire project.

5   Soon enough, we began receiving thousands of text messages. Many volunteers joined the cause after hearing about the need for volunteers via Facebook.

**Geography Background**
During a disaster people use crisis maps to identify where help is needed. Ushahidi is a nonprofit company that provides software that anyone can use to share information during a crisis.

**In Other Words**
**doing my PhD** completing advanced studies
**"digital humanitarians"** people using technology to help others
**24/7** every hour of the day and night

6   On January 19th, just a week after the earthquake, someone from the U.S. Coast Guard emailed us with the following question:

> I am compiling reports from Haiti for the U.S. Coast Guard and Joint Task Force Command Center. Is there someone I can speak with about how better to use the information in Ushahidi?

Several days later, we set up **a dedicated Skype chat with** the Coast Guard to fast-forward the most urgent (and actionable) content that was being added to the Haiti Crisis Map. We were also contacted by an American Search and Rescue team in Port-au-Prince who urgently needed **GPS** coordinators for the locations of trapped individuals.

7   On January 22nd, the U.S. Marine Corps got in touch with us via email.

8   > I am with the U.S. Marine Corps. I am stateside assisting the 22 MEU [Marine Expeditionary Unit] coming off the U.S.S. Bataan [on the Haitian Coast]. We want to use your data to bring aid to the people of Haiti right now. The **USMC** is focusing on Leogane, Grand Goave, and Petit Goave. Is there a way to import your data into **Google Earth or GIS**? We want to make this work for the people of Haiti . . . please let me know **ASAP**!

Haitians unload water from a U.S. military helicopter on January 21, 2010 after the earthquake.

**In Other Words**
**a dedicated Skype chat with** an online video chat only for
**GPS** global mapping
**USMC** United States Marine Corps
**Google Earth or GIS** online mapping services
**ASAP** as soon as possible

9    Five days later, the same contact from the U.S. Marine Corps shared the following by email (which we got permission to make public):

10   I can not overemphasize to you what the work of the Ushahidi/Haiti has provided. It is saving lives every day. I wish I had time to **document to you** every example, but there are too many and our operation is moving too fast. Here is one from the 22 MEU: 'We had data on an area outside of Grand Goave needing help. Today, we sent an assessment team out there to validate their needs and everything checked out. While the team was out there, they found two old women and a young girl with serious injuries from the earthquake; one of the women had critical respiratory issues. They were **evacuated**.'

11   Your site saved these people's lives. I say with confidence that there are 100s of these kinds of stories. The Marine Corps is using your project every second of the day to get aid and assistance to the people that need it most. We did have a **tech barrier** that we had to surmount. The Marines downrange have Google Earth and your site does not work on the ship for them. So, I had Georgia Tech create a bridge from your site to Google Earth.

12   But it is YOUR data and YOUR work that is putting aid and assistance directly on the target and saving lives. Our big gap right now is locating **NGOs** and where they are working. Your site is helping with that. Keep up the good work!! You are making the biggest difference of anything I have seen out there in the open source world.

13   These incredible efforts following the Haiti earthquake demonstrated a huge potential for the future of humanitarian response. Student volunteers in Boston working online with the **Diaspora** using free mapping technology from Africa could help save lives in another country thousands of miles away without ever setting foot in said country. In time, these reactive and organic volunteer-driven efforts in Haiti, and those that followed that same year in Chile, Pakistan, and Russia, led to the launch of the award-winning Standby Volunteer Task Force (SBTF), a global network of 850+ volunteers in more than 80 countries around the world who use their live mapping skills to support humanitarian [and] human rights development and media organizations.

**Key Vocabulary**
• **evacuate** *v.*, to leave, to get out

**In Other Words**
**document to you** provide proof of
**tech barrier** problem with technology
**NGOs** Non-Governmental
  Organizations that provide assistance
**Diaspora** scattering of people

# Compare Across Texts

## Compare Viewpoints

"Volcano!" "Fleeing Katrina," "Earthquake," and "How Crisis Mapping Saved Lives in Haiti" all tell about violent **forces** of nature but from different viewpoints.

## How It Works

**Collect and Organize Information** To compare across texts, organize information in a chart. Consider how the kind of writing affects viewpoint.

| Selection | Kind of Writing | Author's or Character's Viewpoint |
|---|---|---|
| "Volcano!" | science article/nonfiction | objective viewpoint; no opinion |
| "Fleeing Katrina" | journal/nonfiction | |
| "Earthquake" | historical fiction | |
| "How Crisis Mapping Saved Lives in Haiti" | blog/nonfiction | |

Comparison Chart

## Practice Together

**Compare the Information** Analyze the information in the Comparison Chart. First compare the different kinds of writing. Looking at how the types of writing are similar and different will help you to compare viewpoints. Write a paragraph like this one to compare the different kinds of writing.

> The selections tell about different natural disasters. "Volcano!" "Fleeing Katrina," and "How Crisis Mapping Saved Lives in Haiti" are all nonfiction. "Volcano!" is a science article, which is informational text. The other two are nonfiction narratives that tell real-life stories. "Earthquake" is a fictional story that is based on a real event in history.

## Try It!

Copy and complete the chart above. Write a paragraph to compare viewpoints. You may want to use this frame to help you express your comparison.

> Each selection is written from a different viewpoint. The author of "Volcano!" conveys an objective viewpoint by _____. The author's viewpoint in "_____" is _____. He/She uses words and phrases like _____ and _____ to convey his/her viewpoint. He/She also does _____.

**Academic Vocabulary**
- **force** (fors) *noun*
  A **force** is a great power in nature.

# NATURAL FORCES

**GUIDING QUESTION** How should people deal with the forces of nature?

## Content Library

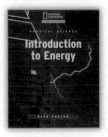

## Leveled Library

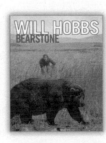

## Reflect on Your Reading

Think back on your reading of the unit selections. Discuss what you did to understand what you read.

**Focus on Reading** **Determine Viewpoints**
In this unit, you learned about viewpoint. Choose a selection. At the top of a card, complete this sentence: *The _____'s viewpoint is to _____.* Explain how you determined the viewpoint. Then explain the viewpoint to a partner.

**Focus Strategy** **Make Connections**
In this unit, you learned to make connections to the reading. Explain to a partner how you will use this strategy in the future.

## Explore the

Throughout this unit, you have been thinking about natural forces. Choose one of these ways to explore the Guiding Question:

- **Discuss** With a group, discuss the Guiding Question. Talk about ways in which people deal with natural disasters.
- **Dramatize** With a group, dramatize a talk show that includes a host, a volcano expert, a hurricane expert, and an earthquake expert.
- **Draw and Tell** If a force of nature were a person, what would it look like to you? Would an earthquake look like a giant that stomps on the ground, for example? Draw a character that represents a force of nature. Share it with classmates and tell about it.

## Book Talk

Which Unit Library book did you choose? Explain to a partner what it taught you about natural forces.

# Creepy
# Classics

4

**GUIDING QUESTION**

# How can a powerful character inspire a range of reactions?

**READ MORE!**

**Content Library**
**Peering Into Darkness**
by Rebecca L. Johnson

**Leveled Library**
**Frankenstein**
by Mary Shelley,
adapted by Larry Weinberg

**The Metamorphosis**
by Franz Kafka, adapted by Peter Kuper

**Othello**
by Julius Lester

**Web Links**
myNGconnect.com

◄ Haunted houses, cemeteries, and bats
are often featured in classic horror films.

# Focus on Reading

## Elements of Fiction

▶ **Plot**
▶ **Characters**
▶ **Setting**

Writers create fictional stories to entertain their readers. They use the **elements** of fiction—**plot**, **characters**, and **setting**—to build their stories.

## Plot: How It Works

The plot is what happens in a story.

- Plots are built around a **conflict**, or problem that the main character faces.
- A plot unfolds in a series of **events**, or episodes. These events affect the character's actions and feelings.
- The **turning point** is the most important event of the story.
- The **resolution** is the event that solves the problem.

Read "The Night Walker" to see examples of the **elements** of fiction and the stages of the plot.

### The Night Walker

The <mark>swamp</mark> smelled rotten in the <mark>night</mark> air. <mark>Isabella</mark> wrinkled her nose. She poked a stick at the piles of green slime in the water. Suddenly, <u>a patch of slime rose up. It was the <mark>Blob</mark></u>!

This terrible creature swallowed everything in its path. Isabella screamed and ran. The slimy Blob slipped out of the swamp and slithered onto the path. As Isabella reached for the handle of her car door, the Blob grasped her foot.

Isabella managed to get the door open. She grabbed the spray bottle of cleaner she always kept in her car. <mark>She blasted the creature with cleaner.</mark> At each squirt, the Blob grew smaller and weaker. In a few minutes, <u>it was just a lifeless puddle.</u> Isabella stood up and smiled. Then she wiped the puddle away with an old towel.

▲ **The Blob lives in the swamp.**

Setting
Character

Conflict

Event and character response

Turning point

Resolution

## Plot: Practice Together

Read "The Night Walker" again, and tell where the events go on this Plot Diagram.

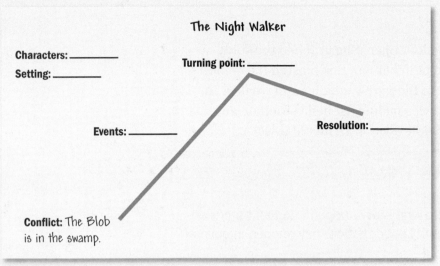

Plot Diagram

## Character: How It Works

Characters are the people or animals that take part in the plot. A writer tells about each character through

- a description of what the character looks like
- the character's actions and words in response to events
- how other characters think about or act toward the character.

See these techniques in action as the writer characterizes the Blob.

> This terrible creature swallowed everything in its path. Isabella screamed and ran. The slimy Blob slipped out of the swamp and slithered onto the path. As Isabella reached for the handle of her car door, the Blob grasped her foot.

Tells about the character directly

Tells how others react to the character

Shows the character's actions in response to events

You can use a Character Description Chart to keep track of what the characters are like.

| Character | What the Character Is Like | How I Know |
|-----------|---------------------------|------------|
| the Blob | terrible | swallows everything in its path<br><br>tries to grab Isabella |

Character Description Chart

## Character: Practice Together

Now read the rest of the story aloud with your class. As you read, listen for the ways the writer characterizes Isabella. After you read, make a Character Description Chart for Isabella.

> Isabella managed to get the door open. She grabbed the spray bottle of cleaner she always kept in her car. She blasted the creature with cleaner. At each squirt, the Blob grew smaller and weaker. In a few minutes, it was just a lifeless puddle. Isabella stood up and smiled. Then she wiped the puddle away with an old towel.

## Setting: How It Works

Setting is the time and place in which the story happens. In most stories, the setting is one place and one time. Longer fiction may happen in several places and times.

See how the writer uses the **elements** of setting in "The Night Walker."

> The swamp smelled rotten in the night air. Isabella wrinkled her nose. She poked a stick at the piles of green slime in the water. Suddenly, a patch of slime rose up. It was the Blob!

The time and place

A normal thing to find in that place

## Setting: Practice Together

Now read a different version of this story aloud with your class. As you read, listen for details about the setting. After you read, complete the activities below the passage.

> The city smelled clean after the evening rain. Isabella made her way through the crowd of people. As she crossed the street, she accidentally stepped in a puddle. Suddenly, something rose from the water. It was the Blob!

Work with a partner to answer these questions.
1. Describe the time and place in the second version.
2. Compare the different settings in these two versions of the story.
3. Predict how the plot of the second version would be different from the first plot.

## Try It!

Read the following passage aloud, and answer the questions about the **elements** of fiction.

1. What is the setting?
2. Who are the characters and what are they like? How do they change in response to story events?
3. What is the conflict?
4. What is the turning point?
5. What is the resolution?

### King Kong Lives

Alfonzo stretched sleepily as the morning sun warmed him. He loved camping in the woods. He had never been to this spot before, so he took time to look around him.

▲ King Kong

When he first saw the creature, he thought it was a mountain in the distance. But then he saw it move. He saw its huge, hairy arms rip up trees like toothpicks. He saw it coming straight for him. Alfonzo knew what this creature was. It was King Kong, the beast that he had seen on the news. Everyone was trying to catch this gigantic, terrible creature.

King Kong crashed through the trees toward Alfonzo. Soon Alfonzo could hear it breathing. He stood frozen in fear.

Suddenly, the tree tops started shaking behind him. Five helicopters came speeding through the sky straight toward King Kong.

King Kong looked up and swung his massive arms at the helicopters. Alfonzo heard several loud pops and then a crash.

The people in the helicopters had hit King Kong with sleeping darts. Now the creature lay sleeping, inches from Alfonzo's feet. The helicopters landed and crews poured out. Within minutes, the crews came down, tied up the creature, and lifted it away.

Alfonzo shook his head in disbelief. Then he packed up his things and started the hike home.

# Focus on Vocabulary

## Use Word Parts

Some English words are made up of parts. These parts include **base words** and **prefixes**. You can use the parts as clues to a word's meaning.

A prefix is a word part that is added to the beginning of a word. It changes the meaning of the base word. The chart shows some common prefixes.

| Prefix | Meaning | Example |
|--------|---------|---------|
| **dis-** | opposite | disagree |
| **im-** | not | impolite |
| **pre-** | before | preview |
| **re-** | again; back | review |

**Common Prefixes**

## How the Strategy Works

When you read, you may come to a word you don't know. Sometimes you can use word parts to figure out the meaning of an unknown word.

1. Look at the surrounding words for clues to the new word's meaning.
2. Break the word into parts. **Identify** word parts you know.

   EXAMPLE    rearrange → re- + arrange

3. Think about the meaning of each word part. If you don't know the base word, look it up in a dictionary.

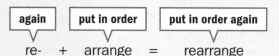

| again | put in order | put in order again |

re-  +  arrange  =  rearrange

4. Put the meanings of the word parts together to understand the whole word. Check that the meaning makes sense in the passage.

Use the strategy to figure out the meaning of each underlined word.

For hundreds of years, people have told stories about the Loch Ness Monster, which some think lives in a lake in Scotland. In modern times, people <u>renamed</u> the monster "Nessie."

Every time people <u>retell</u> the story about Nessie, they describe the monster differently. Some say that Nessie is a giant sea snake. Others say that the monster looks like a dinosaur with fins. One story seems to <u>replace</u> another!

### Strategy in Action

" I see the base word *named*. I know that *named* means 'gave a name' and *re-* means 'again.' So *renamed* means 'gave a name again.' That makes sense."

☑ **REMEMBER** Sometimes you can use the meanings of a prefix and a base word to figure out what the whole word means.

**Academic Vocabulary**
- **identify** (ī-**den**-tu-fī) *verb*
  To **identify** means to find out or to show what something is.

## Practice Together

Read this passage aloud. Look at each underlined word. Find the prefix and the base word. Put their meanings together to figure out the meaning of the underlined word.

# True Monsters

When explorers first came to the deserts of the Southwest, they found a true monster: the Gila monster. This lizard seemed <u>unreal</u> to them. The creature was truly <u>unbelievable</u>.

Gila monsters come out at night to feed on small animals, birds, and eggs. A Gila monster moves slowly, but if its prey takes one <u>misstep</u>, it will get caught. A Gila monster can quickly <u>overpower</u> its prey with a <u>poisonous</u> bite. However, human deaths from Gila monsters are extremely <u>uncommon</u>.

## Try It!

Read this passage on your own. What is the meaning of each underlined word? How do you know?

# A Real Monster

You may think that all monsters are fictional. That is <u>untrue</u>. At least one monster, the giant squid, is based in reality.

After trying and <u>retrying</u> to find a live giant squid, researchers in Japan finally succeeded. They caught a

▲ Scientists caught this young squid in the Pacific Ocean.

24-foot squid. Although it was attached to a fish hook, the giant squid was not <u>inactive</u>. In fact, it was quite strong. It fought hard to <u>untangle</u> itself from the hook.

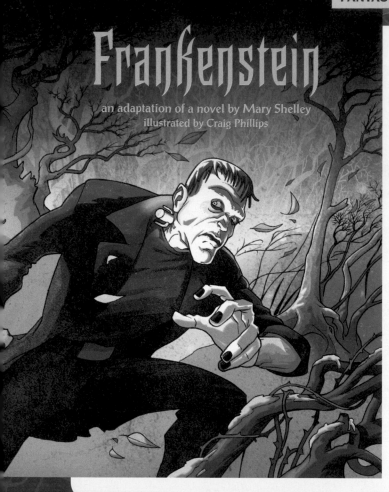

# Frankenstein

an adaptation of a novel by Mary Shelley
illustrated by Craig Phillips

## SELECTION 1 OVERVIEW

▶ **Build Background**

▶ **Language & Grammar**
Describe People and Places
Use Adjectives

▶ **Prepare to Read**
Learn Key Vocabulary
Analyze Character Development

▶ **Read and Write**
**Introduce the Genre**
Fantasy
**Focus on Reading**
Analyze Character Development
**Apply the Focus Strategy**
Visualize
**Critical Thinking**
**Reading Fluency**
Read with Expression
**Vocabulary Review**

**Write About the Guiding Question**

▶ **Connect Across the Curriculum**
**Vocabulary Study**
Use Word Parts
**Literary Analysis**
Analyze Theme
**Language and Grammar**
Describe People and Places
**Writing and Grammar**
Write About a Creepy Situation

# Build Background

## See Familiar Characters

Horror characters like Frankenstein's monster and Godzilla are featured in many stories. What makes them so popular?

**Digital Library**

myNGconnect.com
◉ View the video.

◀ In this model, Godzilla terrorizes a city.

## Connect

**Reaction Chart** Make a chart to show how different story characters make you feel. List the characters from stories, books, and movies. Draw a face to record your reaction. Share your chart and explain it.

| Character | My Feelings |
|---|---|
| Godzilla | ☹ |
| Frankenstein's monster | 😮 |
| | |
| | |

**Reaction Chart**

# Language & Grammar

## Describe People and Places

CD

Look at the picture and listen to the description.
Then describe something in the picture.

**PICTURE PROMPT**

Dear Edwin,

A dark, creepy mansion sits on the hill at the end of the street. A strange old man lives there. He always makes me feel afraid. He wears a long, gray coat and black gloves. He only comes out at night to walk his big dog. His dog has sharp teeth and cruel, yellow eyes.

Be careful,
Alana

| 1 TRY OUT LANGUAGE |
|---|
| 2 LEARN GRAMMAR |
| 3 APPLY ON YOUR OWN |

# Use Adjectives

You can describe people, places, or things with **adjectives**. Use **adjectives** to describe:

- how something looks, sounds, feels, tastes, or smells

    EXAMPLE    The **large** monster growls. His **loud**, **heavy** footsteps scare my **little** sister.

- Add -**er** to many **adjectives** to compare two things.

    EXAMPLE    King Kong is **taller** than Frankenstein.

- Add -**est** to many **adjectives** to compare three or more things.

    EXAMPLE    Godzilla is the **tallest** monster of all.

| To describe one thing | tall |
|---|---|
| To compare two things | taller |
| To compare three or more things | tallest |

- If the adjective ends in a consonant plus **y**, you usually change the **y** to **i** before you add -**er** or -**est**.

    gloom**y̵ⁱ** + -**er** = **gloomier**        craz**y̵ⁱ** + -**est** = **craziest**

## Practice Together

Say each sentence with an appropriate adjective from the box.

| hot    loud    huge    sharper    scarier    highest |
|---|

1. Godzilla is a _____ monster.
2. He is _____ than a giant squid.
3. He has _____, fiery breath.
4. His teeth are _____ than a knife.
5. He can climb Tokyo's _____ building.
6. His _____ roar terrifies the people.

## Try It!

Write each adjective on a card. Read each sentence. Hold up the appropriate adjective card as you say the sentence.

7. The creature lives in a (damp/dampest) cave.
8. The cave is (darker/darkest) than night.
9. It is the (lonelier/loneliest) creature in the world.
10. At night, it creeps out of its (smelly/smellier) cave.
11. It wanders into the (quiet/quieter) village.
12. It looks for a (yummy, yummiest) treat to eat.

▲ Godzilla looks scary.

# Create a Character

## DESCRIBE PEOPLE AND PLACES

Visualize a creepy character and where it lives. Picture details in your mind.
Then draw a picture of it. Give your character a name.

Study your picture. How would you describe the character and place? Jot
down your ideas. Share your drawing and description with a partner.

What comparisons can you make to other creepy characters? Is your
character creepier than Frankenstein's creature? Is it smaller than other
creepy characters?

---

### HOW TO DESCRIBE PEOPLE AND PLACES

**1.** Tell what a person or place is like.

**2.** Give details.

**3.** Use descriptive words.

> What is Old Molly like?

> Old Molly is a crazy woman with long, bony fingers.

---

## USE ADJECTIVES

When you describe people and places, you use **adjectives**. Adjectives help
your listeners picture what you are saying.

**Describe a person:**     Old Molly has **long**, **black** hair.

**Describe a place:**     She lives in a **wooden** shack.

**Make comparisons:**     She is **creepier** than a movie monster.

▲ This woman has bony fingers and large, round eyes.

# Prepare to Read

## Learn Key Vocabulary

**Study the Words** Use the steps below.

1. Pronounce the word. Say it aloud several times. Spell it.
2. Rate your word knowledge.
3. Study the example. Tell more about the word.
4. Practice it. Make the word your own.

### Key Words

**create** (krē-āt) *verb*
▶ page 210

To **create** means to make something new. The artist **creates** a work of art in his studio.
*Synonyms:* **make, produce**

**creature** (krē-chur) *noun*
▶ page 208

A **creature** is a real or imaginary living thing. A dragon is an imaginary **creature**.
*Base Word:* **create**

**destroy** (di-**stroi**) *verb*
▶ page 212

To **destroy** something means to take it apart or to ruin it. Workers **destroy** this building.
*Antonym:* **create**

**evil** (ē-vul) *adjective*
▶ page 210

Something that is **evil** is very bad or harmful. Some people believe rattlesnakes are **evil** because their bite is dangerous.
*Antonym:* **good**

**experiment**
(ik-**spair**-u-munt) *noun* ▶ page 210

An **experiment** is an activity that someone does to test an idea. The students are doing an **experiment** in their science class.

**hideous** (hi-dē-us) *adjective*
▶ page 212

Something that is **hideous** is very ugly. A mask can make someone look **hideous**.
*Antonym:* **beautiful**

**lonely** (lōn-lē) *adjective*
▶ page 208

To be **lonely** means to be alone, without friends. Do you feel **lonely** when your friends are away?
*Base Word:* **lone**

**scientist** (sī-un-tist) *noun*
▶ page 210

A person who studies science is a **scientist**. The **scientist** uses a microscope to study small objects up close.
*Base Word:* **science**

**Practice the Words** With a partner, take turns telling a story using the Key Words.

> **EXAMPLE: PARTNER 1:** Nina wanted to **create** a machine that could walk and talk.
>
> **PARTNER 2:** By mistake, she made a giant **creature**.

# Analyze Character Development

**What Is Character Development?** Usually, main **characters** do not stay the same throughout a book or a movie. As a story progresses, characters change how they think, feel, and act.

Many **elements** in a story can cause a character to change and develop:
- setting, or where and when the story takes place
- events, or what happens to a character
- motivations, or what a character needs and wants

## Reading Strategies
- Plan
- Monitor
- Make Connections
- **Visualize** Imagine the sights, sounds, smells, tastes, and touch of what the author is describing.
- Ask Questions
- Determine Importance
- Make Inferences
- Synthesize

**Look Into the Text**

After many years of study, I had discovered how to bring something to life. I was eager to use what I had learned, so I devoted two years to making a new creature out of bones and body parts from graveyards and slaughterhouses.

At last, my experiment was ready. An enormous, lifeless creature lay on the table in my lab. I thought my creation would show the world what a great scientist I was. I did not know how wrong I was!

"I'm just learning about Dr. Frankenstein. I know he is an eager scientist. I will look for changes in how he thinks, feels, and acts as I read the rest of the story."

## Practice Together

**Begin a Chart** A Beginning-Middle-End Chart can help you analyze how a character changes throughout a story. As you read, list examples to show how story elements cause Dr. Frankenstein to change. This chart has one example from the beginning of the story. Reread the passage above to add information to the Beginning row on the chart.

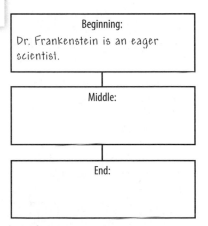

Beginning:
Dr. Frankenstein is an eager scientist.

Middle:

End:

**Beginning-Middle-End Chart**

## Academic Vocabulary

- **element** (e-lu-munt) *noun*
  An **element** is a basic part of a whole.

## Fantasy

Fiction is narrative writing about people, places, and events that the author creates. One kind of fiction is fantasy. Writers of fantasy create magical or unreal **characters** and **events** and make fantastic, imaginary worlds as settings.

Characters' thoughts, feelings, and actions can change in response to the events that happen in a story. As the plot unfolds, keep track of what happens, why it happens, where it happens, and how the characters change because of it.

**Look Into the Text**

That cold November night, I brought my creature to life. I remember the moment his black lips moved. His skin, stretched and sewn together, quivered. He took a rasping breath and opened his watery, yellow eyes.

As you read more about the characters, make pictures in your mind. Pay attention to the feelings that these pictures create in you and how they help you understand the characters.

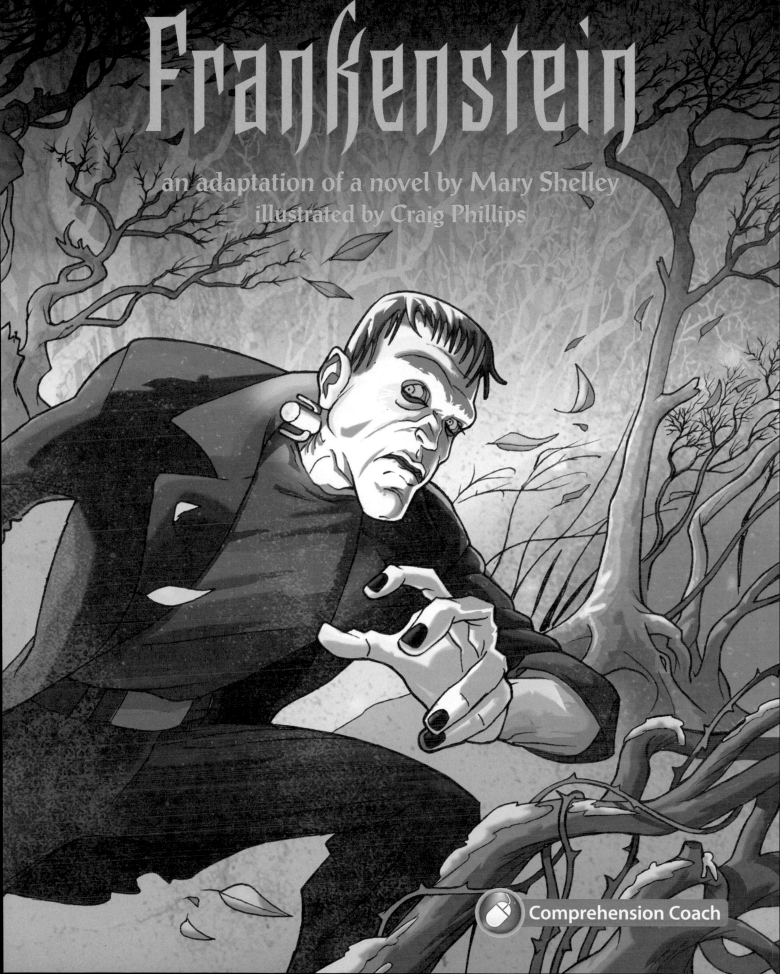

**Set a Purpose**

*Find out about a character named Frankenstein.*

August 19, 17_

My dear sister,

This long **voyage** has been so terribly **lonely**. The chilling frost and snow here in the Arctic completely surround our ship.

Three weeks ago, a remarkable thing happened. We saw a huge, ugly **creature** driving a sled pulled by dogs and racing north. The next morning, we saw a different dogsled drifting toward us on a sheet of ice. The poor dogs were dead, and the **weary** driver was barely alive. He wouldn't **accept** our help until we told him we were **heading** north.

The stranger will tell me his story tomorrow. I will **record it** and send it to you.

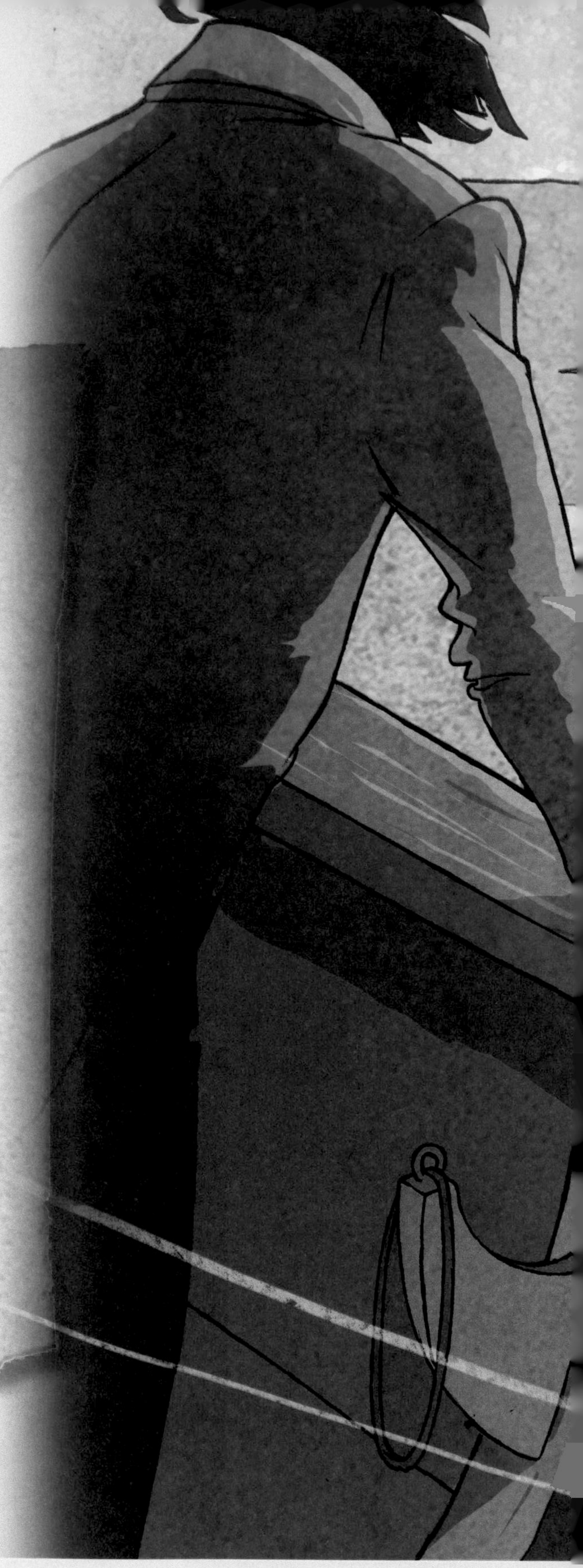

**Key Vocabulary**

**lonely** *adj.*, alone, without friends
**creature** *n.*, a living thing

**In Other Words**

**voyage** trip
**weary** tired
**accept** take; agree to
**heading** going
**record it** write it down

**Geography Background**
The Arctic is the area around the North Pole. It includes northern Canada and Greenland. Traditionally, people used dogsleds to travel across the ice and snow there.

Arctic Circle

## Look Into the Text

1. **Setting** Where and when does the first part of the story take place?
2. **Recall and Interpret** What does the letter say? Why did the man write this?
3. **Word Choice** What mood, or feeling, does the letter have? Which words does the author use to create that mood?

*Predict*
Do the creature and the man
know each other?

# The Stranger's Story

**M**y name is Victor Frankenstein. I **created** an **evil** monster. The terrible things that the creature has done are all because of me. No one else must ever know how to do what I have done— I will **take that secret with me to my grave**.

After many years of study, I had discovered how to bring something to life. I was eager to use what I had learned, so I devoted two years to making a new creature out of bones and body parts from graveyards and **slaughterhouses**.

At last, my **experiment** was ready. An enormous, lifeless creature lay on the table in my lab. I thought my creation would show the world what a great **scientist** I was. I did not know how wrong I was!

That cold November night, I brought my creature to life. I remember the moment his black lips moved. His skin, stretched and sewn together, **quivered**. He took a **rasping** breath and opened his watery, yellow eyes. Then that **repulsive** creature sat up and looked at me.

**Key Vocabulary**
  **create** *v.*, to make something new
  **evil** *adj.*, very bad
  **experiment** *n.*, an activity that
    someone does to test an idea
  **scientist** *n.*, a person who studies
    science

**In Other Words**
  **take that secret with me to my
    grave** never tell that secret
  **slaughterhouses** places where animals
    are killed for meat
  **quivered** shook, moved
  **rasping** scratchy, rough
  **repulsive** ugly

**Look Into the Text**

1. **Confirm Prediction** Was your prediction correct? How do you know? What happened that you did not expect?
2. **Visualize** Describe the **creature**.

Instead of feeling proud, I **was disgusted**. I could not even stand to look at him. So I ran away, asking myself, *What have I done?*

I hid in my room and nervously **paced** the floor, trying to determine what to do. But, because I had been hard at work for so long, I had not **slumbered** for many days, and I soon fell onto my bed and slept.

An odd, gurgling noise woke me up. The terrible creature was standing over me, grinning and making baby noises. He came closer and reached out one of his enormous hands to touch me. I leapt up and ran until I **crumpled** onto the street. A good friend found me and took me to his home. I lay there, sick for several months.

Much later, I learned what had happened to my creature while I was unwell.

## What have I done?

He had wandered the streets. He was a newborn—a **hideous**, giant newborn. He knew nothing, he could not talk, and he did not even understand his own feelings.

People who saw him were terrified. Some people ran away screaming. Others threw stones and bricks at him. One man shot him in the arm.

The frightened, lonely creature hid in **a vacant** shed next to a cottage. He taught himself to speak and read by listening to the family in the cottage. Then he learned that I was his creator.

He found me and begged me for a **companion**. I felt sorry for him, so I agreed to create a wife for him. But when it came time to bring the female creature to life, I couldn't do it. I **destroyed** her instead. He was very angry and promised to make my life as unhappy as his life was. I was now his enemy.

**Key Vocabulary**
**hideous** *adj.*, very ugly
**destroy** *v.*, to take apart, to ruin

**In Other Words**
**was disgusted** felt sick; was shocked
**paced** walked back and forth across
**slumbered** slept
**crumpled** fell down
**a vacant** an empty
**companion** friend

The creature **terrorized** me for many years. First he found and killed my dear brother. Then he killed my best friend. Finally he killed my sweet bride on our wedding night. I **vowed** to stop this horrible beast.

I searched the world for him, and he has led me to this frozen land. But I have become weak from chasing him, and I know I am dying.

Now I realize I was wrong to create the monster and then **abandon him**. Now I know his **misery** is my fault, not his.

**In Other Words**
**terrorized** scared
**vowed** promised
**abandon him** go away from him
**misery** unhappiness

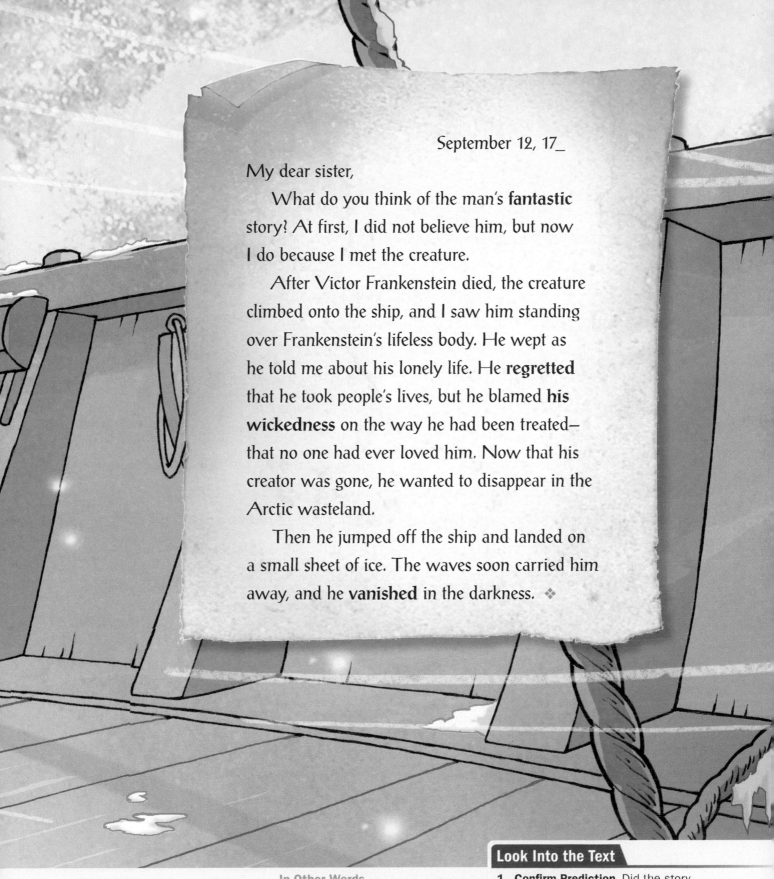

September 12, 17_

My dear sister,

What do you think of the man's **fantastic** story? At first, I did not believe him, but now I do because I met the creature.

After Victor Frankenstein died, the creature climbed onto the ship, and I saw him standing over Frankenstein's lifeless body. He wept as he told me about his lonely life. He **regretted** that he took people's lives, but he blamed **his wickedness** on the way he had been treated— that no one had ever loved him. Now that his creator was gone, he wanted to disappear in the Arctic wasteland.

Then he jumped off the ship and landed on a small sheet of ice. The waves soon carried him away, and he **vanished** in the darkness. ❖

**In Other Words**
**fantastic** amazing, unbelievable
**regretted** was sorry
**his wickedness** the bad things he did
**vanished** disappeared

## Look Into the Text

1. **Confirm Prediction** Did the story end the way you thought it would? Explain what happened that you did not expect.

2. **Narrator's Point of View** Which character tells most of the story? Why is he unable to tell the whole story?

# How Frankenstein Began

by Mary Shelley

People often ask: *How did I think up such a hideous story when I was still a young woman?* Here is how it came about.

In the summer of 1816 my husband and I went to Switzerland. There we became friends with our neighbor, the famous poet Lord Byron.

It was a very wet summer. The rain often kept us in the house for days, so we read ghost stories to pass the time.

One day, Lord Byron suggested, "We will each write our own ghost story." I tried hard to think of a story that would make the reader afraid, but I had no ideas.

One day, I listened to a **conversation** between Lord Byron and my husband. They wondered if a dead person could live again. They wanted to know if body parts could be made, put together, and brought to life.

Mary Wollstonecraft Shelley
1797–1851

*Mary Wollstonecraft Shelley, ca. 1840, Richard Rothwell. Oil on canvas, National Portrait Gallery, London.*

It was very late before we went to bed. I put my head on my pillow, but I did not sleep. Instead, my mind was filled with **vivid images** of pieced-together monsters.

I opened my eyes in terror!! I could not get the dream out of my head. I knew I must try to think of something else. So I thought of my unwritten ghost story. If I could only think of a story that would frighten my reader as much as I had been frightened by my dream!

That's when the idea hit me: I only have to describe the monster in my dream. What terrified me will terrify others.

The next day I announced that I had thought of a story. I began that day and wrote out the details of my dream.

---

**In Other Words**
**conversation** talk
**vivid images** colorful pictures

**Historical Background**
Mary Wollstonecraft Shelley wrote *Frankenstein* when she was nineteen. She was married to Percy Shelley, a well-known poet. Her parents, Mary Wollstonecraft and William Godwin, were also writers.

**Look Into the Text**

1. **Paraphrase** What inspired Mary Shelley to write *Frankenstein*?
2. **Plot and Setting** When and where did this event take place? How did it contribute to the story of Frankenstein?

# Connect Reading and Writing

**Vocabulary**
created
creature
destroys
evil
experiment
hideous
lonely
scientist

## CRITICAL THINKING

1. **SUM IT UP** Use your Beginning-Middle-End Chart to describe how Dr. Frankenstein's character developed throughout the story. Then use your chart to summarize the story.

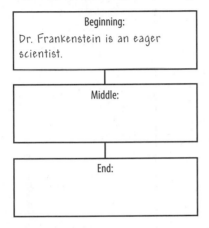

Beginning:
Dr. Frankenstein is an eager scientist.

Middle:

End:

**Beginning-Middle-End Chart**

2. **Compare** Do you think the **hideous** monster in Mary Shelley's dream and story is as frightening today as it was in her time? Why or why not?

3. **Predict** What do you think the **lonely** creature does for the rest of his life? Explain.

4. **Make Judgments** Do you think Dr. Frankenstein is responsible for the **evil** things the **creature** does? Explain. Use examples from the text.

## READING FLUENCY

**Expression** Read the passage on page 567 to a partner. Assess your fluency.

1. My voice never/sometimes/always matched what I read.

2. What I did best in my reading was _____.

## READING STRATEGY

What strategy helped you understand this selection? Tell a partner about it.

## VOCABULARY REVIEW

**Oral Review** Read the paragraph aloud. Add the vocabulary words.

I am a _____ who used to study animals. Last year, I set up an _____ to test ideas about growth. It was wrong! I used a rabbit named Ruff, who used to be a cute, furry little _____. I _____ a _____, ugly monster from him. Ruff Rabbit grew into a 200-pound furball. He is not an _____ monster, but he is dangerous. He hops on cars and _____ them. My friends no longer visit me, so I get _____. I'm busy, though, raising acres of carrots, clover, and alfalfa.

**Written Review** Pretend you knew Dr. Frankenstein before his **experiment**. Write him a letter telling him why he should not **create** the **creature**. Use five vocabulary words.

## WRITE ABOUT THE ⬤ GUIDING QUESTION

### Analyze a Classic Character

Reread the selection. If you saw the **creature**, what feelings would you have? Support your explanation with examples from the text.

# Connect Across the Curriculum

## Use Word Parts

| Prefix | Meaning | Example | Word Meaning |
|---|---|---|---|
| in- | not | inactive | not active |
| de- | do the opposite | defrost | to take the frost off something |
| bi- | two | bicolored | two-colored |

**Academic Vocabulary**
- **locate** (lō-kāt) *verb*
  To **locate** something is to find it.

Many English words are made of word parts, including prefixes and base words. If you know the meaning of the word parts, you can sometimes figure out what the whole word means.

**Combine Word Parts** Figure out the meaning of each word. Look at the chart above. **Locate** the meaning of the prefix. If you don't know the base word, look it up in a dictionary. Put the meanings of the word parts together. Compare your definitions with a partner's. Use a dictionary to confirm.

**1.** incorrect

**2.** decode

**3.** bicycle

**4.** biweekly

**5.** insane

**6.** debug

## Analyze Theme

**Academic Vocabulary**
- **theme** (thēm) *noun*
  A **theme** is the main message of a story.

Usually, a story's **theme** says something important about life or the world, such as "Nature is more powerful than people."

Authors usually don't tell you the **theme**. What the characters do, think, feel, and say can help you identify the **theme**.

Most stories have more than one **theme**. Also, readers interpret **themes** in different ways. Each reader has a personal idea about the **theme**.

**Look for Clues** Review your Beginning-Middle-End Chart about how Dr. Frankenstein changes. Then reread "Frankenstein" and make a similar chart for the creature.

**Put the Clues Together** Look at the clues on your charts and determine what ideas about life or the world you can find.

**State a Theme** Decide what you think the author is trying to tell you. Then write a sentence that states the **theme**.

**Share Your Ideas** With a partner, discuss your interpretation of the **theme**. Do you and your partner have the same idea about the **theme**?

## Describe People and Places

**Class Story** Tell a story about someone lost in a scary place. Have one person start. Take turns adding a sentence. Use adjectives. Continue around the room until the story ends.

> It is the stormiest night of the year.

> A tall girl runs through a dark village.

## Write About a Creepy Situation

**Study the Models** When you write a story or a description, include interesting, descriptive **adjectives** . Adjectives help your readers picture what you are writing about.

**JUST OK**

My brother and I follow a path through the woods. It is the **colder** night of the year. Suddenly, I hear a sound behind me. My brother whispers, "What was that noise?" We turn around and see a pair of eyes in the bushes. It is a wolf!

> This story is a little dull. The writer uses only one descriptive **adjective** and has one wrong form.

**BETTER**

My brother and I follow a **narrow**, **winding** path through the **dark** woods. It is the **coldest** night of the year. Suddenly, I hear a **growling** sound behind me. My brother whispers, "What was that noise?" We turn around and see a pair of **silver** eyes in the bushes. It is a **large**, **gray** wolf! We are **terrified**!

> The writer uses **adjectives** to describe how things look, sound, and feel. The reader thinks: "I can really picture the scene."

**Revise It** Work with a partner to revise the following passage. Add adjectives. Include one comparative or superlative adjective.

A woman lives in this mansion. Every evening she walks in her garden. She wears a cape and carries a candle. A bird sits on her shoulder. At midnight the woman goes inside her house. She puts the candle in that window up there.

▲ A candle sits in the dark, creepy house.

✎ **WRITE ON YOUR OWN** Imagine a creepy situation and describe it. Use descriptive adjectives in your writing.

**REMEMBER**

- Adjectives usually come before nouns.
- **Predicate adjectives** come after forms of *be*.
- Use **-er** or **more** to compare two things and **-est** or **most** to compare three or more.

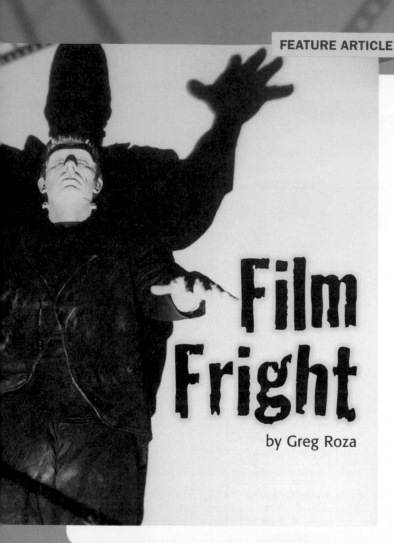

**FEATURE ARTICLE**

# Film Fright

by Greg Roza

## SELECTION 2 OVERVIEW

▶ **Build Background**

▶ **Language & Grammar**
Make Comparisons
Use Adverbs

▶ **Prepare to Read**
Learn Key Vocabulary
Analyze Media

▶ **Read and Write**
**Introduce the Genre**
Feature Article
**Focus on Reading**
Analyze Media
**Apply the Focus Strategy**
Visualize
**Critical Thinking**
**Reading Fluency**
Read with Appropriate Phrasing
**Vocabulary Review**
**Write About the Guiding Question**

▶ **Connect Across the Curriculum**
**Vocabulary Study**
Use Latin and Greek Roots
**Literary Analysis**
Analyze Rhythm in Poetry
**Language and Grammar**
Make Comparisons
**Writing and Grammar**
Write to Compare Creepy Actions

---

## Build Background

### Meet Movie Monsters

Mary Shelley created Frankenstein's monster nearly 200 years ago, and it was terrifying. How does it compare with modern versions?

**Digital Library**

myNGconnect.com
◈ View the video.

◀ This 1940 horror movie features a monster that people now call "Frankenstein."

### Connect

**Describe a Monster** Think of a movie you've seen that includes a monster. Write your thoughts and ideas about what makes the monster scary. Share with a group.

The monster's name:

What makes it scary:

How it was created (for example, with makeup or special effects):

# Language & Grammar

1 TRY OUT LANGUAGE
2 LEARN GRAMMAR
3 APPLY ON YOUR OWN

## Make Comparisons

Listen to the song. Listen again and chime in.

**SONG**

The Wolf Man is not very handsome,
In fact, he's not handsome at all.
In fact, he looks really quite scary,
In Hollywood's *Monster Ball*.

Frankenstein isn't too friendly,
In fact, he's not friendly at all.
In fact, he is scarier than Wolf Man
In Hollywood's *Monster Ball*.

But Frankenstein's Bride is quite pretty.
In fact, she's the prettiest of all.
In fact, there is no one who's prettier
In Hollywood's *Monster Ball*.

# Use Adverbs

- Use an **adverb** to describe a **verb**. Adverbs often end in **-ly**.

  EXAMPLES   The monster's bride **yells loudly**.    (how)
  The Wolf Man **stands there**.            (where)
  Frankenstein **appears immediately**. (when)

- Use an **adverb** to make an adjective or another adverb stronger.

  EXAMPLES   The bride is **really** pretty.
  adjective

- Add **-er** to many **adverbs** to compare two actions.
  Add **-est** to many **adverbs** to compare three or more actions.
  If the **adverb** ends in **-ly**, use **more** to compare two actions and **most** to
  compare three or more actions.

  EXAMPLES   The bride yells **louder** than ever before.
  She stands the **stillest** she has ever stood.
  She backs away **more quietly** than a mouse.
  Her husband rescues her **most earnestly**.

## Practice Together

Say each sentence with an appropriate adverb from the box. Explain
whether the adverb tells how, where, or when about a verb, or whether it
makes an adjective or adverb stronger.

| oddly | really | exactly | there |
| --- | --- | --- | --- |

1. The theater opens _____ at 7:00.
2. We are going _____.
3. The actors are _____ good.
4. They dress _____.

## Try It!

Read each sentence. Write an appropriate adverb
from the box on a card. Hold up the card as you say
the sentence. Does the adverb tell how, where, or
when about the verb? Or does it make an adjective
or adverb stronger?

| tonight | already | skillfully | very |
| --- | --- | --- | --- |

5. We are seeing a movie _____.
6. The actors will say their lines _____.
7. Tonight's film will start _____ soon.
8. The previews are _____ running.

▲ Frankenstein is quite different in each movie.
Sometimes he acts tenderly. Sometimes he behaves
very badly.

# Make a Movie Poster

## MAKE COMPARISONS

Look at the movie poster below and the one on pages 221 and 229. Then create your own poster for a movie monster.

Choose or invent a movie monster. Imagine how your character looks and how it acts. Draw the character on a large piece of paper. Make up a movie title.

Now form a group and compare monsters and their behavior. You may want to use adverbs like *fiercely, more crazily, spookily, wildly, really,* and *very.*

> My monster swims easily through the sewers.

> Yes, but my monster swims more quietly.

## HOW TO MAKE COMPARISONS

1. Tell how two or more things are alike.
2. Tell how two or more things are different.

## USE ADVERBS TO MAKE COMPARISONS

You can use **adverbs** to tell more about a verb and to compare actions.
Add -**er** or use **more** to compare two actions.
Add -**est** or use **most** to compare three or more things.

EXAMPLES     **Tonight**, we're watching a monster movie.

One boy invents **more carefully** than his teacher.

Even so, his monster comes to life the **quickest**.

▲ This movie poster is for two movies: *Son of Frankenstein* and *The Bride of Frankenstein*.

# Prepare to Read

## Learn Key Vocabulary

**Study the Words** Use the steps below.

1. Pronounce the word. Say it aloud several times. Spell it.
2. Rate your word knowledge.
3. Study the example. Tell more about the word.
4. Practice it. Make the word your own.

### Key Words

**actor** (ak-tur) *noun*
▶ page 230

An **actor** is a person who acts in a movie or play. The **actors** are working on a new movie.
*Base Word:* **act**

**character** (kair-ik-tur) *noun*
▶ page 228

A **character** is someone in a story. They acted out the roles of the **characters** in the play.

**classic** (kla-sik) *adjective*
▶ page 232

Something that is **classic** is old but good. **Classic** cars are expensive if they are in good shape.

**fascinated** (fa-su-nā-tud)
*adjective* ▶ page 228

To be **fascinated** means to be very interested in something. The student is **fascinated** by the model.
*Base Word:* **fascinate**

**original** (u-rij-u-nul)
*adjective* ▶ page 229

Something that is **original** is the first of its kind. Mary Shelley's novel is the **original** story of Frankenstein.
*Base Word:* **origin**

**process** (prah-ses) *noun*
▶ page 230

A **process** is a set of actions taken to get a certain result. Workers are part of a **process** for making goods.
*Synonyms:* **system, procedure**

**successful** (suk-ses-ful)
*adjective* ▶ page 228

To be **successful** means to have a good result or to be well liked. The team was **successful** at the science fair.
*Base Word:* **success**

**terror** (tair-ur) *noun*
▶ page 229

To feel **terror** means to have much fear. The man runs away from the bear in **terror**.

**Practice the Words** Make a Study Card for each Key Word. Then compare your cards with a partner's.

> *process*
>
> **What it means:** *a set of actions taken to get a certain result*
>
> **Example:** *a recipe*
>
> **Not an example:** *watching TV*

**Study Card**

# Analyze Media

**What is Media?** Media can be anything used to communicate information. Traditionally, media includes television, radio, film, and printed materials like books and magazines. Today, it also includes Web sites, blogs, podcasts, and other information on the Internet.

You can learn about the same topic from different forms of media. These forms can combine **specific** words, pictures, and sound in different ways to help you understand more about the topic.

## Reading Strategies

- Plan
- Monitor
- Make Connections
- **Visualize** Imagine the sights, sounds, smells, tastes, and feel of what the author is describing.
- Ask Questions
- Determine Importance
- Make Inferences
- Synthesize

### Look Into the Text

" I understand monster movies were very successful in 1931. In the video, I learned that monster movies are the most popular type of horror films. Now I understand that their early success probably made them so popular. "

Movie studios made many popular monster movies from 1920 to 1950. In 1931, Universal Studios released *Dracula* and *Frankenstein*. These films were two of the most successful horror movies of the time. The studios also made movies about other characters. These characters included the Wolf Man, the Invisible Man, and the Creature from the Black Lagoon.

## Practice Together

**Begin a Compare Media Chart** A Compare Media Chart can help you organize your notes about a topic and analyze media. Reread the passage, and add to the chart. Then review your Critical Viewing Guide from "Meet Movie Monsters" and write what you learned from the video in the chart. As you read the feature article, add notes to your chart. Then use what you learned from both forms of media to develop a clear understanding of the topic.

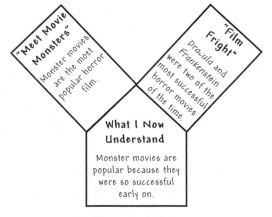

"Meet Movie Monsters"
Monster movies are the most popular horror film.

"Film Fright"
*Dracula* and *Frankenstein* were two of the most successful horror movies of the time.

What I Now Understand
Monster movies are popular because they were so successful early on.

Compare Media Chart

## Academic Vocabulary

- **specific** (spi-**si**-fik) *adjective*
  Something that is **specific** is part of a category of related things.

## Feature Article

A feature article features, or focuses on, one topic. Writers use interesting facts and **descriptive details** to tell about a real-life topic in an entertaining way.

A feature article is print media. You can use what you already know from viewing "Meet Movie Monsters" to help understand the topic.

**Look Into the Text**

> Jack Pierce was a makeup artist. He created the monsters in *Frankenstein Meets the Wolf Man*. Pierce used glue and animal hair to make the Wolf Man.

As you read, analyze how the two forms of media combine words, pictures, and sounds to present information. The descriptive details can help you picture what you read in order to make connections between what you read and what you viewed.

# Film Fright

by Greg Roza

Comprehension Coach

# HISTORY OF HORROR FILMS

The first motion pictures were made in the 1890s. They were usually very short and simple. Some were only thirty seconds long! People were **fascinated** with moving images.

In 1910, Thomas Edison made the movie *Frankenstein*. It was only sixteen minutes. It **terrified moviegoers**, though. In the 1920s, a horror movie revolution began. People made **numerous** silent horror films.

Movie studios made many **popular** monster movies from 1920 to 1950. In 1931, Universal Studios released *Dracula* and *Frankenstein*. These films were two of the most **successful** horror movies of the time. The studios also made movies about other **characters**. These characters included the Wolf Man, the Invisible Man, and the Creature from the Black Lagoon.

**Key Vocabulary**
**fascinated** *adj.*, interested in something
**successful** *adj.*, having a good result; well-liked by many people
**character** *n.*, someone in a story

**In Other Words**
**terrified moviegoers** frightened the people who saw it
**numerous** many
**popular** well-liked

# STUDIO MONSTERS

The studios made several movies about the Frankenstein monster during this time. The **original** one tells about **mad** Dr. Frankenstein. He creates a monster from body parts. Then he brings it to life. The next movie was *The Bride of Frankenstein*. The monster forces Dr. Frankenstein to build him a monster wife. In *The Son of Frankenstein*, Frankenstein's son wakes up the monster. The **terror** begins all over again. *The Ghost of Frankenstein* includes a monster more terrible than ever.

In the 1940s, studios began **teaming up movie monsters**. *Frankenstein Meets the Wolf Man* is an example. It joins the story of Frankenstein's monster with the story of the Wolf Man.

In *The Wolf Man*, Lawrence Talbot tries to save a woman from **a werewolf**. Talbot kills the werewolf. But he is bitten by it. At the next full moon, Talbot turns into the Wolf Man.

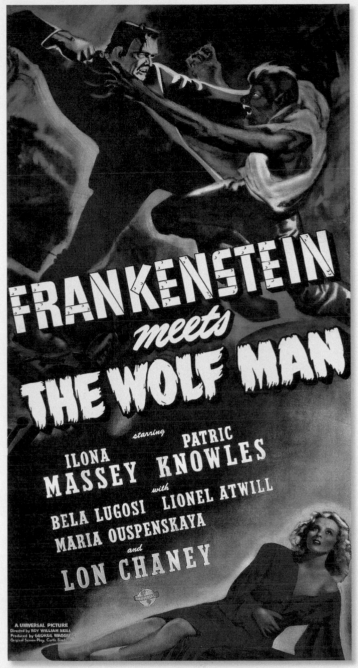

▲ This movie poster shows the classic monster team of the 1940s.

---

**Key Vocabulary**
**original** *adj.*, the first one of its kind
**terror** *n.*, fear

**In Other Words**
**mad** crazy
**teaming up movie monsters** putting different monsters in the same movie
**a werewolf** someone who is part human and part wolf

**Look Into the Text**

1. **Paraphrase** Use your own words to tell the early history of horror movies.
2. **Main Idea and Details** What details show that horror movies were popular?

# THE MEN WHO MADE THE MONSTERS

Jack Pierce was a makeup artist. He created the monsters in *Frankenstein Meets the Wolf Man*. Pierce used glue and animal hair to make the Wolf Man. The makeup was very uncomfortable. The **actors** had to sit still for many hours. It could be a **grueling** experience. The results were **spectacular**, though.

John P. Fulton was a cameraman. He worked on *Frankenstein Meets the Wolf Man*. Fulton used stop-motion photography. This **process** takes a very long time.

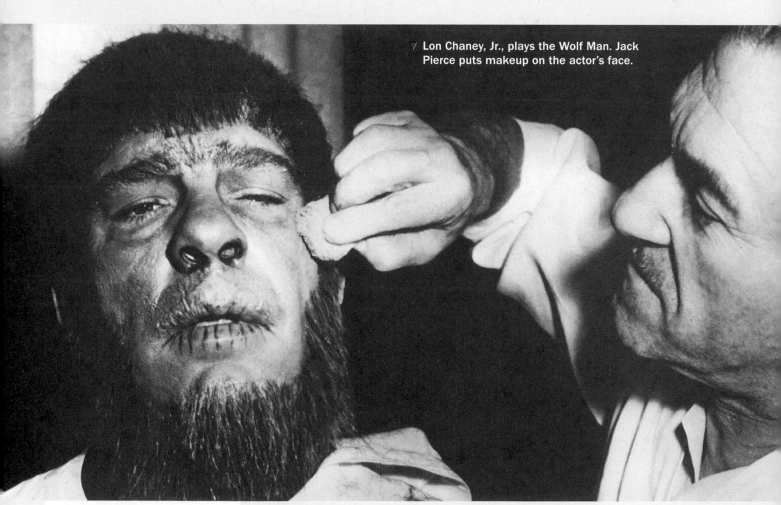

▽ Lon Chaney, Jr., plays the Wolf Man. Jack Pierce puts makeup on the actor's face.

**Key Vocabulary**

**actor** *n.*, a person who acts in a movie or play

**process** *n.*, a set of actions taken to get a certain result

**In Other Words**

**grueling** difficult
**spectacular** wonderful, incredible

Fulton used this **technique** to show Talbot **transforming** into a werewolf. First he filmed the actor without makeup. Then he stopped the camera. Jack Pierce **applied** the first layer of makeup. Then Fulton filmed for a few more seconds. Fulton and Pierce repeated this process many times.

Fulton put all the pieces together. On screen, Talbot turned into the Wolf Man. The transformation on film took ten seconds. The actual process took about six hours!

▲ These photos show how the actor transforms into the Wolf Man.

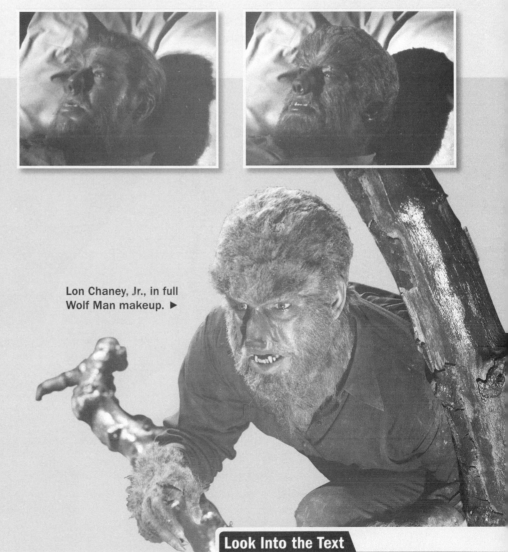

Lon Chaney, Jr., in full Wolf Man makeup. ▶

**In Other Words**
**technique** special way of doing things
**transforming** changing
**applied** put on

**Look Into the Text**

1. **Categorize** Name two jobs people do to make monsters.
2. **Steps in a Process** Tell how John Fulton and Jack Pierce changed an actor into a werewolf.

# THE LEGACY

By the 1950s, U.S. movie studios stopped making these types of monster movies. New horror movies began to take their place. The **classic** monsters were not forgotten, though.

In 1974, Mel Brooks and Gene Wilder made *Young Frankenstein*. They filmed it where the original Frankenstein series was filmed. Their movie is a comedy. It makes fun of the old Frankenstein films. It also **honors** them.

▽ The movie *Young Frankenstein* is a comedy. The actor Gene Wilder plays Dr. Frankenstein. The director, Mel Brooks, is shown at the right.

**Key Vocabulary**
**classic** *adj.*, old but good

**In Other Words**
**honors** shows respect for

## FRANKENSTEIN RETURNS

In 1994, Kenneth Branagh made *Mary Shelley's Frankenstein*. His movie follows the same basic plot as Shelley's novel. In this movie, Frankenstein's monster is not a flat-headed, growling monster. It is **an intelligent and sensitive** creature.

Frankenstein's monster in *Mary Shelley's Frankenstein* is like the character in the classic novel. ▶

## STAMP OF APPROVAL

The movie monsters of the 1930s and '40s have had a lasting effect on popular culture. In 1997, the U.S. Postal Service made the Classic Movie Monsters postage stamps. These stamps also honored the work of makeup artist Jack Pierce.

The work of **these horror movie pioneers** helped make the monsters popular. Because of them, Frankenstein's monster and the Wolf Man continue to be popular today. ❖

▲ The stamp of Frankenstein's monster is one in a series that honors classic movie monsters.

**In Other Words**

**an intelligent and sensitive** a smart and easily upset
**these horror movie pioneers** early makers of horror movies

**Look Into the Text**

1. **Evidence and Conclusion** What information tells you that **classic** monsters were not forgotten?
2. **Compare** How is the movie *Mary Shelley's Frankenstein* like the **original** story?

# FRANKENSTEIN MAKES A SANDWICH
## by Adam Rex

When Frankenstein
prepared to dine
on ham-and-cheese on wheat,

he found, instead,
5  he had no bread
(or mustard, cheese, or meat).

What could he do?
He thought it through
until his brain was sore,

10  And thought he ought
to see what he could
borrow from next door.

**In Other Words**
**prepared to dine on** got ready
to eat
**brain was sore** head hurt

**Cultural Background**
Frankenstein is not the name of
the monster in the original story
by Mary Shelley. The scientist
who created the monster was Dr.
Frankenstein. As this classic story
changed over time, people began
calling the monster Frankenstein.

His neighbors gawked
as Frankie walked
15 the paths up to their porches.

Each time he tried,
the folks inside
would chase him off with torches.

## "A MONSTER! EEK!"
20 the people shrieked.
"Oh, make him go away!"

The angry hordes
unsheathed their swords,
pulled pitchforks out of hay.

25 They threw tomatoes,
pigs, potatoes,
loaves of moldy bread.

And then a thought
struck Frankenstein
30 as pickles struck his head.

**In Other Words**
**gawked** stared
**shrieked** screamed in fear
**hordes unsheathed** groups
   of people took out
**moldy** spoiled, rotten

It's true, at first

he thought the worst:

His neighbors were so rude!

But then he found

35  that on the ground

they'd made a mound of *food*.

He piled it high

and waved good-bye

and shouted, **"Thanks a bunch!"**

40  Then stacked it on

a plate and ate

a big, disgusting lunch. ❖

**In Other Words**
**rude** mean, unkind
**mound** pile

**Look Into the Text**

1. **Rhyme** Which words in this poem rhyme, or sound alike?
2. **Tone** The tone of a poem is what the writer thinks of the topic. What is the tone of this poem? Which words tell you?

# Connect Reading and Writing

actor

characters

classic

fascinated

original

process

successful

terror

## CRITICAL THINKING

1. **SUM IT UP** Compare and discuss your Compare Media Chart with a partner as you summarize the selection.

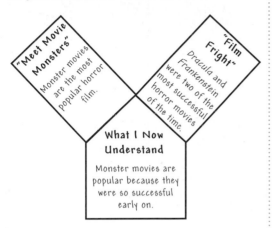

**Meet Movie Monsters"**
Monster movies are the most popular horror film.

**"Film Fright"**
Dracula and Frankenstein were two of the most successful horror movies of the time.

**What I Now Understand**
Monster movies are popular because they were so successful early on.

**Compare Media Chart**

2. **Compare** How is Frankenstein in the poem like the Frankenstein **characters** in the movies? How is he different?

3. **Speculate** Many people go to horror films. Why do you think they are **fascinated** by evil **characters** and **terror**?

4. **Generalize** Think about **classic** monsters in the movies. What traits make these **characters** memorable?

## READING FLUENCY

**Phrasing** Read the passage on page 568 to a partner. Assess your fluency.

1. I did not pause/sometimes paused/ always paused for punctuation.

2. What I did best in my reading was _____.

## READING STRATEGY

What strategy helped you understand this selection? Tell a partner about it.

## VOCABULARY REVIEW

**Oral Review** Read the paragraph aloud. Add the vocabulary words.

Boris Karloff, an _____ in many movies, has played many _____. His role as Frankenstein's monster was his most popular, or _____. Karloff went through the long _____ of putting on monster makeup every day of filming. It created a new look for the creature, unlike the one in the _____ story. Audiences were _____. They were in _____ as they watched the frightening monster. Today, the 1931 movie *Frankenstein* is a _____ movie that people watch on DVD with amusement.

**Written Review** Would you rather be an **actor** or a makeup artist for a horror movie? Write a job description for the job you choose. Use five vocabulary words.

**WRITE ABOUT THE** GUIDING QUESTION

### Analyze a Classic Character
Reread the selection. Why is the **character** of Frankenstein's monster still part of our culture? Support your opinion with evidence from the text.

# Connect Across the Curriculum

## Use Latin and Greek Roots

| Root | Origin | Meaning |
|------|--------|---------|
| dict | Latin | tell |
| gram | Greek | write |
| scrib | Latin | write |
| sect | Latin | cut |
| tele | Greek | far |

**Academic Vocabulary**

• **relate** (ri-lāt) *verb*
   When you **relate** two things, you think about how they are connected.

Greek or Latin roots can make up English words. A root is a central word part that has meaning; however, it cannot stand on its own. If you know the meanings of the word parts, you can figure out the meaning of the word. For example:

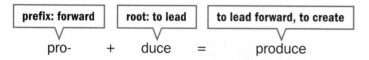

| prefix: forward | root: to lead | to lead forward, to create |
|---|---|---|

pro- + duce = produce

**Use Roots** Define each word. Use the chart above and a dictionary to find the meanings of the word parts and of the words. Discuss how the meaning of each root **relates** to the meaning of the whole word.

**1.** predict    **2.** bisect    **3.** program    **4.** prescribe    **5.** telegram

## Analyze Rhythm in Poetry

**Academic Vocabulary**

• **locate** (lō-kāt) *verb*
   To **locate** something is to find it.

Poetry has **rhythm**, or a pattern of beats. One form of rhythm is **meter**, which is a pattern of stressed and unstressed sounds. To get an idea of what meter is like, make a loud clap and then a soft clap. Continue the pattern of beats. Sound helps communicate the **mood**, or feeling, of a poem. It also helps express a poem's meaning.

**Analyze and Compare** With the class, read "Frankenstein Makes a Sandwich" two times: once silently and another aloud. As you read aloud, clap out the rhythm. **Locate** each stressed sound. Notice that the rhythm is quick and lively.

With a partner, discuss how hearing the poem read aloud compares to reading it silently. First, read the following questions. What do you visualize when you read the poem to yourself? What changed when the poem was read aloud? Why? Is the poem's meaning easier or harder to understand when you read it aloud than when you read it silently? Why? Is the poem's mood serious or silly or something else? How does the rhythm match the mood? Reread the poem silently and aloud. Then discuss each question.

## Make Comparisons

**Share with a Classmate** Imagine being in a monster movie. Tell a classmate what happens and what you do. Use adverbs. Switch roles. Compare your actions with your classmate's.

> I ran away quickly.

> I ran away more quickly than you did!

## Write to Compare Creepy Actions

**Study the Models** When you write, use **adverbs** to tell how, when, or where an action happened or to make an adjective or another adverb stronger.

**NOT OK**

> I think it is scarier when a monster moves **slowly** than when it moves **fast**. Slow movements build suspense. When a monster is **quietly** creeping, I sit at the edge of my seat. I don't know when the monster will leap out! When it does, I scream **more louder** than anyone.

The writer uses **adverbs** sparingly and uses a wrong form to compare actions.

**OK**

> I think it is **much** scarier when a monster moves **slowly** than when it moves **really** **fast**. Slow movements **gradually** build suspense. When a monster is **quietly** creeping **around**, I sit **nervously** at the edge of my seat. I don't know when the monster will **suddenly** leap out! When it does, I scream **louder** than anyone.

The writer fixes the error and uses **adverbs** to add details and to make adjectives and adverbs stronger.

**Revise It** Work with a partner to improve this passage. Add more adverbs that tell how, where, and when.

> The movie begins. A jeep drives along a pitted dirt road. Something growls. The driver stares. Something big and scaly swings from heavy vines. It drops into the jeep.

**WRITE ON YOUR OWN** Write about a scary movie that you have seen. Be sure to include adverbs.

**REMEMBER**
- Use an adverb to describe a verb. Adverbs often end in **-ly**.
- Use an adverb to make an adjective or adverb stronger.

PLAY

# MISTER MONSTER

BY SHIRLEYANN COSTIGAN
ILLUSTRATED BY KEITH GRAVES

# Build Background

## Discuss Plays

In some ways, plays and movies are alike. In other ways, they are different. Look at the photos and talk about how plays are special.

**Digital Library**

myNGconnect.com
⊙ View the images.

▲ Actors perform a play in special costumes.

## Connect

**Quickwrite** Which do you think is more fun to watch, a play or a movie? Why do you think so? Take about three minutes to write your ideas. Save your writing. You may wish to use this frame.

Watching a _____ is better than watching a _____ because _____ .

# Language & Grammar

## Describe an Event or Experience

CD

Look at the photo. Listen to how the people describe the show. Then pretend you are there and describe something.

**PICTURE PROMPT**

▲ The play *Wicked* is based on the characters of the Wicked Witch and the Good Witch from the book *The Wizard of Oz* by L. Frank Baum.

> This show is exciting! The costumes are wonderful.

> The music is wonderful, too. Both actresses sing beautifully.

# Use Participles

You can make your sentences more interesting by adding **participles**.
A **participle** is a verb form that can be used as an adjective.

**EXAMPLES**   The crew put the set on stage. They had **painted** it.
<br>verb

The crew put the **painted** set on stage.
<br>adjective

Then they brought in a platform. The platform was **rolling**.
<br>verb

Then they brought in a **rolling** platform.
<br>adjective

- The **present participles** of regular and irregular verbs end in -**ing**.
- The **past participles** of regular verbs end in -**ed**.
- The **past participles** of irregular verbs usually have a new spelling.

| Regular Verb | Irregular Verb | Present Participle | Past Participle |
|---|---|---|---|
| | break | break**ing** | broken |
| damage | | damag**ing** | damag**ed** |
| determine | | determin**ing** | determin**ed** |
| travel | | travel**ing** | travel**ed** |
| | hide | hid**ing** | hidden |
| | tear | tear**ing** | torn |

## Practice Together

Combine each pair of sentences. Move the underlined participle to tell
about a noun in the other sentence. Say the new sentence.

1. A hotel put up the actors. The actors were <u>traveling</u>.
2. The actors studied their parts. They were <u>determined</u>.
3. Ali fixed the microphones. They were <u>damaged</u>.
4. Jess repaired her script. Someone had <u>torn</u> it.

## Try It!

Write the underlined participle. Combine the sentences and
hold up the participle as you say it in the new sentence.

5. We repair props so we can use them again.
   The props were <u>damaged</u>.
6. I fixed a wand. Someone had <u>broken</u> it.
7. The customer mended a shirt. I had <u>torn</u> it.
8. The witch came out of a trapdoor. It was <u>hidden</u>.

▲ These talented actors are really believable.

# Relive an Experience

## DESCRIBE AN EVENT OR EXPERIENCE

Think of something special that you did. Maybe you went to a party, a big game, or a concert. What was the experience like? List details to help you remember it.

Response Chart

| What was the event? | Who was there? | What did I see and hear? | How did I feel? |
|---|---|---|---|
| a classic car parade | my family and friends; crowds of people | cool cars; the hum of motors; horns honking | excited; interested in all the cars |

Review the details on your chart. Close your eyes and try to relive the experience. Then think about how you would describe it to someone.

## HOW TO DESCRIBE AN EVENT OR EXPERIENCE

1. Tell what happened.
2. Give details.
3. Use descriptive words.

> I saw a classic car parade. The **restored** cars were amazing!

Get together with a partner and describe the event.

## USE PARTICIPLES AND PARTICIPIAL PHRASES

You can make your description more interesting by including **participles** and **participial phrases**.

EXAMPLES    **Sparkling** chrome on the cars dazzled everyone.

**Sitting on the curb**, I cheered for my favorites.

A **decorated** Ford Model T won first prize.

▲ The restored cars move slowly down the street.

# Prepare to Read

## Learn Key Vocabulary

**Study the Words** Use the steps below.

1. Pronounce the word. Say it aloud several times. Spell it.
2. Rate your word knowledge.
3. Study the example. Tell more about the word.
4. Practice it. Make the word your own.

**Rating Scale**

**1 =** I have never seen this word before.

**2 =** I am not sure of the word's meaning.

**3 =** I know this word and can teach the word's meaning to someone else.

### Key Words

**amazed** (u-māzd) *adjective*
▶ page 248

To be **amazed** means to be very surprised. They are **amazed** that the experiment worked so well.

**apply** (u-plī) *verb*
▶ page 248

To **apply** means to ask for or to request something. People often fill out forms when they **apply** for a job.

**audience** (aw-dē-unts) *noun*
▶ page 258

An **audience** is a group of people who watch or listen to something. The **audience** claps during the show.
*Synonyms:* **viewers, crowd**

**commercial** (ku-mur-shul) *noun* ▶ page 254

A **commercial** is an ad on TV or the radio. Most TV **commercials** show products that viewers can buy.
*Synonym:* **advertisement (ad)**

**disappear** (dis-u-pear) *verb*
▶ page 255

To **disappear** means to no longer be seen. When the bell rang, the students left quickly. They **disappeared**.
*Base Word:* **appear**

**mascot** (mas-kot) *noun*
▶ page 248

A **mascot** is a character that represents an organization. This basketball team's **mascot** cheers for the team.

**offstage** (awf-stāj) *adverb*
▶ page 248

To be **offstage** means to be away from the area that people see. The dancer waits **offstage**.
*Base Word:* **stage**
*Related Word:* **onstage**

**response** (ri-sponts) *noun*
▶ page 258

A **response** is what people think or say about something. She raises her hand to give a **response** to the question.
*Synonyms:* **answer, reply**

**Practice the Words** Make a Vocabulary Example Chart for the Key Words. Compare your chart with a partner's.

| Word | Definition | Example from My Life |
|------|-----------|----------------------|
| amazed | very surprised | I am always amazed when I see a full moon. |

Vocabulary Example Chart

# Analyze Character and Plot

**How does the plot affect characters in a story?** Remember that character and plot are important **elements** of fiction. In a story, characters respond to plot episodes. Words that describe the character or tell about what the character says or does reveal how a character changes as the plot moves toward a resolution.

As you read, identify how characters respond to events to help you analyze character and plot.

**Reading Strategies**

- Plan
- Monitor
- Make Connections
- **Visualize** Imagine the sights, sounds, smells, tastes, and touch of what the author is describing.
- Ask Questions
- Determine Importance
- Make Inferences
- Synthesize

**Look Into the Text**

### SCENE ONE

MS. ROSARIO *is pacing nervously in her office. It is 9:00 a.m.*

**MS. ROSARIO.** [*desperate*] I need a mascot for our Monster Sale. The broadcast starts in two hours! There must be at least one monster that needs a job!

> **"**I read that this is Scene One, the beginning of the story. I also see that Ms. Rosario is the character first involved in the plot conflict.**"**

**Begin a Plot Diagram** A Plot Diagram can help you analyze story events and character responses. This Plot Diagram shows the first character mentioned in the story. The plot often starts when a character faces a conflict. Reread the passage above. Determine the conflict in this story, and add it to the Plot Diagram.

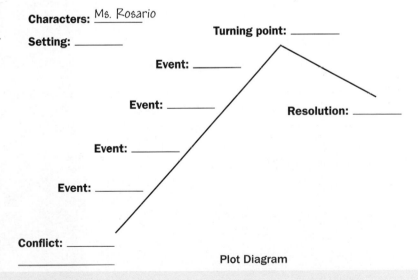

Characters: Ms. Rosario
Setting: _____
Event: _____
Event: _____
Event: _____
Event: _____
Turning point: _____
Resolution: _____
Conflict: _____
_____

Plot Diagram

**Academic Vocabulary**

- **element** (e-lu-ment)
  An **element** is a basic part of a whole.

## Play

A play is a story that is written for actors to perform. Plays have **dialogue**, or the words the characters speak. Plays also have **stage directions** that tell the actors how to look and act.

Look for details about characters in the dialogue and stage directions. Analyzing how characters respond to events can help you to better understand the characters.

**Look Into the Text**

[*MISS PETAL enters. She looks terrified.*] — **stage directions**

**MISS PETAL.** Ms. Rosario, someone is waiting to see you for the mascot job. — **dialogue**

**MS. ROSARIO.** Great! Show him in.

[*MISS PETAL leaves, still looking terrified.*]

Form mental images to visualize how characters think, feel, and act throughout the play. Look for words that describe characters. Picture the detail in your mind or sketch it on paper to make the ideas clear.

# MISTER MONSTER

## BY SHIRLEYANN COSTIGAN
## ILLUSTRATED BY KEITH GRAVES

### CHARACTERS

**MS. ROSARIO**, the manager of Dollar Rite Department Store

**MISS PETAL**, her assistant

**YGOR**, a lab assistant

**VICTOR FRANKENSTEIN**, a scientist

**THE MONSTER**, Dr. Frankenstein's creation

Comprehension Coach

---

**SCENE ONE**

MS. ROSARIO *is **pacing nervously** in her office. It is 9:00 a.m.*

**MS. ROSARIO.** [*desperate*] I need a mascot for our Monster Sale. The **broadcast** starts in two hours! There must be at least one monster that needs a job!

[*MISS PETAL enters. She looks terrified.*]

**MISS PETAL.** Ms. Rosario, someone is waiting to see you for the mascot job.

**MS. ROSARIO.** Great! Show him in.

[*MISS PETAL leaves, still looking terrified.*]

[*YGOR enters, holding a thick rope that is pulled tight. At the other end of the rope is THE MONSTER, hidden **offstage**. MS. ROSARIO stares up at THE MONSTER. She looks **amazed**, then overjoyed.*]

**MS. ROSARIO.** Perfect.

**YGOR.** My name is Ygor Manic. [*points to THE MONSTER, still offstage*] This is my friend Frankensteinz. He wants to **apply** for the job you **advertised**.

**MS. ROSARIO.** [*still staring at THE MONSTER*] Frankensteinz?

**YGOR.** Yes, Frankensteinz is his first name. It's spelled with a *z*.

---

**Key Vocabulary**

**mascot** *n.*, a character that represents an organization

**offstage** *adv.*, away from the area where people can see

**amazed** *adj.*, very surprised

**apply** *v.*, to ask for, to request

**In Other Words**

***pacing nervously*** walking back and forth in a worried way

***desperate*** hopeless

**broadcast** TV show

**advertised** said you had open; are looking to fill

**Cultural Background**

*Ygor* does not appear in the original Frankenstein story. He was created for the movie *Son of Frankenstein*, which was released in 1939. Since then, Ygor has become a regular part of the Frankenstein story.

**MS. ROSARIO.** What is his last name?

**YGOR.** Monster.

[*Offstage*, THE MONSTER *makes a loud* **grunt**. *A cat* **howls**. THE MONSTER *tugs the rope impatiently, pulling* YGOR *toward him.* MS. ROSARIO *pulls the rope back.*]

**YGOR.** No, Frankie! Leave the cat alone! [*turning to* MS. ROSARIO] I think he's hungry. He hasn't eaten since he was born.

[MS. ROSARIO *makes a cell phone call.*]

**MS. ROSARIO.** [*on her cell phone*] Miss Petal, call Cluck-Cluck Chicken. Order a bucket of chicken and a broccoli salad. And **hop to it**, if you love your cat!

[*The rope loosens suddenly.* YGOR *and* MS. ROSARIO *fall to the floor.* MS. ROSARIO *gets up immediately and brushes herself off.*]

**MS. ROSARIO.** [*calmly*] Let's take Mr. Monster to the lunchroom. We can sit down. And I can tell you about the job.

**YGOR.** And how much it pays.

**MS. ROSARIO.** Yes, I can tell you that, too.

**In Other Words**
*grunt* short, low sound
*howls* gives a long, loud cry
**hop to it** make it quick

**Look Into the Text**

1. **Explain** Why does Ygor bring
   Frankensteinz Monster to
   Ms. Rosario's office?
2. **Character's Motive** Why does
   Ms. Rosario tell Miss Petal to
   order lunch?

---

**SCENE TWO**

*Later that morning.* MS. ROSARIO *gives orders to* MISS PETAL, *who takes notes.*

**MS. ROSARIO.** We must hurry. The broadcast begins at 12:30. Call the **makeup department**. Tell them that Mr. Monster looks too scary. They should cover some of **his stitches**. Call **wardrobe**. Say we won't need them.

**MISS PETAL.** [*breathlessly*] Yes, Ms. Rosario.

[*Noises offstage: tin plates clatter.*]

**THE MONSTER.** [*from offstage*] More food!

**YGOR.** [*from offstage*] Eat your broccoli.

[*From offstage,* MISS PETAL's *cat howls.*]

**In Other Words**
**makeup department** people who make actors look good on camera
**his stitches** the sewing marks on him
**wardrobe** the people in charge of Mr. Monster's clothes

**YGOR.** [*from offstage*] No, Frankie!

   Not the cat!

[MS. ROSARIO *and* MISS PETAL *look nervously at each other.*]

**MS. ROSARIO.** And order more chicken.

**MISS PETAL.** Cooked?

**MS. ROSARIO.** [*sounding overwhelmed*]

   Whatever.

**Look Into the Text**

1. **Confirm Prediction** Does the monster get the job? How do you know?

2. **Character's Point of View** Why does Ms. Rosario sound overwhelmed at the end of the scene?

## SCENE THREE

*That afternoon,* MS. ROSARIO *watches a* **commercial** *on TV from her desk. She looks impressed.*

**VOICE OF SALESMAN ON TV.** [*very jolly*]
So, come to Dollar Rite Department Store right away! Discover our **monster bargains**. Shake hands with our monster mascot . . .

**VOICE OF FRANKENSTEINZ ON TV.** More food!

**VOICE OF SALESMAN ON TV.** [*laughing*]
Shake hands if you dare!

[MS. ROSARIO *turns off the TV.* MISS PETAL *enters the office with* DR. FRANKENSTEIN.]

**MISS PETAL.** Ms. Rosario, this gentleman wants to speak with you.

[*She points to the man as she leaves.*]

**DR. FRANKENSTEIN.** [*speaking angrily to* MS. ROSARIO] My name is Dr. Victor Frankenstein. You stole my creation!

**MS. ROSARIO.** [*surprised*] Your what?

**Key Vocabulary**
**commercial** *n.*, an ad on TV or radio

**In Other Words**
**monster bargains** very low sale prices

**DR. FRANKENSTEIN.** My creation! I put him together from a hundred dead bodies! I created him. I did not **give you permission to** use him in your commercial.

[YGOR *enters the office, pulling on the rope.* THE MONSTER *is offstage, at the other end of the rope.*]

**DR. FRANKENSTEIN.** [*pointing at* YGOR] You! You stole my creature to make money!

**YGOR.** We need the money. Do you know how much it will cost to **keep** this monster?

[*As* YGOR *argues with the doctor, he drops the rope mistakenly. The rope* **disappears** .]

**YGOR.** The cost of food alone will **break our backs**!

**DR. FRANKENSTEIN.** That's my problem! I created him. I gave him life!

**Key Vocabulary**
**disappear** *v.*, to no longer be seen

**In Other Words**
**give you permission to** say that you could
**keep** take care of
**break our backs** be very expensive

**YGOR.** Oh, yes, you gave him life. But did you give him love? Did you give him a name? Did you give him breakfast?

[MS. ROSARIO **notices** that the rope is gone.]

**MS. ROSARIO.** Uh, gentlemen? Gentlemen?

[DR. FRANKENSTEIN *and* YGOR *continue to argue, pointing at each other.*]

**DR. FRANKENSTEIN.** You, you . . . listen . . . !

**YGOR.** No, you listen!

**MS. ROSARIO.** [*shouting*] Gentlemen!

**YGOR AND DR. FRANKENSTEIN.** [*turning toward* MS. ROSARIO] What?

**MS. ROSARIO.** He's gone.

**DR. FRANKENSTEIN.** [*looking around*] Oh no!

[YGOR *and* DR. FRANKENSTEIN *both turn toward* MS. ROSARIO.]

**DR. FRANKENSTEIN.** Call the police!

**YGOR.** Call the highway patrol!

**DR. FRANKENSTEIN.** Call the hospital!

**YGOR.** Call the **Recycling Center**!

[*The phone rings.* MS. ROSARIO *answers it. She listens quietly and then hangs up.*]

**MS. ROSARIO.** He's in the lunchroom.

[YGOR *and* DR. FRANKENSTEIN *rush out of the office.* MISS PETAL *enters.*]

**In Other Words**
***notices*** sees, realizes
**Recycling Center** place that
   collects trash to be used again

**MISS PETAL.** Here's the **audience's response** to the commercial. [*reading from her notepad*] **Seventy percent** loved the new mascot. Fifteen percent thought he was just OK. Nine percent thought he was disgusting. Six percent couldn't stop screaming. And . . . oh yeah, Mr. Monster **got two movie offers**.

[*Noises offstage: a loud crash, then the cat howls. MS. ROSARIO smiles and sinks into her chair.*]

**MS. ROSARIO.** [*softly*] A star is born. ❖

**In Other Words**

**Seventy percent** 70 people out of 100

**got two movie offers** was asked to be in two movies

*sinks* slides down

**Look Into the Text**

1. **Conflict** Why does Dr. Frankenstein argue with Ms. Rosario and Ygor?

2. **Confirm Prediction** Was your prediction correct? What happened that you did not expect?

# Connect Reading and Writing

**Vocabulary**

amazed

applied

audience

commercial

disappears

mascot

offstage

response

## CRITICAL THINKING

**1. SUM IT UP** Use your Plot Diagram to analyze character and plot by discussing how the characters responded to events. Then summarize the story to a partner.

Characters: Ms. Rosario

Setting: _____    Turning point: _____

Event: _____

Event: _____    Resolution: _____

Event: _____

Event: _____

Conflict: _____

_____

Plot Diagram

**2. Compare** In the play, what is the **response** of Dr. Frankenstein to his creation? How is this different from the way Dr. Frankenstein acts in Mary Shelley's story?

**3. Explain** How does the action **offstage** add to the humor of the play? Give examples.

**4. Classify** Look back at the reaction of the **audience** to Frankensteinz on page 258. Which group would you be in if you saw the **commercial**?

## READING FLUENCY

**Intonation** Read the passage on page 569 to a partner. Assess your fluency.

**1.** My tone never/sometimes/always matched what I read.

**2.** What I did best in my reading was _____.

## READING STRATEGY

What strategy helped you understand this selection? Tell a partner about it.

## VOCABULARY REVIEW

**Oral Review** Read the paragraph aloud. Add the vocabulary words.

After Act 1 of Frankie's first play, the _____ claps loudly. Frankie's _____ is to look surprised and _____. He smiles as he walks _____ for the break. He remembers when he _____ to drama school to take acting lessons. "I'm so glad I got in," he thinks as he _____ into a dressing room. Then Frankie thinks about the acting job he got in the ad, or _____, based on his acting lessons. The ad was for Chow Down dog food. He wasn't the star, though. The company _____, a dog named Wolf, got all the attention!

**Written Review** Imagine that your favorite monster and Frankensteinz are **mascots** in a **commercial**. Write a paragraph describing the ad. Use five vocabulary words.

 **WRITE ABOUT THE** **GUIDING QUESTION**

**Analyze a Classic Character**

What emotions does this version of Frankenstein inspire in people? Read the selection again, and support your analysis with examples from the text.

# Connect Across the Curriculum

## Vocabulary Study

### Use Word Parts

| Prefix | Meaning | Example | Word Meaning |
|---|---|---|---|
| im- | not | impatiently | not patiently |
| mis- | wrongly | mistakenly | done wrongly |
| over- | a lot or too much | overjoyed | having a lot of joy |

**Academic Vocabulary**
- **identify** (ī-**den**-tu-fī) *verb*
  To **identify** means to find out or to show what something is.

A prefix is a word part that is added at the beginning of a word. It changes the meaning of the base word.

**Define Words** Read each word and **identify** the prefix. Use the chart above to help you define the word.

**1.** overpower    **3.** impossible    **5.** imperfect    **7.** misbehave

**2.** misread    **4.** misjudge    **6.** overcharge    **8.** overreact

Compare your definitions with a partner's. Then look up the words in a dictionary and discuss the definitions.

## Literary Analysis

### Compare Presentations

**Academic Vocabulary**
- **theme** (thēm) *noun*
  A **theme** is the main message of a story.

The **theme** of a play is the same when you read it and when you see it performed live. However, there are differences between the experience of reading a play and watching people act it out. You can compare and contrast to analyze the differences between each version of the story.

Use a Venn Diagram to help you compare and contrast. This Venn Diagram shows one difference between reading the text and watching the play.

**Compare and Contrast** Work with a partner to make your own comparisons. Draw a Venn Diagram on a clean sheet of paper. Review the text of the play "Mister Monster." Think about what you see, or visualize, and hear when you read. Compare and contrast that with what you experienced when you watched and listened to your classmates perform the play live. Add your ideas to the graphic organizer.

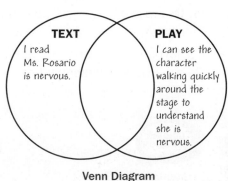

Venn Diagram

## Describe an Event or Experience

**Tell About a Picture** Find a picture of an event, such as a football game or a concert. Describe the event to a partner. Switch roles. Use participles in your descriptions.

> Glaring at the players, the coach stomped onto the field.

## Write About a Performance

**Study the Models** When you tell about a performance, make your sentences interesting. Add participles and participial phrases to provide details and to vary your sentences.

**JUST OK**

> We entered the theater. We did not know if our seats would be good. They were in the balcony. We found our seats. The lights dimmed. The play was starting. Chimney sweeps in black costumes danced on stage.

The reader thinks: "The sentences are too similar, and the details are not interesting."

**BETTER**

> **Entering the theater**, we had no idea how good our seats would be. The balcony, **perched at the top of the theater**, looked far away. We found our seats, **located in the balcony's front row**, as the **dimming** lights announced the play's start. Six chimney sweeps, **dressed in black**, danced on stage. **Seated up high**, we had a perfect view!

This writer uses participial phrases to create interesting, varied sentences. The reader thinks: "The details really help me picture the event."

**Revise It** Look back at the JUST OK passage. Work with a partner to revise it. Use participles and participial phrases to help you write interesting sentences.

✎ **WRITE ON YOUR OWN** Write about a play or another type of performance that you have seen. Be sure to include participles and participial phrases.

**REMEMBER**

Place each phrase near the noun or pronoun It describes.

**Hanging from an umbrella**, Mary Poppins appeared.

She wore a floppy black hat **covered with flowers**.

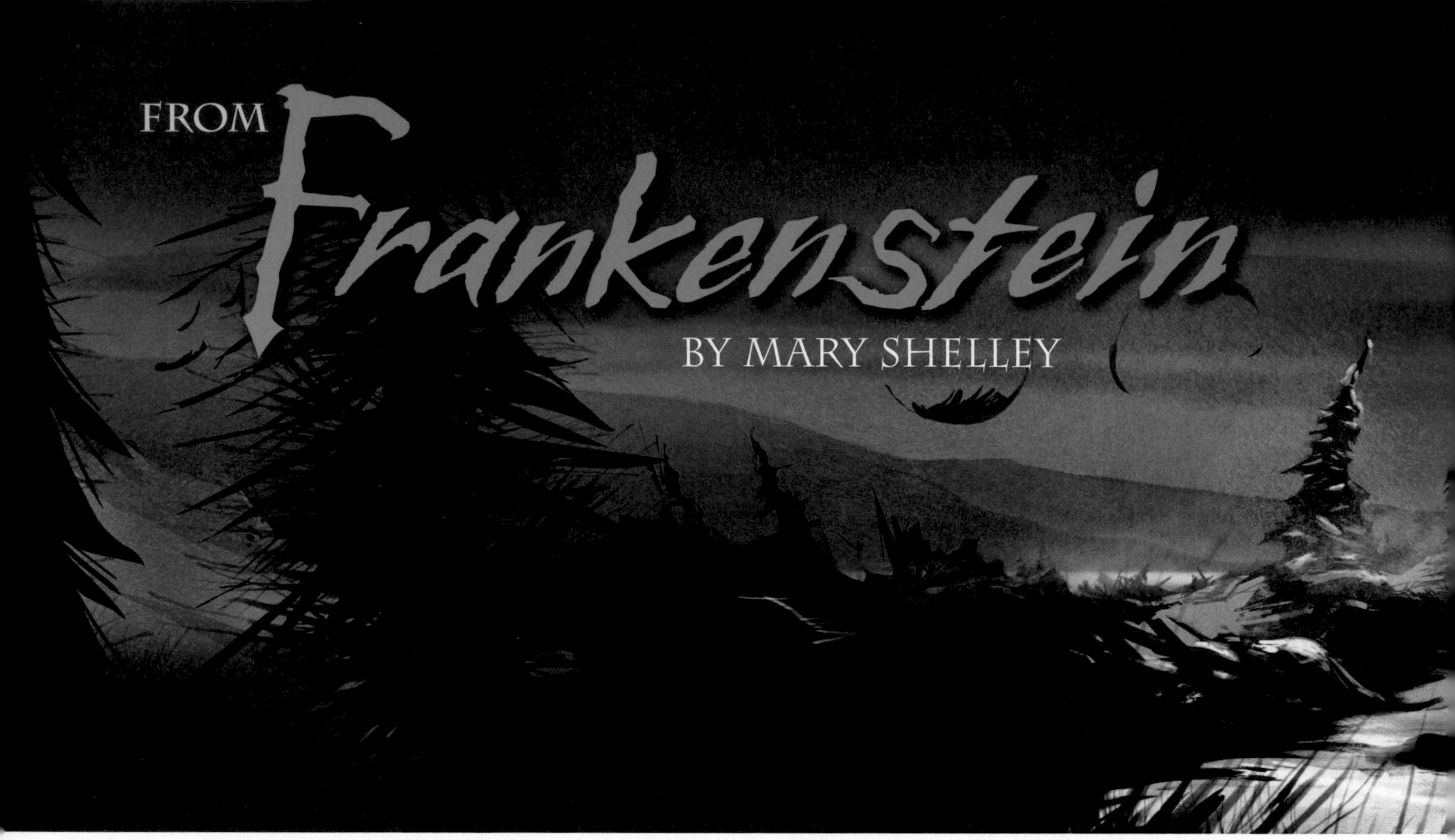

# FROM Frankenstein

## BY MARY SHELLEY

1    The **creature** finished speaking, and fixed his looks upon me in expectation of a reply. But I was bewildered, perplexed and unable to collect my thoughts sufficiently to understand the full extent of what he asked of me. He continued—

2    "You must create a female for me, with whom I can live as a real and feeling human being. This you alone can do; and I demand it of you as a right which you must not refuse to grant to me."

3    The latter part of his tale had **rekindled** in me the anger that had died away while he told me about his peaceful life among the cottagers, and, as he said this, I could no longer **suppress** the rage that burned within me.

4    "I do refuse it," I replied; "and no torture you inflict shall ever make me change my mind. You may make me the most miserable of men, but you shall never make me dishonorable in my own eyes. If I were to create another like yourself, together your wickedness might **desolate** the world! Be gone! I have answered you; you may torture me, but I will never do what you ask."

**Literature Background**
Mary Shelley wrote her novel *Frankenstein* in 1818. A Swiss scientist named Dr. Frankenstein assembles a human being from parts he obtains from dead bodies and brings it back to life by using electricity.

**Key Vocabulary**
- **creature** *n.*, a living thing

**In Other Words**
**rekindled** brought back
**suppress** stop
**desolate** destroy; ruin

5   "You are in the wrong," replied the **fiend**; "and, instead of threatening, I am content to reason with you. I am hateful because I am miserable. Does not **all mankind shun** me and hate me? Even you, my creator, would tear me to pieces, and think it a victory; remember that, and tell me why I should feel sorry for man more than he feels sorry for me? You would not call it murder if you could force me beneath the ice into the water below and **destroy** my being, the work of your own hands. Shall I respect man when he despises me? If others were able to live with me in mutual kindness, then, instead of injury, I would **bestow every benefit upon him** with tears of gratitude at his acceptance. But that cannot be; the human senses are impossible barriers to living in this mutual kindness. Yet I will not submit to their hatred and be their slave. I will **revenge my injuries**: if I cannot inspire love, I will cause fear; and chiefly towards you my greatest enemy, because my creator, do I swear everlasting hatred. Be careful: I will work at your destruction, and not stop until I destroy your heart, so that you shall curse the hour of your birth."

**Key Vocabulary**
- **destroy** *v.*, to take apart, to ruin

**In Other Words**
**fiend** monster
**all mankind shun** everyone ignore
**bestow every benefit upon him** be a great friend
**revenge my injuries** hurt those who hurt me

6   A fiendish rage **animated him** as he said this; his face was wrinkled into contortions too horrible for human eyes to **behold**; but presently he calmed himself and proceeded—

7   "I intended to reason. These human feelings cause me great harm, and you don't realize that you have caused them. If any human being felt emotions of kindness towards me, I should return them an hundred and an hundred **fold**; for that one human being's sake, I would make peace with the whole kind! But I now indulge in dreams of happiness that can never come true. What I ask of you is reasonable and moderate; I demand a creature of another sex, as **hideous** as myself; this satisfaction is small, but it is all

"...IF I CANNOT INSPIRE LOVE, I WILL CAUSE FEAR..."

that I can receive, and it shall content me. It is true we shall be monsters, cut off from all the world; but on that account we shall be more attached to one another. Our lives will not be happy, but they will be harmless, and free from the misery I now feel. Oh! my creator, make me happy; let me feel gratitude towards you for this one benefit! Let me see that I can share these feelings with some existing thing; do not deny me my request!"

8   I was moved. I shuddered when I thought of the possible **consequences** of granting his request; but I felt that there was some justice in his argument. His tale, and the feelings he now expressed, proved him to be a creature **of fine sensations**; and did I not as his maker owe him all the portion of happiness that it was in my power to give to him?

---

**Key Vocabulary**
• **hideous** *adj.*, very ugly

**In Other Words**
**animated him** gave him more energy
**behold** look at
**fold** times
**consequences** results
**of fine sensations** who had feelings

# Compare Across Texts

## Compare Themes

Frankenstein's monster has been featured across many different genres. This character originated in the **classic** monster tale "Frankenstein" by Mary Shelley and appears in adaptations. Frankenstein's monster has also been a character in movies, as discussed in the article "Film Fright," and in poems and plays, such as "Frankenstein Makes a Sandwich" and "Mister Monster." Compare how different genres approach similar **themes**.

## How It Works

**Collect and Organize Ideas** Use a chart to compare **themes**. Add rows for the selections "Film Fright," "Frankenstein Makes a Sandwich," and "Mister Monster." Next to each selection, add the genre, main idea and its most important **theme**.

| Selection | Genre | What It's About | Important Theme |
|---|---|---|---|
| "Frankenstein" | Fantasy | A scientist creates a monster that promises to make him unhappy. | A monster is a dangerous enemy to have. |

Comparison Chart

## Practice Together

Write a paragraph like this one to compare how different genres can approach monster **themes**. Include all the selections.

> The selections all talk about the character Frankenstein's monster in the text. Even though they all have monster themes, each genre has a different approach. For example, the story "Frankenstein" is a fantasy that tells about the dangers of creating a monster. Through the article "Film Fright," we learn about many classic monster movies made in the past.

## Try It!

Write a paragraph to compare two versions or forms of a favorite story. You may want to use this frame to express your ideas.

One of my favorite stories is _____. The genre of one version of the story is _____. It is about _____. The genre of another version of the story is _____. One way the two versions are similar is _____.

**Academic Vocabulary**
- **classic** (kla-sik) *adjective*
  Something that is **classic** is old but good.
- **theme** (thēm) *noun*
  A **theme** is the main message of a story.

# Creepy Classics

**GUIDING QUESTION**

How can a powerful character inspire a range of reactions?

---

**Content Library**

Peering into **Darkness**

Rebecca L. Johnson

---

**Leveled Library**

FRANKENSTEIN

By Mary Shelley
adapted by Larry Weinberg

FRANZ KAFKA

THE METAMORPHOSIS

PETER KUPER

OTHELLO
A NOVEL

JULIUS LESTER

---

# Reflect on Your Reading

Think back on your reading of the unit selections. Discuss what you did to understand what you read.

**Focus on Reading** **Elements of Fiction: Plot, Characters, Setting**

In this unit, you learned about plot, characters, and setting. Choose one of the fiction selections and make a Plot Diagram. Use your diagram to describe the plot, characters, and setting to a partner.

**Focus Strategy** **Visualize**

As you read, you learned to visualize. Explain to a partner how you will use this strategy in the future.

# Explore the GUIDING QUESTION

Throughout this unit, you have been thinking about the characters of classic monster stories. Choose one of these ways to explore the Guiding Question:

- **Discuss** With a group, discuss the Guiding Question. Talk about how you reacted to the characters in the different selections. Which character inspired the most powerful reaction in you? Give details from the text to explain.

- **Create a Character** Imagine you are a movie producer. What character can you create that would inspire strong reactions in people? Draw or make a model of your character and present it to a group. How do your classmates react to it?

- **Role-Play** With a partner, role-play Ms. Rosario, Miss Petal, or Ygor meeting one of the movie monsters from "Film Fright" for the first time.

# Book Talk

Which Unit Library book did you choose? Explain to a partner what it taught you about classic monsters.

# THE
## DRIVE
## TO
# Discover

# How do discoveries change us and the world?

◀ Divers explore Dan's Cave in the Bahamas.

# Focus on Reading

## Text Structure: Main Idea and Details

In fiction and nonfiction, writers **organize** their ideas in different ways. Understanding the organization will help you follow the writer's ideas and remember details.

## How It Works

**In Fiction** Writers of poems do not usually state the **theme,** or main idea. A writer develops the **theme** by providing clues in different parts of the poem. Poems often have a title, and the text is usually **organized** in stanzas, or sets of lines. A poem's title tells about the topic. The stanzas include <u>details</u> that tell more about the **theme.**

> ### *from* Windy Nights
>
> *by Robert Louis Stevenson*
> Whenever the moon and stars are set,
> Whenever the wind is high,
> All night long in the dark and wet,
> A man goes riding by.
> Late in the night when the fires are out,
> Why does he gallop and gallop about?

**Details**

**In Nonfiction** Sometimes writers want to explain something. A writer might state a **main idea** and then provide several <u>details</u> to explain more.

> ### The Grand Canyon Caverns
>
> Scientists have made many discoveries inside the Grand Canyon Caverns. They found prints and bones of the giant ground sloth and now know more about this extinct animal. Scientists have also discovered a dead but well-preserved bobcat and a new type of cave cricket. What will they discover next?

**Main Idea**

**Details**

**Academic Vocabulary**
- **organize** (or-gu-nīz) *verb*
  To **organize** is to put things in a certain order.
- **theme** (thēm) *noun*
  A **theme** is the main message of a story.

## Practice Together

Read the following passages aloud. As you read the poem, listen for details that tell about the theme. As you read the nonfiction passage, listen for the sentence that tells what the text is mostly about.

### *from* Windy Nights

*by Robert Louis Stevenson*

Whenever the trees are crying
aloud,
And ships are tossed at sea,
By, on the highway, low and loud,
By at the gallop goes he.
By at the gallop he goes, and then
By he comes back at the gallop
again.

### A Visit to the Grand Canyon Caverns

Many visitors see fascinating sights as they tour the Grand Canyon Caverns each year. They take an elevator 210 feet down to view the caverns. They enter the main room, which is bigger than a football field. As they explore the caverns, they see Snowball Palace and The Giant's Keyhole. Visitors also learn how the caves were formed during the past 35 million years!

## Try It!

Read the following passages aloud. Is the main idea stated in the text? What details tell about the theme or main idea?

### On Mount Everest

Snow falls. Silently covers my
tracks.
I am alone. One foot
In front of the other.
I climb higher.

Face chapped. Nose red.
Snow blind. Cold.
The summit beckons.
Will I conquer my fear?

The mountain grounds me,
Holds me, supports me.
I walk farther.
A flag will mark my triumph.

### Exploring a Cave

Exploring a cave is a lot of fun, but you must be well-prepared. Caves are dark, so you need a good, strong light. A helmet with a light is best, because it protects your head and leaves your hands free. You should wear waterproof shoes because caves can be wet—some even have streams and waterfalls. Make sure you have warm clothes and plenty of snacks. A backpack is good for carrying these supplies. Most important, never go into a cave alone!

# Focus on Vocabulary

## Use Word Parts

Words that share the same base word look **similar** . But a **prefix** or a **suffix** added to a **base word** makes a word with a different meaning.

**EXAMPLES**

The prefix *re-* means "again."

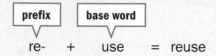

re- + use = reuse

*Reuse* means "to use again."

The suffix *-ful* means "full of."

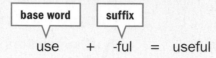

use + -ful = useful

*Useful* means "full of use."

## How the Strategy Works

When you read, you may come to a word you don't know. Look for word parts to help you understand the meaning.

**EXAMPLE** We **reuse** paper bags.

1. Look closely at the word to see if you know any of the parts.
2. Cover any prefixes or suffixes.    **reuse**
3. Think about the meaning of the base word.
4. Uncover any prefixes or suffixes and determine their meanings.
5. Put the meanings of the word parts together to understand the whole word. Be sure the meaning makes sense in the passage.

Use the strategy to figure out the meaning of each underlined word.

> What is it like to climb Mt. Everest, the world's tallest mountain? Samantha Larson, an 18-year-old from California, knows. Samantha, her father, and several <u>helpful</u> guides made the climb in 2007. During the climb, they often had to test and <u>retest</u> their equipment to make sure it was safe. After a month of climbing, they reached the top of the mountain. What a <u>joyful</u> occasion!

**Strategy in Action**

" I see the suffix *-ful* in this word. I'll cover it. There is the base word *help*. I know *-ful* means 'full of.' So *help* + *-ful* means 'full of help.' "

☑ **REMEMBER** You can use the meanings of word parts to figure out the meaning of an unknown word.

**Academic Vocabulary**
- **similar** (si-mu-lur) *adjective*
  Things that are **similar** are almost the same.

## Practice Together

Read this passage aloud. Look at each underlined word. Find the word parts. Put their meanings together to figure out the meaning of the underlined word.

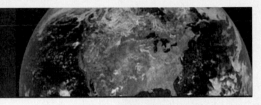

## So Much to Discover on
# EARTH

People have often gone to new places because they want to <u>discover</u> something new. A discovery can be many things. It can be a place that someone sees for the first time. It can be art that was lost for thousands of years. It can even be a new idea.

What lies at the bottom of the ocean? What treasures are hidden deep in the earth? <u>Scientists</u> who ask <u>thoughtful</u> questions like these sometimes find important answers. They write about their findings so people in the world can learn more.

## Try It!

Read this passage aloud. What is the meaning of each underlined word? How do you know?

### Dive into Monterey Bay

Most ocean floors on earth are too deep for a human <u>diver</u> to reach. But in Monterey Bay, a robot travels to the very bottom of the sea to learn about life down deep. This little <u>traveler</u> takes pictures of <u>unusual</u> sea creatures, including one that sends out a glow-in-the-dark

▲ The robot is launched from a research ship.

cloud to scare away its enemies! The robot has also placed a tool on the ocean floor to learn about earthquakes. Scientists are <u>hopeful</u> that they will gather a lot of valuable information from this robot.

# Return to Titanic

by Susan E. Goodman

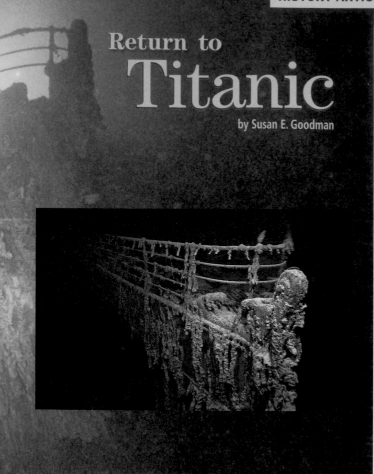

## Build Background

### See Discoveries in Action

What does it feel like to make a discovery?
Robert Ballard knows. In 1985, he discovered
the wreck of *Titanic*. This big, beautiful ship
sank on its first trip in 1912.

### Connect

**Team Brainstorm** You are an explorer on
Robert Ballard's team in 1985. You know that
*Titanic* sank 12,000 feet to the bottom of
the ocean. You want to find *Titanic*, but if you
search for it you will be in danger. What does
your team of explorers decide to do? Why?

**Digital Library**

myNGconnect.com
View the video.

▲ A 1912 postcard shows *Titanic*'s great size.

## Ask for and Give Information

CD

Listen to the chant and the interview.
Chime in on the chant, and role-play the interview.

**CHANT and INTERVIEW**

# Get the Facts

Get the facts. Get them now.
Ask *Who? What? When? Where? Why?* and *How?*

**What** was *Titanic*?

> *Titanic* was a huge ship. It was built in 1912.
> On its first trip, it sank.

**How** did *Titanic* sink?

> *Titanic* sank because it hit an iceberg.
> It broke into two pieces.

**Who** discovered the lost ship?

> Robert Ballard discovered the lost ship.

**Where** was *Titanic* found?

> *Titanic* was found at the bottom of the Atlantic.

**When** did Ballard find the ship?

> Ballard found the ship in 1985. He looked for it
> for many years.

**Why** was *Titanic* famous?

> *Titanic* was famous because it was the biggest ship ever built.

▲ An iceberg in the North Atlantic Ocean

▼ *Titanic*, 1912

# Use Present and Past Tense Verbs

The tense, or time, of a **verb** shows when an action happens.

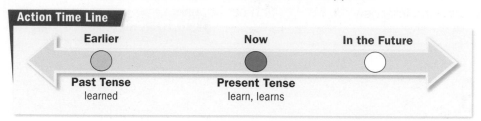

Action Time Line

Earlier · Now · In the Future

Past Tense — learned
Present Tense — learn, learns

- Use the **present tense** to tell about an action that happens now or often.

  EXAMPLES　　Scientists **learn** about the ocean every day. *(happens often)*

  　　　　　　Today, they **look** for an old ship at the bottom of the ocean. *(happens now)*

  Use **-s** at the end of a verb that tells what one other person or thing does.

  EXAMPLE　　My friend **learns** about the ship, too.

- Use the **past tense** to tell about an action that has already happened.

  EXAMPLES　　Yesterday, we **looked** at a video about the ship.

  　　　　　　Last week, we **learned** about the divers on the team.

  Add **-ed** to most verbs when you talk about a past action.

  **learn + -ed = learned　　look + -ed = looked**

## Practice Together

Change the verb in the box to the past tense. Say it. Then say the sentence and add the past tense verb.

1. | call | One diver _____ out, "Let's go!"
2. | jump | Then all the divers _____ into the water.
3. | start | They _____ their search for the old ship.
4. | stay | They _____ together for safety.

## Try It!

Change the verb in the box to the past tense. Write the past tense verb on a card. Then say the sentence and add the past tense verb.

5. | discover | The divers _____ the ship near the shore.
6. | hunt | They _____ for a way in.
7. | open | One diver _____ an old, rusted window.
8. | reach | She _____ inside the window.

▲ Divers discover an old ship.

# Explore the Ocean

## ASK FOR AND GIVE INFORMATION

There is a lot to learn about the ocean. What do you want to find out about it? Do you want to know more about lost ships, animals in the ocean, or how people use the ocean?

Work with a team to complete a question chart. Write six questions, one for each question word.

**Question Chart**

| Question Word | The Answer Will Be | Question |
|---|---|---|
| Who? | a person | Who keeps the treasures from a lost ship? |
| What? | a thing | |
| When? | a time | |
| Where? | a place | |
| Why? | a reason | |
| How? | an explanation | |

Then trade questions with another team. Find out the answers to their questions. Share your questions and answers with the whole group.

## HOW TO ASK FOR AND GIVE INFORMATION

1. When you want information, you ask questions. Start your questions with *Who, What, When, Where, Why,* or *How.*
2. When you give information, you tell your main point and give some details.

How did the divers discover the ship?

They talked to people on the island. An old man pointed to a place on their map.

## USE PRESENT AND PAST TENSE VERBS

When you give information, you may tell about something that happens often. If so, use a verb in the **present tense**. Or you may tell about something that already happened. If so, use a verb in the **past tense**.

**In the Present:** Who **looks** for old ships?
Scientists and treasure hunters **look** for old ships.

**In the Past:** Who **looked** for this old ship?
A scientist **looked** for this ship. He **wanted** to learn more about the ancient culture.

# Prepare to Read

## Learn Key Vocabulary

**Study the Words** Use the steps below.

1. Pronounce the word. Say it aloud several times. Spell it.
2. Rate your word knowledge.
3. Study the example. Tell more about the word.
4. Practice it. Make the word your own.

### Key Words

**alarm** (u-**larm**) *noun*
▶ page 284

An **alarm** warns people of danger. A smoke detector is one kind of **alarm**.

**discover** (dis-**ku**-vur) *verb*
▶ page 286

To **discover** means to find something that is lost or hidden. The boy **discovers** a starfish at the beach.

**explorer** (ik-**splor**-ur) *noun*
▶ page 286

An **explorer** travels somewhere to study something. **Explorers** find out what is special about a new place. *Base Word:* **explore**

**famous** (**fā**-mus) *adjective*
▶ page 282

Something that is **famous** is very well known. Many people have seen the **famous** Statue of Liberty. *Base Word:* **fame**

**ocean** (**ō**-shun) *noun*
▶ page 284

An **ocean** is a large area or body of salt water. **Oceans** cover most of the Earth.

**passenger** (**pa**-sen-jur)
*noun* ▶ page 282

When you ride in a car, boat, or other vehicle, you are a **passenger**. The bus driver took ten **passengers** to the school.

**search** (surch) *verb, noun*
▶ page 286

**1** *verb* When you **search** for something, you look for it. You might **search** for something you lost.
**2** *noun* A **search** is the act of looking for something.

**wreck** (rek) *noun*
▶ page 287

A **wreck** is what is left after a crash. A **shipwreck** is a broken ship that crashed.

**Practice the Words** Make a Study Card for each Key Word. Then compare your cards with a partner's.

> **wreck**
> **What it means:** what is left after a crash
> **Example:** car after an accident
> **Not an example:** new car

Study Card

# Determine Main Idea and Details

**Where Are the Main Idea and Details?** A **main idea** is what a text is mostly about. The main idea is often one of the first sentences in a paragraph. The sentences that follow have **details** that develop the main idea. These details support and explain the main idea.

As you read, look for the sentence that explains what the text is mostly about. Then look for details in the text that build upon the main idea.

**Reading Strategies**

- Plan
- Monitor
- Make Connections
- Visualize
- **Ask Questions** Think actively by asking and answering questions about the text.
- Determine Importance
- Make Inferences
- Synthesize

## Look Into the Text

" The first part of the first sentence tells me what the paragraph is mostly about."

*Titanic* was the largest ship in the world— as long as four city blocks. Many people called it the "wonder ship." It was like a floating palace, with a swimming pool, carved wood, and fancy gold lights . It also had many rich and famous passengers who wanted to be the first to ride on this great ship.

" The second part of the first sentence is a detail. It explains just how big Titanic was."

## Practice Together

**Begin a Main-Idea and Details Chart** A Main-Idea and Details Chart can help you keep track of main ideas and details. This Main-Idea and Details Chart shows the main idea of the paragraph and a detail. Reread the passage above to find other details that tell more about the main idea. Add the details to the chart.

| Main Idea | Details |
|-----------|---------|
| *Titanic* was the largest ship in the world. | It was as long as four city blocks. |

**Main-Idea and Details Chart**

## History Article

A history article tells about real events that happened in the past. Many history articles present information about one event or topic.

The **headings** in the article tell what each part is about. Use the headings as clues to help you determine the main idea. Look for **details** in the text that tell more about the main idea.

Look Into the Text

### A Ship Torn Apart

heading

Soon passengers heard a terrible sound. It was the sound of the ship ripping apart. The ship sank just 20 minutes later with most of the passengers and crew still on board.

As you read, ask questions to help you identify main ideas and details.

# Return to
# Titanic

## by Susan E. Goodman

*Titanic* was meant to be the biggest and best ship of its day, but it sank on its first trip. Yet it is still the best-known boat on Earth.

The broken ship still sits at the bottom of the ocean. ▷

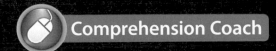

# The Wonder Ship

On April 10, 1912, hundreds of people **packed a dock** in Southampton, England. They came to see *Titanic*, a ship that was about to leave on its first trip. And what a ship it was!

*Titanic* was the largest ship in the world—as long as four city blocks. Many people called it the "wonder ship." It was like a floating **palace**, with a swimming pool, carved wood, and fancy gold lights. It also had many rich and **famous** **passengers** who wanted to be the first to ride on this great ship.

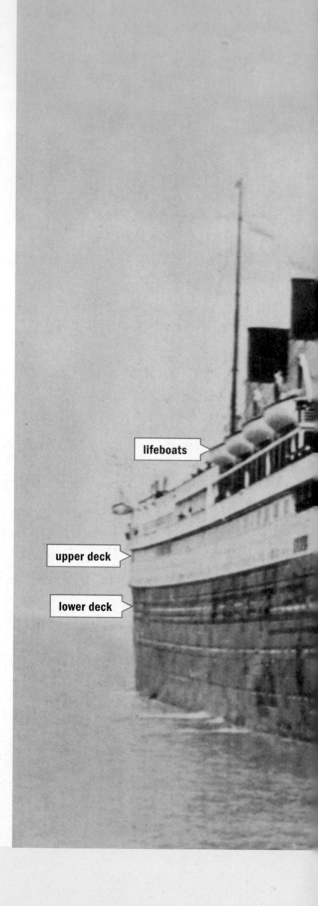

lifeboats

upper deck

lower deck

▲ One of *Titanic's* grand stairways

▼ *Titanic* left England for New York in 1912. Poor passengers had to stay in the lower decks. Only the rich could use the top four decks.

passengers

**Look Into the Text**

1. **Details** What made *Titanic* a floating palace?
2. **Text Features** What information do you learn from the caption on this page?

# Danger Ahead!

*Titanic* **set off for** New York. At first, the ride was like a party. By April 14, the ship was in the middle of the Atlantic **Ocean**. That night, the weather was clear, and stars twinkled against the dark sky. On the ship, people danced late into the night. No one knew that danger was near.

Shortly before midnight, a sailor **on lookout** saw something in the darkness. He knew it could be only one thing. It was an iceberg, a floating mountain of ice. The sailor raised the **alarm**: "Iceberg ahead!" Next, the **crew** tried to turn *Titanic* away from the iceberg, but it was too late. Finally, the ship scraped along the ice.

passengers in a lifeboat

▲ After the ship broke apart, it sank 12,000 feet to the bottom of the ocean.

**Key Vocabulary**
**ocean** *n.*, a large body of salt water
**alarm** *n.*, a signal to warn people of danger

**In Other Words**
**set off for** began sailing to
**on lookout** watching for problems
**crew** workers

# Water Rushes In

The problem did not seem too bad at first. Then water started pouring into the ship, and nothing could stop it. The ship was going to sink!

The crew tried to get help. They shot off fireworks to **attract** the attention of nearby ships. Crew members on those ships thought the fireworks were for fun, so they did not stop to help.

Passengers began climbing into the lifeboats on *Titanic*. Women and children mostly went first, but there was not enough room for everyone. When the last lifeboat was lowered into the water, there were still 1,500 people on the sinking ship.

# A Ship Torn Apart

Soon passengers heard a terrible sound. It was the sound of the ship **ripping apart**. The ship sank just 20 minutes later, with most of the passengers and crew still on board.

▲ A newsboy in London sells papers telling about the **disaster**. The disaster **shocked** people around the world.

**Look Into the Text**

1. **Cause and Effect** Why did the ship sink?
2. **Explain** What happened to the **passengers** when the ship went down?
3. **Inference** Do you think most of the people who lived through the disaster were men or women? How do you know?

## A Boy's Dream

*Titanic* sank to the ocean floor and stayed there for 71 years. Then Robert Ballard set out to find it. As a kid, Ballard had loved reading about *Titanic*. "My dream," he says, "was to find this great ship."

Ballard became an ocean **explorer** and **studied the ocean floor**. Although he made many discoveries, he never forgot his dream: he still wanted to find *Titanic*. People said it was impossible. They said that the shipwreck was too deep, but Ballard did not agree.

## Hunting for *Titanic*

In 1985, Ballard **teamed up** with a French scientist and began his **search** for *Titanic*. The two men sailed to where *Titanic* had sunk. They used **high-tech** tools to **search** the ocean floor. For weeks, they found nothing. Then they sent down Argo, an underwater machine that took pictures and sent them back to the crew.

Argo searched the ocean for a few days without finding anything. Then a big metal object came into view. It was a ship's engine. The team began to cheer. They knew that they had **discovered** *Titanic*!

▼ Robert Ballard and a crew member look at images of *Titanic* from their ship's control room.

**Key Vocabulary**

**explorer** *n.*, a person who goes to a new place to find out about it

**search** *n.*, the act of looking for something; *v.*, to look for something

**discover** *v.*, to find something that is lost or hidden

**In Other Words**

**studied the ocean floor** used tools to learn about the bottom of the ocean

**teamed up** worked

**high-tech** modern

# A Closer Look

Ballard saw the bow, or front, of *Titanic* stuck in mud. He saw cups, beds, shoes, suitcases, and other objects from the ship. It was like visiting a museum. Ballard wanted to see more, but he had run out of time and had to return home.

In 1986, Ballard came back to the ship. This time, he traveled down to the **wreck**, riding in a submersible, which is an underwater craft. He brought a deep-sea robot that was able to look inside the ship.

▲ *Titanic* sank in 1912. Yet some of its windows are still unbroken.

# Saving the Past

As Ballard explored *Titanic*, he took pictures of the shipwreck. He did not take anything away, though. He left things just as they were. Each object helps to tell the sad story of *Titanic*. ❖

▲ This robot took underwater pictures of *Titanic*.

---

**Key Vocabulary**
**wreck** *n.*, what is left of a ship or other vehicle after a crash

**Language Background**
The name *Titanic* comes from the word *titan*, meaning "a giant." With a partner, list other words to describe the gigantic ship.

## Look Into the Text

1. **Summarize** How did Ballard **discover** *Titanic*?
2. **Explain** What did Ballard see as he explored the ship?
3. **Conclusions** Why did Ballard not take anything from *Titanic*?

# Talking with Robert Ballard

Robert Ballard has explored many parts of the ocean. In this interview, he talks about his work.

▲ Robert Ballard

### How did you get interested in ocean exploration?

I always loved the book *Twenty Thousand Leagues Under the Sea* by Jules Verne. It was all I could think about. I wanted to see what was deep in the ocean!

### How did you become an explorer?

My parents wanted me to have a good education. I went to college and studied the ocean. Later, I joined the navy.

### There have been many shipwrecks. What is special about *Titanic*?

*Titanic's* story interests people. The ship was full of people when it sank. Many were scared. Many were brave. Many were also very famous. People want to hear their stories. They want to know how we study the shipwreck.

### Why is it a bad idea to take items from the wreck?

The objects are part of history. Seeing them in place tells a lot. For example, we can learn how the ship sank. That information is lost if you take things away from the wreck.

### What was it like to find *Titanic*? How did you feel?

Finding *Titanic* was **a dream of mine**. So discovering it made me happy.

◄ Ballard found many objects on the wreck, including a passenger's watch.

**In Other Words**
**a dream of mine** one of my goals in my life

**Look Into the Text**

1. **Viewpoint** According to Ballard, what makes *Titanic's* story interesting?
2. **Judgment** Was Ballard right to leave all the items with the wreck? Why or why not? Use details from the interview to support your answer.

# Connect Reading and Writing

**Vocabulary**
alarm
discover
explorer
famous
ocean
passengers
search
wreck

## CRITICAL THINKING

1. **SUM IT UP** Use your Main-Idea and Details Chart to explain how Ballard explored the **ocean** to find *Titanic*.

| Main Idea | Details |
|---|---|
| *Titanic* was the largest ship in the world. | It was as long as four city blocks. |

**Main-Idea and Details Chart**

2. **Analyze** Describe *Titanic* to a friend. Use details from the text to give a clear picture. Tell why *Titanic* is **famous** .

3. **Conclusion** Which picture best shows why so many people wanted to **search** for *Titanic*? Support your conclusion.

4. **Interpret** Robert Ballard says, "Information is lost if you take things away from the **wreck** ." Do you agree? Why or why not?

## READING FLUENCY

**Intonation** Read the passage on page 570 to a partner. Assess your fluency.

1. My tone never/sometimes/always matched what I read.

2. What I did best in my reading was _____ .

## READING STRATEGY

What strategy helped you understand this selection? Tell a partner about it.

## VOCABULARY REVIEW

**Oral Review** Read the paragraph aloud. Add the vocabulary words.

Most ships are safe, but some ships face terrible danger. Sometimes there is no warning or _____ and a ship crashes into rocks. The ship may sink into the _____. The _____ may lose their lives. People may _____ for the _____ of a lost ship for many years before they _____ it. An _____ who studies a well-known, or _____, shipwreck can learn new information.

**Written Review** Imagine you are an **explorer** , diving to see the **wreck** of *Titanic*. Write a journal entry about it. Use five vocabulary words.

 **WRITE ABOUT THE** (GUIDING QUESTION)

**Explore the Drive to Discover**
Why do you think Robert Ballard put his life in danger to **discover** *Titanic*? Read the selection again. Support your opinion with examples from the text.

# Connect Across the Curriculum

## Use Word Parts

| Word Part | Meaning |
|---|---|
| **dis-** | the opposite of |
| **un-** | not |
| **-able** | having the quality of; can be done |
| **-er, -or** | one who |
| **-ful** | full of |

**Academic Vocabulary**
- **similar** (si-mu-lur) *adjective*
  Things that are **similar** are almost the same.

Words that share the same base word can look **similar**. But a prefix or a suffix changes the meaning of the base word. For example:

- *pack* means "to put things in a container."
- *packer* means "someone who packs," because the suffix -*er* means "one who."
- *unpack* means "to take things out of a container." Explain how the meanings of the word parts add up to this definition.

**Figure Out Word Meanings** Work with a partner. Cover the prefix or suffix in each word. Find the base word. Uncover the prefix. What does it mean? Then put the meanings together and write the meaning of the word.

| | | | |
|---|---|---|---|
| **1.** sailor | **3.** explorer | **5.** lovable | **7.** visitor |
| **2.** disappear | **4.** unclear | **6.** comfortable | **8.** hopeful |

## Compare Texts: Events

Important historical events are often explained in different ways. Comparing how one event is explained in two different texts gives readers a more complete understanding of what happened.

**Identify and Compare** Use your Main-Idea and Details Charts to identify the events discussed in "Talking with Robert Ballard" and "Return to the *Titanic*." Identify the main ideas that are the same in both texts. Compare the details that each text uses to explain these ideas. Find details that are in both texts. Look at the differences. What main ideas and details are in only one text?

**Discuss** How does your understanding change when you compare what is explained in both texts versus only one? What additional questions do you have? Present your findings to the class.

## Ask for and Give Information

**Role-Play** With a group, act out a news conference with explorers of *Titanic*. Some of you ask questions as news reporters. The explorers answer. Use past tense verbs. Trade roles.

> *Where did you search?*

> *We searched the part of the Atlantic Ocean near New York.*

---

**Writing and Grammar**

## Write About the Past

**Study the Models** When you write about an event that already happened, you use verbs in the past tense. Once you choose a verb tense for your writing, stick with it.

**NOT OK**

> I **walk** through the door of the museum and **looked** at a boat that was 1000 years old! I **wanted** to know if it was real. So I **tap** on the side of the boat and **touched** the surface.

**This writer confuses the reader by switching between past tense and present tense.**

**OK**

> I **walked** through the door of the museum and **looked** at a boat that was 1000 years old! I **wanted** to know if it was real. So I **tapped** on the side of the boat and **touched** the surface.

**This writer sticks to the past tense.**

**WRITE ON YOUR OWN** Write about something you discovered when you were younger. Pay attention to the tense of your verbs. Check your verbs for correct spelling, too.

**REMEMBER**
- Use the past tense to tell about something that already happened.
- Many past tense verbs end in -**ed**.
  learn**ed**   walk**ed**

### Spelling Rules

**1.** Often, you just have to add -**ed**.

**look + -ed = looked**   The guard **looked** right at me.

**2.** If a verb ends in silent **e**, drop the **e** before you add -**ed**.

**like + -ed = liked**   He **liked** his job.

**3.** If the verb has one syllable and ends in one vowel and one consonant, double the consonant.

**plan + n + -ed = planned**   He **planned** to walk to the museum.

**4.** If the verb ends in a consonant + **y**, change the **y** to **i**. Then add -**ed**.

**study + i/y ed = studied**   He **studied** ways to protect old ships.

# The Forgotten Treasure

### an adaptation of a Nigerian folk tale

Extended Family, 2006, Jimoh Buraimoh. Beads on board, Via Mundi Gallery, Atlanta, Georgia.

## SELECTION 2 OVERVIEW

▶ **Build Background**

▶ **Language & Grammar**
**Engage in Discussion**
**Use Verb Tense:**
*Be* and *Have*

▶ **Prepare to Read**
**Learn Key Vocabulary**
**Determine Theme**

▶ **Read and Write**
**Introduce the Genre**
Folk Tale
**Focus on Reading**
Determine Theme
**Apply the**
**Focus Strategy**
Ask Questions
**Critical Thinking**
**Reading Fluency**
Read with Expression
**Vocabulary Review**
**Write About the**
**Guiding Question**

▶ **Connect Across the Curriculum**
**Vocabulary Study**
Use Word Parts
**Literary Analysis**
Compare Texts: Theme
**Language and Grammar**
Engage in Discussion
**Writing and Grammar**
Write About the Past

# Build Background

## Connect

**Anticipation Guide** Think about an object that is really important to you. What would you do if you lost it? Tell whether you agree or disagree with these statements.

| | Agree | Disagree |
|---|---|---|
| **1.** I would never forget about it. I would keep on looking and remembering, even after many years. | _____ | _____ |
| **2.** I don't worry about what is lost. I would find something new. | _____ | _____ |

**Anticipation Guide**

## Meet a Griot

"The Forgotten Treasure" takes place in Nigeria. Nigeria has a long history of oral storytelling by griots. These storytellers, poets, and wandering musicians travel across the country, singing traditional songs and telling tales like this one.

> **Digital Library**
> **myNGconnect.com**
> 👁 View the video.

Nigeria

**Nigeria is in West Africa.** ▲

# Language & Grammar

## Engage in Discussion

CD

Listen to the chant and chime in. Then listen to a discussion. In a discussion, you discover other people's ideas—agreeing with some and disagreeing with others. You share your own ideas, too.

**CHANT and DISCUSSION**

## Talk It Over

Hear what others have to say.

You'll understand much more that way!

Focus on the topic—

That's what it's all about!

When it's your turn to speak,

Get the main points out.

1 TRY OUT LANGUAGE
2 LEARN GRAMMAR
3 APPLY ON YOUR OWN

# Use Verb Tense: *Be* and *Have*

The tense of a verb tells when an action happens. The verbs *be* and *have* use special forms to tell about the **present** and the **past**.

**Forms of *Be***

| Present Tense | Past Tense |
|---|---|
| I **am** | I **was** |
| you **are** | you **were** |
| he, she, or it **is** | he, she, or it **was** |
| we **are** | we **were** |
| they **are** | they **were** |

**Forms of *Have***

| Present Tense | Past Tense |
|---|---|
| I **have** | I **had** |
| you **have** | you **had** |
| he, she, or it **has** | he, she, or it **had** |
| we **have** | we **had** |
| they **have** | they **had** |

Use the correct form of the verb.

EXAMPLES  **Forms of *be***

**Present:**  He **is** interested in folk tales.

**Past:**  He **was** interested in folk tales.

**Present:**  We **are** in eighth grade.

**Past:**  We **were** in seventh grade.

EXAMPLES  **Forms of *have***

**Present:**  Our class **has** many students.

**Past:**  Last year, our class **had** only a few students.

**Present:**  The students **have** lots of stories to tell.

**Past:**  Last year, we even **had** a folk tale festival.

▲ The friends have a lot of stories to share.

## Practice Together

Say each sentence. Then say it again and change the verb to the past tense.

1. I <u>am</u> interested in folk tales.
2. Ana and I <u>are</u> storytellers.
3. We <u>have</u> a favorite story.
4. It <u>is</u> a tale from Mexico.

## Try It!

Say each sentence. Write the past tense of the underlined verb on a card. Then say the sentence and add the past tense verb.

5. We <u>have</u> a folk tale performance.
6. Ana <u>has</u> the best voice!
7. I <u>am</u> good at different sounds.
8. The show <u>is</u> a success.

# Discuss Stories

## ENGAGE IN DISCUSSION

Are stories really that important? Discuss your ideas with a group.

### HOW TO ENGAGE IN DISCUSSION

1. Give your ideas. Include examples to support them.
2. Ask and answer questions.
3. Show you are listening to other people's ideas. Respect their opinions.

> Stories are fun to hear, but I'm not sure they are that important.

> That's interesting. Why do you think that?

Remember that everyone can have different ideas. When you discuss ideas, you are just sharing what you think. Other people may agree or disagree.

## USE VERB TENSE: *BE* AND *HAVE*

When you discuss ideas, be sure to use the correct form of *be* and *have*.

**In the Present:**  I **am** a big fan of stories! Stories **are** important. I **have** a great book of fables. Each fable **has** a moral, or lesson. One moral **is** "There **is** always another side of the story."

**In the Past:**  When I **was** little, I **had** a book of stories. They **were** all scary. The book **had** scary pictures in it, too. I **had** bad dreams from those stories! I **was** happy to give the book to my older cousin.

# Prepare to Read

## Learn Key Vocabulary

**Study the Words** Use the steps below.

1. Pronounce the word. Say it aloud several times. Spell it.
2. Rate your word knowledge.
3. Study the example. Tell more about the word.
4. Practice it. Make the word your own.

**Rating Scale**

**1** = I have never seen this word before.

**2** = I am not sure of the word's meaning.

**3** = I know this word and can teach the word's meaning to someone else.

### Key Words

**beautiful** (byū-ti-ful)
*adjective* ▶ page 302

Something that is **beautiful** is very pretty. The flowers are **beautiful**.
*Base Word:* **beauty**

**forest** (for-ust) *noun*
▶ page 301

A **forest** is a place that has lots of trees.
*Synonym:* **woods**

**forget** (fur-get) *verb*
▶ page 300

When you **forget** something, you stop thinking about it. The boy leaves without his shoes. He **forgets** them.
*Past tense:* **forgot**
*Past participle:* **forgotten**

**locate** (lō-kāt) *verb*
▶ page 304

To **locate** something is to find it. The woman tries to **locate** something she lost.

**loss** (laws) *noun*
▶ page 301

When you no longer have something important, you feel the **loss**. A terrible **loss** is the death of a loved one.

**remember** (ri-mem-bur)
*verb* ▶ page 300

When you **remember** something, you think of it again later. The man goes to the monument and **remembers** his friend who died.

**skeleton** (ske-lu-tun) *noun*
▶ page 304

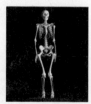

A **skeleton** is the set of bones in an animal or a person. The model shows a human **skeleton**.

**treasure** (tre-zhur) *noun*
▶ page 300

A **treasure** is something very special and important. These decorated eggs are **treasures**.

**Practice the Words** Work with a partner. Write a question using two Key Words. Answer your partner's question. Use at least one Key Word in your answer. Keep going until you have used all of the Key Words twice.

| Questions | Answers |
|---|---|
| Do you remember how to locate your house? | Yes. I will never forget my address. |

# Determine Theme

**Reading Strategies**
- Plan
- Monitor
- Make Connections
- Visualize
- **Ask Questions** Think actively by asking and answering questions about the text.
- Determine Importance
- Make Inferences
- Synthesize

**How Do Readers Determine Theme?** The **theme** of a story is its main message. The message says something important about life or the world. Writers usually don't state the **theme**. One way to determine the **theme** is to look for clues in the title, the setting, the thoughts and actions of the characters, and the plot.

As you read, look for clues that you can use to determine the **theme**.

> **Look Into the Text**

**" The title is one place I can look for clues to use to determine the theme."**

## The Forgotten Treasure

Once there was a hunter who lived with his wife and their four sons. Each son had eyes like shiny black stones. The hunter looked at his sons and smiled. "Some men have gold, but my sons are better than gold. They are my treasures."

Every morning, the hunter said to his family, "You are all my treasures. If you care about me, remember me always."

## Practice Together

**Begin a Theme Chart** Use a Theme Chart to collect the clues you discover. First, think about the title of the selection. What message do the words tell you?

Each box shows an element of the story. Reread the passage above, and add a clue about the characters to the Theme Chart. As you read the story, continue adding clues and think about what they tell you.

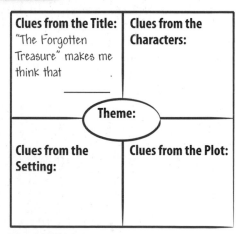

Theme Chart

**Academic Vocabulary**
- **theme** (thēm) *noun*
  A **theme** is the main message of a story.

## Folk Tale

A folk tale is a story that has been told and retold for many years. The words and actions of the **characters** , or people in the story, show what is important.

In a folk tale, the characters' **thoughts, words, and actions** are details that can provide clues to the theme. Look for the theme by analyzing the characters and other elements of the story.

**Look Into the Text**

Once there was a hunter who lived with his wife and their four sons. Each son had eyes like shiny black stones. The hunter looked at his sons and smiled. "Some men have gold, but my sons are better than gold."

As you read, ask questions about elements of the folk tale to help you determine theme.

# The Forgotten Treasure

## an adaptation of a Nigerian folk tale

*Extended Family*, 2006, Jimoh Buraimoh. Beads on board, Via Mundi Gallery, Atlanta, Georgia.

▲ **Critical Viewing: Design** How is this family portrait like others you have seen? How is it different?

Once there was a hunter who lived with his wife and their four sons. Each son had eyes like shiny black stones. The hunter looked at his sons and smiled. "Some men have gold, but my sons are better than gold. They are my **treasures**."

The hunter's wife was going to have a fifth baby. Sometimes she could feel it kick. "It will be another boy," she would say. "Another **fine** boy, just like his brothers."

Every morning, the hunter said to his family, "You are all my treasures. If you care about me, **remember** me always."

Every morning, his sons would say, "Father, we do not need to remember you. Every day you go out, but every day you come back. You are always here, so how could we ever **forget** you?"

*African Hunter*, 2002, Emmanuel Yeboa. Oils and batik on calico, courtesy of Novica, Los Angeles.

▲ **Critical Viewing: Character** Which character in the folk tale could this be? Explain.

**Key Vocabulary**

**treasure** *n.*, something that has great value or importance

**remember** *v.*, to keep in mind; to think of again

**forget** *v.*, to stop thinking about someone or something

**In Other Words**

**fine** good

One day, the hunter went out into the **forest** with **his spear, his bow, and his arrows**. At the end of the day, he did not come home. His wife and his four sons stayed up all night waiting for him, but still he didn't come home. A week passed but still he did not come home. His wife and his sons cried for their **loss**.

Weeks went by, but the hunter did not come home. His wife and his four sons dried their tears.

A month went by and the hunter still did not come home. His wife and his four sons forgot about him. They forgot all about the hunter with his spear, his bow, and his arrows.

Many months went by. The new baby boy was born, and he was just like his brothers. The baby grew. First, he **crawled**. Then he walked. But he did not play.

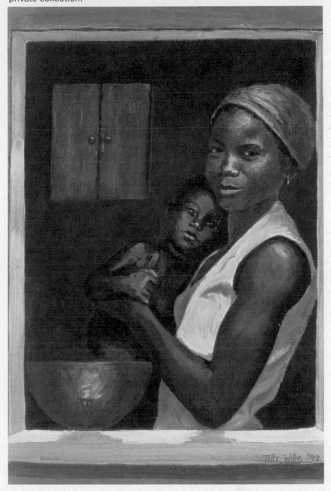

*Through the Window*, 1992, Tilly Willis. Oil on canvas, private collection.

▲ **Critical Viewing: Character** Which sentence in the folk tale do you think goes best with this painting? Explain why you think so.

**Look Into the Text**

1. **Vocabulary** The father says that his sons are his "**treasures**." What does he mean?
2. **Sequence** What happens when the hunter does not come home? What happens a month later?

Every day, the mother gave the little boy a shiny stone or a **beautiful** feather, but the boy would not even look at it. Every day, the brothers took turns trying to find him something nice. One day it was a colorful leaf. Another day it was a smooth red shell. Still another day it was a sparkling spider web. But the boy would not look at the gifts.

"I want our treasure," said the little boy.

His family laughed. "We have no treasure!" they said in **response**. "We are just an ordinary family."

The little boy looked at his mother and told her again, "I want our treasure!"

"Little one," said the mother, with a smile. "Today you want a treasure. Tomorrow you will forget and want something good to eat. That is how it is with little ones."

The little boy, whose eyes were like shiny black stones, looked at his four brothers. "I want our treasure," he said. "Don't you want our treasure, too?"

**They covered their faces with their hands**. "Oh! Our treasure! We forgot him! We forgot all about him! He went into the forest and never came home."

The mother said, "My sons, you must find your father."

The next morning, the four brothers set off together into the forest. First, they found a spear on the ground. Then they found the bow and arrows. Next, they found the hunter's white bones, which were almost covered by fallen leaves.

**Key Vocabulary**
**beautiful** *adj.*, very pretty

**In Other Words**
**response** answer
**They covered their faces with their hands.** They felt ashamed, or bad about themselves.

*African Sunset*, 2005, Angela Ferreira. Oil on canvas, collection of the artist.

▲ **Critical Viewing: Setting** Describe the setting of this painting.

**Look Into the Text**

1. **Confirm Prediction** Was your prediction correct? What happened that you did not expect?

2. **Inference** Why doesn't the little boy want the gifts from his mother and brothers?

3. **Cause and Effect** What causes the brothers to **remember** their father?

And so the sons **located** their father, but how could they help him? The first brother said, "It's a good thing I know how to bring the bones together!" As he sang over his father's bones, the bones jumped up and made a **skeleton**.

The second brother said, "It's a good thing I know how to put skin on the bones!" As he sang over his father's skeleton, skin covered the bones.

The third brother said, "It's a good thing I know how to put life into the body!" As he sang over his father's body, the hunter's heart began to beat.

Egungun costume and mask, Nigerian Yoruba culture.

▲ **Critical Viewing: Design** What details make this object like a painting? How is the object different from a painting?

**Key Vocabulary**
**locate** *v.*, to find exactly where something or someone is
**skeleton** *n.*, all the bones of an animal or person

The fourth brother said, "It's a good thing I know how to make the body move!" As he sang to his father's heart, the hunter sat up and looked around.

"Where have I been?" the father asked. His sons answered, "You were lost, but we have found you."

The father smiled at his sons. "You are my treasures," he said. Then he picked up his spear, his bow, and his arrows and went home with his sons.

At first, the wife was happy to see her husband. Then she looked away from him **in shame**. "You were gone for so long that we forgot you," she said.

**"You are my treasures."**

The hunter smiled at his wife. "You are my treasure," he said. He sat down by the fire, picked up a knife and a lump of wood, and began to **carve**. His sons watched him. He carved all night. He carved for a week. He carved for a month. He carved for a year.

The hunter made the most beautiful carving that his wife and sons had ever seen. The carving showed every animal in the forest. It showed every tree and every flower.

The father looked at his family. "This carving is for the one who saved my life," he said.

**In Other Words**
**in shame** because she felt bad
**carve** cut shapes onto the wood

▲ **Critical Viewing: Character** What are the characters in this painting like?

His wife said, "Then it is mine. I sent your sons to find you."

The first brother said, "No, it is mine. I put your bones back together."

The second brother said, "No, it is mine. I put skin back on your bones."

The third brother said, "No, it is mine. I made your heart beat again."

The fourth brother said, "No, it is mine. I made you move again."

The hunter looked at them all. He smiled and shook his head. "No," he said. "This is for the little one. He is the one who remembered me. As long as a person is remembered and treasured by someone, he is not really lost." The hunter lifted the fifth son onto his knee. Then he put the beautiful carving into his son's hands. ❖

## Stories and Storytellers

Charlotte Blake Alston

No one knows who made up "The Forgotten Treasure," but people have been telling stories like it for thousands of years. In West Africa, a storyteller is called a *griot* (**grē-ō**). Stories are not written down, so griots must be able to remember them all. Griots are also the keepers of history.

Today, many American storytellers tell stories aloud. **Charlotte Blake Alston** gathers folk tales from West Africa. She visits schools to share the stories. Alston uses the "power of the voice" when she performs.

### Look Into the Text

1. **Confirm Prediction** Was your prediction about the hunter coming home correct?
2. **Plot** How does the fifth son save his father's life?

# There Is No Word for Goodbye

### by Mary Tall Mountain

Sokoya, I said, looking through
    the net of wrinkles into
    wise black pools
    of her eyes.
5  What do you say in Athabaskan
    when you leave each other?
    What is the word
    for goodbye?
  A shade of feeling rippled
10  the wind-tanned skin.
    Ah, nothing, she said,
    watching the river flash.
She looked at me close.
    We just say, Tlaa. That means,
15  See you.
    We never leave each other.
    When does your mouth
    say goodbye to your heart?

She touched me light
20  as a bluebell.
    You forget when you leave us,
    You're so small then.
    We don't use that word.
We always think you're coming back,
25  but if you don't,
    we'll see you some place else.
    You understand.
    There is no word for goodbye.

**In Other Words**

**Sokoya** Aunt (in Athabaskan)
**Athabaskan** your Native American
  language
**rippled** moved
**bluebell** flower

## Look Into the Text

1. **Inference** Is Sokoya young or old? Find details that support your answer.
2. **Interpret** What does Sokoya mean when she says, "When does your mouth say goodbye to your heart?"

# Connect Reading and Writing

**Vocabulary**
beautiful
forest
forget
located
loss
remember
skeletons
treasures

## CRITICAL THINKING

1. **SUM IT UP** Use your Theme Chart to retell the folk tale. Be sure to explain the theme in your retelling.

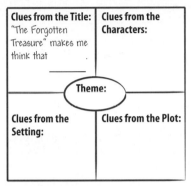

| Clues from the Title: | Clues from the Characters: |
|---|---|
| "The Forgotten Treasure" makes me think that _____ . | |
| Theme: | |
| Clues from the Setting: | Clues from the Plot: |

Theme Chart

2. **Explain** Look again at the Anticipation Guide on page 292. Do you want to change your responses? With a group, discuss if you prefer to **remember** or **forget** about something you lose. Tell why.

3. **Compare** Tell about the **loss** and the discovery in "The Forgotten Treasure" and "There Is No Word for Goodbye."

4. **Analyze** Why does the father put so much care into the **beautiful** carving?

## READING FLUENCY

**Expression** Read the passage on page 571 to a partner. Assess your fluency.

1. My voice never/sometimes/always matched what I read.

2. What I did best in my reading was _____ .

## READING STRATEGY

What strategy helped you understand this selection? Tell a partner about it.

## VOCABULARY REVIEW

**Oral Review** Read the paragraph aloud. Add the vocabulary words.

I dreamed I found _____ jewels, gold, and other _____ in the woods. I put them in a paper bag, which I lost. I was upset about my _____ . I tried to _____ where I had last seen the bag. I looked near every tree in the _____ . The branches looked like bones, or _____ . At last, I _____ the bag. I will never _____ about that dream!

**Written Review** Write a paragraph that tells about a **treasure** of your own. Use at least five vocabulary words in your paragraph. Then draw a picture of your treasure.

**WRITE ABOUT THE** GUIDING QUESTION

**Explore Personal Discoveries**
Choose a character from "The Forgotten Treasure." Tell how the discovery of the father changed the character. Have you ever made a discovery like that? Give examples from the text and your life.

# Connect Across the Curriculum

## Vocabulary Study

### Use Word Parts

| Suffix | Meaning |
|--------|---------|
| -er, -or | one who |
| -ful | full of |
| -ous | full of, having |
| -y | like, having that quality |

**Academic Vocabulary**
- **record** (ri-**kord**) *verb*
  To **record** means to put something in writing.

Adding a suffix to a base word, changes the meaning.

[base word] [suffix]

color   +   -ful   =   colorful

The suffix *-ful* means "full of," so *colorful* means "full of color."

**Spelling Rules**

**1.** If the suffix begins with a consonant, only change base words that end in *-y*.

hope + -ful = hopeful     beauty + -ful = beautiful

**2.** If the suffix begins with a vowel, you may need to make a change.

fame + -ous = famous     shine + -y = shiny     hunt + -er = hunter

**Build Words** Add a suffix to each base word. Use the chart above. **Record** the new word and use it in a sentence.

**1.** courage     **3.** plenty     **5.** carve     **7.** visit
**2.** dirt        **4.** work       **6.** danger    **8.** faith

## Literary Analysis

### Compare Texts: Theme

**Academic Vocabulary**
- **sequence** (sē-kwens) *noun*
  The **sequence** of events is the order in which the events happen.

Stories and poems can have similar themes, even if they are about different characters, happen in different settings, or have a different **sequence**, or order, of plot events.

**Compare Literary Elements** Use the Theme Charts you completed for "The Forgotten Treasure" and "There Is No Word for Goodbye." Identify any literary elements, such as character actions and **sequence** of events, that are similar in both texts and any that are different.

**Analyze Similar Themes** With a partner, discuss the themes you wrote on your charts. How are the themes similar? What literary elements in the story were different? How does this affect the theme? Share your findings with the class.

## Engage in Discussion

**Group Talk** Imagine that the family in "The Forgotten Treasure" did not listen to the youngest son. What do you think might have happened? Use present and past tense verbs in your discussion.

> I agree with you. I felt bad for the youngest son, too. What did you think about the family?

## Write About the Past

**Study the Models** At almost any age, people make personal discoveries. When writers tell about a discovery, they let the reader know when things happen.

**NOT OK**

Last year, I **am** very shy. I was afraid to speak in front of the class or to join groups. Then a new student came to our class. She **has** no friends. I **decide** to say hello. I discovered that I was not so shy after all! Soon, Dana and I were good friends.

> The writer uses some **present tense** verbs to tell about the past. The reader is confused: "I can't tell if the narrator is still shy."

**OK**

When I **was** a little kid, I **was** different from a lot of my friends. They **screamed** when they **saw** big, ugly bugs, but I just **wanted** to learn more about them. I **collected** insects and **studied** them. One day I **learned** about entomology, or the study of insects. I **was** so excited! Today, I **work** at a university. I **am** an entomologist.

> The reader can tell from **past tense verbs** when things happened.

> This part is about today, so the writer uses the **present tense**.

**Revise It** Look back at the NOT OK passage. Work with a partner to revise it. Fix verb tenses so they don't confuse readers.

**WRITE ON YOUR OWN** Write about a personal discovery of your own. Use correct verb tenses.

**REMEMBER**

|  | Regular Verbs | | Forms of *Be* | | | Forms of *Have* | |
|---|---|---|---|---|---|---|---|
| **Present Tense** | discover | learn | am | is | are | have | has |
| **Past Tense** | discover**ed** | learn**ed** | was | was | were | had | had |

# Mysteries
## of the Ancient Past
### by Reyna Eisenstark

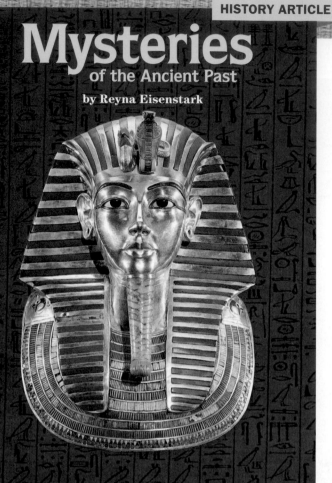

## SELECTION 3 OVERVIEW

▶ **Build Background**

▶ **Language & Grammar**
Define and Explain
Use Past Tense Verbs

▶ **Prepare to Read**
Learn Key Vocabulary
Determine Main Idea and Details

▶ **Read and Write**
Introduce the Genre
History Article
Focus on Reading
Determine Main Idea and Details
Apply the Focus Strategy
Ask Questions
Critical Thinking
Reading Fluency
Read with Appropriate Phrasing
Vocabulary Review
Write About the Guiding Question

▶ **Connect Across the Curriculum**
**Vocabulary Study**
Use Word Parts
**Research/Speaking**
Research Pyramids
**Language and Grammar**
Define and Explain
**Writing and Grammar**
Write About the Past and Present

## Build Background

### Discuss the Ancient Past

Scientists discover many things when they dig up the past. Look at the illustration, and think about what it reveals about life in ancient Egypt.

**Digital Library**     **myNGconnect.com**
🔄 View the images.

▲ Ancient Egyptians grew crops.

### Connect

**KWL Chart**  Tell what you know about ancient Egyptians. Write your ideas in column 1 of a KWL Chart. In column 2, write what you want to learn about ancient Egyptians. Use column 3 to list what you learned after reading.

| WHAT I KNOW | WHAT I WANT TO KNOW | WHAT I LEARNED |
|---|---|---|
| The ancient Egyptians built the Pyramids. | Why were they built? | |

**KWL Chart**

# Language & Grammar

## Define and Explain

Study the photo and listen to the explanation.
Then explain something else in the picture.

**PICTURE PROMPT**

archaeologist

skeleton

hand tool

An archaeologist studies human life in the past. Archaeologists often use hand tools. They dig up old buildings, pots, and bones. They work slowly and carefully so they do not break anything.

1 TRY OUT LANGUAGE
2 LEARN GRAMMAR
3 APPLY ON YOUR OWN

# Use Past Tense Verbs

The tense of a verb tells when an action happens.
- Add **-ed** to most verbs to show that an action already happened.
- Use special **past tense** forms for irregular verbs.

| Present | Past | Example in the Past |
|---------|------|---------------------|
| do, does | did | I **did** my research on pyramids. |
| go, goes | went | I **went** to the library. |
| feel | felt | At first I **felt** tired. |
| know | knew | I **knew** nothing about pyramids. |
| see | saw | Then I **saw** pictures of them. |
| tell | told | "This is interesting," I **told** myself. |

## Practice Together

Say each sentence. Choose the past tense form of the verb.

1. Last year, my parents (did/do) something amazing.
2. They (go/went) to Egypt.
3. Mom and Dad (felt/feel) so excited.
4. They (see/saw) some pyramids.
5. They (told/tell) us all about them.
6. We never (know/knew) that pyramids could be so interesting.
7. Mom and Dad (told/tell) us that they want to go back to Egypt some day.

## Try It!

Say each sentence. Write the past tense form of the verb on a card. Then hold up the card as you say the sentence with the past tense verb.

8. The professor (went/goes) to Egypt every year.
9. He (does/did) research on life in the past.
10. He (saw/sees) bones and old buildings.
11. He (went/goes) to many interesting places.
12. He (felt/feels) excited about his job.
13. He (knows/knew) a lot about life long ago.
14. He (tells/told) us all about it.
15. We (saw/see) his photos, too.

▲ Scientists went to this site to study bones.

# Describe a Favorite Topic

## DEFINE AND EXPLAIN

What do you enjoy? Tell a partner about a game, sport, or other topic that you know well. Define the difficult words.

First, use a Word Web to gather the important words that go with the topic. Here is a Word Web about Egypt.

**Word Web**

Decide which words you may need to define for your partner. Write the meanings. Use a dictionary if you need help.

Then talk with a partner. When you give your explanation, define at least one word.

## HOW TO DEFINE AND EXPLAIN

1. **Define:** Tell what the word means.
2. **Explain:** Give details and examples to make the definition clear.

> A mummy is a body that has been treated so it doesn't fall apart. A mummy is wrapped in cloth. In ancient Egypt, the dead were made into mummies.

## USE VERB TENSES

Be sure to use the correct verb tense when you speak. When you define something, you can use the **present tense verbs** *is* or *are*.

EXAMPLES    The Nile **is** an important river in Egypt.
The pyramids **are** special buildings in Egypt.

When you give an explanation, you may tell about something that already happened. If so, use **past tense verbs**.

EXAMPLES    Last year, I **went** to a museum. I **saw** a mummy up close.
It **was** covered in cloth. The guide **told** us that the mummy **was** 2000 years old.

## Learn Key Vocabulary

**Study the Words** Use the steps below.

1. Pronounce the word. Say it aloud several times. Spell it.
2. Rate your word knowledge.
3. Study the example. Tell more about the word.
4. Practice it. Make the word your own.

**Rating Scale**

**1** = I have never seen this word before.

**2** = I am not sure of the word's meaning.

**3** = I know this word and can teach the word's meaning to someone else.

### Key Words

**ancient** (ānt-shunt) *adjective*
▶ page 320

If something is **ancient**, it is very old. People built this **ancient** temple long ago.
*Antonym:* **new**

**archaeologist**
(ar-kē-**ah**-lu-jist) *noun* ▶ page 322

An **archaeologist** studies the way people lived in the past. Bones, buildings, and tools help **archaeologists** learn about the past.
*Base Word:* **archaeology**

**artifact** (ar-ti-fakt) *noun*
▶ page 323

An **artifact** is an object, or the remains of one, that represents a culture. An old statue is an **artifact**.

**bury** (bair-ē) *verb*
▶ page 327

To **bury** means to place in the ground. The dog **buries** a bone.
*Synonym:* **cover**

**civilization**
(si-vu-lu-**zā**-shun) *noun* ▶ page 320

A **civilization** is the culture of a specific place, time, or group of people. Greece has a very old **civilization**.

**clue** (klü) *noun*
▶ page 320

A **clue** is a piece of information that leads to a solution. The man looks for **clues** to the crime.
*Synonyms:* **hint, sign**

**pyramid** (pear-u-mid) *noun*
▶ page 320

A **pyramid** is a building with a square base and four sides that are triangles. This **pyramid** is in Egypt.

**tomb** (tüm) *noun*
▶ page 324

A **tomb** is a grave, or a special place for the body of a dead person. This is the inside of a **tomb** in Italy.

**Practice the Words** Work with a partner to complete an Expanded Meaning Map for each Key Word.

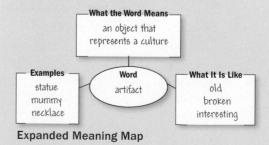

**Expanded Meaning Map**

# Determine Main Idea and Details

**How Is Writing Organized?** Nonfiction writers begin with a topic, or what the text discusses. Writers **organize** the text so the ideas are clear to readers. They state the central or **main idea**—what they want to say about the topic—and then give **details** about the main idea.

As you read, look for information that helps you analyze the main idea and details.

**Reading Strategies**

- Plan
- Monitor
- Make Connections
- Visualize
- **Ask Questions** Think actively by asking and answering questions about the text.
- Determine Importance
- Make Inferences
- Synthesize

## Look Into the Text

### Digging Up the Past

Archaeologists study objects from the past to learn about the people who made or used those objects  and left them behind when they died. Archaeologists gather clues in many places. They look in old buildings. They also look for objects buried under the ground.

**"**The writer states the main idea at the beginning of the section and in the heading.**"**

**"**I read to find what details tell more about the main idea.**"**

## Practice Together

**Begin a Main-Idea Chart** A Main-Idea Chart can help you keep track of the main idea and details of each section of a text. The first two boxes of this Main-Idea Chart include information from the first paragraph of the passage above. Reread the passage to add to the Main-Idea Chart.

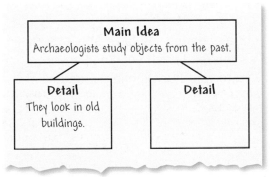

**Main-Idea Chart**

Main Idea
Archaeologists study objects from the past.

Detail
They look in old buildings.

Detail

---

**Academic Vocabulary**

- **organize** (or-gu-nīz) *verb*
  To **organize** is to put things in a certain order.

## History Article

A history article is nonfiction. It tells about something that happened in the past. The headings show what each section is about.

The paragraphs in a history article often tell about one **main idea.** They include **details** to support the main idea. By analyzing the main idea and its supporting details in each section, you will better understand the topic of the selection as a whole.

**Look Into the Text**

### Objects from Long Ago

The objects that archaeologists study are called artifacts. Artifacts are clues that tell archaeologists how people lived in ancient times.

Think of a question you have about the main idea as you read each section. Look for answers to your question in the details of the sentences or paragraphs following the main idea.

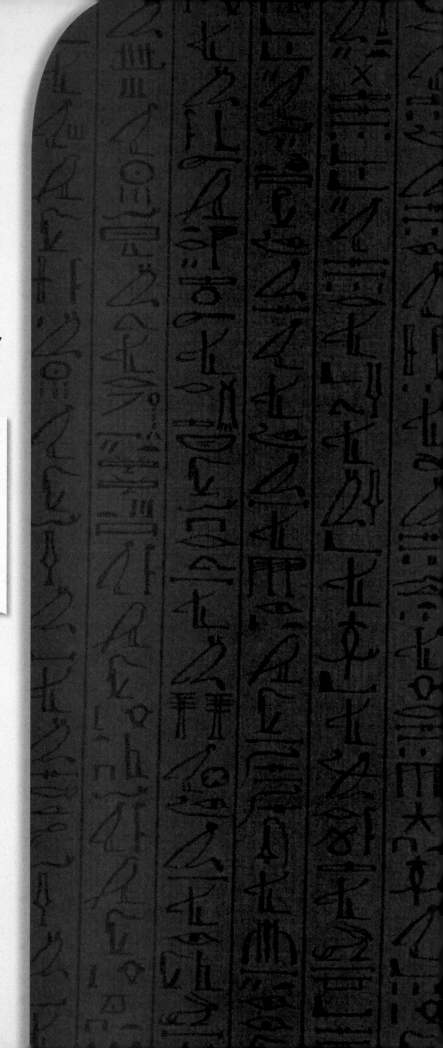

# Mysteries
## of the Ancient Past

by Reyna Eisenstark

Comprehension Coach

# Discovering the Past in
# ANCIENT EGYPT

Egypt

**Ancient** Egypt was home to a great **civilization**. The people who lived there left **clues** about how they lived. One clue is the **pyramids**, buildings that have stood in the desert for thousands of years.

Who built the pyramids, and why did they build them? What lies inside these mysterious buildings? These are some of the questions that scientists and **historians** try to answer.

**Key Vocabulary**

**ancient** *adj.*, very old

**civilization** *n.*, the culture of a specific place, time, or group

**clue** *n.*, a piece of information that leads to a solution

**pyramid** *n.*, a building with a square base and four triangular sides

# Digging Up the Past

**Archaeologists** study objects from the past to learn about the people who made or used those objects and left them behind when they died. Archaeologists gather clues in many places. They look in old buildings. They also look for objects buried under the ground. Archaeologists often have to dig to find what they are looking for.

A worker is cleaning the dirt from this ancient Egyptian carving. ▶

**Key Vocabulary**

**archaeologist** *n.*, a scientist who studies the way that people lived long ago

# Objects from Long Ago

The objects that archaeologists study are called **artifacts**. Artifacts are clues that tell archaeologists how people lived in ancient times.

Artifacts can take many shapes. Old toys and games are artifacts. Statues and other art objects, baskets, bowls, and **mummies** are also artifacts. When artifacts are broken, archaeologists try to put the pieces back together.

◄ This little statue of a hippo is an artifact from ancient Egypt.

Ancient Egyptians made this mummy of a cat long ago. ►

## Look Into the Text

1. **Main Idea and Details** What do scientists want to know about the **pyramids**?
2. **Vocabulary** What does an **archaeologist** do? Cite details from the text.

# A Search Begins

When Howard Carter was still a teenager, he traveled thousands of miles from his home in England to Egypt. As he did so, he **traveled back thousands of years in time**.

Carter became an archaeologist and continued to work in Egypt. He was searching for an ancient **tomb**. He knew that inside the tomb he would find clues about a time long ago.

▲ Howard Carter made important discoveries about King Tut.

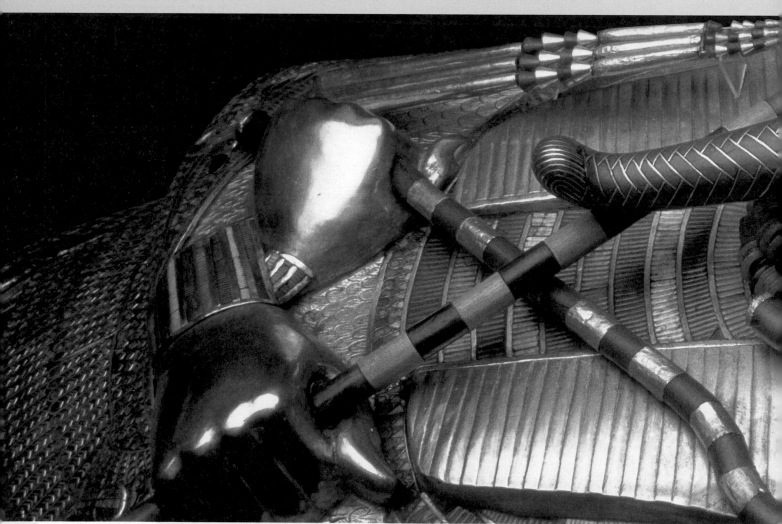

**Key Vocabulary**
**tomb** *n.*, a grave

**In Other Words**
**traveled back thousands of years in time** learned about what life was like thousands of years ago

▼ King Tut was a teenager when he died. This is a detail, or part, of the **coffin** in which his body was placed.

**In Other Words**
**coffin** container

## Look Into the Text

1. **Explain** Who was Howard Carter?
2. **Inference** Read the caption and study the photo on this page. How do you think **ancient** Egyptians felt about King Tut? Explain.

# ANCIENT EGYPT

Mediterranean
Sea

Nile River

Red
Sea

EGYPT

■ Archaeological Sites

⚠ **Interpret the Map** Where are most of the archaeological sites located?

**In Other Words**

**Archaeological Sites** Places
where archaeologists think ancient
people stayed for a period of time
and left artifacts

# Lost Treasures

Ancient Egyptians **buried** their dead kings in special tombs. Some tombs were in pyramids. Others were in the Valley of the Kings. Many archaeologists wanted to find these tombs so they could study the valuable artifacts inside. Often, though, when they opened the tombs there was nothing left inside, because people had stolen the treasures long before.

▲ Archaeologists dig for artifacts.

# Looking for King Tut

Howard Carter had a plan. He read stories of Egypt's history. He learned about a leader named Tutankhamun, or King Tut. No one knew where King Tut was buried, though.

Carter wanted to look for King Tut's tomb. He decided to look in the Valley of the Kings. Carter got a map of the valley and marked the tombs that had already been found. Carter thought King Tut's tomb might be nearby. He began to dig in 1917.

▲ Carter and his team dig in search of King Tut's tomb.

**Key Vocabulary**

**bury** *v.*, to place in the ground

**Look Into the Text**

1. **Main Idea and Details** What was special about the Valley of the Kings?
2. **Cause and Effect** How did Carter decide where to look for King Tut's tomb?

A statue of young King Tut ▷

## Stairs to a Door

Carter searched for many years. At first he found nothing. But he kept looking. He was determined to find King Tut's tomb. On November 4, 1922, his luck changed. Carter's team discovered a step that was cut into some rock.

The team kept digging. Soon they found fifteen more steps. The steps led to an ancient doorway. The door seemed to be **sealed**. It had the name Tutankhamun written on it.

▲ Carter and his team entered the tomb through this door.

## The Room Beyond

The team took nearly three weeks to clear the staircase. Carter slowly made a hole in the door. He was **stunned** by what he found. Through the door was a series of rooms. One room held King Tut's mummy. Other rooms were filled with artifacts that had been buried with King Tut thousands of years before.

▲ The Egyptians believed that this statue would protect King Tut.

**In Other Words**
**sealed** closed tight
**stunned** amazed

# The Glint of Gold!

The ancient tomb held more than 3,500 artifacts. It held jewels, statues, paintings, and lots of gold. King Tut's coffin was solid gold. The dead king had a gold mask and throne, too.

Howard Carter carefully studied all of these artifacts, which showed the great riches of Egyptian kings. They also gave clues about life in ancient Egypt. It took Carter **a decade** to finish work on King Tut's tomb.

▲ Howard Carter uses a brush to clean an artifact.

# A Famous King

King Tut died more than 3,000 years ago and **reigned** for only a decade or so. He had little **claim to fame**. He is well-known today, though, simply because of Howard Carter's amazing discovery.

King Tut's tomb has taught us a lot about life in ancient Egypt. For example, it proves that ancient Egyptians believed in life after death. It also shows that people honored their king. And it shows the great riches of the ancient Egyptian civilization. ❖

King Tut's gold throne ▶

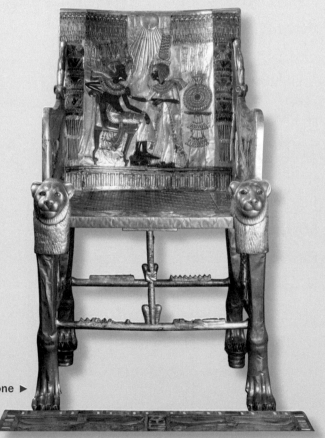

**In Other Words**
**a decade** ten years
**reigned** was king
**claim to fame** reason to be famous

**Look Into the Text**

1. **Explain** Why is King Tut famous today?
2. **Summarize** What does King Tut's tomb teach us about life in **ancient** Egypt?

# Connect Reading and Writing

Vocabulary

ancient

archaeologists

artifact

buried

civilization

clues

pyramid

tomb

## CRITICAL THINKING

1. **SUM IT UP** Use your Main-Idea Chart to explain the main idea and details from "Mysteries of the Ancient Past" and summarize the selection to a partner.

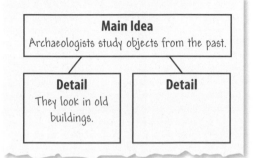

**Main Idea**
Archaeologists study objects from the past.

**Detail**
They look in old buildings.

**Detail**

Main-Idea Chart

2. **Explain** Return to the KWL Chart you made on page 312. Write what you learned about **pyramids** in column 3. Discuss your chart with a group.

3. **Interpret** How do **artifacts** give us **clues** about people of the past?

4. **Infer** Why do you think it took Carter so long to work on King Tut's **tomb**?

## READING FLUENCY

**Phrasing** Read the passage on page 572 to a partner. Assess your fluency.

1. I did not pause/sometimes paused/ always paused for punctuation.

2. What I did best in my reading was _____ .

## READING STRATEGY

What strategy helped you understand this selection? Tell a partner about it.

## VOCABULARY REVIEW

**Oral Review** Read the paragraph aloud. Add the vocabulary words.

A museum had a very old statue from the grave, or _____, of a dead king. The handmade object, or _____, was beautiful. It had been created during the time of a great _____. One day the _____ statue was stolen from the museum. Some _____ and other scientists decided to search for it. They solved the mystery by looking for _____ to follow. They found the statue, where it was _____ underground, near the base of a _____.

**Written Review** Imagine you are an **archaeologist**. Write a paragraph to tell about your work. Use at least four vocabulary words in your paragraph.

**WRITE ABOUT THE** GUIDING QUESTION

### Explore Discoveries of the Past

How do the discoveries of Howard Carter's team of **archaeologists** change us and the world? Read the selection again and look for details that support your answer.

# Connect Across the Curriculum

## Use Word Parts

| Prefix | Meaning |
|--------|---------|
| **dis-** | the opposite of |
| **mid-** | middle |
| **mis-** | wrongly |
| **pre-** | before |
| **super-** | above |

**Academic Vocabulary**
- **record** (ri-**kord**) *verb*
  To **record** means to put something in writing.

A prefix can be added to the beginning of a base word. It changes the word's meaning.

[ **prefix** ]     [ **base word** ]

mis-  +  judge  =  misjudge

The prefix *mis-* means "wrongly," so *misjudge* means "to judge wrongly."

**Build Words** Start with a base word and then add a prefix from the list to make a new word. **Record** each new word you make. Keep the spelling of the prefix and the base word the same. Say what the new word means, and use it in a sentence.

**1.** star      **3.** way      **5.** agree      **7.** cook

**2.** night     **4.** trust    **6.** spell      **8.** market

## Research Pyramids

**Academic Vocabulary**
- **fact** (**fakt**) *noun*
  A **fact** is a piece of information that is true.

**❶ Conduct Research** Learn some **facts** about pyramids. Find out how they were built and what is inside of them. Take notes about an aspect of the pyramids that interests you.

**Internet** myNGconnect.com
- 🔗 Take a virtual tour inside a pyramid.
- 🔗 Read about some important pyramids.
- 🔗 Study diagrams of pyramids.

**❷ Prepare a Presentation** Put the information you learned into words to help you understand and share about the topic. Use your notes to help you prepare an oral report. Decide which facts to tell about and how to organize them. Then think of an interesting introduction, or way to begin your talk. Create a good conclusion, or ending. Briefly sum up what you said.

**❸ Present Your Findings** Practice giving your talk. Then tell your classmates what you learned.

## Define and Explain

**Be an Expert** Work with a partner. List the technical terms in the selection. Take turns choosing a term to define. Tell what it means and give an example. Use past tense verbs when it makes sense.

> Artifacts are objects made by people. A toy or a bowl can be an artifact.

---

**Writing and Grammar**

## Write About the Past and Present

**Study the Models** When you write about a discovery, it's important to let your readers know when it happened and how it affects people today.

**NOT OK**

> Some archaeologists **go** to Egypt. They **bring** special tools for digging up artifacts. Some workers **find** a large tomb. Today, scientists **study** the artifacts and **learn** about ancient Egypt.

This is not OK because the writer uses **present tense** to tell about the past.

**OK**

> Some archaeologists **went** to Egypt. They **brought** special tools for digging up artifacts. Some workers **found** a large tomb. Today, scientists **study** the artifacts and **learn** about ancient Egypt.

The writer uses **past tense** to tell what happened and **present tense** to tell how the discovery connects to today.

**Add Sentences** Think of two sentences to add to the OK model above. Be sure to use the correct tense.

**WRITE ON YOUR OWN** Choose a moment in history that you know about. Write about it, and tell how it connects to something that is happening today. Pay attention to the verb tenses.

**REMEMBER**

Add -**ed** to most verbs to show past tense. Some verbs use special forms to show action in the past.

|  | Regular Verbs | | Irregular Verbs | | | | | |
|---|---|---|---|---|---|---|---|---|
| **Present Tense** | discover | study | bring | find | go | know | see | take |
| **Past Tense** | discover**ed** | stud**ied** | brought | found | went | knew | saw | took |

# The Power of Mysteries

by Alan Lightman

1   I believe in the power of the unknown. I believe that a sense of the unknown **propels us** in all of our creative activities, from science to art.

2   When I was a child, after bedtime I would often get out of my bed in my pajamas, go to the window and stare at the stars. I had so many questions. How far away were those tiny points of light? Did space go on forever and ever, or was there some end to space, some giant edge? And if so, what lay beyond the edge?

3   Another of my childhood questions: Did time go on forever? I looked at pictures of my parents and grandparents and tried to imagine their parents, and so on, back through the generations, back and back through time. Looking out of my bedroom window into the vastness of space, time seemed to stretch forward and backward without end, **engulfing** me, engulfing my parents and great-grandparents, the entire history of earth. Does time go on forever? Or is there some beginning of time? And if so, what came before?

4   When I grew up, I became a professional **astrophysicist**. Although I never answered any of these questions, they continued to challenge me, to haunt me, to drive me in my scientific research, to cause me to live on tuna fish and no sleep for days at a time while I was obsessed with a science problem. These same questions, and questions like them, challenge and haunt the leading scientists of today.

5   Einstein once wrote that "the most **beautiful** experience we can have is the mysterious. It is the fundamental emotion which **stands at the cradle of** true art and true science." What did Einstein mean by "the mysterious?" I don't think he meant that science is full of unpredictable or unknowable or supernatural forces. I think that he meant a sense of awe, a sense that there are things larger than us, that we do not have all the answers at this moment. A sense that we can stand right at the boundary between known and unknown and gaze into that cavern and be exhilarated rather than frightened.

**Key Vocabulary**
- **beautiful** *adj.*, very pretty; amazing

**In Other Words**
**propels us** pushes us forward
**engulfing** surrounding
**astrophysicist** person who studies the way objects move in space
**stands at the cradle of** is the starting point for learning about

**Historical Background**
Albert Einstein was a famous and award-winning physicist.

6  Scientists are happy, of course, when they find answers to questions. But scientists are also happy when they become stuck, when they **discover** interesting questions that they cannot answer. Because that is when their imaginations and creativity are **set on fire**. That is when the greatest progress occurs.

"...the most beautiful experience we can have is the mysterious."

7  One of the **Holy Grails** in physics is to find the so-called "theory of everything," the final theory that will **encompass all the fundamental laws of nature**. I, for one, hope that we never find that final theory. I hope that there are always things that we don't know—about the physical world as well as about ourselves. I believe in the creative power of the unknown. I believe in the exhilaration of standing at the boundary between the known and the unknown. I believe in the unanswered questions of children.

**Key Vocabulary**
- **discover** *v.*, to find something that is lost or hidden

**In Other Words**
**set on fire** truly inspired
**Holy Grails** greatest quests, or searches
**encompass all the fundamental laws of nature** answer all of our questions about the universe

▲ The Horsehead Nebula is a dark nebula, or interstellar cloud. Its swirling gases are in the form of a horse head. It is about 1500 light years from Earth.

# Compare Across Texts

## Compare Important Ideas

"Return to *Titanic*," "The Forgotten Treasure," "Mysteries of the Ancient Past," and "The Power of Mysteries" tell about people who **discover** things. Compare the ideas in the texts.

## How It Works

**Collect and Organize Ideas** To compare ideas across several texts, **organize** them in a chart. List two or three questions to get the big ideas.

| Big Idea Question | Return to Titanic | The Forgotten Treasure | Mysteries of the Ancient Past | The Power of Mysteries |
|---|---|---|---|---|
| 1. Do discoveries make a difference? | The discovery of Titanic helped explain why it sank. | The discovery of the father taught that family is important. | The discovery of artifacts helped explain the past. | Discoveries can solve science problems. |
| 2. Why do people try to make discoveries? | | | | |

Comparison Chart

## Practice Together

**Compare the Ideas** Study the answers for each question. Turn the question into a statement. Then explain how ideas are alike or different. Here is a summary for question 1.

> All of the selections show that discoveries make a difference. Each discovery gave people information about events, people, and the past. "The Power of Mysteries" tells how discoveries solve problems.

## Try It!

Make a chart to collect answers to question 2. Summarize them. You may want to use this frame to help you express your comparison.

> All of the selections show why people try to make discoveries. In "Return to *Titanic*," people want _____. In "The Forgotten Treasure," people want _____, and in "Mysteries of the Ancient Past," they want _____. In "The Power of Mysteries," people want to _____ about _____.

**Academic Vocabulary**

- **discover** (dis-**ku**-vur) *verb*
  To **discover** means to find out something you didn't know before.
- **organize** (**or**-gu-nīz) *verb*
  To **organize** is to put things in a certain order.

THE
DRIVE
TO
# Discover

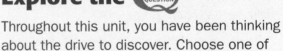 How do discoveries change us and the world?

## Content Library

## Leveled Library

## Reflect on Your Reading

Think back on your reading of the unit selections. Discuss what you did to understand what you read.

**Focus on Reading** **Text Structure: Main Idea and Details**

In this unit, you learned about some ways writers structure a text. Choose a selection from the unit, and draw a diagram or other graphic that shows its structure. It could be a chart or even a picture. Use your drawing to explain the structure of the selection to a partner.

**Focus Strategy** **Ask Questions**

As you read the selections, you learned to ask and answer questions. Explain to a partner how you will use this strategy in the future.

## Explore the

Throughout this unit, you have been thinking about the drive to discover. Choose one of these ways to explore the Guiding Question:

- **Discuss** With a group, discuss the Guiding Question. Remember, there can be many answers. What's yours? Give details from the selections that support your idea.
- **Role-Play** Imagine if people or characters from two different selections could meet and discuss the Guiding Question. With a partner, role-play their discussion. For example, what would Robert Ballard and Howard Carter say to each other?
- **Draw** Create a visual interpretation of your answer to the Guiding Question.

## Book Talk

Which Unit Library book did you choose? Explain to a partner what it taught you about discoveries.

# STRUGGLE FOR FREEDOM

# 6

# How far should people go for the sake of freedom?

◀ A sculpture in Howick, South Africa honoring Nelson Mandela stands on the exact spot where he was arrested.

# Focus on Reading

## Text Structure: Cause and Effect

A common text structure authors use is **cause and effect**. A cause is the reason something happens. An effect is what happens as a result of the cause. Effects often become causes of something else that happens. Writers use cause and effect to explain why things happen.

### How It Works

Before reading, preview the text to figure out how the writer **arranged** the information and ideas. This will help you follow the text.

**Clue words** can help you determine if a writer used **cause** and **effect** as a text structure. As you read, look for causes and effects. In fiction, causes can be important plot events. These causes are steps toward the final effect. The setting, or where a story takes place, can have an effect on plot events. Plot events and setting can be described in a sentence, paragraph, chapter, or whole section. Read this example.

### Fight for Freedom

Sanjana lived in a country that was ruled by the king of another country. The king did not pay the farmers enough for their grain. Because of this, people wanted to fight him.

Sanjana did not believe war was the right way to gain freedom, so she encouraged people to stop selling grain to the kingdom. If people did not feed the king, then he might change how he was treating people.

As a result, the king got angry. He burned crops and increased taxes. But Sanjana encouraged the people not to give up. The people did not pay their taxes. They planted secret gardens and disobeyed the king for many years.

Finally, since the king was not getting what he wanted, he made a peaceful agreement with the people. Everyone was glad they had followed Sanjana's plan. Consequently, they asked her to be the leader of the farmers.

**Cause and Effect Clue Words**

| | |
|---|---|
| as a result | if/then |
| because | led to |
| because of | since |
| caused | so |
| consequently | therefore |

The setting of this story, a country ruled by a king of another country, effects plot events. The people of Sanjana's country want to fight the king because he rules unfairly.

**Academic Vocabulary**
- **arrange** (u-rānj) *verb*
  To **arrange** means to put things in a certain order.

## Practice Together

Read the following passage aloud. As you read, listen for clues that help you identify cause-and-effect relationships. Think about how these relationships help explain why things happen and help develop ideas in the text.

### Gandhi in South Africa

When he was a young man, Mohandas Gandhi worked as a lawyer in South Africa, where many people from India lived and worked. He thought the laws there treated Indians unfairly and often harshly. Gandhi reasoned that if a law was unjust, then it was OK to break that law. He therefore urged people to break unfair laws. Indians followed his advice. As a result, South Africa changed its laws and gave Indians more rights.

When Gandhi returned to India, he saw unfair laws there. So he began to lead peaceful protests in India. Consequently, the laws in India changed, too.

▲ Gandhi helped change unfair laws in South Africa in the early 1900s.

## Try It!

Read the following passage aloud. What are the causes and effects? How do you know? How do these causes and effects help develop the ideas in the text?

### Peaceful Protests

Henry David Thoreau is a famous American writer of the nineteenth century. He wrote that if each person acts peacefully against an unfair law, then the law eventually would be changed.

Mohandas Gandhi read Thoreau's essays and agreed with them. Therefore, he used the ideas in his fight for civil rights.

Later, because of Thoreau and Gandhi, Martin Luther King, Jr., led peaceful protests in the United States. He encouraged African Americans to protest against unfair laws. These protests led to new laws that were more fair.

▲ The ideas of Thoreau inspired Mohandas Gandhi and Martin Luther King, Jr.

# Focus on Vocabulary

## Use Context Clues for Unfamiliar Words

On-page clues to the meaning of a word are called **context** clues. There are several different kinds of **context** clues.

| Type of Clue | What It Does | Signal Words | Example |
|---|---|---|---|
| Definition clue | Explains the word directly in the text | *is, are, was, called, refers to, means* | **Slavery** *refers to* people owning other people and forcing them to work. |
| Restatement clue | Gives the meaning in a different way, usually after a comma | *or* | American slaves were **emancipated**, *or* freed, in 1865. |
| Synonym clue | Gives a word or phrase that means almost the same thing | *also, like* | *Like* other farm workers, the **laborers** picked cotton. |
| Antonym clue | Gives a word or phrase that means almost the opposite of the word | *but, unlike* | **Enslaved** people, *unlike* free people, cannot leave their jobs. |
| Example clue | Gives an example of what the word means | *for example, including, such as* | When slaves ran away, they faced **punishment**, *such as* beatings. |

## How the Strategy Works

When you read, you may come to a word that you don't know. Look for **context** clues to help you figure out the meaning.

1. Read the words nearby, and look for signal words.
2. Predict what the word means.
3. Try out your predicted meaning to see if it makes sense.
4. Check the word's meaning in a dictionary.

Use the strategy to figure out the meaning of each underlined word.

Where Arianna lived, soldiers <u>monitored</u>, or watched, everyone all the time. The soldiers did <u>unjust</u> things, such as taking food from Arianna's restaurant without paying for it. Her brother was <u>incarcerated</u> for a small crime, but others were left free for the same crime. Arianna and her family wanted a better life. They became <u>refugees</u>, which means they went to a new country to be free.

**Strategy in Action**

" I see the word *or* after *monitored*. It could be a signal word for a restatement clue. *Monitored* could mean 'watched.' That makes sense. "

☑ **REMEMBER** You can use **context** clues to figure out the meanings of unfamiliar words.

**Academic Vocabulary**
- **context** (kon-tekst) *noun*
  **Context** refers to the parts nearby that help explain the meaning.

## Practice Together

Read this passage aloud. Look at each underlined word. Use **context** clues to figure out its meaning.

### A Divided Country

When Chang was a child, his country was <u>divided</u> into two parts: the North and the South. Each part of the country had its own government. Chang and his family lived in the South. People were free there, unlike the North, where they were <u>restricted</u>. The two areas fought for many years. Finally, the North was <u>victorious</u> and took control of the entire country. Chang and his family <u>fled</u>, or left, the country in search of freedom.

## Try It!

Read this passage aloud. What is the meaning of each underlined word? How can you tell?

### Fight for Freedom

Joseph and his family lived on a rich, <u>prosperous</u> island in the Caribbean. When he was young, he was free. When he grew up, a new government controlled the island. People who were born in the country and were <u>native</u> to it, like Joseph and his family, were forced to work for no pay.

Joseph and his family should have been protected from <u>abuse</u>, but they received unfair treatment. Finally, they <u>rebelled</u>. They fought the government for many years and finally won. They began a new government. They gave their free, <u>independent</u> country a new name.

# Escaping to Freedom

by Daniel Schulman

## SELECTION 1 OVERVIEW

- **Build Background**
- **Language & Grammar**
  Summarize
  Use Nouns in the Subject and Predicate
- **Prepare to Read**
  Learn Key Vocabulary
  Text Structure: Cause and Effect
- **Read and Write**
  Introduce the Genre
  Biography
  Focus on Reading
  Text Structure: Cause and Effect
  Apply the Focus Strategy
  Determine Importance
  Critical Thinking
  Reading Fluency
  Read with Intonation
  Vocabulary Review
  Write About the Guiding Question

- **Connect Across the Curriculum**
  Vocabulary Study
  Use Context Clues
  Listening/Speaking
  Dramatize a Song
  Language and Grammar
  Summarize
  Writing and Grammar
  Write About Freedom

# Build Background

## Learn About Slavery

Until the mid-1800s, many landowners in the Americas used slave labor on their farms. Life was very hard for the enslaved people.

**Digital Library**    myNGconnect.com
> View the video.

▲ Slave houses in 1860

## Connect

**Discussion** What traits did people need if they wanted to help enslaved people reach safety? Brainstorm and make a list. Then tell which traits you have.

Traits
1. Courage
2. Ability to keep secrets
3. Concern about people
4. Ability to solve problems

# Language & Grammar

## Summarize

Listen to a formal presentation. Then listen to a summary of the presentation.

**FORMAL PRESENTATION and SUMMARY**

## The Underground Railroad

> The Underground Railroad was not a real railroad. It was a system of trails for slaves in America who ran away. The slaves followed the trails to Canada, where slavery was illegal.

Summary of "The Underground Railroad"

The Underground Railroad was a system of trails that helped runaway slaves in America escape to Canada.

# Use Nouns in the Subject and Predicate

Remember, a complete sentence has a subject and a predicate.

The runaway slaves  wanted freedom.
    subject              predicate

- Often, the most important word in the subject is a **noun**.

  EXAMPLE    The runaway **slaves** wanted freedom.

- A **noun** can also be the object of an action verb. To find the object, turn the verb into a question: "Wanted what?"

  EXAMPLE    The runaway slaves **wanted** **freedom**.
                          verb      object

- Many English sentences follow this pattern: subject → verb → object.

  EXAMPLE    Many **people** in the North **opposed** **slavery**.
              subject            verb      object

## Practice Together

Say each sentence. Tell whether the underlined noun is a subject or an object.

1. Slave traders captured people in Africa.
2. Ships carried some captives to America.
3. Colonists bought the slaves.
4. Many enslaved people tended crops in the fields.
5. Other captives did chores inside houses.

## Try It!

Read each sentence. Write *subject* or *object* on a card for the underlined noun. Hold up the card as you say the sentence.

6. Many people hated slavery.
7. Some of these people helped runaways.
8. These brave Americans joined a special organization.
9. Members of the organization secretly helped the enslaved people.
10. The runaways received food.
11. The tired people also received shelter.
12. Often, the assistance saved their lives.

▲ Enslaved people pick cotton.

# Tell About a Topic

**SUMMARIZE**

You learned facts about the Underground Railroad on page 345. Review what you learned. Then think about other facts you may already know about the topic.

List facts you know about the Underground Railroad.

The Underground Railroad
1. People helped slaves escape to the North.
2. It was dangerous.
3. Slaves and their helpers could be punished.

Review your notes. Think about the information. When you feel ready, tell the information to a partner.

Now listen as your partner summarizes what you said. Switch roles.

## HOW TO SUMMARIZE A PRESENTATION

1. Identify the topic.
2. Identify the main idea, or what the presentation mostly says about the topic.
3. Stay focused on what is important. Leave out details that are interesting but not important.

People gave food to the hungry, tired runaways. They gave them safe places to rest or sleep during the day.

People gave the runaways food and shelter.

**USE PRECISE NOUNS**

When you make a presentation or summarize ideas, state the information clearly. Use precise **nouns** in the subjects and predicates of your sentences.

**Not Precise:** A **woman** helped other **people**.

**Precise:** **Harriet Tubman** helped other escaping **slaves**.

# Prepare to Read

## Learn Key Vocabulary

**Study the Words** Use the steps below.

1. Pronounce the word. Say it aloud several times. Spell it.
2. Rate your word knowledge.
3. Study the example. Tell more about the word.
4. Practice it. Make the word your own.

### Key Words

**assist** (u-sist) *verb*
▶ page 356

To **assist** means to help. The father **assists** his son with an assignment when he has trouble understanding it.

**capture** (kap-chur) *noun*
▶ page 354 *verb* ▶ page 357

**1** *verb* To **capture** means to take by force. The farmer **captured** a raccoon. **2** *noun* A **capture** is the act of catching something. Soon after the **capture**, he released the raccoon.

**escape** (is-kāp) *verb* ▶ page 352 *noun* ▶ page 355

**1** *verb* To **escape** means to get away. People **escaped** the burning building. **2** *noun* An **escape** is the act of getting away from something. We heard about their successful **escape**.

**freedom** (frē-dum) *noun*
▶ page 352

**Freedom** is the state of being free, or not limited. The bird was released and given **freedom**.

**reward** (ri-word) *noun*
▶ page 354

Lost Dog

3 year-old male Pug
Answers to the name of "Curley"
If found, call (123) 456-7891

REWARD OFFERED

A **reward** is money given for helping someone. We offered a **reward** to anyone who could find our lost dog.

**right** (rīt) *noun*
▶ page 352

A **right** is the power a person has because of a country's rules. In 1920 American women got the **right** to vote.

**slave** (slāv) *noun*
▶ page 352

A **slave** is someone who belongs to another person and who works without pay. Owners forced **slaves** to work.

**travel** (tra-vul) *verb*
▶ page 354

To **travel** means to go from one place to another place. People can **travel** over land by car, train, or wagon.

**Practice the Words** Write a sentence for each Key Word. Include context clues. Copy the sentences, but put a blank in place of the Key Word. Ask a partner to fill in the words.

The owner forced the _____ to work in the fields.

# Text Structure: Cause and Effect

**How Is Writing Organized?** Some nonfiction writers use **cause** and **effect** to structure, or **arrange**, their ideas. They use the structure to explain why something happens and how one event leads to another.

Sometimes a single cause has more than one effect. Sometimes two or more causes lead to one effect.

**Reading Strategies**

· Plan
· Monitor
· Make Connections
· Visualize
· Ask Questions
· **Determine Importance**
  Focus your attention on the author's most significant ideas and information.
· Make Inferences
· Synthesize

### Look Into the Text

" The first sentence is a reason or cause."

Until 1865, most African Americans were not free. They were slaves with no rights. Their owners forced them to work without pay. They could be sold and sent far away from their families. Many African Americans decided their only chance for freedom was to escape.

## Practice Together

**Make a Diagram** You can use a Cause-and-Effect Diagram to show how events are related. This diagram shows one of the causes that led to the effect. Reread the passage above, and add causes to the Cause-and-Effect Diagram.

| Cause | | Effect |
|---|---|---|
| Most African Americans were not free. | → | African Americans decided their only chance for freedom was escape. |
| **Cause** | → | |
| **Cause** | → | |

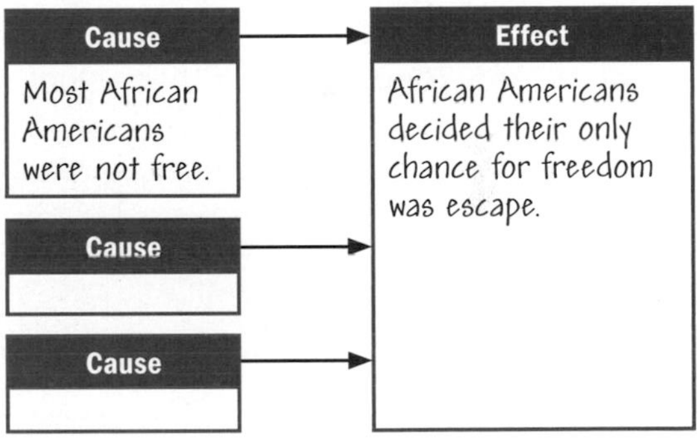

Cause-and-Effect Diagram

**Academic Vocabulary**

● **arrange** (u-rānj) *verb*
  To **arrange** means to put things in a certain order.

## Biography

A biography is the story of a person's life, written by another person. In biographies, writers often use a **cause**-and-**effect** text structure to show why events happened in a person's life.

One day Henson learned some troubling news. He learned that Riley planned to sell him. . . .

Henson could not accept this, so he made a plan for his family to escape.

> clue word

As you read, look for **clue words** that signal cause-and-effect events. These important events will help you summarize the biography.

# Escaping to Freedom

## by Daniel Schulman

Until 1865, most African Americans were not free. They were **slaves** with no **rights**. Their owners forced them to work without pay. They could be sold and sent far away from their families. Many African Americans decided their only chance for **freedom** was to **escape**.

## Bonds of Slavery

In 1830, Josiah Henson was 41 years old. A life of slavery was all he had ever known. Born in Maryland, Henson was taken from his family as a child. He was bought and sold many times.

Henson lived on a plantation, or large farm, in Kentucky. He had a wife and four children. He tried to buy his way out of slavery, but his owner, Amos Riley, tricked him. Riley kept the money that Henson paid for his freedom, but he did not let Henson go.

## Bad News

One day Henson learned some **troubling news**. He learned that Riley planned to sell him. Henson would have to move to Louisiana, and he might never see his wife and children again! Henson could not **accept** this, so he made a plan for his family to escape.

▲ Josiah Henson in later life

Many men, women, and children worked as slaves on large farms like this one.

## Historical Background

Slavery was not common in North America until 1793. That is when Eli Whitney invented a cotton gin. This machine made cotton a popular crop. Many people used slaves to work on their farms. In 1865, the Thirteenth Amendment made slavery against the law in the United States.

Cotton gin

### Look Into the Text

1. **Paraphrase** What was Henson's life like? Tell about it in your own words.
2. **Cause and Effect** What happened that made Henson decide to **escape** from the Riley farm?

# The Path to Freedom

One dark night, Henson and his family left their home. He carried his two youngest children in a backpack. The family **boarded** a small boat and crossed the Ohio River into Indiana.

Once in Indiana, the family had to move slowly. They had to be careful not to be seen. Some slave owners **offered** **rewards** for the **capture** of escaped slaves. If the family was found, they might be returned to Riley. To make sure no one saw them, Henson's family often **traveled** at night and slept during the day.

**100 DOLLARS**

# REWARD!

Ranaway from the subscriber on the 27th of July, my Black Woman, named

## EMILY,

Seventeen years of age, well grown, black color, has a whining voice. She took with her one dark calico and one blue and white dress, a red corded gingham bonnet; a white striped shawl and slippers. I will pay the above reward if taken near the Ohio river on the Kentucky side, or **THREE HUNDRED DOLLARS**, if taken in the State of Ohio, and delivered to me near Lewisburg, Mason County, Ky.     **THO'S. H. WILLIAMS.**
August 4, 1853.

▲ Some slave owners posted signs that offered rewards for the capture of runaway slaves.

**Key Vocabulary**

**reward** *n.*, the money given for helping someone else

**capture** *n.*, the act of catching and keeping a person or animal

**travel** *v.*, to go from one place to another place

**In Other Words**

**boarded** got into
**offered** said they would pay

# Free at Last

The family traveled by wagon, by boat, and on foot. They traveled toward Canada, where slavery was not allowed. Along the way, people helped the family. Some people gave them food, and others hid them in barns.

The family **set foot** in Canada more than a month after their **daring** escape. The first words that Henson **exclaimed** when he got there were, "I am free!"

▲ People led escaped slaves through forests and other places on the path to freedom.

▲ People hid escaped slaves in wagons and other secret places.

**In Other Words**

**set foot** arrived
**daring** brave and dangerous
**exclaimed** said

## Look Into the Text

1. **Cause and Effect** Why did the family have to **travel** slowly?
2. **Conclusion** Why did the family travel to Canada?

# Freedom Train

How was Henson's family able to make the trip to freedom? They traveled by the Underground Railroad, which was not really a railroad and did not go underground, either. The Underground Railroad was a set of paths made of people who helped slaves run away.

People along the Underground Railroad **assisted** runaways. They gave them food and a place to stay. They carried runaways closer to freedom in boats or wagons.

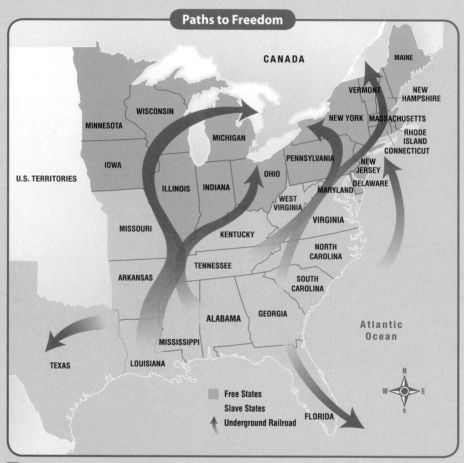

**Paths to Freedom**

CANADA

MAINE
VERMONT
NEW HAMPSHIRE
NEW YORK
MASSACHUSETTS
RHODE ISLAND
CONNECTICUT
PENNSYLVANIA
NEW JERSEY
DELAWARE
MARYLAND
WEST VIRGINIA
VIRGINIA
NORTH CAROLINA
SOUTH CAROLINA
GEORGIA
FLORIDA

WISCONSIN
MINNESOTA
MICHIGAN
IOWA
U.S. TERRITORIES
ILLINOIS
INDIANA
OHIO
MISSOURI
KENTUCKY
TENNESSEE
ARKANSAS
ALABAMA
MISSISSIPPI
LOUISIANA
TEXAS

Atlantic Ocean

- Free States
- Slave States
- Underground Railroad

▲ **Interpret the Map** Choose one path of the Underground Railroad. Name all the states it went through.

**Key Vocabulary**
**assist** *v.*, to help

**Historical Background**
The Underground Railroad helped between 40,000 and 100,000 slaves escape. Some people, like Harriet Tubman, escaped and then returned to the southern states to help others find freedom.

# Secret Paths to Freedom

The Underground Railroad was secret. We do not know all of the paths that people traveled, but we do know that the Underground Railroad helped many slaves escape to freedom. Some **journeys** took a month. Others took a year or more. Some runaways were **captured** or died along the way. The Underground Railroad shows how far people will go for freedom. ❖

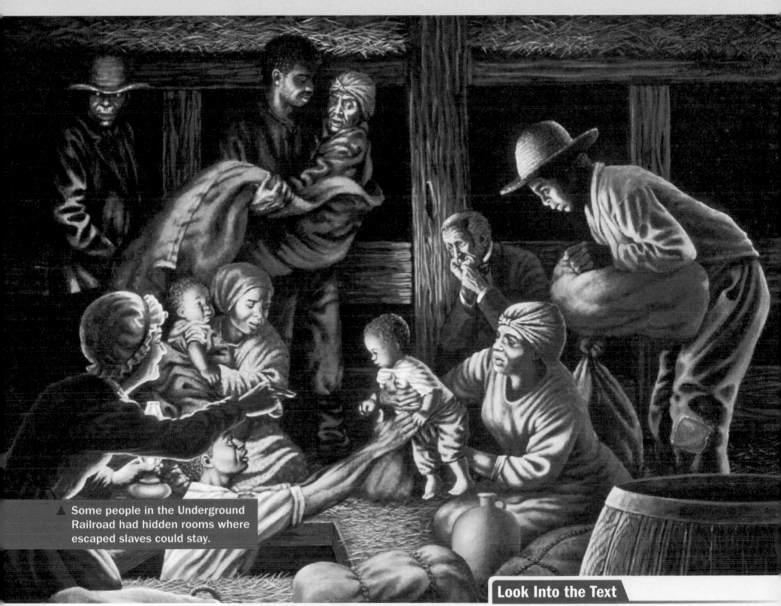

▲ Some people in the Underground Railroad had hidden rooms where escaped slaves could stay.

**Key Vocabulary**
**capture** *v.*, to take by force

In Other Words
**journeys** trips

**Look Into the Text**
1. **Summarize** What was the Underground Railroad?
2. **Explain** What did enslaved people and those who helped them risk by using the Underground Railroad?

# Follow the Drinking Gourd
**A Traditional Song**

Follow the drinking gourd!

Follow the drinking gourd!

For the old man is a-waiting for to carry you to freedom

If you follow the drinking gourd.

5  When the sun comes back and the first quail calls,

Follow the drinking gourd.

For the old man is a-waiting for to carry you to freedom

If you follow the drinking gourd.

**In Other Words**

**a-waiting for to carry** waiting
  to take
**quail** bird

**Background Note**

A gourd is a hard-shelled fruit. Some
dry gourds can be used like a cup.
The pattern of stars called the Big
Dipper looks like a drinking gourd.
People can use the Big Dipper to
find their way north at night because
it points to the North Star.

**Look Into the Text**

1. **Metaphor** What do you think the
   "old man" represents in this song?
2. **Mood** The mood of a song is the
   feeling the writer gives it. What is
   the mood of this song?

# Connect Reading and Writing

Vocabulary
assisted
capture
escape
freedom
rewards
rights
slaves
traveled

## CRITICAL THINKING

1. **SUM IT UP** Use your Cause-and-Effect Diagrams to summarize the selection.

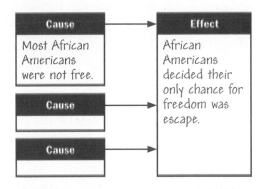

**Cause-and-Effect Diagram**

2. **Interpret** Suppose you lived in the 1830s and saw a poster offering a **reward** for a runaway **slave**. How would you react? Explain why.

3. **Describe** How would you describe people who joined the Underground Railroad to **assist** **slaves**? Give three adjectives.

4. **Infer** Look at the map on page 356. Do you think it was easier for Henson to **escape** than for many other **slaves**? Explain.

## READING FLUENCY

**Intonation** Read the passage on page 573 to a partner. Assess your fluency.

1. My tone never/sometimes/always matched what I read.

2. What I did best in my reading was _____.

## READING STRATEGY

What strategy helped you understand this selection? Tell a partner about it.

## VOCABULARY REVIEW

**Oral Review** Read the paragraph aloud. Add the vocabulary words.

> To _____ from slavery, Josiah Henson _____ to Canada, which did not allow slavery. In Canada, African Americans had the same _____, or legal powers, as other citizens. Enslaved people who avoided _____ and reached Canada got their liberty, or _____. Although many owners offered _____, Canada would not return escaped _____. Henson then _____ former slaves.

**Written Review** Imagine that you live in the past and that you **travel** from town to town to speak out against slavery. Write your speech. Use at least five vocabulary words.

**WRITE ABOUT THE** GUIDING QUESTION

**Explore the Struggle for Freedom**
How does "Follow the Drinking Gourd" go with "**Escaping** to **Freedom**"? Reread both texts. Find examples in each one to support your ideas.

## Vocabulary Study

### Use Context Clues

> **Academic Vocabulary**
> • **context** (kon-tekst) *noun*
>   **Context** refers to the parts nearby that help explain the meaning.

A **definition clue** explains an unfamiliar word directly in the text.
A **restatement clue** gives the meaning in a different way.

Look at the **context** clues in this sentence from "Escaping to Freedom."
Notice how the phrase "or large farm" restates the meaning of *plantation*.

> EXAMPLE    Henson lived on a <u>plantation</u>, or large farm, in Kentucky.

**Figure Out Word Meanings** Use **context** clues to figure out the meaning of each underlined word. Write a definition of the word.

**1.** The slaves had many <u>hardships</u>, or difficulties, in their lives.

**2.** The Underground Railroad <u>enabled</u>, or allowed, many slaves to escape.

**3.** <u>Underground</u> often refers to something that is secret.

**4.** A <u>conductor</u> on the Underground Railroad was a person who led slaves to safety.

## Listening/Speaking

### Dramatize a Song

DRAMA

> **Academic Vocabulary**
> • **interpret** (in-**tur**-prut) *verb*
>   To **interpret** means to explain or tell what something means.

**Read and Interpret** Reread the traditional song "Follow the Drinking Gourd."
Notice that the lyrics include some unusual words and phrases that we do
not use every day. **Interpret** the words and phrases in the lyrics and think
of words and phrases people might use today to express the same idea.

**Discuss the Song** With a group, discuss how the unusual words and
phrases affect the song. What mood, or feeling, do they give the song?

**Prepare and Present** Plan to give a dramatic reading of the song. Show
how you **interpret** the song. Use actions and facial expressions that match
the words. Practice a few times. Speak clearly and loudly. Use a tone that
expresses the song.

## Summarize

**Pair Talk** Work with a partner to summarize one section of "Escaping to Freedom." Use subject and object pronouns correctly. Share your summary with the class.

> We read the first section, "Bonds of Slavery."

> Josiah Henson was a slave in Kentucky. He tried to buy his freedom. Josiah's owner took the money but didn't release him.

## Write About Freedom

**Study the Models** When you write about an important topic like freedom, you want your readers to understand all your ideas. Use pronouns correctly so that your readers know whom or what you are talking about.

### NOT OK

> Jonathan Walker was born in 1799. **Him** opposed slavery strongly. Walker worked hard to try to stop **them**. Once, Walker helped seven slaves escape. **They** sailed from Florida to freedom in the Bahamas. The authorities caught Walker and punished **us**. The incident did not stop **they**, however. For many years, **them** traveled around America and spoke out against slavery.

The reader thinks: **"I'm confused. The writer confuses subject and object pronouns and makes other mistakes with pronouns."**

### OK

> My aunt and my grandmother came to the United States from Saudi Arabia. **They** were amazed at all the freedom here. In Saudi Arabia, **they** could not drive a car or have a job. Everyone expected **them** to stay home most of the time. Now my aunt has a job. **She** works as an Arabic language teacher. Aunt Nadia loves **it**. **She** teaches **us** Arabic, too!

This writer uses correct **subject pronouns** and **object pronouns**. It's easy to tell whom the writer is talking about.

**Revise It** Look back at the NOT OK passage. Work with a partner to revise it. Fix subject, object, and unclear pronouns.

**WRITE ON YOUR OWN** Write about something you have done or would like to do to improve the rights or freedoms of others. Use subject and object pronouns correctly.

### REMEMBER

|                  | Singular |     |     |     |    | Plural |     |      |
|------------------|----------|-----|-----|-----|----|--------|-----|------|
| **Subject Pronouns** | I    | you | he  | she | it | we     | you | they |
| **Object Pronouns**  | me   | you | him | her | it | us     | you | them |

# Brave Butterflies
### by Susan Blackaby

Butterfly, 1978. Tamás Galambos. Oil on canvas, private collection.

## SELECTION 2 OVERVIEW

▶ **Build Background**

▶ **Language & Grammar**

Make Comparisons

Use Pronouns in the Subject and Predicate

▶ **Prepare to Read**

Learn Key Vocabulary

Text Structure: Cause and Effect

▶ **Read and Write**

Introduce the Genre
Short Story

Focus on Reading
Text Structure:
Cause and Effect

Apply the
Focus Strategy
Determine Importance

Critical Thinking

Reading Fluency
Read with Expression

Vocabulary Review

Write About the
Guiding Question

▶ **Connect Across the Curriculum**

Vocabulary Study
Use Context Clues

Literary Analysis
Analyze the Topic

Language and Grammar
Make Comparisons

Writing and Grammar
Write About
a New Home

# Build Background

## Tour an Island Country

The Dominican Republic is an island in the Caribbean Sea. The country has an interesting past and present.

**Digital Library**  **myNGconnect.com**
● View the video.

▲ **A port on the island of the Dominican Republic**

## Connect

**T Chart** What do you think of the Dominican Republic? What would you like and dislike? Work with a group. List positive and negative impressions of the Dominican Republic.

| Positive | Negative |
|----------|----------|
| climate mountains | poverty politics |

**T Chart**

# Compare Homes

## MAKE COMPARISONS

People have many different kinds of homes, and you can compare them.
Try one of these ideas:

- Compare your home with another home or an imaginary home.
- Compare your current home with one you used to live in.
- Compare the two most unusual homes you have seen.

Start your comparison with a Venn Diagram. In the outside sections, tell how the homes are different. In the center section, tell how the homes are the same or similar.

**Venn Diagram**

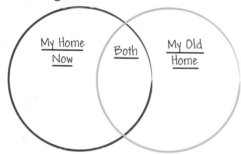

▲ This unusual house was built to look like a car.

Use your diagram to organize your ideas about the two homes. Then share your comparison with a group.

## HOW TO MAKE COMPARISONS

1. Tell how things are alike. Use words like *all*, *both*, *the same*, *similar*, and *too*.
2. Tell how things are different. Use words like *differ*, *different*, *only* and *but*.

> My new home is smaller than my old one, but it has a pretty garden.

## USE PRONOUNS CORRECTLY

When you make your comparison, be sure to use the correct **subject pronouns** and **object pronouns** .

EXAMPLE    **My parents** sold our **house** in Venezuela.
           **They** didn't need **it** anymore.

If it is hard to tell which noun a **pronoun** refers back to, replace the pronoun with a noun or rewrite the sentence.

Odette and Sal visit relatives in Haiti. ~~They~~ Their relatives dress colorfully.

# Prepare to Read

## Learn Key Vocabulary

**Study the Words** Use the steps below.

1. Pronounce the word. Say it aloud several times. Spell it.
2. Rate your word knowledge.
3. Study the example. Tell more about the word.
4. Practice it. Make the word your own.

### Key Words

**arrest** (u-rest) *verb*
▸ page 370

To **arrest** means to put someone in jail. A police officer **arrests** a suspect and puts handcuffs on him.

**dictator** (dik-tā-tur) *noun*
▸ page 370

A **dictator** is a person who leads a country without sharing power. Most **dictators** do not allow others to make decisions for the country.

**hopeful** (hōp-ful) *adjective*
▸ page 376

Someone who is **hopeful** is full of good thoughts about what will happen. This girl is **hopeful** about winning the contest.

**journal** (jur-nul) *noun*
▸ page 370

A **journal** is a record of someone's thoughts, feelings, and actions. Some people write in their **journal** almost every day.

**organize** (or-gu-nīz) *verb*
▸ page 370

To **organize** means to plan and set up something. The man **organizes** the people to support a cause.

**politics** (pah-lu-tiks) *noun*
▸ page 373

**Politics** is the business of government. Members of Congress talk about issues of national and international **politics**.

**rescue** (res-kyū) *noun*
▸ page 377

A **rescue** is the act of saving someone or something from danger. The **rescue** was daring and successful.

**violent** (vī-u-lunt) *adjective*
▸ page 373

Something that is **violent** uses force. **Violent** storms like tornadoes can damage buildings and kill people.
*Synonyms:* **cruel, fierce**
*Antonyms:* **peaceful, gentle**

**Practice the Words** Make a Frayer Model for each Key Word. Then compare your maps with a partner's.

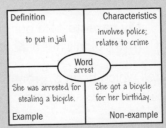

| Definition | Characteristics |
|---|---|
| to put in jail | involves police; relates to crime |
| | Word<br>arrest | |
| She was arrested for stealing a bicycle. | She got a bicycle for her birthday. |
| Example | Non-example |

**Frayer Model**

# Text Structure: Cause and Effect

**How Is Writing Organized?** You often read about causes and effects in stories. Sometimes a situation leads to a character taking action. The action is the effect, or the result of the cause. Sometimes an effect influences another event later in the story.

**Reading Strategies**
- Plan
- Monitor
- Make Connections
- Visualize
- Ask Questions
- **Determine Importance**
  Focus your attention on the author's most significant ideas and information.
- Make Inferences
- Synthesize

### Look Into the Text

Kiki, that rascal, had escaped when I opened the door. She scampered across the lawn and slipped into the Garcías' yard.

I followed her and searched the bushes next to the house. . . . I was about to call to her when I heard two men's voices drifting through the open window . . .

" Because the door opened, the cat escaped and ran into the neighbor's yard. I will keep reading to see how this action influences what happens later.**"**

## Practice Together

**Use a Cause-and-Effect Chain**
A Cause-and-Effect Chain helps **demonstrate** how some events influence other events. Begin by writing the first cause in the first box. Write the effect in the next box, and so on. Reread the second paragraph above, and add to the Cause-and-Effect Chain.

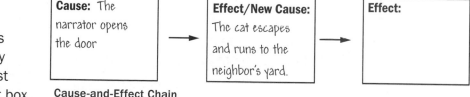
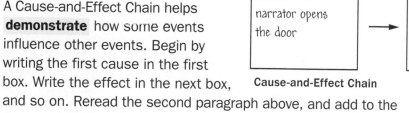

Cause: The narrator opens the door → Effect/New Cause: The cat escapes and runs to the neighbor's yard. → Effect:

**Cause-and-Effect Chain**

**Academic Vocabulary**
- **demonstrate** (de-mun-strāt) *verb*
  To **demonstrate** means to prove or make clear.

## Short Story

A short story is a kind of narrative fiction. The actions of the characters make up the plot. Short stories often have a **cause** -and- **effect** structure. The reason for each character's action is a cause. What happens because of the action is an effect.

**Look Into the Text**

At dinner I couldn't eat. My stomach churned, and my throat felt raw. Papi chatted with Carlos about baseball as if he didn't have a care in the world. Mami, always on the alert, reached over and felt my forehead.

As you read, look for causes and effects and other important details that tell you more about the plot and the main ideas of the story.

# Brave Butterflies

## by Susan Blackaby

Butterfly, 1978, Tamás Galambos. Oil on canvas, private collection.

▲ **Critical Viewing: Design** Why do you think the artist made the butterfly In this painting larger than the leaves?

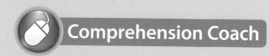

Comprehension Coach

## "Kitty . . . Here, kitty kitty . . ."

Kiki, that rascal, had escaped when I opened the door. She **scampered** across the lawn and slipped into the Garcías' yard.

I followed her and searched the bushes next to the house. When I finally **spotted** her, I had to bend low to reach her. She pawed at my outstretched fingers. I was about to call to her when I heard two men's voices drifting through the open window above my head. They were talking about my father. I froze.

"Alberto Pérez is involved," said Mr. García. "He has been seen with those who are foolish enough to **organize** in the name of *Las Mariposas*. I've heard he keeps a **journal** about their activities. It's only a matter of time until we **arrest** him. In the meantime, I'm **keeping my eye on** him."

"Why should we wait?" the other voice asked. "We should get our hands on that journal now. Think of the reward!" he said.

García laughed. "There's no harm in conducting a surprise search. It's a good way to find out what information he has."

I was stunned! I never suspected that Mr. García was a member of the secret police!

---

**Key Vocabulary**

  **dictator** *n.*, a person who leads a country completely

  **organize** *v.*, to plan and set up

  **journal** *n.*, a record of one's thoughts and feelings

  **arrest** *v.*, to put someone in jail

**In Other Words**

**scampered** ran
**spotted** found
**keeping my eye on** watching

**Historical Background**

*Las Mariposas* (the Butterflies) was the code name for the three Mirabal sisters who opposed the dictator, Rafael Trujillo. They were killed on November 25, 1960. In their memory, November 25 is International Day for the Elimination of Violence Against Women.

The voices became **muffled** as the men moved through the house, and I heard the front door open. I stayed in my hiding place until I saw Mr. García and the other man drive away. Then I scooped up Kiki and sneaked back home.

*Home*, 2006, Elizabeth Rosen. Acrylic on wood, collection of the artist.

▲ **Critical Viewing: Setting** How does this image relate to the setting of the story? Explain.

**In Other Words**
**muffled** hard to understand

At dinner I couldn't eat. My stomach **churned**, and my throat felt raw. Papi chatted with Carlos about baseball as if **he didn't have a care in the world**. Mami, always on the alert, reached over and felt my forehead. Her thin fingers tipped my chin to the light. I looked into her eyes and saw the fear and worry that I had not recognized before.

"Early bedtime for you," she said.

Normally I would **protest**. I had just turned thirteen, and Mami still treated me like a child. But now I simply nodded, not trusting myself to speak.

*Madre Protectora II*, 2007, Felix Berroa. Acrylic and oil on canvas, collection of the artist.

▲ **Critical Viewing: Character** How do these people feel about each other? Why do you think that?

**In Other Words**

**churned** was upset
**he didn't have a care in the world** nothing was wrong
**protest** disagree

I awoke in the middle of the night and looked outside. A dim light **flickered** in one of the Garcías' windows, a watchful eye spying on us. In the **study**, I could hear Papi and Mami talking in low whispers. I tiptoed down the hallway and stood in the shadows.

"Alberto, please, you must be more careful," Mami pleaded. "Getting involved in **politics** is risky. Think of our friends who have gone to prison or disappeared. Think of the Mirabal sisters. **We could suffer the same fate.**"

"I am thinking of them," said Papi. "I am thinking of the courage that the Mirabals—those brave *Mariposas*—

> "... you must be more careful," Mami pleaded.

showed in standing up to the dictator. And I am thinking of our children's future. Just imagine what it would be like to live in freedom."

"But Alberto, these are **violent** and dangerous times," said Mami. "Everyone in the Dominican Republic is **caught in an iron grip of fear**. I share your dream, but I'm afraid of what could happen."

"And I'm afraid of what could happen if we do nothing," said Papi.

I tiptoed back to my room and curled up with Kiki under my chin. I didn't sleep for a long time, and when I did, I dreamed of butterflies, their wings flickering in the sunshine.

**Key Vocabulary**
**politics** *n.*, the business of government
**violent** *adj.*, using force

**In Other Words**
**flickered** shone
**study** office
**We could suffer the same fate.** The same thing could happen to us.
**caught in an iron grip of fear** very scared

**Look Into the Text**

1. **Paraphrase** What does the girl learn at the García house? What does she learn in her own house?
2. **Cause and Effect** Why does the girl go to bed early?
3. **Inference** Why does the girl dream of butterflies?

**A week later,** Mr. García **carried out his threat**. When Carlos and I got home from school, the car I had seen before was parked out in front of the Garcías' house. Once we were safely inside, I grabbed Carlos's arm and hurried him into the kitchen, where Mami was cooking.

"Mr. García is going to search the house," I said. "Is Papi's journal here?"

Mami looked startled. Then she answered, "Yes, Ana, but it is well hidden. I don't know where it is."

"I do," I said.

I hurried to Papi's study and pulled up the loose **floorboard** underneath the desk.

The thin, worn notebook was wrapped in cloth.

"Carlos, quick," I said. "Hand me your baseball bat."

I was replacing the floorboard when Mr. García pounded on the door. Carlos answered and then stepped aside as Mr. García and several of the men in his **squad** entered the house. Mami came from the kitchen, wiping her hands on her apron.

"Good evening, Mrs. Pérez." Mr. García smiled, but his eyes were as cold as steel.

"Good evening," said Mami. "If you're looking for Alberto, I'm afraid he isn't here."

"Oh, we know that, Mrs. Pérez," said Mr. García. "He was seen leaving the university just a little while ago.

**In Other Words**
**carried out his threat** did what he
 said he was going to do
**floorboard** part of the floor
**squad** group

*Journey*, 2000, Rafael Lopez. Acrylic on canvas, collection of the artist.

▲ **Critical Viewing: Mood** How does this image make you feel? Why?

Unless he stops somewhere on the way home, he should be here in fifteen or twenty minutes."

"I'm sure he will come straight home," said Mami.

"We will soon see," said Mr. García. "In the meantime, my men will have a look around." Mami, Carlos, and I sat in the dining room while Mr. García's men opened drawers and cupboards. They pulled the books off the bookshelf and threw the pillows off the furniture.

"So, Carlos," sneered Mr. García, "I hear that you are the fourth Alou brother. I suppose you are **hopeful** that you will be asked to **play ball** in the United States in a few years."

"Yes sir," said Carlos, twirling his baseball bat between his knees.

Just then Kiki danced across the floor. We watched as she **swatted** a big wad of tape between her paws. One flick sent it tumbling under a **bureau**.

Mr. García frowned.

I held my breath.

Papi came through the door, right on time.

> "... my men will have a look around."

**Key Vocabulary**
   **hopeful** *adj.*, full of good thoughts about what will happen

**In Other Words**
**play ball** be on a professional baseball team
**swatted** hit
**bureau** set of drawers

**Historical Background**
Brothers Matty, Felipe, and Jesus Alou all moved from the Dominican Republic to the United States to play professional baseball. One season they all played for the San Francisco Giants. Then they played for different teams. Felipe went on to become a baseball manager.

Late that night, when the police were finally gone, Papi came into my room.

"You were very brave, Ana," he said. "Carlos and Mami tell me that you were the one who came to the **rescue**."

"We all did, Papi," I said. "Carlos wrapped your notebook around the handle of his bat and Mami helped me retape it. Even Kiki helped. She hid the old tape under the bureau."

"But you knew what was coming," said Papi. "You **hover around** us, watching and waiting."

"Kind of like a butterfly," I said. ❖

*Vegetation*, 1978, Tamás Galambos. Oil on canvas, private collection.

⬛ **Critical Viewing: Design** What details do you notice in the painting? How do they affect the overall feeling?

**Look Into the Text**

1. **Confirm Prediction** Was your prediction correct? What happened that you did not expect?
2. **Paraphrase** How does Ana come to the **rescue**?

# Farah Ahmedi

by Libby Lewis

Farah Ahmedi was born in Afghanistan. Although her country was at war, she had a happy life with her father, mother, brothers, and sisters.

But when Farah was seven years old, something terrible happened. As she crossed a field, she stepped on a **land mine**, and it exploded. Farah survived, but she lost her left leg. She had to get a **prosthetic** leg to help her walk.

Then, two years later, a bomb hit her house. It killed her father and sisters.

A few months later, her brothers left home and were never heard from again.

Farah and her mother were alone.

At this time, the laws in Afghanistan said women could not go anywhere in public without a male relative. Farah and her mother could not go to work, school, or even the store.

Farah and her mother decided they had to leave their country in order to be free.

They crossed into Pakistan by walking over the mountains. The path was steep, and it was a risk with Farah's prosthetic leg. But she did not let it slow her down.

Farah and her mother made it safely to Pakistan. After many more hardships, they came to the United States.

Today, Farah and her mother live in Illinois. She works with an international group that clears **minefields** around the world. She also runs a foundation to help other **amputees**.

"I lost my leg, I lost my family, I am out from my country, but I never gave up," Farah says. "And I will keep going."

**In Other Words**

**land mine** bomb
**prosthetic** false, artificial
**minefields** areas with bombs
**amputees** people who have lost body parts

**Look Into the Text**

1. **Explain** Why did Farah and her mother walk over the mountains to Pakistan?
2. **Character** What kind of person is Farah Ahmedi? What details make you think this?

# Connect Reading and Writing

**Vocabulary**

arrest

dictator

hopeful

journal

organize

politics

rescue

violent

## CRITICAL THINKING

1. **SUM IT UP** Use your Cause-and-Effect Chains to summarize the selection.

| Cause: The narrator opens the door | → | Effect/New Cause: The cat escapes and runs to the neighbor's yard. | → | Effect: |

**Cause-and-Effect Chain**

2. **Speculate** Do you think Mr. García will ever **arrest** Ana's father? Explain.

3. **Generalize** Think about what you read about the **dictator** in this story and what you know about other **dictators**. Tell two things that are true for all or most dictators.

4. **Compare** Both Ana and Farah experienced **violent** situations. Do you think one situation was worse than the other? Explain.

## READING FLUENCY

**Expression** Read the passage on page 574 to a partner. Assess your fluency.

1. My voice never/sometimes/always matched what I read.

2. What I did best in my reading was _____.

## READING STRATEGY

What strategy helped you understand this selection? Tell a partner about it.

## VOCABULARY REVIEW

**Oral Review** Read the paragraph aloud. Add the vocabulary words.

Alberto Pérez keeps a _____ about some people who are active in _____. Those heroes try to come to the _____, to save their country from Trujillo's iron grip. Trujillo was the _____ of the Dominican Republic from 1930 to 1961. If people tried to _____ against him, the police could _____ them. Police actions could be mean and _____. In May 1961, Trujillo himself was murdered, but problems continued. Not until many years later, when fair elections began, could people begin to be _____ about the future.

**Written Review** Imagine that you are living in the Dominican Republic during the 1950s and are **organizing** against the government. Write a report. Use five vocabulary words.

 **WRITE ABOUT THE** GUIDING QUESTION

### Explore the Struggle for Freedom
What do you think the Pérez family is willing to do for the sake of freedom from the **dictator**? Use details from the text to support your response.

## Use Context Clues

**Academic Vocabulary**
- **explain** (ik-splān) *verb*
  When you **explain** an idea, you make it clear so people can understand it.

When you come to an unfamiliar word in the text, you can look for context clues that **explain** the meaning. A **synonym clue** gives a word or phrase that means almost the same as the unfamiliar word. An **antonym clue** gives a word or phrase that means the opposite of the unfamiliar word.

**Figure Out the Meaning** Tell the meaning of each underlined word. **Explain** how you used the context clues.

1. I never <u>suspected</u> that Mr. García was a member of the secret police. It was unbelievable!

2. "You must be more careful," Mami pleaded. "Getting involved in politics is <u>risky</u>."

3. Mami looked <u>startled</u> at first, but then tried to calm herself.

4. Mr. García <u>sneered</u> and made fun of Carlos's dreams of playing baseball.

## Analyze the Topic

**Academic Vocabulary**
- **topic** (tah-pik) *noun*
  A **topic** is the subject of a piece of writing or of a discussion.

Different writers can write about the same **topic**. Compare the information that different authors present to learn more about the **topic**.

**Begin a Chart** The **topic** of "Brave Butterflies" and the biography of Farah Ahmedi is life under a cruel government. Use a Comparison Chart to compare how the two selections discuss this **topic**.

| Selection | Kind of Writing | Information |
|---|---|---|
| "Brave Butterflies" | fiction short story | Dominicans were afraid of the government. |
| "Farah Ahmedi" | | |

Comparison Chart

**Analyze Topics** Use your charts to analyze the two selections. Why do you think the authors chose the genres they did to discuss the **topic**? What did you learn about life under a cruel government?

## Make Comparisons

**Compare and Share** Compare the experience of the Pérez family with the experiences of enslaved Americans seeking freedom. Share your comparison with a partner. Use pronouns correctly.

> Ana's family is afraid of being arrested or killed by the secret police. Runaway slaves were afraid of being caught.

## Write About a New Home

**Study the Models** When you write about personal experiences, you want readers to be interested. Vary your sentences and use pronouns to take the place of nouns. Be sure to use the right pronouns so readers won't get confused.

**NOT OK**

Two years ago, my parents and I arrived in New York. Our relatives met my parents and me at the airport. My relatives took my parents and me to their house. My parents and I stayed there for several months before finding an apartment. The apartment was not very big, but we liked the apartment. The apartment was not far from our relatives' house. My parents and I got to see our relatives often.

> The writer repeats the same words, and the sentences sound too similar. The reader thinks: "I can't understand this."

**OK**

Two years ago, my parents and I arrived in New York. Our relatives met **us** at the airport. Where do you think **they** took **us**? To their house! **We** stayed there for several months before finding an apartment. Our apartment wasn't very big, but we liked **it**. Best of all, **it** was close to our relatives' house, and **we** got to see **them** often.

> The writer uses a mix of nouns and pronouns as well as different kinds of sentences. The writing is more interesting.

**Add Sentences** Think of two sentences to add to the OK model above. Use subject pronouns and object pronouns correctly.

✏️ **WRITE ON YOUR OWN** Think about a time in your life when you moved to a new place or thought about moving. Write about the experience. Pay attention to subject and object pronouns.

**REMEMBER**

|  | Singular |  |  |  |  | Plural |  |  |
|---|---|---|---|---|---|---|---|---|
| **Subject Pronouns** | I | you | he | she | it | we | you | they |
| **Object Pronouns** | me | you | him | her | it | us | you | them |

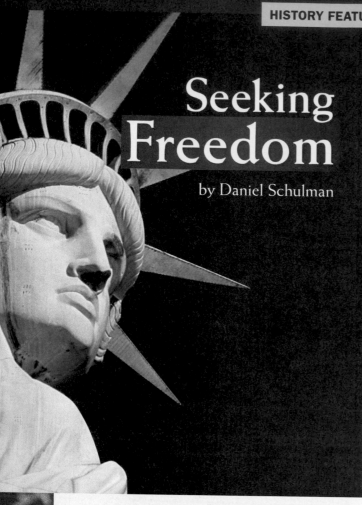

# Seeking Freedom

by Daniel Schulman

# Build Background

## Connect

**Anticipation Guide** What will people do for freedom? Tell whether you agree or disagree with each statement.

| | Agree | Disagree |
|---|---|---|
| **1.** It is OK to break the law if you are fighting for human rights. | _____ | _____ |
| **2.** People should be willing to give up their rights in exchange for safety and security. | _____ | _____ |

Anticipation Guide

## Talk About Rights

People all over the world have certain needs and wants. Look at the photos, and discuss how people stand up for their rights.

**Digital Library**  **myNGconnect.com**
🔊 View the images.

▲ **Journalists fight for rights in Pakistan.**

# Language & Grammar

1 TRY OUT LANGUAGE
2 LEARN GRAMMAR
3 APPLY ON YOUR OWN

## Express Opinions CD

Listen to the information. Then listen to the opinions.
What do you think?

**INFORMATION and OPINIONS**

Myanmar is a country in Southeast Asia. For many years, people there were not allowed to express their opinions in public about the government or to vote for their own government.

In September of 2007, thousands of people marched in the streets of Myanmar. They protested peacefully against the government. The government arrested many people. Some people were beaten or even killed.

> In my opinion, all people should have the freedom to say what they think about their government.

# Use Reflexive and Intensive Pronouns

- Use a **reflexive pronoun** to talk about the same person or thing twice in the same sentence.

    EXAMPLES  I prepared **myself** for an interview.
    The **President** introduced **himself**.

- Use an **intensive pronoun** to provide emphasis or make something stronger.

    EXAMPLES  I **myself** phoned the President.
    The **President himself** returned my call.

| Reflexive and Intensive Pronouns | |
| --- | --- |
| **Singular** | **Plural** |
| myself | ourselves |
| yourself | yourselves |
| himself | themselves |
| herself | |
| itself | |

## Practice Together

Read each sentence. Choose the correct pronoun. Say the sentence again. Then tell whether the pronoun is a reflexive or an intensive pronoun.

1. People should speak up for **(themselves/yourself)**
2. I **(itself/myself)** am afraid to speak up.
3. Carlos prepared by studying by **(himself/ourselves)**.
4. Sarah forced **(herself/myself)** to speak up.
5. Our founders **(himself/themselves)** want us to speak up.

## Try It!

Read each sentence. Write the correct pronoun on a card. Hold up the card as you say the sentence. Then tell whether the pronoun is a reflexive or an intensive pronoun.

6. The wall **(herself/itself)** was strong.
7. We write laws for **(myself/ourselves)**.
8. I prepared **(myself/itself)** for the debate.
9. The protesters covered **(himself/themselves)** in flags.
10. The dictator **(myself/himself)** admitted his guilt.
11. Can you interview them **(myself/yourself)**?
12. Adam read the speech to **(himself/herself)**.

▲ The people of Berlin knocked down the Berlin Wall themselves.

# Discuss Ideas About Freedom

## EXPRESS OPINIONS

Imagine that you live in a country that does not allow its citizens to be free. How far would you go to fight for your rights? What would you do?

As a class, form two groups. With your group, brainstorm a list of tasks and dangers that someone might face in the fight for human rights. Write the list in your own notebook. Check off the tasks and dangers you would be willing to face.

| Tasks and Dangers | Yes or No? |
|---|---|
| 1. Go to prison | |
| 2. Face armed soldiers | |
| 3. Risk death | |

Now have a "fishbowl" discussion with the other group. Form a circle with your chairs. Face inward, toward the center of the circle. The other group forms a circle around you. The outside group listens as your group members exchange opinions about fighting for human rights.

Switch positions and listen to the other group's discussion. How is it different from your group's discussion?

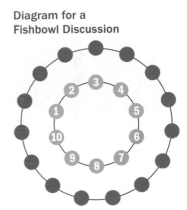

Diagram for a
Fishbowl Discussion

## How to EXPRESS OPINIONS

**1.** Tell what you think about something.
Use expressions like *I think*, *I believe*,
*In my opinion*, and *For me*.

**2.** If you have the same opinion as someone else, you can say "I agree." If you have a different opinion, you can say "I disagree."

*In my opinion, freedom is more important than anything else.*

*I agree.*

## USE REFLEXIVE AND INTENSIVE PRONOUNS CORRECTLY

When you express opinions, you can add emphasis with **intensive pronouns**. Use a **reflexive pronoun** when the actor and receiver of the action are the same.

EXAMPLES  Most people don't want to find **themselves** in jail.
But I would protest in the streets **myself** if I needed to!

# Prepare to Read

## Learn Key Vocabulary

**Study the Words** Use the steps below.

1. Pronounce the word. Say it aloud several times. Spell it.
2. Rate your word knowledge.
3. Study the example. Tell more about the word.
4. Practice it. Make the word your own.

**Rating Scale**

**1** = I have never seen this word before.

**2** = I am not sure of the word's meaning.

**3** = I know this word and can teach the word's meaning to someone else.

### Key Words

**government**
(gu-vurn-munt) *noun* ▶ page 390

The people who control the country according to certain laws are the **government**. Washington, DC, is the center of the U.S. **government**.

**law** (law) *noun*
▶ page 390

The **law** is a country's rules. A police officer reminds people to follow the **law**.

**leader** (lē-dur) *noun*
▶ page 392

A **leader** is a person in charge of others. The **leader** of our hiking club decides which trail we will take.

**opinion** (u-pin-yun) *noun*
▶ page 391

An **opinion** is a belief or a view about a topic. My friends share their **opinions** about fashion.

**protest** (prō-test) *verb*
▶ page 395 *noun* ▶ page 396

**1** *verb* To **protest** means to make a statement against an idea. The students **protested** against school spending cuts. **2** *noun* A **protest** is a display of strong feelings.

**public** (pu-blik) *noun*
▶ page 398

When you are in **public**, you are in an area that is open to others. Even though we held our family gathering in **public**, the setting felt private.

**responsibility**
(ri-spont-su-**bi**-lu-tē) *noun* ▶
page 390

A **responsibility** is something you should do because it is right. It is my **responsibility** to walk the dog every day.

**system** (sis-tum) *noun*
▶ page 394

A **system** is a way of doing things. An assembly line is a factory **system** that usually saves time and money.

**Practice the Words** Work with a partner to complete an Expanded Meaning Map for each Key Word.

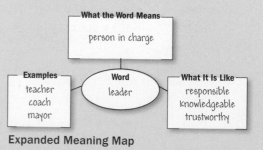

**What the Word Means**
person in charge

**Examples**
teacher
coach
mayor

**Word**
leader

**What It Is Like**
responsible
knowledgeable
trustworthy

**Expanded Meaning Map**

# Text Structure: Cause and Effect

**How Is Writing Organized?** Nonfiction texts often **demonstrate** cause-and-effect relationships. Words and phrases such as *because*, *the reason*, *since*, and *as a result* signal cause and effect. Writers use cause and effect to organize their writing and to explain why things happen.

As you read, pay attention to **clue words** that help you analyze cause and effect.

**Reading Strategies**

- Plan
- Monitor
- Make Connections
- Visualize
- Ask Questions
- **Determine Importance**
  Focus your attention on the author's most significant ideas and information.
- Make Inferences
- Synthesize

## Look Into the Text

> Millions of people have left their homes in search of freedom. Often they want freedom to practice their religion or the freedom to pick their leaders.

What is one reason why people might move to another place?

## Practice Together

**Begin a Cause-and-Effect Chart** A Cause-and-Effect Chart can help you **demonstrate** how events and ideas in a text are related. This Cause-and-Effect Chart shows an effect and one related cause from the passage above. Reread the passage, and add at least one more cause to the chart.

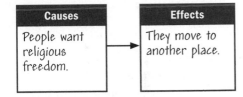

| Causes | Effects |
|---|---|
| People want religious freedom. | They move to another place. |

**Cause-and-Effect Chart**

**Academic Vocabulary**

- **demonstrate** (de-mun-strāt) *verb*
  To **demonstrate** means to prove or make clear.

## History Feature

History features tell about real people and real events from the recent past or long ago. History features often contain **cause**-and-**effect** relationships about important events and ideas.

**Look Into the Text**

> Some countries do not have laws that protect people's freedom. What do people in those countries do to find freedom?
>
> Sometimes people leave their homes.

Determine what is important to you as you read. Look for answers to why certain events happen and what you want to know about the topic of each section.

# Seeking Freedom

## by Daniel Schulman

Throughout history, people have searched for freedom and found it in different ways.

 Comprehension Coach

# A Plan for Freedom

The people who built the **government** of the United States more than 200 years ago knew that freedom was important. They wrote on paper their ideas for a free country. This paper is the Constitution, and it explains how the government should work. Part of the Constitution is the Bill of Rights. It lists freedoms that all Americans share.

People who have freedom also have **responsibilities**. One responsibility is knowing that others have rights, too. We should not hurt others or break the **law**, but we are free to make choices.

▼ This shows the beginning of the U.S. Constitution. The actual document, including the Bill of Rights, is several pages. Some additional laws, or amendments, have been added more recently.

## Key Vocabulary

**government** *n.*, the people who control the country according to certain laws

**responsibility** *n.*, something you should do because it is right

**law** *n.*, a country's rules

## Historical Background

The Constitution explains the powers of the U.S. government. It became law in 1789. The Bill of Rights contains the first ten amendments, or changes, to the Constitution. The amendments protect the rights of every U.S. citizen. They were added in 1791.

# Some Freedoms in the Bill of Rights

## Freedom of Speech

People can say what they think, without fear. This means people can disagree with one another or the government about what should be done.

## Freedom of the Press

**News reporters** can tell the news as they see it. This helps people understand events and form their own **opinions**.

## Freedom of Religion

People can choose their religion. In free countries, there are often many different religions.

---

**Key Vocabulary**
**opinion** *n.*, a belief or view about a topic

**In Other Words**
**News reporters** People who write news stories

**Look Into the Text**

1. **Explain** What does it mean to have **responsibilities** as well as rights?
2. **Interpret** What are some of the freedoms that U.S. citizens share?

# Seeking Freedom

Some countries do not have laws that protect people's freedoms. What do people in those countries do to find freedom?

Sometimes people leave their homes. They might move to a country with more freedom, but this can be very hard. People who move to a new country might have to learn a new language and way of life.

# Reasons to Leave Home

Millions of people have left their homes in search of freedom. Often they want freedom to practice their religion or the freedom to pick their **leaders**. People move for freedom of speech and freedom of the press. People also move because they want a better education or jobs.

## People Who Have Moved for Freedom

**English, 1600s**
The Pilgrims began to leave for the Americas in 1620. They left England because they were not allowed to practice their religion.

**Germans, 1930s**
Many Germans, especially Jews, left Germany because of a **cruel** government. They moved to other countries to find freedom.

**Key Vocabulary**
**leader** *n.*, a person in charge of others

**In Other Words**
**cruel** mean and hurtful

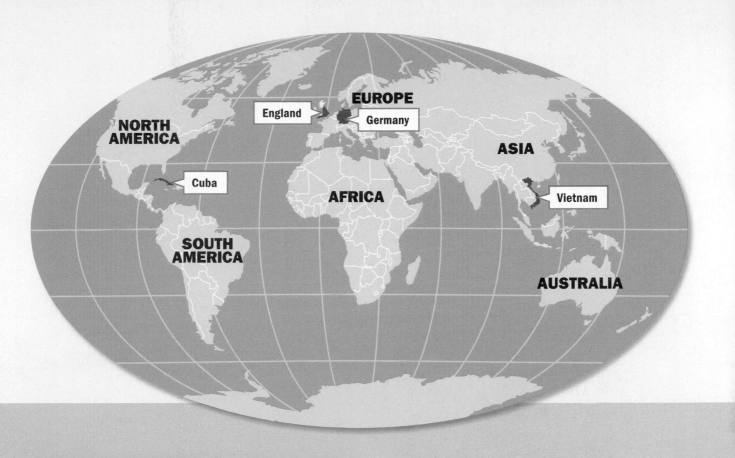

## Cubans, 1960s

Many Cubans left their island country in the 1960s. They left because their government did not allow them to pick their leaders.

## Vietnamese, 1970s

Many people from Vietnam left to escape war. People there were also not free to speak out or to choose their work.

### Look Into the Text

1. **Categorize** What are four reasons why people might leave their home countries?

2. **Compare and Contrast** The Pilgrims started to leave England in 1620, and many Vietnamese left Vietnam in the 1970s. How were their reasons for leaving alike and different?

Seeking Freedom **393**

▲ Nelson Mandela spent 27 years in jail for speaking about freedom.

AFRICA

South Africa

# Working for Freedom at Home

People do not always leave their country to find freedom. Sometimes they struggle for it at home. That happened in South Africa. About 20 years ago, South Africa had a **system** called apartheid, which means "separation." Apartheid was a set of unfair laws. These laws took away freedoms from some people because of the color of their skin.

Nelson Mandela fought against apartheid. He was even **jailed** for speaking out, but he won! Apartheid laws were changed. Like many others, Mandela thought freedom was **worth fighting** for.

**Key Vocabulary**
  **system** *n.*, a way of doing things

**In Other Words**
  **jailed** put in jail
  **worth fighting** important enough to fight

# Students Speak Out

In 1989, thousands of Chinese students gathered in Tiananmen Square in Beijing, China, to **peacefully protest** unfair laws. They wanted more freedom from their government.

The students did not **succeed** because China's government sent in the army to stop the students. Hundreds of students were killed. People in China still do not have many freedoms.

ASIA

China

▲ Students in Tiananmen Square carried signs asking for fair laws.

**Key Vocabulary**
**protest** *v.*, to make a strong statement against an idea or action

**In Other Words**
**peacefully** quietly and calmly
**succeed** get what they wanted

**Look Into the Text**
1. **Vocabulary** What is apartheid? What clues in the text help you know the definition?
2. **Cause and Effect** What happened when students **protested** in Tiananmen Square?

# The Right to Vote

People in the United States have struggled for the freedom we have now. For many years women could not vote, and they did not have the same rights as men.

Women who wanted to vote began to join together. They held meetings and **protests**. Some were even **arrested** and jailed. On August 26, 1920, women in the United States finally **gained** the right to vote.

▲ This Suffrage Badge was produced around 1910 to encourage women to fight for the right to vote.

▲ In the early 1900s, women protested to gain the right to vote. This photo shows Mrs. Herbert Carpenter leading a march on Fifth Avenue in New York City to gain women's rights.

**Key Vocabulary**
  **protest** n., a display of strong feelings against an idea or action

**In Other Words**
  **arrested** taken away by the police
  **gained** won, got

# Freedom for All

African Americans in the United States did not always have the same freedoms as other Americans. Many were kept from voting. Some were not allowed to go to good schools. Others were not allowed to use or enjoy the same things as white people.

In the 1960s, people protested. They said African Americans should have the same rights as all Americans. These protests helped change the laws.

▲ On August 28, 1963, Dr. Martin Luther King, Jr., spoke to more than 200,000 people during the March on Washington to demand equal rights for all citizens.

## Look Into the Text

1. **Conclusion** Why did many American women **protest** against the **government** in the early 1900s?

2. **Compare and Contrast** Why did African Americans **protest** in the 1960s? How were their goals similar to and different from the goals of women in the early 1900s?

# The Search for Freedom Continues

Today freedom is spreading around the world. **Until recently**, people in Afghanistan had very few freedoms. Women were not allowed to go to school or work, and they could not be seen in **public**. Men were **punished** or killed if they did not follow the government's rules.

Countries around the world helped the people of Afghanistan. Now they have important rights and a new **constitution**.

It says that citizens have the right to vote. They can choose who will stand up and speak for them. The new constitution says that girls can go to school. It also says that women can work and move freely in public.

All around the world, people **seek** freedom to make their own choices. ❖

▼ Girls in Afghanistan now have the right to go to school.

ASIA

Afghanistan

**In Other Words**
**Until recently** Not many years ago
**punished** hurt
**constitution** list of rules that says what can happen in the country
**seek** look for; try to get

## Look Into the Text

1. **Evidence and Conclusion** What are two examples that freedom is spreading around the world?

2. **Main Idea and Details** Use details from the selection to explain how things are better for women in Afghanistan now.

# Connect Reading and Writing

### Vocabulary

governments

laws

leaders

opinion

protests

public

responsibility

systems

## CRITICAL THINKING

1. **SUM IT UP** Use your Cause-and-Effect Chart to describe how selection events and ideas are related. Then summarize the selection with a partner.

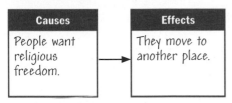

| Causes | | Effects |
|---|---|---|
| People want religious freedom. | → | They move to another place. |

**Cause-and-Effect Chart**

2. **Explain** What can people do if the **leaders** or **laws** of their country are unjust? Support your ideas with examples from the text.

3. **Infer** The U.S. **government** is based on the Constitution. Why do you think this document has worked so well for more than 200 years?

4. **Analyze** Review your Anticipation Guide on page 382. Do you want to change your **opinions**? Discuss in a group.

## READING FLUENCY

**Phrasing** Read the passage on page 575 to a partner. Assess your fluency.

1. I did not pause/sometimes paused/ always paused for punctuation.

2. What I did best in my reading was _____.

## READING STRATEGY

What strategy helped you understand this selection? Tell a partner about it.

## VOCABULARY REVIEW

**Oral Review** Read the paragraph aloud. Add the vocabulary words.

Mohandas Gandhi and Martin Luther King, Jr., believed that the people who ran their _____ had made rules, or _____, that failed to protect everyone. Their countries' political _____, or ways of doing things, needed to change. Gandhi and King took _____ for forcing change. They spoke in _____, not just in private, about unjust conditions and became great _____ for people. They organized peaceful marches and _____ to help create change. In the _____ of many people, Gandhi and King are heroes of freedom.

**Written Review** Think of a **responsibility** that someone has in a free country. Write a paragraph about it. Use at least five vocabulary words.

### WRITE ABOUT THE (GUIDING QUESTION)

**Explore the Struggle for Freedom**
Why is freedom worth fighting for? Reread the selection and write your **opinion** about the worth of freedom. Use evidence from the text.

# Connect Across the Curriculum

## Use Context Clues

> **Academic Vocabulary**
> • **context** (kon-tekst) *noun*
>   **Context** refers to the parts nearby that help explain the meaning.

An **example clue** illustrates the meaning of another word in the text. The words *for example*, *including*, and *such as* signal an example clue.

**Figure Out Word Meanings** Work with a partner. Use **context** clues to figure out the meaning of each underlined word. Write the definition, and check it in a dictionary.

**1.** Many people want <u>liberties</u> such as freedom of speech, freedom of religion, and freedom of the press.

**2.** Some people take <u>drastic</u> actions, such as crossing the ocean in a small boat, to find freedom.

**3.** People may have many <u>hurdles</u> in a new country, including learning a new language and way of life.

**4.** People have to make <u>adjustments</u> to a new place. For example, they may be able to see friends and family only occasionally.

## Distinguish Facts From Opinion

> **Academic Vocabulary**
> • **fact** (fakt) *noun*
>   A **fact** is a piece of information that is true.

Nonfiction texts give **facts** about ideas and events. Sometimes nonfiction writers include opinions to express their own points of view about certain ideas. They also may report other people's opinions.

A **fact** is a statement that can be proved as true or false. Numbers and dates often signal statements of **fact**.

An opinion is a statement of what a person thinks or believes. Opinions often include signal words like *think*, *believe*, *want* or *like* or descriptive words such as *good, wise,* or *foolish*.

**Find Facts and Opinions** Reread "Seeking Freedom." Identify **facts** and opinions. List them in a Fact-and-Opinion Chart. Include specific examples to show how the author conveyed facts or his point of view.

## Express Opinions

**Group Share** With a group, discuss the
different stories in "Seeking Freedom."
Which part did you find the most interesting?
Take turns sharing opinions and commenting on the
ideas of others. Use reflexive and intensive pronouns correctly.

> I myself found the part about Nelson Mandela's life to be the most inspiring.

> African Americans stood up for themselves. That inspired me the most.

## Write About Human Rights

**Study the Models** When you write about important ideas, you can add
clarity and emphasis by using reflexive and intensive pronouns.

**JUST OK**

> Martin Luther King, Jr., is one of America's heroes.
> His efforts were important. He wrote many speeches. His
> speeches helped to create positive change. King inspired
> African Americans to stand up for their rights. My friends
> and I are very lucky that Martin Luther King, Jr., spoke up
> for the rights of everyone. I talk about this all the time.

> **The writer doesn't give specifics. Also, he claims to talk about this a lot, but the piece doesn't express his passion.**

**MUCH STRONGER**

> I **myself** believe that Martin Luther King, Jr., is one
> of America's heroes. His efforts to change conditions for
> African Americans were very important. He spoke for
> **himself** and all people in his speeches. His speech, "I Have
> a Dream," helped to create positive change. King inspired
> African Americans **themselves** to stand up for the rights
> due them. My friends and I consider **ourselves** very lucky
> that Martin Luther King, Jr., spoke up for the rights of
> everyone. I express **myself** about this often.

> **The writer has added specifics. And now the reader can feel his passion. The reader understands why the writer talks about Dr. King a lot.**

**Add Sentences** With a partner, think of two sentences to add to the MUCH
STRONGER model above. Use a reflexive pronoun in one and an
intensive pronoun in the other.

**✎ WRITE ON YOUR OWN** Imagine your family is fighting
for human rights. Describe what happens. Include reflexive
and intensive pronouns.

> **REMEMBER**
> - Use reflexive pronouns to refer twice to the same person or thing in the same sentence. Use an intensive pronoun to add emphasis.
> - Avoid mistakes with reflexive and intensive pronouns.
>   **themselves**
>   They found ~~theirselves~~ in a tricky situation.
>   **himself**
>   Ahmad read the speech silently to ~~hisself~~.

# From
# HARRIET TUBMAN
# CONDUCTOR
# — on the —
# UNDERGROUND RAILROAD

## BY ANN PETRY

1   In December 1851, when Harriet Tubman started out with the **band of fugitives** that she planned to take to Canada, she had been in the **vicinity** of the plantation for days, planning the trip, carefully selecting the **slaves** that she would take with her.

2   She had announced her arrival in the slave quarter by singing the forbidden spiritual—"Go down, Moses, 'way down to Egypt Land"—singing it softly outside the door of a slave cabin, late at night. The husky voice was beautiful even when it was barely more than a **murmur** borne on the wind.

3   Once she had made her presence known, word of her coming spread from cabin to cabin. The slaves whispered to each other, ear to mouth, mouth to ear, "Moses is here." "Moses has come." "Get ready. Moses is back again." The ones who had agreed to go North with her put ashcake and salt herring in an old bandanna, hastily tied it into a bundle, and then waited patiently for the signal that meant it was time to start.

4   There were eleven in this party, including one of her brothers and his wife. It was the largest group that she had ever conducted, but she was determined that more and more slaves should know what **freedom** was like.

5   She had to take them all the way to Canada. The Fugitive Slave **Law** was no longer a great many **incomprehensible words** written down on the country's law books. The new law had become a reality. It was Thomas Sims, a boy, picked up on the streets of Boston at night and shipped back to Georgia. It was Jerry and Shadrach, **arrested** and jailed with no warning.

## Key Vocabulary

- **slave** *n.*, someone who belongs to another and works without pay
- **freedom** *n.*, the state of being free, or not limited
- **law** *n.*, a country's rules
- **arrest** *v.*, to put someone in jail

## In Other Words

**band of fugitives** group of escaping slaves
**vicinity** area
**murmur** whisper
**incomprehensible words** words you can't understand

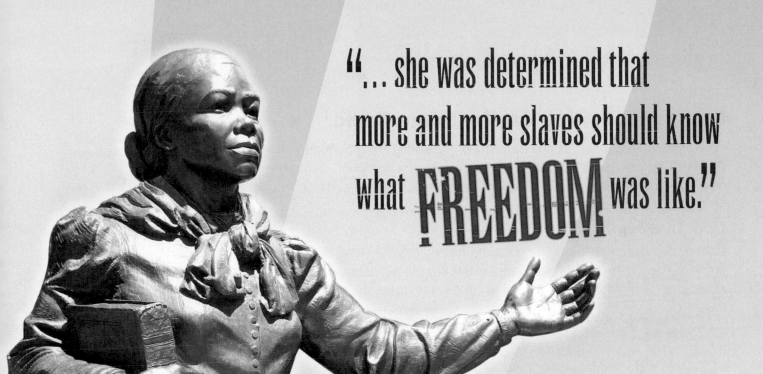

# "... she was determined that more and more slaves should know what FREEDOM was like."

6 She had never been in Canada. The route beyond Philadelphia was strange to her. But she could not let the runaways who accompanied her know this. As they walked along she told them stories of her own first flight, she kept painting **vivid** word pictures of what it would be like to be free.

7 But there were so many of them this time. She knew moments of doubt when she was half afraid, and kept looking back over her shoulder, imagining that she heard **the sound of pursuit**. They would certainly be **pursued**. Eleven of them. Eleven thousand dollars' worth of flesh and bone and muscle that belonged to Maryland planters. If they were caught, the eleven runaways would be whipped and sold South, but she—she would probably be hanged.

◄ "Step On Board," by Fern Cunningham in 1999 is a sculpture in Harriet Tubman Park, Boston, MA.

**Historical Background**
Moses was a Hebrew prophet whose story is told in the Old Testament book of the Bible. Moses led Hebrew slaves to freedom.

**In Other Words**
**vivid** detailed
**the sound of pursuit** people chasing them
**pursued** chased after

# Compare Across Texts

## Compare Writing on the Same Topic

"Escaping to Freedom," "Brave Butterflies," "Seeking Freedom," and "Harriet Tubman" all tell about people's struggles for **freedom**. Compare how writing about the topic of **freedom** is different in these texts.

### How It Works

**Collect and Organize Ideas**  To compare ideas across several texts, organize them in a Comparison Chart. What are the big ideas in the selections? What details does each writer include about the topic?

| Writing about Freedom | Escaping to Freedom | Brave Butterflies | Seeking Freedom | Harriet Tubman |
|---|---|---|---|---|
| big ideas | how Matthew Henson gained freedom | how Ana saves her father from being arrested | how different people have gained freedom | how a former slave helped others gain freedom |
| details | | | | |

Comparison Chart

### Practice Together

**Study and Compare the Ideas**  Analyze how the selections talk about **freedom** . Then write a paragraph that compares them. Here is a paragraph that compares the big ideas in the selections.

> The four selections are all about the topic of freedom. "Escaping to Freedom" tells how Matthew Henson gained freedom. "Brave Butterflies" tells how Ana saves her father from being arrested. "Seeking Freedom" explains how different groups of people have gained freedom. "Harriet Tubman" describes how a former slave helped others gain freedom.

### Try It!

Complete the Comparison Chart. Then use the ideas to write a paragraph that compares the details. You may want to use this frame.

The four selections are all about freedom. In "Escaping to Freedom," the author tells _____ . An example is _____ . In "Brave Butterflies," the main character tells _____ . An example is _____ . In "Seeking Freedom," the author describes _____ . An example is _____ . In "Harriet Tubman," we learn _____ . An example is _____ .

**Academic Vocabulary**
- **freedom** (frē-dum) *noun*
  If you have **freedom**, you are not limited in what you do.

# STRUGGLE FOR FREEDOM

**How far should people go for the sake of freedom?**

**Content Library**

**Leveled Library**

## Reflect on Your Reading

Think back on your reading of the unit selections. Discuss what you did to understand what you read.

**Focus on Reading**  **Text Structure: Cause and Effect** In this unit, you learned how writers use cause and effect to organize their ideas. Choose a selection from the unit, and make a Cause-and-Effect Chain that shows how the text is organized. Use your graphic to explain the organization to a partner.

**Focus Strategy**  **Determine Importance** As you read the selections, you learned to summarize, identify main ideas and details, and determine what is important. Explain to a partner how you will use this strategy in the future.

## Explore the

Throughout this unit, you have been thinking about freedom. Choose one way to explore the Guiding Question:

- **Discuss** With a group, discuss the Guiding Question. Talk about personal qualities, such as vision, courage, or an ability to plan, that can help people in the struggle for human rights.
- **Create a Journal** Imagine that you live in a country with a terrible dictator. Write a journal of your experiences. Explain what you will do for freedom.
- **Draw** Create a visual interpretation of your answer to the Guiding Question. Explain to a partner how your artwork is a picture of your response.

## Book Talk

Which Unit Library book did you choose? Explain to a partner what it taught you about the need for freedom.

# Star
# Power

# 7

## What can we learn from the stars?

**READ MORE!**

**Content Library**
**Missions in Space**
by Stephen Currie

**Leveled Library**
**The War of the Worlds**
by H.G. Wells,
adapted by Mary Ann Evans

**Stargirl**
by Jerry Spinelli

**The Man Who Went to the
Far Side of the Moon**
by Bea Uusma Schyffert

**Web Links**
 myNGconnect.com

◀ Two tails made of stars, gas, and dust are a
result of the Antennae Galaxies colliding.

# Focus on Reading

## Analyze Argument

An argument begins with claims. Claims are statements that give the author's viewpoint on a topic. Authors use evidence to support their claims. They also give reasons to explain how their evidence connects to their claim. They should use relevant information in their evidence and reasons. The purpose of an argument is to change the reader's viewpoint or to bring about action from the reader.

## How It Works

Before you read a text, preview it to determine the topic. The argument is usually related to that topic.

To **evaluate** an argument, look carefully at the reasons and evidence used to support it. An author may give examples, statements from experts, or photographs to prove that something is true. However, an author may make some claims that are not valid, or that are not supported by reasons and evidence. In this example, the author argues that the U.S. space program is important. **Evaluate** the claims. Decide which are supported by reasons and evidence.

### Bold Frontiers

In 1961, President Kennedy announced an exciting plan: "I believe that this nation should commit itself to achieving the goal . . . of landing a man on the moon and returning him safely to the earth."

The United States met the goal. In 1969, men walked on the moon for the first time.

Now it is time for our country to become fearless again! We need to put citizens like us on the moon. This is an amazing time in history. We should be able to move humans across the solar system.

We landed people on the moon. We must become bold again!

Loaded words make readers feel emotions such as anger, fear, and pride. These words show the author's viewpoint and they support his purpose, but they do not support claims.

" This statement is a valid fact. It supports the argument and can be proven."

" This statement is an opinion. It is not supported, so it is not valid."

## Practice Together

Read the following passage aloud. Find the argument. What evidence does the author use to support the argument?

### Kids in Space, Now!

If there can be a Teacher-in-Space program, then there should be a Kids-in-Space program. We kids want to enjoy the amazing thrill and excitement of zooming into space. Kids from all over the country would try out. We're already experts at going to school, so we can easily spend a year in a training program to go into space. We study science and math, two important subjects for space travel. The thrill of flying into space in a space shuttle would be too fantastic to miss.

▲ Kids at space camp love the challenge of space training.

## Try It!

Read the following passage aloud. Can the evidence be proved? How do you know? Does the photo support the argument? Why or why not?

### Junk Yard in the Sky

Since 1957, people have put more than 5,000 satellites in space. These machines float above Earth. They help us talk to each other, track weather, and study space. But only about 600 are being used. The rest are junk. And some of it is dangerous, zooming along at thousands of miles per hour! It could be life-threatening to astronauts. The U.S. Space Command tracks this space junk so that it doesn't run into the path of active satellites. What a waste of time and effort! If we can launch rockets and set up space stations, then we should be able to pick up all of that garbage. Let's get someone to clean it up!

▲ This computer-made image shows all the junk being tracked around Earth.

# Focus on Vocabulary

## Use Context Clues for Multiple-Meaning Words

Many English words have more than one meaning. They are called **multiple-meaning words**. In the dictionary, the different meanings are numbered.

> EXAMPLE    I made a **table** with facts about the planets.
> I worked at the kitchen **table**.

Sometimes one meaning is technical, or specific to the topic or field of study. The kind of text you are reading can help you decide which meaning is **appropriate**. For example, a scientific article might describe tables that support an argument. These tables would most likely refer to the second meaning.

**table** (tā-bul) *noun* **1** a piece of furniture with a flat top, supported by legs **2** information arranged in rows and columns

**Dictionary Entry**

## How the Strategy Works

The best way to figure out the **appropriate** meaning of an unknown multiple-meaning word is to use context clues. Follow these steps:

1. Look at other words in the sentence.
2. Read the sentences that come before and after to find more clues.
3. Use the clues to determine a meaning that makes sense.
4. Replace the word with the meaning, and say the sentence. If it does not make sense, look in a dictionary for more meanings.

Use the strategy to figure out the meaning of each underlined word.

Stars in the night sky look like tiny <u>points</u> of light. The North Star, however, is more than a twinkling dot. Throughout history, people have used the North Star to determine which direction is north. This bright star is located in a group of stars called the Little Dipper. It is at the <u>tip</u> of the handle of the dipper. It shines above the North Pole, the most northern <u>point</u> on Earth.

"Tonight we will follow the North Star to freedom," the woman whispered. The boy was <u>shocked</u>. He hadn't expected this announcement for another month. He <u>darted</u> across the field toward his cabin. The sun was already setting. He threw food and a blanket into a sack and hurried back out the door.

### Strategy in Action

" The words *tiny* and *dot* in the first two sentences are clues. They tell me that *points* probably means 'small spots.' "

### Strategy in Action

" The phrase *hadn't expected this* is a clue. It tells me that *shocked* probably means 'surprised.' I think the writer chose this word because it sets a serious and anxious tone. "

☑ **REMEMBER** You can use context clues to figure out the **appropriate** meaning of a multiple-meaning word.

**Academic Vocabulary**

• **appropriate** (u-prō-prē-ut) *adjective*
If something is **appropriate**, it is correct for the situation.

## Practice Together

Read this passage aloud. Look at each underlined word. Use context clues to figure out the correct meaning of the multiple-meaning word.

# Light Show

Are you a <u>fan</u> of the night sky? On clear, starry nights, do you like to look up at the sparkling <u>show</u>? Ancient people liked to look at the sky. They noticed that groups of stars formed shapes and <u>figures</u>.

Over time, people learned more and more about the night sky. They invented <u>instruments</u>, like the telescope, to study distant objects in the sky.

Today, people continue to explore the sky to learn about the universe. They also enjoy <u>just</u> looking up at the twinkling, <u>bright</u> lights!

## Try It!

Read this passage aloud. What is the meaning of each underlined word? How do you know?

### Colorful Planets

The planets come in a rainbow of colors. Earth usually appears <u>light</u> blue with <u>patches</u> of white in photos. What about some of the other planets? Mars is fiery <u>orange</u> and red. Venus and Saturn tend to be pale yellow. Jupiter, the largest planet, has orange and white <u>bands</u>.

▲ The red-orange color of Mars comes from the rusty soil and dust on its surface.

# The Earth Under Sky Bear's Feet

### Native American Poems of the Land

by Joseph Bruchac
illustrations by Thomas Locker

## Build Background

## See Constellations

In the past, people noticed that some stars seemed to form patterns or shapes in the sky. These are called constellations. People gave each constellation a name, such as Orion or Leo, and created stories about the characters.

## Connect

**Group Discussion** What do you know about the constellations? Share stories or other information you may know about them. Then vote on your favorite constellation picture. Explain your choice.

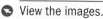
Digital Library

myNGconnect.com
🔍 View the images.

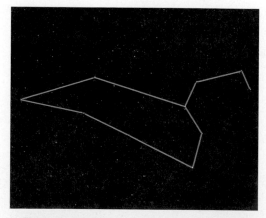

▲ This constellation is known as Leo, the lion.

# Language & Grammar

1 TRY OUT LANGUAGE
2 LEARN GRAMMAR
3 APPLY ON YOUR OWN

## Describe

Look at the picture and listen to the description.
Then describe something in the picture.

PICTURE PROMPT

# What Is It Like?

> It is so clear tonight. I wish you could see the stars. They look like diamonds scattered across the sky.

Language & Grammar **413**

# Use Possessive Nouns

Use a **possessive noun** to show that someone or something owns, or possesses, something.

| | How to Make the Noun Possessive | Examples |
|---|---|---|
| **One Owner** | Add **'s** | The sky**'s** display fascinates us. |
| **More Than One Owner** | Add **'** if the noun ends in **-s** | The stars**'** and planets**'** colors vary. |
| | Add **'s** if the noun does not end in **-s** | People**'s** ideas about stars and planets have changed over time. |

EXAMPLE    The skies **of nighttime** glisten. **Nighttime's** skies glisten.

EXAMPLE    The stars **of the skies** form curious shapes. The **skies'** stars form curious shapes.

## *Practice Together*

Change the words in each box to form a phrase with a possessive noun. Say the phrase. Then say the complete sentence.

1. | roof of the elementary school |  The _____ is a great place for stargazing.

2. | telescope of a teacher |  A _____ lets kids see the stars.

3. | excitement of the children |  The _____ led to more nighttime field trips.

4. | support of their parents |  The _____ helped to buy a second telescope.

5. | group of middle school students |  Now, a _____ has one on their roof.

## *Try It!*

Change the words in each box to form a phrase with a possessive noun. Write the phrase on a card. Then say the sentence with the phrase.

6. | sky in the desert |  The _____ is very clear at night.

7. | telescopes of astronomers |  _____ are often put in the desert.

8. | lights of cities |  _____ make it hard to see stars.

9. | group of women |  My mom's _____ camped in the desert to see them.

10. | shapes of galaxies |  "We even saw several _____," she told me.

▲ The telescope's features let the woman study the sky.

# Tell About the Sky

## DESCRIBE

Pretend that you are sitting under a starry sky. Close your eyes and imagine it. What do you see and hear? What do you feel and smell?

Make a list of words and phrases that tell about the scene.

1. black sky
2. bright stars
3. bugs chirping
4. cold air on my skin
5. the wind in the trees

Use your list to help you create a description. Then describe the sky to a partner.

## HOW TO DESCRIBE

1. Tell what something or someone is like.
2. Give details.
3. Use descriptive words.

The forest's scent had a syrupy sweetness.

## USE POSSESSIVE NOUNS

**Possessive nouns** can help you provide details. Remember that things can possess other things.

EXAMPLES    The **evening's** breeze calmed as night arrived.

The **children's** voices gave way to silence.

And then, the **crickets'** chirps filled the broad stillness.

▲ The stars' display is magnificent in the mountains.

# Prepare to Read

## Learn Key Vocabulary

**Study the Words** Use the steps below.

1. Pronounce the word. Say it aloud several times. Spell it.
2. Rate your word knowledge.
3. Study the example. Tell more about the word.
4. Practice it. Make the word your own.

### Key Words

**advice** (ud-vīs) *noun*
▶ page 426

**Advice** is a suggestion or an idea that helps someone decide what to do. Family members can give you **advice** when you have a problem.

**continue** (kun-tin-yū) *verb*
▶ page 422

To **continue** means to keep going. The highway **continues** for miles.
*Synonyms:* **go on, last**
*Antonym:* **discontinue**

**hunter** (hun-tur) *noun*
▶ page 422

A **hunter** is a person who looks for wild animals to capture or kill. A skilled **hunter** may use a bow and arrows to hunt.

**remain** (ri-mān) *verb*
▶ page 424

To **remain** means to stay in the same place. The dog is learning to **remain** in one spot when told.
*Synonym:* **stay**
*Antonym:* **leave**

**roam** (rōm) *verb*
▶ page 420

To **roam** means to wander or to travel without any particular place to go. Wild animals **roam** freely.
*Synonyms:* **stray, drift**

**scatter** (ska-tur) *verb*
▶ page 424

To **scatter** means to throw or drop many things over a wide area. The leaves **scatter** across the street.
*Synonyms:* **spread, toss, sprinkle**

**tale** (tāl) *noun*
▶ page 422

A **tale** is a story. The children enjoy listening to the **tale**.
*Synonym:* **story**

**track** (trak) *noun*
▶ page 422

A **track** is a footprint or a mark left by something as it moves over a surface. When you look at animal **tracks**, you can tell what kind of animal was in the area.

**Practice the Words** Work with a partner. Write a question using at least one Key Word. Answer your partner's question using a different Key Word. Keep going until you have used each word twice.

| Questions | Answers |
|---|---|
| What did the hunters find? | They found deer tracks. |
| | |

# Analyze Characters' Viewpoints

**What Do Characters Think?** Characters, like people, have viewpoints. What they say, how they act, and even what they think give readers clues about their viewpoints. What other characters say about a character may also provide clues.

To analyze viewpoints, ask questions about the characters and their actions to determine what they think.

Each character may have a different viewpoint.

**Reading Strategies**

- Plan
- Monitor
- Make Connections
- Visualize
- Ask Questions
- Determine Importance
- **Make Inferences**
  When the author does not say something directly, use what you know to figure out what the author means.
- Synthesize

### Look Into the Text

"Does Sky Bear see everything from up there? Does she hear what we say?"

"*Hen*, Granddaughter. As she travels the sky this whole earth is stretched beneath her feet. Listen. I will share with you some of the stories our old people tell about what Sky Bear sees and hears through the night."

" Why does Grandmother say this? These stories are important to her, and she wants to explain what the old people thought of Sky Bear."

## Practice Together

**Begin a Chart** A Character's Viewpoint Chart can help you analyze the viewpoints of characters in a story. This chart shows what Grandmother said. The reader used this clue to determine Grandmother's viewpoint. Reread the passage, and add to the chart.

| Character | What the Character Says, Does, or Thinks | Character's Viewpoint |
|---|---|---|
| Grandmother | says she will share some stories their old people tell about Sky Bear | The stories are important to her. |
|  |  |  |

Character's Viewpoint Chart

## Myth

A myth is a fictional narrative that explains something about the world. A myth usually gives a supernatural, or nonscientific, explanation for something in nature.

In this selection, Grandmother tells three myths that explain how star patterns formed. Just like people, not all characters see this event in the same way. Use **what the characters say** and how they act to determine their viewpoints.

Look Into the Text

"*Hen*, Granddaughter. As she travels the sky this whole earth is stretched beneath her feet. Listen. I will share with you some of the stories our old people tell about what Sky Bear sees and hears through the night."

As you read, make inferences to determine characters' viewpoints. Combine what you know with what you read about the characters.

# The Earth Under Sky Bear's Feet

## Native American Poems of the Land

by Joseph Bruchac

illustrations by Thomas Locker

 Comprehension Coach

Grandmother sat in front of the lodge. The small girl beside her watched. The old woman's strong hands finished the weaving of the ash splint basket. The glow of the setting sun reflected from the surface of the river. Autumn leaves **swirled** in the **current**.

"*Akhsotha*," the girl said. "My grandmother, we must go into the lodge before it is dark. I'm afraid of the night."

Grandmother shook her head. "*Iah*, if we go in too soon, we will not see Sky Bear." Grandmother looked up into the sky. The pattern of stars that shaped the Great Bear was bright. "Soon she will **roam** around the skyland."

"Does Sky Bear see everything from up there? Does she hear what we say?"

"*Hen*, Granddaughter. As she travels the sky this whole earth is stretched beneath her feet. Listen. I will share with you some of the stories our old people tell about what Sky Bear sees and hears through the night."

**Key Vocabulary**
roam *v.*, to wander or travel

**In Other Words**
**swirled** turned around and around
**current** flow of the river water
*Akhsotha* My grandmother
  (in Mohawk)
*Iah* No (in Mohawk)
*Hen* Yes (in Mohawk)

**Cultural Background**

The characters in this tale are Iroquois, a native people from New York state. The grandmother is making a basket with thin strips of ash wood. The strips are called *splints*. The characters speak Mohawk, one of several Iroquois languages.

**Look Into the Text**

1. **Explain** Why does Grandmother want to stay outside longer?
2. **Character's Point of View** Why does Grandmother want to tell her granddaughter stories about Sky Bear?

Most people have seen the Big Dipper. Native Americans call this star pattern Sky Bear. The Mohawk people tell this **tale** of how Sky Bear formed.

# Sky Bear

Long ago,
three **hunters** and their little dog
found the **tracks** of a giant bear.
They followed those tracks
5   all through the day
and even though it was almost dark
they did not stop, but **continued** on.
They saw that bear now, climbing up
a hill, which **glittered**
10  with new-fallen snow.
They ran hard to catch it,
but the bear was too fast.
They ran and they ran, climbing
up and up until one of the hunters said,
15  "Brothers, look down."
They did and saw they
were high above Earth.
That bear was Sky Bear,
running on through the stars.
20  Look up now
and you will see her,
**circling** the sky.

**Key Vocabulary**

**tale** *n.*, a story
**hunter** *n.*, someone who hunts wild animals
**track** *n.*, a mark left by something; a footprint
**continue** *v.*, to keep going

**In Other Words**

**glittered** was shiny
**circling** going in a circle around

**Look Into the Text**

1. **Recall and Interpret** Based on this **tale**, how was the Big Dipper formed?

2. **Figurative Language** When the **hunters** see Sky Bear "running through the stars," what picture do you see in your mind? Is this a good way to describe what they see? Explain.

The Earth Under Sky Bear's Feet **423**

The Cochiti Pueblo of New Mexico tell this brief story.
It explains how all star patterns formed.

# The Scattered Stars

Why are the stars
scattered all through the sky?
Sky Bear says it happened long ago,
when the people came
5   from the underworld.
Our Mother, the Mother
of All the People,
gave one little girl named *Ko-tci-man-yo*
a bag made of white cotton
10  for her to carry.
Do not open this bag, Our Mother said.
But as they walked for many days,
*Ko-tci-man-yo* felt that bag grow heavy.

One night, when they stopped,
15  *Ko-tci-man-yo* climbed up to a hill
where no one could see her,
and then she untied the many knots
to take just one small look inside.
But when she loosened the last knot,
20  the bag popped open
and bright things began to escape
to the sky.

*Ko-tci-man-yo* quickly closed that bag,
but only a few of the stars remained
25  to be placed in patterns in the sky.
All the others scattered.
They are still that way
because of her curiosity.

**Key Vocabulary**
**scatter** *v.*, to throw or drop
   many things over a wide area
**remain** *v.*, to stay in the same
   place

**In Other Words**
**came from the underworld** first
   came to the land
**cotton** cloth, fabric
**knots** places where the bag was
   tied
**loosened** untied
**of her curiosity** she was curious

**Look Into the Text**

1. **Summarize** According to this Cochiti **tale**, how did star patterns form?

2. **Cause and Effect** Why does the girl open the bag? What happens when she does?

This Lenape story tells about a group of seven stars. The Lenape people are from the Eastern Woodlands of the United States.

# The Seven Mateinnu

Long ago, seven **wise men**
lived among the people.
They knew so much that everyone
was always asking them for **advice** .

5  They grew so tired that
they decided to hide from the people,
and **turned themselves
into** seven big stones.
But before too long,
10  the people found them,
and because they were stones,
they had to sit and listen
to everyone ask for help.

They tried a second time to hide,
15  and turned into seven cedar trees.
But once again,
the people found them,
and because they were **rooted**,
they still had to listen.

20  At last they **accepted**
that they could not hide.
They changed themselves
into seven stars dancing in the middle
of the sky.

25  Each night the people look up to them
and see the answers to their questions
in the light of those stars. ❖

**Key Vocabulary**

**advice** *n.*, ideas that help
someone decide what to do

**In Other Words**

**wise men** men who gave good
advice
**turned themselves into** became
**rooted** attached to the ground
**accepted** knew it was true

**Look Into the Text**

1. **Problem and Solution** Why do the
   seven wise men want to hide? How
   do they solve the problem?
2. **Personification** How are the wise
   men still like people after they turn
   into rocks, trees, and stars? How
   are they different?

"There can be as much to see in the living night as in the more familiar light of day."

—Joseph Bruchac

## About the Author

Joseph Bruchac

**Joseph Bruchac** (1942– ) is a storyteller and a poet. He loves nature and the stories about nature that he learned from his Native American ancestors. Bruchac believes that everything in nature has its own story to tell.

Bruchac tells readers, "keep listening, listen to the voices of others, listen to the sounds of nature around us, and listen to your heart. Everything is there."

# Connect Reading and Writing

Vocabulary

advice

continues

hunter

remains

roams

scatter

tale

tracks

## CRITICAL THINKING

1. **SUM IT UP** Choose one myth. Use your Character's Viewpoint Chart to retell the **tale** to a partner.

| Character | What the Character Says, Does, or Thinks | Character's Viewpoint |
|---|---|---|
| Grandmother | says she will share some stories their old people tell about Sky Bear | The stories are important to her. |
| | | |

Character's Viewpoint Chart

2. **Infer** Why did people use stories long ago to explain mysteries such as why stars are **scattered** across the sky?

3. **Analyze** What does "The Seven Mateinnu" tell you about people and their need to seek **advice** about the world? Use examples from the text.

4. **Generalize** Why do people **continue** to tell old myths?

## READING FLUENCY

**Expression** Read the passage on page 576 to a partner. Assess your fluency.

1. My voice never/sometimes/always matched what I read.

2. What I did best in my reading was _____.

## READING STRATEGY

What strategy helped you understand this selection? Tell a partner about it.

## VOCABULARY REVIEW

**Oral Review** Read the paragraph aloud. Add the vocabulary words.

Here is a short _____: A deer family _____ the fields. The father deer, a buck, sees something moving in the grass ahead. He signals his family to _____. They quickly take his _____. The buck stays, or _____, and watches as a _____ comes near. The buck runs, leaving _____ in the dirt. He leaps into the sky. The buck _____ in this way, leaping from star to star. Whenever you see a shooting star, the buck is running.

**Written Review** Look back at the illustrations of the stars in the selection. Write a caption for each picture. Use at least four vocabulary words.

 **WRITE ABOUT THE** **GUIDING QUESTION**

### Explore the Power of the Stars

Why do people look for patterns in the stars and then create **tales** about those patterns? Support your explanation with examples from the text.

# Connect Across the Curriculum

## Use Context Clues

**Academic Vocabulary**
- **appropriate** (u-**prō**-prē-ut) *adjective*
  If something is **appropriate**, it is correct for the situation.

Use a dictionary to find definitions for words that have multiple meanings. Use the context clues as hints to help you find the **appropriate** meaning.

**hide** (**hīd**) *verb* **1** to go where no one can see you   *noun* **2** an animal's skin

**knot** (**not**) *noun* **1** the tied ends of rope or string   **2** unit used to measure a ship's speed

**lodge** (**loj**) *verb* **1** to become fixed in one place and not move   *noun* **2** a small house or cabin

**tracks** (**traks**) *noun* **1** the rails a train rides on   **2** marks left by an animal

Dictionary Entries

**Determine Meanings** Find each of these words in the selection. Determine which meaning applies in the text. Use context clues.

**1.** lodge, p. 420   **2.** tracks, p. 422   **3.** knot, p. 424   **4.** hide, p. 426

## Analyze Mood and Tone

**Academic Vocabulary**
- **discuss** (di-**skus**) *verb*
  When you **discuss** something, you talk about it.

All writing has a **mood** and **tone**. The author's word choice helps to set the mood and tone of a text. The mood of a text is the feeling you get when you read it. The tone of a text is the author's attitude toward the topic.

In "The Scattered Stars" on p. 424, the author's word choice sets the mood and tone. "Just one small look" and "popped open" give the writing a mood of childlike wonder. This writer has a respectful tone as he explains reasons for *Ko-tci-man-yo*'s actions.

**Analyze a Myth** With a partner, choose another myth. **Discuss** how the author's word choice impacts the mood and tone. Give examples.

## Describe

**Describe a Picture** Look back at the illustrations for the three myths. Decide which one is your favorite. Then describe it. Use possessive nouns to add clarity to your description.

> Even the hunter's dog saw the bear in the sky.

## Write About a Character in Space

**Study the Models** When you write a story, provide details to make your story come to life. Use possessive nouns correctly to show ownership.

**JUST OK**

Jade stared down at the **planets'** outline. She could see **Hestias** landscape. It was her **parents'** decision to move to Hestia. But Jade wasn't sure the people would accept her.

> The writer doesn't give enough details to paint a clear picture. The writer also needs to correct mistakes with possessive nouns.

**BETTER**

Jade stared through a porthole. The **planet's** outline was coming into view below her. The **window's** view was limited. Even so, she could see **Hestia's** purple oceans and orange mountains. It had been her **parents'** decision to move to one of the **galaxy's** distant planets. But here on Hestia, would the **people's** government welcome her? Jade wasn't sure.

> Here, the writer uses possessive nouns correctly and adds details that make the writing more interesting.

**Add Sentences** Think of two sentences to add to the BETTER model above. Try to include at least one possessive noun.

**WRITE ON YOUR OWN** Imagine a character who is traveling in space. Write about what happens. Use possessive nouns correctly.

**REMEMBER**

Add **'s** or **'** to a noun to show ownership.
the ocean**'s** color
her parents**'** idea
the children**'s** worries

▲ The astronaut's suit keeps him safe.

# A Universe of Stars

by Ellen Fried

# Build Background

## Meet an Astronomer

Astronomers are scientists who study the stars, the planets, and other objects in space. Famous astronomers like Galileo Galilei have helped us understand the universe.

**Digital Library**

myNGconnect.com
◉ View the video.

◀ Unlike others of his time, Galileo Galilei believed the Earth moved around the sun.

## Connect

**KWLS Chart** What do you know about the stars and space? What would you like to know? Create a KWLS Chart. Fill in the last two columns after you read the selection.

| WHAT I KNOW | WHAT I WANT TO KNOW | WHAT I LEARNED | WHAT I STILL WANT TO LEARN |
|---|---|---|---|
| The sun is a star. | How big is the sun? | | |

KWLS Chart

# Language & Grammar

## Define and Explain

CD

Study the images and listen to the explanation.
Then explain something about one of the images.

**PICTURE PROMPT**

In 2006, NASA launched New Horizons, a spacecraft that will study Pluto and the Kuiper belt. The Kuiper belt is a group of icy objects outside the orbit of Neptune. Astronomers believe that studying these objects will help them better understand how our solar system began.

Charon, one of Pluto's moons

Pluto

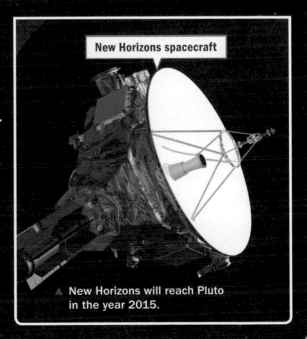

New Horizons spacecraft

▲ New Horizons will reach Pluto in the year 2015.

**1 TRY OUT LANGUAGE**
**2 LEARN GRAMMAR**
**3 APPLY ON YOUR OWN**

# Use Possessive Adjectives and Pronouns

Possessive adjectives and possessive pronouns show ownership.
A **possessive adjective** identifies who owns or has something. It comes before a noun. A **possessive pronoun** names the thing owned and who owns or has it. It stands alone.

| Possessive Adjectives | my | your | his | her | our | their |
|---|---|---|---|---|---|---|
| Possessive Pronouns | mine | yours | his | hers | ours | theirs |

EXAMPLES
We call **our** solar system's star the sun.
Of all the stars in the galaxy, the sun is **ours**.

Galileo used **his** telescope to watch the night sky.
One early design for the telescope was **his**.

## Practice Together

Choose the possessive adjective or a possessive pronoun to complete each sentence correctly.

1. Kayla brought _____ telescope to the park.
2. None of the other kids brought _____.
3. Kayla's telescope is only strong enough to see things in _____ solar system.
4. Still, all the kids were happy to use _____.

## Try It!

Read each sentence. Write a possessive adjective or possessive pronoun from the chart on a card. Then hold up the card as you say the full sentence.

5. May I look through _____ telescope?
6. I don't have _____ because I left it at home.
7. Is that object in the sky _____ moon?
8. NASA has huge telescopes. Imagine looking through one of _____.
9. Working for NASA is one of _____ dreams.
10. Is it one of _____?

▲ Other solar systems have planets, too. Jupiter, seen here through a telescope, is one of ours.

# Explain Something About Space

## DEFINE AND EXPLAIN

What do you know about space? Tell a partner something you know about a planet, a spacecraft, an astronomer, or a similar topic.

First, review the information in your science textbook or another source. Make an outline to organize your thoughts.

**Outline**

I. The Solar System
  A. the sun
  B. planets that orbit the sun
    1. Mercury
    2. Venus
    3. Earth
    4. Mars
    5. Jupiter
    6. Saturn
    7. Uranus
    8. Neptune

Check your outline to see if there are any words or phrases you may need to define for your partner. Write their meanings on your outline. If you need help with the definitions, use a dictionary.

Explain the information to your partner. Define the difficult words.

## HOW TO DEFINE AND EXPLAIN

**1.** Define: As you give information, tell the meaning of any difficult words or phrases.
**2.** Explain: Give more details or examples to make the definition clear.

> To orbit means to move around an object. Earth orbits the sun.

## USE POSSESSIVE ADJECTIVES AND PRONOUNS

When you give an explanation, be sure to correctly use any **possessive adjectives** and **possessive pronouns**.

EXAMPLES    NASA has landed several of **their** Rovers on Mars.
                   Curiosity is one of **theirs**.

# Prepare to Read

## Learn Key Vocabulary

**Study the Words** Use the steps below.

1. Pronounce the word. Say it aloud several times. Spell it.
2. Rate your word knowledge.
3. Study the example. Tell more about the word.
4. Practice it. Make the word your own.

### Key Words

**distance** (dis-tunts) *noun*
▸ page 441

**Distance** is the area between two points. The **distance** between Earth and the sun is 93 million miles.

**orbit** (or-but) *verb*
▸ page 445

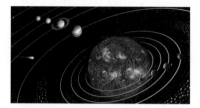

To **orbit** means to move in an almost circular path around another object. It takes Earth about 365 days to **orbit** the sun.

**space** (spās) *noun*
▸ page 440

**Space** is the area beyond Earth. Scientists send special ships into **space** to learn about other planets and the moon.

**telescope** (te-lu-skōp) *noun*
▸ page 443

A **telescope** is a tool you can look through to make faraway things look bigger. You can use a **telescope** to look at the moon.

**temperature** (tem-pur-chur) *noun* ▸ page 444

The **temperature** is how hot or cold something is. We measure **temperature** using a thermometer.

**unit** (yū-nit) *noun*
▸ page 442

A **unit** is a certain amount used in measuring. An inch is a common **unit** used to measure small objects.

**universe** (yū-nu-vurs) *noun*
▸ page 440

The **universe** is everywhere and includes Earth, all other planets, and all stars.

**vary** (vair-ē) *verb*
▸ page 444

To **vary** means to be different from others. Snowflakes **vary** from one another so that no two are alike.

**Practice the Words** Make a Frayer Model for each Key Word. Then compare your models with a partner's.

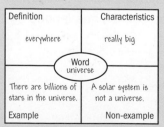

| Definition | Characteristics |
|---|---|
| everywhere | really big |
| There are billions of stars in the universe. | A solar system is not a universe. |
| Example | Non-example |

Word: universe

**Frayer Model**

# Analyze Author's Purpose

**Why Do Authors Write?** Before authors write, they think about what to tell readers and why. Their purpose, or reason, for writing helps them decide on the genre, or form of writing, to use. Authors write to inform, persuade, entertain, or explain.

If you know the author's purpose, it can help you **evaluate** the text. For example, if the author's purpose is to inform, you can decide if you learned something from the text. To determine the author's purpose, look at the **elements** and details in the text.

### Reading Strategies

- Plan
- Monitor
- Make Connections
- Visualize
- Ask Questions
- Determine Importance
- **Make Inferences**
  When the author does not say something directly, use what you know to figure out what the author means.
- Synthesize

## Look Into the Text

If you stand outside on a clear, dark night, far away from any city lights, you may see a pale band of light stretching across the sky. The band of light is the Milky Way. The glow is from a huge number of stars.

Long ago, people could use only their eyes to study the sky. Over time, more powerful tools have allowed us to look farther and farther out into the universe. We've learned so much about space, but there is *much* more left to explore.

" The author explains how powerful tools have helped people learn more about space. "

## Practice Together

**Begin a Chart** When analyzing author's purpose, a T Chart is a helpful tool to use to list details in the text. This T Chart shows the author's purpose and the detail that helped reveal it. Reread the passage above, and add to the T Chart.

| "A Universe of Stars" | "The Astronomer" |
|---|---|
| Purpose: to inform and explain | Purpose: |
| explanations | |

**T Chart**

### Academic Vocabulary

- **evaluate** (i-**val**-yu-wāt) *verb*
  To **evaluate** means to judge something's value or worth.
- **element** (e-lu-munt) *noun* An **element** is a basic part of a whole.

## Science Article

A science article gives information about the world around us. It contains many facts and **scientific terms**.

An author's purpose for writing a science article is to inform and explain. As you read, look for elements and details that reveal the author's purpose.

**Look Into the Text**

> Each star is a giant, fiery ball of gases. Our sun is a star. It is made mostly of hydrogen and helium gases. The sun is extremely hot. Huge columns of gas sometimes leap from the surface.

Read carefully to make sure that you understand the facts presented and the terms used by the author. Make inferences by putting together what the author explains and what you already know to fill in missing information.

# A Universe
## of
# Stars

by Ellen Fried

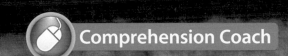

# The Night Sky

If you stand outside on a clear, dark night, far away from any city lights, you may see a **pale band** of light stretching across the sky. The band of light is the Milky Way. The **glow** is from a huge number of stars.

Long ago, people could use only their eyes to study the sky. Over time, more powerful tools have allowed us to look farther and farther out into the universe. We've learned so much about space, but there is *much* more **left** to explore.

On dark and cloudless nights, people can view the stars. ▷

---

**Key Vocabulary**

**universe** *n.*, everywhere, including Earth, the planets, and the stars

**space** *n.*, the area beyond Earth

**In Other Words**

**pale band** light-colored strip
**glow** soft, steady light
**left** still

# What Is a Star?

In the night sky, stars look like tiny diamonds **fastened** to the ceiling. They seem peaceful, timeless, and unchanging. In reality, stars are huge. They are scattered through **vast distances** in space. They're not timeless but are always changing, and those changes can be **violent**.

Each star is a giant, **fiery** ball of gases. Our sun is a star. It is made mostly of hydrogen and helium gases. The sun is **extremely** hot. Huge columns of gas sometimes **leap** from the surface.

Our sun is so big that a million Earths could fit inside it. More than a hundred Earths could stretch side by side across it. Other stars look much smaller than our sun, but that is because they are much farther away from us than the sun is.

▼ Hot streams of gas leap from the surface of the sun.

**In Other Words**
**fastened** stuck
**vast** large, great
**violent** strong, forceful
**fiery** burning
**extremely** very
**leap** jump

## Look Into the Text

1. **Simile** How are stars "like tiny diamonds fastened to the sky"? How is this comparison not true?
2. **Summarize** What is a star?

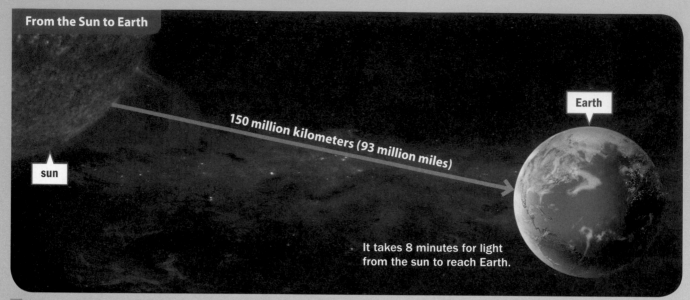

From the Sun to Earth

150 million kilometers (93 million miles)

sun

Earth

It takes 8 minutes for light from the sun to reach Earth.

▲ Interpret the Diagram What does 150 million kilometers or 93 million miles represent?

# Measuring the Universe

Distances in space are so great that scientists use a special **unit** to measure them. This unit of measurement is based on how fast light travels.

Light is the fastest moving thing we know. It takes about 8 minutes for light to travel from the sun to Earth. That's a distance of 150 million kilometers (93 million miles). You might say that the sun is 8 light-minutes from Earth.

It takes years for the light from other stars to reach us. We use a unit called a light-year to measure the distance between Earth and those other stars. A light-year is the distance that light travels in a year.

We cannot travel to the stars. We cannot even send **space probes** that far away. To learn about other stars, scientists study the light and other energy that travels through space and reaches us on Earth.

**Key Vocabulary**
  **unit** *n.*, a certain amount used in measuring

**In Other Words**
  **space probes** spacecraft without people

# Scoping the Sky

Long ago, people studied the stars just by eye. They noticed that stars seem to move across the sky and that groups of stars **formed patterns**. They gave names to the patterns. A group of stars that forms a pattern is a constellation. Knowing the constellations helped people travel at night.

In the 1600s scientists started using **telescopes** to look at the sky. Since then, telescopes have become more powerful. They allow us to see things that are very far away. Other tools let us study the light that telescopes **collect**.

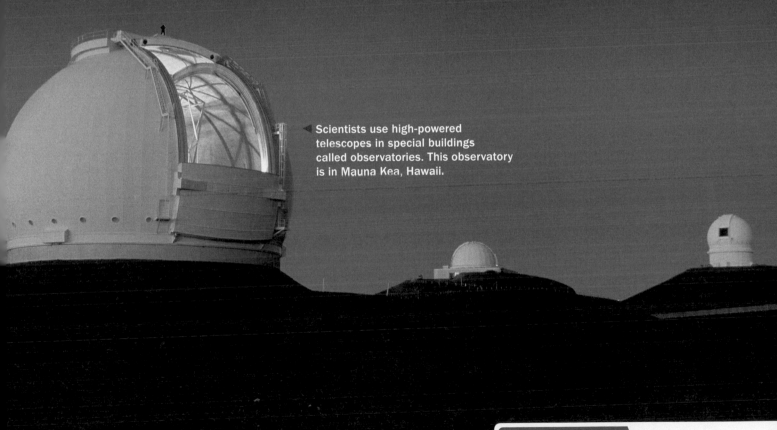

◄ Scientists use high-powered telescopes in special buildings called observatories. This observatory is in Mauna Kea, Hawaii.

---

**Key Vocabulary**

**telescope** *n.*, a tool you can look through to make faraway things look bigger

**In Other Words**

**formed patterns** looked like shapes
**collect** bring together in one place

**Look Into the Text**

1. **Explain** What **unit** do scientists use to measure **distances** in **space**? Explain what it means.

2. **Compare and Contrast** What is different about how people studied the stars long ago and the way they study them now? What is the same?

# Star Variety

Stars **vary** greatly in how much light they give off. Our sun looks bright only because it is so close. Some stars give off thousands of times more light than the sun. Other stars give off much less light.

Stars also give off different colors of light. Our sun gives off mostly yellow light. Some stars give off mostly red light. Others give off mostly white or blue light.

The surface **temperature** of stars varies, too. The surface temperature of our sun is about 5,500°C (10,000°F). Some stars are much hotter. Others are only half as hot. Usually, the hotter a star is, the brighter it is. This isn't always true, though.

Also, stars vary in size. **Dwarf** stars are small compared to other stars. Giant stars are very large. The sun is a smaller star.

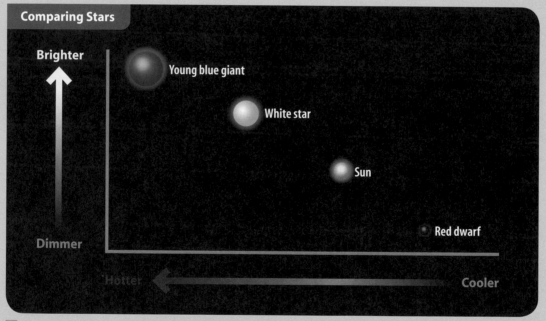

**Comparing Stars**

Brighter

Young blue giant

White star

Sun

Red dwarf

Dimmer

Hotter

Cooler

▲ **Interpret the Chart** Which is hotter, a young blue giant star or a red dwarf star?

**Key Vocabulary**
**vary** *v.*, to be different from others
**temperature** *n.*, how hot or cold something is

**In Other Words**
**Dwarf** Small

# Our Place in Space

The universe is huge, and our place in it is small. Earth is just one of the planets that **orbit** the sun. The sun is just one of a great many stars in the Milky Way, and the Milky Way is just one of more than a hundred billion **galaxies** in space.

There is so much more to learn about stars and the universe. The more we study the night sky, the more we will uncover. ❖

A telescope in space took this photo of the universe. It shows galaxies stretching out over billions of light-years.

**Key Vocabulary**
**orbit** *v.*, to move in a path around another object

**In Other Words**
**galaxies** groups of stars

**Look Into the Text**

1. **Categorize** Name three ways that stars vary.
2. **Evidence and Conclusion** Why does the author say that our place in the **universe** is small? What details support this idea?

# THE ASTRONOMER

### BY AESOP

There was once a famous **astronomer** who attracted many visitors. Scientists came from far and wide to listen to him speak about the night sky.

One clear night, the astronomer took some visitors for a walk. He described each planet and named each constellation, but he did not watch where he was going.

Suddenly, the astronomer stumbled, fell forward, and landed face down in a muddy **ditch**. He slowly got up. His clothes were wet and his body was **bruised**.

The poor man limped back to the road. There, clear as day, was a rock in the path.

A visitor **remarked**, "You see great things in the sky, but you should see the small things at your feet, too."

**MORAL:** As you think about the great things in life, don't **ignore** the small things.

**In Other Words**
**astronomer** scientist who studied the stars
**ditch** hole in the ground
**bruised** hurt
**remarked** said
**ignore** forget about

### Look Into the Text

1. **Cause and Effect** Why did the astronomer fall down? What happened after he fell?
2. **Paraphrase** Restate the moral, or lesson, of this fable.

# Connect Reading and Writing

Vocabulary
distances
orbit
space
telescopes
temperatures
unit
universe
vary

## CRITICAL THINKING

1. **SUM IT UP** With a partner, use your T Charts to explain the author's purpose and summarize each selection.

| "A Universe of Stars" | "The Astronomer" |
|---|---|
| Purpose: to inform and explain | Purpose: |
| explanations | |

**T Chart**

2. **Speculate** Review the information on page 441 about the size of the sun. Then look at page 444. About how many Earths could fit in a young blue giant?

3. **Compare** "A Universe of Stars" and "The Astronomer" both tell about scientists studying the **universe**. Do the authors feel the same way about this topic? Explain.

4. **Infer** How have **telescopes** changed our understanding of the **universe**?

## READING FLUENCY

**Phrasing** Read the passage on page 577 to a partner. Assess your fluency.

1. I did not pause/sometimes paused/ always paused for punctuation.

2. What I did best in my reading was _____.

## READING STRATEGY

What strategy helped you understand this selection? Tell a partner about it.

## VOCABULARY REVIEW

**Oral Review** Read the paragraph aloud. Add the vocabulary words.

Scientists use a variety of tools and methods to study the stars and other objects in _____. They use a _____ of measurement called the light-year to determine the vast _____ to some stars. Scientists look through _____ and launch rockets. Rockets carry probes that gather data about the _____. Rockets also place satellites that _____ Earth. The purpose of satellites can _____. For example, some satellites gather _____ and other weather data.

**Written Review** Imagine that you have just discovered an object in **space** such as a new planet. Write a description of it using five vocabulary words.

 **WRITE ABOUT THE** **GUIDING QUESTION**

### Explore the Power of the Stars

Do you think it is important to study the **universe**? Why or why not? Support your opinion with evidence from the text.

# Connect Across the Curriculum

## Use Context Clues

**Academic Vocabulary**
- **appropriate** (u-prō-prē-ut) *adjective*
  If something is **appropriate**, it is correct for the situation.

You can use context clues to figure out the **appropriate** meaning of a multiple-meaning word. Then check the definition using a dictionary.

> The full moon looks <u>odd</u> behind the clouds.

> **odd** (od) *adjective* **1** strange or unusual **2** not able to be divided by two

Dictionary Entry

The sentence is about the moon. This context helps you figure out the **appropriate** meaning of *odd*: The moon looks strange behind the clouds.

**Define Words** Find each of these words on page 440. Write the context clues. Then look up the word in a dictionary, and copy the **appropriate** definition.

**1.** stand  **2.** clear  **3.** band  **4.** left

---

## Analyze Style

**Academic Vocabulary**
- **style** (stī-ul) *noun*
  A **style** is a certain way of expressing an idea.

An author's **style** is the way the author expresses an idea. A children's book author may write in short, rhyming sentences. A science author may write in long sentences full of technical terms that are specific to the topic.

**Analyze a Passage** Read the first paragraph on p. 441 from "A Universe of Stars." Look at the words the author uses. Are they descriptive, everyday, or technical? Are important words repeated? Then look at the sentences. How do they begin? What is the length of each sentence?

**Choose Another Selection** Look back at a selection you read before. Analyze the author's **style** for that selection using the questions above. Take notes on what you find and discuss with a partner.

## Define and Explain

**Partner Share** Look in the selection for a difficult word or phrase that you learned. Then share with a partner. Define the difficult term. Explain its meaning. Use possessive adjectives and pronouns correctly.

> A light-minute is the distance that light travels in one minute. Its trip from the sun to Earth takes about eight minutes.

## Write About an Adventure

**Study the Models** When you write about an adventure, include details and dialogue. This will make your work interesting for readers. Use possessive adjectives and pronouns correctly.

**JUST OK**

The spacecraft was lost in space. One of **it's** instruments had failed. "Contact a nearby spacecraft," said the captain. "Tell them we're in trouble. Maybe they can help."

> The reader thinks: **"This story isn't very exciting. It needs details to make it seem real. It also has a possessive mistake."**

**MUCH BETTER**

The spacecraft was adrift in the Pinwheel Galaxy. All **its** positioning devices had stopped working. Keifer shouted to **his** mate, "Get a message to Ship X-11. Tell Tsang Ying that our GPS just failed. Ask if they can use **theirs** to locate **our** position."

"Can't do," Taro shouted. " **My** transmitter has failed!"

> The writer adds details and characters' names. The writer also adds clarity by using **possessives** correctly.

**Add Sentences** Think of two sentences to add to the MUCH BETTER model above. Use at least one possessive adjective or pronoun correctly.

✎ **WRITE ON YOUR OWN** Write about an adventure on a real planet or an imaginary planet. Include details. Use possessives correctly.

> **REMEMBER**
>
> A **possessive adjective** comes before a noun.
>
> A **possessive pronoun** stands alone.

◄ This image shows an imaginary planet.

# Not-So-Starry Nights

**Light Pollution Turns Night into Day**

by Sharon Guynup

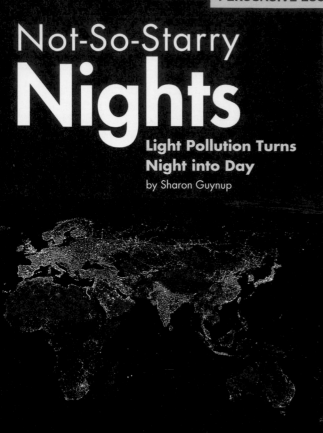

# Build Background

## Connect

**Anticipation Guide** What do you think about the environment? Tell whether you agree or disagree with these statements.

|  | Agree | Disagree |
|---|---|---|
| 1. Environmental problems hurt humans more than animals. | _____ | _____ |
| 2. Outdoor lighting is not a problem for wildlife. | _____ | _____ |
| 3. Most electricity is produced in a way that doesn't harm the environment. | _____ | _____ |

Anticipation Guide

## Learn About Night Lights

About a century ago, people in the United States could see hundreds of twinkling stars at night. Today, artificial lights in cities make it difficult to see most of the stars at night.

**Digital Library**

**myNGconnect.com**
⬧ View the video.

▲ Artificial lights block our view of the stars.

# Language & Grammar

## Persuade

Listen to the chant. Listen again and join in.
Then listen to a persuasive argument.

**CHANT and PERSUASIVE ARGUMENT**

## What Is It Worth?

A tossed bottle,
A thrown cup,
Polluted water—
Clean it up!

What is it worth
To us on Earth
To clean our atmosphere?
We must reduce the garbage
That pollutes the land and air!

Language and Grammar, continued

1 TRY OUT LANGUAGE
2 LEARN GRAMMAR
3 APPLY ON YOUR OWN

# Use Prepositions and Prepositional Phrases

**Prepositions** show how two objects or ideas are related.

- Some show location:
  We sat **on** the bench.
  The stars were **above** us.

- Some show direction:
  Mom came **through** the door.
  She walked **up** the stairs.

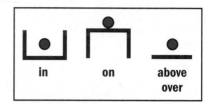

in      on      above
                over

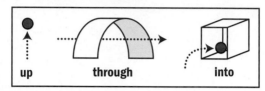

up          through          into

- Some show time: We saw some constellations **at** nine o'clock.
- Some show origin: That constellation is **from** a Greek myth.

- A **prepositional phrase** is a group of words. It begins with a **preposition** and ends with a **noun** or an **object pronoun**.

  EXAMPLES    The planets travel **around** the **sun**.

  Stars and planets are interesting **to me**.

| Object Pronouns | |
|---|---|
| **Singular** | **Plural** |
| me | us |
| you | you |
| him, her, it | them |

## Practice Together

Complete the underlined prepositional phrases. Add a preposition or an object pronoun as needed. Say the sentence.

**1.** There are two telescopes _____ the roof of our school.

**2.** We each got to look _____ the telescopes.

**3.** Our school is _____ the desert away from lights.

**4.** I saw Saturn and the rings around _____.

**5.** I found two constellations and counted the stars in _____.

## Try It!

Read each incomplete sentence. On a card, write a preposition or an object pronoun to complete the prepositional phrase. Then hold up the card as you say the sentence.

**6.** Do you like to sleep _____ the stars?

**7.** I do, but only if my dog sleeps beside _____.

**8.** You should try it _____ a clear night.

**9.** Thousands of stars twinkle _____ your head.

**10.** The constellations spin around _____ all night.

▲ Thousands of stars twinkle over my head.

# Give a Persuasive Speech

## PERSUADE

Think about the chant on page 451. What would you do to improve the environment? What is Earth worth to you? How important is it to you?

Work in small groups. Discuss environmental problems and solutions. Record your ideas on a chart.

**Idea Chart**

| Problem | Action Needed | Why It's Important |
|---|---|---|
| People are cutting down forests faster than new trees can grow. | use less paper, recycle paper | Forests provide homes for animals. Forests protect soil from washing away. |
| The air is polluted. | | |
| People are overfishing. | | |

Focus on one problem. Then write a speech to persuade others to help solve the problem.

## HOW TO PERSUADE

**1.** State your opinion.

**2.** Give reasons for your opinion.

**3.** Use persuasive words like *must*, *have to*, and *should*.

**4.** Tell why your opinion or plan of action is important.

**5.** Tell how it will help others.

> We should use shopping bags made of cloth. This will help save trees.

After you finish the speech, decide which group member will present it to the class.

## USE PREPOSITIONAL PHRASES

When you try to persuade people, you need to use effective and interesting sentences. Using **prepositional phrases** adds interest and convincing details to your sentences.

**Not as Interesting:**  We must stop overfishing.

**More Interesting:**  We must stop the overfishing **in our oceans, rivers, and lakes** .

# Prepare to Read

## Learn Key Vocabulary

**Study the Words** Use the steps below.

1. Pronounce the word. Say it aloud several times. Spell it.
2. Rate your word knowledge.
3. Study the example. Tell more about the word.
4. Practice it. Make the word your own.

**Rating Scale**

**1 =** I have never seen this word before.

**2 =** I am not sure of the word's meaning.

**3 =** I know this word and can teach the word's meaning to someone else.

### Key Words

**benefit** (be-nu-fit) *noun*
▸ page 458

A **benefit** is something that is helpful. Fresh air and exercise are two **benefits** of hiking.

**environment**
(in-vī-run-munt) *noun* ▸ page 460

An **environment** is the area where plants and animals live and grow. Plants grow well in a healthy **environment**.

**migrate** (mī-grāt) *verb*
▸ page 462

To **migrate** means to move from one place to another. These birds **migrate** to a warm climate for the winter.

**pollution** (pu-lü-shun) *noun*
▸ page 458

**Pollution** is waste that harms nature. Trash is one form of **pollution**.

**protect** (pru-tekt) *verb*
▸ page 463

To **protect** means to keep safe. The mother bird **protects** her chicks from danger.
*Synonym:* **save**

**reduce** (ri-düs) *verb*
▸ page 465

To **reduce** means to have fewer or less of something. The box is too heavy for her to carry, so her friend helps **reduce** the heavy load.
*Antonym:* **increase**

**release** (ri-lēs) *verb*
▸ page 460

To **release** means to let out. When you **release** an animal into the wild, you let it go free.

**wasted** (wāst-ud) *adjective*
▸ page 460

Something that is **wasted** is not needed. Food that you throw away instead of eating is **wasted**.

**Practice the Words** Make a chart to tell how you feel about each word. Is your response positive, negative, or neither? Explain. Compare your chart with a partner's and discuss.

| Word | Positive (+) Negative (-) Neither (=) | Reason |
|------|------|------|
| release | + | I think it is good to release animals. |

**Connotation Chart**

# Analyze Argument and Evidence

**How Are Arguments Supported?** Authors of nonfiction text often state an argument, or their position or belief about a topic. They may use words such as *must* and *should* to make specific claims. Then authors give evidence or reasons to support their position. They use relevant information. For example, they may give facts, examples, statements from experts, or photographs to prove that something is true.

As you read, identify arguments stated in the text and **analyze** whether they are supported by reasons and evidence.

### Reading Strategies

- Plan
- Monitor
- Make Connections
- Visualize
- Ask Questions
- Determine Importance
- **Make Inferences**
  When the author does not say something directly, use what you know to figure out what the author means.
- Synthesize

### Look Into the Text

A star-filled sky is a magnificent sight. It is also an important part of our lives. By studying the sky, we learn about our place in the universe.

Animals also need the night sky. Some animals use the stars to find their way. Others depend on the dark to feel safe.

" The author states her belief that a star-filled sky is important to our lives. I will read on to look for reasons that support her argument. "

## Practice Together

**Begin an Argument Chart** An Argument Chart can help you analyze arguments and evidence in a text. This Argument Chart shows the first argument the author makes. Reread the passage above to determine whether the argument is supported by reasons or evidence, and add information to the Argument Chart.

| Argument | Support (Yes/No) | Evidence |
|---|---|---|
| A star-filled sky is an important part of our lives. | | |
| | | |

Argument Chart

## Academic Vocabulary

- **analyze** (a-nu-līz) *verb*
  To **analyze** means to break down information into parts to understand it better.

# Persuasive Essay

A persuasive essay is a short piece of nonfiction writing about one subject.
The author's purpose is to convince you of something. The author states an argument and supports it with evidence, such as **facts and examples**.

Analyzing the claims an author makes helps you to separate unsupported arguments from those supported by reasons.

**Look Into the Text**

> About one-third of all lighting in the United States is wasted. Wasted light costs billions of dollars per year. It also harms the environment.
> Electricity comes from power plants.... Power plants burn coal, which pollutes the air.

Make inferences as you read to better understand the author's arguments.
Use information from the text combined with what you know to build on your inferences.

# Not-So-Starry Nights

## Light Pollution Turns Night into Day

by Sharon Guynup

This photo from space shows how bright the lights from cities are.

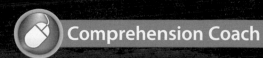 Comprehension Coach

# The Sky as a Natural Resource

A star-filled sky is a magnificent sight. It is also an important part of our lives. By studying the sky, we learn about our place in the universe.

Animals also need the night sky. Some animals use the stars to **find their way**. Others depend on the dark to feel safe.

This natural **wonder**, like many others, is in danger from human activity. Light **pollution** is changing our view of the night. We must change our ways, or we will lose the **benefits** of the starry sky.

# History of the Problem

One hundred years ago, everyone **had a twinkling view of** the night sky. At that time, people could see about 1,500 stars. Today, only one in ten Americans has a beautiful, starry view. People in cities see a glowing orange sky and just a few dozen stars instead.

Astronomers were the first to notice the growing problem of light pollution. They began to realize it in the 1970s. They were shocked when they looked into their telescopes and saw that some of the stars and planets that they had studied were gone. They were still there, of course, but city lights made them impossible to see.

Nights started to get brighter more than a century ago. The first long-lasting light bulb was invented in 1879. Companies began to **install** electric power lines across the country. More and more people used electricity for lighting.

At the same time, the population grew. Many people moved to the United States. In 1900, there were 76 million Americans. There are more than 300 million today. More people now live in cities and suburbs, and their lights create light pollution.

---

**Key Vocabulary**

**pollution** *n.*, waste that harms nature

**benefit** *n.*, something that is helpful

**In Other Words**

**find their way** know which direction to go

**wonder** resource

**had a twinkling view of** could see stars in

**install** put up

▲ This photo was taken on August 14, 2003. It shows the night sky over Ontario, Canada, **during a blackout**.

▲ This photo was taken the next night. It shows how the night sky looks when there are many lights on.

**In Other Words**

**during a blackout** when electricity was not available

**Science Background**

A lightbulb uses electricity to heat a thin strip of material that glows brightly. The material lasts a long time before it burns out. The glass bulb is filled with a mostly harmless gas.

**Look Into the Text**

1. **Author's Viewpoint** How does the author feel about a starry night sky? Cite evidence from the text.
2. **Evidence and Conclusion** How did astronomers first learn about light **pollution**?

# What Causes Light Pollution?

Light pollution is caused by excess light that is **beamed** into the sky. The extra light shines from houses, office buildings, streetlights, and sports fields. It reflects onto low clouds, causing a sky glow that **blots out** the stars.

Bad **light fixtures** cause much of the problem. Most of the **murky** glow in the night sky is **wasted** light, according to David Crawford. He is the director of the International Dark-Sky Association, an organization that is working to stop light pollution. Crawford says that lights should point at the ground, not at the sky.

About one-third of all lighting in the United States is wasted. Wasted light costs billions of dollars per year. It also harms the **environment**.

Electricity comes from power plants. Half of the country's power plants burn coal, which pollutes the air. The power plants **release** sulfur dioxide and carbon dioxide. Sulfur dioxide creates harmful acid rain. Carbon dioxide traps heat near the Earth's surface, causing global warming.

**Key Vocabulary**
**wasted** *adj.*, not needed
**environment** *n.*, the area where plants and animals live and grow
**release** *v.*, to let out

**In Other Words**
**beamed** sent
**blots out** makes it hard to see
**light fixtures** streetlights, spotlights, and other sources of light
**murky** dull

The more electricity people use, the more power plants have to produce. That means more air pollution.

**Science Background**

Sunlight heats Earth's surface. Some heat goes out into space, but most stays close to Earth. Gases, including carbon dioxide, soak up the heat. As more gases are released into the air, they keep more and more heat close to Earth. Earth becomes warmer than usual.

**Look Into the Text**

1. **Cause and Effect** How does **wasted** light cause light **pollution**?
2. **Evaluating Sources** Do you have the same viewpoint as Mr. Crawford? Why or why not? Support your answer with information from the text.

# Animals at Risk

Light pollution also harms wildlife. "Animals depend on patterns of light and dark," says Travis Longcore. He is an **ecologist** with the Urban Wildlands Group. According to Longcore, lighting up the night changes the way animals **behave**.

Light pollution has the worst effect on birds. Many birds **migrate** at night and use the stars like street signs to find their way. Bright lights sometimes confuse birds in flight. Lights from buildings and towers attract the birds. The birds **veer off course**, and sometimes whole **flocks** of birds crash.

▲ Millions of migratory birds crash into buildings each year and die. The birds in this photo were all killed in Toronto, Canada, while migrating one year.

**Key Vocabulary**
**migrate** *v.*, to move from one place to another

**In Other Words**
**ecologist** environmental scientist
**behave** act
**veer off course** fly in the wrong direction
**flocks** groups

In 1954, a flock of birds followed the spotlights at a U.S. Air Force base in Georgia. They flew straight into the ground. About 50,000 birds died.

Hundreds of **bird species** in North America die from light pollution. Some of these species are **endangered**, as Michael Mesure explains. Mesure is president of Canada's Fatal Light Awareness Program. His group helps **protect** migrating birds.

**Key Vocabulary**
**protect** *v.*, to keep safe

**In Other Words**
**bird species** types of birds
**endangered** rare, at risk of dying out

**Look Into the Text**
1. **Explain** How can light **pollution** harm birds that **migrate** at night?
2. **Viewing** How does the photo of the birds illustrate the ideas in the text?

# Turtles in Danger

Light pollution is also bad for other **nocturnal animals**. Female sea turtles come **ashore** at night and lay their eggs in the sand.

Beach hotels want people to enjoy the outdoors at night. They light up the beaches. But turtles do not feel safe on brightly lighted beaches. They will not come to shore to lay their eggs.

Turtles must be allowed to nest each year. There are only seven species of sea turtles, and all of them are endangered. It is important for them to lay eggs.

**Hatchlings** need a dark night sky, too, just as the female turtles do. When baby turtles hatch, they need to crawl to the water. Starlight and moonlight shining on the water pull them toward the sea. Light coming from land leads them the wrong way. As a result, the turtles wander into streets and parking lots and get lost. There, they **risk getting run over** by cars.

▼ Sea turtle hatchlings crawl toward the water.

**In Other Words**

**nocturnal animals** animals that are active at night

**ashore** onto the beach

**Hatchlings** Baby turtles

**risk getting run over** are in danger of being killed

# Taking Back the Night

We need to stop light pollution. It is an easy problem to fix, says Crawford.

Cities need to use lamps that don't waste light. Special streetlights can shine light directly downward. **Individuals** and businesses must use fewer lights. We need to leave many parking lots and office buildings dark at night.

Some states have already passed lighting laws. Hundreds of communities have, too. Miami and other cities have already bought new streetlights. Toronto is trying to **reduce** city lights during bird migration season.

These steps will help, but everyone needs to help stop this problem. "**At the flick of a switch**, this problem could disappear," says Mesure. ❖

## About the Author

**Sharon Guynup**

**Sharon Guynup** (1958– ) is a science writer, editor, and photographer. She especially enjoys writing about nature. Guynup's stories have appeared in many science magazines. She travels all over the world for her assignments.

"Hiking deep in the rainforest or snorkeling along coral reefs gave me a deep love of nature," Guynup says. "Much of my work explores ways we need to protect wildlife—and this beautiful planet we all share."

---

**Key Vocabulary**
**reduce** *v.*, to have fewer of something

**In Other Words**
**Individuals** People
**At the flick of a switch** By turning lights off

**Look Into the Text**

1. **Paraphrase** Use your own words to tell why light **pollution** is bad for turtles.
2. **Interpret** How can lighting laws **reduce** the problem of light **pollution**?

# Preserving the Rural Environment

by Anthony Arrigo

**Snyderville Basin, Utah** – Ten years ago, county officials acted to preserve our view of the beautiful, star-filled night skies.

They set up laws for outdoor lighting. The laws say all outdoor lights must be directed downward. **Flood lights** are not allowed.

Unfortunately, people did not pay much attention to the laws. Now our **basin** is flooded with light.

The county must start **enforcing** the lighting laws.

And since the county created the problem, it should help fix it.

Homeowners who replace their bad lights within a year should pay 50 percent of the cost. The county should pay the rest.

People who wait a year to buy new lights should pay 75 percent. Those who wait for more than two years should pay the whole amount.

We must act now. We must prevent our beautiful area from becoming another **blemish** along the **interstate**.

Snyderville Basin at night

## In Other Words

**Flood lights** Lights that shine up into the sky
**basin** valley
**enforcing** making people follow
**blemish** ugly mark
**interstate** road, highway

## Look Into the Text

1. **Main Idea and Details** What problem in Snyderville Basin is this editorial about?
2. **Author's Claim** What reason does the author give to support his view that the county should fix the problem?

# Connect Reading and Writing

Vocabulary
benefit
environment
migrate
pollution
protect
reduce
released
wasted

## CRITICAL THINKING

1. **SUM IT UP** Use your Argument Chart to trace the author's arguments and evidence. Then work with a partner to summarize the text.

| Argument | Support (Yes/No) | Evidence |
|---|---|---|
| A star-filled sky is an important part of our lives. | | |
| | | |

**Argument Chart**

2. **Analyze** Look again at your Anticipation Guide about the **environment** from page 450. Evaluate your answers. Discuss your thinking with a group.

3. **Synthesize** How is the problem of **wasted** light connected to animals?

4. **Compare** Compare the author's purpose for the two texts. Which text is more persuasive? Explain.

## READING FLUENCY

**Intonation** Read the passage on page 578 to a partner. Assess your fluency.

1. My tone never/sometimes/always matched what I read.

2. What I did best in my reading was _____.

## READING STRATEGY

What strategy helped you understand this selection? Tell a partner about it.

## VOCABULARY REVIEW

**Oral Review** Read the paragraph aloud. Add the vocabulary words.

I found a sick bird. When it got better, I _____ it into the air. That night, I saw a program on TV about light _____. I learned how unused, or _____, light not only harms the _____, but also confuses birds. As birds _____, they use the stars to guide them. Artificial lights can cause them to go the wrong way. I want to help and _____ birds, so I wrote a letter to the mayor. I said that the city should find out if it shines too much light at night. If it does, it should _____ the glow. I explained why this would be a big _____ to the birds in our area.

**Written Review** Imagine that your city passed laws against **wasted** light. What would the sky look like? Write a description. Use four vocabulary words.

## WRITE ABOUT THE GUIDING QUESTION

**Explore the Power of the Stars**
Is lighting up the night sky worth the **benefit** to humans, or is it too harmful to the **environment**? Write a persuasive paragraph to explain what you think. Use examples from the text.

# Connect Across the Curriculum

## Vocabulary Study

## Use Context Clues

**Academic Vocabulary**
- **locate** (lō-kāt) *verb*
  To **locate** something is to find it.

**Jargon** is specialized language used by members of a particular group, such as scientists, musicians, or chefs. The underlined word below has a special meaning. **Locate** context clues to figure it out.

> Most asteroids—small, rocky objects in space—are in the asteroid <u>belt</u> between Mars and Jupiter.

> **belt** (belt) *noun* **1** a strip of material worn around the waist   **2** an area full of a particular thing

**Dictionary Entry**

The context clues *asteroid, Mars,* and *Jupiter* help you determine that the second definition fits the text.

**Define Words** With a partner, look in the text for each word below that is used to talk about electricity. **Locate** clues to determine the correct meaning. Then find the word in a dictionary. Copy the definition that fits the text.

**1.** lines, p. 458   **2.** fixtures, p. 460   **3.** power, p. 460   **4.** plants, p. 460

## Research/Media

## Analyze Media

MEDIA & TECHNOLOGY

**Academic Vocabulary**
- **evaluate** (i-**val**-yu-wāt) *verb*
  To **evaluate** means to judge something's value or worth.

People do not always agree about environmental issues. How do you know what to believe when you hear or see messages in the media?

**❶ Conduct Research** Find out about an environmental issue. Look for articles or ads in magazines or other media, including the Internet.

**❷ Study the Argument** **Evaluate** the article or ad for evidence or facts that can be proved. Also look for clues that make specific claims or express opinions. List important details. What audience do you think the writer wants to persuade?

**❸ Discuss Your Findings** Share the article or ad and your notes. How effective is the article or ad? How well does it work for the audience?

## Persuade

**Role-Play** Work in a group of three. The citizen wants more laws to protect the environment. The business owner does not want more laws. They both try to persuade the mayor. Use prepositional phrases in your role-play.

> Looking at the lake, I saw trash in the water.

# Write About the Night Sky

**Study the Models** When you write about the night sky, make your sentences interesting. Add details to give readers a clearer picture of what you mean, and vary your sentences. Use prepositional phrases to help.

**NOT OK**

> My family went camping last summer. We drove to the mountains. We arrived at night. We were amazed by the sky. We had never seen so many stars! The twinkling stars seemed to wink at us.

The reader thinks: "The sentences are too much the same, and the details are not interesting."

**OK**

> Sitting **outside our tent** one night, we saw an amazing sight. There **above us** was a shooting star! It looked like a ball **of fire with a glowing tail**. The star, dragging a thin stream **of light behind it**, zoomed **through the sky**. Thrilled **by the sight**, I clapped my hands and shouted, "Wow!"

This writer uses **prepositional phrases** to create interesting sentences. The reader thinks: "The details really help me picture the star."

**Revise It** Look back at the NOT OK passage. Work with a partner to revise it. Use prepositional phrases to add details and interest.

**WRITE ON YOUR OWN** Write about something you have seen in the night sky. Use prepositional phrases to help you write interesting sentences.

**REMEMBER**

A prepositional phrase tells more about another word in the sentence.

We saw two meteors shoot **across the night sky**.

You can see more stars **on a night with a crescent moon**.

# John F. Kennedy's Speech on Going to the Moon

## BY JOHN F. KENNEDY

1   If we are to win the battle that is now going on around the world between freedom and **tyranny**, the dramatic achievements in **space** which occurred in recent weeks should have made clear to us all, as did the **Sputnik** in 1957, the impact of this adventure on the minds of men everywhere, who are attempting to make a determination of which road they should take. Since early in my term, our efforts in space have been under review. With the advice of the Vice President, who is Chairman of the National Space Council, we have examined where we are strong and where we are not, where we may succeed and where we may not. Now it is time to take longer strides—time for a great new American **enterprise**—time for this nation to take a clearly leading role in space achievement, which in many ways may hold the key to our future on earth.

2   I believe we possess all the resources and talents necessary. But the facts of the matter are that we have never made the national decisions or **marshaled** the national resources required for such leadership. We have never specified long-range goals on an urgent time schedule, or managed our resources and our time so as to insure their fulfillment.

3   Recognizing the head start obtained by the Soviets with their large rocket engines, which gives them many months of lead time, and recognizing the likelihood that they will exploit this lead for some time to come in still more impressive successes, we nevertheless are required to make new efforts on our own. For while we cannot guarantee that we shall one day be first, we can guarantee that any failure to make this effort will make us last. We take an additional risk by making it in full view of the world, but as shown by the **feat of astronaut Shepard**, this very risk enhances our stature when we are successful. But this is not merely a race. Space is open to us now; and our eagerness to share its meaning is not governed by the efforts of others. We go into space because whatever mankind must undertake, free men must fully share.

**Key Vocabulary**
- **space** *n.*, the area beyond Earth

**In Other Words**
**tyranny** unjust government
**Sputnik** Soviet space satellite
**enterprise** project
**marshaled** arranged properly
**feat of astronaut Shepard** fact that astronaut Alan Shepard was the first American to travel into space

4   I therefore ask the Congress, above and beyond the increases I have earlier requested for space activities, to provide the funds, which are needed to meet the following national goal[s]:

5   First, I believe that this nation should commit itself to achieving the goal, before this decade is out, of landing a man on the moon and returning him safely to the earth. No single space project in this period will be more impressive to mankind, or more important for the long-range exploration of space; and none will be so difficult or expensive to accomplish. We propose to accelerate the development of the appropriate lunar spacecraft. We propose to develop **alternate liquid and solid fuel boosters**, much larger than any now being developed, until certain, which is superior. We propose additional funds for other engine development and for **unmanned explorations**—explorations which are particularly important for one purpose which this nation will never overlook: the survival of the man who first makes this daring flight. But in a very real sense, it will not be one man going to the moon—if we **make this judgment affirmatively**, it will be an entire nation. For

"I believe we should go to the moon."

all of us must work to put him there.

6   It is a most important decision that we make as a nation. But all of you have lived through the last four years and have seen the significance of space and the adventures in space, and no one can predict with certainty what the ultimate meaning will be of mastery of space.

7   I believe we should go to the moon. But I think every citizen of this country as well as the Members of the Congress should consider the matter carefully in making their judgment, to which we have given attention over many weeks and months, because it is a **heavy burden**, and there is no sense in agreeing or desiring that the United States take an affirmative position in outer space, unless we are prepared to do the work and bear the burdens to make it successful. If we are not, we should decide today and this year.

8   New objectives and new money cannot solve these problems. They could in fact, **aggravate them further**—unless every scientist, every engineer, every serviceman, every technician, contractor, and civil servant gives his personal pledge that this nation will move forward, with the full speed of freedom, in the exciting adventure of space.

**In Other Words**

**alternate liquid and solid fuel boosters** other ways to power spacecraft
**unmanned explorations** space exploration without human astronauts

**make this judgment affirmatively** decide to explore space
**heavy burden** important decision
**aggravate them further** make them worse

# Compare Across Texts

## Compare Arguments

The selections "Not-So-Starry Nights," "Preserving the Rural Environment," and "John F. Kennedy's Speech on Going to the Moon" all discuss the power of the stars. Each selection contains arguments and claims that are supported with **facts** or other types of evidence.

## How It Works

**Collect and Organize Ideas** To **compare** arguments across texts, organize information in a chart. List the genre, main argument, and types of support used as evidence.

|  | Not-So-Starry Nights | Preserving the Rural Environment | John F. Kennedy's Speech on Going to the Moon |
|---|---|---|---|
| Genre | persuasive essay | editorial |  |
| Main Argument | We must stop light pollution. |  |  |
| Evidence | facts, examples, photographs |  |  |

Comparison Chart

## Practice Together

**Write a Comparison** Use the information from your chart to **compare** the selections. First, tell how the selections are similar or related. Then explain the unique argument each selection makes and how each author supports that argument. Finally, share whether you think the author makes valid claims.

> All of the selections are persuasive texts. In "Not-So-Starry Nights," the author believes we must stop light pollution. She uses facts, examples, and photographs to support her claims. I think many of her claims are valid.

## Try It!

Review the information in your completed chart. Write a report that **compares** the arguments of all three selections. Use this frame as a guide.

All three selections are _____. The main argument in "_____" is _____.
The author uses _____ as evidence.
I think the claims are _____. I believe the claims in "_____" are best supported.

**Academic Vocabulary**

- **fact** (fakt) *noun*
  A **fact** is a piece of information that is true.
- **compare** (kum-**pair**) *verb*
  When you **compare** two things, you think about how they are alike and different.

# Star Power

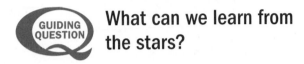

**GUIDING QUESTION**

## What can we learn from the stars?

**Content Library**

**Leveled Library**

 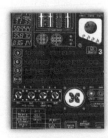 

## Reflect on Your Reading

Think back on your reading of the unit selections. Discuss what you did to understand what you read.

**Focus on Reading** **Analyze Arguments**

In this unit, you learned to analyze arguments. Choose a selection. At the top of a card, complete this sentence: *The author's argument is _____.* Tell about the evidence the author used to support his or her argument. Then explain the author's argument to a partner.

**Focus Strategy** **Make Inferences**

As you read, you learned to make inferences. Explain to a partner how you will use this strategy.

## Explore the

In this unit, you have been thinking about stars. Choose one way to explore the Guiding Question:

- **Discuss** With a group, discuss the Guiding Question. Use what you know from your own life and details from the selections to support your ideas.

- **Draw** Create a visual interpretation of your answer to the Guiding Question. Explain to a partner how your artwork answers the Guiding Question.

- **Write and Share** Write your own star myth. Or research something you would like to know about the stars and write a brief report. Share your story or report with a group. Then post your work in the classroom for others to read.

## Book Talk

Which Unit Library book did you choose? Explain to a partner what it taught you about star power.

# ART
## AND
# SOUL

8

GUIDING
QUESTION
Q

# What do we learn about people from their artful expressions?

**READ MORE!**

◀ In Seattle, Washington, passersby stop to admire a chalk drawing of Boticelli's painting *Venus*.

# Focus on Reading

## Text Features

▶ **In Fiction**
▶ **In Nonfiction**

Writers use text features in fiction and nonfiction to show information in a different way. They **select** the best features to add to their writing to help readers better understand the text. For example, many writers use photos, illustrations, diagrams and charts to show information in a visual way.

## How It Works

Before you read, look at the text features to see how the text is organized. As you read, use the features to help guide you through the text.

**Text Features in Fiction** The **titles** of stories and novels often tell what the story is about. **Paragraphs** separate the ideas in a story into understandable parts. Fiction often has **illustrations**, which help readers visualize the characters and events.

**Text Features in Nonfiction** Like fiction, nonfiction texts have titles and paragraphs. They often have other kinds of text features, too. Look at the **headings** and the **photo** and **caption** in this nonfiction text. Think about how this information adds to your understanding of the topic and text.

### Origami
> The title tells what the text is about.

Origami is the Japanese art of paper folding. It is more than 400 years old. Artist Robert J. Lang has been doing origami since he was six. He is a master of the art.

#### Origami As Art
Lang can create many shapes. He can form flowers, birds, frogs, butterflies, and other creatures. He also makes origami shapes of buildings, including the Empire State Building.

#### Origami As Science
> A heading tells the main idea of a section.

Using math and computers for origami has brought it to a new level. Scientists can use origami to help design medical and safety devices. Lang used it to help design a giant telescope.

**Photos and captions give extra information or help explain the text.**

▲ Lang makes a figure of two dancers from two rectangular sheets of paper.

**Academic Vocabulary**
● **select** (su-**lekt**) *verb*
To **select** something means to choose it.

## Practice Together

Read the following passage aloud. As you read, look for text features that the writer used to organize the text to aid understanding.

### Louis Armstrong

#### Early Days

Louis Armstrong was born in New Orleans in 1901. He showed musical talent early. He was a street performer as a kid. He danced and sang for pennies. Then he got his first horn. He soon became known as a great jazz player.

#### New Jazz

After becoming famous in New Orleans, Armstrong traveled to Chicago to play jazz and then to New York City. Before long, he was playing music around the world. Armstrong was a technical master and a creative genius. No one could match his spirit, but many musicians copied his style.

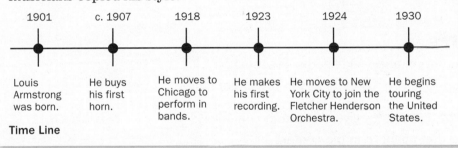

| 1901 | c. 1907 | 1918 | 1923 | 1924 | 1930 |
|------|---------|------|------|------|------|
| Louis Armstrong was born. | He buys his first horn. | He moves to Chicago to perform in bands. | He makes his first recording. | He moves to New York City to join the Fletcher Henderson Orchestra. | He begins touring the United States. |

**Time Line**

## Try It!

Read the following passage aloud. What text features did the writer use? How do they help guide you through the text?

### Public Expression

#### Painting on Walls

*Graffiti* means words or pictures drawn on public buildings. It has been around since paintings were drawn on cave walls. Today, many people see graffiti as a crime. Graffiti artists often work at night to avoid being caught. They write names, messages, or symbols.

▲ Murals decorate buildings in Philadelphia.

#### Murals

When does painting a building become art and not a crime? For many years, Philadelphia had a big graffiti problem. Then the city tried something new—a mural-making program. The program director invited graffiti artists to help paint murals. The program has been very successful.

# Focus on Vocabulary

## Go Beyond the Literal Meaning

Writers choose their words carefully. **Figurative language** consists of words and phrases that have meanings outside of what the words mean by themselves. Figurative language includes idioms, metaphors, and connotative meanings.

An **idiom** is a group of words that, together, **communicate** a different meaning than what the words mean by themselves. For example, *David is **out of shape*** means "David needs to exercise."

A **metaphor** compares two unlike things. Metaphors often say that one thing *is* the other. For example, *Your hand is an **ice cube*** means "Your hand is cold."

A **connotative meaning** is what a word implies or suggests. Similar words **communicate** different meanings. Connotations can emphasize ideas or emotions. For example, using the word *excited* instead of *happy* gives readers a better idea of how a person might feel about an event.

## How the Strategy Works

Use context to understand unknown phrases and figures of speech.

EXAMPLE      Tish can be loud. She often shouts **at the top of her lungs**.

1. Look at sentences nearby. See if they give clues to the meaning.
2. Predict a literal meaning that might fit in the context.
3. Reread the sentence to see if your definition makes sense. If it does not, ask someone to explain the phrase.

Use the strategy to figure out the meaning of each underlined phrase.

> My best friend's father is a <u>talented</u> gardener. People say that he <u>has a green thumb</u>. He certainly can make plants <u>thrive</u>! Every year he enters the garden show. This year, his entry <u>stole the spotlight</u>. It won first prize. It was so amazing!

☑ **REMEMBER** Use context to figure out the meaning of figurative language.

**Strategy in Action**

" The first sentence says that he is a talented gardener. The word *talented* emphasizes how well he gardens. It sounds like *having a green thumb* means 'he is a good gardener.' That meaning makes sense. "

**Academic Vocabulary**
- **communicate** (ku-myū-nu-kāt) *verb*
  When you **communicate**, you share information.

## Practice Together

Read this passage aloud. Look at each underlined word or phrase. Use context to figure out the meaning.

## Develop Your Talent

Everyone has talent of some kind. Some people are talented artists or musicians. Others are good at sports. Skateboarding, for example, might be a <u>piece of cake</u> for those people!

Some people have no talent for sports. Instead, they might be <u>excellent</u> at solving problems. Their talent is to <u>think outside the box</u>!

Once you find your talent, you need to develop it. You have to <u>feed and water it</u> by practicing often. You also should listen to people's advice for how to <u>improve</u>. Sometimes that can be <u>hard to swallow</u>. But when you see the results, you will feel good about your success. Then you can <u>pat yourself on the back</u>!

## Try It!

Read this passage aloud. What is the meaning of each underlined word or phrase? How do you know? How does the author's use of figurative language emphasize the ideas?

## The Cure

Arturo felt <u>down in the dumps.</u> He had no energy. He could not <u>put his finger on it</u>, but he just did not feel right. Then he remembered he had not played music for <u>eons</u>. Music was <u>the best medicine</u>. It always made him feel <u>superior</u>.

▲ Arturo plays a trombone.

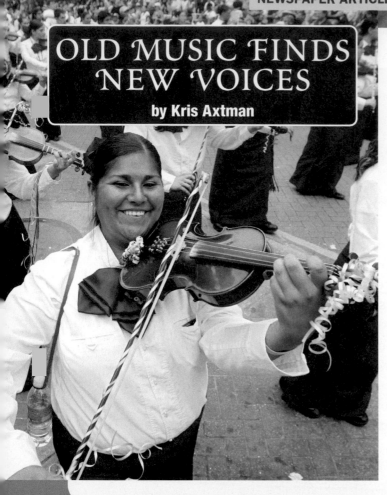

# OLD MUSIC FINDS NEW VOICES

### by Kris Axtman

## SELECTION 1 OVERVIEW

▷ **Build Background**

▷ **Language & Grammar**
Use Appropriate Language
Use Complete Sentences

▷ **Prepare to Read**
Learn Key Vocabulary
Analyze News Media

▷ **Read and Write**
**Introduce the Genre**
Newspaper Article
**Focus on Reading**
Analyze News Media
**Apply the Focus Strategy**
Synthesize
**Critical Thinking**
**Reading Fluency**
Read with Appropriate Phrasing
**Vocabulary Review**
**Write About the Guiding Question**

▷ **Connect Across the Curriculum**
**Vocabulary Study**
Interpret Metaphors
**Listening/Speaking**
Recite Songs
**Language and Grammar**
Use Appropriate Language
**Writing and Grammar**
Write About Music

# Build Background

## Explore the Arts

Artists express their ideas and feelings through their art. They also express their culture. Take a look at some artful expressions from around the world.

## Connect

**Quickwrite** How do you express yourself? Do you write, draw, sing, play an instrument, play a sport? Take three minutes to write your answer. You will refer to it later.

**Digital Library**

**myNGconnect.com**
◐ View the video.

▲ Mexican dancers and musicians perform at a concert in Hawaii.

# Language & Grammar

1 **TRY OUT LANGUAGE**
2 **LEARN GRAMMAR**
3 **APPLY ON YOUR OWN**

## Use Appropriate Language

CD

Listen to three different people talk about the painting.
How are their word choices and expressions different?

**PICTURE PROMPT**

Vahine No Te Tiare (Woman with a Flower), 1891.
Paul Gauguin. Oil on canvas, Ny Carlsberg Glyptotek, Copenhagen, Denmark.

To my left you'll see the portrait *Woman with a Flower* by Paul Gauguin. He painted it in 1891 when he was living in Tahiti.

Look at this painting. It's called *Woman with a Flower* because she's holding a flower in her hand.

Wow! Look at this painting by Paul Gauguin. I love the colors.

Language & Grammar **481**

# Use Complete Sentences

Remember, a complete sentence has two parts: the **subject** and the **predicate** .

EXAMPLE　　**The artist**　**paints brightly tinted images on canvas.**

- A **statement** is a sentence that tells something. In a statement, the subject usually comes before the predicate.

EXAMPLE　　**The name of this celebrated artist**　**is Paul Gauguin.**

- A **simple sentence** is a sentence with one subject and one predicate.

EXAMPLE　　**Many of Gauguin's paintings**　**tell stirring stories of island culture.**

## Practice Together

Say each group of words. Add a subject or a predicate. Say the complete sentence. Then name the subject and the predicate in the sentence.

1. love art.
2. Every weekend in October we
3. The frame around the painting
4. express many feelings.
5. paints pictures of tree-covered mountains.
6. The paintings in most cities' museums
7. is a good artist.
8. My favorite distinguished artist

## Try It!

Read each group of words. Write a subject or a predicate on a card. Hold up the card as you say the complete sentence. Then name the subject and the predicate in the sentence.

9. makes animated clay pots.
10. His studio in Manhattan
11. loves to sing.
12. are in a museum.
13. Those beautiful paintings
14. creates artwork from recycled objects.
15. Her well-trained voice
16. The recital hall near the subway

▲ Sol LeWitt created this colorful sculpture near the park.

# Make a Presentation

## USE APPROPRIATE LANGUAGE

We all express ourselves in different ways. Think about how you express yourself. Do you like to draw or paint? Do you act, sing, or play an instrument? Interview a partner. Start by listing interview questions like these:

| Questions |
|---|
| How do you express yourself? |
| Why do you enjoy . . . ? |
| When did you start . . . ? |
| Where did you learn . . . ? |

Take notes as your partner answers the questions. Then use your notes to prepare a presentation for the class. Before you give your presentation, consider the way you spoke during the interview. Then consider the language you will use when you speak to the class.

## HOW TO USE APPROPRIATE LANGUAGE

**1.** Use words that match the audience and the occasion.
  • Use formal language when you give a presentation. Formal language is proper and polite.
  • Use informal language when you talk with a friend. Informal language uses familiar expressions and ordinary, everyday words.

**2.** Use appropriate facial expressions, body language, tone, and volume.
  • In a formal situation, look serious. Stand up straight. Make eye contact. Speak loudly and clearly enough for the audience to hear you.
  • In an informal situation, you can act more relaxed and less serious. You can speak with more emotion.

> Good afternoon, everyone. Today I would like to tell you about Ahmad.

## USE COMPLETE SENTENCES

When you give your presentation, be sure to use complete sentences. Remember, a complete sentence has a **subject** and a **predicate**.

EXAMPLE     **Ahmad** **writes poems in Arabic**.

# Prepare to Read

## Learn Key Vocabulary

**Study the Words** Use the steps below.

1. Pronounce the word. Say it aloud several times. Spell it.
2. Rate your word knowledge.
3. Study the example. Tell more about the word.
4. Practice it. Make the word your own.

### Key Words

**approve** (u-prüv) *verb*
▶ page 488

To **approve** means to think something is good or right. The teacher **approves** the work I did.

**career** (ku-rear) *noun*
▶ page 489

A **career** is a job someone trains for and does full-time. This man went to veterinary school and now has a **career** working with animals.

**competition**
(kom-pu-**ti**-shun) *noun* ▶ page 489

A **competition** is a contest. The runners are in **competition** to win the race or to improve their time.
*Synonyms:* **game, challenge**

**concert** (kont-surt) *noun*
▶ page 489

A **concert** is an event where people play music for an audience. The orchestra is giving a **concert**.
*Synonyms:* **show, performance**

**instrument** (int-stru-munt)
*noun* ▶ page 491

An **instrument** is something you play to make music. Guitars and violins are both stringed **instruments**.

**preserve** (pri-**zurv**) *verb*
▶ page 490

To **preserve** means to save. The grandmother **preserves** a special tradition by sharing it with her granddaughter.
*Synonym:* **protect**

**roots** (rüts) *noun*
▶ page 488

**Roots** are a person's family traditions and culture. My family is from India. I am so proud of my Indian **roots**.

**support** (su-port) *verb*
▶ page 490

To **support** means to help. People **support** friends and family when they encourage or comfort each other.
*Synonym:* **assist**

**Practice the Words** Make a Vocabulary Example Chart for each Key Word. Then compare your chart with a partner's.

| Word | Definition | Example from My Life |
|---|---|---|
| approve | to think something is good or right | My teacher approved the plans for my project. |

**Vocabulary Example Chart**

# Analyze News Media

**What Is in an Article?** Articles in news publications **report** facts about events. Facts are statements that can be proved as true or false. Dates, places, and data suggest facts. Articles can include opinions, too. Most opinion statements use words like *think, believe,* or *like.*

As you read, think about what topic or issue the reporter wants you to focus your attention on. Analyze the facts and opinions in the article to form an opinion about the topic or issue.

**Reading Strategies**

- Plan
- Monitor
- Make Connections
- Visualize
- Ask Questions
- Determine Importance
- Make Inferences
- **Synthesize** Bring together ideas gained from texts and blend them into a new understanding.

### Look Into the Text

Many Mexican American teens are thinking about careers in mariachi. Schools offer courses in mariachi music, and competitions are spreading across the country as more and more Hispanic teens become interested in their culture.

"I like to tell stories," says Victoria Acosta, who won competitions even before she was a teen. "When I'm singing, it's like I'm telling a story. There are sad songs, and happy songs, and love songs. There are all different kinds of stories to tell."

❝ I can check this statement. I think it's a fact. ❞

## Practice Together

**Begin a Chart** A Fact and Opinion Chart can help you analyze news media. This chart shows a fact from the passage and how the fact contributes to the reader's understanding of the topic. Reread the passage above, and add to the chart.

| What I Read | Fact or Opinion | What It Makes Me Think |
|---|---|---|
| Schools offer courses in mariachi music. | fact | I will learn more about how important mariachi music is. |

**Fact and Opinion Chart**

### Academic Vocabulary

- **report** (ri-**port**) *verb*
  When you **report** on an event, you describe what happened.

## Newspaper Article

Newspaper articles provide facts about recent topics and events. The reporter's purpose is to inform readers.

A newspaper article begins with a **headline**, which tells what the article is about and grabs the reader's interest. A **deck** is a short introduction to the article, which often includes what the author wants the reader to know or learn. A **byline** identifies the writer of the article.

A reporter uses facts and opinions in an article. Analyze these statements to understand what the author wants you to know about the topic or event.

**Look Into the Text**

# Old Music Finds New Voices ← headline

*Mexico's traditional mariachi music is a hit again—with Hispanic youngsters in the United States. It connects them to their roots.* ← deck

by Kris Axtman ← byline

As you read, combine details and your experience to draw conclusions.

# OLD MUSIC FINDS NEW VOICES

## by Kris Axtman

High school group Mariachi Nuevo Santander from Roma, Texas, performs in Atlanta, Georgia.

# Old Music Finds New Voices

*Mexico's traditional mariachi music is **a hit** again — with Hispanic youngsters in the United States. It connects them to their **roots**.*

**by Kris Axtman**
Staff writer of *The Christian Science Monitor*

**San Antonio** - Virginia Stille can't decide on the right shade of lipstick. She doesn't want anything too bright, but the color must be bright enough to show up on stage.

"What about this one, Mom?" she calls.

Mom **approves**, and Virginia puts on the lipstick. Just as she's about to stand up, someone asks her to sing.

Now, that's something Virginia is not **indecisive** about.

She begins slowly: "*Rebozo, Rebozo.*" Then she sings more quickly: "*de Santa María.*"

**Key Vocabulary**

**roots** *n.*, a person's family traditions and culture

**approve** *v.*, to think something is good or right

**In Other Words**

**a hit** popular
**indecisive** unsure
***Rebozo, Rebozo . . . de Santa María*** Shawl, shawl . . . of Santa María (in Spanish)

At thirteen-years-old, Virginia has just won the Mariachi Vargas Extravaganza. She **competed** against hundreds of young people, and now she is preparing for an evening **concert**.

"I hope to keep on singing and one day do it **professionally**," Virginia says. "I want to **make it big**."

While it may be hard to imagine a mariachi singer making a lot of money, mariachi is growing more popular in the United States. Plus, mariachi is **hip** with the youngsters here.

Many Mexican American teens are thinking about **careers** in mariachi. Schools offer courses in mariachi music, and **competitions** are spreading across the country as more and more Hispanic teens become interested in their culture.

"I like to tell stories," says Victoria Acosta, who won competitions even before she was a teen. "When I'm singing, it's like I'm telling a story. There are sad songs, and happy songs, and love songs. There are all different kinds of stories to tell."

Valerie Vargas and her group Mariachi Las Altenas win a competition in Houston, Texas.

**Key Vocabulary**

**concert** *n.*, an event where people play music for an audience

**career** *n.*, a job someone trains for and does full-time

**competition** *n.*, a contest

**In Other Words**

**competed** took part in the contest
**professionally** as my job
**make it big** become famous
**hip** popular at this time

## Look Into the Text

1. **Details** What evidence shows that mariachi is becoming more popular in the US? Give two details from the text.

2. **Explain** What does Victoria Acosta like about mariachi?

When Victoria was just 4 years old, she fell in love with mariachi music. She **begged** her parents for lessons.

A member of the all-female group Mariachi Altenas performs in Little Rock, Arkansas.

Her parents **supported** her. "We need to do our part to **preserve** our culture," says her father, Ruben Acosta. He is a **fifth-generation Mexican American**. "Mariachi music is so beautiful. We want to make sure it doesn't die out."

Spanish is not spoken in many homes like the Acostas'. Both parents only know a little of the language. Their children are learning Spanish for the first time through mariachi music.

Maria Elena Gonzales tells about the song she just sang. "It's about a shepherd who sings to his sheep," she says. "I don't really know Spanish, so I think that's what it's about."

Her family speaks Spanish when they are together. Maria Elena says she never paid attention. "I guess I never really wanted to know what they were saying."

She and her best friend, Lizzette Abreu, began learning mariachi songs just two years ago. "I grew to love it," says Lizzette. She is dressed in white lace-up boots and a white ***traje de charro***. This is a female style of the mariachi suit. "When I sing, I feel like I am in Mexico."

**Key Vocabulary**
**support** *v.*, to help
**preserve** *v.*, to save

**In Other Words**
**begged** asked
**fifth-generation Mexican American**
 person whose great-great grandparents
 came to the U.S. from Mexico
***traje de charro*** cowboy costume
 (in Spanish)

A young musician tunes his *guitarrón* with the help of a friend. This special type of guitar plays low notes. It is used mostly in mariachi music.

Her mother was surprised at Lizzette's interest in mariachi. Lucila Ruiz moved to Houston 37 years ago from Mexico City. "When she used to listen to mariachi music in her room, I told her: '[Turn] it off. We're from here now,'" says Ms. Ruiz. "But I could see she really felt it in her heart, and so I'm proud of her."

When Jorge Perez first started to play mariachi, he says, "I had to learn to like the music." He puts on his felt hat and grabs his **instrument**. "My grandpa used to play the guitar and sing. When he found out I was playing in a mariachi band, it surprised him a lot."

"Don't ask me why, but when I'm playing, I feel a lot closer to my Mexican roots." ❖

**Look Into the Text**

1. **Cause and Effect** According to the text, what are some Mexican-American teens learning as a result of studying mariachi?

2. **Text Features** What additional information does the caption tell you about a *guitarrón*?

# When I Sing/ Cuando Canto

## by Juanita Ulloa

When I sing, I see the sky
    and its color becomes more beautiful.
When I sing, I feel inspired and my soul
    fills with love.

5  When I sing, I fly high and my wings
    are made of light.
I feel inspired when I sing
    with love.
That's why I sing, because
10  it's my passion.

*Cuando canto, veo el cielo*
    *y es mas bello su color.*
*Cuando canto, me emociono y en mi*
    *alma hay solo amor.*

5  *Cuando canto, vuelo alto y mis alas*
    *son de luz.*
*Yo me siento inspirada cuando canto*
    *con amor.*
*Es por eso que canto, porque*
10  *es mi pasión.*

## About the Songwriter

Juanita Ulloa

**Juanita Ulloa** was 8 years old when her family moved to Mexico City. "My dad would take me to hear mariachi bands. I remember those powerful voices and how their musice would just soar."

Juanita Ulloa studied music at Yale University and U.C.--Berkeley. She is now a Professor of Music at Texas State University. She performs worldwide as an Operachi solo singer and songwriter. She solos (or "performs as a soloist") nationwide with top symphonies and mariachi groups. She has eight prize-winning recordings and three songbooks, including five bilingual ones for children.

**In Other Words**
**inspired** like I want to do something important
**my passion** something I really love to do

**Look Into the Text**
1. **Metaphor** What does the singer mean when she says, "I fly high and my wings are made of light"?
2. **Interpret** What is this song about? What message does the singer want to give people?

# Connect Reading and Writing

Vocabulary
approve
career
competition
concert
instrument
preserve
roots
support

## CRITICAL THINKING

1. **SUM IT UP** Compare your Fact and Opinion Chart with a partner's chart. Discuss how the author used facts and opinions in the article. Then use your chart to sum up the selection.

| What I Read | Fact or Opinion | What It Makes Me Think |
|---|---|---|
| Schools offer courses in mariachi music. | fact | I will learn more about how important mariachi music is. |

**Fact and Opinion Chart**

2. **Describe** Use details in the photos and the text to describe what a mariachi performer typically wears during a **competition**.

3. **Generalize** The performers in the selection like to feel close to their **roots**. Do you think this is true for others who perform ethnic music in the United States? Explain.

4. **Compare** How do the mariachi musicians and Juanita Ulloa feel about their music? How can feelings like these help **preserve** mariachi music?

## READING FLUENCY

**Phrasing** Read the passage on page 579 to a partner. Assess your fluency.

1. I did not pause/sometimes paused/ always paused for punctuation.

2. What I did best in my reading was _____.

## READING STRATEGY

What strategy helped you understand this selection? Tell a partner about it.

## VOCABULARY REVIEW

**Oral Review** Read the paragraph aloud. Add the vocabulary words.

There are many ways to keep, or _____, the customs of a culture. One way is to study folk dancing and make it a profession, or _____. Some people have selected Irish step dancing. American square dancing is also popular and has its _____ in step dancing. The fiddle, a fun and lively _____, is used with both forms of dance. My friends _____ of my interest in folk dancing. They will _____ me by coming to my next _____. At my last _____, I got a silver medal!

**Written Review** Imagine that you want a **career** as a mariachi performer. Write a list of goals. Use four vocabulary words.

 **WRITE ABOUT THE** **GUIDING QUESTION**

### Explore Art and Soul

Why is music an important way for people to express themselves? **Support** your ideas with examples from the selection and your own life.

# Connect Across the Curriculum

## Interpret Metaphors

> **Academic Vocabulary**
> - **interpret** (in-**tur**-prut) *verb*
>   To **interpret** means to explain or tell what something means.

A metaphor compares two things that are not really alike. Metaphors often suggest that one thing is another thing or that it has the qualities of something else. The speaker of "When I Sing" compares herself to a bird.

> When I sing, I fly high and my wings are made of light.

Singing makes the speaker feel like she is flying. Her wings are not really made of light. They just feel like they have no substance, or matter.

**Interpret Metaphors** Find each metaphor in the passage below. Explain what two things it compares and how you **interpret** it. Discuss how it helps you understand the text.

> When I play my guitar, my fingers are butterflies. They float on the strings. The music becomes a satin blanket. I sway my head in the sea of music.

## Recite Songs

MUSIC

> **Academic Vocabulary**
> - **select** (su-**lekt**) *verb*
>   To **select** something means to choose it.

**Choose a Song** **Select** a short song or poem that you know well and that you can share. **Select** one that is meaningful to you. Songs or poems that have rhyming words and a strong rhythm, or beat, are easier to memorize. Memorize the poem or song lyrics. Practice reciting it with feeling.

**Share Your Song** Recite your poem or song lyrics to a group. Tell the title and the name of the songwriter or poet. Use good speaking skills.

**Compare** Discuss the poems and songs with your group. How was listening different from reading the poem? Did your opinion of the poem change? Compare the rhythm and rhyme when you heard it and when you read it.

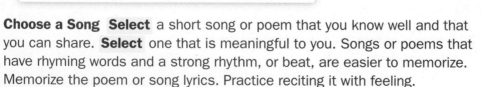

## Use Appropriate Language

**Role-Play** Work with a partner. Imagine you
are one of the singers or musicians in the
selection. Your partner discusses your music
with you as a friend and then as a reporter from a serious
news program. Switch roles. Speak in complete sentences.

> Mr. Perez, what do you like most about mariachi music?

> I feel a connection to Mexico when I play.

## Write About Music

**Study the Models** When you write about music you like, you want to share
your ideas. Be sure to use complete sentences so your readers do not
become confused.

**NOT OK**

> Bluegrass music began in the southern United States. Some
> common bluegrass instruments. Banjo, guitar, and fiddle. A blend of
> English, Irish, Scottish, and African American music. It is sometimes
> called "mountain music." Because early bluegrass musicians wrote
> songs about their life in the mountains and the country.

**The writer confuses the reader by using fragments instead of complete sentences.**

**OK**

> Bluegrass music began in the southern United States. **Some
> common bluegrass instruments** **include the banjo, guitar,
> and fiddle**. **Bluegrass** **is a blend of English, Irish,
> Scottish, and African American music**. It is sometimes called
> "mountain music" because early bluegrass musicians wrote songs
> about their life in the mountains and the country.

**The writer fixes fragments by adding missing subjects and missing verbs in predicates.**

**Revise It** Work with a partner to revise this passage.
Fix the fragments.

> Mariachi is music from Mexico. Very popular now among young
> people. Learning to sing and play the songs. Mexican American
> kids are especially interested in this traditional music. They learn
> the words to the old songs in Spanish. Although many of them
> do not speak Spanish at home.

✏️ **WRITE ON YOUR OWN** What kind of music do you
like? Write a paragraph about it. Make sure every sentence
expresses a complete thought.

**REMEMBER**

To fix a fragment, you can
• add a **subject** or a **predicate**
• combine sentences.

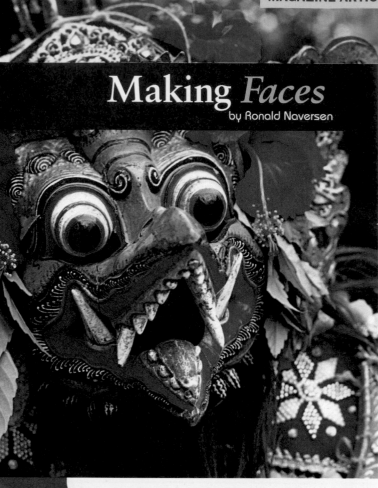

# Making *Faces*
### by Ronald Naversen

## SELECTION 2 OVERVIEW

- ▶ **Build Background**

- ▶ **Language & Grammar**
  - Use Appropriate Language
  - Use Compound Sentences

- ▶ **Prepare to Read**
  - Learn Key Vocabulary
  - Analyze Author's Purpose and Tone

- ▶ **Read and Write**
  - **Introduce the Genre**
  - Magazine Article
  - **Focus on Reading**
  - Analyze Author's Purpose and Tone
  - **Apply the Focus Strategy**
  - Synthesize
  - **Critical Thinking**
  - **Reading Fluency**
  - Read with Intonation

- **Vocabulary Review**
- **Write About the Guiding Question**

- ▶ **Connect Across the Curriculum**
  - **Vocabulary Study**
  - Analyze Idioms
  - **Research/Speaking**
  - Explore Ancient Greek Drama
  - **Language and Grammar**
  - Use Appropriate Language
  - **Writing and Grammar**
  - Write About Your Interests

## Build Background

### Talk About Costumes

Costumes change the way you look and feel. Look at the photos. Make a list of reasons that people wear costumes or masks.

**Digital Library**

**myNGconnect.com**
  ◉ View the images.

◀ A costumed performer gets ready for a festival in Japan.

### Connect

**Class Survey** Find out the most common reasons that people wear masks or special clothing. Survey the class. Use a chart to record the results.

| Did you wear a mask or special clothing . . . ? | Responses | Total |
|---|---|---|
| to perform a play or dance | ‖‖ ∕∕∕ | 8 |
| as a uniform | | |
| to a dress-up party | | |
| for a certain holiday | | |

**Survey Tally**

# Language & Grammar

1 **TRY OUT LANGUAGE**
2 **LEARN GRAMMAR**
3 **APPLY ON YOUR OWN**

## Use Appropriate Language  CD

Listen to the actors. Listen to the people in the audience.
Notice the differences in their word choices and expressions.

**PICTURE PROMPT**

## At the Theater

> Monkey King, you must come with us.

> I will not come, and you cannot force me!

▲ Actors perform the story of the Monkey King, a popular story from China.

> I like their costumes, and their makeup is great!

> I agree!

# Use Compound Sentences

An **independent clause** expresses a complete thought. It can stand alone as a sentence. When you join two independent clauses, you make a **compound sentence**.

The words *and*, *but*, and *or* are **conjunctions**. They join the two clauses. A comma (**,**) comes before the conjunction.

> EXAMPLE   **Leon puts on the green mask** , **and** **I put on the blue one** .

- Use *and* to join similar or related ideas.

  > EXAMPLE   Jorge cuts out the mask, **and** Maya paints it.

- Use *but* to join different or opposite ideas.

  > EXAMPLE   Tessa thinks the mask is scary, **but** I think it looks funny.

- Use *or* to show a choice.

  > EXAMPLE   You can wear the mask, **or** you can hang it on a wall.

## Practice Together

Say each pair of sentences. Combine them with *and*, *but*, or *or* to make a compound sentence. Say the sentence.

1. People wear masks during celebrations. They have parades.
2. Some masks are old. Other masks are new.
3. Do you like traditional masks? Do you prefer new ones?
4. A mask might be made of paper. A mask might be made of wood.
5. Some masks are supposed to scare people. People still enjoy them.

▲ This is a Day of the Dead mask, and it is from Mexico City.

## Try It!

Read each pair of sentences. Combine the pair using *and*, *but*, or *or* to make a compound sentence. Write the conjunction on a card. Then hold up the card as you say the sentence.

6. I might wear a clown mask for the parade. I might wear a tiger mask.
7. My father bought a dancer's mask in Guatemala. He bought a theater mask in Japan.
8. You can buy a carnival mask in Puerto Rico. You can find one on the Internet.
9. We have three African masks on our living room wall. They are all handmade.
10. I like all the masks. My favorite is the long, thin one with the surprised expression.

# Talk About It!

## USE APPROPRIATE LANGUAGE

People who like masks sometimes collect them. What interests you? What do you collect, or what would you like to collect?

With a group, talk about your ideas. Find out what your classmates are interested in, too. Do any of them have collections? Record the information on a chart.

**Class Chart**

| Name | Collects . . . | Wants to collect . . . | Why? |
|------|----------------|------------------------|------|
| Sonja | | coins from around the world | She wants to have one coin from every country. |
| Henry | comic books | | He wants to be an artist. |

As a group, prepare a formal presentation about what you discussed. Choose one person in the group to give the presentation to the class.

## HOW TO USE APPROPRIATE LANGUAGE

1. When you talk to your classmates in a small group, use informal language. Relax and be casual. Speak in a normal tone of voice.
2. When you give a presentation in front of a large group, use formal language. Stand up straight. Look serious. Make eye contact with the audience. Speak loudly and clearly.

> I collect comic books, but I want to collect baseball cards.

> The members of my group have many interests, and those interests are all different.

## USE COMPOUND SENTENCES

Use the **conjunctions** and, but, and or to combine some of the sentences in your presentation. Your talk will sound better and will be more interesting.

**Just OK:** Boris collects postcards. He always buys some when he goes on vacation. He asks other people to send postcards to him.

**Better:** Boris collects postcards. He always buys some when he goes on vacation, **and** he asks other people to send postcards to him.

# Prepare to Read

## Learn Key Vocabulary

**Study the Words** Use the steps below.

1. Pronounce the word. Say it aloud several times. Spell it.
2. Rate your word knowledge.
3. Study the example. Tell more about the word.
4. Practice it. Make the word your own.

### Key Words

**belief** (bu-lēf) *noun*
▶ page 505

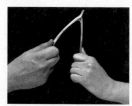

A **belief** is a feeling that something is true or right. One **belief** is that your wish comes true if you break a wishbone and get the bigger part.

**carve** (karv) *verb*
▶ page 505

To **carve** means to cut shapes from a material like stone or wood. The artist uses sharp tools to **carve** this sculpture.
*Synonym:* **cut**

**collect** (ku-lekt) *verb*
▶ page 504

To **collect** means to gather things of interest. This boy **collects** stamps.

**costume** (kos-tüm) *noun*
▶ page 512

A **costume** is a set of clothes that someone wears to look like another person. You can dress up in a **costume** for a special occasion.

**decorate** (de-ku-rāt) *verb*
▶ page 506

To **decorate** means to add things to make something look better. The baker **decorates** the fancy dessert.

**design** (di-zīn) *noun*
▶ page 511

A **design** is a drawing or a pattern. The tiles are placed so they form a colorful **design**.

**mask** (mask) *noun*
▶ page 504

A **mask** is something a person wears to hide his or her face. The girl will wear a **mask** to a dress-up party.

**perform** (pur-form) *verb*
▶ page 508

To **perform** means to dance, sing, act, or play music for an audience. Students **perform** on stage for special events.

**Practice the Words** Work with a partner. Write a question using two Key Words. Answer your partner's question using a different Key Word. Keep going until you have used all of the words twice.

| Questions | Answers |
|---|---|
| Where will you wear the mask that you carved from wood? | I will wear it to perform. |

# Analyze Author's Purpose and Tone

**How Are Purpose and Tone Related?** An author may want to inform, entertain, or persuade readers. The author's **purpose** often determines the **tone**. Tone is the author's attitude toward the topic. The words an author uses help readers determine the tone.

- To entertain readers, the author's tone may be friendly and cheerful. The author may use everyday language, and descriptive words.
- To inform readers, the author's tone may be serious. The author may use words that are specific, accurate, and technical.
- To persuade readers, the author's tone may be strong and forceful. The author may use words like *must* or *should*.

Sometimes an author has more than one purpose. In this case, the writing may have more than one tone.

As you read, **identify** the author's purpose for writing by looking for the words the author uses to create tone.

## Reading Strategies

- Plan
- Monitor
- Make Connections
- Visualize
- Ask Questions
- Determine Importance
- Make Inferences

  **Synthesize** Bring together ideas gained from texts and blend them into a new understanding.

## Look Into the Text

My young neighbor was shocked. It was her first visit to my house, and everywhere she turned, another strange face stared back at her. There were big faces and small faces. Some were bright, and others were plain. At last, she said, "You really have an interesting place here!"

" *Shocked* makes me think the girl looks around with her mouth open. I get a better picture of how the girl feels than if the author used the word *interested*. "

## Practice Together

**Begin a Chart** An Author's Purpose Chart can help you analyze the author's purpose and tone of a text. This chart shows words and phrases the author chose and the tone and purpose that they convey. Reread the passage above, and add to the Author's Purpose Chart.

| Word Choice | Tone | Purpose |
|---|---|---|
| shocked; strange face | friendly | to entertain |

**Author's Purpose Chart**

## Key Vocabulary
- **identify** (ī-den-tu-fī) *verb*
  To **identify** means to find out or to show what something is.

## Magazine Article

Most magazine articles are nonfiction. Many have **headings** to divide the text into readable parts. Articles also use **photos** and **captions** to make the text more interesting and to help readers understand more about the topic.

Magazine articles can be written about an author's experiences, using *I* and *me*. They can be written to entertain or to inform. Match tone and purpose as you read. **Specific language** and **punctuation** are clues to how the author feels about the events.

**Look Into the Text**

My *Collection*  — heading

I collect masks, so my house is filled with them. I have about 150. Masks amaze me with their power. They change how people look and act!

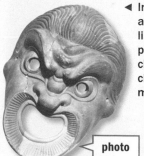

◄ In ancient Greece, actors wore masks like this one. They played different characters by changing their masks. — caption

photo

As you read, bring together different ideas to create generalizations.

# Making *Faces*

## by Ronald Naversen

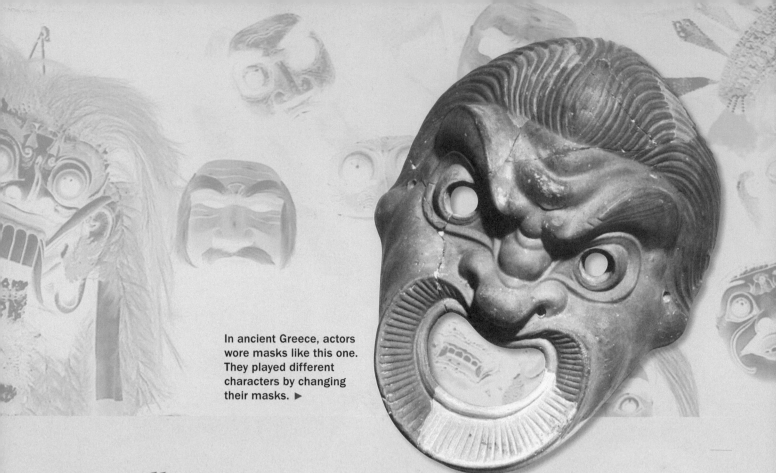

In ancient Greece, actors wore masks like this one. They played different characters by changing their masks. ▶

# My Collection

My young neighbor was shocked. It was her first visit to my house, and everywhere she **turned**, another strange face stared back at her. There were big faces and small faces. Some were bright, and others were plain. At last, she said, "You really have an interesting place here!"

I **collect masks**, so my house is filled with them. I have about 150. Masks amaze me with their power. They change how people look and act!

I take trips to study masks. In Greece, I watched people make masks that were just like masks used **in ancient times**. Back then, actors wore masks in plays. Different masks helped actors play more than one part.

My trip to Romania was great, too. There I saw masks change people into hairy, wild men. To celebrate the start of spring, people put on these masks and then run through the streets.

**Key Vocabulary**
**collect** *v.*, to gather things of interest
**mask** *n.*, something a person wears to hide his or her face

**In Other Words**
**turned** looked
**in ancient times** a long time ago

# Full of *Spirit*

One of my favorite trips was to Bali. It is an island in Indonesia that is famous for its wooden masks. There I learned how to **carve** wooden masks.

Carving masks is hard work. After the masks are carved, artists paint them with many colors. They use 15 to 20 **coats** of paint to get each mask just right. Some artists add hair or jewels.

The masks are used in plays about good and evil. People in Bali believe that the character's **spirit** lives in each mask. Wearing masks helps people act as those characters.

Many cultures have similar **beliefs** about the power of masks.

An actor from Bali wears a mask in a play. The mask helps the actor show the spirit of the character. ▷

**Key Vocabulary**
**carve** *v.*, to cut shapes from a material like stone or wood
**belief** *n.*, a feeling that something is true or right

**In Other Words**
**coats** layers
**spirit** life force

**Look Into the Text**

1. **Author's Point of View** Why does the author think that **masks** have power?
2. **Steps in a Process** How does an artist in Bali make a wooden **mask**? List three steps in order.

# Festival *Faces*

People in Bhutan, a small **nation** in Asia, use masks to tell stories, too. The people there hold festivals to keep evil spirits away and bring good **fortune**.

At the festivals, dancers wear masks that show spirits, **demons**, and other characters. The masks are carved out of wood, and then they are painted and **decorated**.

The audience knows each character by its mask. That helps people follow the stories. These dances tell favorite tales from their religion, known as Buddhism. These stories tell how to lead a good life.

A masked dancer from Bhutan performs a jumping dance. ▶

Festival dancers in Bhutan wear masks that help the audience follow the story. ▶

**Key Vocabulary**
**decorate** *v.*, to add things to make something look better

**In Other Words**
**nation** country
**fortune** luck
**demons** evil creatures, monsters

**Cultural Background**
Buddhism is a religion and a set of beliefs. A Buddhist is someone who follows the ideas of Siddhartha Gautama, a prince and teacher who lived in India and Nepal about 2500 years ago. Buddhism spread through Asia and the rest of the world.

**Look Into the Text**

1. **Details** How do people in Bhutan use **masks** at festivals?

2. **Recall and Interpret** Why does each character have its own **mask**? How does this help the audience?

# Facing *Change*

The Dogon people live in West Africa. They make many different kinds of masks that **differ** from village to village. Some masks are twice as tall as a man. Others look like cloth bags covered with shells. Some have tall, thin wood pieces on top. Some are simple wooden faces.

Masks are especially important for rituals that honor the dead. Dancers **perform** in masks when someone dies. They dance on the roof of the person's house to show respect for the dead person.

The Dogon also wear masks to dance at festivals. Doing so helps keep Dogon traditions alive. That's important to many Dogon, since the world keeps changing, and they don't want their ways to die out.

The Dogon wear masks at festivals. The masks are an important part of their tradition. ▶

**Key Vocabulary**
**perform** *v.*, to dance, sing, act, or play music for an audience

**In Other Words**
**differ** are different

# Wearing the *Wolf*

Masks are not the only way that people make faces. Some people put paint or ink on their faces to change the way they look.

The Northern Arapaho people in Wyoming do that. They wear paint and **headgear** to look like wolves.

The wolf is special to them because the Northern Arapaho see wolves as teachers.

Watching wolves taught them to hunt and showed them how to share food.

Now the Arapaho honor wolves with dances they perform at **gatherings** called powwows. Face paint helps dancers **look the part**.

▼ A Northern Arapaho man wears a wolf headdress and face paint. He is ready for a powwow, or gathering.

**In Other Words**
**headgear** special hats
**gatherings** meetings
**look the part** seem like wolves

## Look Into the Text

1. **Summarize** How does a Dogon dancer show respect for someone who dies?
2. **Viewing** Look at the photo of the Northern Arapaho man. Describe how he has made himself look like a wolf.

▼ Face paint helps the Karo people stand out from neighboring groups.

# Standing *Out*

The Karo are a people from the East African country of Ethiopia who also paint themselves.

They live near a larger group of people. Since both groups speak similar languages, the Karo could easily blend into the larger group and lose their culture.

Instead, they want to **stand out**. To do so, they **smear** white and yellow paint on their faces. Sometimes they add dots and lines. Their face paint says, "Look at me. I am proud to be Karo!"

**In Other Words**
**stand out** be different
**smear** spread, wipe

# Read My *Face*

The Maori are a people in New Zealand. To them, **designs** on a face tell a story. One side of a man's face tells about his father's family, and the other side tells about his mother's family. Women also wear these designs. But they do not have as many as men.

Maori face decorations **are permanent**. Artists cut the designs into the skin. Then they put color into the cuts to make blue-black marks.

The process takes a long time and is very painful, yet the Maori accept the pain because the designs are signs **of belonging to** the group.

▼ The Maori wear permanent designs on their faces. The designs tell about a person's family.

**In Other Words**

**are permanent** do not come off
**of belonging to** that they are a part of

**Look Into the Text**

1. **Compare and Contrast** How are face painting **designs** similar for the Karo and Maori? How are they different?
2. **Analyze** What clues tell you that face **designs** are important to the Maori people?

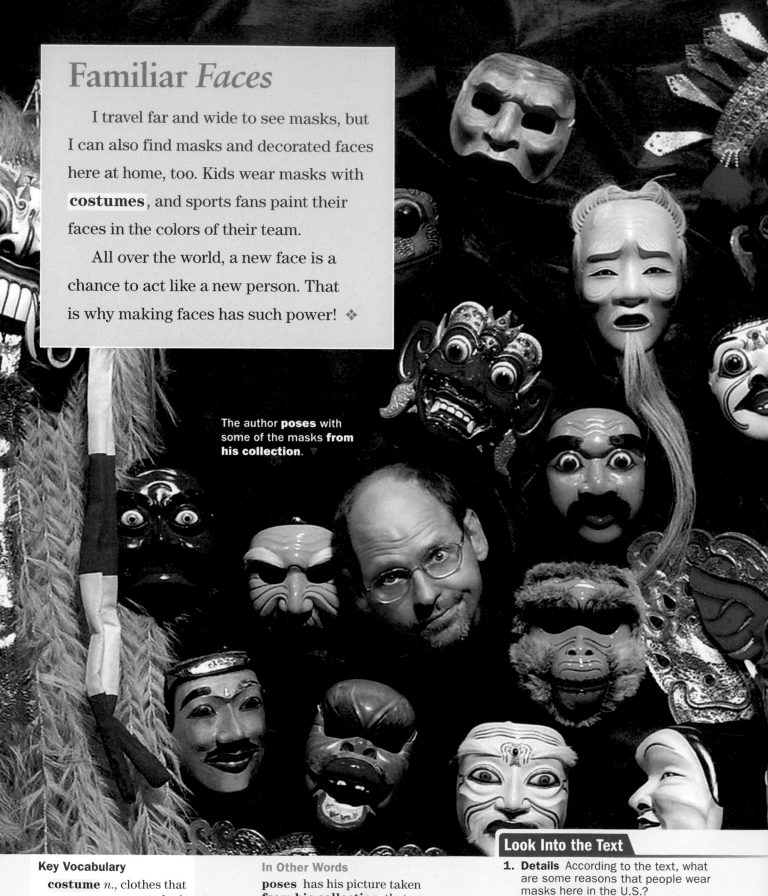

# Familiar *Faces*

I travel far and wide to see masks, but I can also find masks and decorated faces here at home, too. Kids wear masks with **costumes**, and sports fans paint their faces in the colors of their team.

All over the world, a new face is a chance to act like a new person. That is why making faces has such power! ❖

The author **poses** with some of the masks **from his collection**. ▽

**Key Vocabulary**
**costume** *n.*, clothes that someone wears to look like another person

## Look Into the Text

1. **Details** According to the text, what are some reasons that people wear masks here in the U.S.?
2. **Word Choice** What does the author mean by the phrase "a new face" in the first sentence of the last paragraph?

# Connect Reading and Writing

## Vocabulary
beliefs

carve

collect

costumes

decorated

design

masks

perform

## CRITICAL THINKING

**1. SUM IT UP** Discuss your Author's Purpose Chart with a partner. Use your chart to summarize the article.

| Word Choice | Tone | Purpose |
|---|---|---|
| shocked; strange face | friendly | to entertain |

Author's Purpose Chart

**2. Analyze** Why do you think many people make **masks** to express their **beliefs** about important matters like good and evil and death?

**3. Draw Conclusions** The author **collects** **masks** from around the world. What does this activity say about him?

**4. Explain** The Karo and the Maori **decorate** their faces with **designs** for a special reason. What is it?

## READING FLUENCY

**Intonation** Read the passage on page 580 to a partner. Assess your fluency.

**1.** I did not pause/sometimes paused/ always paused for punctuation.

**2.** What I did best in my reading was _____.

## READING STRATEGY

What strategy helped you understand this selection? Tell a partner about it.

## VOCABULARY REVIEW

**Oral Review** Read the paragraph aloud. Add the vocabulary words.

Some Native American groups in the Northwest make _____ to wear on their faces and _____ to wear as special clothing. One dance they _____ is called the Winter Dance. The masks are _____ with different colors. Artists cut, or _____, masks inside of masks. The _____ on the outside is an animal and on the inside is a human. The masks are based on the powerful _____ of the Native Americans. Because the masks are unusual, many people _____ them.

**Written Review** Choose a **belief** you have, such as a belief in friendship or hard work. Draw a **mask** that expresses your belief. Then write a description of the mask. Use five vocabulary words.

## WRITE ABOUT THE GUIDING QUESTION

**Explore Artful Expressions**

What did you learn about the **beliefs** of some mask makers from reading this selection? Include examples from the selection in your response.

# Connect Across the Curriculum

## Analyze Idioms

> **Academic Vocabulary**
> • **communicate** (ku-**myū**-nu-kāt) *verb*
> When you **communicate**, you share
> information.

An **idiom** is a group of words that, together, **communicates** a meaning that
is different from what the words mean by themselves.

> *My brother* makes a face *when he has to come inside to do his homework.*

The context explains that "to make a face" means to change expression.

**Interpret Idioms** Use context clues to determine what each underlined
phrase **communicates** . Then use the idiom to express your own ideas.

**1.** When the author travels, he keeps an eye out for interesting masks.

**2.** He looks for unusual masks that stand out from others.

**3.** It costs him an arm and a leg to buy a rare and valuable mask.

**4.** Once he lost a mask, and he turned his place upside down to find it.

HISTORY

## Explore Ancient Greek Drama

> **Academic Vocabulary**
> • **element** (e-lu-munt) *noun*
> An **element** is a basic part of a whole.

Many ancient Greek plays written 2,500 years ago are still performed today.
Movies and TV use **elements** of ancient Greek drama.

**Research a Topic** Choose a question to find out more about this connection:

• What characters in movies or TV shows are based on characters from
  ancient Greek drama? How are the stories similar and different?

• What was the *chorus* in ancient Greek drama? How is this **element**
  used today?

• What were ancient Greek stages, costumes, and props like? How
  are these **elements** different today? Use the text features in books,
  magazines, and on the Internet to locate information. Find reviews of
  plays, movies, and TV. Watch TV episodes and movies that have
  **elements** of ancient Greek drama to answer the question you chose.

**Plan and Give Your Report** Gather information for an oral report. Include
facts and details that will interest listeners. Find or create visuals, such as
pictures, maps, or charts. Use them as you deliver your report.

## Use Appropriate Language

**Act It Out** With a group, create a short play to present to the class. Use the masks you made on page 513. Present your play, and then discuss it with the audience. Use appropriate language for each occasion. Use some compound sentences.

> We wrote this play "The Sisters," and we hope you enjoy it.

## Write About Your Interests

**Study the Models** When you write about something you enjoy doing, you can make your writing more interesting by using a blend of short and long sentences.

**NOT OK**

> Masks are beautiful, and I love to make them, and I enjoy wearing them. I wear my own masks in parades or at parties, I let other kids wear them, too. My friends love my masks, and sometimes they try to make their own masks, and they ask me what to do. I show them the materials they will need, I explain all the steps to them.

The sentences go on and on. The reader thinks: "I can't understand this."

**OK**

> Masks are beautiful. I love to make them, and I enjoy wearing them. I wear my own masks in parades or at parties, and I let other kids wear them, too. My friends love my masks. Sometimes they try to make their own masks, but they always ask me what to do. I show them the materials they will need, and I explain all the steps to them.

The sentences are different lengths, and the text flows smoothly. There are no run-on sentences.

**Revise It** Work with a partner to revise this passage. Fix run-on sentences or overly long sentences.

> I collect stamps and I have relatives in South America and they send me letters and postcards. They always choose the most interesting stamps, some of the stamps have photos of famous people on them, some show famous buildings. I also belong to a stamp club and we meet once a month and we share our stamp collections with one another.

**REMEMBER**
- A **conjunction** joins the two clauses in a compound sentence.
- Usually, a comma (,) comes before the conjunction:

    I have a hat collection, **and** my brother collects rocks.

✎ **WRITE ON YOUR OWN** Write about something you do that expresses your personality and interests. Include short and long sentences. Watch out for run-on sentences.

# Wings

Written and illustrated by
**Christopher Myers**

## SELECTION 3 OVERVIEW

▶ **Build Background**

▶ **Language & Grammar**
Retell a Story
Use Complex Sentences

▶ **Prepare to Read**
Learn Key Vocabulary
Analyze Plot

▶ **Read and Write**
**Introduce the Genre**
Short Story
**Focus on Reading**
Analyze Plot
**Apply the Focus Strategy**
Synthesize
**Critical Thinking**
**Reading Fluency**
Read with Expression
**Vocabulary Review**
**Write About the Guiding Question**

▶ **Connect Across the Curriculum**
**Vocabulary Study**
Analyze Similes
**Literary Analysis**
Compare Characters
**Language and Grammar**
Retell a Story
**Writing and Grammar**
Write About Myths

# Build Background

## Explore Flying Machines

Look at pictures of early flying machines. How do you think they worked?

**Digital Library**

myNGconnect.com
◉ View the images.

◀ A pilot tries to take off in his glider.

## Connect

**Sort Drawings** What kind of flying machine would you invent? Make a sketch of it. Then, as a group, form categories based on how the inventions look or move. Sort the sketches.

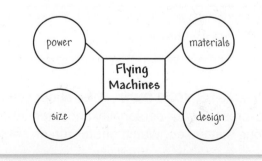

Category Web

# Language & Grammar

**1 TRY OUT LANGUAGE**
**2 LEARN GRAMMAR**
**3 APPLY ON YOUR OWN**

## Retell a Story

Listen to the rap. Listen again and chime in.
Then listen to a story and a retelling of the story.

**RAP and STORY**

## Let Me Tell It!

Let me tell the story
Because I know how it goes.
I'll introduce the setting
And the heroes.
I'll tell all the events
For as far as they extend,
Because I like the story,
Especially the end.

◄ In the story, the girl
dreams she is flying.

1 TRY OUT LANGUAGE
2 LEARN GRAMMAR
3 APPLY ON YOUR OWN

# Use Complex Sentences

- A clause has a **subject** and a **verb**. An **independent clause** can stand alone as a sentence.

  EXAMPLE **The girl** **runs** fast.
  <u>independent clause</u>

- A **dependent clause** also has a **subject** and a **verb**. It cannot stand alone because it begins with a **conjunction**. *After, although, because, before, since, until,* and *when* are conjunctions.

  EXAMPLE **because** **she** **wants** to escape
  <u>dependent clause</u>

- You can use a conjunction to link a dependent clause to an independent clause. The new sentence is complete, and it is called a **complex sentence**.

  EXAMPLE **The girl** **runs** fast **because** **she** **wants** to escape.
  <u>independent clause</u>       <u>dependent clause</u>

- If the dependent clause comes first, use a **comma** after the dependent clause.

  EXAMPLE **Because** **she** **wants** to escape, **the girl** **runs** fast.
  <u>dependent clause</u>       <u>independent clause</u>

## Practice Together

Match each independent clause in column 1 to a dependent clause in column 2. Say the complex sentence.

1. I have wanted to fly
2. I can't fly
3. my father can fly.
4. he felt like a bird.
5. I will learn to hang glide

a. Although he doesn't have wings,
b. when I am old enough.
c. After he took hang gliding lessons,
d. because I don't have wings.
e. since I was a small child.

▲ **When they learn how to hang glide, people can enjoy the feeling of flying.**

## Try It!

Match each independent clause in column 1 to a dependent clause in column 2. Write the complex sentence on a card. Hold up the card as you say the sentence.

6. I flew in an airplane
7. I would like to be a pilot
8. you have to get a lot of training.
9. I have been interested in aviation
10. I may go to flight school.

a. since I was little.
b. because it is an exciting job.
c. when I went to visit my uncle.
d. Before you can fly a plane,
e. Unless I get interested in something else,

# Tell What Happened

## RETELL A STORY

Did you enjoy the rap and the story you listened to on page 517? How would you retell the story? What would you say?

First, think about what happened. Make a time line to help you remember which event happened first, next, and so on.

**Time Line**

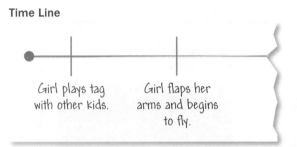

Girl plays tag with other kids.

Girl flaps her arms and begins to fly.

Look at the events on your time line. Think about how you could tell each part in your own words. Practice your version of the story. Be sure to tell the events in the right order.

Now retell the story to a partner. Speak with enthusiasm. Use facial expressions to show emotions and gestures to show action. You may even want to act out parts of the story.

## HOW TO RETELL A STORY

1. Recall the sequence of events.
2. Say the events in your own words. Use words that tell time order.
3. Speak clearly and with expression.
4. Use facial expressions and gestures.

> The girl was running very fast because the boy was chasing her. She started to do this (flaps arms).

## USE COMPLEX SENTENCES

When you retell your story, use **complex sentences** to express some of the actions and events. This will show how events are related. It will also make your story sound smooth.

**Simple Sentences:**   The girl was very surprised.
                        She floated up into the air.

**Complex Sentence:**   The girl was very surprised when she floated up
                        into the air.

# Prepare to Read

## Learn Key Vocabulary

**Study the Words** Use the steps below.

1. Pronounce the word. Say it aloud several times. Spell it.
2. Rate your word knowledge.
3. Study the example. Tell more about the word.
4. Practice it. Make the word your own.

**Rating Scale**

**1** = I have never seen this word before.

**2** = I am not sure of the word's meaning.

**3** = I know this word and can teach the word's meaning to someone else.

### Key Words

**complain** (kum-plān) *verb*
▸ page 524

To **complain** means to say that you are unhappy about something. I **complained** that it was not fair I had to take out the trash by myself.

**drift** (drift) *verb*
▸ page 526

To **drift** means to move along slowly in the air or on water. She **drifts** down the river, carried along by the current.
*Synonym:* **float**

**droop** (drüp) *verb*
▸ page 526

To **droop** means to hang down. The branches of the tree **droop** to the ground.
*Synonyms:* **bend, sink**

**impressed** (im-prest) *verb*
▸ page 526

If you are **impressed**, you are strongly affected by something. The audience is very **impressed** by the musicians.

**proud** (prowd) *adjective*
▸ page 524

If you are **proud**, you are feeling happy about yourself. I felt **proud** when I won the prize.
*Antonym:* **ashamed**

**struggle** (stru-gul) *verb*
▸ page 526

To **struggle** means to try hard. I **struggle** to beat my uncle at arm wrestling.
*Synonyms:* **work, fight**

**useless** (yūs-lus) *adjective*
▸ page 524

If something is **useless**, it is of no use. A broken cell phone is **useless**.
*Antonym:* **useful**

**whisper** (whis-pur) *verb*
▸ page 524

To **whisper** means to speak very quietly. I **whisper** the secret to my friend so no one else can hear.
*Antonym:* **shout**

**Practice the Words** Make a Key Vocabulary Chart for the Key Words. Compare your chart with a partner's.

| Word | Synonyms | Definition | Sentence or Picture |
|------|----------|------------|---------------------|
| complain | protest | to say something is wrong | I complain about getting up at 5 in the morning. |

**Key Vocabulary Chart**

# Analyze Plot

**How Is Writing Sequenced?** The **plot** of a story is the **series** of events or episodes that happen. The story often starts with an **exposition, or introduction.** Often the plot involves a problem to be solved. The events build up to the **climax**, or most intense part. The final events finish the story and resolve the problem.

As you read, identify important events that move a story forward and help you analyze the plot.

### Reading Strategies
- Plan
- Monitor
- Make Connections
- Visualize
- Ask Questions
- Determine Importance
- Make Inferences
- **Synthesize** Bring together ideas gained from texts and blend them into a new understanding.

**Look Into the Text**

# Wings

"Look at that strange boy!"

Everyone from the neighborhood is pointing fingers and watching the sky.

"How's he doing that?"

They stretch their necks and shake their heads.

Ikarus Jackson, a new boy on my block, is flying above the rooftops.

> The author states the exposition, or introduction, to the story.

## Practice Together

**Begin a Plot Diagram** A Plot Diagram can help you analyze plot events and how characters respond in a text. This Plot Diagram shows the exposition introduced by the author.

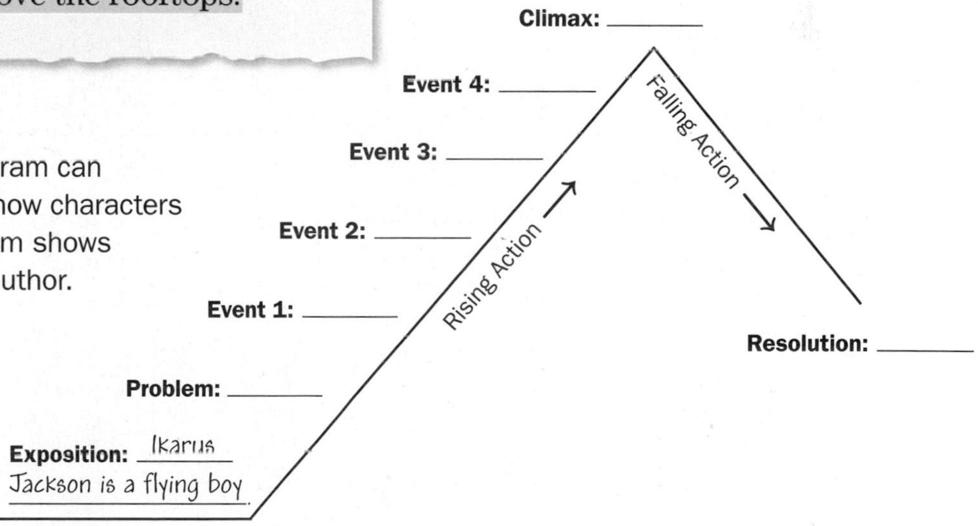

Climax: _____

Event 4: _____

Event 3: _____

Event 2: _____

Event 1: _____

Rising Action

Falling Action

Resolution: _____

Problem: _____

Exposition: _Ikarus Jackson is a flying boy_.

**Plot Diagram**

## Academic Vocabulary

- **series** (**sear**-ēz) *noun*
  A **series** is a group of related things that are put in a certain order.

# Short Story

A short story is brief narrative fiction. It often focuses on one event or a short series of episodes. You learn about the characters through the events of the plot.

Analyzing **plot events** can help you better understand how the story unfolds and how **characters** can change from beginning to end.

**Look Into the Text**

Ikarus Jackson, the fly boy, came to my school last Thursday. His long, strong, proud wings followed wherever he went.

> plot event

The whole school was staring eyes and wagging tongues. They whispered about his wings and his hair and his shoes. Like they whisper about how quiet I am.

Comparing across texts is one way to synthesize. As you read "Wings," write notes. Then do the same for "Icarus and Daedalus." When you've finished reading both selections, note the similarities and differences between plot events.

# Wings

Written and illustrated by
**Christopher Myers**

"Look at that strange boy!"

Everyone from the neighborhood is pointing fingers and watching the sky.

"How's he doing that?"

They stretch their necks and shake their heads.

Ikarus Jackson, a new boy on my block, is flying above the rooftops. He is swooping and diving, looping past people's windows and over the crowd.

I don't think he's strange.

Ikarus Jackson, the fly boy, came to my school last Thursday. His long, strong, **proud** wings followed wherever he went.

The whole school was **staring eyes and wagging tongues**. They **whispered** about his wings and his hair and his shoes. Like they whisper about how quiet I am.

# Look at that strange boy!

Our teacher **complained** that the other kids couldn't help but gawk and stare. He said that Ikarus's wings blocked the blackboard and made it hard for the students to pay attention.

The teacher told Ikarus to leave class until he could **figure out** what to do with his wings. He left the room quietly, dragging his feathers behind him. One boy **snickered**.

At recess the snicker grew into a giggle and spread across the playground. Soon all the kids were laughing at Ikarus Jackson's "**useless**" wings. I thought that if he flew just once everyone would stop laughing. Ikarus looked up, flapped his wings a couple of times, then jumped into the air.

**Key Vocabulary**
**proud** *adj.*, feeling happy about yourself
**whisper** *v.*, to speak very quietly
**complain** *v.*, to say you are unhappy about something
**useless** *adj.*, of no use

**In Other Words**
**staring eyes and wagging tongues** looking at him and talking about him
**figure out** decide
**snickered** laughed

**Look Into the Text**

1. **Narrator's Point of View** Who is telling the story? What clues in the story and the picture help you know?
2. **Problem and Solution** What is Ikarus's problem?

**Predict**
***How will Ikarus react to the way others treat him?***

He swept through the schoolyard like a slow-motion instant replay. But the other kids were not **impressed**. One girl grabbed the basketball. A boy stuffed the handball in his pocket. Somebody nagged, "Nobody likes a **show-off**."

Their words sent Ikarus **drifting** into the sky, away from the glaring eyes and the pointing fingers.

I waited for them to point back at me as I watched Ikarus float farther and farther away.

Walking home from school, I knew how he felt, how lonely he must be. Maybe I should have said something to those mean kids.

*I knew how he felt . . .*

I ran through the streets with my eyes to the sky, searching the clouds for Ikarus.

He **struggled** to stay in the air. His wings **drooped** and his head hung low. He landed heavily on the edge of a building and sat with the pigeons. Pigeons don't **make fun of people**.

A policeman passing by blew his whistle.

"You with the wings, come down from there! **Stay yourself** on the ground. You'll get in trouble. You'll get hurt."

It seemed to me Ikarus was already in trouble and hurt. Could the policeman put him in jail for flying, for being too different?

**Key Vocabulary**
**impressed** *v.*, strongly affected by something
**drift** *v.*, to move along slowly in the air
**struggle** *v.*, to try hard
**droop** *v.*, to hang down

**In Other Words**
**show-off** person who tries to get attention
**make fun of people** cause people to feel hurt
**Stay yourself** Get down

**Look Into the Text**

1. **Character's Viewpoint** How is Ikarus feeling at this point? How can you tell? Cite evidence from the text.

2. **Confirm Prediction** Was your prediction correct? What happened that you did not expect?

*Predict*
**What will happen to Ikarus now?**

When the neighborhood kids saw the policeman yelling at him, they **exploded** with laughter. Ikarus dropped to the ground.

"Stop!" I cried. "Leave him alone." And they did.

I called to Ikarus and he **sailed** closer to me. I told him what someone should have long ago: "Your flying is beautiful."

For the first time, I saw Ikarus smile. At that moment I forgot about the kids who had laughed at him and me. I was just glad that Ikarus had found his wings again.

"Look at that amazing boy!" I called to all the people on the street as I pointed to my new friend Ikarus **swirling** through the sky. ❖

**In Other Words**
**exploded** burst out loudly
**sailed** flew
**swirling** flying in circles

# About the Author

**Christopher Myers**

**Christopher Myers** has been around storytellers his entire life. His grandfather was a great storyteller. His father, Walter Dean Myers, is an award-winning author.

Christopher Myers is a writer and an illustrator. He began by drawing pictures for his father's books. Now he writes and illustrates his own stories. Myers says that he was different growing up. He wants kids to know that it's OK to be different. He says, "The things that make you *you* are the things that you need to be proud of. [They] are the things . . . to be celebrated."

## Look Into the Text

1. **Confirm Prediction** Did you predict what happened to Ikarus? What happened that you did not expect?
2. **Character's Motive** Why does the narrator shout "Look at that amazing boy!"?

# ICARUS AND DAEDALUS
## a Greek myth

When the famous builder, Daedalus, went to Crete, he built an amazing **labyrinth** for the king. It had twists and turns. It had **corridors that coiled** in dizzy circles like the spirals on a seashell.

King Minos hid the Minotaur, a creature with a bull's head and a man's body, in the **maze**.

Every seven years, the king did something horrible. He fed youths from Athens to the Minotaur. A man named Theseus wanted to stop this terrible practice, so he entered the maze and killed the beast. Daedalus had told him how to escape from the maze.

King Minos was angry, and he locked Daedalus and his son, Icarus, in a tower.

From the tower, Icarus watched the seabirds **whirl** over the water every day. One day a thought came to Daedalus. He and Icarus could fly to freedom!

Father and son began to gather feathers

**In Other Words**
**laybrinth** place with twisting passages
**corridors that coiled** hallways that turned
**maze** confusing passages
**whirl** fly quickly in circles

from the birds that landed at their window. When Daedalus had a pile of feathers, he **stitched** them together, and he used candle wax to fasten the ends. Then he attached the wings to **harnesses** that he had cleverly made from his sandals.

Icarus helped his father with his harness. Then he put on his own set of wings. Just before their escape, Daedalus warned his son, "You must not fly too high. The sun will melt the wax."

The two men **soared** out over the sea. Icarus fluttered his wings joyfully. He felt like a leaf playing in the wind. As he flapped higher and higher, he forgot his father's warning.

Suddenly a drop of hot wax trickled down his arm. A feather dropped from one wing. More feathers **wafted** down like snow.

"Fly lower, Icarus!" Daedalus shouted. But it was too late. He watched helplessly

**In Other Words**
**stitched** joined, sewed
**harnesses** straps
**soared** flew smoothly
**wafted** floated

as his son drifted away, out of sight.

Daedalus whirled high and low searching for Icarus. He **skimmed above** the sea, calling his son's name. Soon he spotted **dozens** of feathers floating sadly on the waves.

Daedalus flew to the island of Sicily where he built a **temple** in honor of his beautiful son, Icarus. ❖

## Greek Myths

Myths are stories about events that happened long ago. Many myths tell how things in nature came to be. Others explain why people do things in a certain way.

Some myths tell the adventures of gods or famous people from long ago. Most heroes in myths were brave warriors, but Daedalus was an architect and inventor. No one knows if he was a real person. If he was, he may have built some of the oldest buildings in Greece.

Greek myths are still popular. The stories continue to be told in plays, movies, books, poems, and art.

**In Other Words**
**skimmed above** flew close to
**dozens** a lot
**temple** building to honor a god or hero

**Look Into the Text**

1. **Explain** Tell how Daedalus plans to escape from the tower with his son.
2. **Cause and Effect** Why does Daedalus tell Icarus not to fly too close to the sun? What happens when Icarus forgets this warning?

# Connect Reading and Writing

## Vocabulary
complains
drifts
droop
impressed
proud
struggles
useless
whispers

## CRITICAL THINKING

**1. SUM IT UP** Use your Plot Diagram to show how you analyzed plot events and then to share a summary with a partner.

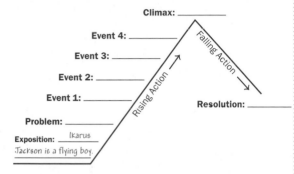

Climax: _____
Event 4: _____
Event 3: _____
Event 2: _____
Event 1: _____
Problem: _____
Exposition: _Ikarus Jackson is a flying boy._
Rising Action
Falling Action
Resolution: _____

Plot Diagram

**2. Infer** "Wings" is about a boy who **struggles** because he is different. What is the author's message? Support your answer with examples.

**3. Paraphrase** Why did Icarus **drift** out of his father's sight? Use your own words to tell what happened.

**4. Speculate** Do you think the teacher, the policeman, and the kids in "Wings" will be **impressed** with Ikarus at the end of the story? Explain.

## READING FLUENCY

**Expression** Read the passage on page 581 to a partner. Assess your fluency.

**1.** My voice never/sometimes/always matched what I read.

**2.** What I did best in my reading was _____.

## READING STRATEGY

What strategy helped you understand this selection? Tell a partner about it.

## VOCABULARY REVIEW

**Oral Review** Read the paragraph aloud. Add the vocabulary words.

Zephyr is a great trapeze artist. He is a _____ member of a circus troupe that performs around the world. Zephyr practices every day. He never _____ about the hard work. He _____ to improve at every practice session. Sometimes when he has trouble doing a new trick, his spirits _____. He _____ quietly to himself, "I can't do this. It's _____!" But everyone else is _____ with Zephyr's talent. He swings, swirls, and _____ through the air like a beautiful bird.

**Written Review** Imagine yourself flying over a city or an ocean. Write a paragraph. Tell what thoughts would come to you as you **drift** through the sky. Use five vocabulary words.

## WRITE ABOUT THE GUIDING QUESTION

### Explore Art and Soul
How does Ikarus Jackson **struggle** to express himself? What artful expression does he make? Use details from "Wings" to explain your answer.

# Connect Across the Curriculum

## Analyze Similes

> **Academic Vocabulary**
> • **compare** (kum-**pair**) *verb*
>   When you **compare** two things, you think
>   about how they are alike and different.

A **simile** is one kind of figurative language. It **compares** two unlike things, usually with the words *like*, *as*, or *than*.

> EXAMPLE    He swept through the schoolyard <u>like a slow-motion instant replay</u>.

This simile **compares** the way Ikarus moves to a sports replay. This helps you imagine how Ikarus moves with slow, repeated movements.

**Interpret Similes** Find similes with a partner. Complete the chart.

| Simile | What It Compares | How They're Alike |
|---|---|---|
| like the spirals on a seashell, p. 530 | | |
| like a leaf playing in the wind, p. 531 | | |
| like snow, p. 531 | | |

**Simile Chart**

## Compare Characters

> **Academic Vocabulary**
> • **interpret** (in-**tur**-prut) *verb*
>   To **interpret** means to explain or tell what
>   something means.

When writers refer to a person, place, or thing that is not described in the text, it is called an **allusion**. Readers have to **interpret** the allusion.

> EXAMPLE    Dillon, a real Superman, finished his homework, walked the dog, and made dinner all before seven o'clock.

The author alludes to Superman to tell about Dillon's character.

**Compare Characters** The name of the main character in "Wings" is an allusion to the myth about Icarus. **Interpret** the allusion:

• How are the two characters, Ikarus and Icarus, alike?
• What does the allusion communicate about the theme?
• How is the theme approached differently in the story and in the myth?
• How does the allusion help you understand the story?

## Retell a Story

**Partner Story Exchange** With a partner, take turns retelling the myth. Speak clearly. Use gestures and facial expressions. Tell events in order. Include some complex sentences.

> Daedalus and Icarus were locked in a tower because Daedalus made the king angry.

## Write About Myths

**Study the Models** When you write a myth, keep your readers interested by using a variety of sentences. Mix short, simple sentences with compound and complex sentences.

**NOT OK**

> Ajit read about Icarus and Daedalus. He wanted to read another myth. He went online. He found a Web site with myths from all over the world. He printed out a story about a flying horse named Pegasus. He loved the story. He wanted to read an illustrated version of it. He hurried to the library. It was still open.

**The writer uses too many short sentences.**

**OK**

> **After** Ajit read about Icarus and Daedalus, he wanted to read another myth. He went online **and** found a Web site with myths from all over the world. He printed out a story about a flying horse named Pegasus. He loved the story, **but** he wanted to read an illustrated version of it. He hurried to the library **since** it was still open.

**The writer uses conjunctions to combine sentences.**

**Revise It** Work with a partner to revise the following passage. Fix fragments. Use conjunctions to combine sentences.

> Mount Olympus is in the sky. It is beautiful. Because the Greek gods live there. One day, a man named Bellerophon tried to ride Pegasus to Mount Olympus. When the mighty god Zeus saw Bellerophon. He became angry. Zeus made an insect sting Pegasus. Bellerophon fell off Pegasus's back.

▲ Pegasus

**REMEMBER**

- Use conjunctions to combine sentences.
- A compound sentence uses the conjunctions **and**, **but**, or **or**.

    Daedalus made wings, **and** he escaped.
- A complex sentence uses conjunctions like **because**, **since**, or **when**.

    Daedalus made wings **because** he wanted to escape.

✎ **WRITE ON YOUR OWN** Think of a myth you have read, or create your own. Write it, using short and long sentences.

# Pas de Trois

by Sandy Asher

"You cannot,"
it's been said,
"separate the dancer
from the dance."

5　Sculptors
step away,
poets
put down their pens;
their work **endures**.

10　Hands
that pluck the strings
of a harp
are neither instrument
nor **celestial song**.

15　But no dance exists
without its dancer.

To my eye, this line
**choreographs**:
glissade,
20　arabesque,
tombé,
pirouette…
Strength, balance,
energy and rhythm
25　draw me in.
A dance is clearly **intended**.

Between us
appears
the dancer.

**In Other Words**

**endures** lives on
**celestial song** song of the heavens
**choreographs** designs a dance
**intended** meant to be

▲ **Critical Viewing**  How is the painting like dance? According to the poem, how is it not like dance?

**Cultural Background**
Ballet is a type of dance that
includes specific positions and
movements.

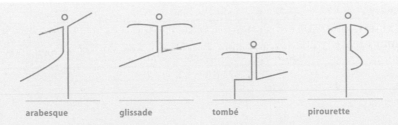

arabesque          glissade          tombé          pirouette

# Compare Across Texts

## Compare Themes

"Old Music Finds New Voices," "Making Faces," "Wings," and "Pas de Trois" tell about how people **communicate** with expressions of art. Compare the themes and topics in these texts.

## How It Works

**Collect and Organize Ideas** Work with a group. Think about the author's messages, or themes, for each selection. Remember that selections often have more than one theme or more than one topic within a theme. Collect your ideas in a chart.

| Old Music Finds New Voices | Making Faces | Wings | Pas de Trois |
|---|---|---|---|
| People express themselves through playing music. | People express themselves through making and wearing masks. | People express themselves with their unique abilities. | People express themselves most uniquely through dancing. |

Comparison Chart

## Practice Together

**Study and Explain** Choose one theme from each selection. Then write a comparison paragraph. First, write a sentence that tells how all the themes are similar or related. Then tell how each is unique, or different from the others. Here is a comparison paragraph for one set of themes.

> "Old Music Finds New Voices," "Making Faces," "Wings," and "Pas de Trois" all tell how people express themselves. In "Old Music Finds New Voices," people tell stories with music. People in "Making Faces" wear masks to act out stories. In "Wings," a boy expresses himself by flying. The poet in "Pas de Trois" thinks dancers are unique artists.

## Try It!

Write a comparison paragraph about another set of themes you collected. You may want to use this frame to help you express your comparison.

One theme of the three selections is _____. In "Old Music Finds New Voices," _____. In "Making Faces," _____. In "Wings," _____. In "Pas de Trois," _____.

**Academic Vocabulary**
- **communicate** (ku-**myū**-nu-kāt) *verb*
  When you **communicate**, you share information.

# ART AND SOUL

**What do we learn about people from their artful expressions?**

---

**Content Library**

---

**Leveled Library**

## Reflect on Your Reading

Think back on your reading of the unit selections. Discuss what you did to understand what you read.

**Focus on Reading**   **Text Features**

In this unit, you studied the text features in a newspaper article, a magazine article, and a short story. List as many features as you can. Then explain to a partner how each feature helped you understand the information in the selections.

**Focus Strategy**   **Synthesize**

As you read, you learned how to synthesize information. Explain to a partner how you will use this strategy in the future.

## Explore the

Throughout this unit, you have been learning about artful expressions. Choose one of these ways to explore the Guiding Question:

- **Discuss** With a group, discuss what you have learned about how people use art to express themselves. Give supporting details from the selections.
- **Share Your Art** Think about an art form that expresses who you are, such as playing an instrument or telling jokes. Describe your art to a group, and show an example of it.
- **Display Art** Show an example of art that you like. Tell how it expresses the artist's culture or personal beliefs and feelings.

## Book Talk

Which Unit Library book did you choose? Explain to a partner what it taught you about expressions of art.

# Resources

## Reading Handbook

# Reading Strategies

## What Are Reading Strategies?

Reading strategies are hints or tips. You can use these tips to help you become a better reader. Reading strategies help you understand what you read. They can be used before, during, and after you read.

### Plan and Monitor

### What is this strategy about?

- previewing and planning
- asking questions and setting a purpose for reading
- making and checking predictions
- checking that you understand what you read

### How do I PLAN?

**Plan** your reading *before* you read. To plan, **preview**, or look at what you will read. Previewing helps you learn what the text is about. After you preview, **think about the text**. What **questions** do you have? Use your questions to **set a purpose for reading**. Your purpose tells you **why** you will read the text.

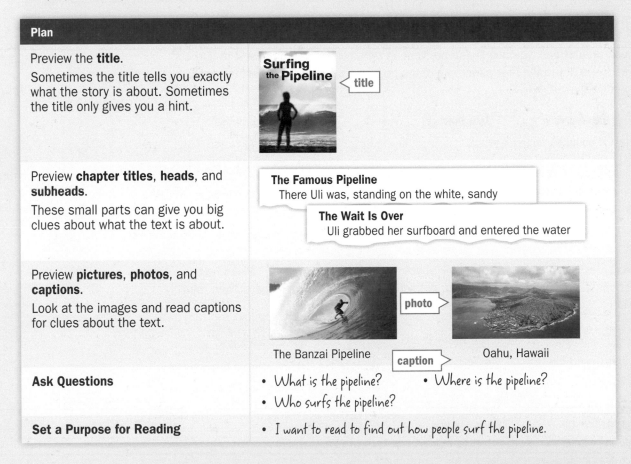

| Plan | |
|---|---|
| Preview the **title**. Sometimes the title tells you exactly what the story is about. Sometimes the title only gives you a hint. | **Surfing the Pipeline** ◁ title |
| Preview **chapter titles**, **heads**, and **subheads**. These small parts can give you big clues about what the text is about. | **The Famous Pipeline** There Uli was, standing on the white, sandy **The Wait Is Over** Uli grabbed her surfboard and entered the water |
| Preview **pictures**, **photos**, and **captions**. Look at the images and read captions for clues about the text. | photo ▷ The Banzai Pipeline   caption ▷   Oahu, Hawaii |
| Ask Questions | • What is the pipeline?   • Where is the pipeline? • Who surfs the pipeline? |
| Set a Purpose for Reading | • I want to read to find out how people surf the pipeline. |

# How do I MAKE PREDICTIONS?

A **prediction** is a careful guess about what will happen in the text. Making predictions about a text will help you understand what you read. To make a prediction:

- **preview** information
- ask **questions**
- think about what you **already know**

| Predict | |
|---|---|
| **Preview Information** | • The word "Surfing" is in the title.<br>• A picture shows Hawaii. |
| **Ask Questions** | • What is this story about?<br>• What is the pipeline? |
| **I Already Know . . .** | • I know many people surf in the ocean.<br>• I've seen a movie about people surfing on big waves. |
| **Make Predictions** | • The text is about surfing.<br>• This pipeline is a place to surf. It is in Hawaii. |

# How do I CHECK PREDICTIONS?

To **check predictions**, you see if your predictions were correct. Read the text to find out what happens. Read the first paragraph of the text. Use a **Prediction Chart** to check your predictions.

| Prediction | Is It Correct? | How Do You Know? |
|---|---|---|
| The text is about surfing. | yes | • title is "Surfing the Pipeline"<br>• The Banzai Pipeline is a famous place to surf. |
| This pipeline is a place to surf. It is in Hawaii. | yes | • Uli stands on the white, sandy shores of Oahu, Hawaii.<br>• The famous Banzai Pipeline is right in front of her. |

After you read the first paragraph, think about the text. What happened? **Make new predictions** about the text. Record your predictions in your prediction chart. Then read the rest of "Surfing the Pipeline" to see if your predictions are correct.

| Prediction | Is It Correct? | How Do You Know? |
|---|---|---|
| Uli wants to surf the Banzai Pipeline. | yes | • She is at the starting point to begin surfing.<br>• She has waited for this day for a long time. |
| Surfing the Banzai Pipeline will be hard for Uli. | Not yet, but I think it will be. | • Uli uses all her energy to swim to the starting point. |

# Surfing the Pipeline

**Prediction:** Uli wants to surf the Banzai Pipeline.

Uli stands on the white, sandy shores of Oahu, Hawaii. The famous Banzai Pipeline is right in front of her. The Banzai Pipeline is a special place. It is one of the most difficult places to surf in the world. It is also a dangerous place to surf. Uli looks out and sees twelve-foot waves. She watches the tall waves crash loudly.

Uli had been waiting for this day for a long time. She is ready.

**Check Prediction:** This part of the text shows my prediction is correct.

**Prediction:** Surfing the Banzai Pipeline will be hard for Uli.

Uli grabs her surfboard and enters the water. The waves are strong. Uli uses all of her energy to swim. She swims to the surfing location. She sees rocks sticking up in the water. Uli finally finds the perfect starting point. She waits anxiously to begin surfing.

**Check:** This part of the text shows my prediction is correct.

The Banzai Pipeline

Oahu, Hawaii

## How do I MONITOR MY READING?

When you **monitor your reading**, you are making sure that you understand what you read. Use these monitoring strategies to help you.

| Strategy | How to Use It |
|---|---|
| Reread | Reread means read again. Reread the text that you don't understand. First, reread it silently. Then reread it aloud. Continue reading until you understand the text better. |
| Use Vocabulary Resources | Find a word that you do not know in a dictionary or thesaurus. You can also ask a classmate what the word means.<br><br>". . . dangerous places to surf . . ." I'm not sure what "surf" means. I'll look in a dictionary.<br><br>Dictionary |
| Read On and Use Context Clues | Find the text that you don't understand. Then keep reading. What does the rest of the text tell you? Are there words or phrases that help you understand?<br><br>". . . looks out and sees twelve-foot waves . . ." Maybe "surf" means riding ocean waves. |
| Change Your Reading Speed | Read slowly when something is confusing or difficult.<br><br>SLOW — Reading Speed — FAST<br>Confusing or Difficult Text — Easier Text |
| Change Your Purpose for Reading | Think of your purpose for reading. Do you have a new reason for reading?<br><br>I wanted to find out how people surf the pipeline. Now I want to read to see if Uli actually surfs it! |

# How Do I Organize Information?

**Graphic organizers** are tools. Use graphic organizers to **record your ideas**. They can also help you **remember information**. Choose an organizer that matches the type of information you need to organize.

## How to Use Graphic Organizers

Before you read, you can use graphic organizers to prepare for better comprehension. For example, use a **KWL Chart** to record your prior knowledge about the topic.

**KWL Chart**

| WHAT I KNOW | WHAT I WANT TO KNOW | WHAT I LEARNED |
|---|---|---|
| | | |

As you read, use a variety of graphic organizers such as diagrams and charts to help keep track of your thinking. Take notes about any ideas or vocabulary that confuse you. Writing down ideas keeps you actively involved in your reading. It also can help clear up any confusion you may have about information in a selection.

Use graphic organizers to capture your thoughts and to help you remember information based on how it was described in the text or based on the text structure. Here are some more examples of graphic organizers:

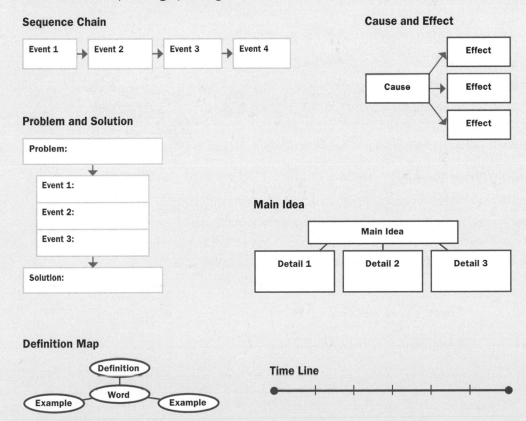

**Sequence Chain**

Event 1 → Event 2 → Event 3 → Event 4

**Cause and Effect**

Cause → Effect
Cause → Effect
Cause → Effect

**Problem and Solution**

Problem:
Event 1:
Event 2:
Event 3:
Solution:

**Main Idea**

Main Idea
Detail 1 | Detail 2 | Detail 3

**Definition Map**

Definition — Word — Example / Example

**Time Line**

## Visualize

## What is this strategy about?

- creating mental images
- using all your senses

## How do I VISUALIZE?

When you **visualize,** you use your imagination to help you understand what you read. You can use the writer's words to create pictures in your mind.

Sensory words help you visualize.

### My Favorite Car Is a Truck

My name is Steven. I've been working hard and saving money all summer. I finally have enough money for a down payment on a new car. My father took me to the dealership to pick out a new car. I found my favorite vehicle. It was a red, shiny truck with gleaming wheels. I climbed inside and looked around. The brown seats were sparkling clean, and the truck still had that new car smell. I put the key in the ignition and turned it on. The quiet hum of the engine made me so happy.

## How to Visualize Using Sketches

- **Before Reading** Look at any illustrations or graphics.
- **Read the Text** Pay attention to descriptive words that help you imagine events, places, and people.
- **Draw the Events** Sketch pictures to show what is happening.

## How to Visualize Using Your Senses

- **Look for Words** Find words that tell how things look, sound, smell, taste, and feel.
- **Add What You Know** As you read, think about your own experiences. Add what you know to the information in the text.
- **Create a Picture in Your Mind** What do you hear, feel, see, smell, and taste?

| | |
|---|---|
| **I smell:** new-car smell | **I hear:** engine humming |
| **I see:** red, shiny truck | **I feel:** texture of the seats, the key |

## Determine Importance

### What is this strategy about?

- finding the most important ideas in the text
- putting the ideas in your own words

### How do I DETERMINE IMPORTANCE?

When you **determine importance**, you find the most important details or ideas in the text. Then you state the main idea in your own words.

Look at the picture below. What is the most important idea in this picture? Use an Idea Web to help you organize information. Write details about the picture in the circles. Then use the details to find the most important idea.

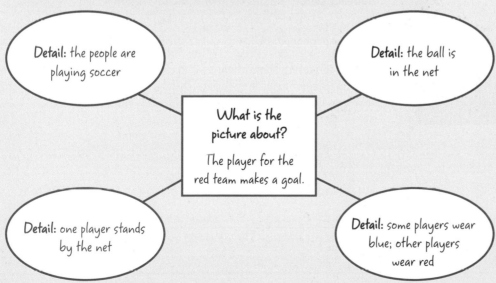

Detail: the people are playing soccer

Detail: the ball is in the net

**What is the picture about?**

The player for the red team makes a goal.

Detail: one player stands by the net

Detail: some players wear blue; other players wear red

## Make Connections

### What is this strategy about?

- thinking about what you know
- thinking about what you have experienced

### How do I MAKE CONNECTIONS?

When you **make connections**, you think about how the text connects to other things. As you read, think about what the text says, what you already know, and how it connects.

Look at the picture below. What connections can you make to **yourself**?

**The picture shows:** A person speaking

**I already know:** Speaking in front of people can be scary.

**I have experienced:** In class, I had to give a speech. I was so nervous!

**Picture-to-self connection:** I was nervous during my speech. But this person is smiling. Maybe I should try to smile more during speeches.

Look at the picture below. What connections can you make to the **picture** above?

**The picture shows:** A person speaking

**I already know:** The speaker in the picture above is smiling.

**I have experienced:** When I smile, I feel less nervous.

**Picture-to-picture connection:** This speaker is not smiling. He does not look happy. But he does not look nervous. Each speaker has a different way of speaking.

What connections can you make to the **world**?

**Picture-to-world connection:** Speaking is important. A lot of people have to speak in their jobs. On TV, I see people running for president speaking. They have to be good speakers to get the votes that they need.

## Make Inferences

### What is this strategy about?

This strategy is about making guesses using

- what you already know
- what you have experienced
- facts and details from the text

### How do I MAKE INFERENCES?

When you **make inferences**, you guess what the text is about. To make guesses, you use what is in the text. You use what you already know. You also use your own experiences.

Look at the picture below. Make inferences about the people in the picture. Use what you know, what you have experienced, and what you see in the picture. What message does the picture below tell you?

| Inferences | | |
|---|---|---|
| I see . . . | I know . . . | So I think . . . |
| a woman, man, and two children | My parents used to take me outside when I was younger. We went to the park. | This is a family playing in the snow park. |
| they are laughing | I laugh a lot when I play with my younger brother. | The family is happy. They would not laugh if they were unhappy. |

### Ask Questions

## What is this strategy about?

- learning new information
- figuring out what is important
- checking that you understand what you read

## How do I ASK QUESTIONS?

**Asking questions** helps you find information that you might have missed. Use **a question word** such as *Who, What, When, Where, Why,* or *How.* Use the **text**, **photographs**, or other **visuals** to answer your questions.

Look at the picture below. Ask questions about the picture. Use question words. Then find the answers. You can find the answers in the picture or using what you already know.

| Question Words | Questions | Answers |
| --- | --- | --- |
| Who | Who is in the picture? | There are many people in the picture. Some people look like children. Some people are adults. |
| What | What is happening in the picture? | The people are laughing. They are eating food. |
| When | When did this take place? | I don't know when the party took place. But there is a cake. The picture might have been taken on someone's birthday. |
| Where | Where are they? | It looks like they are at a party. The party is at someone's house. |
| Why | Why are the people together? | The people are celebrating someone's birthday. |

## Questions to Yourself

Asking **yourself** questions can help you learn new information. Asking questions can also help you understand what is happening in the text. There are many ways that asking questions can help you take control of your reading.

| Ask Yourself Questions to . . . | Example Questions |
|---|---|
| understand something that is confusing. | • What are the people in the story doing?<br>• Why is this detail important?<br>• Who is this person?<br>• How can I figure out what this word means? |
| keep track of what is happening. | • What happened after the character went to school?<br>• Where did this event take place? |
| think about what you know. | • Do I agree with what the text is saying?<br>• Have I ever experienced something like this before?<br>• What do I already know about this topic? |

## Questions to the Author

Sometimes, you may have questions about what the **author** is trying to tell you in a text. Ask questions, and then try to answer them by reading the text.

| Ask the Author Questions to . . . | Example Questions |
|---|---|
| understand what the author is trying to tell you. | • What is the author trying to say in this part of the text?<br>• Does the author explain his or her ideas clearly?<br>• What is the author talking about?<br>• Can I find facts that support the author's ideas? |

Asking questions is a good way to make sure you're actively thinking—before, during, and after reading.

## Synthesize

### What is this strategy about?

- finding the most important ideas
- putting the ideas in your own words
- combining what you have just learned with what you already know and responding

### How do I SYNTHESIZE?

Reading is like putting a puzzle together. There are many different parts that come together to make up the whole selection. When you **synthesize**, you put the pieces together as you read. You draw conclusions, make generalizations, and compare. You combine new information with what you already know to create an original idea or form new understandings.

Look at the picture below. Use what you see and what you know to draw conclusions. What new idea or understanding do you have?

| Drawing Conclusions | | |
|---|---|---|
| I see . . . | I know . . . | So I think . . . |
| a bird eating a piece of a plastic bag | Ocean animals can be hurt by trash left on the beach. | By keeping our beaches clean, we can protect ocean animals. |

Read this passage and the text that follows to help you understand how to make generalizations about what you read.

## Sea Turtle Hatchlings

Sea turtles are beautiful ocean animals that are endangered. Sea turtle hatchlings have a long journey from the nest to the water. When sea turtle hatchlings come out from eggs they try to quickly make their way to the water's edge. They must escape dangers such as birds, dogs, beach vehicles, and people. Scientists estimate that only one in 1,000 hatchlings will survive to become an adult sea turtle.

| Make Generalizations | |
|---|---|
| **Look for the message of the selection.** | Sea turtles are endangered. |
| **Think About What You Know** | I know people and groups work to help sea turtles in trouble. |
| **Make a generalization** | By helping sea turtle hatchlings get safely in the water, there will be a better chance of survival. |

## How to Compare Texts

Comparing two or more texts helps you combine ideas, draw conclusions, and synthesize. When you compare texts you figure out how texts are the same and how they are different. Read the chart below to help you understand how to compare texts.

| Compare Texts |
|---|
| **Think about something you have already read.** |
| **Think about what you are reading right now.** |
| **Compare how the texts are the same and how they are different.** |

# Reading Fluency

## What Is Reading Fluency?

Reading fluency is the ability to read smoothly and expressively with clear understanding. Fluent readers are able to better understand and enjoy what they read. Use the strategies that follow to build your fluency in these four key areas:

- accuracy and rate
- phrasing
- intonation
- expression

## How to Improve Accuracy and Rate

Accuracy is the correctness of your reading. Rate is the speed of your reading.

How to read accurately:

- Use correct pronunciation.
- Emphasize correct syllables.
- Recognize most words.

How to read with proper rate:

- Match your reading speed to what you are reading. For example, if you are reading an exciting story, read slightly faster. If you are reading a sad story, read slightly slower.
- Recognize and use punctuation.

Test your accuracy and rate:

- Choose a text you are familiar with, and practice reading it aloud or silently multiple times.
- Keep a dictionary with you while you read, and look up words you do not recognize.
- Use a watch or clock to time yourself while you read a passage.
- Ask a friend or family member to read a passage for you, so you know what it should sound like.

Use the formula below to measure a reader's accuracy and rate while reading aloud. For passages to practice with, see **Reading Fluency Practice**, pp. 558–581.

| Accuracy and Rate Formula | | |
|---|---|---|
| _____ | − _____ | = _____ |
| words attempted in one minute | number of errors | words correct per minute (wcpm) |

# How to Improve Intonation

Intonation is the rise and fall in the pitch or tone of your voice as you read aloud. Pitch and tone both mean the highness or lowness of the sound.

How to read with proper intonation:

- Change the sound of your voice to match what you are reading.
- Make your voice flow, or sound smooth while you read.
- Make sure you are pronouncing words correctly.
- Raise the sound of your voice for words that should be stressed, or emphasized.
- Use proper rhythm and meter.
- Use visual clues. (see box below)

| Visual Clue and Meaning | Example | How to Read It |
|---|---|---|
| **Italics:** draw attention to a word to show special importance | She is *smart*. | Emphasize "smart." |
| **Dash:** shows a quick break in a sentence | She is—smart. | Pause before saying "smart." |
| **Exclamation:** can represent energy, excitement, or anger | She is smart! | Make your voice louder at the end of the sentence. |
| **All capital letters:** can represent strong emphasis, or yelling | SHE IS SMART. | Emphasize the whole sentence. |
| **Bold facing:** draws attention to a word to show importance | She is **smart**. | Emphasize "smart." |
| **Question mark:** shows curiosity or confusion | She is smart? | Raise the pitch of your voice slightly at the end of the sentence. |

Use the rubric below to measure how well a reader uses intonation while reading aloud. For intonation passages, see **Reading Fluency Practice**, pp. 558–581.

| Intonation Rubric | | |
|---|---|---|
| **1** | **2** | **3** |
| The reader's tone does not change. The reading all sounds the same. | The reader's tone changes sometimes to match what is being read. | The reader's tone always changes to match what is being read. |

# How to Improve Phrasing

Phrasing is how you use your voice to group words together.

How to read with proper phrasing:

- Use correct rhythm and meter by not reading too fast or too slow.
- Pause for key words within the text.
- Make sure your sentences have proper flow and meter, so they sound smooth instead of choppy.
- Make sure you sound like you are reading a sentence instead of a list.
- Use punctuation to tell you when to stop, pause, or emphasize. (see box below)

| Punctuation | How to Use It |
|---|---|
| . period | stop at the end of the sentence |
| , comma | pause within the sentence |
| ! exclamation point | emphasize the sentence and pause at the end |
| ? question mark | emphasize the end of the sentence and pause at the end |
| ; semicolon | pause within the sentence between two related thoughts |
| : colon | pause within the sentence before giving an example or explanation |

One way to practice phrasing is to copy a passage, then place a slash (/), or pause mark, within a sentence where there should be a pause. One slash (/) means a short pause. Two slashes (//) mean a longer pause, such as a pause at the end of a sentence.

Read aloud the passage below, pausing at each pause mark. Then try reading the passage again without any pauses. Compare how you sound each time.

There are many ways / to get involved in your school / and community. // Joining a club / or trying out for a sports team / are a few of the options. // Volunteer work can also be very rewarding. // You can volunteer at community centers, / nursing homes, / or animal shelters. //

Use the rubric below to measure how well a reader uses phrasing while reading aloud. For phrasing passages, see **Reading Fluency Practice**, pp. 558–581.

| Phrasing Rubric | | |
|---|---|---|
| **1** | **2** | **3** |
| Reading is choppy. There are usually no pauses for punctuation. | Reading is mostly smooth. There are some pauses for punctuation. | Reading is very smooth. Punctuation is being used properly. |

# How to Improve Expression

Expression in reading is how you use your voice to express feeling.

How to read with proper expression:

- Match the sound of your voice to what you are reading. For example, read louder and faster to show strong feeling. Read slower and quieter to show sadness or seriousness.
- Match the sound of your voice to the genre. For example, read a fun, fictional story using a fun, friendly voice. Read an informative, nonfiction article using an even tone and a more serious voice.
- Avoid speaking in monotone, which is using only one tone in your voice.
- Pause for emphasis and exaggerate letter sounds to match the mood or theme of what you are reading.

Practice incorrect expression by reading this sentence without changing the tone of your voice: *I am so excited!*

Now read the sentence again with proper expression: *I am so excited!* The way you use your voice while reading can help you to better understand what is happening in the text.

For additional practice, read the sentences below aloud with and without changing your expression. Compare how you sound each time.

- I am very sad.
- That was the most *boring* movie I have ever seen.
- We won the game!

Use the rubric below to measure how well a reader uses expression while reading aloud. For expression passages, see **Reading Fluency Practice**, pp. 558–581.

**Expression Rubric**

| 1 | 2 | 3 |
|---|---|---|
| The reader sounds monotone. The reader's voice does not match the subject of what is being read. | The reader is making some tone changes. Sometimes, the reader's voice matches what is being read. | The reader is using proper tones and pauses. The reader's voice matches what is being read. |

## Practice Intonation: "Growing Together"

Intonation is the rise and fall in the pitch or tone of your voice as you read aloud. Use this passage to practice reading with proper intonation. Print a copy of this passage from **myNGconnect.com** to help you monitor your progress.

He stands up as I run to him. I cry angry tears.

A moment like this comes for every immigrant child.

It is hard to leave a home you know. It is even harder to make another place home. Everything is new. Everything is strange. Everything is different.

I tell Papi how I feel.

"I hate it here! I am not like them, and they are not like me!" I say to him.

Papi pulls out a handkerchief and hands it to me.

My father, the gardener, looks at me intently for a few moments. Then he asks, "Carmita, do you remember our mango tree in Cuba?"

"Yes," I sniff. I am curious now.

"Do you know what it means to graft a tree?"

I nod. "You take a branch from one tree and attach it to another tree. The branch and the tree grow together. Right?"

"*Sí*, that is right," Papi says.

My father tells me that I am like a branch from that Cuban mango tree. He says Georgia is like the magnolia tree. I must wait. Eventually, the mango and magnolia will grow together.

From "Growing Together," page 16

## Practice Expression: "Kids Like Me"

Expression in reading is how you use your voice to express feeling. Use this passage to practice reading with proper expression. Print a copy of this passage from myNGconnect.com to help you monitor your progress.

**Q: What advice do you have for people who move to the United States?**

**Eunji:** Ask many questions. That way, you learn about the person you are talking to. You can also learn about American culture.

**Hewan:** Quickly make friends in order to learn the language and culture. With their help, it is easier to settle into a new country. Friends can also make it easier to adjust to the different customs and ideas.

**Liban:** Be yourself. That is the main thing. Do not put yourself down. Do not let anybody put you down. Work hard. Talk to people. Ask for help if you need it. Say what you want to say (other than bad words).

**Adib:** Play sports to meet new people. Make an effort to be social and talk with people in your classes. This is hard at first.

**Anne Rose:** Get involved in everything you can. The more things you get into, the more opportunities you have to learn, understand, and appreciate life.

**Manuel:** I have one piece of advice. Don't be lazy!

From "Kids Like Me," page 32

## Practice Phrasing: "Familiar Places"

Phrasing is how you use your voice to group words together. Use this passage to practice reading with proper phrasing. Print a copy of this passage from myNGconnect.com to help you monitor your progress.

Familiar sounds can make a new place feel like home.

When a language is new to you, the words can look so different. Sometimes it is nice to see your native language.

Korean people who move to Koreatown agree. In Koreatown, you can find words in English and Korean. Read the *hangul* signs. Buy a book in Korean. Find a Korean newspaper.

Familiar words can make a new place feel like home.

Everyone likes to celebrate! There are always many reasons to have fun. Some celebrations are more familiar, though.

Every September, the people of Little Italy hold a festival. Look at the decorations and watch the parade. Then eat *cannoli* while you dance and sing Italian songs.

Familiar celebrations can make a new place feel like home.

Familiar foods, sounds, and celebrations can make you feel at home in a new neighborhood. As new people move in, the neighborhood will continue to change and become their home, too.

From "Familiar Places," page 48

## Practice Expression: "The Secret Water"

Expression in reading is how you use your voice to express feeling. Use this passage to practice reading with proper expression. Print a copy of this passage from myNGconnect.com to help you monitor your progress.

Then the Voice of the Mountain shouts, "Shu Fa, you told my secret! Now you must live in my river forever."

Shu Fa cries. She begs the Voice to let her say goodbye to her family. The Voice grumbles, "Go, but you must return here tonight."

Shu Fa runs back to the village. "What can I do?" she asks herself. "I do not want to live in the river!" She decides to tell Uncle about the problem.

Uncle thinks for a few minutes. Then he says, "I have a plan."

Uncle works all day to carve a statue out of stone. The statue looks just like Shu Fa. He thinks the statue will trick the Voice of the Mountain.

"I just need one thing," Uncle tells Shu Fa. He cuts Shu Fa's long, white hair and attaches it to the statue. Then he places the statue in the river. Water flows over the statue. It carries the white hair over the mountain like a waterfall.

The Voice of the Mountain sees the statue. It says, "Hello, Shu Fa!"

The trick worked!

From "The Secret Water," page 76

## Practice Phrasing: "How Do We Use Water?"

Phrasing is how you use your voice to group words together. Use this passage to practice reading with proper phrasing. Print a copy of this passage from **myNGconnect.com** to help you monitor your progress.

An incredible amount of water covers Earth. Look at a globe. The blue area represents the water. There are about 200 billion liters (53 billion gallons) of water for each person on Earth!

There is not always enough water to drink, however.

Most of Earth's water is salty ocean water. Salt water is fine for sea creatures. But it is not fine for humans and most other animals.

Only 3 percent of Earth's water is fresh water. Fresh water is an important resource that we need every day.

We need to drink fresh water to live. All day, we lose water from our bodies. We lose it when we sweat and when we get rid of waste. We drink water to replace the water we lose.

From "How Do We Use Water?," page 92

## Practice Intonation: "Water at Work"

Intonation is the rise and fall in the pitch or tone of your voice as you read aloud. Use this passage to practice reading with proper intonation. Print a copy of this passage from <u>myNGconnect.com</u> to help you monitor your progress.

At 5 a.m. it is still dark outside. But Kevin Aiken has been awake for an hour. Kevin is a farmer. He grows cherries near Wenatchee, Washington. In the orchard, Kevin stops at an irrigation pipe. He turns a big wheel on the pipe. Water spouts from sprinklers under the cherry trees.

This area does not have enough rainfall to grow fruit trees. Instead, Kevin uses water from the Columbia River to water the trees. Pumps move the river water to the cherry trees.

Farther down the Columbia River is the city of Pasco, Washington. Roberto López plays basketball at his school there. Roberto stops for a drink of water. The water in the water fountain comes from the Columbia River.

Before the water reaches Roberto's school, though, it has to be cleaned. People cannot safely drink water directly from rivers. The water is treated at a water treatment plant first.

From "Water at Work," page 108

## Practice Phrasing: "Volcano!"

Phrasing is how you use your voice to group words together. Use this passage to practice reading with proper phrasing. Print a copy of this passage from MyNGconnect.com to help you monitor your progress.

About 1,500 of Earth's volcanoes are active. An active volcano is one that can erupt lava.

Some volcanoes make runny lava. The lava flows fast, like pancake batter. It piles up in thin layers. Over time, it forms low, wide mountains.

Other volcanoes erupt thick lava. It flows slowly, like toothpaste. It piles up in thick layers. Over time, it forms tall, steep mountains.

Volcanoes are found all over Earth. Some form on land. Others rise up from the bottom of the ocean.

Most volcanoes are near the Pacific Ocean. They form a circle of volcanoes known as the Ring of Fire.

These volcanoes are found in areas where big pieces of Earth's surface, or plates, meet. Many volcanoes are formed along such plate boundaries.

From "Volcano!," page 134

## Practice Expression: "Fleeing Katrina"

Expression in reading is how you use your voice to express feeling. Use this passage to practice reading with proper expression. Print a copy of this passage from myNGconnect.com to help you monitor your progress.

I went home. But it wasn't home. Home isn't really there anymore.

Mud was caked everywhere on the ground. Things were brown and gray, not green as they used to be. It was like I stepped into some other reality. This wasn't the St. Bernard I remembered.

We turned into my neighborhood, and it was strange. Usually, I see green grass, green bushes, green shrubs, and trees. Now, the salt water had killed all of those things. It was brown now, an old, dry brown.

Dad stopped the truck in the middle of the street, and we spilled out.

When mom walked onto the porch and looked through the front room door, I knew she wasn't expecting what she saw. And the smell was horrible. Mold and rotten food and mud scents mixing together.

From "Fleeing Katrina," page 152

## Practice Intonation: "Earthquake"

Intonation is the rise and fall in the pitch or tone of your voice as you read aloud. Use this passage to practice reading with proper intonation. Print a copy of this passage from **myNGconnect.com** to help you monitor your progress.

In the early dawn, confused and frightened, we gathered at Portsmouth Square. All of Chinatown must have been there.

"You must go to Golden Gate Park!" shouted the policeman.

"The city is on fire. Go quickly now!"

Dark smoke hurt our eyes. Gritty dust filled the air, our mouths and noses, too.

The earth shook again. We stopped, and watched in fear as buildings crumbled around us.

Elder Brother, Younger Brother, and I cleared a path for the cart carrying MaMa and PoPo and our belongings.

We were hot and thirsty until we shed the extra clothing and drank some cold tea.

In the early-morning rush to leave, we had not eaten anything.

PoPo gave us crackers and dried fruit.

Up the steep hills, across the city, we pushed and pulled the heavy cart.

From "Earthquake," page 172

## Practice Expression: "Frankenstein"

Expression in reading is how you use your voice to express feeling. Use this passage to practice reading with proper expression. Print a copy of this passage from **myNGconnect.com** to help you monitor your progress.

My name is Victor Frankenstein. I created an evil monster. The terrible things that the creature has done are all because of me. No one else must ever know how to do what I have done—I will take that secret with me to my grave.

After many years of study, I had discovered how to bring something to life. I was eager to use what I had learned, so I devoted two years to making a new creature out of bones and body parts from graveyards and slaughterhouses.

At last, my experiment was ready. An enormous, lifeless creature lay on the table in my lab. I thought my creation would show the world what a great scientist I was. I did not know how wrong I was!

From "Frankenstein," page 206

## Practice Phrasing: "Film Fright"

Phrasing is how you use your voice to group words together. Use this passage to practice reading with proper phrasing. Print a copy of this passage from myNGconnect.com to help you monitor your progress.

The first motion pictures were made in the 1890s. They were usually very short and simple. Some were only thirty seconds long! People were fascinated with moving images.

In 1910, Thomas Edison made the movie *Frankenstein*. It was only sixteen minutes. It terrified moviegoers, though. In the 1920s, a horror movie revolution began. People made numerous silent horror films.

Movie studios made many popular monster movies from 1920 to 1950. In 1931, Universal Studios released *Dracula* and *Frankenstein*. These films were two of the most successful horror movies of the time. The studios also made movies about other characters. These characters included the Wolf Man, the Invisible Man, and the Creature from the Black Lagoon.

From "Film Fright," page 226

## Practice Intonation: "Mister Monster"

Intonation is the rise and fall in the pitch or tone of your voice as you read aloud. Use this passage to practice reading with proper intonation. Print a copy of this passage from **myNGconnect.com** to help you monitor your progress.

**DR. FRANKENSTEIN.** [*speaking angrily to* MS. ROSARIO] My name is Dr. Victor Frankenstein. You stole my creation!

**MS. ROSARIO.** [*surprised*] Your what?

**DR. FRANKENSTEIN.** My creation! I put him together from a hundred dead bodies! I created him. I did not give you permission to use him in your commercial.

[YGOR *enters the office, pulling on the rope.* THE MONSTER *is offstage, at the other end of the rope.*]

**DR. FRANKENSTEIN.** [*pointing at* YGOR] You! You stole my creature to make money!

**YGOR.** We need the money. Do you know how much it will cost to keep this monster?

[*As* YGOR *argues with the doctor, he drops the rope mistakenly. The rope disappears.*]

**YGOR.** The cost of food alone will break our backs!

**DR. FRANKENSTEIN.** That's my problem! I created him. I gave him life!

**YGOR.** Oh, yes, you gave him life. But did you give him love? Did you give him a name? Did you give him breakfast?

From "Mister Monster," page 246

## Practice Intonation: "Return to *Titanic*"

Intonation is the rise and fall in the pitch or tone of your voice as you read aloud. Use this passage to practice reading with proper intonation. Print a copy of this passage from **myNGconnect.com** to help you monitor your progress.

*Titanic* was the largest ship in the world—as long as four city blocks. Many people called it the "wonder ship." It was like a floating palace, with a swimming pool, carved wood, and fancy gold lights. It also had many rich and famous passengers who wanted to be the first to ride on this great ship.

*Titanic* set off for New York. At first, the ride was like a party. By April 14, the ship was in the middle of the Atlantic Ocean. That night, the weather was clear, and stars twinkled against the dark sky. On the ship, people danced late into the night. No one knew that danger was near.

Shortly before midnight, a sailor on lookout saw something in the darkness. He knew it could be only one thing. It was an iceberg, a floating mountain of ice. The sailor raised the alarm : "Iceberg ahead!" Next, the crew tried to turn *Titanic* away from the iceberg, but it was too late. Finally, the ship scraped along the ice.

The problem did not seem too bad at first. Then water started pouring into the ship, and nothing could stop it. The ship was going to sink!

From "Return to *Titanic*," page 280

## Practice Expression: "The Forgotten Treasure"

Expression in reading is how you use your voice to express feeling. Use this passage to practice reading with proper expression. Print a copy of this passage from myNGconnect.com to help you monitor your progress.

Once there was a hunter who lived with his wife and their four sons. Each son had eyes like shiny black stones. The hunter looked at his sons and smiled. "Some men have gold, but my sons are better than gold. They are my treasures."

The hunter's wife was going to have a fifth baby. Sometimes she could feel it kick. "It will be another boy," she would say. "Another fine boy, just like his brothers."

Every morning, the hunter said to his family, "You are all my treasures. If you care about me, remember me always."

Every morning, his sons would say, "Father, we do not need to remember you. Every day you go out, but every day you come back. You are always here, so how could we ever forget you?"

From "The Forgotten Treasure," page 298

## Practice Phrasing: "Mysteries of the Ancient Past"

Phrasing is how you use your voice to group words together. Use this passage to practice reading with proper phrasing. Print a copy of this passage from **myNGconnect.com** to help you monitor your progress.

Who built the pyramids, and why did they build them? What lies inside these mysterious buildings? These are some of the questions that scientists and historians try to answer.

Archaeologists study objects from the past to learn about the people who made or used those objects and left them behind when they died. Archaeologists gather clues in many places. They look in old buildings. They also look for objects buried under the ground. Archaeologists often have to dig to find what they are looking for.

The objects that archaeologists study are called artifacts. Artifacts are clues that tell archaeologists how people lived in ancient times.

Artifacts can take many shapes. Old toys and games are artifacts. Statues and other art objects, baskets, bowls, and mummies are also artifacts. When artifacts are broken, archaeologists try to put the pieces back together.

From "Mysteries of the Ancient Past," page 318

## Practice Intonation: "Escaping to Freedom"

Intonation is the rise and fall in the pitch or tone of your voice as you read aloud. Use this passage to practice reading with proper intonation. Print a copy of this passage from myNGconnect.com to help you monitor your progress.

One dark night, Henson and his family left their home. He carried his two youngest children in a backpack. The family boarded a small boat and crossed the Ohio River into Indiana.

Once in Indiana, the family had to move slowly. They had to be careful not to be seen. Some slave owners offered rewards for the capture of escaped slaves. If the family was found, they might be returned to Riley. To make sure no one saw them, Henson's family often traveled at night and slept during the day.

The family traveled by wagon, by boat, and on foot. They traveled toward Canada, where slavery was not allowed. Along the way, people helped the family. Some people gave them food, and others hid them in barns.

The family set foot in Canada more than a month after their daring escape. The first words that Henson exclaimed when he got there were, "I am free!"

From "Escaping to Freedom," page 350

## Practice Expression: "Brave Butterflies"

Expression in reading is how you use your voice to express feeling. Use this passage to practice reading with proper expression. Print a copy of this passage from **myNGconnect.com** to help you monitor your progress.

I awoke in the middle of the night and looked outside. A dim light flickered in one of the Garcías' windows, a watchful eye spying on us. In the study, I could hear Papi and Mami talking in low whispers. I tiptoed down the hallway and stood in the shadows.

"Alberto, please, you must be more careful," Mami pleaded. "Getting involved in politics is risky. Think of our friends who have gone to prison or disappeared. Think of the Mirabal sisters. We could suffer the same fate."

"I am thinking of them," said Papi. "I am thinking of the courage that the Mirabals—those brave Mariposas—showed in standing up to Trujillo. And I am thinking of our children's future. Just imagine what it would be like to live in freedom."

From "Brave Butterflies," page 368

## Practice Phrasing: "Seeking Freedom"

Phrasing is how you use your voice to group words together. Use this passage to practice reading with proper phrasing. Print a copy of this passage from myNGconnect.com to help you monitor your progress.

Some countries do not have laws that protect people's freedoms. What do people in those countries do to find freedom?

Sometimes people leave their homes. They might move to a country with more freedom, but this can be very hard. People who move to a new country might have to learn a new language and way of life.

Millions of people have left their homes in search of freedom. Often they want freedom to practice their religion or the freedom to pick their leaders. People move for freedom of speech and freedom of the press. People also move because they want a better education or jobs.

From "Seeking Freedom," page 388

## Practice Expression: "The Earth Under Sky Bear's Feet"

Expression in reading is how you use your voice to express feeling. Use this passage to practice reading with proper expression. Print a copy of this passage from myNGconnect.com to help you monitor your progress.

Long ago,

three hunters and their little dog

found the tracks of a giant bear.

They followed those tracks

all through the day

and even though it was almost dark

they did not stop, but continued on.

They saw that bear now, climbing up

a hill, which glittered

with new-fallen snow.

They ran hard to catch it,

but the bear was too fast.

They ran and they ran, climbing

up and up until one of the hunters said,

"Brothers, look down."

They did and saw they

were high above Earth.

That bear was Sky Bear,

running on through the stars.

Look up now

and you will see her,

circling the sky.

From "The Earth Under Sky Bear's Feet," page 418

## Practice Phrasing: "A Universe of Stars"

Phrasing is how you use your voice to group words together. Use this passage to practice reading with proper phrasing. Print a copy of this passage from myNGconnect.com to help you monitor your progress.

If you stand outside on a clear, dark night, far away from any city lights, you may see a pale band of light stretching across the sky. The band of light is the Milky Way. The glow is from a huge number of stars.

Long ago, people could use only their eyes to study the sky. Over time, more powerful tools have allowed us to look farther and farther out into the universe. We've learned so much about space, but there is *much* more left to explore.

In the night sky, stars look like tiny diamonds fastened to the ceiling. They seem peaceful, timeless, and unchanging. In reality, stars are huge. They are scattered through vast distances in space. They're not timeless but are always changing, and those changes can be violent.

From "A Universe of Stars," page 438

## Practice Intonation: "Not-So-Starry Nights"

Intonation is the rise and fall in the pitch or tone of your voice as you read aloud. Use this passage to practice reading with proper intonation. Print a copy of this passage from **myNGconnect.com** to help you monitor your progress.

Astronomers were the first to notice the growing problem of light pollution. They began to realize it in the 1970s. They were shocked when they looked into their telescopes and saw that some of the stars and planets that they had studied were gone. They were still there, of course, but city lights made them impossible to see.

Nights started to get brighter more than a century ago. The first long-lasting lightbulb was invented in 1879. Companies began to install electric power lines across the country. More and more people used electricity for lighting.

At the same time, the population grew. Many people moved to the United States. In 1900, there were 76 million Americans. There are more than 300 million today. More people now live in cities and suburbs, and their lights create light pollution.

From "Not-So-Starry Nights," page 456

## Practice Phrasing: "Old Music Finds New Voices"

Phrasing is how you use your voice to group words together. Use this passage to practice reading with proper phrasing. Print a copy of this passage from myNGconnect.com to help you monitor your progress.

Many Mexican American teens are thinking about careers in mariachi. Schools offer courses in mariachi music, and competitions are spreading across the country as more and more Hispanic teens become interested in their culture.

"I like to tell stories," says Victoria Acosta, who won competitions even before she was a teen. "When I'm singing, it's like I'm telling a story. There are sad songs, and happy songs, and love songs. There are all different kinds of stories to tell."

When Victoria was just 4 years old, she fell in love with mariachi music. She begged her parents for lessons.

Her parents supported her. "We need to do our part to preserve our culture," says her father, Ruben Acosta. He is a fifth-generation Mexican American. "Mariachi music is so beautiful. We want to make sure it doesn't die out."

From "Old Music Finds New Voices," page 486

## Practice Intonation: "Making Faces"

Intonation is the rise and fall in the pitch or tone of your voice as you read aloud. Use this passage to practice reading with proper intonation. Print a copy of this passage from **myNGconnect.com** to help you monitor your progress.

My young neighbor was shocked. It was her first visit to my house, and everywhere she turned, another strange face stared back at her. There were big faces and small faces. Some were bright, and others were plain. At last, she said, "You really have an interesting place here!"

I collect masks, so my house is filled with them. I have about 150. Masks amaze me with their power. They change how people look and act!

I take trips to study masks. In Greece, I watched people make masks that were just like masks used in ancient times. Back then, actors wore masks in plays. Different masks helped actors play more than one part.

My trip to Romania was great, too. There I saw masks change people into hairy, wild men. To celebrate the start of spring, people put on these masks and then run through the streets.

From "Making Faces," page 502

## Practice Expression: "Wings"

Expression in reading is how you use your voice to express feeling. Use this passage to practice reading with proper expression. Print a copy of this passage from myNGconnect.com to help you monitor your progress.

I ran through the streets with my eyes to the sky, searching the clouds for Ikarus.

He struggled to stay in the air. His wings drooped and his head hung low.

He landed heavily on the edge of a building and sat with the pigeons. Pigeons don't make fun of people.

A policeman passing by blew his whistle.

"You with the wings, come down from there! Stay yourself on the ground. You'll get in trouble. You'll get hurt."

It seemed to me Ikarus was already in trouble and hurt. Could the policeman put him in jail for flying, for being too different?

When the neighborhood kids saw the policeman yelling at him, they exploded with laughter. Ikarus dropped to the ground.

"Stop!" I cried. "Leave him alone." And they did.

From "Wings," page 522

# Glossary

The definitions in this glossary are for words as they are used in the selections in this book. Use the Pronunciation Key below to help you use each word's pronunciation. Then read about the parts of an entry.

## Pronunciation Key

| Symbols for Consonant Sounds | | | | Symbols for Short Vowel Sounds | | Symbols for R-controlled Sounds | | Symbols for Variant Vowel Sounds | |
|---|---|---|---|---|---|---|---|---|---|
| b | box | p | pan | a | hat | ar | barn | ah | father |
| ch | chick | r | ring | e | bell | air | chair | aw | ball |
| d | dog | s | bus | i | chick | ear | ear | oi | boy |
| f | fish | sh | fish | o | box | ir | fire | ow | mouse |
| g | girl | t | hat | u | bus | or | corn | oo | book |
| h | hat | th | earth | | | ur | girl | ü | fruit |
| j | jar | th | father | **Symbols for Long Vowel Sounds** | | | | | |
| k | cake | v | vase | | | | | **Miscellaneous Symbols** | |
| ks | box | w | window | ā | cake | | | | |
| kw | queen | wh | whale | ē | key | | | shun | fraction |
| l | bell | y | yarn | ī | bike | | | chun | question |
| m | mouse | z | zipper | ō | goat | | | zhun | division |
| n | pan | zh | treasure | yū | mule | | | | |
| ng | ring | | | | | | | | |

## • Academic Vocabulary

Certain words in this glossary have a red dot indicating that they are academic vocabulary words. These are the words that you will use as you study many different subjects in school.

## Parts of an Entry

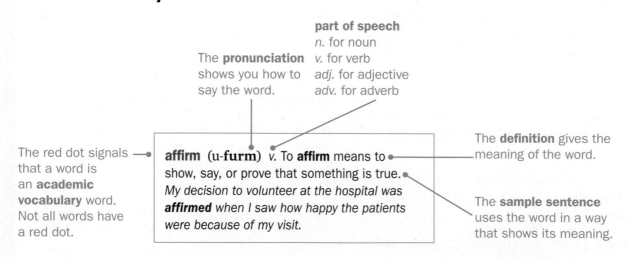

part of speech
*n.* for noun
The **pronunciation**   *v.* for verb
shows you how to   *adj.* for adjective
say the word.   *adv.* for adverb

The red dot signals that a word is an **academic vocabulary** word. Not all words have a red dot.

**affirm** (u-**furm**) *v.* To **affirm** means to show, say, or prove that something is true. *My decision to volunteer at the hospital was affirmed when I saw how happy the patients were because of my visit.*

The **definition** gives the meaning of the word.

The **sample sentence** uses the word in a way that shows its meaning.

## A

**active** (**ak**-tiv) *adj.* Something that is **active** is likely to move or to show action. *Children are **active** when they run and play games outside.*

**actor** (**ak**-tur) *n.* An **actor** is a person who acts in a movie or play. *The **actors** are working on a new movie.*

• **adjust** (u-**just**) *v.* To **adjust** means to change in order to become comfortable with something. *I hope I can **adjust** to my new school.*

**advice** (ad-**vīs**) *n.* **Advice** is a suggestion or an idea that helps someone decide what to do. *Family members can give you **advice** when you have a problem.*

**agree** (u-**grē**) *v.* When you **agree** with someone, you have the same ideas. *A handshake shows that people **agree** to something.*

**alarm** (u-**larm**) *n.* An **alarm** warns people of danger. *A smoke detector is one kind of **alarm**.*

**alive** (u-**līv**) *adj.* Something that is living is **alive**. *The girl looks happy to be **alive**.*

**amazed** (u-**māzd**) *adj.* To be **amazed** means to be very surprised. *They are **amazed** that the experiment worked so well.*

**amount** (u-**mount**) *n.* An **amount** is the total number or quantity. *There is a large **amount** of wood in this pile.*

• **analyze** (**a**-nu-līz) *v.* To **analyze** means to break down information into parts to understand it better. *Our science class will **analyze** cell structures using a microscope.*

**ancient** (**ānt**-shunt) *adj.* If something is **ancient**, it is very old. *People built this **ancient** temple long ago.*

**angry** (**ang**-grē) *adj.* When you are **angry**, you are mad at someone or something. *An **angry** leopard hisses a warning.*

• **apply** (u-**plī**) *v.* To **apply** means to ask for or to request something. *People often fill out forms when they **apply** for a job.*

• **appreciate** (u-**prē**-shē-āt) *v.* To **appreciate** means to care about something or someone. *A boy gives flowers to his mom to show that he **appreciates** her.*

• **Academic Vocabulary**

• **appropriate** (u-**prō**-prē-ut) *adj.* If something is **appropriate**, it is correct for the situation. *Lisa's blue dress is **appropriate** to wear to the wedding.*

**approve** (u-**prüv**) *v.* To **approve** means to think something is good or right. *The teacher **approves** the work I did.*

**archaeologist** (ar-kē-ah-lu-jist) *n.* An **archaeologist** studies the way people lived in the past. *Bones, buildings, and tools help **archaeologists** learn about the past.*

• **arrange** (u-**rānj**) *v.* To **arrange** means to put things in a certain order. *The librarian will **arrange** the books on the shelves at the library.*

**arrest** (u-**rest**) *v.* To **arrest** means to put someone in jail. *When police officers **arrest** a suspect, they may use handcuffs.*

**arrive** (u-**rīv**) *v.* To **arrive** means to reach a place. *A plane **arrives** at an airport.*

**artifact** (**ar**-ti-fakt) *n.* An **artifact** is an object, or the remains of one, that represents a culture. *An old statue is an **artifact**.*

• **assist** (u-**sist**) *v.* To **assist** means to help. *The father **assists** his son with an assignment when he has trouble understanding it.*

**audience** (**aw**-dē-unts) *n.* An **audience** is a group of people who watch or listen to something. *The **audience** claps during the show.*

• **available** (u-**vā**-lu-bul) *adj.* When something is **available**, it is here and ready for use. *Fresh fruit is **available** in the summer.*

## B

**beautiful** (**byū**-ti-ful) *adj.* Something that is **beautiful** is very pretty. *The flowers are **beautiful**.*

• **belief** (bu-**lēf**) *n.* A **belief** is a feeling that something is true or right. *One **belief** is that your wish comes true if you break a wishbone and get the bigger part.*

• **benefit** (**ben**-e-fit) *n.* A benefit is something that is helpful. *Fresh air and exercise are two **benefits** of hiking.*

**bury** (**bair**-ē) *v.* To **bury** means to place in the ground. *The dog **buries** a bone.*

# Glossary

## C

**capture** (**kap**-chur) **1** *v.* To **capture** means to take by force. *The farmer captured a raccoon.* **2** *n.* A **capture** is the act of catching something. *Soon after the capture, he released the raccoon.*

**career** (ku-**rear**) *n.* A **career** is a job someone trains for and does full-time. *This man went to veterinary school and now has a career working with animals.*

**carefully** (**kair**-foo-lē) *adv.* To act **carefully** means to act with care. *You should carry the eggs carefully so they do not break.*

**carve** (**karv**) *v.* To **carve** means to cut shapes from a material like stone or wood. *The artist used sharp tools to carve a sculpture.*

• **category** (**ka**-tu-gor-ē) *n.* A **category** is a group of items that are related in some way. *Cheetahs and leopards belong to the same category of big cats.*

**change** (**chānj**) *n.* A **change** is something new and different. *A sudden change in weather can surprise people!*

**character** (**kair**-ik-tur) *n.* A **character** is someone in a story. *He acted out the role of the main character in the play.*

**civilization** (si-vu-lu-**zā**-shun) *n.* A **civilization** is the culture of a specific place, time, or group of people. *Greece has a very old civilization.*

• **classic** (**kla**-sik) *adj.* Something that is **classic** is old but good. *Classic cars are expensive if they are in good shape.*

**clue** (**klü**) *n.* A **clue** is a piece of information that leads to a solution. *A police detective looks for clues to the crime.*

• **collapse** (ku-**laps**) *v.* To **collapse** means to fall down. *The old building collapsed.*

**commercial** (ku-**mur**-shul) *n.* A **commercial** is an ad on TV or the radio. *Most TV commercials show products that viewers can buy.*

• **communicate** (ku-**myū**-ni-kāt) *v.* When you **communicate**, you share information. *The pilot used the loud speaker to communicate with the passengers.*

• **community** (ku-**myū**-ni-tē) *n.* A **community** is a place where people live, work, and carry out their daily lives. *Some communities have outdoor markets.*

• **compare** (kum-**pair**) *v.* When you **compare** two things, you think about how they are alike and different. *I would like to compare the apple pie to the blueberry pie to find out which one tastes better.*

**competition** (kom-pe-**ti**-shun) *n.* A **competition** is a contest. *The runners are in competition to win the race or to improve their time.*

**complain** (kum-**plān**) *v.* To **complain** means to say that you are unhappy about something. *I complained that it was not fair I had to take out the trash by myself.*

**concert** (**kont**-surt) *n.* A **concert** is an event where people play music for an audience. *The orchestra is giving a concert.*

**confused** (kun-**fyūzd**) *adj.* To be **confused** means to be unsure or not clear. *We could not follow the recipe because we were confused by the instructions.*

• **context** (**kon**-tekst) *n.* **Context** refers to the parts nearby that help explain the meaning. *Paul knows to use the context to help him understand what a new word means.*

**continue** (kun-**tin**-yū) *v.* To **continue** means to keep going. *The highway continues for miles.*

**costume** (**kos**-tüm) *n.* A **costume** is a set of clothes that someone wears to look like another person. *You can dress up in a costume for a special occasion.*

• **create** (krē-**āt**) *v.* To **create** means to make something new. *The artist creates a work of art in his studio.*

**creature** (**krē**-chur) *n.* A **creature** is a real or imaginary living thing. *A dragon is an imaginary creature.*

**crop** (**krop**) *n.* **Crops** are plants that farmers grow. *Corn, beans, and peaches are different crops.*

• **culture** (**kul**-chur) *n.* The ideas and way of life for a group of people make up their **culture**. *Baseball and jazz are both part of American culture.*

• **Academic Vocabulary**

**curious** (**kyoor**-ē-us) *adj.* If you are **curious**, you want to know more about something. *A **curious** person shows interest in things.*

## D

**dangerous** (**dān**-jur-us) *adj.* Something that is **dangerous** is not safe. *It is **dangerous** to walk barefoot near broken glass. You could cut yourself.*

**decorate** (**de**-ku-rāt) *v.* To **decorate** means to add things to make something look better. *The baker **decorates** the fancy dessert.*

• **define** (dē-**fīn**) *v.* When you **define** something, you tell what it means. *I have to **define** eight new words for homework.*

• **demonstrate** (**de**-mun-strāt) *v.* To **demonstrate** means to prove or make clear. *As the team coach, Mike **demonstrates** how to kick the soccer ball.*

**depend** (dē-**pend**) *v.* When you **depend** on something, you need it. *Babies **depend** on their parents for everything.*

• **design** (di-**zīn**) *n.* A **design** is a drawing or a pattern. *The tiles are placed so they form a colorful **design** on the surface.*

**destroy** (di-**stroi**) *v.* To **destroy** something means to take it apart or to ruin it. *Workers **destroyed** the old building.*

**dictator** (**dik**-tā-tur) *n.* A **dictator** is a person who leads a country without sharing power. *Most **dictators** do not allow others to make decisions for the country.*

**different** (**dif**-er-ent) *adj.* Something that is **different** is not the same. *A red flower in a field of orange tulips is **different** from the others.*

**disappear** (dis-u-**pear**) *v.* To **disappear** means to no longer be seen. *When the bell rang, the students left quickly. They **disappeared**.*

• **discover** (dis-**ku**-vur) *v.* To **discover** means to find something that is lost or hidden. *The boy **discovers** a starfish at the beach.*

• **discuss** (di-**skus**) *v.* When you **discuss** something, you talk about it. *My teacher likes to **discuss** the classroom rules every morning.*

• **Academic Vocabulary**

**distance** (**dis**-tunts) *n.* **Distance** is the area between two points. *The **distance** between Earth and the sun is 93 million miles.*

**drift** (**drift**) *v.* To **drift** means to move along slowly in the air or on water. *She **drifts** down the river on a raft, carried along by the current.*

**droop** (**drüp**) *v.* To **droop** means to hang down. *The branches of the tree **droop** to the ground.*

## E

**earthquake** (**urth**-kwāk) *n.* An **earthquake** is a sudden shaking of the earth. *Strong **earthquakes** cause damage to roads and buildings.*

**electricity** (ē-lek-**tri**-si-tē) *n.* **Electricity** is a form of energy. *Lamps and computers use **electricity** to work.*

• **element** (**e**-le-ment) *n.* An **element** is a basic part of a whole. *Pitching is one **element** of a baseball game.*

• **environment** (en-**vī**-run-ment) *n.* An **environment** is the area where plants and animals live and grow. *Plants grow well in a healthy **environment**.*

• **equipment** (ē-**kwip**-ment) *n.* Tools or machines for a certain use are **equipment**. *Hospitals have **equipment** for treating people who are sick or hurt.*

**erupt** (ē-**rupt**) *v.* To **erupt** means to break open or shoot out suddenly. *When a volcano **erupts**, lava and ash shoot out.*

**escape** (es-**kāp**) **1** *v.* To **escape** means to get away. *People **escaped** the burning building.* **2** *n.* An **escape** is the act of getting away from something. *We heard about their successful **escape**.*

**evacuate** (ē-va-**kyū**-āt) *v.* To **evacuate** means to leave or to get out. *The woman **evacuated** the building when the fire alarm rang.*

• **evaluate** (ē-**val**-yu-wāt) *v.* To **evaluate** means to judge something's value or worth. *The coach will **evaluate** all students who want to play basketball.*

**evil** (ē-vul) *adj.* Something that is **evil** is very bad or harmful. *Some people believe rattlesnakes are **evil** because their bite is dangerous.*

**experiment** (eks-**spair**-i-ment) *n.* An **experiment** is an activity that someone does to test an idea. *The students are doing an **experiment** in their science class.*

• **explain** (eks-**splān**) *v.* When you **explain** an idea, you make it clear so people can understand it. *Lucy **explains** the rules of the game to her sister.*

**explorer** (eks-**splor**-ur) *n.* An **explorer** travels somewhere to study something. ***Explorers** find out what is special about a new place.*

### F

• **fact** (fakt) *n.* A **fact** is a piece of information that is true. *It is a proven **fact** that Earth revolves around the sun.*

**familiar** (fu-**mil**-yur) *adj.* Something that is **familiar** is already known. *He was happy to see a **familiar** face at the party.*

**famous** (**fā**-mus) *adj.* Something that is **famous** is very well known. *Many people have seen the **famous** Statue of Liberty.*

**fascinated** (**fa**-su-**nā**-tud) *adj.* To be **fascinated** means to be very interested in something. *The student is **fascinated** by the model.*

**festival** (**fes**-tu-vul) *n.* A **festival** is a special event or party. *Dancers perform at the **festival**.*

**flow** (flō) *v.* To **flow** means to move freely. *A river **flows** without stopping.*

• **force** (fors) **1** *v.* To **force** means to push. *Too much weight **forces** the ice loose.* **2** *n.* A **force** is a great power in nature. *The **force** sent ice flying.*

**forest** (**for**-ust) *n.* A **forest** is a place that has lots of trees. *Many **forests** have been cut down to make room for new buildings.*

**forget** (for-**get**) *v.* When you **forget** something, you stop thinking about it. *The boy leaves without his shoes. He **forgets** them.*

**fortunate** (**for**-chu-nut) *adj.* Someone who is **fortunate** is lucky. *The family is **fortunate** that their house did not burn in the fire.*

• **freedom** (**frē**-dum) *n.* If you have **freedom** you are not limited in what you do. *The bird was released and given **freedom**.*

**frightened** (**frī**-tund) *adj.* To be **frightened** is to be afraid or scared. *When I'm **frightened** at the movies, I cover my face with my hands.*

**future** (**fyū**-chur) *n.* The **future** is what will happen in the time to come. *I am going to a concert at some time in the near **future**.*

### G

• **generate** (**je**-nu-rāt) *v.* To **generate** means to make something. *Windmills **generate** energy that people can use.*

• **globe** (glōb) *n.* A **globe** is a model of Earth. *A **globe** shows the shape of the land. The blue represents oceans.*

**goods** (goodz) *n.* **Goods** are things that people buy and sell. *Stores sell **goods**. For this meaning, **goods** is always plural.*

**government** (**gu**-vurn-munt) *n.* The people who control the country according to certain laws are the **government**. *Washington, DC, is the center of the U.S. **government**.*

### H

**hideous** (**hi**-dē-us) *adj.* Something that is **hideous** is very ugly. *A mask can make someone look **hideous**.*

**hopeful** (**hōp**-ful) *adj.* Someone who is **hopeful** is full of good thoughts about what will happen. *The girl is **hopeful** about winning the contest.*

**hunter** (**hun**-tur) *n.* A **hunter** is a person who looks for wild animals to capture or kill. *A skilled **hunter** may use a bow and arrows to hunt.*

**hurricane** (**hur**-u-kān) *n.* A **hurricane** is an ocean storm with strong winds. *From space, a **hurricane** looks like a spiral of white clouds.*

• **Academic Vocabulary**

## I

- **identify** (ī-**den**-tu-fī) *v.* To **identify** means to find out or to show what something is. *Some scientists try to identify how germs make people sick.*

- **immigrant** (**i**-mu-grunt) *n.* An **immigrant** is a person who comes to live in a new country. *Immigrants say a pledge, or promise, when they become citizens.*

**impressed** (im-**prest**) *adj.* If you are **impressed**, you are strongly affected by something. *The audience was very impressed by the talented musicians.*

**instrument** (**int**-stru-munt) *n.* An **instrument** is something you play to make music. *Guitars and violins are both stringed instruments.*

- **interpret** (in-**tur**-prut) *v.* To **interpret** means to explain or tell what something means. *Paul has to interpret the directions for me.*

## J

**journal** (**jur**-nul) *n.* A **journal** is a record of someone's thoughts, feelings, and actions. *Some people write in their journal almost every day.*

## L

**law** (**law**) *n.* The **law** is a country's rules. *A police officer reminds people to follow the law.*

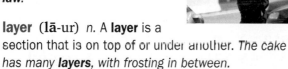

**layer** (**lā**-ur) *n.* A **layer** is a section that is on top of or under another. *The cake has many layers, with frosting in between.*

**leader** (**lē**-dur) *n.* A **leader** is a person in charge of others. *The leader of our hiking club decides which trail we will take.*

**learn** (**lurn**) *v.* To **learn** means to know about a subject by studying or practicing it. *You can learn many things by reading.*

**leave** (**lēv**) *v.* When you **leave** a place, you go away from it. *A bird leaves its nest to find food.*

**levee** (le-**vē**) *n.* A **levee** is a structure that keeps a river from flooding. *If rainfall is heavy for a long time, a river could rise and the water could spill over the levee.*

- **locate** (lō-**kāt**) *v.* To **locate** something is to find it. *The woman tried to locate her missing purse.*

**lonely** (**lōn**-lē) *adj.* To be **lonely** means to be alone, without friends. *Do you feel lonely when your friends are away?*

**loss** (**laws**) *n.* When you no longer have something important, you feel the **loss**. *A terrible loss is the death of a loved one.*

## M

**mascot** (**mas**-kot) *n.* A **mascot** is a character that represents an organization. *The basketball team's mascot cheers for the team.*

**mask** (**mask**) *n.* A **mask** is something a person wears to hide his or her face. *The girl will wear a mask to a dress-up party.*

**material** (mu-**tear**-ē-ul) *n.* **Materials** are things you need to make a product or to do a project. *Paint and brushes are materials you need for painting.*

- **migrate** (**mī**-grāt) *v.* To **migrate** means to move from one place to another. *Some birds migrate to a warm climate for the winter.*

## N

- **narrative** (**nair**-u-tiv) **1** *adj.* **Narrative** writing tells a story. **2** *n.* A **narrative** tells a story. *My narrative about life in another country won first place in the narrative writing contest.*

**native** (**nā**-tiv) *adj.* Something that belongs to you because of where you were born is **native** to you. *People wave flags from their native countries.*

**necessity** (ni-**se**-su-tē) *n.* A **necessity** is an item that someone needs. *Food and water are the most basic necessities of life.*

**neighborhood** (**nā**-bur-hood) *n.* A **neighborhood** is a place where people live and work together. *Most families know each other in our neighborhood in Boston.*

• **Academic Vocabulary**

## O

**ocean** (ō-shun) *n.* An **ocean** is a large area or body of salt water. *Oceans cover most of Earth.*

**offstage** (awf-**stāj**) *adv.* To be **offstage** means to be at the side of the stage. *The dancer waits offstage and gets ready to perform.*

**opinion** (u-**pin**-yun) *n.* An **opinion** is a belief or a view about a topic. *My friends share their opinions about fashion.*

**opportunity** (ah-pur-**tü**-nu-tē) *n.* An **opportunity** is a good chance to do something. *A sign in the window tells about a job opportunity at the restaurant.*

**orbit** (**or**-but) *v.* To **orbit** means to move in an almost circular path around another object. *It takes Earth about 365 days to orbit the sun.*

**ordinary** (**or**-du-nair-ē) *adj.* An **ordinary** thing is plain. *The brown box looks ordinary.*

• **organize** (**or**-gu-nīz) *v.* To **organize** means to plan and set up something. *The leader organizes the people to support a cause.*

**original** (u-**rij**-u-nul) *adj.* Something that is **original** is the first of its kind. *Mary Shelley's novel is the original story of Frankenstein.*

## P

**passenger** (**pa**-sen-jur) *n.* When you ride in a car, boat, or other vehicle, you are a **passenger**. *The bus driver took ten passengers to the school.*

**perfect** (**pur**-fikt) *adj.* Something that is **perfect** is just right. *The girl made a perfect dive into the water.*

**perform** (pur-**form**) *v.* To **perform** means to dance, sing, act, or play music for an audience. *Students perform on stage for special events.*

**plan** (plan) *n.* A **plan** is an idea about how to do something. *The architect's drawings show the plans for building a new house.*

**politics** (**pah**-lu-tiks) *n.* **Politics** is the business of government. *Members of Congress talk about issues of national and international politics.*

**pollution** (pu-**lü**-shun) *n.* **Pollution** is waste that harms nature. *Trash is one form of pollution.*

**population** (pah-pyu-**lā**-shun) *n.* **Population** means the number of people who live somewhere. *Many people live in New York City. It has a large population.*

**power** (**pow**-ur) *n.* **Power** is energy that makes things work. *A dam collects water to use as a source of power.*

**prepare** (pri-**pair**) *v.* To **prepare** means to get ready. *Dad is preparing vegetables for dinner tonight.*

**preserve** (pri-**zurv**) *v.* To **preserve** means to save. *A grandmother preserves a family tradition by sharing it with her granddaughter.*

**problem** (**prah**-blum) *n.* A **problem** is something that is wrong. A **problem** needs to be solved or fixed. *The driver has a problem because his truck is stuck in the mud.*

**process** (**prah**-ses) *n.* A **process** is a set of actions taken to get a certain result. *Making homemade jam is a difficult process.*

**protect** (pru-**tekt**) *v.* To **protect** means to keep safe. *The mother bird protects her chicks from danger.*

**protest** (**prō**-test) **1** *v.* To **protest** means to make a statement against an idea. *The students protested against school spending cuts.* **2** *n.* A **protest** is a display of strong feelings. *The students led a protest.*

**proud** (prowd) *adj.* If you are **proud**, you are feeling happy about yourself. *I felt proud when I won the prize.*

**public** (**pu**-blik) *n.* When you are in **public**, you are in an area that is open to others. *Even though we held our family gathering in public, the setting felt private.*

**pyramid** (**pear**-u-mid) *n.* A **pyramid** is a building with a square base and four sides that are triangles. *Egypt has many ancient pyramids.*

• **Academic Vocabulary**

## R

**rainfall** (rān-fawl) *n.* **Rainfall** is the total rain, snow, or sleet that falls in a period of time. *There has been a lot of rainfall this year.*

• **record** (ri-**kord**) *v.* To **record** means to put something in writing. *The weather scientist records how much rain falls in one month.*

**reduce** (ri-**düs**) *v.* To **reduce** means to have fewer or less of something. *The box was too heavy for her to carry so her friend helped in order to reduce the heavy load.*

• **relate** (ri-**lāt**) *v.* When you **relate** two things, you think about how they are connected. *Boats and trains both relate to the topic of transportation.*

**relative** (**re**-lu-tiv) *n.* A family member is a **relative**. *The mother and daughter are relatives.*

• **release** (ri-**lēs**) *v.* To **release** means to let out. *When you release an animal into the wild, you let it go free.*

**remain** (ri-**mān**) *v.* To **remain** means to stay in the same place. *My dog is learning to remain in one spot when I tell him.*

**remember** (ri-**mem**-bur) *v.* When you **remember** something, you think of it again later. *A soldier went to the monument to remember his friend who died.*

• **report** (ri-**port**) *v.* When you **report** on an event, you describe what happened. *I will report the lost dog to the police.*

**rescue** (**res**-kyū) *n.* A **rescue** is the act of saving someone or something from danger. *The rescue was daring and successful.*

• **resource** (**rē**-sors) *n.* A **resource** is something that people need and use. *Air, soil, and water are natural resources.*

• **response** (ri-**sponts**) *n.* A **response** is what people think or say about something. *She raises her hand to give a response to the question.*

**responsibility** (ri-spont-su-**bi**-lu-tē) *n.* A **responsibility** is something you should do because it is right. *It is my responsibility to walk the dog every day.*

**reward** (ri-**ward**) *n.* A **reward** is money given for helping someone. *We offered a reward to anyone who could find our lost dog.*

**right** (rīt) *n.* A **right** is the power a person has because of a country's rules. *In 1920 American women got the right to vote.*

**roam** (rōm) *v.* To **roam** means to wander or to travel without any particular place to go. *Wild animals roam freely.*

**roots** (rüts) *n.* **Roots** are a person's family traditions and culture. *My family is from India. I am so proud of my Indian roots.*

## S

**safely** (**sāf**-lē) *adv.* To do something **safely** is to do it without danger. *The girl worked safely by protecting her eyes from the chemicals.*

**scatter** (**ska**-tur) *v.* To **scatter** means to throw or drop many things over a wide area. *The leaves scatter across the street.*

**scientist** (**sī**-un-tist) *n.* A person who studies science is a **scientist**. *The scientist uses a microscope to study small objects up close.*

**search** (surch) **1** *v.* When you **search** for something, you look for it. *You might search for something you lost.* **2** *n.* A **search** is also the act of looking for something. *We organized a search for the missing dog.*

**secret** (**sē**-krut) **1** *adj.* Something that is **secret** is hidden from others. **2** *n.* A **secret** is something you hide from others. *Can you keep a secret?*

• **select** (su-**lekt**) *v.* To **select** something means to choose it. *You may select five books to borrow from the library.*

• **Academic Vocabulary**

## Glossary

- **series** (sear-ēz) *n.* A **series** is a group of related things that are put in a certain order. *There is a concert **series** for children in the park this summer.*

- **sequence** (sē-kwens) *n.* The **sequence** of events is the order in which the events happen. *Sarah must remember the right **sequence** of numbers to open her lock.*

   **severe** (su-vear) *adj.* Something that is **severe** is very serious or dangerous. *Dad could not read because he had a **severe** headache.*

   **shelter** (shel-tur) *n.* A **shelter** is a place where people can safely stay. *An umbrella provides **shelter** from the rain.*

- **similar** (si-mu-lur) *adj.* Things that are **similar** are almost the same. *Oranges and tangerines are **similar** fruits.*

   **skeleton** (ske-lu-tun) *n.* A **skeleton** is the set of bones in an animal or a person. *The model shows a human **skeleton**.*

   **slave** (slāv) *n.* A **slave** is someone who belongs to another person and who works without pay. *Owners forced **slaves** to work.*

- **space** (spās) *n.* **Space** is the area beyond Earth. *Scientists send special ships into **space** to learn about other planets and the moon.*

- **specific** (spi-si-fik) *adj.* Something that is **specific** is exact. *Dr. Gonzales gave **specific** directions about which medicine to take.*

   **statue** (sta-chü) *n.* A **statue** is a model of a person or thing. *The monument has a **statue** of Abraham Lincoln.*

   **strange** (strānj) *adj.* Something that is **strange** is not familiar. *The reflection in this mirror is **strange**. I look so much taller.*

- **structure** (struk-chur) *n.* **Structure** is the way something is organized or put together. *The **structure** of the building is strong.*

   **struggle** (stru-gul) *v.* To **struggle** means to try hard. *I **struggle** to beat my uncle at arm wrestling.*

- **style** (stī-ul) *n.* A **style** is a certain way of expressing an idea. *Salsa is one **style** of dance.*

   **successful** (suk-ses-ful) *adj.* To be **successful** means to have a good result or to be well liked. *The team was **successful** at the science fair.*

- **support** (su-port) *v.* To **support** means to help. *People **support** friends and family when they encourage or comfort each other.*

   **surface** (sur-fus) *n.* The **surface** is the outside part of something. *The **surface** of the lake is calm.*

   **system** (sis-tum) *n.* A **system** is a way of doing things. *An assembly line is a factory **system** that usually saves time and money.*

## T

   **tale** (tāl) *n.* A **tale** is a story. *The children enjoy listening to the **tale**.*

   **telescope** (te-lu-skōp) *n.* A **telescope** is a tool you can look through to make faraway things look bigger. *You can use a **telescope** to look at the moon.*

   **temperature** (tem-pur-chur) *n.* The **temperature** is how hot or cold something is. *We measure **temperature** using a thermometer.*

   **terror** (tair-ur) *n.* To feel **terror** means to have much fear. *The frightened man runs away from the bear in **terror**.*

- **theme** (thēm) *n.* A **theme** is the main message of a story. *The **theme** of the school play is to always ask for help when you need it.*

   **tomb** (tüm) *n.* A **tomb** is a grave, or a special place for the body of a dead person. *The inside of the **tomb** looked almost like someone's living room.*

- **topic** (tah-pik) *n.* A **topic** is the subject of a piece of writing or of a discussion. *Meg's teacher said the **topic** for the day was how to write complete sentences.*

- **Academic Vocabulary**

**track** (trak) *n.* A **track** is a footprint or a mark left by something as it moves over a surface. *When you look at animal **tracks**, you can tell what kind of animal was in the area.*

• **tradition** (tru-**di**-shun) *n.* A **tradition** is an activity or belief that people share for many years. *It is a **tradition** for our family to celebrate Kwanzaa every December.*

**travel** (**tra**-vul) *v.* To **travel** means to go from one place to another place. *People can **travel** over land by car, train, or wagon.*

**treasure** (**tre**-zhur) *n.* A **treasure** is something very special and important. *The old gold coins are part of a famous **treasure**.*

**treat** (trēt) *v.* When you **treat** something, you change it. *You can use a special cleaner to **treat** a stain on clothing.*

## U

**understand** (un-dur-**stand**) *v.* To **understand** something is to know it well. *A teacher who **understands** a math problem can explain it to the students.*

**unit** (**yū**-nit) *n.* A **unit** is a certain amount used in measuring. *An inch is a common **unit** used to measure small objects.*

**universe** (**yū**-nu-vurs) *n.* The **universe** is everywhere and includes Earth, all other planets, and all stars.

**untouched** (un-**tucht**) *adj.* Something that is **untouched** is not changed or hurt in any way. *Few areas of the world have been **untouched** by humans.*

**useless** (**yūs**-lus) *adj.* If something is **useless**, it is of no use. *A broken cell phone is **useless**.*

## V

**value** (**val**-yū) *n.* A **value** is something that people care about. *Respect is an important **value** in Japan.*

• **vary** (**vair**-ē) *v.* To **vary** means to be different from others. *Snowflakes **vary** from one another so that no two are alike.*

**village** (**vi**-lij) *n.* A **village** is a very small town. *Not many people live in farming **villages**, where homes are separated by large areas of land.*

**violent** (**vī**-u-lunt) *adj.* Something that is **violent** uses force. ***Violent** storms like tornadoes can damage buildings and kill people.*

**volcano** (vol-**kā**-nō) *n.* A **volcano** is an opening in Earth from which lava, ash, and steam escape. *The state of Hawaii has several **volcanoes**.*

## W

**warning** (**wor**-ning) *n.* A **warning** is a sign that something bad may happen. *The road sign gives us a **warning** that a railroad crossing is ahead.*

**wasted** (**wāst**-ud) *adj.* Something that is **wasted** is not needed. *Food that you throw away instead of eating is **wasted**.*

**whisper** (**whis**-pur) *v.* To **whisper** means to speak very quietly. *I **whisper** the secret to my friend so no one else can hear.*

**worry** (**wur**-ē) *v.* To **worry** about something means to feel unhappy and afraid about what may happen. *People often **worry** when they are late.*

**wreck** (rek) *n.* A **wreck** is what is left after a crash. *A **shipwreck** is a broken ship that crashed.*

• **Academic Vocabulary**

# • Academic Vocabulary Master Word List

| | | | |
|---|---|---|---|
| adaptation | convince | globe | refer |
| adjust | couple | identify | reflect |
| adjustment | create | illustrate | region |
| affect | credit | image | relate |
| aid | culture | immigrant | release |
| amend | data | impact | report |
| analyze | debate | individual | research |
| appeal | decision | inevitable | resource |
| application | define | integrate | response |
| apply | definition | interpret | result |
| appreciate | demonstrate | involve | role |
| approach | describe | issue | route |
| appropriate | design | job | section |
| area | despite | judgment | select |
| arrange | device | literal | sequence |
| assignment | discover | locate | series |
| assist | discuss | location | similar |
| associate | distinguish | logical | situation |
| assume | effect | media | solve |
| attach | effectively | migrate | space |
| available | element | model | specific |
| awareness | emerge | modify | structure |
| belief | encounter | narrative | style |
| benefit | energy | negative | summarize |
| bond | ensure | obvious | support |
| capable | environment | organize | survive |
| category | equipment | origin | symbol |
| challenge | establish | original | team |
| chapter | evaluate | outcome | technical |
| characteristic | evidence | perspective | technique |
| classic | exact | plan | technology |
| collapse | experiment | position | temporary |
| communicate | expert | positive | theme |
| community | explain | predict | topic |
| compare | express | presentation | tradition |
| compound | fact | process | trait |
| concentrate | feature | professional | unique |
| conflict | focus | promote | vary |
| connect | force | propaganda | |
| connotation | freedom | purpose | |
| context | goal | react | |
| contrast | generate | record | |

• Words in red appear in Level A.

# Literary Terms

## A

**Alliteration** The repetition of the same sounds (usually consonants) at the beginning of words that are close together. **Example:** Molly makes magnificent mousse, though Pablo prefers pecan pie.

> See also **Repetition**

**Allusion** A key form of literary language, in which one text makes the reader think about another text that was written before it. Allusion can also mean a reference to a person, place, thing, or event that is not specifically named. **Example:** When Hannah wrote in her short story that vanity was the talented main character's "Achilles heel," her teacher understood that Hannah was referring to a character in a Greek myth. So, she suspected that the vanity of the main character in Hannah's short story would prove to be the character's greatest weakness.

> See also **Connotation; Literature; Poetry**

**Argument** A type of writing or speaking that supports a position or attempts to convince the reader or listener. Arguments include a claim that is supported by reasons and evidence.

> See also **Claim; Reason; Evidence**

**Article** A short piece of nonfiction writing on a specific topic. Articles appear in newspapers and magazines.

> See also **Expository nonfiction; Nonfiction**

**Autobiography** The story of a person's life, written by that person. **Example:** Mahatma Gandhi wrote an autobiography titled *Gandhi: An Autobiography: The Story of My Experiments With Truth*.

> See also **Diary; Journal; Personal narrative**

## B

**Biographical fiction** A fictional story that is based on real events in the life of a real person. **Example:** Although the book *Farmer Boy* by Laura Ingalls Wilder is about her husband's childhood, the conversations between characters are from the author's imagination. They are based on what she thought the characters might have said at the time.

> See also **Biography; Fiction**

**Biography** The story of a person's life, written by another person.

> See also **Autobiography; Biographical fiction**

## C

**Character** A person, an animal, or an imaginary creature in a work of fiction.

> See also **Characterization; Character traits**

**Characterization** The way a writer creates and develops a character. Writers use a variety of ways to bring a character to life: through descriptions of the character's appearance, thoughts, feelings, and actions; through the character's words; and through the words or thoughts of other characters.

> See also **Character; Character traits; Motive**

**Character traits** The special qualities of personality that writers give their characters.

> See also **Character; Characterization**

**Claim** A statement that clearly identifies an author's ideas or opinion.

> See also **Argument; Reason; Evidence**

**Climax** The turning point or most important event in a plot.

> See also **Falling action; Plot; Rising action**

**Complication** See **Rising action**

**Conflict** The main problem faced by a character in a story or play. The character may be involved in a struggle against nature, another character, or society. The struggle may also be between two elements in the character's mind.

> See also **Plot**

**Connotation** The feelings suggested by a word or phrase, apart from its dictionary meaning. **Example:** The terms "used car" and "previously owned vehicle" have different connotations. To most people, the phrase "previously owned vehicle" sounds better than "used car."

> See also **Denotation; Poetry**

## D

**Denotation** The dictionary meaning of a word or phrase. Denotation is especially important in functional texts and other types of nonfiction used to communicate information precisely.

> See also **Connotation; Functional text; Nonfiction**

**Descriptive language** Language that creates a "picture" of a person, place, or thing—often using words that appeal to the five senses: sight, hearing, touch, smell, and taste. **Example:** The bright, hot sun beat down on Earth's surface. Where once a vibrant lake cooled the skin of hippos and zebras, only thin, dry cracks remained, reaching across the land like an old man's fingers, as far as the eye could see. The smell of herds was gone, and only silence filled the space.

> See also **Imagery**

**Dialogue** What characters say to each other. Writers use dialogue to develop characters, move the plot forward, and add interest. In most writing, dialogue is set off by quotation marks; in play scripts, however, dialogue appears without quotation marks.

**Diary** A book written by a person about his or her own life as it is happening. Unlike an autobiography, a diary is not usually meant to be published. It is made up of entries that are written shortly after events occur. The person writing a diary often expresses feelings and opinions about what has happened.

# Literary Terms

**Drama** A kind of writing in which a plot unfolds in the words and actions of characters performed by actors.
*See also* **Genre; Play; Plot**

## E

**Essay** A short piece of nonfiction, normally in prose, that discusses a single topic without claiming to do so thoroughly. Its purpose may be to inform, entertain, or persuade.
*See also* **Nonfiction; Photo-essay; Topic**

**Evidence** Information provided to support a claim.
*See also* **Argument; Claim; Reasons**

**Exposition** The rising action of a story in which characters and the problems they face are introduced.
*See also* **Rising action**

**Expository nonfiction** Writing that gives information and facts. It is usually divided into sections that give information about subtopics of a larger topic.
*See also* **Article; News feature; Nonfiction; Report; Textbook; Topic**

**Exaggeration** Figurative language that makes things seem bigger than they really are in order to create a funny image in the reader's mind. **Example:** My eyes are so big they pop out of my face when I get surprised or angry.
*See also* **Figurative language; Hyperbole**

## F

**Fable** A brief fictional narrative that teaches a lesson about life. Many fables have animals instead of humans as characters. Fables often end with a short, witty statement of their lesson. **Example:** "The Tortoise and the Hare" is a famous fable in which a boastful, quick-moving hare challenges a slow-moving tortoise to a race. Because the overconfident hare takes a nap during the race, the tortoise wins. The moral of the fable is that slow and steady wins the race.
*See also* **Fiction; Folk tale**

**Fairy tale** *See* **Fantasy; Folk tale**

**Falling action** The actions and events in a plot that happen after the climax. Usually, the major problem is solved in some way, so the remaining events serve to bring the story to an end.
*See also* **Climax; Conflict; Plot, Rising action**

**Fantasy** Fiction in which imaginary worlds differ from the "real" world outside the text. Fairy tales, science fiction, and fables are examples of fantasy.
*See also* **Fable; Fiction**

**Fiction** Narrative writing about imaginary people, places, things, or events.
*See also* **Biographical fiction; Fable; Fantasy; Folk tale; Historical fiction; Myth; Novel; Realistic fiction; Short story**

**Figurative language** The use of a word or phrase to say one thing and mean another. Figurative language is especially important in literature and poetry because it gives writers a more effective way of expressing what they mean than using direct, literal language. **Example:** Upon receiving her monthly bills, Victoria complained that she was "drowning in debt."
*See also* **Exaggeration; Hyperbole; Idiom; Imagery; Literature; Metaphor; Personification; Poetry; Simile; Symbol**

**Folk tale** A short, fictional narrative shared orally rather than in writing, and thus partly changed through its retellings before being written down. Folk tales include myths, legends, fables, ghost stories, and fairy tales.
*See also* **Fable; Legend; Myth**

**Folklore** The collection of a people's beliefs, customs, rituals, spells, songs, sayings, and stories as shared mainly orally rather than in writing.
*See also* **Folk tale; Legend; Myth**

**Functional text** Writing in which the main purpose is to communicate the information people need to accomplish tasks in everyday life. **Examples:** résumés, business letters, technical manuals, and the help systems of word-processing programs.

## G

**Genre** A type or class of literary works grouped according to form, style, and/or topic. Major genres include fictional narrative prose (such as short stories and most novels), nonfiction narrative prose (such as autobiographies, diaries, and journals), drama, poetry, and the essay.
*See also* **Essay; Fiction; Literature; Nonfiction; Poetry; Prose; Style; Topic**

## H

**Hero** or **Heroine** In myths and legends, a man or woman of great courage and strength who is celebrated for his or her daring feats.
*See also* **Legend; Myth**

**Historical fiction** Fiction based on events that actually happened or on people who actually lived. It may be written from the point of view of a "real" or an imaginary character, and it usually includes invented dialogue.
*See also* **Fiction**

**Hyperbole** Figurative language that exaggerates, often to the point of being funny, to emphasize something. **Example:** When his mother asked how long he had waited for the school bus that morning, Jeremy grinned and said, "Oh, not long. Only about a million years."
*See also* **Exaggeration; Figurative language**

## I

**Idiom** A phrase or expression that means something different from the word or words' dictionary meanings. Idioms cannot be translated word for word into another language because an idiom's meaning is not the same as that of the individual words that make it up. **Example:** "Mind your p's and q's" in English means to be careful, thoughtful, and behave properly.

**Imagery** Figurative language that communicates sensory experience. Imagery can help the reader imagine how people, places, and things look, sound, taste, smell, and feel. It can also make the reader think about emotions and ideas that commonly go with certain sensations. Because imagery appeals to the senses, it is sometimes called *sensory language*.

> *See also* **Descriptive language; Figurative language; Symbol**

**Interview** A discussion between two or more people in which questions are asked and answered so that the interviewer can get information. The record of such a discussion is also called an interview.

## J

**Jargon** Specialized language used by people to describe things that are specific to their group or subject. **Example:** *Mouse* in a computer class means "part of a computer system," not "a rodent."

**Journal** A personal record, similar to a diary. It may include accounts of actual events, stories, poems, sketches, thoughts, essays, a collection of interesting information, or just about anything the writer wishes to include.

> *See also* **Diary**

## L

**Legend** A very old story, usually written about a hero or heroine or to explain something in nature. Legends are mostly fiction, but some details may be true.

> *See also* **Folk tale; Hero or Heroine; Myth**

**Literature** Works written as prose or poetry.

> *See also* **Poetry; Prose**

## M

**Metaphor** A type of figurative language that compares two unlike things by saying that one thing is the other thing. **Example:** Dhara says her grandfather can be a real mule when he doesn't get enough sleep.

> *See also* **Figurative language; Simile; Symbol**

**Meter** The patterning of language into regularly repeating units of rhythm. Language patterned in this way is called *verse*. By varying the rhythm within a meter, the writer can heighten the reader's attention to what is going on in the verse and reinforce meaning.

> *See also* **Poetry; Rhythm**

**Mood** The overall feeling or atmosphere a writer creates in a piece of writing.

> *See also* **Tone**

**Motive** The reason a character has for his or her thoughts, feelings, actions, or words. **Example:** Maria's motive for bringing cookies to her new neighbors was to learn what they were like.

> *See also* **Characterization**

**Myth** A fictional narrative, often a folk tale, that tells of supernatural events as a way of explaining natural events and their relation to human life. Myths commonly involve gods, goddesses, monsters, and superhuman heroes or heroines.

> *See also* **Folk tale; Hero** or **Heroine; Legend**

## N

**Narrative writing** Writing that gives an account of a set of real or imaginary events (the story), which the writer selects and arranges in a particular order (the plot). Narrative writing includes nonfiction works such as news articles, autobiographies, and journals, as well as fictional works such as short stories, novels, and plays.

> *See also* **Autobiography; Fiction; Journal; Narrator; Nonfiction; Plot; Story**

**Narrator** Someone who gives an account of events. In fiction, the narrator is the teller of a story (as opposed to the real author, who invented the narrator as well as the story). Narrators differ in how much they participate in a story's events. In a first-person narrative, the narrator is the "I" telling the story. In a third-person narrative, the narrator is not directly involved in the events and refers to characters by name or as *he*, *she*, *it*, or *they*. Narrators also differ in how much they know and how much they can be trusted by the reader.

> *See also* **Character; Point of view**

**News feature** A nonfiction article that gives facts about real people and events.

> *See also* **Article; Expository nonfiction; Nonfiction**

**Nonfiction** Written works about events or things that are not imaginary; writing other than fiction.

> *See also* **Autobiography; Biography; Diary; Essay; Fiction; Journal; Personal narrative; Photo-essay; Report; Textbook**

**Novel** A long, fictional narrative, usually in prose. Its length enables it to have more characters, a more complicated plot, and a more fully developed setting than shorter works of fiction.

> *See also* **Character; Fiction; Plot; Prose; Setting; Short story**

## O

**Onomatopoeia** The use of words that imitate the sounds they refer to. **Examples:** *buzz, slam, hiss*

# Literary Terms

## P

**Personal narrative** An account of a certain event or set of events in a person's life, written by that person.
    *See also* **Autobiography; Diary; Journal**

**Personification** Figurative language that describes animals, things, or ideas as having human traits. **Examples:** In the movie *Babe* and in the book *Charlotte's Web*, the animals are all personified.
    *See also* **Figurative language**

**Persuasive writing** Writing that attempts to get someone to do or agree to something by appealing to logic or emotion. Persuasive writing is used in advertisements, editorials, and political speeches.

**Photo-essay** A short nonfiction piece made up of photographs and captions. The photographs are as important as the words in presenting information.
    *See also* **Essay; Nonfiction**

**Play** A work of drama, especially one written to be performed on a stage. **Example:** Lorraine Hansberry's *A Raisin in the Sun* was first performed in 1959.
    *See also* **Drama**

**Plot** The pattern of events and situations in a story or play. Plot is usually divided into four main parts: *conflict* (or *problem*), *rising action* (or *exposition* or *complication*), *climax*, and *falling action* (or *resolution*).
    *See also* **Climax; Conflict; Drama; Falling action; Fiction; Rising action; Story**

**Poetry** A form of literary expression that uses line breaks for emphasis. Poems often use connotation, imagery, metaphor, symbol, allusion, repetition, and rhythm. Word patterns in poetry include rhythm or meter, and often rhyme and alliteration.
    *See also* **Alliteration; Connotation; Figurative language; Meter; Repetition; Rhyme; Rhythm**

**Point of view** The position from which the events of a story seem to be observed and told. A first-person point of view tells the story through what the narrator knows, experiences, concludes, or can find out by talking to other characters. A third-person point of view may be *omniscient*, giving the narrator unlimited knowledge of things, events, and characters, including characters' hidden thoughts and feelings. Or it may be *limited* to what one or a few characters know and experience. **Example** of First-Person Point of View: I'm really hungry right now, and I can't wait to eat my lunch. **Example** of Third-Person Limited Point of View: Olivia is really hungry right now and she wants to eat her lunch. **Example** of Third-Person Omniscient Point of View: Olivia is really hungry right now and she wants to eat her lunch. The other students are thinking about their weekend plans. The teacher is wondering how she will finish the lesson before the bell rings.
    *See also* **Character; Fiction; Narrator**

**Propaganda** A type of persuasion that twists or doesn't tell the whole truth. Types of propaganda include *glittering generalities* (using impressive words to skip past the truth), *transfers* (using appealing ideas or symbols that aren't directly related to the topic), *testimonials* (using the words of famous people), *plain folks* (showing that a product or idea has the same values as the audience), *bandwagon* (claiming that everyone else is doing it), and *name calling*.
    *See also* **Persuasive writing**

**Prose** A form of writing in which the rhythm is less regular than that of verse and more like that of ordinary speech.
    *See also* **Poetry; Rhythm**

**Proverb** A short saying that expresses a general truth. Proverbs are found in many different languages and cultures. **Example:** An apple a day keeps the doctor away.

**Purpose** An author's reason for writing. Most authors write to entertain, inform, or persuade. **Example:** An author's purpose in an editorial is to persuade the reader to think or do something.
    *See also* **Expository nonfiction; Narrative writing; Persuasive writing**

## R

**Realistic fiction** Fiction in which detailed handling of imaginary settings, characters, and events produces a lifelike illusion of a "real" world. **Example:** Although Upton Sinclair's *The Jungle* is a work of fiction, the author's graphic, detailed descriptions of the slaughterhouse workers' daily lives led to real changes in the meatpacking industry.
    *See also* **Fiction**

**Reason** A logical explanation that connects a piece of evidence to a writer or speaker's claim.
    *See also* **Argument; Claim; Evidence**

**Repetition** The repeating of individual vowels and consonants, syllables, words, phrases, lines, or groups of lines. Repetition can be used because it sounds pleasant, to emphasize the words in which it occurs, or to help tie the parts of a text into one structure. It is especially important in creating the musical quality of poetry, where it can take such forms as alliteration and rhyme.
    *See also* **Alliteration; Poetry; Rhyme**

**Report** A usually short piece of nonfiction writing on a particular topic. It differs from an essay in that it normally states only facts and does not directly express the writer's opinions.
    *See also* **Essay; Nonfiction; Topic**

**Resolution** See **Falling action**

**Rhyme** The repetition of ending sounds in different words. Rhymes usually come at the end of lines of verse, but they may also occur within a line. **Examples:** *look, brook, shook*

>   *See also* **Poetry; Repetition; Rhyme scheme**

**Rhyme scheme** The pattern of rhymed line endings in a work of poetry or a stanza. It can be represented by giving a certain letter of the alphabet to each line ending on the same rhyme. **Example:** Because the end word of every other line rhymes in the following poem, the rhyme scheme is *abab*:

Winter night falls quick (a)
The pink sky gone, blackness overhead (b)
Looks like the snow will stick (a)
Down the street and up the hill I tread (b)

>   *See also* **Poetry; Rhyme; Stanza**

**Rhythm** The natural rise and fall, or "beat," of language. Rhythm is present in all language, including speech and prose, but it is most obvious in poetry.

>   *See also* **Meter; Poetry; Prose**

**Rising action** The part of a plot that presents actions or events that lead to the climax.

>   *See also* **Climax; Conflict; Exposition; Falling action; Plot**

## S

**Setting** The time and place in which the events of a story occur.

**Short story** A brief, fictional narrative. Like the novel, it organizes the action, thought, and dialogue of its characters into a plot. But it tends to focus on fewer characters and to center on a single event.

>   *See also* **Character; Fiction; Novel; Plot; Story**

**Simile** A type of figurative language that compares two unlike things by using a word or phrase such as *like, as, than, similar to, resembles,* or *seems*. **Examples:** The tall, slim man had arms as willowy as a tree's branches. The woman's temper is like an unpredictable volcano.

>   *See also* **Figurative language; Metaphor**

**Song lyrics** Words meant to be sung. Lyrics have been created for many types of songs, including love songs, religious songs, work songs, sea chanties, and children's game songs. Lyrics for many songs were shared orally for generations before being written down. Not all song lyrics are lyrical like poems; some are the words to songs that tell a story. Not all poems called songs were written to be sung.

>   *See also* **Folklore; Poetry**

**Speech** A message on a specific topic, spoken before an audience; also, spoken (not written) language.

**Stanza** A group of lines that forms a section of a poem and has the same pattern (including line lengths, meter, and usually rhyme scheme) as other sections of the same poem. In printed poems, stanzas are separated from each other by a space.

>   *See also* **Meter; Poetry; Rhyme scheme**

**Story** A series of events (actual or imaginary) that can be selected and arranged in a certain order to form a narrative or dramatic plot. It is the raw material from which the finished plot is built. Although there are technical differences, the word *story* is sometimes used in place of *narrative*.

>   *See also* **Drama; Plot**

**Style** The way a writer uses language to express the feelings or thoughts he or she wants to convey. Just as no two people are alike, no two styles are exactly alike. A writer's style results from his or her choices of vocabulary, sentence structure and variety, imagery, figurative language, rhythm, repetition, and other resources.

>   *See also* **Figurative language; Genre; Imagery; Repetition; Rhythm**

**Symbol** A word or phrase that serves as an image of some person, place, thing, or action but that also calls to mind some other, usually broader, idea or range of ideas. **Example:** An author might describe doves flying high in the sky to symbolize peace.

>   *See also* **Figurative language; Imagery**

## T

**Textbook** A book prepared for use in schools for the study of a subject.

**Theme** The underlying message or main idea of a piece of writing. It expresses a broader meaning than the topic of the piece.

>   *See also* **Topic**

**Tone** A writer's or speaker's attitude toward his or her topic or audience or toward him- or herself. A writer's tone may be positive, negative, or neutral. The words the writer chooses, the sentence structure, and the overall pattern of words convey the intended tone.

>   *See also* **Connotation; Figurative language; Literature; Mood; Rhythm; Topic**

**Topic** What or who is being discussed in a piece of writing; the subject of the piece.

>   *See also* **Theme**

# Index of Skills

## G

**Generalizations, make** 237, 379, 429, 493, 553

**Genre**
biography 350, 378, 402
blog 186
essay 334
expository nonfiction 48
fable 446
fantasy 206
feature article 226
folk tale 298
historical fiction 172
history article 280, 318
history feature 388
interview 32, 288
journal 152
legend 76
magazine article 502, 522
myth 418, 530, 532
newspaper article 486
online news brief 118
personal narrative 16, 216
persuasive essay 456
play 246
poetry 22, 234, 308, 536
science article 134, 438
science fiction 262
short story 58, 368, 522
social science article 92, 102, 108
song and poem 358, 492
speech 470

**Glossary** 184, 582

**Grammar**
clauses 498, 518
conjunctions 498, 499, 515, 535
participles 242, 243
sentence 12, 25, 44, 88, 89, 101, 346, 364, 482, 483, 495, 498, 499, 515, 518, 519, 535
subject-verb agreement 104, 105
*see also Adjectives, Adverbs, Conjunctions, Nouns, Prepositions, Pronouns, Verbs*

**Graphic organizers**
argument chart 455, 467
attribute web 151, 163
author's purpose chart 501, 513
beginning-middle-end chart 205
category web 516
cause-and-effect chart 133, 349, 359, 367, 379, 387, 399
character description chart 171, 183, 195

character viewpoint chart 417, 429
class chart 499
classification chart 128
comparison chart 62, 120, 190, 225, 237, 266, 336, 380, 404, 472, 538
conclusion chart 47, 551
connotation chart 454
expanded meaning map 106, 170, 316, 386
fact-and-opinion chart 485, 493
fact web 143
generalization chart 552
idea chart 169, 453
idea web 105, 546
KWL chart 102, 312, 432
main-idea chart 5, 91, 107, 279, 317, 331
plot diagram 195, 245, 259, 521, 533
problem-and-solution chart 75, 83
question chart 29, 277
reaction chart 200
response chart 73, 243
survey chart 86
survey tally 496
T chart 362, 437, 447
theme chart 297, 309
time line 519
Venn diagram 260, 365
word map 132, 366, 436

## I

**Ideas and feelings, express** 11, 13, 25

**Idiom** 478, 514

**Importance, determine** 4, 5, 31, 349, 367, 387, 405, 546

**Independent Reading** *see Content library, Digital library, Leveled library*

**Infer** 5, 38, 47, 81, 83, 99, 115, 143, 183, 285, 303, 308, 325, 331, 359, 373, 399, 417, 429, 437, 447, 455, 473, 533, 548

**Information, give** 87, 89, 101, 275, 277, 291

**Internet** 1, 10, 26, 42, 65, 70, 86, 100, 102, 116, 123, 128, 146, 164, 166, 193, 200, 220, 240, 269, 274, 292, 312, 332, 339, 344, 362, 382, 407, 412, 432, 450, 475, 480, 496, 516,

**Interpret** 23, 53, 83, 209, 289, 308, 331, 359, 360, 391, 423, 465, 492, 494, 507, 514, 534

chart 37, 97, 444
diagram 442
graph 98
map 34, 326, 356

**Interview** 32, 35–38

## J

**Judgments, make** 55, 143, 217, 288

## K

**Key vocabulary** 14, 18, 19, 20, 23, 30, 34, 35, 36, 37, 38, 39, 46, 50, 51, 52, 53, 54, 55, 60, 71, 74, 78, 80, 82, 83, 90, 94, 96, 97, 98, 99, 106, 111, 112, 113, 114, 115, 119, 132, 136, 137, 138, 140, 142, 143, 150, 154, 156, 159, 160, 162, 163, 170, 174, 176, 177, 182, 183, 186, 189, 204, 208, 210, 212, 217, 224, 228, 229, 230, 232, 237, 244, 248, 254, 255, 258, 259, 262, 263, 264, 278, 282, 284, 286, 287, 289, 296, 300, 301, 302, 304, 309, 316, 320, 322, 323, 324, 327, 331, 334, 335, 348, 352, 354, 355, 356, 357, 359, 366, 370, 373, 376, 377, 379, 386, 390, 391, 392, 394, 395, 396, 398, 399, 402, 416, 420, 422, 424, 426, 429, 436, 440, 441, 442, 443, 444, 445, 447, 454, 458, 460, 462, 463, 465, 467, 484, 488, 489, 490, 491, 493, 500, 501, 504, 505, 506, 508, 511, 512, 513, 520, 524, 526, 533

## L

**Language & Grammar** 11, 13, 25, 27, 29, 41, 43–45, 57, 71, 73, 85, 87–89, 101, 103–105, 117, 129–131, 145, 147–149, 165, 167–169, 185, 201–203, 219, 221–223, 239, 241–243, 261, 275–277, 291, 293–295, 311, 313–315, 333, 345–347, 361, 363–365, 381, 383–385, 401, 413–415, 431, 433–435, 449, 451–453, 469, 481–483, 495, 497–499, 515, 517–519, 535

**Language, use appropriate** 481, 483, 495, 497, 499, 515

**Leveled library** 1, 63, 65, 121, 123, 191, 193, 267, 269, 337, 339, 405, 407, 473, 475, 539

**Listening/Speaking**
ask questions 63
book talk 63, 121, 191, 267, 337, 405, 473, 539

compare tales across cultures 84
discussion 63, 121, 129, 131, 145, 191, 267, 337, 405, 473, 539
dramatize 191, 360
draw and tell 63, 191, 405, 473
recite songs 494
report 121
role-play 267, 337
share your art 539
write and share 121, 405, 473
**Literary Analysis**
characters 534
compare events 290
facts from opinion 400
mood and tone 430
narrator's point of view 24
presentations 260
rhythm in poetry 238
style 464
text structure 41, 56
theme 218, 310
topic 380
**Literary terms** 593

## M

**Main idea and details** 19, 51, 53, 56, 66, 91, 92, 95, 97, 99, 107–108, 111, 142, 229, 270–271, 279–280, 317–318, 323, 327, 337, 398, 466
**Media/Speaking** 164
**Media**
analyze media 225
digital library 1, 10, 26, 42, 65, 70, 86, 102, 128, 146, 166, 200, 220, 240, 274, 292, 312, 339, 344, 362, 382, 407, 412, 432, 450, 480, 496, 516
Research/Media 144
use the Internet for research 116
viewing 35, 82, 114, 142, 463, 509
**Metaphor** 21, 358, 478, 492, 494
**Modifiers** *see Adjectives, Adverbs*
**Monitor reading** 2, 15, 75–76, 91, 107, 121, 544
**Mood** 358, 430
**Multiple-meaning words** 8–9, 40, 410–411, 448

## N

**Narrator's point of view** 19, 24, 182, 215, 525
**Needs and wants, express** 71, 73, 85

**Nouns** 346
plural 72, 73, 85
possessive 414, 415, 431
precise 347

## O

**Opinion** 383, 385, 401

## P

**Paraphrase** 55, 82, 163, 179, 216, 229, 353, 373, 377, 446, 465, 533
**Participles** 242, 243
**Personification** 427
**Perspective** 527
**Persuade** 437, 451, 453, 468–469
**Plan and monitor** 2, 15, 541–544
**Plot** 216, 233, 245, 259, 267, 307
climax 521
conflict 194–195, 197, 245, 258
events 66, 75, 120, 194–195, 206, 245, 521–522
exposition 521
problem 75, 76, 82
resolution 75, 194–195, 197, 245
turning point 194–195, 197, 245
**Poetic elements**
rhyme 236
rhythm 238
tone 236
**Point of view** 19, 24, 62, 124–125, 151, 152, 163, 171, 172, 179, 182, 190, 191, 288, 417, 418, 421
**Predict**
confirm predictions 2, 16, 21, 79, 81, 159, 162, 182, 211, 215, 253, 258, 303, 307, 377, 527, 529
preview and predict 2, 15, 20, 80, 82, 115, 159, 160, 180, 210, 212, 217, 252, 254, 302, 304, 374, 526, 528, 541, 542, 543
**Prefixes** 198–199, 218, 260, 272–273, 290, 332
**Prepositions** 452, 453, 454, 469
**Problem and solution** 157, 427, 525
**Pronouns**
intensive 384, 385, 401
object 361, 364, 365, 381, 452
plural 384
possessive 434, 435, 449
reflexive 384, 385, 401
singular 384
subject 130, 131, 148, 149, 361, 364, 365, 381

**Punctuation**
commas 515, 518
endmarks 12, 44, 57

## R

**Reading Fluency**
accuracy 554
expression 39, 83, 163, 217, 309, 379, 429, 533, 557, 559, 561, 565, 567, 571, 574, 576, 581
intonation 23, 115, 183, 259, 289, 359, 467, 513, 555, 558, 563, 566, 569, 570, 573, 578, 580
phrasing 55, 99, 143, 237, 331, 399, 447, 493, 556, 560, 562, 564, 568, 572, 575, 577, 579
prosody *see expression and intonation*
rate 554
**Reading Strategies** 2, 23, 39, 55, 83, 99, 115, 143, 163, 183, 217, 237, 259, 289, 309, 331, 359, 379, 399, 429, 447, 467, 493, 513, 533, 541–553
ask questions 4, 31, 279, 297, 317, 549–550
determine importance 4, 5, 31, 349, 367, 387, 546
make connections 3, 31, 133, 151, 547
make inferences 5, 417, 437, 455, 548
plan and monitor 2, 15, 75, 91, 107, 541–544
synthesize 6, 485, 501, 521, 551–553
visualize 3, 15, 205, 225, 245, 545
**Recall** 209, 423, 507
**Reference sources**
dictionary 40, 56
glossary 184
index 184
Internet 10, 26, 42, 65, 70, 86, 100, 102, 116, 123, 128, 144, 146, 164, 166, 193, 200, 220, 240, 269, 274, 292, 312, 332, 339, 344, 362, 382, 407, 412, 432, 450, 475, 480, 496, 516
**Research/Media**
projects 144, 468
skills 144, 468
**Research/Speaking**
projects 116, 184, 332, 514
skills 116, 332, 494, 514

**Research/Writing**
  projects 100
  skills 100
**Retell a story** 517, 519, 535
**Role play** 267
**Roots of words** 238

## S

**Sentences**
  command 44, 45
  complete 88, 89, 101,
    346, 482, 483, 495
  complex 518, 519, 535
  compound 498, 499, 535
  fragment 495, 535
  predicate 88, 89, 101, 346,
    364, 482, 483, 495
  question 28, 29
  run-on 515
  simple 519
  statement 12, 28, 29, 44, 45
  subject 88, 89, 101, 346,
    364, 482, 483, 495, 518
**Sequence** 141, 301
**Set a Purpose** 2, 15, 18, 78, 154,
  175, 208, 248, 300, 370, 524, 541
**Setting** 179, 196–197, 209, 216, 267
**Shades of meaning** 478
**Simile** 441, 534
**Speaking/Listening** *see*
  *Listening/Speaking*
**Speculate** 379, 447, 533
**Spelling** 72, 85, 242, 291
**Steps in a process** 113, 231, 505
**Study and explain** 538
**Style** 22, 448
**Subject-verb agreement** 104, 105
**Suffixes** 126–127, 164,
  184, 272–273, 290, 310
**Summarize** 4, 5, 23, 31, 39, 83, 99,
  115, 139, 143, 157, 163, 183, 217, 237,
  259, 287, 289, 330, 331, 345, 347,
  357, 359, 361, 379, 399, 425, 429,
  441, 447, 467, 493, 509, 513, 533
**Synonyms** 68, 100, 116, 342–343, 380
**Synthesize** 6, 47, 115, 467,
  485, 501, 521, 539, 551–553

## T

**Technology**
  Comprehension Coach 17, 33, 49,
    77, 93, 109, 135, 153, 173, 207,
    227, 247, 281, 299, 319, 351, 369,
    389, 419, 439, 457, 487, 503, 523
**Text features** 539
  caption 92, 283, 476, 491, 541
  charts 37, 97, 444
  diagrams 134, 442
  graphs 98
  headings 108, 280, 476–477, 541
  illustrations 476
  labels 134
  maps 34, 138, 154, 326, 356
  paragraph 476
  photo 92, 142, 476, 541, 549
  pictures 82, 541
  subhead 541
  title 134, 476–477, 541
**Text structures** 40, 56,
  270–271, 337, 340–341, 349,
  350, 367, 368, 387, 405
**Theme** 218, 260, 270–271,
  297, 298, 310
**Tone** 430, 501

## U

**Unfamiliar words** 342–343

## V

**Verbs**
  helping 168, 169
  *is* 12, 13, 25
  past participle 242
  past tense 276, 277, 291, 294,
    295, 311, 314, 315, 333
  present participle 242
  present tense 276, 277, 291,
    294, 295, 311, 315, 333
  *to be* 294, 295, 311
  *to have* 294, 295, 311
**Viewing**
  critical see Critical viewing;
    Media/viewing
**Visualize** 3, 15, 205, 211,
  225, 245, 267, 545
**Vocabulary** 301, 323, 342–343, 395
  academic *see Academic*
    *vocabulary*

key *see Key vocabulary*
review vocabulary 23, 39, 55, 83,
  99, 115, 143, 163, 183, 217, 237,
  259, 289, 309, 331, 359, 379, 399,
  429, 447, 467, 493, 513, 533
use a graphic organizer 30, 41, 68,
  74, 106, 116, 132, 225, 244, 245,
  315, 342, 366, 367, 436, 519, 520
**Vocabulary study**
  antonyms 116
  connotation 478
  context clues 8–9, 24, 40,
    56, 342–343, 360, 380, 400,
    410–411, 430, 448, 468
  idioms 478, 514
  Latin and Greek roots 238
  metaphors 478, 492, 494
  multiple-meaning
    words 8–9, 410–411
  similes 534
  synonyms 100, 116
  unfamiliar words 342–343
  word categories 84
  word parts 164, 184

## W

**Word categories** 84
**Word choice** 209
**Word origins** 244
**Word parts**
  base words 126, 164, 184, 198–199,
    218, 260, 272–273, 290, 310, 332
  compound words 126, 144
  figurative language 478–
    479, 494, 514, 534
  prefixes 198–199, 218, 260,
    272–273, 290, 332
  suffixes 126–127, 164, 184,
    272–273, 290, 310
**Write about the Guiding
  Question** 23, 39, 55, 83, 99,
  115, 143, 163, 183, 217, 237, 259,
  289, 309, 331, 359, 379, 399,
  429, 447, 467, 493, 513, 533
**Writing and Grammar** 25, 41, 57,
  85, 101, 117, 121, 145, 165, 185, 219,
  239, 261, 291, 311, 333, 361, 381, 401,
  431, 449, 469, 473, 495, 515, 535

# Index of Authors and Titles

# Index of Art and Artists

## Acknowledgments, continued from page ii

Grateful acknowledgement is also given for permission to provide audio recordings of literature and informational text selections included in this book.

**Anthony Arrigo:** "Preserving the Rural Environment" by Anthony Arrigo from www.starrynightlights.com. Used by permission of the author.

**Sandy Asher:** "Pas de Trois" by Sandy from *Heart to Heart: New Poems Inspired by Twentieth-Century American Art*, edited by Jan Greenberg. Copyright © by Sandy Asher. Reprinted by permission of the author.

**Blue Cloud Quarterly:** "There Is No Word for Goodbye" from *There is No Word for Goodbye* by Mary Tall Mountain. Copyright © 1981 by Mary Tall Mountain. Published by Blue Cloud Quarterly, Marvin, South Dakota. Used by permission. A special thank you to The American Indian Resource Center at the County of Los Angeles Public Library in Huntington Park.

**California State University Bakersfield:** From "California Odyssey: The 1930's Migration to the Southern San Joaquin Valley" an oral history interview of Ethel Oleta Wever Belezzuoli by Stacey Jagels. Copyright © 1981 by California State University Bakersfield. Used by permission.

**The Christian Science Monitor:** Adapted from "Old Music Finds New Voices" by Kris Axtma from the *Christian Science Monitor*, January 9, 2002. Copyright © 2002 the Christian Science Monitor. Reprinted by permission of the Christian Science Monitor. All rights reserved.

**Farrar, Straus and Giroux, LLC.:** Excerpt from *Earthquake* by Milly Lee, illustrations by Yangsook Choi. Text copyright © 2001 by Milly Lee, illlustrations © 2001 by Yangsook Choi. Reprinted by permissions of Farrar, Straus and Giroux, LLC.

**Henry Holt and Company:** "The Power of Mysteries" by Alan Lightman, from *This I Believe: The Personal Philosophies of Remarkable Men and Women*, edited by Jay Allison and Dan Gediman. Copyright © 2006 by This I Believe, Inc. Reprinted by permission of Henry Holt and Company, LLC.

**Houghton Mifflin Harcourt:** Excerpt from *Frankenstein Makes a Sandwich* by Adam Rex. Copyright © 2006 by Adam Rex. Reproduced by permission of Houghton Mifflin Harcourt Publishing Company. All rights reserved.

**Intercultural Press:** Excerpt adapted from *Kids Like Me: Voices of the Immigrant Experience* Adapted by Judith M. Blohm and Terri Lapinsky. Copyright © 2006 by Judith M. Blohm and Terri Lapinsky. Reprinted by permission of Intercultural Press, a Nicholas Brealey Publishing Company, Boston, MA.

**National Geographic Society:** Adaptation of "The Power of a Radically Affordable Irrigation Pump" by Sandra Postel from *National Geographic Newswatch*. Copyright © 2012 by the National Geographic Society. Reprinted by permission of the National Geographic Society.

Excerpt from "How Crisis Mapping Saved Lives in Haiti" from the blog by Patrick Meier. Copyright © 2010 by the National Geographic Society. Reprinted by permission of the National Geographic Society.

**Penguin Group (USA), Inc.:** "The Earth Under Sky Bear's Feet," "Sky Bear," "The Scattered Stars",, and "The Seven Mateinuu," from *The Earth Under Sky Bear's Feet: Native American Poems of the Land* text by Joseph Bruchac, illustrations by Thomas Locker. Text copyright © 1995 by Joseph Bruchac, illustrations © by Thomas Locker. Used

by permission of Philomel Books, A Division of Penguin Young Readers Group, a Member of Penguin Group (USA) Inc. All rights reserved.

**Rosen Publishing Group, Inc.:** Excerpt from *Frankenstein Meets the Wolf Man* by Greg Roza. Copyright 2007 by the Rosen Publishing Group, 29 East 21st Street, New York, NY, 10010. Reprinted with permission.

**Russell & Volkening, Inc.:** Excerpt from *Harriet Tubman: Conductor on the Underground Railroad* by Ann Petry. Copyright © 1955 by Ann Petry, renewed 1983 by Ann Petry. Reprinted by permission of Russell & Volkening as agents for the author's estate.

**Scholastic, Inc.:** Excerpt from *Wings* by Christopher Myers. Scholastic Inc./Scholastic Press. Copyright © 2000 by Christopher Myers. Reprinted by permission.

Excerpt from *Call Me Maria*, by Judith Ortiz Cofer. Copyright © 2004 by Judith Ortiz Cofer. Reprinted by permission.

**The Tattoo:** "Caught in the Rain" from "Hurricane Journal" by Samantha Perez. Copyright © 2005 by The Tattoo. Reprinted with the permission of The Tattoo international teen newspaper.

**Ulloa Productions/ Vocal Power Productions:** "Cuando canto/ When I Sing" by Jaunita Ulloa from *Juanita: Mujeres y Mariachi*. Copyright © Ulloa Productions. All rights Reserved. Used by permission.

**Janet Wong:** "When I Grow Up" from *A Suitcase Full of Seaweed* by Janet S. Wong. Copyright © 1996 by Janet S. Wong. Reprinted with the permission of the author.

## Photography

**Cover** ©Patrick Endres/Visuals Unlimited/Corbis. **iii** ©Jeff Greenberg/The Image Works. **iii** ©John Kobal Foundation/Moviepix/Getty Images. **iii** ©Kenneth Garrett/National Geographic. **iii** ©Mark Newman/Lonely Planet Images/Getty Images. **vi** ©Rieger Bertrand/hemis.fr/Getty Images. **viii** ©chanwit whanset/Shutterstock. **xiv** ©Rieger Bertrand/hemis.fr/Getty Images. **xiv** ©National Geographic Stock. **xvi, xviii** ©Cengage Learning. **xx** ©Ethan Welty/Aurora/Getty Images. **xxii** ©AP Photo/Eric Gay. **xxii** ©Roger Ressmeyer/Eureka Premium/Corbis. **xxiv** ©Patricia Correia Gallery. **1** ©Rieger Bertrand/hemis.fr/Getty Images. **3** ©Palemale. **4** ©karamysh/Shutterstock.com. **9** ©Bob Jacobson/keepsake RF/Corbis. **10** ©David Diaz/Cengage Learning. **10** ©JAMES L. STANFIELD/National Geographic Stock. **11** ©Neil Emmerson/Robert Harding World Imagery/Corbis. **12** ©Wolfgang Kaehler. **12** ©Oberhäuser/Caro/Alamy. **14** ©Brian Drouin/National Geographic Image Collection. **14** ©David Mcnew/Getty Images. **14** ©Michael Durham/Getty Images. **14** ©Peter Mason/Taxi/Getty Images. **14** ©David Tipling/Alamy. **14** ©Frances Roberts/Alamy. **17** ©David Diaz. **22** ©Datacraft/sozaijiten/Age Fotostock. **25** ©amana images inc./Alamy. **26** ©Jane Sterrett. **26** ©Tom McCarthy/Photo Network/Alamy. **27** ©Danita Delimont/Alamy. **28** ©Michael Newman/PhotoEdit. **29** ©Tim Hall/Taxi/Getty Images. **30** ©Ace Stock Limited/Alamy. **30** ©Drew Hallowell/Getty Images. **30** ©James Sugar/National Geographic Image Collection. **30** ©Jon Feingersh/Getty Images. **30** ©Lars Klove/The Image Bank/Getty Images. **30** ©Randy Faris/Cardinal/Corbis. **30** ©DigitalStock/Corbis. **32–33, 35–37** ©Jane Sterrett. **37** ©Joseph Clark/Photodisc/Getty Images. **38** ©Jane Sterrett. **42** ©Jose Fuste Raga/Corbis. **42** ©Jose Fuste Raga/Corbis. **42** ©Robert Holmes/Corbis. **43** ©Richard T. Nowitz/Corbis. **44**

©Jeff Greenberg/PhotoEdit. **45** ©fotog/Tetra Images/AGE Fotostock. **46** ©Adam Pretty/Staff/Getty Images Sport/Getty Images. **46** ©Jeff Pullen/The Bridgeman Art Library/Getty Images. **46** ©Larry Dale Gordon/The Image Bank/Getty Images. **46** ©Mark Adams/Getty Images. **46** ©Mitchell Funk/Photographer's Choice/Getty Images. **46** ©Photodisc/Getty Images. **46** ©Rob Reichenfeld/Dorling Kindersley/Getty Images. **46** ©Sam Kittner/National Geographic Image Collection. **48–49** ©Jose Fuste Raga/Corbis. **50** ©AP Photo/Lauren Victoria Burke. **50** ©John Dominis/Time Life Pictures/Getty Images. **51** ©Sandy Felsenthal/Corbis. **52** ©Jeff Greenberg/The Image Works. **53** ©Nik Wheeler/Corbis. **54** ©Bob Krist/Corbis. **62** ©David Diaz/Cengage Learning. **62** ©Jane Sterrett. **62** ©Jose Fuste Raga/Corbis. **64–65** ©Chanwit Whanset/Shutterstock.com. **67** ©TAYLOR S. KENNEDY/National Geographic Stock. **69** ©Mark Newman/Lonely Planet Images/Getty Images. **69** ©Richard Cummins/Corbis. **70** ©Jean and Mou-sien Tseng. **70** ©Paul Conklin/PhotoEdit. **74** ©Dann Tardif/LWA/Corbis. **74** ©David Madison/The Image Bank/Getty Images. **74** ©Image Source/Getty Images. **74** ©JOEL SARTORE/National Geographic Stock. **74** ©RICHARD NOWITZ/National Geographic Stock. **74** ©TODD GIPSTEIN/National Geographic Stock. **74** ©Zigy Kaluzny/Stone/Getty Images. **74** ©eclypse78/Shutterstock.com. **76–77** ©Jean and Mou-sien Tseng. **78** ©FoodShapes/PunchStock. **86** ©Ocean/Corbis. **86** ©Stephen Frink/Photographers Choice/Getty Images. **86** ©Digital Stock/Corbis. **87** ©imagewerks/Getty Images. **87** ©Walt Curlee. **88** ©MICHAEL FAY/National Geographic Stock. **90** ©Brian Drouin/National Geographic Image Collection. **90** ©Image Source/Getty Images. **90** ©IRA BLOCK/National Geographic Stock. **90** ©Nicole Duplaix/National Geographic Image Collection. **90** ©PAUL DAMIEN/National Geographic Stock. **90** ©PRIIT VESILIND/National Geographic Stock. **90** ©ROY TOFT/National Geographic Stock. **90** ©Steve Wisbauer/Photodisc/Getty Images. **92** © Royalty-Free/Corbis. **92–93** ©Brian Hagiwara/Brand X/Corbis. **92–96** ©Reed Kaestner/Corbis. **94** ©Mark Mawson/Robert Harding World Imagery/Getty Images. **94** ©Rick Doyle/Corbis. **94–95** ©Ocean/Corbis. **94–95** ©Digital Stock/Corbis/MG. **94–95** ©Mark Mawson/Robert Harding World Imagery/Getty Images. **95** ©Stockbyte/Getty. **96** ©Bill Barksdale/AgStock Images/Corbis. **96–97** ©Ocean/Corbis. **97** ©Lester Lefkowitz/Stone/Getty Images. **98** ©Kaml Kishore/Reuters/Corbis. **98** ©Ocean/Corbis. **102** ©IC Productions/The Image Bank/Getty Images. **102** ©Ryan Fox/Lonely Planet Images/Getty Images. **102** ©Sky Light Pictures/Shutterstock.com. **103** ©Robert Harding Picture Library/Alamy Images. **104** ©Brent Stirton/Staff/Getty Images News/Getty Images. **105** ©Medioimages/Photodisc/Getty Images. **106** ©Bill Hatcher/National Geographic/Getty Images. **106** ©Christina Kennedy/PhotoEdit. **106** ©Derek Croucher/Photographer's Choice/Getty Images. **106** ©Nicholas Prior/Taxi/Getty Images. **106** ©SARAH LEEN/National Geographic Stock. **106** ©Sheer Photo Inc/Photographer's Choice/Getty Images. **106** ©SKIP BROWN/National Geographic Stock. **106** ©Andersen Ross/Blend Images/Corbis. **108–109** ©Ryan Fox/Lonely Planet Images/Getty Images. **110** ©Fotokostic/Shutterstock.com. **111** ©Michael Dechev/Shutterstock.com. **112** ©Richard Gross/Corbis. **113** ©Matthew Mcvay/Corbis. **114** ©Bruce Forster/Stone/Getty Images. **118–119** ©Courtesy International Development Enterprises. **120** ©Jean and Mou-sien Tseng. **120** ©Ocean/Corbis. **120** ©Ryan Fox/Lonely Planet Images/Getty Images. **122–123** ©Sigurdur H. Stefnisson. **125** ©Bettmann/Corbis. **127** ©HMS Group Inc/Getty Images. **127** ©Mario Tama/Getty

Images News/Getty Images. **128** ©LOOK Die Bildagentur der Fotografen GmbH/Alamy. **128** ©Martin Rietze/Westend61 GmbH/Alamy. **128** ©Steve Raymer/National Geographic. **129** ©Schafer & Hill/Stone/Getty Images. **130** ©Martin Gray/National Geographic. **131** ©Karen Kasmauski/National Geographic. **132** ©Brian Gordon Green/National Geographic Stock. **132** ©Carsten Peter/National Geographic. **132** ©Catherine Karnow/National Geographic Image collection. **132** ©Chris Johns/National Geographic. **132** ©Frank Lukasseck/ Terra/Corbis. **132** ©Jose Luis Pelaez Inc/Blend Images/Getty Images. **132** ©Pixtal/PunchStock. **132** ©Westend61/Jupiter Images. **132** ©Jupiterimages Brand X/Alamy. **134–135** ©LOOK Die Bildagentur der Fotografen GmbH/Alamy. **136** ©Carsten Peter/National Geographic/Getty Images. **138** ©G. Brad Lewis/Getty Images. **139** ©Steve Satushek/Photographer's Choice/Getty Images. **140** ©Gary L. Rosenquist. **140** ©Gary L. Rosenquist. **140** ©Gary L. Rosenquist. **140** ©InterNetwork Media/Photodisc/Getty Images. **141** ©Jim Richardson/National Geographic. **141** ©Mark Moffett/Minden Pictures/Getty Images. **142** ©Philippe Bourseiller. 144 Yuri Arcuri/Shutterstock. **146** ©NOAA/ZUMA/Corbis Wire/Corbis. **146** ©Otis Imboden/National Geographic Stock. **146** ©Tom Fox/Dallas Morning News/Corbis. **147** ©Margo Silver/Photonica World/Getty Images. **148** ©Warren Faidley/Corbis. **150** ©Brian Drouin/National Geographic Image Collection. **150** ©Harold F Pierce/NASA. **150** ©Joel Sartore/National Geographic. **150** ©Juan Silva/The Image Bank/Getty Images. **150** ©Karen Kasmauski/National Geographic. **150** ©Kay Blaschke/Stock4B/Getty Images. **150** ©Corbis/Superstock. **150** ©Stacy Gold/National Geographic. **150** ©Steve Hix/Somos Images/Corbis. **152–153** ©Tom Fox/Dallas Morning News/Corbis. **155** ©Chris Jordan Photographic Arts. **155** ©NASA/Corbis. **155** ©NOAA/ZUMA/Corbis Wire/Corbis. **156–157** ©Warren Faidley/Corbis. **158** ©Jerry Grayson/Helifilms Australia PTY Ltd/Getty Images. **158** ©Robert Polidori. **161** ©Marianna Day Massey/ZUMA/Corbis. **161** ©Robert Polidori. **162** ©Ed Kashi/Corbis. **162** ©The Tattoo. **162** ©Yellow Dog Productions/Taxi/Getty Images. **164** ©Yuri Arcuri/Shutterstock. **166** ©InterNetwork Media/Photodisc/Getty Images. **166** ©Peter Dazeley/Stone/Getty Images. 166 Text and Illustrations from *Earthquake* by Milly Lee. Illustrated by Yangsook Choi. Text ©2001 by Milly Lee. Illustrations ©2001 by Yangsook Choi. Reprinted by permissions of Farrar Straus and Giroux LLC. **167** ©Reuters/Corbis. **168** ©Creativ Studio Heinemann/Getty Images. **168** ©Lauren Nicole/Digital Vision/Getty Images. **168** ©Sheer Photo Inc/Photodisc/Getty Images. **170** ©Bruce Forster/Stone/Getty Images. **170** ©Image Source/Corbis. **170** ©Ira Block/National Geographic. **170** ©Karen Kasmauski/National Geographic. **170** ©Lucas Tange/cultura/Corbis. **170** ©PictureNet/Corbis. **170** ©Todd Gipstein/National Geographic. **170** ©Liz Garza Williams/Cengage Learning. **172–173** Text and Illustrations from *Earthquake* by Milly Lee. Illustrated by Yangsook Choi. Text ©2001 by Milly Lee. Illustrations ©2001 by Yangsook Choi. Reprinted by permissions of Farrar Straus and Giroux LLC. **174** ©Frederic Lewis/Getty Images. **174** ©Ted Streshinsky/Corbis. **175–182** Text and Illustrations from *Earthquake* by Milly Lee. Illustrated by Yangsook Choi. Text ©2001 by Milly Lee. Illustrations ©2001 by Yangsook Choi. Reprinted by permissions of Farrar Straus and Giroux LLC. **185** ©Winfield Parks/National Geographic Stock. **186** ©Joe Raedle/Getty Images News/Getty Images. **187** Courtesy Ushahidi. **188** ©Erin Oberholtzer/U.S. Navy/Getty Images. **190** ©LOOK Die Bildagentur der Fotografen GmbH/Alamy. **190** Text and Illustrations from

*Earthquake* by Milly Lee. Illustrated by Yangsook Choi. Text ©2001 by Milly Lee. Illustrations ©2001 by Yangsook Choi. Reprinted by permissions of Farrar Straus and Giroux LLC. **190** ©Tom Fox/Dallas Morning News/Corbis. **192–193** ©Jason Lugo/E+/Getty Images. **194** ©Theo Allofs/Stone/Getty Images. **197** ©Guy Crittenden/Photographer's Choice/Getty Images. **199** ©AP Photo/Tsunemi. **199** ©Tim Flach/Stone/Getty Images. **200** ©Gary Nolton/Stone/Getty Images. **200** ©Christian Aslund/Lonely Planet Images/Getty Images. **201** ©Daniele Montella. **202** ©TriStar Pictures/Everett Collection. **203** ©Willie Rodger/The Bridgeman Art Library/Getty Images. **204** ©Joel Sartore/National Geographic. **204** ©Joel Sartore/National Geographic Stock. **204** ©Malcolm Fife/Photographer's Choice/Getty Images. **204** ©Milton Montenegro/Photodisc/Getty Images. **204** ©Richard Lewisohn/Digital Vision/Getty Images. **204** ©Steve Winter/National Geographic. **204** ©Sydney Hastings/National Geographic Stock. **204** (cr) ©Franz-Marc Frei/Corbis. **216** ©The Granger Collection NYC. **219** ©Jan Hakan Dahlstrom/Photonica/Getty Images. **220** ©John Kobal Foundation/Getty Images. **220, 226** ©John Kobal Foundation/Moviepix/Getty Images. **221** ©Tim Gabor. **221** ©George B Diebold/Lithium/AGE Fotostock. **222** ©Lisette Le Bon/SuperStock. **223** ©Bettmann/Corbis. **224** ©Galen Rowell/Terra/Corbis. **224** ©James L. Stanfield/National Geographic. **224** ©Jose Pelaez/Corbis. **224** ©Maria Stenzel/National Geographic. **224** ©Randy Faris/Corbis. **224** ©The Print Collector/Heritage-Images/Imagestate. **224** ©DreamPictures/Shannon Faulk/Jupiter Images. **224** ©fStop/Alamy. **226** ©John Kobal Foundation/Getty Images. **228** ©Bettmann/Corbis. **229** ©Pictorial Press Ltd/Alamy. **230** ©Everett Collection. **231** ©1943 Universal Pictures. **231** ©1943 Universal Pictures. **231** ©1943 Universal Pictures. **231** ©John Kobal Foundation/Getty Images. **232** ©20th Century Fox Film Corp/Everett Collection. **233** ©Everett Collection. **233** ©Mike Nelson/AFP/Getty Images. **234–236** *Frankenstein Makes a Sandwich* ©2006 by Adam Rex. Reproduced by permission of Houghton Mifflin Harcourt Publishing Company. **240** ©Keith Graves/Cengage Learning. **240** ©Wayne Eastep/Photographer's Choice/Getty Images. **241** ©Joan Marcus Photography. **242** ©Robbie Jack/Corbis. **243** ©Universal Images Group/Getty. **244** ©Barry Rosenthal/Taxi/Getty Images. **244** ©Brand X Pictures/Jupiter Images. **244** ©Emmanuel Faure/Stone/Getty Images. **244** ©Holos/Taxi/Getty Images. **244** ©Jonathan Daniel/Getty Images Sport/Getty Images. **244** ©Keith Brofsky/UpperCut Images/Getty Images. **244** ©Ronnie Kaufman/Bridge/Corbis. **244** ©Steve Raymer/National Geographic. **249** (inset) ©Underwood & Underwood/Corbis. **266** ©Craig Phillips. **266** ©John Kobal Foundation/Getty Images. **268–269** ©National Geographic Stock. **268–269** ©WES C. SKILES/National Geographic. **271** ©Ladislav Janicek/Corbis. **273** ©EMORY KRISTOF/National Geographic Image Collection. **273** ©Emory Kristof/National Geographic Image Collection. **273** ©Kevin Horgan/Stone/Getty Images. **274** ©Institute for Exploration/University of Rhode Island & Mystic Aquarium. **274** ©National Museums Northern Ireland. **275** ©Paul Souders/Corbis. **275** ©The Mariners' Museum/Corbis. **276** ©M. Timothy O'Keefe/Alamy. **278** ©Don Hammond/Design Pics/Corbis. **278** ©epa/Corbis. **278** ©Michael Blann/Getty Images. **278** ©Moodboard/Corbis. **278** ©Ocean/Corbis. **278** ©Pixland/Corbis. **278** ©Tom Grill/Spirit/Corbis. **278** ©Kryssia Campos/Flickr/Getty Images. **280–281** ©Institute for Exploration/University of Rhode Island & Mystic Aquarium. **281** ©Institute for Exploration/University of Rhode Island &

Mystic Aquarium. **282** ©Bureau L.A. Collection/Sygma/Corbis. **282–283** ©Getty Images. **284** Illustration by Ken Marschall ©1992 from *Titanic: An Illustrated History* a Hyperion/Madison Press Book. **285** ©Topical Press Agency/Getty Images. **287** ©Institute for Exploration / Institute for Archaeological Oceanography. **287** Institute for Exploration/University of Rhode Island & Mystic Aquarium. **288** ©Bruce Dale/National Geographic Stock. **288** ©PRIIT VESILIND/National Geographic Stock. **292** ©Via Mundi Gallery. **293** ©Photodisc/SW Productions/Getty Images. **294** ©Steve Hix/Somos Images/Corbis. **295** ©Dana White/PhotoEdit. **296** ©AP Photo/Mike Derer. **296** ©Ed Taylor/Taxi/Getty Images. **296** ©Frans Lemmens/The Image Bank/Getty Images. **296** ©Kaz Chiba/Photodisc/Getty Images. **296** ©Mark Scott/Photodisc/Getty Images. **296** ©Michele Constantini/ PhotoAlto Agency RF Collections/Getty Images. **296** ©O. Louis Mazzatenta/National Geographic Image Collection. **296** ©Shannon Fagan/Stone+/Getty Images. **299** ©Via Mundi Gallery. **300** ©Courtesy of Novica Los Angeles. **301** ©Willis Tilly (Contemporary Artist)/Private Collection/The Bridgeman Art Library. **303** ©Angela Ferreira. **304** Courtesy of Hamill Gallery Boston. **305** Courtesy of Hamill Gallery Boston. **306** Courtesy of Nzalamba Art Works Los Angeles. **307** ©Annie Tiberio Cameron/DC Artists Management. **312** ©Stapleton Collection/Corbis. **312** The funerary mask of Tutankhamun (c.1370–1352 BC) c.1336–1327 BC New Kingdom (gold inlaid with semi-precious stones) Egyptian 18th Dynasty (c.1567–1320 BC)/Egyptian National Museum Cairo Egypt/Giraudon/The Bridgeman Art Library. **313** ©Cardinal/Corbis. **313** ©SISSE BRIMBERG/National Geographic Stock. **316** ©Adam Jones/Digital Vision/Getty Images. **316** ©AP Photo/Hasan Jamali. **316** ©AP Photo/Marco Ugarte. **316** ©Buena Vista Images/Photodisc/Getty Images. **316** ©David Cattanach/Alamy. **316** ©David Muir/Getty Images. **316** ©Martin Child/Getty Images. **316** ©Oppenheim Bernhard/Stone+/Getty Images. **318–319** ©Planet Art: Ancient Egypt. **319** The funerary mask of Tutankhamun (c.1370–1352 BC) c.1336–1327 BC New Kingdom (gold inlaid with semi-precious stones) Egyptian 18th Dynasty (c.1567–1320 BC)/Egyptian National Museum Cairo Egypt/Giraudon/©The Bridgeman Art Library. **320–321** ©Paul Hardy/Corbis. **322–323** ©KENNETH GARRETT/National Geographic Image Collection. **323** ©Erich Lessing/Art Resource NY. **323** ©Louvre Paris France/Bridgeman Art Library. **324** ©Bettmann/Corbis. **324–325** ©Kenneth Garrett/National Geographic. **327** ©Roger Viollet Paris/Bridgeman Art Library. **327** ©Ron Watts/Corbis. **328** 'Dummy' of the young Tutankhamun (c.1370–52 BC) wearing a compromise between the crown of the kings of Lower Egypt and the headdress of Nefertiti (painted & stuccoed wood) (see 148193) Egyptian 18th Dynasty (c.1567–1320 BC)/Egyptian National Museum Cairo Egypt/©The Bridgeman Art Library. **329** ©Bridgeman Art Library. **329** ©Harry Burton/The Granger Collection NY. **330** ©Griffith Institute Oxford. **330** ©Sandro Vannini/Corbis. **334–335** ©Corey Ford/Stocktrek Images/Getty Images. **336** ©Institute for Exploration/University of Rhode Island & Mystic Aquarium. **336** ©Institute for Exploration/University of Rhode Island & Mystic Aquarium. **336** The funerary mask of Tutankhamun (c.1370–1352 BC) c.1336–1327 BC New Kingdom (gold inlaid with semi-precious stones) Egyptian 18th Dynasty (c.1567–1320 BC)/Egyptian National Museum Cairo Egypt/Giraudon/©The Bridgeman Art Library. **336** ©Via Mundi Gallery. **338–339** ©Andrew Wilson/Demotix/Corbis. **341** ©Hulton Archive/Getty Images. **341** ©Hulton Archive/Getty Images. **343** ©Adalberto Rios Szalay/Sexto Sol/Getty Images. **343** ©Albert

Normandin/Masterfile. **344** ©Hulton Archive/
Getty Images. **344** ©Janice Northcutt Huse. **344**
©Masterfile. **345** ©Michael Newman/PhotoEdit.
**346** ©Hulton Archive/Getty Images. **348** ©Azure
Computer & Photo Services/Animals Animals. **348**
©Brian Drouin/National Geographic Image
Collection. **348** ©Creatas Images/Creatas/Jupiter
Images. **348** ©Historical/Corbis. **348** ©Karan
Kapoor/The Image Bank/Getty Images. **348**
©Michael Melford/National Geographic Stock. **348**
©National Photo Company/Corbis. **348** ©Spencer
Platt/Edit/Getty Images. **350–351** ©Comstock/
Fotosearch.com. **350–351** ©Janice Northcutt
Huse. **352** ©C Squared Studios/Photodisc. **352**
©Janice Northcutt Huse. **353** ©Bettmann/Corbis.
**353** ©Henry P. Moore/The New York Historical
Society. **354** The Ohio Historical Society Archives
Library. **354–355** ©SuperStock /SuperStock. **355**
©Levi Coffin House. **357** ©Janice Northcutt Huse.
**358** ©2007 Masterfile Corporation. **358** ©Dave
King/Dorling Kindersley. **362** ©ACE STOCK
LIMITED/Alamy. **363** ©Bertrand Gardel/hemis.fr/
Getty Images. **363** ©Dave G. Houser/Corbis. **364**
©John Miller/Robert Harding World Imagery/Getty
Images. **365** ©FRANZ NEUMAYR/AFP/Getty
Images. **366** ©Carsten Peter/National Geographic/
Getty Images. **366** ©Image Source/Jupiter Images.
**366** ©JOHN GURZINSKI/AFP/Getty Images. **366**
©ML Harris/Getty Images. **366** ©ML Harris/
Iconica/Getty Images. **366** ©Stephen St John/
National Geographic Image Collection. **366**
©Victor Mikhailovich Vasnetsov/The Bridgeman
Art Library/Getty Images. **366** ©Frances Twitty/
E+/Getty Images. **377** ©Tamas Galambos private
collection/Bridgeman Art Library. **378** ©David
Bartolomi. **378** ©Ric Ergenbright/Corbis. **382**
©Arif Ali/Stringer/AFP/Getty Images. **382**
©Charlie Drevstam/Johner Images Royalty-Free/
Getty Images. **382** ©Mitchell Funk/The Image
Bank/Getty Images. **383** ©AFP/Getty Images.
**384** ©GERARD MALIE/AFP/Getty Images. **386**
©Antonio Morraxi/Getty Images. **386** ©AP Photo/
Ron Edmonds. **386** ©Digital Vision/Getty Images.
**386** ©H. EDWARD KIM/National Geographic
Stock. **386** ©Lars Klove Photo Service/Getty
Images. **386** ©Lyndon Beddoe/Alamy. **386**
©Michael Siluk/Photo Library. **386** ©Simon
Marcus/Corbis. **386** ©Lisa Stirling/Digital Vision/
Getty Images. **388–389** ©Mitchell Funk/The
Image Bank/Getty Images. **390** ©Joseph Sohm/
Visions of America/Corbis. **391** ©Bob Daemmrich/
PhotoEdit. **391** ©David Young-Wolff/PhotoEdit.
**391** ©Steve Raymer/Corbis. **392** ©Michael
Schwarz. **392** ©Press Association Incorporated/
Corbis. **393** ©Bettmann/Corbis. **393** ©Colin
Braley/Reuters Photo Archive/NewsCom. **394**
©David Turnley/Corbis. **394–395** Jacques
Langevin/Sygma/Corbis. **396** ©Bettmann/Corbis.
**396** ©Mary Evans/THE WOMENS LIBRARY/The
Image Works. **397** ©Francis Miller/Time Life
Pictures/Getty Images. **398** ©Patrick Robert/
Sygma/Corbis. **403** ©Glenn Leblanc/Photolibrary/
Getty Images. **404** ©Janice Northcutt Huse. **404**
©Mitchell Funk/The Image Bank/Getty Images.
**406–407** ©ESA and NASA/National Geographic.
**409** Compliments of Cape Kennedy Space Center
Visitor Complex. **409** Compliments of NASA
Orbital Debris Program Office. **411** NASA ESA and
A Nota (STScI/ESA). **411** ©Stocktrek/Corbis/
Houghton Mifflin Harcourt. **412** ©JTB Photo
Communications Inc/Alamy Images. **412** ©Larry
Landolfi/Science Source/Photo Researchers. **412**
©Thomas Locker. **413** ©Motofish Images/Corbis.
**413** ©Robert Llewellyn/Corbis. **414** ©Robert
Atanasovski/AFP/Getty Images. **415** ©sagir/
Shutterstock. **416** ©Image Source Pink/Getty
Images. **416** ©Bill Hatcher/National Geographic
Stock. **416** ©Camille Tokerud/Stone/Getty Images.
**416** ©David Young-Wolff/Photographer's Choice/
Getty Images. **416** ©RAYMOND GEHMAN/
National Geographic Stock. **416** ©Robert Ross/
Getty Images. **416** ©TNT Magazine/Alamy. **416**
©Tyrone Turner/National Geographic Stock.

**418–419** ©Stocktrek/Photodisc/Getty Images.
**428** ©Michael Greenlar/The Image Works. **428**
©Thomas Locker. **431** ©Digital Vision/Getty
Images. **432** ©Hulton Archive/Getty Images. **432**
©NASA/Jpl-Caltech/Eureka/Corbis. **432** ©Roger
Ressmeyer/Encyclopedia/Corbis. **433** ©Jason
Reed/Photodisc/Getty Images. **433** NASA Jet
Propulsion Laboratory/(NASA-JPL). **434** ©Trip/
Art Directors & TRIP/Alamy. **436** ©AFP/Getty
Images. **436** ©Barry Tessman/National Geographic
Stock. **436** ©Comstock Premium/Jupiterimages/
Alamy Images. **436** ©Jozsef Szentpeteri/National
Geographic Image Collection. **436** NASA. **436**
©Peter Cade/Iconica/Getty Images. **436** ©W.E.
GARRETT/National Geographic Stock. **438–439**
©Roger Ressmeyer/Encyclopedia/Corbis. **440**
©Steve Cole/Photographer's Choice/Getty Images.
**441** ©Soho/NASA/Jpl-Caltech/Corbis. **442**
©Panoramic Images/Getty Images. **443** ©Roger
Ressmeyer/Eureka Premium/Corbis. **445** NASA
and A. Riess. **449** ©Purestock/Getty Images. **450**
NASA Goddard Space Flight Center. **450** ©Owaki/
Kulla/Terra/Corbis. **450** ©Robert Llewellyn/
Comet/Corbis. **451** ©Denis Scott/Corbis. **451**
©Tyrone Turner/National Geographic. **454**
©Digital Vision/Alamy Images. **454** ©Karen
Kasmauski/National Geographic Stock. **454**
©Pixland/Corbis. **454** ©Raymond Gehman/
National Geographic Stock. **454** ©Raymond
Gehman/National Geographic Stock. **454** ©Saeed
Khan/Afp/Getty Images. **454** ©Skip Brown/
National Geographic Stock. **454** ©Millard H Sharp/
Photo Researchers/Getty Images. **454** ©Andrés/
Shutterstock.com. **454** ©Pixland/Corbis. **456–557**
NASA Goddard Space Flight Center. **459** ©Todd
Carlson. **461** ©Stephen Simpson/Creatas/Jupiter
Images. **462–463** ©Mark Thiessen/National
Geographic. **464** ©iconsight/Alamy. **465** ©Sharon
Guynup. **466** ©Brad Mischler Photography. **468**
©Yuri Arcuri/Shutterstock. **470** NASA/JPL/USGS.
**470** ©AP Photo. **471** NASA. **474–475** ©Ethan
Welty/Aurora/Getty Images. **476** ©Robert J. Lang.
**477** ©2003 City of Philadelphia Mural Arts
Program/ Donald Gensler. Photo by Jack Ramsdale.
**479** ©Drew Kelly Photography/Crush/Corbis. **479**
©Muntz/Taxi/Getty Images. **480** ©AP Photo/Eric
Gay. **480** ©AP Photo/Paul Spinelli. **481** ©Steve
Bjorkman. **482** ©Barry Winiker/Index Stock
Imagery/Photo Library. **484** ©AMY WHITE & AL
PETTEWAY/National Geographic Stock. **484** ©Bill
Frymire/Alamy Images. **484** ©Brooke Slezak/The
Image Bank/Getty Images. **484** ©Erich Auerbach/
Getty Images. **484** ©Getty Images. **484** ©Image
Source/Getty Images. **484** ©John Gichigi/Getty
Images Sport/Getty Images. **484** ©Walter Hodges/
Stone/Getty Images. **486–847** ©AP Photo/Eric
Gay. **488** ©Mariachi Vargas Extravaganza.
**488–489** ©Don Klumpp/The Image Bank/Getty
Images. **489** ©AP Photo/The Houston Chronicle
Melissa Phillip. **490** ©AP Photo/David Quinn.
**490–491** ©Don Klumpp/The Image Bank/Getty
Images. **491** ©AP Photo/Jeff Geissler. **492** ©Stuart
Westmorland/Documentary/Corbis. **492** ©Vocal
Power Productions. **496** ©Ernst Haas/Getty
Images. **496** ©J.D.Heaton/Picture Finders/Age
Fotostock. **497** ©Dean Conger/Corbis. **498** ©age
fotostock/SuperStock. **500** ©Bilderlounge/Tips
RF/beyond fotomedia/Jupiter Images. **500** ©Bruce
Dale/National Geographic Stock. **500** ©Cro
Magnon/Alamy. **500** ©Dana White/PhotoEdit.
**500** ©Jupiterimages/Creatas/Alamy Images. **500**
©Michael Newman/PhotoEdit. **500** ©Raul Touzon/
National Geographic Stock. **500** ©Tim Pannell/
Cardinal/Corbis. **502** ©Dmitri Kessel/Time & Life
Pictures/Getty Images. **502–503** ©J.D.Heaton/
Picture Finders/Age Fotostock. **504** ©David
Samuel Robbins/Photographers Choice/Getty
Images. **504** ©Dmitri Kessel/Time & Life Pictures/
Getty Images. **505** ©Hilarie Kavanagh/Stone. **506**
©David Samuel Robbins/Photographer's Choice/
Getty Images. **506–507** ©Ernst Haas/Getty
Images. **508** ©Eric Meola/The Image Bank/Getty
Images. **509** ©Kevin R. Morris/Corbis. **510** ©Gavin

Hellier/Robert Harding World Imagery/Getty
Images. **511** ©Frans Lanting/Corbis. **511** ©Mike
Powell/Stone/Getty Images. **512** ©Jeff Garner,
Southern Illinois University Carbondale. **516**
©Imagno/Hulton Archive/Getty Images. **516–517**
©Hiroshi Higuchi/Photographer's Choice/Getty
Images. **517** ©Michael Hitoshi/Stone+/Getty
Images. **518** ©Skip Brown/National Geographic
Stock. **520** ©Ed Bock/Corbis. **520** ©Jason
Edwards/National Geographic Stock. **520** ©Phil
Cawley/Alamy. **520** ©Randy Faris/Bridge/Corbis.
**520** ©Rich Reid/National Geographic Stock. **520**
©Tim Pannell/Cardinal/Corbis. **520** ©TOMASZ
TOMASZEWSKI/National Geographic Stock. **524,
529** ©Gail Armstrong. **529** ©Scholastic Inc.
**530–532** ©Gail Armstrong. **535** ©Ron Brown/
SuperStock. **536–537** ©Christie's Images/Corbis.
**538** ©AP Photo/Eric Gay. **538** ©J.D.Heaton/
Picture Finders/Age Fotostock. **538** ©Christie's
Images/Corbis. **552** ©Francois Loubser/
Shutterstock.com. **583** ©Bill Frymire/Alamy
Images. **583** ©Martin Child/Getty Images. **584**
©Sydney Hastings/National Geographic Stock.
**585** ©Rich Reid/National Geographic Stock.
**586** ©Brian Drouin/National Geographic Image
Collection. **586** ©Joel Sartore/National Geographic
Stock. **587** ©Lyndon Beddoe/Alamy. **588** ©Steve
Raymer/National Geographic. **589** ©Image Source
Pink/Getty Images. **589** ©IRA BLOCK/National
Geographic Stock. **590** ©Ed Taylor/Taxi/Getty
Images. **590** ©Randy Faris/Corbis. **591** ©Stacy
Gold/National Geographic Illustration.

## Illustration

**134, 137, 209** Precision Graphics. **206–211,
213–215** Craig Phillips. **246–258** Keith Graves.
**292, 320, 394–395, 397–398** Mapping
Specialists. **419–423, 425, 427** Thomas
Locker. **446** Igor Oleynikov. **516, 522–523,
525, 527–528, 538** Christopher Myers.

## Fine Art

**368–369** *Butterfly* ©1978 Tamas Galambos.
Oil on canvas private collection/Bridgeman Art
Library/Superstock. **371** *Home* ©2006 Elizabeth
Rosen. Acrylic on wood collection of the artist
courtesy of Morgan Gaynin Inc. New York.
**372** *Madre Protectora II* ©2007 Felix Berroa.
Acrylic and oil on canvas collection of the artist
courtesy of Hummingbird Lane Art Gallery
Dahlonega Georgia. **375** *Journey* ©2000 Rafael
Lopez. Acrylic on canvas collection of the artist.
**404** *Butterfly* ©1978 Tamas Galambos. Oil on
canvas private collection/Bridgeman Art Library/
Superstock. **481** *Vahine No Te Tiare (Woman
with a Flower)*, 1891, Paul Gauguin (1848–1903).
Oil on canvas. Ny Carlsberg Glyptotek Copenhagen
Denmark/©The Bridgeman Art Library.

# Common Core State Standards

**Unit Launch**

| Pages | Lesson | Code | Standards Text |
|---|---|---|---|
| **0–1** | **Unit Opener** | SL.6.1 | Engage effectively in a range of collaborative discussions (one-on-one, in groups, and teacher-led) with diverse partners on grade 6 topics, texts, and issues, building on others' ideas and expressing their own clearly. |
| **2–7** | **Focus on Reading**<br>Reading Strategies: Plan, Monitor, Make Connections, Visualize, Ask Questions, Determine Importance, Make Inferences, Synthesize | RL.6.1 | Cite textual evidence to support analysis of what the text says explicitly as well as inferences drawn from the text. |
| | | RL.6.2 | Determine a theme or central idea of a text and how it is conveyed through particular details; provide a summary of the text distinct from personal opinions or judgments. |
| | **Literary Analysis**<br>Comprehend Text, Use Text Evidence, Use Context Clues | RL.6.4 | Determine the meaning of words and phrases as they are used in a text, including figurative and connotative meanings; analyze the impact of a specific word choice on meaning and tone. |
| | | RL.6.10 | By the end of the year, read and comprehend literature, including stories, dramas, and poems, in the grades 6–8 text complexity band proficiently, with scaffolding as needed at the high end of the range. |
| | | RI.6.1 | Cite textual evidence to support analysis of what the text says explicitly as well as inferences drawn from the text. |
| | | RI.6.2 | Determine a central idea of a text and how it is conveyed through particular details; provide a summary of the text distinct from personal opinions or judgments. |
| | | RI.6.10 | By the end of the year, read and comprehend literary nonfiction in the grades 6–8 text complexity band proficiently, with scaffolding as needed at the high end of the range. |
| **8–9** | **Focus on Vocabulary**<br>Use Context Clues for Multiple-Meaning Words | RL.6.4 | Determine the meaning of words and phrases as they are used in a text, including figurative and connotative meanings; analyze the impact of a specific word choice on meaning and tone. |
| | | RI.6.4 | Determine the meaning of words and phrases as they are used in a text, including figurative, connotative, and technical meanings. |
| | | L.6.4 | Determine or clarify the meaning of unknown and multiple meaning words and phrases based on grade 6 reading and content, choosing flexibly from a range of strategies. |
| | | L.6.4.a | Determine or clarify the meaning of unknown and multiple-meaning words and phrases based on grade 6 reading and content, choosing flexibly from a range of strategies.<br>Use context (e.g., the overall meaning of a sentence or paragraph; a word's position or function in a sentence) as a clue to the meaning of a word or phrase. |
| | | L.6.4.c | Determine or clarify the meaning of unknown and multiple-meaning words and phrases based on grade 6 reading and content, choosing flexibly from a range of strategies.<br>Consult reference materials (e.g., dictionaries, glossaries, thesauruses), both print and digital, to find the pronunciation of a word or determine or clarify its precise meaning or its part of speech. |
| | | L.6.4.d | Determine or clarify the meaning of unknown and multiple-meaning words and phrases based on grade 6 reading and content, choosing flexibly from a range of strategies.<br>Verify the preliminary determination of the meaning of a word or phrase (e.g., by checking the inferred meaning in context or in a dictionary). |

# Common Core State Standards, continued

**Selection 1 Growing Together**

| Pages | Lesson | Code | Standards Text |
|---|---|---|---|
| **10** | **Connect** | SL.6.1.c | Engage effectively in a range of collaborative discussions (one-on-one, in groups, and teacher-led) with diverse partners on grade 6 topics, texts, and issues, building on others' ideas and expressing their own clearly.<br><br>Pose and respond to specific questions with elaboration and detail by making comments that contribute to the topic, text, or issue under discussion. |
| | | SL.6.2 | Interpret information presented in diverse media and formats (e.g., visually, quantitatively, orally) and explain how it contributes to a topic, text, or issue under study. |
| **11–13** | **Language & Grammar**<br>Express Ideas and Feelings | SL.6.1 | Engage effectively in a range of collaborative discussions (one-on-one, in groups, and teacher-led) with diverse partners on grade 6 topics, texts, and issues, building on others' ideas and expressing their own clearly. |
| | Use Statements with<br>*Am, Is,* and *Are* | L.6.1 | Demonstrate command of the conventions of standard English grammar and usage when writing or speaking. |
| **14** | **Key Vocabulary** | RI.6.4 | Determine the meaning of words and phrases as they are used in a text, including figurative, connotative, and technical meanings. |
| | | L.6.4 | Determine or clarify the meaning of unknown and multiple-meaning words and phrases based on grade 6 reading and content, choosing flexibly from a range of strategies. |
| **15** | **Reading Strategy**<br>Plan, Monitor, and Visualize | RI.6.1 | Cite textual evidence to support analysis of what the text says explicitly as well as inferences drawn from the text. |
| | **Literary Analysis**<br>Use Text Evidence | RI.6.10 | By the end of the year, read and comprehend literary nonfiction in the grades 6–8 text complexity band proficiently, with scaffolding as needed at the high end of the range. |
| **16–22** | **Reading Selection** | RL.6.1 | Cite textual evidence to support analysis of what the text says explicitly as well as inferences drawn from the text. |
| | | RL.6.6 | Explain how an author develops the point of view of the narrator or speaker in a text. |
| | | RI.6.1 | Cite textual evidence to support analysis of what the text says explicitly as well as inferences drawn from the text. |
| | | RI.6.10 | By the end of the year, read and comprehend literary nonfiction in the grades 6–8 text complexity band proficiently, with scaffolding as needed at the high end of the range. |
| | | L.6.5 | Demonstrate understanding of figurative language, word relationships, and nuances in word meanings. |
| | | L.6.5.a | Demonstrate understanding of figurative language, word relationships, and nuances in word meanings.<br><br>Interpret figures of speech (e.g., personification) in context. |
| **23** | **Connect Reading and Writing**<br>Critical Thinking | RI.6.2 | Determine a central idea of a text and how it is conveyed through particular details; provide a summary of the text distinct from personal opinions or judgments. |
| | Vocabulary Review | L.6.6 | Acquire and use accurately grade-appropriate general academic and domain-specific words and phrases; gather vocabulary knowledge when considering a word or phrase important to comprehension or expression. |
| | Write About the GQ | W.6.9 | Draw evidence from literary or informational texts to support analysis, reflection, and research. |
| | | W.6.10 | Write routinely over extended time frames (time for research, reflection, and revision) and shorter time frames (a single sitting or a day or two) for a range of discipline-specific tasks, purposes, and audiences. |

**Selection 1 Growing Together,** continued

| Pages | Lesson | Code | Standards Text |
|---|---|---|---|
| **24** | **Vocabulary Study**<br>Use Context Clues | L.6.4.a | Determine or clarify the meaning of unknown and multiple-meaning words and phrases based on grade 6 reading and content, choosing flexibly from a range of strategies.<br>Use context (e.g., the overall meaning of a sentence or paragraph; a word's position or function in a sentence) as a clue to the meaning of a word or phrase. |
| | | L.6.4.c | Determine or clarify the meaning of unknown and multiple-meaning words and phrases based on grade 6 reading and content, choosing flexibly from a range of strategies.<br>Consult reference materials (e.g., dictionaries, glossaries, thesauruses), both print and digital, to find the pronunciation of a word or determine or clarify its precise meaning or its part of speech. |
| | | L.6.4.d | Determine or clarify the meaning of unknown and multiple-meaning words and phrases based on grade 6 reading and content, choosing flexibly from a range of strategies.<br>Verify the preliminary determination of the meaning of a word or phrase (e.g., by checking the inferred meaning in context or in a dictionary). |
| **24** | **Literary Analysis**<br>Analyze Narrator's Point of View | RI.6.6 | Determine an author's point of view or purpose in a text and explain how it is conveyed in the text. |
| **25** | **Language and Grammar**<br>Express Ideas and Feelings | SL.6.1 | Engage effectively in a range of collaborative discussions (one-on-one, in groups, and teacher-led) with diverse partners on grade 6 topics, texts, and issues, building on others' ideas and expressing their own clearly. |
| **25** | **Writing and Grammar**<br>Write About Someone You Know | L.6.1 | Demonstrate command of the conventions of standard English grammar and usage when writing or speaking. |
| | | W.6.3.d | Write narratives to develop real or imagined experiences or events using effective technique, relevant descriptive details, and well-structured event sequences.<br>Use precise words and phrases, relevant descriptive details, and sensory language to convey experiences and events. |

**Selection 2 Kids Like Me**

| Pages | Lesson | Code | Standards Text |
|---|---|---|---|
| **26** | **Connect** | SL.6.2 | Interpret information presented in diverse media and formats (e.g., visually, quantitatively, orally) and explain how it contributes to a topic, text, or issue under study. |
| **27–29** | **Language & Grammar**<br>Ask and Answer Questions | L.6.1 | Demonstrate command of the conventions of standard English grammar and usage when writing or speaking. |
| | | SL.6.1.c | Engage effectively in a range of collaborative discussions (one-on-one, in groups, and teacher-led) with diverse partners on grade 6 topics, texts, and issues, building on others' ideas and expressing their own clearly.<br>Pose and respond to specific questions with elaboration and detail by making comments that contribute to the topic, text, or issue under discussion. |
| | Questions and Statements | L.6.1 | Demonstrate command of the conventions of standard English grammar and usage when writing or speaking. |
| **30** | **Key Vocabulary** | RI.6.4 | Determine the meaning of words and phrases as they are used in a text, including figurative, connotative, and technical meanings. |
| | | L.6.4 | Determine or clarify the meaning of unknown and multiple-meaning words and phrases based on grade 6 reading and content, choosing flexibly from a range of strategies. |
| **31** | **Reading Strategy**<br>Make Connections, Ask Questions, and Determine Importance | RI.6.1 | Cite textual evidence to support analysis of what the text says explicitly as well as inferences drawn from the text. |
| | **Literary Analysis**<br>Use Text Evidence, Determine Main Idea | RI.6.2 | Determine a central idea of a text and how it is conveyed through particular details; provide a summary of the text distinct from personal opinions or judgments. |

# Common Core State Standards, continued

Selection 2 Kids Like Me, continued

| Pages | Lesson | Code | Standards Text |
|---|---|---|---|
| 32–38 | Reading Selection | RI.6.1 | Cite textual evidence to support analysis of what the text says explicitly as well as inferences drawn from the text. |
| | | RI.6.7 | Integrate information presented in different media or formats (e.g., visually, quantitatively) as well as in words to develop a coherent understanding of a topic or issue. |
| | | RI.6.10 | By the end of the year, read and comprehend literary nonfiction in the grades 6–8 text complexity band proficiently, with scaffolding as needed at the high end of the range. |
| 39 | Connect Reading and Writing Critical Thinking | RI.6.2 | Determine a central idea of a text and how it is conveyed through particular details; provide a summary of the text distinct from personal opinions or judgments. |
| | | SL.6.1.d | Engage effectively in a range of collaborative discussions (one-on-one, in groups, and teacher-led) with diverse partners on grade 6 topics, texts, and issues, building on others' ideas and expressing their own clearly. |
| | | | Review the key ideas expressed and demonstrate understanding of multiple perspectives through reflection and paraphrasing. |
| | Vocabulary Review | L.6.6 | Acquire and use accurately grade-appropriate general academic and domain-specific words and phrases; gather vocabulary knowledge when considering a word or phrase important to comprehension or expression. |
| | Write About the GQ | W.6.9 | Draw evidence from literary or informational texts to support analysis, reflection, and research. |
| | | W.6.10 | Write routinely over extended time frames (time for research, reflection, and revision) and shorter time frames (a single sitting or a day or two) for a range of discipline-specific tasks, purposes, and audiences. |
| 40 | Vocabulary Study Use Context Clues | RI.6.4 | Determine the meaning of words and phrases as they are used in a text, including figurative, connotative, and technical meanings. |
| | | L.6.4 | Determine or clarify the meaning of unknown and multiple-meaning words and phrases based on grade 6 reading and content, choosing flexibly from a range of strategies. |
| | | L.6.4.a | Determine or clarify the meaning of unknown and multiple-meaning words and phrases based on grade 6 reading and content, choosing flexibly from a range of strategies. |
| | | | Use context (e.g., the overall meaning of a sentence or paragraph; a word's position or function in a sentence) as a clue to the meaning of a word or phrase. |
| | | L.6.4.c | Determine or clarify the meaning of unknown and multiple-meaning words and phrases based on grade 6 reading and content, choosing flexibly from a range of strategies. |
| | | | Consult reference materials (e.g., dictionaries, glossaries, thesauruses), both print and digital, to find the pronunciation of a word or determine or clarify its precise meaning or its part of speech. |
| | | L.6.4.d | Determine or clarify the meaning of unknown and multiple-meaning words and phrases based on grade 6 reading and content, choosing flexibly from a range of strategies. |
| | | | Verify the preliminary determination of the meaning of a word or phrase (e.g., by checking the inferred meaning in context or in a dictionary). |
| 40 | Literary Analysis Analyze Text Structure: Compare and Contrast | RI.6.5 | Analyze how a particular sentence, paragraph, chapter, or section fits into the overall structure of a text and contributes to the development of the ideas. |
| 41 | Language and Grammar Ask and Answer Questions | SL.6.1.c | Engage effectively in a range of collaborative discussions (one-on-one, in groups, and teacher-led) with diverse partners on grade 6 topics, texts, and issues, building on others' ideas and expressing their own clearly. |
| | | | Pose and respond to specific questions with elaboration and detail by making comments that contribute to the topic, text, or issue under discussion. |

**Selection 2 Kids Like Me,** continued

| Pages | Lesson | Code | Standards Text |
|---|---|---|---|
| **41** | **Writing and Grammar** <br> Write a Message | W.6.3.d | Write narratives to develop real or imagined experiences or events using effective technique, relevant descriptive details, and well-structured event sequences. <br><br> Use precise words and phrases, relevant descriptive details, and sensory language to convey experiences and events. |
| | | L.6.1 | Demonstrate command of the conventions of standard English grammar and usage when writing or speaking. |

**Selection 3 Familiar Places**

| Pages | Lesson | Code | Standards Text |
|---|---|---|---|
| **42** | **Connect** | SL.6.2 | Interpret information presented in diverse media and formats (e.g., visually, quantitatively, orally) and explain how it contributes to a topic, text, or issue under study. |
| **43–45** | **Language & Grammar** <br> Give Commands | SL.6.1 | Engage effectively in a range of collaborative discussions (one-on-one, in groups, and teacher-led) with diverse partners on grade 6 topics, texts, and issues, building on others' ideas and expressing their own clearly. |
| | | L.6.1 | Demonstrate command of the conventions of standard English grammar and usage when writing or speaking. |
| | Use Statements and Commands | L.6.3.a | Use knowledge of language and its conventions when writing, speaking, reading, or listening. <br><br> Vary sentence patterns for meaning, reader/listener interest, and style. |
| **46** | **Key Vocabulary** | RI.6.4 | Determine the meaning of words and phrases as they are used in a text, including figurative, connotative, and technical meanings. |
| | | L.6.4 | Determine or clarify the meaning of unknown and multiple-meaning words and phrases based on grade 6 reading and content, choosing flexibly from a range of strategies. |
| **47** | **Reading Strategy** <br> Make Inferences; Synthesize <br> **Literary Analysis** <br> Make Inferences | RI.6.1 | Cite textual evidence to support analysis of what the text says explicitly as well as inferences drawn from the text. |
| **48–54** | **Reading Selection** | RI.6.1 | Cite textual evidence to support analysis of what the text says explicitly as well as inferences drawn from the text. |
| | | RI.6.2 | Determine a central idea of a text and how it is conveyed through particular details; provide a summary of the text distinct from personal opinions or judgments. |
| | | RI.6.10 | By the end of the year, read and comprehend literary nonfiction in the grades 6–8 text complexity band proficiently, with scaffolding as needed at the high end of the range. |
| **55** | **Connect Reading and Writing** <br> Critical Thinking | RI.6.2 | Determine a central idea of a text and how it is conveyed through particular details; provide a summary of the text distinct from personal opinions or judgments. |
| | Vocabulary Review | L.6.6 | Acquire and use accurately grade-appropriate general academic and domain-specific words and phrases; gather vocabulary knowledge when considering a word or phrase important to comprehension or expression |
| | Write About the GQ | W.6.9 | Draw evidence from literary or informational texts to support analysis, reflection, and research. |
| | | W.6.10 | Write routinely over extended time frames (time for research, reflection, and revision) and shorter time frames (a single sitting or a day or two) for a range of discipline-specific tasks, purposes, and audiences. |

# Common Core State Standards, continued

**Selection 3 Familiar Places,** continued

| Pages | Lesson | Code | Standards Text |
|---|---|---|---|
| **56** | **Vocabulary Study**<br>Use Context Clues | RI.6.4 | Determine the meaning of words and phrases as they are used in a text, including figurative, connotative, and technical meanings. |
| | | L.6.4 | Determine or clarify the meaning of unknown and multiple-meaning words and phrases based on grade 6 reading and content, choosing flexibly from a range of strategies. |
| | | L.6.4.a | Determine or clarify the meaning of unknown and multiple-meaning words and phrases based on grade 6 reading and content, choosing flexibly from a range of strategies.<br>Use context (e.g., the overall meaning of a sentence or paragraph; a word's position or function in a sentence) as a clue to the meaning of a word or phrase. |
| | | L.6.4.c | Determine or clarify the meaning of unknown and multiple-meaning words and phrases based on grade 6 reading and content, choosing flexibly from a range of strategies.<br>Consult reference materials (e.g., dictionaries, glossaries, thesauruses), both print and digital, to find the pronunciation of a word or determine or clarify its precise meaning or its part of speech. |
| | | L.6.4.d | Determine or clarify the meaning of unknown and multiple-meaning words and phrases based on grade 6 reading and content, choosing flexibly from a range of strategies.<br>Verify the preliminary determination of the meaning of a word or phrase (e.g., by checking the inferred meaning in context or in a dictionary). |
| **56** | **Literary Analysis**<br>Analyze Text Structure: Main Idea | RI.6.2 | Determine a central idea of a text and how it is conveyed through particular details; provide a summary of the text distinct from personal opinions or judgments. |
| **57** | **Language and Grammar**<br>Give Commands | SL.6.1 | Engage effectively in a range of collaborative discussions (one-on-one, in groups, and teacher-led) with diverse partners on grade 6 topics, texts, and issues, building on others' ideas and expressing their own clearly. |
| | | L.6.3.a | Use knowledge of language and its conventions when writing, speaking, reading, or listening.<br>Vary sentence patterns for meaning, reader/listener interest, and style. |
| **57** | **Writing and Grammar**<br>Write About a Special Event | W.6.3.d | Write narratives to develop real or imagined experiences or events using effective technique, relevant descriptive details, and well-structured event sequences.<br>Use precise words and phrases, relevant descriptive details, and sensory language to convey experiences and events. |
| | | L.6.3.a | Use knowledge of language and its conventions when writing, speaking, reading, or listening.<br>Vary sentence patterns for meaning, reader/listener interest, and style. |
| **58–61** | **Close Reading** | RL.6.10 | By the end of the year, read and comprehend literature, including stories, dramas, and poems, in the grades 6–8 text complexity band proficiently, with scaffolding as needed at the high end of the range. |

## Compare Across Texts

| | | | |
|---|---|---|---|
| **62** | **Compare Points of View** | RL.6.6 | Explain how an author develops the point of view of the narrator or speaker in a text. |
| | | RI.6.6 | Determine an author's point of view or purpose in a text and explain how it is conveyed in the text. |

**Unit Wrap-Up**

| Pages | Lesson | Code | Standards Text |
|---|---|---|---|
| 63 | **Reflect on Your Reading**<br>**Explore the GQ/Book Talk** | W.6.10 | Write routinely over extended time frames (time for research, reflection, and revision) and shorter time frames (a single sitting or a day or two) for a range of discipline-specific tasks, purposes, and audiences. |
| | | SL.6.1 | Engage effectively in a range of collaborative discussions (one-on-one, in groups, and teacher-led) with diverse partners on grade 6 topics, texts, and issues, building on others' ideas and expressing their own clearly. |
| | | SL.6.1.c | Engage effectively in a range of collaborative discussions (one-on-one, in groups, and teacher-led) with diverse partners on grade 6 topics, texts, and issues, building on others' ideas and expressing their own clearly.<br>Pose and respond to specific questions with elaboration and detail by making comments that contribute to the topic, text, or issue under discussion. |
| | | SL.6.1.d | Engage effectively in a range of collaborative discussions (one-on-one, in groups, and teacher-led) with diverse partners on grade 6 topics, texts, and issues, building on others' ideas and expressing their own clearly.<br>Review the key ideas expressed and demonstrate understanding of multiple perspectives through reflection and paraphrasing. |
| | | SL.6.5 | Include multimedia components (e.g., graphics, images, music, sound) and visual displays in presentations to clarify information. |

**Unit 2   Water for Life**

**Unit Launch**

| Pages | Lesson | Code | Standards Text |
|---|---|---|---|
| 64–65 | **Unit Opener** | SL.6.1 | Engage effectively in a range of collaborative discussions (one-on-one, in groups, and teacher-led) with diverse partners on grade 6 topics, texts, and issues, building on others' ideas and expressing their own clearly. |
| 66–67 | **Focus on Reading**<br>Analyze Events and Ideas | RL.6.3 | Describe how a particular story's or drama's plot unfolds in a series of episodes as well as how the characters respond or change as the plot moves toward a resolution. |
| | | RI.6.3 | Analyze in detail how a key individual, event, or idea is introduced, illustrated, and elaborated in a text (e.g., through examples or anecdotes). |
| 68–69 | **Focus on Vocabulary**<br>Relate Words | RL.6.4 | Determine the meaning of words and phrases as they are used in a text, including figurative and connotative meanings; analyze the impact of a specific word choice on meaning and tone. |
| | | RI.6.4 | Determine the meaning of words and phrases as they are used in a text, including figurative, connotative, and technical meanings. |
| | | L.6.4 | Determine or clarify the meaning of unknown and multiple-meaning words and phrases based on grade 6 reading and content, choosing flexibly from a range of strategies. |
| | | L.6.5.b | Demonstrate understanding of figurative language, word relationships, and nuances in word meanings.<br>Use the relationship between particular words (e.g., cause/effect, part/whole, item/category) to better understand each of the words. |
| | | L.6.5.c | Demonstrate understanding of figurative language, word relationships, and nuances in word meanings.<br>Distinguish among the connotations (associations) of words with similar denotations (definitions) (e.g., *stingy, scrimping, economical, unwasteful, thrifty*). |

# Common Core State Standards, continued

**Selection 1 The Secret Water**

| Pages | Lesson | Code | Standards Text |
|---|---|---|---|
| **70** | **Connect** | SL.6.2 | Interpret information presented in diverse media and formats (e.g., visually, quantitatively, orally) and explain how it contributes to a topic, text, or issue under study. |
| **71–73** | **Language & Grammar** <br> Express Needs and Wants | SL.6.1 | Engage effectively in a range of collaborative discussions (one-on-one, in groups, and teacher-led) with diverse partners on grade 6 topics, texts, and issues, building on others' ideas and expressing their own clearly. |
| | Use Nouns | L.6.1 | Demonstrate command of the conventions of standard English grammar and usage when writing or speaking. |
| | | L.6.2.b | Demonstrate command of the conventions of standard English capitalization, punctuation, and spelling when writing. <br> Spell correctly. |
| **74** | **Key Vocabulary** | RL.6.4 | Determine the meaning of words and phrases as they are used in a text, including figurative and connotative meanings; analyze the impact of a specific word choice on meaning and tone. |
| | | L.6.4 | Determine or clarify the meaning of unknown and multiple-meaning words and phrases based on grade 6 reading and content, choosing flexibly from a range of strategies. |
| **75** | **Reading Strategy** <br> Monitor: Clarify Ideas | RL.6.1 | Cite textual evidence to support analysis of what the text says explicitly as well as inferences drawn from the text. |
| | **Literary Analysis** <br> Analyze Plot | RL.6.3 | Describe how a particular story's or drama's plot unfolds in a series of episodes as well as how the characters respond or change as the plot moves toward a resolution. |
| **76–82** | **Reading Selection** | RL.6.1 | Cite textual evidence to support analysis of what the text says explicitly as well as inferences drawn from the text. |
| | | RL.6.10 | By the end of the year, read and comprehend literature, including stories, dramas, and poems, in the grades 6–8 text complexity band proficiently, with scaffolding as needed at the high end of the range. |
| **83** | **Connect Reading and Writing** <br> Critical Thinking | RL.6.1 | Cite textual evidence to support analysis of what the text says explicitly as well as inferences drawn from the text. |
| | | RL.6.2 | Determine a theme or central idea of a text and how it is conveyed through particular details; provide a summary of the text distinct from personal opinions or judgments. |
| | Vocabulary Review | L.6.6 | Acquire and use accurately grade-appropriate general academic and domain-specific words and phrases; gather vocabulary knowledge when considering a word or phrase important to comprehension or expression. |
| | Write About the GQ | W.6.9 | Draw evidence from literary or informational texts to support analysis, reflection, and research. |
| | | W.6.10 | Write routinely over extended time frames (time for research, reflection, and revision) and shorter time frames (a single sitting or a day or two) for a range of discipline-specific tasks, purposes, and audiences. |
| **84** | **Vocabulary Study** <br> Create Word Categories | RL.6.4 | Determine the meaning of words and phrases as they are used in a text, including figurative and connotative meanings; analyze the impact of a specific word choice on meaning and tone. |
| | | L.6.5.b | Demonstrate understanding of figurative language, word relationships, and nuances in word meanings. <br> Use the relationship between particular words (e.g., cause/effect, part/whole, item/category) to better understand each of the words. |

**Selection 1 The Secret Water, continued**

| Pages | Lesson | Code | Standards Text |
|---|---|---|---|
| 84 | **Listening and Speaking**<br>Compare Tales Across Cultures | RL.6.3 | Describe how a particular story's or drama's plot unfolds in a series of episodes as well as how the characters respond or change as the plot moves toward a resolution. |
| | | RL.6.9 | Compare and contrast texts in different forms or genres (e.g., stories and poems; historical novels and fantasy stories) in terms of their approaches to similar themes and topics. |
| 85 | **Language and Grammar**<br>Express Needs and Wants | SL.6.1 | Engage effectively in a range of collaborative discussions (one-on-one, in groups, and teacher-led) with diverse partners on grade 6 topics, texts, and issues, building on others' ideas and expressing their own clearly. |
| 85 | **Writing and Grammar**<br>Write About a Situation | W.6.3.d | Write narratives to develop real or imagined experiences or events using effective technique, relevant descriptive details, and well-structured event sequences.<br>Use precise words and phrases, relevant descriptive details, and sensory language to convey experiences and events. |

**Selection 2 How Do We Use Water?**

| Pages | Lesson | Code | Standards Text |
|---|---|---|---|
| 86 | **Connect** | RI.6.7 | Integrate information presented in different media or formats (e.g., visually, quantitatively) as well as in words to develop a coherent understanding of a topic or issue. |
| | | SL.6.2 | Interpret information presented in diverse media and formats (e.g., visually, quantitatively, orally) and explain how it contributes to a topic, text, or issue under study. |
| 87–89 | **Language & Grammar**<br>Give Information<br><br>Use Complete Sentences | L.6.1 | Demonstrate command of the conventions of standard English grammar and usage when writing or speaking. |
| | | SL.6.1.a | Engage effectively in a range of collaborative discussions (one-on-one, in groups, and teacher-led) with diverse partners on grade 6 topics, texts, and issues, building on others' ideas and expressing their own clearly.<br>Come to discussions prepared, having read or studied required material; explicitly draw on that preparation by referring to evidence on the topic, text, or issue to probe and reflect on ideas under discussion. |
| | | L.6.1 | Demonstrate command of the conventions of standard English grammar and usage when writing or speaking. |
| 90 | **Key Vocabulary** | RI.6.4 | Determine the meaning of words and phrases as they are used in a text, including figurative, connotative, and technical meanings. |
| | | L.6.4 | Determine or clarify the meaning of unknown and multiple-meaning words and phrases based on grade 6 reading and content, choosing flexibly from a range of strategies. |
| 91 | **Reading Strategy**<br>Monitor: Clarify Vocabulary | RI.6.1 | Cite textual evidence to support analysis of what the text says explicitly as well as inferences drawn from the text. |
| | **Literary Analysis**<br>Analyze Main Idea and Detail | RI.6.3 | Analyze in detail how a key individual, event, or idea is introduced, illustrated, and elaborated in a text (e.g., through examples or anecdotes). |

# Common Core State Standards, continued

**Selection 2 How Do We Use Water?, continued**

| Pages | Lesson | Code | Standards Text |
|---|---|---|---|
| 92–98 | **Reading Selection** | RI.6.1 | Cite textual evidence to support analysis of what the text says explicitly as well as inferences drawn from the text. |
| | | RI.6.2 | Determine a central idea of a text and how it is conveyed through particular details; provide a summary of the text distinct from personal opinions or judgments. |
| | | RI.6.3 | Analyze in detail how a key individual, event, or idea is introduced, illustrated, and elaborated in a text (e.g., through examples or anecdotes). |
| | | RI.6.7 | Integrate information presented in different media or formats (e.g., visually, quantitatively) as well as in words to develop a coherent understanding of a topic or issue. |
| | | RI.6.10 | By the end of the year, read and comprehend literary nonfiction in the grades 6–8 text complexity band proficiently, with scaffolding as needed at the high end of the range. |
| 99 | **Connect Reading and Writing**<br>Critical Thinking | RI.6.2 | Determine a central idea of a text and how it is conveyed through particular details; provide a summary of the text distinct from personal opinions or judgments. |
| | Vocabulary Review | L.6.6 | Acquire and use accurately grade-appropriate general academic and domain-specific words and phrases; gather vocabulary knowledge when considering a word or phrase important to comprehension or expression. |
| | Write About the GQ | W.6.9 | Draw evidence from literary or informational texts to support analysis, reflection, and research. |
| | | W.6.10 | Write routinely over extended time frames (time for research, reflection, and revision) and shorter time frames (a single sitting or a day or two) for a range of discipline-specific tasks, purposes, and audiences. |
| 100 | **Vocabulary Study**<br>Use Synonyms | RI.6.4 | Determine the meaning of words and phrases as they are used in a text, including figurative, connotative, and technical meanings. |
| | | SL.6.1.a | Engage effectively in a range of collaborative discussions (one-on-one, in groups, and teacher-led) with diverse partners on grade 6 topics, texts, and issues, building on others' ideas and expressing their own clearly.<br><br>Come to discussions prepared, having read or studied required material; explicitly draw on that preparation by referring to evidence on the topic, text, or issue to probe and reflect on ideas under discussion. |
| | | SL6.4 | Present claims and findings, sequencing ideas logically and using pertinent descriptions, facts, and details to accentuate main ideas or themes; use appropriate eye contact, adequate volume, and clear pronunciation. |
| | | L.6.4.c | Determine or clarify the meaning of unknown and multiple-meaning words and phrases based on grade 6 reading and content, choosing flexibly from a range of strategies.<br><br>Consult reference materials (e.g. dictionaries, glossaries, thesauruses), both print and digital, to find the pronunciation of a word or determine or clarify its precise meaning or its part of speech. |
| | | L.6.5.c | Demonstrate understanding of figurative language, word relationships, and nuances in word meanings.<br><br>Distinguish among the connotations (associations) of words with similar denotations (definitions) (e.g., *stingy, scrimping, economical, unwasteful, thrifty*). |
| 101 | **Language and Grammar**<br>Give Information | SL.6.1.a | Come to discussions prepared, having read or studied required material; explicitly draw on that preparation by referring to evidence on the topic, text, or issue to probe and reflect on ideas under discussion. |

## Selection 2 How Do We Use Water?, continued

| Pages | Lesson | Code | Standards Text |
|---|---|---|---|
| **101** | **Writing and Grammar**<br>Write About Water | W.6.3.d | Write narratives to develop real or imagined experiences or events using effective technique, relevant descriptive details, and well-structured event sequences.<br><br>Use precise words and phrases, relevant descriptive details, and sensory language to convey experiences and events. |
| | | L.6.1 | Demonstrate command of the conventions of standard English grammar and usage when writing or speaking. |

## Selection 3 Water at Work

| Pages | Lesson | Code | Standards Text |
|---|---|---|---|
| **102** | **Connect** | RI.6.7 | Integrate information presented in different media or formats (e.g., visually, quantitatively) as well as in words to develop a coherent understanding of a topic or issue. |
| | | SL.6.2 | Interpret information presented in diverse media and formats (e.g., visually, quantitatively, orally) and explain how it contributes to a topic, text, or issue under study. |
| **103–105** | **Language & Grammar**<br>Elaborate<br>Make Subjects and Verbs Agree | L.6.1 | Demonstrate command of the conventions of standard English grammar and usage when writing or speaking. |
| **106** | **Key Vocabulary** | RI.6.4 | Determine the meaning of words and phrases as they are used in a text, including figurative, connotative, and technical meanings. |
| | | L.6.4 | Determine or clarify the meaning of unknown and multiple-meaning words and phrases based on grade 6 reading and content, choosing flexibly from a range of strategies. |
| **107** | **Reading Strategy**<br>Monitor: Clarify Vocabulary | RI.6.1 | Cite textual evidence to support analysis of what the text says explicitly as well as inferences drawn from the text. |
| | **Literary Analysis**<br>Analyze Main Idea and Details | RI.6.3 | Analyze in detail how a key individual, event, or idea is introduced, illustrated, and elaborated in a text (e.g., through examples or anecdotes). |
| **108–114** | **Reading Selection** | RI.6.1 | Cite textual evidence to support analysis of what the text says explicitly as well as inferences drawn from the text. |
| | | RI.6.2 | Determine a central idea of a text and how it is conveyed through particular details; provide a summary of the text distinct from personal opinions or judgments. |
| | | RI.6.10 | By the end of the year, read and comprehend literary nonfiction in the grades 6–8 text complexity band proficiently, with scaffolding as needed at the high end of the range. |
| | | L.6.4.a | Determine or clarify the meaning of unknown and multiple-meaning words and phrases based on grade 6 reading and content, choosing flexibly from a range of strategies.<br><br>Use context (the overall meaning of a sentence or paragraph; a word's position or function in a sentence) as a clue to the meaning of a word or phrase. |
| **115** | **Connect Reading and Writing**<br>Critical Thinking | RI.6.2 | Determine a central idea of a text and how it is conveyed through particular details; provide a summary of the text distinct from personal opinions or judgments. |
| | | RI.6.1 | Cite textual evidence to support analysis of what the text says explicitly as well as inferences drawn from the text. |
| | Vocabulary Review | L.6.6 | Acquire and use accurately grade-appropriate general academic and domain-specific words and phrases; gather vocabulary knowledge when considering a word or phrase important to comprehension or expression. |

# Common Core State Standards, continued

## Unit 2   Water for Life, continued

### Selection 3 Water at Work, continued

| Pages | Lesson | Code | Standards Text |
|---|---|---|---|
| | Write About the GQ | W.6.9 | Draw evidence from literary or informational texts to support analysis, reflection, and research. |
| | | W.6.10 | Write routinely over extended time frames (time for research, reflection, and revision) and shorter time frames (a single sitting or a day or two) for a range of discipline-specific tasks, purposes, and audiences. |
| 116 | Vocabulary Study<br>Use Synonyms and Antonyms | L.6.5.b | Demonstrate understanding of figurative language, word relationships, and nuances in word meanings.<br>Use the relationship between particular words (e.g., cause/effect, part/whole, item/category) to better understand each of the words. |
| 116 | Research/Speaking<br>Discuss Hydroelectric Power | SL.6.3 | Delineate a speaker's argument and specific claims, distinguishing claims that are supported by reasons and evidence from claims that are not. |
| 117 | Language and Grammar<br>Elaborate | SL.6.1.a | Engage effectively in a range of collaborative discussions (one-on-one, in groups, and teacher-led) with diverse partners on grade 6 topics, texts, and issues, building on others' ideas and expressing their own clearly.<br>Come to discussions prepared, having read or studied required material; explicitly draw on that preparation by referring to evidence on the topic, text, or issue to probe and reflect on ideas under discussion. |
| 117 | Writing and Grammar<br>Write About a Day at a River | L.6.1 | Demonstrate command of the conventions of standard English grammar and usage when writing or speaking. |
| | | W.6.3.d | Write narratives to develop real or imagined experiences or events using effective technique, relevant descriptive details, and well-structured event sequences.<br>Use precise words and phrases, relevant descriptive details, and sensory language to convey experiences and events. |
| 118–119 | Close Reading | RI.6.10 | By the end of the year, read and comprehend literary nonfiction in the grades 6–8 text complexity band proficiently, with scaffolding as needed at the high end of the range. |

### Compare Across Texts

| | | | |
|---|---|---|---|
| 120 | Compare Ideas | RL.6.3 | Describe how a particular story's or drama's plot unfolds in a series of episodes as well as how the characters respond or change as the plot moves toward a resolution. |
| | | RI.6.3 | Analyze in detail how a key individual, event, or idea is introduced, illustrated, and elaborated in a text (e.g., through examples or anecdotes). |

### Unit Wrap-Up

| | | | |
|---|---|---|---|
| 121 | Reflect on Your Reading | RL.6.3 | Describe how a particular story's or drama's plot unfolds in a series of episodes as well as how the characters respond or change as the plot moves toward a resolution. |
| | | RI.6.3 | Analyze in detail how a key individual, event, or idea is introduced, illustrated, and elaborated in a text (e.g., through examples or anecdotes). |
| | Explore the GQ/Book Talk | SL.6.5 | Include multimedia components (e.g., graphics, images, music, sound) and visual displays in presentations to clarify information. |

## Unit 3   Natural Forces

### Unit Launch

| | | | |
|---|---|---|---|
| 122–123 | Unit Opener | SL.6.1 | Engage effectively in a range of collaborative discussions (one-on-one, in groups, and teacher led) with diverse partners on grade 6 topics, texts, and issues, building on others' ideas and expressing their own clearly. |

**Unit Launch,** continued

| Pages | Lesson | Code | Standards Text |
|---|---|---|---|
| **124–125** | **Focus on Reading**<br>Determine Viewpoint | RL.6.6 | Explain how an author develops the point of view of the narrator or speaker in a text. |
| | | RI.6.6 | Determine an author's point of view or purpose in a text and explain how it is conveyed in the text. |
| **126–127** | **Focus on Vocabulary**<br>Use Word Parts | L.6.4 | Determine or clarify the meaning of unknown and multiple-meaning words and phrases based on grade 6 reading and content, choosing flexibly from a range of strategies. |
| | | L.6.4.b | Determine or clarify the meaning of unknown and multiple-meaning words and phrases based on grade 6 reading and content, choosing flexibly from a range of strategies.<br>Use common, grade-appropriate Greek or Latin affixes and roots as clues to the meaning of a word (e.g., *audience, auditory, audible*). |
| | | L.6.6 | Acquire and use accurately grade-appropriate general academic and domain-specific words and phrases; gather vocabulary knowledge when considering a word or phrase important to comprehension or expression. |

**Selection 1 Volcano!**

| Pages | Lesson | Code | Standards Text |
|---|---|---|---|
| **128** | **Connect** | RI.6.7 | Integrate information presented in different media or formats (e.g., visually, quantitatively) as well as in words to develop a coherent understanding of a topic or issue. |
| | | SL.6.2 | Interpret information presented in diverse media and formats (e.g., visually, quantitatively, orally) and explain how it contributes to a topic, text, or issue under study. |
| **129–131** | **Language & Grammar**<br>Engage in Conversation | SL.6.1 | Engage effectively in a range of collaborative discussions (one-on-one, in groups, and teacher-led) with diverse partners on grade 6 topics, texts, and issues, building on others' ideas and expressing their own clearly. |
| | Use Subject Pronouns | L.6.1.a | Demonstrate command of the conventions of standard English grammar and usage when writing or speaking.<br>Ensure that pronouns are in the proper case (subjective, objective, possessive). |
| **132** | **Key Vocabulary** | RI.6.4 | Determine the meaning of words and phrases as they are used in a text, including figurative, connotative, and technical meanings. |
| | | L.6.4 | Determine or clarify the meaning of unknown and multiple-meaning words and phrases based on grade 6 reading and content, choosing flexibly from a range of strategies. |
| **133** | **Reading Strategy**<br>Make Connections | RI.6.1 | Cite textual evidence to support analysis of what the text says explicitly as well as inferences drawn from the text. |
| | **Literary Analysis**<br>Analyze Text Structure: Cause and Effect | RI.6.5 | Analyze how a particular sentence, paragraph, chapter, or section fits into the overall structure of a text and contributes to the development of the ideas. |
| **134–142** | **Reading Selection** | RI.6.1 | Cite textual evidence to support analysis of what the text says explicitly as well as inferences drawn from the text. |
| | | RI.6.2 | Determine a central idea of a text and how it is conveyed through particular details; provide a summary of the text distinct from personal opinions or judgments. |
| | | RI.6.5 | Analyze how a particular sentence, paragraph, chapter, or section fits into the overall structure of a text and contributes to the development of the ideas. |
| | | RI.6.7 | Integrate information presented in different media or formats (e.g., visually, quantitatively) as well as in words to develop a coherent understanding of a topic or issue. |
| | | RI.6.10 | By the end of the year, read and comprehend literary nonfiction in the grade 6–8 text complexity band proficiently, with scaffolding as needed at the high end of the range. |

# Common Core State Standards, continued

**Selection 1 Volcano!, continued**

| Pages | Lesson | Code | Standards Text |
|---|---|---|---|
| **143** | **Connect Reading and Writing**<br>Critical Thinking | RI.6.1 | Cite textual evidence to support analysis of what the text says explicitly as well as inferences drawn from the text. |
| | | RI.6.2 | Determine a central idea of a text and how it is conveyed through particular details; provide a summary of the text distinct from personal opinions or judgments. |
| | Vocabulary Review | L.6.6 | Acquire and use accurately grade-appropriate general academic and domain-specific words and phrases; gather vocabulary knowledge when considering a word or phrase important to comprehension or expression. |
| | Write About the GQ | W.6.9 | Draw evidence from literary or informational texts to support analysis, reflection, and research. |
| | | W.6.10 | Write routinely over extended time frames (time for research, reflection, and revision) and shorter time frames (a single sitting or a day or two) for a range of discipline-specific tasks, purposes, and audiences. |
| **144** | **Vocabulary Study**<br>Use Word Parts | L.6.4.b | Determine or clarify the meaning of unknown and multiple-meaning words and phrases based on grade 6 reading and content, choosing flexibly from a range of strategies.<br>Use common, grade-appropriate Greek or Latin affixes and roots as clues to the meaning of a word (e.g., *audience, auditory, audible*). |
| **144** | **Research/Media**<br>Report On a Volcano | SL.6.4 | Present claims and findings, sequencing ideas logically and using pertinent descriptions, facts, and details to accentuate main ideas or themes; use appropriate eye contact, adequate volume, and clear pronunciation. |
| | | SL.6.5 | Include multimedia components (e.g., graphics, images, music, sound) and visual displays in presentations to clarify information. |
| **145** | **Language and Grammar**<br>Engage in Conversation | SL.6.1 | Engage effectively in a range of collaborative discussions (one-on-one, in groups, and teacher-led) with diverse partners on grade 6 topics, texts, and issues, building on others' ideas and expressing their own clearly. |
| **145** | **Writing and Grammar**<br>Write About an Interesting Place | W.6.3.d | Write narratives to develop real or imagined experiences or events using effective technique, relevant descriptive details, and well-structured event sequences.<br>Use precise words and phrases, relevant descriptive details, and sensory language to convey experiences and events. |
| | | L.6.1.a | Demonstrate command of the conventions of standard English grammar and usage when writing or speaking.<br>Ensure that pronouns are in the proper case (subjective, objective, possessive). |
| | | L.6.1.c | Demonstrate command of the conventions of standard English grammar and usage when writing or speaking.<br>Recognize and correct inappropriate shifts in pronoun number and person. |

**Selection 2 Fleeing Katrina**

| Pages | Lesson | Code | Standards Text |
|---|---|---|---|
| **146** | **Connect** | RI.6.7 | Integrate information presented in different media or formats (e.g., visually, quantitatively) as well as in words to develop a coherent understanding of a topic or issue. |
| | | SL.6.2 | Interpret information presented in diverse media and formats (e.g., visually, quantitatively, orally) and explain how it contributes to a topic, text, or issue under study. |

**Selection 2 Fleeing Katrina,** continued

| Pages | Lesson | Code | Standards Text |
|---|---|---|---|
| 147–149 | **Language & Grammar**<br>Ask and Answer Questions | L.6.1.a | Demonstrate command of the conventions of standard English grammar and usage when writing or speaking.<br>Ensure that pronouns are in the proper case (subjective, objective, possessive). |
| | | L.6.1.c | Demonstrate command of the conventions of standard English grammar and usage when writing or speaking.<br>Recognize and correct inappropriate shifts in pronoun number and person. |
| | **Use Correct Subject Pronouns** | L.6.1.d | Demonstrate command of the conventions of standard English grammar and usage when writing or speaking.<br>Recognize and correct vague pronouns (i.e., ones with unclear or ambiguous antecedents). |
| | | SL.6.1.c | Engage effectively in a range of collaborative discussions (one-on-one, in groups, and teacher-led) with diverse partners on grade 6 topics, texts, and issues, building on others' ideas and expressing their own clearly.<br>Pose and respond to specific questions with elaboration and detail by making comments that contribute to the topic, text, or issue under discussion. |
| 150 | **Key Vocabulary** | RI.6.4 | Determine the meaning of words and phrases as they are used in a text, including figurative, connotative, and technical meanings. |
| | | L.6.4 | Determine or clarify the meaning of unknown and multiple-meaning words and phrases based on grade 6 reading and content, choosing flexibly from a range of strategies. |
| 151 | **Reading Strategy**<br>Make Connections | RI.6.1 | Cite textual evidence to support analysis of what the text says explicitly as well as inferences drawn from the text. |
| | **Literary Analysis**<br>Analyze Author's Viewpoint | RI.6.6 | Determine an author's point of view or purpose in a text and explain how it is conveyed in the text. |
| 152–162 | **Reading Selection** | RI.6.1 | Cite textual evidence to support analysis of what the text says explicitly as well as inferences drawn from the text. |
| | | RI.6.2 | Determine a central idea of a text and how it is conveyed through particular details; provide a summary of the text distinct from personal opinions or judgments. |
| | | RI.6.10 | By the end of the year, read and comprehend literary nonfiction in the grades 6–8 text complexity band proficiently, with scaffolding as needed at the high end of the range. |
| 163 | **Connect Reading and Writing**<br>Critical Thinking | RI.6.2 | Determine a central idea of a text and how it is conveyed through particular details; provide a summary of the text distinct from personal opinions or judgments. |
| | Vocabulary Review | L.6.6 | Acquire and use accurately grade-appropriate general academic and domain-specific words and phrases; gather vocabulary knowledge when considering a word or phrase important to comprehension or expression. |
| | Write About the GQ | W.6.9 | Draw evidence from literary or informational texts to support analysis, reflection, and research. |
| | | W.6.10 | Write routinely over extended time frames (time for research, reflection, and revision) and shorter time frames (a single sitting or a day or two) for a range of discipline-specific tasks, purposes, and audiences. |
| 164 | **Vocabulary Study**<br>Use Word Parts | L.6.4.b | Determine or clarify the meaning of unknown and multiple-meaning words and phrases based on grade 6 reading and content, choosing flexibly from a range of strategies.<br>Use common, grade-appropriate Greek or Latin affixes and roots as clues to the meaning of a word (e.g.,*audience, auditory, audible*). |

# Common Core State Standards, continued

**Selection 2 Fleeing Katrina,** continued

| Pages | Lesson | Code | Standards Text |
|---|---|---|---|
| **164** | **Media/Speaking**<br>Compare Media Accounts | RI.6.7 | Integrate information presented in different media or formats (e.g., visually, quantitatively) as well as in words to develop a coherent understanding of a topic or issue. |
| | | SL.6.2 | Interpret information presented in diverse media and formats (e.g., visually, quantitatively, orally) and explain how it contributes to a topic, text, or issue under study. |
| | | SL.6.1.c | Engage effectively in a range of collaborative discussions (one-on-one, in groups, and teacher-led) with diverse partners on grade 6 topics, texts, and issues, building on others' ideas and expressing their own clearly.<br>Pose and respond to specific questions with elaboration and detail by making comments that contribute to the topic, text, or issue under discussion. |
| **165** | **Writing and Grammar**<br>Write About A Natural Disaster | W.6.3.d | Write narratives to develop real or imagined experiences or events using effective technique, relevant descriptive details, and well-structured event sequences.<br>Use precise words and phrases, relevant descriptive details, and sensory language to convey experiences and events. |
| | | L.6.1.c | Demonstrate command of the conventions of standard English grammar and usage when writing or speaking.<br>Recognize and correct inappropriate shifts in pronoun number and person. |
| | | L.6.1.d | Demonstrate command of the conventions of standard English grammar and usage when writing or speaking.<br>Recognize and correct vague pronouns (i.e., ones with unclear or ambiguous antecedents). |

**Selection 3 Earthquake**

| Pages | Lesson | Code | Standards Text |
|---|---|---|---|
| **166** | **Connect** | SL.6.2 | Interpret information presented in diverse media and formats (e.g., visually, quantitatively, orally) and explain how it contributes to a topic, text, or issue under study. |
| **167–169** | **Language & Grammar**<br>Give Advice | L.6.1 | Demonstrate command of the conventions of standard English grammar and usage when writing or speaking. |
| | Use Helping Verbs | SL.6.1 | Engage effectively in a range of collaborative discussions (one-on-one, in groups, and teacher-led) with diverse partners on grade 6 topics, texts, and issues, building on others' ideas and expressing their own clearly. |
| **170** | **Key Vocabulary** | RL.6.4 | Determine the meaning of words and phrases as they are used in a text, including figurative and connotative meanings; analyze the impact of a specific word choice on meaning and tone. |
| | | L.6.4 | Determine or clarify the meaning of unknown and multiple-meaning words and phrases based on grade 6 reading and content, choosing flexibly from a range of strategies. |
| **171** | **Reading Strategy**<br>Make Connections | RL.6.1 | Cite textual evidence to support analysis of what the text says explicitly as well as inferences drawn from the text. |
| | **Literary Analysis**<br>Analyze Characters' Viewpoints | RL.6.6 | Explain how an author develops the point of view of the narrator or speaker in a text. |

**Selection 3 Earthquake, continued**

| Pages | Lesson | Code | Standards Text |
|---|---|---|---|
| **172–182** | **Reading Selection** | RL.6.1 | Cite textual evidence to support analysis of what the text says explicitly as well as inferences drawn from the text. |
| | | RL.6.6 | Explain how an author develops the point of view of the narrator or speaker in a text. |
| | | RL.6.10 | By the end of the year, read and comprehend literature, including stories, dramas, and poems, in the grades 6–8 text complexity band proficiently, with scaffolding as needed at the high end of the range |
| **183** | **Connect Reading and Writing** Critical Thinking | RL.6.1 | Cite textual evidence to support analysis of what the text says explicitly as well as inferences drawn from the text. |
| | | RL.6.2 | Determine a theme or central idea of a text and how it is conveyed through particular details; provide a summary of the text distinct from personal opinions or judgments. |
| | Vocabulary Review | L.6.6 | Acquire and use accurately grade-appropriate general academic and domain-specific words and phrases; gather vocabulary knowledge when considering a word or phrase important to comprehension or expression. |
| | Write About the GQ | W.6.9 | Draw evidence from literary or informational texts to support analysis, reflection, and research. |
| | | W.6.10 | Write routinely over extended time frames (time for research, reflection, and revision) and shorter time frames (a single sitting or a day or two) for a range of discipline-specific tasks, purposes, and audiences. |
| **184** | **Vocabulary Study** Use Word Parts | L.6.4.b | Determine or clarify the meaning of unknown and multiple-meaning words and phrases based on grade 6 reading and content, choosing flexibly from a range of strategies. Use common, grade-appropriate Greek or Latin affixes and roots as clues to the meaning of a word (e.g., *audience, auditory, audible*). |
| **184** | **Research/Speaking** Research Earthquakes | SL.6.1.a | Engage effectively in a range of collaborative discussions (one-on-one, in groups, and teacher-led) with diverse partners on grade 6 topics, texts, and issues, building on others' ideas and expressing their own clearly. Come to discussions prepared, having read or studied required material; explicitly draw on that preparation by referring to evidence on the topic, text, or issue to probe and reflect on ideas under discussion. |
| | | SL.6.4 | Present claims and findings, sequencing ideas logically and using pertinent descriptions, facts, and details to accentuate main ideas or themes; use appropriate eye contact, adequate volume, and clear pronunciation. |
| **185** | **Language and Grammar** Give Advice | SL.6.1 | Engage effectively in a range of collaborative discussions (one-on-one, in groups, and teacher-led) with diverse partners on grade 6 topics, texts, and issues, building on others' ideas and expressing their own clearly. |
| **185** | **Writing and Grammar** Write Advice | L.6.1 | Demonstrate command of the conventions of standard English grammar and usage when writing or speaking. |
| | | W.6.3.d | Write narratives to develop real or imagined experiences or events using effective technique, relevant descriptive details, and well-structured event sequences. Use precise words and phrases, relevant descriptive details, and sensory language to convey experiences and events. |
| **186–189** | **Close Reading** | RI.6.10 | By the end of the year, read and comprehend literary nonfiction in the grades 6–8 text complexity band proficiently, with scaffolding as needed at the high end of the range. |

# Common Core State Standards, continued

## Compare Across Texts

| Pages | Lesson | Code | Standards Text |
|---|---|---|---|
| **190** | **Compare Viewpoints** | RL.6.6 | Explain how an author develops the point of view of the narrator or speaker in a text. |
| | | RI.6.6 | Determine an author's point of view or purpose in a text and explain how it is conveyed in the text. |

## Unit Wrap-Up

| Pages | Lesson | Code | Standards Text |
|---|---|---|---|
| **191** | **Reflect on Your Reading** | RL.6.1 | Cite textual evidence to support analysis of what the text says explicitly as well as inferences drawn from the text. |
| | | RL.6.6 | Explain how an author develops the point of view of the narrator or speaker in a text. |
| | | RI.6.1 | Cite textual evidence to support analysis of what the text says explicitly as well as inferences drawn from the text. |
| | | RI.6.6 | Determine an author's point of view or purpose in a text and explain how it is conveyed in the text. |
| | **Explore the GQ/Book Talk** | SL.6.1.c | Engage effectively in a range of collaborative discussions (one-on-one, in groups, and teacher-led) with diverse partners on grade 6 topics, texts, and issues, building on others' ideas and expressing their own clearly. Pose and respond to specific questions with elaboration and detail by making comments that contribute to the topic, text, or issue under discussion |
| | | SL.6.1.d | Engage effectively in a range of collaborative discussions (one-on-one, in groups, and teacher-led) with diverse partners on grade 6 topics, texts, and issues, building on others' ideas and expressing their own clearly. Review the key ideas expressed and demonstrate understanding of multiple perspectives through reflection and paraphrasing. |

## Unit 4 Creepy Classics

### Unit Launch

| Pages | Lesson | Code | Standards Text |
|---|---|---|---|
| **192–193** | **Unit Opener** | SL.6.1 | Engage effectively in a range of collaborative discussions (one-on-one, in groups, and teacher-led) with diverse partners on grade 6 topics, texts, and issues, building on others' ideas and expressing their own clearly. |
| **194–197** | **Focus on Reading** Elements of Fiction | RL.6.3 | Describe how a particular story's or drama's plot unfolds in a series of episodes as well as how the characters respond or change as the plot moves toward a resolution. |
| **198–199** | **Focus on Vocabulary** Use Word Parts | RI.6.4 | Determine the meaning of words and phrases as they are used in a text, including figurative, connotative, and technical meanings. |
| | | L.6.4 | Determine or clarify the meaning of unknown and multiple-meaning words and phrases based on grade 6 reading and content, choosing flexibly from a range of strategies. |
| | | L.6.4.b | Determine or clarify the meaning of unknown and multiple-meaning words and phrases based on grade 6 reading and content, choosing flexibly from a range of strategies. Use common, grade-appropriate Greek or Latin affixes and roots as clues to the meaning of a word (e.g., *audience, auditory, audible*). |

### Selection 1 Frankenstein

| Pages | Lesson | Code | Standards Text |
|---|---|---|---|
| **200** | **Connect** | SL.6.2 | Interpret information presented in diverse media and formats (e.g., visually, quantitatively, orally) and explain how it contributes to a topic, text, or issue under study. |

**Selection 1 Frankenstein,** continued

| Pages | Lesson | Code | Standards Text |
|---|---|---|---|
| 201–203 | **Language & Grammar**<br>Describe People and Place | SL.6.1 | Engage effectively in a range of collaborative discussions (one-on-one, in groups, and teacher-led) with diverse partners on grade 6 topics, texts, and issues, building on others' ideas and expressing their own clearly. |
| | Use Adjectives | L.6.1 | Demonstrate command of the conventions of standard English grammar and usage when writing or speaking. |
| 204 | **Key Vocabulary** | RL.6.4 | Determine the meaning of words and phrases as they are used in a text, including figurative and connotative meanings; analyze the impact of a specific word choice on meaning and tone. |
| | | L.6.4 | Determine or clarify the meaning of unknown and multiple-meaning words and phrases based on grade 6 reading and content, choosing flexibly from a range of strategies. |
| 205 | **Reading Strategy**<br>Visualize: Identify Emotional Responses | RL.6.4 | Determine the meaning of words and phrases as they are used in a text, including figurative and connotative meanings; analyze the impact of a specific word choice on meaning and tone. |
| | **Literary Analysis**<br>Analyze Character Development | RL.6.3 | Describe how a particular story's or drama's plot unfolds in a series of episodes as well as how the characters respond or change as the plot moves toward a resolution. |
| 206–216 | **Reading Selection** | RL.6.1 | Cite textual evidence to support analysis of what the text says explicitly as well as inferences drawn from the text. |
| | | RL.6.4 | Determine the meaning of words and phrases as they are used in a text, including figurative and connotative meanings; analyze the impact of a specific word choice on meaning and tone. |
| | | RL.6.6 | Explain how an author develops the point of view of the narrator or speaker in a text. |
| | | RL.6.10 | By the end of the year, read and comprehend literature, including stories, dramas, and poems, in the grades 6–8 text complexity band proficiently, with scaffolding as needed at the high end of the range. |
| 217 | **Connect Reading and Writing**<br>Critical Thinking | RL.6.2 | Determine a theme or central idea of a text and how it is conveyed through particular details; provide a summary of the text distinct from personal opinions or judgments. |
| | Vocabulary Review | L.6.6 | Acquire and use accurately grade-appropriate general academic and domain-specific words and phrases; gather vocabulary knowledge when considering a word or phrase important to comprehension or expression. |
| | Write About the GQ | W.6.9 | Draw evidence from literary or informational texts to support analysis, reflection, and research. |
| | | W.6.10 | Write routinely over extended time frames (time for research, reflection, and revision) and shorter time frames (a single sitting or a day or two) for a range of discipline-specific tasks, purposes, and audiences. |
| 218 | **Vocabulary Study**<br>Use Word Parts | L.6.4.b | Determine or clarify the meaning of unknown and multiple-meaning words and phrases based on grade 6 reading and content, choosing flexibly from a range of strategies.<br>Use common, grade-appropriate Greek or Latin affixes and roots as clues to the meaning of a word (e.g., *audience, auditory, audible*). |
| 218 | **Literary Analysis**<br>Analyze Theme | SL.6.1.d | Engage effectively in a range of collaborative discussions (one-on-one, in groups, and teacher-led) with diverse partners on grade 6 topics, texts, and issues, building on others' ideas and expressing their own clearly.<br>Review the key ideas expressed and demonstrate understanding of multiple perspectives through reflection and paraphrasing. |
| | | RL.6.2 | Determine a theme or central idea of a text and how it is conveyed through particular details; provide a summary of the text distinct from personal opinions or judgments. |

# Common Core State Standards, continued

## Selection 1 Frankenstein, continued

| Pages | Lesson | Code | Standards Text |
|---|---|---|---|
| 219 | **Language and Grammar**<br>Describe People and Places | SL.6.1 | Engage effectively in a range of collaborative discussions (one-on-one, in groups, and teacher-led) with diverse partners on grade 6 topics, texts, and issues, building on others' ideas and expressing their own clearly. |
| 219 | **Writing and Grammar**<br>Write About a Creepy Situation | L.6.1 | Demonstrate command of the conventions of standard English grammar and usage when writing or speaking. |
| | | W.6.3.d | Write narratives to develop real or imagined experiences or events using effective technique, relevant descriptive details, and well-structured event sequences.<br>Use precise words and phrases, relevant descriptive details, and sensory language to convey experiences and events. |

## Selection 2 Film Fright

| Pages | Lesson | Code | Standards Text |
|---|---|---|---|
| 220 | **Connect** | RI.6.7 | Integrate information presented in different media or formats (e.g., visually, quantitatively) as well as in words to develop a coherent understanding of a topic or issue. |
| | | SL.6.2 | Interpret information presented in diverse media and formats (e.g., visually, quantitatively, orally) and explain how it contributes to a topic, text, or issue under study. |
| 221–223 | **Language & Grammar**<br>Make Comparisons | SL.6.1 | Engage effectively in a range of collaborative discussions (one-on-one, in groups, and teacher-led) with diverse partners on grade 6 topics, texts, and issues, building on others' ideas and expressing their own clearly. |
| | Use Adverbs | L.6.1 | Demonstrate command of the conventions of standard English grammar and usage when writing or speaking. |
| 224 | **Key Vocabulary** | RI.6.4 | Determine the meaning of words and phrases as they are used in a text, including figurative, connotative, and technical meanings. |
| | | L.6.4 | Determine or clarify the meaning of unknown and multiple-meaning words and phrases based on grade 6 reading and content, choosing flexibly from a range of strategies. |
| 225 | **Reading Strategy**<br>Visualize: Form Mental Images | RI.6.4 | Determine the meaning of words and phrases as they are used in text, including figurative, connotative, and technical meanings. |
| | **Literary Analysis**<br>Analyze Media | RI.6.7 | Integrate information presented in different media or formats (e.g., visually, quantitatively) as well as in words to develop a coherent understanding of a topic or issue. |
| 226–236 | **Reading Selection** | RI.6.1 | Cite textual evidence to support analysis of what the text says explicitly as well as inferences drawn from the text. |
| | | RI.6.10 | By the end of the year, read and comprehend literary nonfiction in the grades 6–8 text complexity band proficiently, with scaffolding as needed at the high end of the range. |
| 237 | **Connect Reading and Writing**<br>Critical Thinking | RI.6.2 | Determine a central idea of a text and how it is conveyed through particular details; provide a summary of the text distinct from personal opinions or judgments. |
| | Vocabulary Review | L.6.6 | Acquire and use accurately grade-appropriate general academic and domain-specific words and phrases; gather vocabulary knowledge when considering a word or phrase important to comprehension or expression. |
| | Write About the GQ | W.6.9 | Draw evidence from literary or informational texts to support analysis, reflection, and research. |
| | | W.6.10 | Write routinely over extended time frames (time for research, reflection, and revision) and shorter time frames (a single sitting or a day or two) for a range of discipline-specific tasks, purposes, and audiences. |

## Selection 2 Film Fright, continued

| Pages | Lesson | Code | Standards Text |
|---|---|---|---|
| **238** | **Vocabulary Study**<br>Use Latin and Greek Roots | L.6.4.b | Determine or clarify the meaning of unknown and multiple-meaning words and phrases based on grade 6 reading and content, choosing flexibly from a range of strategies.<br>Use common, grade-appropriate Greek or Latin affixes and roots as clues to the meaning of a word (e.g., *audience, auditory, audible*). |
| | | L.6.6 | Acquire and use accurately grade-appropriate general academic and domain-specific words and phrases; gather vocabulary knowledge when considering a word or phrase important to comprehension or expression. |
| **238** | **Literary Analysis**<br>Analyze Rhythm in Poetry | RL.6.7 | Compare and contrast the experience of reading a story, drama, or poem to listening to or viewing an audio, video, or live version of the text, including contrasting what they "see" and "hear" when reading the text to what they perceive when they listen or watch. |
| **239** | **Language and Grammar**<br>Make Comparisons | SL.6.1 | Engage effectively in a range of collaborative discussions (one-on-one, in groups, and teacher-led) with diverse partners on grade 6 topics, texts, and issues, building on others' ideas and expressing their own clearly. |
| **239** | **Writing and Grammar**<br>Write to Compare Creepy Actions | W.6.3.d | Write narratives to develop real or imagined experiences or events using effective technique, relevant descriptive details, and well-structured event sequences.<br>Use precise words and phrases, relevant descriptive details, and sensory language to convey experiences and events. |
| | | L.6.1 | Demonstrate command of the conventions of standard English grammar and usage when writing or speaking. |

## Selection 3 Mister Monster

| Pages | Lesson | Code | Standards Text |
|---|---|---|---|
| **240** | **Connect** | SL.6.1.d | Engage effectively in a range of collaborative discussions (one-on-one, in groups, and teacher-led) with diverse partners on grade 6 topics, texts, and issues, building on others' ideas and expressing their own clearly.<br>Review the key ideas expressed and demonstrate understanding of multiple perspectives through reflection and paraphrasing. |
| | | SL.6.2 | Interpret information presented in diverse media and formats (e.g., visually, quantitatively, orally) and explain how it contributes to a topic, text, or issue under study. |
| **241–243** | **Language & Grammar**<br>Describe an Event or Experience | SL.6.1 | Engage effectively in a range of collaborative discussions (one-on-one, in groups, and teacher-led) with diverse partners on grade 6 topics, texts, and issues, building on others' ideas and expressing their own clearly. |
| | Use Participles | L.6.2.a | Demonstrate command of the conventions of standard English capitalization, punctuation, and spelling when writing.<br>Use punctuation (commas, parentheses, dashes) to set off nonrestrictive/parenthetical elements. |
| | | L.6.3.a | Use knowledge of language and its conventions when writing, speaking, reading, or listening<br>Vary sentence patterns for meaning, reader/listener interest, and style. |
| **244** | **Key Vocabulary** | RI.6.4 | Determine the meaning of words and phrases as they are used in a text, including figurative, connotative, and technical meanings. |
| | | L.6.4 | Determine or clarify the meaning of unknown and multiple-meaning words and phrases based on grade 6 reading and content, choosing flexibly from a range of strategies. |

# Common Core State Standards, continued

| Pages | Lesson | Code | Standards Text |
|---|---|---|---|
| **245** | **Reading Strategy**<br>Visualize: Form Mental Images | RL.6.3 | Describe how a particular story's or drama's plot unfolds in a series of episodes as well as how the characters respond or change as the plot moves toward a resolution. |
| | **Literary Analysis**<br>Analyze Character and Plot | RL.6.4 | Determine the meaning of words and phrases as they are used in a text, including figurative and connotative meanings; analyze the impact of a specific word choice on meaning and tone. |
| **246–258** | **Reading Selection** | RL.6.1 | Cite textual evidence to support analysis of what the text says explicitly as well as inferences drawn from the text. |
| | | RI.6.10 | By the end of the year, read and comprehend literary nonfiction in the grades 6–8 text complexity band proficiently, with scaffolding as needed at the high end of the range. |
| **259** | **Connect Reading and Writing**<br>Critical Thinking | RL.6.2 | Determine a theme or central idea of a text and how it is conveyed through particular details; provide a summary of the text distinct from personal opinions or judgments. |
| | Vocabulary Review | L.6.6 | Acquire and use accurately grade-appropriate general academic and domain-specific words and phrases; gather vocabulary knowledge when considering a word or phrase important to comprehension or expression |
| | Write About the GQ | W.6.9 | Draw evidence from literary or informational texts to support analysis, reflection, and research. |
| | | W.6.10 | Write routinely over extended time frames (time for research, reflection, and revision) and shorter time frames (a single sitting or a day or two) for a range of discipline-specific tasks, purposes, and audiences. |
| **260** | **Vocabulary Study**<br>Use Word Parts | L.6.4 | Determine or clarify the meaning of unknown and multiple-meaning words and phrases based on grade 6 reading and content, choosing flexibly from a range of strategies. |
| | | L.6.4.b | Determine or clarify the meaning of unknown and multiple-meaning words and phrases based on grade 6 reading and content, choosing flexibly from a range of strategies.<br>Use common, grade-appropriate Greek or Latin affixes and roots as clues to the meaning of a word (e.g., *audience, auditory, audible*). |
| | | L.6.6 | Acquire and use accurately grade-appropriate general academic and domain-specific words and phrases; gather vocabulary knowledge when considering a word or phrase important to comprehension or expression. |
| **260** | **Literary Analysis**<br>Compare Presentations | RL.6.7 | Compare and contrast the experience of reading a story, drama, or poem to listening to or viewing an audio, video, or live version of the text, including contrasting what they "see" and "hear" when reading the text to what they perceive when they listen or watch. |
| **261** | **Language and Grammar**<br>Describe an Event or Experience | SL.6.1 | Engage effectively in a range of collaborative discussions (one-on-one, in groups, and teacher-led) with diverse partners on grade 6 topics, texts, and issues, building on others' ideas and expressing their own clearly. |
| **261** | **Writing and Grammar**<br>Write About a Performance | W.6.3.d | Write narratives to develop real or imagined experiences or events using effective technique, relevant descriptive details, and well-structured event sequences.<br>Use precise words and phrases, relevant descriptive details, and sensory language to convey experiences and events. |
| | | L.6.2.a | Demonstrate command of the conventions of standard English capitalization, punctuation, and spelling when writing.<br>Use punctuation (commas, parentheses, dashes) to set off nonrestrictive/parenthetical elements. |
| | | L.6.3.a | Use knowledge of language and its conventions when writing, speaking, reading, or listening.<br>Vary sentence patterns for meaning, reader/listener interest, and style. |

**Selection 3 Mister Monster, continued**

| Pages | Lesson | Code | Standards Text |
|---|---|---|---|
| 262–265 | **Close Reading** | RL.6.10 | By the end of the year, read and comprehend literature, including stories, dramas, and poems, in the grades 6–8 text complexity band proficiently, with scaffolding as needed at the high end of the range. |
| 266 | **Compare Themes** | RL.6.9 | Compare and contrast texts in different forms or genres (e.g., stories and poems; historical novels and fantasy stories) in terms of their approaches to similar themes. |

**Unit Wrap-Up**

| Pages | Lesson | Code | Standards Text |
|---|---|---|---|
| 267 | **Reflect on Your Reading** | RL.6.3 | Describe how a particular story's or drama's plot unfolds in a series of episodes as well as how the characters respond or change as the plot moves toward a resolution. |
| | | RL.6.4 | Determine the meaning of words and phrases as they are used in a text, including figurative and connotative meanings; analyze the impact of a specific word choice on meaning and tone. |
| | | RI.6.10 | By the end of the year, read and comprehend literary nonfiction in the grades 6-8 text complexity band proficiently, with scaffolding as needed at the high end of the range. |
| | **Explore the GQ/Book Talk** | SL.6.1.c | Engage effectively in a range of collaborative discussions (one-on-one, in groups, and teacher-led) with diverse partners on grade 6 topics, texts, and issues, building on others' ideas and expressing their own clearly.<br><br>Pose and respond to specific questions with elaboration and detail by making comments that contribute to the topic, text, or issue under discussion. |
| | | SL.6.1.d | Engage effectively in a range of collaborative discussions (one-on-one, in groups, and teacher-led) with diverse partners on grade 6 topics, texts, and issues, building on others' ideas and expressing their own clearly.<br><br>Review the key ideas expressed and demonstrate understanding of multiple perspectives through reflection and paraphrasing. |

## Unit 5   The Drive to Discover

**Unit Launch**

| Pages | Lesson | Code | Standards Text |
|---|---|---|---|
| 268–269 | **Unit Opener** | SL.6.1 | Engage effectively in a range of collaborative discussions (one-on-one, in groups, and teacher led) with diverse partners on grade 6 topics, texts, and issues, building on others' ideas and expressing their own clearly. |
| 270–271 | **Focus on Reading**<br>Text Structure: Main Idea and Details | RL.6.5 | Analyze how a particular sentence, chapter, scene, or stanza fits into the overall structure of a text and contributes to the development of the theme, setting, or plot. |
| | | RI.6.5 | Analyze how a particular sentence, paragraph, chapter, or section fits into the overall structure of a text and contributes to the development of the ideas. |
| 272–273 | **Focus on Vocabulary**<br>**Use Word Parts** | RI.6.4 | Determine the meaning of words and phrases as they are used in a text, including figurative, connotative, and technical meanings. |
| | | L.6.4 | Determine or clarify the meaning of unknown and multiple-meaning words and phrases based on grade 6 reading and content, choosing flexibly from a range of strategies. |
| | | L.6.4.b | Determine or clarify the meaning of unknown and multiple-meaning words and phrases based on grade 6 reading and content, choosing flexibly from a range of strategies.<br><br>Use common, grade-appropriate Greek or Latin affixes and roots as clues to the meaning of a word (e.g., *audience, auditory, audible*). |
| | | L.6.6 | Acquire and use accurately grade-appropriate general academic and domain-specific words and phrases; gather vocabulary knowledge when considering a word or phrase important to comprehension or expression. |

# Common Core State Standards, continued

**Selection 1 Return to Titanic**

| Pages | Lesson | Code | Standards Text |
|---|---|---|---|
| 274 | **Connect** | SL.6.2 | Interpret information presented in diverse media and formats (e.g., visually, quantitatively, orally) and explain how it contributes to a topic, text, or issue under study. |
| 275–277 | **Language & Grammar**<br>Ask for and Give Information<br>Use Present and Past Tense Verbs | SL.6.1.c | Pose and respond to specific questions with elaboration and detail by making comments that contribute to the topic, text, or issue under discussion. |
| | | L.6.1 | Demonstrate command of the conventions of standard English grammar and usage when writing or speaking. |
| | | L.6.2.b | Demonstrate command of the conventions of standard English capitalization, punctuation, and spelling when writing.<br>Spell correctly. |
| 278 | **Key Vocabulary** | RI.6.4 | Determine the meaning of words and phrases as they are used in a text, including figurative, connotative, and technical meanings. |
| | | L.6.4 | Determine or clarify the meaning of unknown and multiple-meaning words and phrases based on grade 6 reading and content, choosing flexibly from a range of strategies. |
| 279 | **Reading Strategy**<br>Ask Questions: Self Question | RI.6.1 | Cite textual evidence to support analysis of what the text says explicitly as well as inferences drawn from the text. |
| | **Literary Analysis**<br>Determine Main Idea and Details | RI.6.2 | Determine a central idea of a text and how it is conveyed through particular details; provide a summary of the text distinct from personal opinions or judgments. |
| | | RI.6.5 | Analyze how a particular sentence, paragraph, chapter, or section fits into the overall structure of a text and contributes to the development of the ideas. |
| 280–288 | **Reading Selection** | RI.6.1 | Cite textual evidence to support analysis of what the text says explicitly as well as inferences drawn from the text. |
| | | RI.6.2 | Determine a central idea of a text and how it is conveyed through particular details; provide a summary of the text distinct from personal opinions or judgments. |
| | | RI.6.10 | By the end of the year, read and comprehend literary nonfiction in the grades 6–8 text complexity band proficiently, with scaffolding as needed at the high end of the range. |
| 289 | **Connect Reading and Writing**<br>Critical Thinking | RI.6.2 | Determine a central idea of a text and how it is conveyed through particular details; provide a summary of the text distinct from personal opinions or judgments. |
| | Vocabulary Review | L.6.6 | Acquire and use accurately grade-appropriate general academic and domain-specific words and phrases; gather vocabulary knowledge when considering a word or phrase important to comprehension or expression. |
| | Write About the GQ | W.6.9 | Draw evidence from literary or informational texts to support analysis, reflection, and research. |
| | | W.6.10 | Write routinely over extended time frames (time for research, reflection, and revision) and shorter time frames (a single sitting or a day or two) for a range of discipline-specific tasks, purposes, and audiences. |
| 290 | **Vocabulary Study**<br>**Use Word Parts** | L.6.4.b | Determine or clarify the meaning of unknown and multiple-meaning words and phrases based on grade 6 reading and content, choosing flexibly from a range of strategies.<br>Use common, grade-appropriate Greek or Latin affixes and roots as clues to the meaning of a word (e.g., *audience, auditory, audible*). |
| | | L.6.6 | Acquire and use accurately grade-appropriate general academic and domain-specific words and phrases; gather vocabulary knowledge when considering a word or phrase important to comprehension or expression. |

**Selection 1 Return to Titanic, continued**

| Pages | Lesson | Code | Standards Text |
|---|---|---|---|
| 290 | **Literary Analysis** **Compare Events** | RI.6.9 | Compare and contrast one author's presentation of events with that of another (e.g., a memoir written by and a biography on the same person). |
| 291 | **Language and Grammar** Ask for and Give Information | SL.6.1.c | Engage effectively in a range of collaborative discussions (one-on-one, in groups, and teacher-led) with diverse partners on grade 6 topics, texts, and issues, building on others' ideas and expressing their own clearly. Pose and respond to specific questions with elaboration and detail by making comments that contribute to the topic, text, or issue under discussion. |
| 291 | **Writing and Grammar** Write About the Past | W.6.3.d | Write narratives to develop real or imagined experiences or events using effective technique, relevant descriptive details, and well-structured event sequences. Use precise words and phrases, relevant descriptive details, and sensory language to convey experiences and events. |
| | | L.6.1 | Demonstrate command of the conventions of standard English grammar and usage when writing or speaking. |
| | | L.6.2.b | Demonstrate command of the conventions of standard English capitalization, punctuation, and spelling when writing. Spell correctly. |

**Selection 2 The Forgotten Treasure**

| Pages | Lesson | Code | Standards Text |
|---|---|---|---|
| 292 | **Connect** | SL.6.2 | Interpret information presented in diverse media and formats (e.g., visually, quantitatively, orally) and explain how it contributes to a topic, text, or issue under study. |
| 293–295 | **Language & Grammar** Engage in Discussion Use Verb Tense: *Be* and *Have* | L.6.1 | Demonstrate command of the conventions of standard English grammar and usage when writing or speaking. |
| | | SL.6.1 | Engage effectively in a range of collaborative discussions (one-on-one, in groups, and teacher-led) with diverse partners on grade 6 topics, texts, and issues, building on others' ideas and expressing their own clearly. |
| | | SL.6.1.b | Engage effectively in a range of collaborative discussions (one-on-one, in groups, and teacher-led) with diverse partners on grade 6 topics, texts, and issues, building on others' ideas and expressing their own clearly. Follow rules for collegial discussions, set specific goals and deadlines, and define individual roles as needed. |
| | | L.6.1 | Demonstrate command of the conventions of standard English grammar and usage when writing or speaking. |
| 296 | **Key Vocabulary** | RL.6.4 | Determine the meaning of words and phrases as they are used in a text, including figurative and connotative meanings; analyze the impact of a specific word choice on meaning and tone. |
| | | L.6.4 | Determine or clarify the meaning of unknown and multiple-meaning words and phrases based on grade 6 reading and content, choosing flexibly from a range of strategies. |
| 297 | **Reading Strategy** Ask Questions: Find Answers to Your Questions **Literary Analysis** Determine Theme | RL.6.1 | Cite textual evidence to support analysis of what the text says explicitly as well as inferences drawn from the text. |
| | | RL.6.2 | Determine a theme or central idea of a text and how it is conveyed through particular details; provide a summary of the text distinct from personal opinions or judgments. |

# Common Core State Standards, continued

## Selection 2 The Forgotten Treasure, continued

| Pages | Lesson | Code | Standards Text |
|---|---|---|---|
| 298–308 | **Reading Selection** | RL.6.1 | Cite textual evidence to support analysis of what the text says explicitly as well as inferences drawn from the text. |
| | | RL.6.3 | Describe how a particular story's or drama's plot unfolds in a series of episodes as well as how the characters respond or change as the plot moves toward a resolution. |
| | | RL.6.4 | Determine the meaning of words and phrases as they are used in a text, including figurative and connotative meanings; analyze the impact of a specific word choice on meaning and tone. |
| | | RL.6.10 | By the end of the year, read and comprehend literature, including stories, dramas, and poems, in the grades 6–8 text complexity band proficiently, with scaffolding as needed at the high end of the range. |
| | | SL.6.2 | Interpret information presented in diverse media and formats (e.g., visually, quantitatively, orally) and explain how it contributes to a topic, text, or issue under study. |
| 309 | **Connect Reading and Writing**<br>Critical Thinking | RL.6.2 | Determine a theme or central idea of a text and how it is conveyed through particular details; provide a summary of the text distinct from personal opinions or judgments. |
| | Vocabulary Review | L.6.6 | Acquire and use accurately grade-appropriate general academic and domain-specific words and phrases; gather vocabulary knowledge when considering a word or phrase important to comprehension or expression. |
| | Write About the GQ | W.6.9 | Draw evidence from literary or informational texts to support analysis, reflection, and research. |
| | | W.6.10 | Write routinely over extended time frames (time for research, reflection, and revision) and shorter time frames (a single sitting or a day or two) for a range of discipline-specific tasks, purposes, and audiences. |
| 310 | **Vocabulary Study**<br>Use Word Parts | L.6.4.b | Determine or clarify the meaning of unknown and multiple-meaning words and phrases based on grade 6 reading and content, choosing flexibly from a range of strategies.<br><br>Use common, grade-appropriate Greek or Latin affixes and roots as clues to the meaning of a word (e.g., *audience, auditory, audible*). |
| | | L.6.6 | Acquire and use accurately grade-appropriate general academic and domain-specific words and phrases; gather vocabulary knowledge when considering a word or phrase important to comprehension or expression. |
| 310 | **Literary Analysis**<br>Compare Theme | RL.6.9 | Compare and contrast texts in different forms or genres (e.g., stories and poems; historical novels and fantasy stories) in terms of their approaches to similar themes and topics. |
| 311 | **Language and Grammar**<br>Engage in Discussion | SL.6.1 | Engage effectively in a range of collaborative discussions (one-on-one, in groups, and teacher-led) with diverse partners on grade 6 topics, texts, and issues, building on others' ideas and expressing their own clearly. |
| 311 | **Writing and Grammar**<br>Write About the Past | W.6.3.d | Write narratives to develop real or imagined experiences or events using effective technique, relevant descriptive details, and well-structured event sequences.<br><br>Use precise words and phrases, relevant descriptive details, and sensory language to convey experiences and events. |
| | | L.6.1 | Demonstrate command of the conventions of standard English grammar and usage when writing or speaking. |

## Selection 3 Mysteries of the Ancient Past

| Pages | Lesson | Code | Standards Text |
|---|---|---|---|
| 312 | **Connect** | SL.6.2 | Interpret information presented in diverse media and formats (e.g. visually, quantitatively, orally) and explain how it contributes to a topic, text, or issue under study. |

**Selection 3 Mysteries of the Ancient Past, continued**

| Pages | Lesson | Code | Standards Text |
|---|---|---|---|
| 313–315 | **Language & Grammar**<br>Define and Explain | SL.6.1 | Engage effectively in a range of collaborative discussions (one-on-one, in groups, and teacher-led) with diverse partners on grade 6 topics, texts, and issues, building on others' ideas and expressing their own clearly. |
|  | Use Past Tense Verbs | L.6.1 | Demonstrate command of the conventions of standard English grammar and usage when writing or speaking. |
| 316 | **Key Vocabulary** | RI.6.4 | Determine the meaning of words and phrases as they are used in a text, including figurative, connotative, and technical meanings. |
| 317 | **Reading Strategy**<br>Ask Questions:<br>Find Answers to Your Questions | RI.6.1 | Cite textual evidence to support analysis of what the text says explicitly as well as inferences drawn from the text. |
|  | **Literary Analysis**<br>Determine Main Idea and Details | RI.6.2 | Determine a central idea of a text and how it is conveyed through particular details; provide a summary of the text distinct from personal opinions or judgments. |
| 318–330 | **Reading Selection** | RI.6.1 | Cite textual evidence to support analysis of what the text says explicitly as well as inferences drawn from the text. |
|  |  | RI.6.2 | Determine a central idea of a text and how it is conveyed through particular details; provide a summary of the text distinct from personal opinions or judgments. |
|  |  | RI.6.4 | Determine the meaning of words and phrases as they are used in a text, including figurative, connotative, and technical meanings. |
|  |  | RI.6.10 | By the end of the year, read and comprehend literary nonfiction in the grades 6–8 text complexity band proficiently, with scaffolding as needed at the high end of the range. |
|  |  | SL.6.2 | Interpret information presented in diverse media and formats (e.g., visually, quantitatively, orally) and explain how it contributes to a topic, text, or issue under study. |
| 331 | **Connect Reading and Writing**<br>Critical Thinking | RI.6.2 | Determine a central idea of a text and how it is conveyed through particular details; provide a summary of the text distinct from personal opinions or judgments. |
|  |  | RI.6.1 | Cite textual evidence to support analysis of what the text says explicitly as well as inferences drawn from the text. |
|  | Vocabulary Review | L.6.6 | Acquire and use accurately grade-appropriate general academic and domain-specific words and phrases; gather vocabulary knowledge when considering a word or phrase important to comprehension or expression |
|  | Write About the GQ | W.6.9 | Draw evidence from literary or informational texts to support analysis, reflection, and research. |
|  |  | W.6.10 | Write routinely over extended time frames (time for research, reflection, and revision) and shorter time frames (a single sitting or a day or two) for a range of discipline-specific tasks, purposes, and audiences. |
| 332 | **Vocabulary Study**<br>**Use Word Parts** | L.6.4.b | Determine or clarify the meaning of unknown and multiple-meaning words and phrases based on grade 6 reading and content, choosing flexibly from a range of strategies.<br>Use common, grade-appropriate Greek or Latin affixes and roots as clues to the meaning of a word (e.g., *audience, auditory, audible*). |
|  |  | L.6.6 | Acquire and use accurately grade-appropriate general academic and domain-specific words and phrases; gather vocabulary knowledge when considering a word or phrase important to comprehension or expression. |
| 332 | **Research/Speaking**<br>Research Pyramids | RI.6.7 | Integrate information presented in different media or formats (e.g., visually, quantitatively) as well as in words to develop a coherent understanding of a topic or issue. |

# Common Core State Standards, continued

## Selection 3 Mysteries of the Ancient Past, continued

| Pages | Lesson | Code | Standards Text |
|---|---|---|---|
| 333 | **Language and Grammar**<br>Define and Explain | SL.6.1 | Engage effectively in a range of collaborative discussions (one-on-one, in groups, and teacher-led) with diverse partners on grade 6 topics, texts, and issues, building on others' ideas and expressing their own clearly. |
| 333 | **Writing and Grammar**<br>Write About the Past and Present | L.6.1 | Demonstrate command of the conventions of standard English grammar and usage when writing or speaking. |
| | | L.6.2.b | Demonstrate command of the conventions of standard English capitalization, punctuation, and spelling when writing.<br>Spell correctly. |
| | | W.6.3.d | Write narratives to develop real or imagined experiences or events using effective technique, relevant descriptive details, and well-structured event sequences.<br>Use precise words and phrases, relevant descriptive details, and sensory language to convey experiences and events. |
| 334–335 | **Close Reading** | RI.6.10 | By the end of the year, read and comprehend literary nonfiction in the grades 6–8 text complexity band proficiently, with scaffolding as needed at the high end of the range. |

### Compare Across Texts

| | | | |
|---|---|---|---|
| 336 | **Compare Important Ideas** | RL.6.9 | Compare and contrast texts in different forms or genres (e.g., stories and poems; historical novels and fantasy stories) in terms of their approaches to similar themes and topics. |
| | | RI.6.1 | Cite textual evidence to support analysis of what the text says explicitly as well as inferences drawn from the text. |

### Unit Wrap

| | | | |
|---|---|---|---|
| 337 | **Reflect on Your Reading** | RL.6.1 | Cite textual evidence to support analysis of what the text says explicitly as well as inferences drawn from the text. |
| | | RL.6.5 | Analyze how a particular sentence, chapter, scene, or stanza fits into the overall structure of a text and contributes to the development of the theme, setting, or plot. |
| | | RI.6.1 | Cite textual evidence to support analysis of what the text says explicitly as well as inferences drawn from the text. |
| | | RI.6.5 | Analyze how a particular sentence, paragraph, chapter, or section fits into the overall structure of a text and contributes to the development of the ideas. |
| | **Explore the GQ/Book Talk** | SL.6.1 | Engage effectively in a range of collaborative discussions (one-on-one, in groups, and teacher led) with diverse partners on grade 6 topics, texts, and issues, building on others' ideas and expressing their own clearly. |

# Unit 6   Struggle for Freedom

## Unit Launch

| Pages | Lesson | Code | Standards Text |
|---|---|---|---|
| **338–339** | **Unit Opener** | SL.6.1 | Engage effectively in a range of collaborative discussions (one-on-one, in groups, and teacher-led) with diverse partners on grade 6 topics, texts, and issues, building on others' ideas and expressing their own clearly. |
| **340–341** | **Focus on Reading** Text Structure: Cause and Effect | RL.6.5 | Analyze how a particular sentence, chapter, scene, or stanza fits into the overall structure of a text and contributes to the development of the theme, setting, or plot. |
| | | RI.6.5 | Analyze how a particular sentence, paragraph, chapter, or section fits into the overall structure of a text and contributes to the development of the ideas. |
| **342–343** | **Focus on Vocabulary** Use Context Clues for Unfamiliar Words | RI.6.4 | Determine the meaning of words and phrases as they are used in a text, including figurative, connotative, and technical meanings. |
| | | L.6.4 | Determine or clarify the meaning of unknown and multiple-meaning words and phrases based on grade 6 reading and content, choosing flexibly from a range of strategies. |
| | | L.6.4.a | Determine or clarify the meaning of unknown and multiple-meaning words and phrases based on grade 6 reading and content, choosing flexibly from a range of strategies. Use context (e.g., the overall meaning of a sentence or paragraph; a word's position or function in a sentence) as a clue to the meaning of a word or phrase. |

## Selection 1 Escaping to Freedom

| Pages | Lesson | Code | Standards Text |
|---|---|---|---|
| **344** | **Connect** | SL.6.2 | Interpret information presented in diverse media and formats (e.g., visually, quantitatively, orally) and explain how it contributes to a topic, text, or issue under study. |
| **345–347** | **Language & Grammar** Summarize Use Nouns in the Subject and Predicate | L.6.1 | Demonstrate command of the conventions of standard English grammar and usage when writing or speaking. |
| | | SL.6.1.d | Engage effectively in a range of collaborative discussions (one-on-one, in groups, and teacher-led) with diverse partners on grade 6 topics, texts, and issues, building on others' ideas and expressing their own clearly. Review the key ideas expressed and demonstrate understanding of multiple perspectives through reflection and paraphrasing. |
| | | L.6.1 | Demonstrate command of the conventions of standard English grammar and usage when writing or speaking. |
| **348** | **Key Vocabulary** | RI.6.4 | Determine the meaning of words and phrases as they are used in a text, including figurative, connotative, and technical meanings. |
| | | L.6.4 | Determine or clarify the meaning of unknown and multiple-meaning words and phrases based on grade 6 reading and content, choosing flexibly from a range of strategies. |
| **349** | **Reading Strategy** Determine Importance | RI.6.2 | Determine a central idea of a text and how it is conveyed through particular details; provide a summary of the text distinct from personal opinions or judgments. |
| | **Literary Analysis** Text Structure | RI.6.5 | Analyze how a particular sentence, paragraph, chapter, or section fits into the overall structure of a text and contributes to the development of the ideas. |
| **350–358** | **Reading Selection** | RL.6.1 | Cite textual evidence to support analysis of what the text says explicitly as well as inferences drawn from the text. |
| | | RI.6.1 | Cite textual evidence to support analysis of what the text says explicitly as well as inferences drawn from the text. |
| | | RI.6.10 | By the end of the year, read and comprehend literary nonfiction in the grades 6–8 text complexity band proficiently, with scaffolding as needed at the high end of the range. |

# Common Core State Standards, continued

| Pages | Lesson | Code | Standards Text |
|---|---|---|---|
| 359 | **Connect Reading and Writing**<br>Critical Thinking | RI.6.1 | Cite textual evidence to support analysis of what the text says explicitly as well as inferences drawn from the text. |
| | | RI.6.2 | Determine a central idea of a text and how it is conveyed through particular details; provide a summary of the text distinct from personal opinions or judgments. |
| | Vocabulary Review | L.6.6 | Acquire and use accurately grade-appropriate general academic and domain-specific words and phrases; gather vocabulary knowledge when considering a word or phrase important to comprehension or expression. |
| | Write About the GQ | W.6.9 | Draw evidence from literary or informational texts to support analysis, reflection, and research. |
| | | W.6.10 | Write routinely over extended time frames (time for research, reflection, and revision) and shorter time frames (a single sitting or a day or two) for a range of discipline-specific tasks, purposes, and audiences. |
| 360 | **Vocabulary Study**<br>Use Context Clues | RI.6.4 | Determine the meaning of words and phrases as they are used in a text, including figurative, connotative, and technical meanings. |
| | | L.6.4.a | Determine or clarify the meaning of unknown and multiple-meaning words and phrases based on grade 6 reading and content, choosing flexibly from a range of strategies.<br>Use context (e.g., the overall meaning of a sentence or paragraph; a word's position or function in a sentence) as a clue to the meaning of a word or phrase. |
| | | L.6.6 | Acquire and use accurately grade-appropriate general academic and domain-specific words and phrases; gather vocabulary knowledge when considering a word or phrase important to comprehension or expression. |
| 360 | **Listening and Speaking**<br>Dramatize a Song | RL.6.7 | Compare and contrast the experience of reading a story, drama, or poem to listening to or viewing an audio, video, or live version of the text, including contrasting what they "see" and "hear" when reading the text to what they perceive when they listen or watch. |
| | | SL.6.1.d | Engage effectively in a range of collaborative discussions (one-on-one, in groups, and teacher-led) with diverse partners on grade 6 topics, texts, and issues, building on others' ideas and expressing their own clearly.<br>Review the key ideas expressed and demonstrate understanding of multiple perspectives through reflection and paraphrasing. |
| | | SL.6.4 | Present claims and findings, sequencing ideas logically and using pertinent descriptions, facts, and details to accentuate main ideas or themes; use appropriate eye contact, adequate volume, and clear pronunciation. |
| 361 | **Language and Grammar**<br>Summarize | SL.6.1.d | Engage effectively in a range of collaborative discussions (one-on-one, in groups, and teacher-led) with diverse partners on grade 6 topics, texts, and issues, building on others' ideas and expressing their own clearly.<br>Review the key ideas expressed and demonstrate understanding of multiple perspectives through reflection and paraphrasing. |
| 361 | **Writing and Grammar**<br>Write About Freedom | W.6.3.d | Write narratives to develop real or imagined experiences or events using effective technique, relevant descriptive details, and well-structured event sequences.<br>Use precise words and phrases, relevant descriptive details, and sensory language to convey experiences and events. |
| | | L.6.1.a | Demonstrate command of the conventions of standard English grammar and usage when writing or speaking.<br>Ensure that pronouns are in the proper case (subjective, objective, possessive). |
| | | L.6.1.c | Demonstrate command of the conventions of standard English grammar and usage when writing or speaking.<br>Recognize and correct inappropriate shifts in pronoun number and person. |

**Selection 2 Brave Butterflies**

| Pages | Lesson | Code | Standards Text |
|---|---|---|---|
| **362** | **Connect** | SL.6.2 | Interpret information presented in diverse media and formats (e.g., visually, quantitatively, orally) and explain how it contributes to a topic, text, or issue under study. |
| **363–365** | **Language & Grammar**<br>Make Comparisons | SL.6.1 | Engage effectively in a range of collaborative discussions (one-on-one, in groups, and teacher-led) with diverse partners on grade 6 topics, texts, and issues, building on others' ideas and expressing their own clearly. |
| | | L.6.1.a | Demonstrate command of the conventions of standard English grammar and usage when writing or speaking.<br>Ensure that pronouns are in the proper case (subjective, objective, possessive). |
| | | L.6.1.c | Demonstrate command of the conventions of standard English grammar and usage when writing or speaking.<br>Recognize and correct inappropriate shifts in pronoun number and person. |
| | Use Pronouns in the Subject and Predicate | L.6.1.d | Demonstrate command of the conventions of standard English grammar and usage when writing or speaking.<br>Recognize and correct vague pronouns (i.e., ones with unclear or ambiguous antecedents). |
| **366** | **Key Vocabulary** | RL.6.4 | Determine the meaning of words and phrases as they are used in a text, including figurative and connotative meanings; analyze the impact of a specific word choice on meaning and tone. |
| | | L.6.4 | Determine or clarify the meaning of unknown and multiple-meaning words and phrases based on grade 6 reading and content, choosing flexibly from a range of strategies. |
| **367** | **Reading Strategy**<br>Determine Importance | RL.6.2 | Determine a theme or central idea of a text and how it is conveyed through particular details; provide a summary of the text distinct from personal opinions or judgments. |
| | **Literary Analysis**<br>Text Structure: Cause and Effect | RL.6.5 | Analyze how a particular sentence, chapter, scene, or stanza fits into the overall structure of a text and contributes to the development of the theme, setting, or plot. |
| **368–378** | **Reading Selection** | RL.6.1 | Cite textual evidence to support analysis of what the text says explicitly as well as inferences drawn from the text. |
| | | RL.6.10 | By the end of the year, read and comprehend literature, including stories, dramas, and poems, in the grades 6–8 text complexity band proficiently, with scaffolding as needed at the high end of the range. |
| | | RI.6.1 | Cite textual evidence to support analysis of what the text says explicitly as well as inferences drawn from the text. |
| | | SL.6.1.d | Engage effectively in a range of collaborative discussions (one-on-one, in groups, and teacher-led) with diverse partners on grade 6 topics, texts, and issues, building on others' ideas and expressing their own clearly.<br>Review the key ideas expressed and demonstrate understanding of multiple perspectives through reflection and paraphrasing. |

# Common Core State Standards, continued

**Selection 2 Brave Butterflies, continued**

| Pages | Lesson | Code | Standards Text |
|---|---|---|---|
| 379 | **Connect Reading and Writing**<br>Critical Thinking | RL.6.2 | Determine a theme or central idea of a text and how it is conveyed through particular details; provide a summary of the text distinct from personal opinions or judgments. |
| | Vocabulary Review | L.6.6 | Acquire and use accurately grade-appropriate general academic and domain-specific words and phrases; gather vocabulary knowledge when considering a word or phrase important to comprehension or expression. |
| | Write About the GQ | W.6.9 | Draw evidence from literary or informational texts to support analysis, reflection, and research. |
| | | W.6.10 | Write routinely over extended time frames (time for research, reflection, and revision) and shorter time frames (a single sitting or a day or two) for a range of discipline-specific tasks, purposes, and audiences. |
| 380 | **Vocabulary Study**<br>Use Context Clues | RL.6.4 | Determine the meaning of words and phrases as they are used in a text, including figurative and connotative meanings; analyze the impact of a specific word choice on meaning and tone. |
| | | L.6.4.a | Determine or clarify the meaning of unknown and multiple-meaning words and phrases based on grade 6 reading and content, choosing flexibly from a range of strategies.<br>Use context (e.g., the overall meaning of a sentence or paragraph; a word's position or function in a sentence) as a clue to the meaning of a word or phrase |
| | | L.6.6 | Acquire and use accurately grade-appropriate general academic and domain-specific words and phrases; gather vocabulary knowledge when considering a word or phrase important to comprehension or expression. |
| 380 | **Literary Analysis**<br>Analyze the Topic | SL.6.1.a | Engage effectively in a range of collaborative discussions (one-on-one, in groups, and teacher-led) with diverse partners on grade 6 topics, texts, and issues, building on others' ideas and expressing their own clearly.<br>Come to discussions prepared, having read or studied required material; explicitly draw on that preparation by referring to evidence on the topic, text, or issue to probe and reflect on ideas under discussion. |
| 381 | **Language and Grammar**<br>Make Comparisons | SL.6.1 | Engage effectively in a range of collaborative discussions (one-on-one, in groups, and teacher-led) with diverse partners on grade 6 topics, texts, and issues, building on others' ideas and expressing their own clearly. |
| 381 | **Writing and Grammar**<br>Write About A New Home | W.6.3.d | Write narratives to develop real or imagined experiences or events using effective technique, relevant descriptive details, and well-structured event sequences.<br>Use precise words and phrases, relevant descriptive details, and sensory language to convey experiences and events. |
| | | L.6.3.a | Use knowledge of language and its conventions when writing, speaking, reading, or listening.<br>Vary sentence patterns for meaning, reader/listener interest, and style. |
| | | L.6.1.a | Demonstrate command of the conventions of standard English grammar and usage when writing or speaking.<br>Ensure that pronouns are in the proper case (subjective, objective, possessive). |

**Selection 3 Seeking Freedom**

| Pages | Lesson | Code | Standards Text |
|---|---|---|---|
| 382 | **Connect** | SL.6.1.d | Engage effectively in a range of collaborative discussions (one-on-one, in groups, and teacher-led) with diverse partners on grade 6 topics, texts, and issues, building on others' ideas and expressing their own clearly.<br>Review the key ideas expressed and demonstrate understanding of multiple perspectives through reflection and paraphrasing. |
| | | SL.6.2 | Interpret information presented in diverse media and formats (e.g., visually, quantitatively, orally) and explain how it contributes to a topic, text, or issue under study. |

**Selection 3 Seeking Freedom,** continued

| Pages | Lesson | Code | Standards Text |
|---|---|---|---|
| 383–385 | **Language & Grammar**<br>Express Opinions | SL.6.1 | Engage effectively in a range of collaborative discussions (one-on-one, in groups, and teacher-led) with diverse partners on grade 6 topics, texts, and issues, building on others' ideas and expressing their own clearly. |
| | Use Reflexive and Intensive Pronouns | L.6.1.b | Demonstrate command of the conventions of standard English grammar and usage when writing or speaking.<br>Use intensive pronouns (e.g., myself, ourselves). |
| 386 | **Key Vocabulary** | RI.6.4 | Determine the meaning of words and phrases as they are used in a text, including figurative, connotative, and technical meanings. |
| | | L.6.4 | Determine or clarify the meaning of unknown and multiple-meaning words and phrases based on grade 6 reading and content, choosing flexibly from a range of strategies. |
| 387 | **Reading Strategy**<br>Determine Importance | RI.6.2 | Determine a central idea of a text and how it is conveyed through particular details; provide a summary of the text distinct from personal opinions or judgments |
| | | L.6.6 | Acquire and use accurately grade-appropriate general academic and domain-specific words and phrases; gather vocabulary knowledge when considering a word or phrase important to comprehension or expression. |
| | **Literary Analysis**<br>Text Structure: Cause and Effect | RI.6.5 | Analyze how a particular sentence, paragraph, chapter, or section fits into the overall structure of a text and contributes to the development of the ideas. |
| 388–398 | **Reading Selection** | RI.6.1 | Cite textual evidence to support analysis of what the text says explicitly as well as inferences drawn from the text. |
| | | RI.6.10 | By the end of the year, read and comprehend literary nonfiction in the grades 6–8 text complexity band proficiently, with scaffolding as needed at the high end of the range. |
| 399 | **Connect Reading and Writing**<br>Critical Thinking | RI.6.1 | Cite textual evidence to support analysis of what the text says explicitly as well as inferences drawn from the text. |
| | | RI.6.2 | Determine a central idea of a text and how it is conveyed through particular details; provide a summary of the text distinct from personal opinions or judgments. |
| | Vocabulary Review | L.6.6 | Acquire and use accurately grade-appropriate general academic and domain-specific words and phrases; gather vocabulary knowledge when considering a word or phrase important to comprehension or expression |
| | Write About the GQ | W.6.9 | Draw evidence from literary or informational texts to support analysis, reflection, and research. |
| | | W.6.10 | Write routinely over extended time frames (time for research, reflection, and revision) and shorter time frames (a single sitting or a day or two) for a range of discipline-specific tasks, purposes, and audiences. |
| 400 | **Vocabulary Study**<br>Use Context Clues | RI.6.4 | Determine the meaning of words and phrases as they are used in a text, including figurative, connotative, and technical meanings. |
| | | L.6.4.a | Determine or clarify the meaning of unknown and multiple-meaning words and phrases based on grade 6 reading and content, choosing flexibly from a range of strategies.<br>Use context (e.g., the overall meaning of a sentence or paragraph; a word's position or function in a sentence) as a clue to the meaning of a word or phrase. |
| | | L.6.6 | Acquire and use accurately grade-appropriate general academic and domain-specific words and phrases; gather vocabulary knowledge when considering a word or phrase important to comprehension or expression. |

# Common Core State Standards, continued

**Selection 3 Seeking Freedom, continued**

| Pages | Lesson | Code | Standards Text |
|---|---|---|---|
| **400** | **Literary Analysis**<br>Distinguish Facts From Opinion | RI.6.6 | Determine an author's point of view or purpose in a text and explain how it is conveyed in the text. |
| | | L.6.6 | Acquire and use accurately grade-appropriate general academic and domain-specific words and phrases; gather vocabulary knowledge when considering a word or phrase important to comprehension or expression. |
| **401** | **Language and Grammar**<br>Express Opinions | SL.6.1 | Engage effectively in a range of collaborative discussions (one-on-one, in groups, and teacher-led) with diverse partners on grade 6 topics, texts, and issues, building on others' ideas and expressing their own clearly. |
| **401** | **Writing and Grammar**<br>Write About Human Rights | L.6.1.b | Demonstrate command of the conventions of standard English grammar and usage when writing or speaking.<br>Use intensive pronouns (e.g., myself, ourselves). |
| | | W.6.3.d | Write narratives to develop real or imagined experiences or events using effective technique, relevant descriptive details, and well-structured event sequences.<br>Use precise words and phrases, relevant descriptive details, and sensory language to convey experiences and events. |
| **402–403** | **Close Reading** | RI.6.10 | By the end of the year, read and comprehend literary nonfiction in the grades 6–8 text complexity band proficiently, with scaffolding as needed at the high end of the range. |

## Compare Across Texts

| Pages | Lesson | Code | Standards Text |
|---|---|---|---|
| **404** | **Compare Writing on the Same Topic** | RI.6.7 | Integrate information presented in different media or formats (e.g., visually, quantitatively) as well as in words to develop a coherent understanding of a topic or issue. |

## Unit Warp

| Pages | Lesson | Code | Standards Text |
|---|---|---|---|
| **405** | **Reflect on Your Reading** | RL.6.2 | Determine a theme or central idea of a text and how it is conveyed through particular details; provide a summary of the text distinct from personal opinions or judgments. |
| | | RL.6.5 | Analyze how a particular sentence, chapter, scene, or stanza fits into the overall structure of a text and contributes to the development of the theme, setting, or plot. |
| | | RI.6.2 | Determine a central idea of a text and how it is conveyed through particular details; provide a summary of the text distinct from personal opinions or judgments. |
| | | RI.6.5 | Analyze how a particular sentence, paragraph, chapter, or section fits into the overall structure of a text and contributes to the development of the ideas. |
| | **Explore the GQ/Book Talk** | W.6.10 | Write routinely over extended time frames (time for research, reflection, and revision) and shorter time frames (a single sitting or a day or two) for a range of discipline-specific tasks, purposes, and audiences. |

## Unit 7 Star Power

### Unit Launch

| Pages | Lesson | Code | Standards Text |
|---|---|---|---|
| **406–407** | **Unit Opener** | SL.6.1 | Engage effectively in a range of collaborative discussions (one-on-one, in groups, and teacher-led) with diverse partners on grade 6 topics, texts, and issues, building on others' ideas and expressing their own clearly. |
| **408–409** | **Focus on Reading**<br>Analyze Argument | RI.6.8 | Trace and evaluate the argument and specific claims in a text, distinguishing claims that are supported by reasons and evidence from claims that are not. |
| **410–411** | **Focus on Vocabulary**<br>Use Context Clues for Multiple-Meaning Words | RL.6.4 | Determine the meaning of words and phrases as they are used in a text, including figurative and connotative meanings; analyze the impact of a specific word choice on meaning and tone. |
| | | RI.6.4 | Determine the meaning of words and phrases as they are used in a text, including figurative, connotative, and technical meanings. |
| | | L.6.4 | Determine or clarify the meaning of unknown and multiple-meaning words and phrases based on grade 6 reading and content, choosing flexibly from a range of strategies. |
| | | L.6.4.a | Determine or clarify the meaning of unknown and multiple-meaning words and phrases based on grade 6 reading and content, choosing flexibly from a range of strategies.<br>Use context (e.g., the overall meaning of a sentence or paragraph; a word's position or function in a sentence) as a clue to the meaning of a word or phrase. |
| | | L.6.4.c | Determine or clarify the meaning of unknown and multiple-meaning words and phrases based on grade 6 reading and content, choosing flexibly from a range of strategies.<br>Consult reference materials (e.g., dictionaries, glossaries, thesauruses), both print and digital, to find the pronunciation of a word or determine or clarify its precise meaning or its part of speech. |
| | | L.6.4.d | Determine or clarify the meaning of unknown and multiple-meaning words and phrases based on grade 6 reading and content, choosing flexibly from a range of strategies.<br>Verify the preliminary determination of the meaning of a word or phrase (e.g., by checking the inferred meaning in context or in a dictionary). |

### Selection 1 The Earth Under Sky Bear's Feet

| Pages | Lesson | Code | Standards Text |
|---|---|---|---|
| **412** | **Connect** | SL.6.1.d | Engage effectively in a range of collaborative discussions (one-on-one, in groups, and teacher-led) with diverse partners on grade 6 topics, texts, and issues, building on others' ideas and expressing their own clearly.<br>Review the key ideas expressed and demonstrate understanding of multiple perspectives through reflection and paraphrasing. |
| | | SL.6.2 | Interpret information presented in diverse media and formats (e.g., visually, quantitatively, orally) and explain how it contributes to a topic, text, or issue under study. |
| **413–415** | **Language & Grammar**<br>Describe | SL.6.1 | Engage effectively in a range of collaborative discussions (one-on-one, in groups, and teacher-led) with diverse partners on grade 6 topics, texts, and issues, building on others' ideas and expressing their own clearly. |
| | Use Possessive Nouns | L.6.1 | Demonstrate command of the conventions of standard English grammar and usage when writing or speaking. |
| | | L.6.2 | Demonstrate command of the conventions of standard English capitalization, punctuation, and spelling when writing. |

# Common Core State Standards, continued

**Selection 1 The Earth Under Sky Bear's Feet,** continued

| Pages | Lesson | Code | Standards Text |
|---|---|---|---|
| **416** | **Key Vocabulary** | RL.6.4 | Determine the meaning of words and phrases as they are used in a text, including figurative and connotative meanings; analyze the impact of a specific word choice on meaning and tone. |
| | | L.6.4 | Determine or clarify the meaning of unknown and multiple-meaning words and phrases based on grade 6 reading and content, choosing flexibly from a range of strategies. |
| **417** | **Reading Strategy** Make Inferences | RL.6.1 | Cite textual evidence to support analysis of what the text says explicitly as well as inferences drawn from the text. |
| | **Literary Analysis** Analyze Characters' Viewpoints | RL.6.6 | Explain how an author develops the point of view of the narrator or speaker in a text. |
| **418–428** | **Reading Selection** | RL.6.1 | Cite textual evidence to support analysis of what the text says explicitly as well as inferences drawn from the text. |
| | | RL.6.10 | By the end of the year, read and comprehend literature, including stories, dramas, and poems, in the grades 6–8 text complexity band proficiently, with scaffolding as needed at the high end of the range. |
| | | L.6.5 | Demonstrate understanding of figurative language, word relationships, and nuances in word meanings. |
| | | L.6.5.a | Demonstrate understanding of figurative language, word relationships, and nuances in word meanings. Interpret figures of speech (e.g., personification) in context. |
| **429** | **Connect Reading and Writing** Critical Thinking | RL.6.1 | Cite textual evidence to support analysis of what the text says explicitly as well as inferences drawn from the text. |
| | | RL.6.2 | Determine a theme or central idea of a text and how it is conveyed through particular details; provide a summary of the text distinct from personal opinions or judgments. |
| | Vocabulary Review | L.6.6 | Acquire and use accurately grade-appropriate general academic and domain-specific words and phrases; gather vocabulary knowledge when considering a word or phrase important to comprehension or expression. |
| | Write About the GQ | W.6.9 | Draw evidence from literary or informational texts to support analysis, reflection, and research. |
| | | W.6.10 | Write routinely over extended time frames (time for research, reflection, and revision) and shorter time frames (a single sitting or a day or two) for a range of discipline-specific tasks, purposes, and audiences. |
| **430** | **Vocabulary Study** Use Context Clues | L.6.4.a | Determine or clarify the meaning of unknown and multiple-meaning words and phrases based on grade 6 reading and content, choosing flexibly from a range of strategies. Use context (e.g., the overall meaning of a sentence or paragraph; a word's position or function in a sentence) as a clue to the meaning of a word or phrase. |
| | | L.6.4.c | Determine or clarify the meaning of unknown and multiple-meaning words and phrases based on grade 6 reading and content, choosing flexibly from a range of strategies. Consult reference materials (e.g., dictionaries, glossaries, thesauruses), both print and digital, to find the pronunciation of a word or determine or clarify its precise meaning or its part of speech. |
| | | L.6.4.d | Determine or clarify the meaning of unknown and multiple-meaning words and phrases based on grade 6 reading and content, choosing flexibly from a range of strategies. Verify the preliminary determination of the meaning of a word or phrase (e.g., by checking the inferred meaning in context or in a dictionary). |

**Selection 1 The Earth Under Sky Bear's Feet, continued**

| Pages | Lesson | Code | Standards Text |
|---|---|---|---|
| **430** | **Literary Analysis**<br>Analyze Mood and Tone | RL.6.4 | Determine the meaning of words and phrases as they are used in a text, including figurative and connotative meanings; analyze the impact of a specific word choice on meaning and tone. |
| | | SL.6.1.a | Engage effectively in a range of collaborative discussions (one-on-one, in groups, and teacher-led) with diverse partners on grade 6 topics, texts, and issues, building on others' ideas and expressing their own clearly.<br>Come to discussions prepared, having read or studied required material; explicitly draw on that preparation by referring to evidence on the topic, text, or issue to probe and reflect on ideas under discussion. |
| | | SL.6.1.d | Engage effectively in a range of collaborative discussions (one-on-one, in groups, and teacher-led) with diverse partners on grade 6 topics, texts, and issues, building on others' ideas and expressing their own clearly.<br>Review the key ideas expressed and demonstrate understanding of multiple perspectives through reflection and paraphrasing. |
| **431** | **Language and Grammar**<br>Describe | SL.6.1 | Engage effectively in a range of collaborative discussions (one-on-one, in groups, and teacher-led) with diverse partners on grade 6 topics, texts, and issues, building on others' ideas and expressing their own clearly. |
| **431** | **Writing and Grammar**<br>Write About a Character in Space | W.6.3.d | Write narratives to develop real or imagined experiences or events using effective technique, relevant descriptive details, and well-structured event sequences.<br>Use precise words and phrases, relevant descriptive details, and sensory language to convey experiences and events. |
| | | L.6.1 | Demonstrate command of the conventions of standard English grammar and usage when writing or speaking. |
| | | L.6.2 | Demonstrate command of the conventions of standard English capitalization, punctuation, and spelling when writing. |

**Selection 2 A Universe of Stars**

| Pages | Lesson | Code | Standards Text |
|---|---|---|---|
| **432** | **Connect** | SL.6.2 | Interpret information presented in diverse media and formats (e.g., visually, quantitatively, orally) and explain how it contributes to a topic, text, or issue under study. |
| **433–435** | **Language & Grammar**<br>Define and Explain | SL.6.1 | Engage effectively in a range of collaborative discussions (one-on-one, in groups, and teacher-led) with diverse partners on grade 6 topics, texts, and issues, building on others' ideas and expressing their own clearly. |
| | Use Possessive Adjectives and Pronouns | L.6.1.a | Demonstrate command of the conventions of standard English grammar and usage when writing or speaking.<br>Ensure that pronouns are in the proper case (subjective, objective, possessive). |

# Common Core State Standards, continued

**Selection 2 A Universe of Stars, continued**

| Pages | Lesson | Code | Standards Text |
|---|---|---|---|
| **436** | **Key Vocabulary** | RI.6.4 | Determine the meaning of words and phrases as they are used in a text, including figurative, connotative, and technical meanings. |
| | | L.6.4 | Determine or clarify the meaning of unknown and multiple-meaning words and phrases based on grade 6 reading and content, choosing flexibly from a range of strategies. |
| **437** | **Reading Strategy** Make Inferences | RI.6.1 | Cite textual evidence to support analysis of what the text says explicitly as well as inferences drawn from the text. |
| | **Literary Analysis** Analyze Author's Purpose | RI.6.6 | Determine an author's point of view or purpose in a text and explain how it is conveyed in the text. |
| **438–446** | **Reading Selection** | RL.6.1 | Cite textual evidence to support analysis of what the text says explicitly as well as inferences drawn from the text. |
| | | RI.6.1 | Cite textual evidence to support analysis of what the text says explicitly as well as inferences drawn from the text. |
| | | RI.6.4 | Determine the meaning of words and phrases as they are used in a text, including figurative, connotative, and technical meanings. |
| | | RI.6.10 | By the end of the year, read and comprehend literary nonfiction in the grades 6–8 text complexity band proficiently, with scaffolding as needed at the high end of the range. |
| | | SL.6.1.d | Engage effectively in a range of collaborative discussions (one-on-one, in groups, and teacher-led) with diverse partners on grade 6 topics, texts, and issues, building on others' ideas and expressing their own clearly. Review the key ideas expressed and demonstrate understanding of multiple perspectives through reflection and paraphrasing. |
| | | L.6.5 | Demonstrate understanding of figurative language, word relationships, and nuances in word meanings. |
| | | L.6.5.a | Demonstrate understanding of figurative language, word relationships, and nuances in word meanings. Interpret figures of speech (e.g., personification) in context. |
| **447** | **Connect Reading and Writing** Critical Thinking | RI.6.1 | Cite textual evidence to support analysis of what the text says explicitly as well as inferences drawn from the text. |
| | | RI.6.2 | Determine a central idea of a text and how it is conveyed through particular details; provide a summary of the text distinct from personal opinions or judgments. |
| | Vocabulary Review | L.6.6 | Acquire and use accurately grade-appropriate general academic and domain-specific words and phrases; gather vocabulary knowledge when considering a word or phrase important to comprehension or expression. |
| | Write About the GQ | W.6.9 | Draw evidence from literary or informational texts to support analysis, reflection, and research. |
| | | W.6.10 | Write routinely over extended time frames (time for research, reflection, and revision) and shorter time frames (a single sitting or a day or two) for a range of discipline-specific tasks, purposes, and audiences. |

**Selection 2 A Universe of Stars, continued**

| Pages | Lesson | Code | Standards Text |
|---|---|---|---|
| **448** | **Vocabulary Study**<br>Use Context Clues | L.6.4.a | Determine or clarify the meaning of unknown and multiple-meaning words and phrases based on grade 6 reading and content, choosing flexibly from a range of strategies.<br>Use context (e.g., the overall meaning of a sentence or paragraph; a word's position or function in a sentence) as a clue to the meaning of a word or phrase. |
| | | L.6.4.c | Determine or clarify the meaning of unknown and multiple-meaning words and phrases based on grade 6 reading and content, choosing flexibly from a range of strategies.<br>Consult reference materials (e.g., dictionaries, glossaries, thesauruses), both print and digital, to find the pronunciation of a word or determine or clarify its precise meaning or its part of speech. |
| | | L.6.4.d | Determine or clarify the meaning of unknown and multiple-meaning words and phrases based on grade 6 reading and content, choosing flexibly from a range of strategies.<br>Verify the preliminary determination of the meaning of a word or phrase (e.g., by checking the inferred meaning in context or in a dictionary). |
| **448** | **Literary Analysis**<br>Analyze Style | RI.6.4 | Determine the meaning of words and phrases as they are used in a text, including figurative, connotative, and technical meanings. |
| | | SL.6.1.a | Engage effectively in a range of collaborative discussions (one-on-one, in groups, and teacher-led) with diverse partners on grade 6 topics, texts, and issues, building on others' ideas and expressing their own clearly.<br>Come to discussions prepared, having read or studied required material; explicitly draw on that preparation by referring to evidence on the topic, text, or issue to probe and reflect on ideas under discussion. |
| | | SL.6.1.d | Engage effectively in a range of collaborative discussions (one-on-one, in groups, and teacher-led) with diverse partners on grade 6 topics, texts, and issues, building on others' ideas and expressing their own clearly.<br>Review the key ideas expressed and demonstrate understanding of multiple perspectives through reflection and paraphrasing. |
| **449** | **Language and Grammar**<br>Define and Explain | SL.6.1 | Engage effectively in a range of collaborative discussions (one-on-one, in groups, and teacher-led) with diverse partners on grade 6 topics, texts, and issues, building on others' ideas and expressing their own clearly. |
| **449** | **Writing and Grammar**<br>Write About an Adventure | W.6.3.d | Write narratives to develop real or imagined experiences or events using effective technique, relevant descriptive details, and well-structured event sequences.<br>Use precise words and phrases, relevant descriptive details, and sensory language to convey experiences and events. |
| | | L.6.1.a | Demonstrate command of the conventions of standard English grammar and usage when writing or speaking.<br>Ensure that pronouns are in the proper case (subjective, objective, possessive). |
| | | L.6.1.e | Demonstrate command of the conventions of standard English grammar and usage when writing or speaking.<br>Recognize variations from standard English in their own and others' writing and speaking, and identify and use strategies to improve expression in conventional language. |

**Selection 3 Not-So-Starry Nights**

| Pages | Lesson | Code | Standards Text |
|---|---|---|---|
| **450** | **Connect** | SL.6.2 | Interpret information presented in diverse media and formats (e.g., visually, quantitatively, orally) and explain how it contributes to a topic, text, or issue under study. |

# Common Core State Standards, continued

**Selection 3 Not-So-Starry Nights,** continued

| Pages | Lesson | Code | Standards Text |
|-------|--------|------|----------------|
| 451–453 | **Language & Grammar**<br>Persuade | SL.6.1 | Engage effectively in a range of collaborative discussions (one-on-one, in groups, and teacher-led) with diverse partners on grade 6 topics, texts, and issues, building on others' ideas and expressing their own clearly. |
|  | Use Prepositions | L.6.1 | Demonstrate command of the conventions of standard English grammar and usage when writing or speaking. |
| 454 | **Key Vocabulary** | RI.6.4 | Determine the meaning of words and phrases as they are used in a text, including figurative, connotative, and technical meanings. |
|  |  | L.6.4 | Determine or clarify the meaning of unknown and multiple-meaning words and phrases based on grade 6 reading and content, choosing flexibly from a range of strategies. |
| 455 | **Reading Strategy**<br>Make Inferences | RI.6.1 | Cite textual evidence to support analysis of what the text says explicitly as well as inferences drawn from the text. |
|  | **Literary Analysis**<br>Analyze Argument and Evidence | RI.6.8 | Trace and evaluate the argument and specific claims in a text, distinguishing claims that are supported by reasons and evidence from claims that are not. |
| 456–466 | **Reading Selection** | RI.6.1 | Cite textual evidence to support analysis of what the text says explicitly as well as inferences drawn from the text. |
|  |  | RI.6.8 | Trace and evaluate the argument and specific claims in a text, distinguishing claims that are supported by reasons and evidence from claims that are not. |
|  |  | RI.6.10 | By the end of the year, read and comprehend literary nonfiction in the grades 6–8 text complexity band proficiently, with scaffolding as needed at the high end of the range. |
| 467 | **Connect Reading and Writing**<br>Critical Thinking | RI.6.2 | Determine a central idea of a text and how it is conveyed through particular details; provide a summary of the text distinct from personal opinions or judgments. |
|  |  | SL.6.1.d | Engage effectively in a range of collaborative discussions (one-on-one, in groups, and teacher-led) with diverse partners on grade 6 topics, texts, and issues, building on others' ideas and expressing their own clearly.<br>Review the key ideas expressed and demonstrate understanding of multiple perspectives through reflection and paraphrasing. |
|  | Vocabulary Review | L.6.6 | Acquire and use accurately grade-appropriate general academic and domain-specific words and phrases; gather vocabulary knowledge when considering a word or phrase important to comprehension or expression |
|  | Write About the GQ | W.6.9 | Draw evidence from literary or informational texts to support analysis, reflection, and research. |
|  |  | W.6.10 | Write routinely over extended time frames (time for research, reflection, and revision) and shorter time frames (a single sitting or a day or two) for a range of discipline-specific tasks, purposes, and audiences. |
| 468 | **Vocabulary Study**<br>Use Context Clues | RI.6.4 | Determine the meaning of words and phrases as they are used in a text, including figurative, connotative, and technical meanings. |
| 468 | **Research/Media**<br>Analyze Media | RI.6.7 | Integrate information presented in different media or formats (e.g., visually, quantitatively) as well as in words to develop a coherent understanding of a topic or issue. |
|  |  | RI.6.8 | Trace and evaluate the argument and specific claims in a text, distinguishing claims that are supported by reasons and evidence from claims that are not. |
| 469 | **Language and Grammar**<br>Persuade | SL.6.1 | Engage effectively in a range of collaborative discussions (one-on-one, in groups, and teacher-led) with diverse partners on grade 6 topics, texts, and issues, building on others' ideas and expressing their own clearly. |

**Selection 3 Not-So-Starry Nights,** continued

| Pages | Lesson | Code | Standards Text |
|---|---|---|---|
| **469** | **Writing and Grammar** **Write About the Night Sky** | W.6.3.d | Write narratives to develop real or imagined experiences or events using effective technique, relevant descriptive details, and well-structured event sequences. Use precise words and phrases, relevant descriptive details, and sensory language to convey experiences and events. |
| | | L.6.1 | Demonstrate command of the conventions of standard English grammar and usage when writing or speaking. |
| | | L.6.3.a | Use knowledge of language and its conventions when writing, speaking, reading, or listening. Vary sentence patterns for meaning, reader/listener interest, and style. |
| **470–471** | **Close Reading** | RI.6.10 | By the end of the year, read and comprehend literary nonfiction in the grades 6–8 text complexity band proficiently, with scaffolding as needed at the high end of the range. |

**Compare Across Texts**

| Pages | Lesson | Code | Standards Text |
|---|---|---|---|
| **472** | **Compare Arguments** | RI.6.8 | Trace and evaluate the argument and specific claims in a text, distinguishing claims that are supported by reasons and evidence from claims that are not. |

**Unit Wrap**

| Pages | Lesson | Code | Standards Text |
|---|---|---|---|
| **473** | **Reflect on Your Reading** | RL.6.1 | Cite textual evidence to support analysis of what the text says explicitly as well as inferences drawn from the text. |
| | | RI.6.1 | Cite textual evidence to support analysis of what the text says explicitly as well as inferences drawn from the text. |
| | | RI.6.8 | Trace and evaluate the argument and specific claims in a text, distinguishing claims that are supported by reasons and evidence from claims that are not. |
| | **Explore the GQ/Book Talk** | W.6.10 | Write routinely over extended time frames (time for research, reflection, and revision) and shorter time frames (a single sitting or a day or two) for a range of discipline-specific tasks, purposes, and audiences. |
| | | SL.6.1.d | Engage effectively in a range of collaborative discussions (one-on-one, in groups, and teacher-led) with diverse partners on grade 6 topics, texts, and issues, building on others' ideas and expressing their own clearly. Review the key ideas expressed and demonstrate understanding of multiple perspectives through reflection and paraphrasing. |
| | | SL.6.5 | Include multimedia components (e.g., graphics, images, music, sound) and visual displays in presentations to clarify information. |

# Common Core State Standards, continued

## Unit Launch

| Pages | Lesson | Code | Standards Text |
|---|---|---|---|
| 474–475 | Unit Opener | SL.6.1 | Engage effectively in a range of collaborative discussions (one-on-one, in groups, and teacher-led) with diverse partners on grade 6 topics, texts, and issues, building on others' ideas and expressing their own clearly. |
| 476–477 | Focus on Reading<br>Analyze Text Features | RI.6.7 | Integrate information presented in different media or formats (e.g., visually, quantitatively) as well as in words to develop a coherent understanding of a topic or issue. |
| 478–479 | Focus on Vocabulary<br>Go Beyond the Literal Meaning | RL.6.4 | Determine the meaning of words and phrases as they are used in a text, including figurative and connotative meanings; analyze the impact of a specific word choice on meaning and tone. |
| | | RI.6.4 | Determine the meaning of words and phrases as they are used in a text, including figurative, connotative, and technical meanings. |
| | | L.6.5 | Demonstrate understanding of figurative language, word relationships, and nuances in word meanings. |
| | | L.6.5.a | Demonstrate understanding of figurative language, word relationships, and nuances in word meanings.<br>Interpret figures of speech (e.g., personification) in context. |
| | | L.6.5.c | Demonstrate understanding of figurative language, word relationships, and nuances in word meanings.<br>Distinguish among the connotations (associations) of words with similar denotations (definitions) (e.g., *stingy, scrimping, economical, unwasteful, thrifty*). |

## Selection 1 Old Music Finds New Voices

| Pages | Lesson | Code | Standards Text |
|---|---|---|---|
| 480 | Connect | SL.6.2 | Interpret information presented in diverse media and formats (e.g., visually, quantitatively, orally) and explain how it contributes to a topic, text, or issue under study. |
| 481–483 | Language & Grammar<br>Use Appropriate Language | SL.6.6 | Adapt speech to a variety of contexts and tasks, demonstrating command of formal English when indicated or appropriate. |
| | Use Complete Sentences | L.6.1 | Demonstrate command of the conventions of standard English grammar and usage when writing or speaking. |
| | | L.6.1.e | Demonstrate command of the conventions of standard English grammar and usage when writing or speaking.<br>Recognize variations from standard English in their own and others' writing and speaking, and identify and use strategies to improve expression in conventional language. |
| 484 | Key Vocabulary | RI.6.4 | Determine the meaning of words and phrases as they are used in a text, including figurative, connotative, and technical meanings. |
| | | L.6.4 | Determine or clarify the meaning of unknown and multiple-meaning words and phrases based on grade 6 reading and content, choosing flexibly from a range of strategies. |
| 485 | Reading Strategy<br>Synthesize | RI.6.1 | Cite textual evidence to support analysis of what the text says explicitly as well as inferences drawn from the text. |
| | Literary Analysis<br>Analyze News Media | SL.6.2 | Interpret information presented in diverse media and formats (e.g., visually, quantitatively, orally) and explain how it contributes to a topic, text, or issue under study. |
| 486–492 | Reading Selection | RI.6.1 | Cite textual evidence to support analysis of what the text says explicitly as well as inferences drawn from the text. |
| | | RI.6.10 | By the end of the year, read and comprehend literary nonfiction in the grades 6–8 text complexity band proficiently, with scaffolding as needed at the high end of the range. |

**Selection 1 Old Music Finds New Voices,** continued

| Pages | Lesson | Code | Standards Text |
|---|---|---|---|
| **493** | **Connect Reading and Writing**<br>Critical Thinking | RI.6.2 | Determine a central idea of a text and how it is conveyed through particular details; provide a summary of the text distinct from personal opinions or judgments. |
| | Vocabulary Review | L.6.6 | Acquire and use accurately grade-appropriate general academic and domain-specific words and phrases; gather vocabulary knowledge when considering a word or phrase important to comprehension or expression. |
| | Write About the GQ | W.6.9 | Draw evidence from literary or informational texts to support analysis, reflection, and research. |
| | | W.6.10 | Write routinely over extended time frames (time for research, reflection, and revision) and shorter time frames (a single sitting or a day or two) for a range of discipline-specific tasks, purposes, and audiences. |
| **494** | **Vocabulary Study**<br>Interpret Metaphors | RI.6.4 | Determine the meaning of words and phrases as they are used in a text, including figurative, connotative, and technical meanings. |
| | | L.6.5 | Demonstrate understanding of figurative language, word relationships, and nuances in word meanings. |
| | | L.6.5.a | Demonstrate understanding of figurative language, word relationships, and nuances in word meanings.<br>Interpret figures of speech (e.g., personification) in context. |
| | | L.6.6 | Acquire and use accurately grade-appropriate general academic and domain-specific words and phrases; gather vocabulary knowledge when considering a word or phrase important to comprehension or expression. |
| **494** | **Listening and Speaking**<br>Recite Songs | RL.6.7 | Compare and contrast the experience of reading a story, drama, or poem to listening to or viewing an audio, video, or live version of the text, including contrasting what they "see" and "hear" when reading the text to what they perceive when they listen or watch. |
| | | SL.6.4 | Present claims and findings, sequencing ideas logically and using pertinent descriptions, facts, and details to accentuate main ideas or themes; use appropriate eye contact, adequate volume, and clear pronunciation. |
| | | L.6.6 | Acquire and use accurately grade-appropriate general academic and domain-specific words and phrases; gather vocabulary knowledge when considering a word or phrase important to comprehension or expression. |
| **495** | **Language and Grammar**<br>Use Appropriate Language | SL.6.6 | Adapt speech to a variety of contexts and tasks, demonstrating command of formal English when indicated or appropriate. |
| **495** | **Writing and Grammar**<br>Write About Music | L.6.1 | Demonstrate command of the conventions of standard English grammar and usage when writing or speaking. |
| | | L.6.1.e | Demonstrate command of the conventions of standard English grammar and usage when writing or speaking.<br>Recognize variations from Standard English in their own and others' writing and speaking, and identify and use strategies to improve expression in conventional language. |
| | | W.6.3.d | Write narratives to develop real or imagined experiences or events using effective technique, relevant descriptive details, and well-structured event sequences.<br>Use precise words and phrases, relevant descriptive details, and sensory language to convey experiences and events. |

# Common Core State Standards, continued

**Selection 2 Making Faces**

| Pages | Lesson | Code | Standards Text |
|---|---|---|---|
| 496 | Connect | SL.6.2 | Interpret information presented in diverse media and formats (e.g., visually, quantitatively, orally) and explain how it contributes to a topic, text, or issue under study. |
| 497–499 | Language & Grammar<br>Use Appropriate Language | SL.6.6 | Adapt speech to a variety of contexts and tasks, demonstrating command of formal English when indicated or appropriate. |
| | Use Compound Sentences | L.6.3.a | Use knowledge of language and its conventions when writing, speaking, reading, or listening. Vary sentence patterns for meaning, reader/listener interest, and style. |
| 500 | Key Vocabulary | RI.6.4 | Determine the meaning of words and phrases as they are used in a text, including figurative, connotative, and technical meanings. |
| | | L.6.4 | Determine or clarify the meaning of unknown and multiple-meaning words and phrases based on grade 6 reading and content, choosing flexibly from a range of strategies. |
| 501 | Reading Strategy<br>Synthesize | RI.6.1 | Cite textual evidence to support analysis of what the text says explicitly as well as inferences drawn from the text. |
| | | RI.6.4 | Determine the meaning of words and phrases as they are used in a text, including figurative, connotative, and technical meanings. |
| | Literary Analysis<br>Analyze Author's Purpose and Tone | RI.6.6 | Determine an author's point of view or purpose in a text and explain how it is conveyed in the text. |
| | | L.6.5.c | Demonstrate understanding of figurative language, word relationships, and nuances in word meanings. Distinguish among the connotations (associations) of words with similar denotations (definitions) (e.g., *stingy, scrimping, economical, unwasteful, thrifty*). |
| 502–512 | Reading Selection | RI.6.1 | Cite textual evidence to support analysis of what the text says explicitly as well as inferences drawn from the text. |
| | | RI.6.10 | By the end of the year, read and comprehend literary nonfiction in the grades 6–8 text complexity band proficiently, with scaffolding as needed at the high end of the range. |
| 513 | Connect Reading and Writing<br>Critical Thinking | RI.6.2 | Determine a central idea of a text and how it is conveyed through particular details; provide a summary of the text distinct from personal opinions or judgments. |
| | Vocabulary Review | L.6.6 | Acquire and use accurately grade-appropriate general academic and domain-specific words and phrases; gather vocabulary knowledge when considering a word or phrase important to comprehension or expression. |
| | Write About the GQ | W.6.9 | Draw evidence from literary or informational texts to support analysis, reflection, and research. |
| | | W.6.10 | Write routinely over extended time frames (time for research, reflection, and revision) and shorter time frames (a single sitting or a day or two) for a range of discipline-specific tasks, purposes, and audiences. |
| 514 | Vocabulary Study<br>Analyze Idioms | RI.6.4 | Determine the meaning of words and phrases as they are used in a text, including figurative, connotative, and technical meanings. |
| | | L.6.5 | Demonstrate understanding of figurative language, word relationships, and nuances in word meanings. |
| | | L.6.5.a | Demonstrate understanding of figurative language, word relationships, and nuances in word meanings. Interpret figures of speech (e.g., personification) in context. |

## Selection 2 Making Faces, continued

| Pages | Lesson | Code | Standards Text |
|---|---|---|---|
| 514 | **Research/ Speaking**<br>**Explore Ancient Greek Drama** | RI.6.7 | Integrate information presented in different media or formats (e.g., visually, quantitatively) as well as in words to develop a coherent understanding of a topic or issue. |
| | | SL.6.4 | Present claims and findings, sequencing ideas logically and using pertinent descriptions, facts, and details to accentuate main ideas or themes; use appropriate eye contact, adequate volume, and clear pronunciation. |
| | | SL.6.5 | Include multimedia components (e.g., graphics, images, music, sound) and visual displays in presentations to clarify information. |
| 515 | **Language and Grammar**<br>Use Appropriate Language | SL.6.6 | Adapt speech to a variety of contexts and tasks, demonstrating command of formal English when indicated or appropriate. |
| 515 | **Writing and Grammar**<br>Write About Your Interests | W.6.3.d | Write narratives to develop real or imagined experiences or events using effective technique, relevant descriptive details, and well-structured event sequences.<br>Use precise words and phrases, relevant descriptive details, and sensory language to convey experiences and events. |
| | | L.6.3.a | Use knowledge of language and its conventions when writing, speaking, reading, or listening.<br>Vary sentence patterns for meaning, reader/listener interest, and style. |
| | | L.6.1.e | Demonstrate command of the conventions of standard English grammar and usage when writing or speaking.<br>Recognize variations from standard English in their own and others' writing and speaking, and identify and use strategies to improve expression in conventional language. |

## Selection 3 Wings

| Pages | Lesson | Code | Standards Text |
|---|---|---|---|
| 516 | **Connect** | SL.6.2 | Interpret information presented in diverse media and formats (e.g., visually, quantitatively, orally) and explain how it contributes to a topic, text, or issue under study. |
| 517–519 | **Language & Grammar**<br>Retell a Story | SL.6.4 | Present claims and findings, sequencing ideas logically and using pertinent descriptions, facts, and details to accentuate main ideas or themes; use appropriate eye contact, adequate volume, and clear pronunciation. |
| | Use Complex Sentences | L.6.2 | Demonstrate command of the conventions of standard English capitalization, punctuation, and spelling when writing. |
| | | L.6.2.a | Demonstrate command of the conventions of standard English capitalization, punctuation, and spelling when writing.<br>Use punctuation (commas, parentheses, dashes) to set off nonrestrictive/ parenthetical elements. |
| | | L.6.3.a | Use knowledge of language and its conventions when writing, speaking, reading, or listening.<br>Vary sentence patterns for meaning, reader/listener interest, and style. |
| 520 | **Key Vocabulary** | RL.6.4 | Determine the meaning of words and phrases as they are used in a text, including figurative and connotative meanings; analyze the impact of a specific word choice on meaning and tone. |
| | | L.6.4 | Determine or clarify the meaning of unknown and multiple-meaning words and phrases based on grade 6 reading and content, choosing flexibly from a range of strategies. |
| 521 | **Reading Strategy**<br>Synthesize | RL.6.1 | Cite textual evidence to support analysis of what the text says explicitly as well as inferences drawn from the text. |
| | **Literary Analysis**<br>Analyze Plot | RL.6.3 | Describe how a particular story's or drama's plot unfolds in a series of episodes as well as how the characters respond or change as the plot moves toward a resolution. |

# Common Core State Standards, continued

| Pages | Lesson | Code | Standards Text |
|---|---|---|---|
| **522–532** | **Reading Selection** | RL.6.1 | Cite textual evidence to support analysis of what the text says explicitly as well as inferences drawn from the text. |
| | | RL.6.10 | By the end of the year, read and comprehend literature, including stories, dramas, and poems, in the grades 6–8 text complexity band proficiently, with scaffolding as needed at the high end of the range. |
| **533** | **Connect Reading and Writing** Critical Thinking | RL.6.1 | Cite textual evidence to support analysis of what the text says explicitly as well as inferences drawn from the text. |
| | | RL.6.2 | Determine a theme or central idea of a text and how it is conveyed through particular details; provide a summary of the text distinct from personal opinions or judgments. |
| | Vocabulary Review | L.6.6 | Acquire and use accurately grade-appropriate general academic and domain-specific words and phrases; gather vocabulary knowledge when considering a word or phrase important to comprehension or expression |
| | Write About the GQ | W.6.9 | Draw evidence from literary or informational texts to support analysis, reflection, and research. |
| | | W.6.10 | Write routinely over extended time frames (time for research, reflection, and revision) and shorter time frames (a single sitting or a day or two) for a range of discipline-specific tasks, purposes, and audiences. |
| **534** | **Vocabulary Study** Analyze Similes | RL.6.4 | Determine the meaning of words and phrases as they are used in a text, including figurative and connotative meanings; analyze the impact of a specific word choice on meaning and tone. |
| | | L.6.5 | Demonstrate understanding of figurative language, word relationships, and nuances in word meanings. |
| | | L.6.5.a | Demonstrate understanding of figurative language, word relationships, and nuances in word meanings. Interpret figures of speech (e.g., personification) in context. |
| **534** | **Literary Analysis** Compare Characters | RL.6.3 | Describe how a particular story's or drama's plot unfolds in a series of episodes as well as how the characters respond or change as the plot moves toward a resolution. |
| | | RL.6.9 | Compare and contrast texts in different forms or genres (e.g., stories and poems; historical novels and fantasy stories) in terms of their approaches to similar themes and topics. |
| **535** | **Language and Grammar** Retell a Story | SL.6.4 | Present claims and findings, sequencing ideas logically and using pertinent descriptions, facts, and details to accentuate main ideas or themes; use appropriate eye contact, adequate volume, and clear pronunciation. |
| **535** | **Writing and Grammar** Write About Myths | L.6.2 | Demonstrate command of the conventions of standard English capitalization, punctuation, and spelling when writing. |
| | | L.6.2.a | Demonstrate command of the conventions of standard English capitalization, punctuation, and spelling when writing. Use punctuation (commas, parentheses, dashes) to set off nonrestrictive/parenthetical elements. |
| | | L.6.3.a | Use knowledge of language and its conventions when writing, speaking, reading, or listening. Vary sentence patterns for meaning, reader/listener interest, and style. |
| | | W.6.3.d | Write narratives to develop real or imagined experiences or events using effective technique, relevant descriptive details, and well-structured event sequences. Use precise words and phrases, relevant descriptive details, and sensory language to convey experiences and events. |

### Selection 3 Wings, continued

| Pages | Lesson | Code | Standards Text |
|---|---|---|---|
| 536–537 | Close Reading | RL.6.10 | By the end of the year, read and comprehend literature, including stories, dramas, and poems, in the grades 6–8 text complexity band proficiently, with scaffolding as needed at the high end of the range. |

### Compare Across Texts

| Pages | Lesson | Code | Standards Text |
|---|---|---|---|
| 538 | Compare Themes | RL.6.9 | Compare and contrast texts in different forms or genres (e.g., stories and poems; historical novels and fantasy stories) in terms of their approaches to similar themes and topics. |

### Unit Wrap-Up

| Pages | Lesson | Code | Standards Text |
|---|---|---|---|
| 539 | Reflect on Your Reading | RL.6.1 | Cite textual evidence to support analysis of what the text says explicitly as well as inferences drawn from the text. |
| | | RI.6.1 | Cite textual evidence to support analysis of what the text says explicitly as well as inferences drawn from the text. |
| | Explore the GQ/Book Talk | SL.6.1 | Engage effectively in a range of collaborative discussions (one-on-one, in groups, and teacher-led) with diverse partners on grade 6 topics, texts, and issues, building on others' ideas and expressing their own clearly. |
| | | SL.6.1.c | Engage effectively in a range of collaborative discussions (one-on-one, in groups, and teacher-led) with diverse partners on grade 6 topics, texts, and issues, building on others' ideas and expressing their own clearly. Pose and respond to specific questions with elaboration and detail by making comments that contribute to the topic, text, or issue under discussion. |
| | | SL.6.1.d | Engage effectively in a range of collaborative discussions (one-on-one, in groups, and teacher-led) with diverse partners on grade 6 topics, texts, and issues, building on others' ideas and expressing their own clearly. Review the key ideas expressed and demonstrate understanding of multiple perspectives through reflection and paraphrasing. |

### Reading Handbook

| Pages | Lesson | Code | Standards Text |
|---|---|---|---|
| 541–545 | Plan and Monitor | RL.6.1 | Cite textual evidence to support analysis of what the text says explicitly as well as inferences drawn from the text. |
| | | RI.6.1 | Cite textual evidence to support analysis of what the text says explicitly as well as inferences drawn from the text. |
| | | RI.6.10 | By the end of the year, read and comprehend literary nonfiction in the grades 6–8 text complexity band proficiently, with scaffolding as needed at the high end of the range. |
| 546 | Visualize | RI.6.1 | Cite textual evidence to support analysis of what the text says explicitly as well as inferences drawn from the text. |
| 547 | Determine Importance | RI.6.2 | Determine a central idea of a text and how it is conveyed through particular details; provide a summary of the text distinct from personal opinions or judgments. |
| 548 | Make Connections | RL.6.1 | Cite textual evidence to support analysis of what the text says explicitly as well as inferences drawn from the text. |
| | | RI.6.1 | Cite textual evidence to support analysis of what the text says explicitly as well as inferences drawn from the text. |

# Common Core State Standards, continued

**Reading Handbook, continued**

| Pages | Lesson | Code | Standards Text |
|-------|--------|------|----------------|
| **549** | **Make Inferences** | RL.6.1 | Cite textual evidence to support analysis of what the text says explicitly as well as inferences drawn from the text. |
| **550–551** | **Ask Questions** | RI.6.6 | Determine an author's point of view or purpose in a text and explain how it is conveyed in the text. |
| **552-553** | **Synthesize** | RI.6.1 | Cite textual evidence to support analysis of what the text says explicitly as well as inferences drawn from the text. |

The five-story, red brick apartment building at 253 East Tenth Street in New York City has been standing for more than a century. In 1900, one of the twenty small apartments in the building was occupied by thirty-nine-year-old Julius Streicher, Christine Streicher, age thirty-three, and their four young children. The Streichers were immigrants, having come in 1885 from their native Germany to New York, where they met and married.

The Streichers probably considered themselves successful. Julius operated a small clothing shop a few blocks from his apartment; Christine stayed at home, raised the children, and did housework. Like most people in the country at that time, neither Julius nor Christine had graduated from high school, and they worked for ten to twelve hours a day, six days a week. Their income—average in the United States for that time—was about $35 a month or about $425 a year. (In today's dollars, that would be slightly more than $8,000, which would put the family well below today's poverty line.) They spent almost half of their income for food; most of the rest went for rent.

Today, Dorothy Sabo resides at 253 East Tenth Street, living alone in the same apartment where the Streichers spent much of their lives. Now eighty-seven, she is retired from a career teaching art at a nearby museum. In many respects, Sabo's life has been far easier than the life the Streichers knew. For one thing, when the Streichers lived there, the building had no electricity (people used kerosene lamps and candles) and no running water (Christine Streicher spent most of every Monday doing laundry, using water she carried from a public fountain at the end of the block). There were no telephones, no television, and of course no computers. Today, Dorothy Sabo takes such conveniences for granted. Although she is hardly rich, her pension and Social Security are several times as much (in constant dollars) as the Streichers earned.

Sabo has her own worries. She is concerned about the environment and often speaks out about global warming. But a century ago, if the Streichers and their neighbors were concerned about "the environment," they probably would have meant the smell coming up from the street. At a time when motor vehicles were just beginning to appear in New York City, carriages, trucks, and trolleys were all pulled by horses—thousands of them. These animals dumped 60,000 gallons of urine and 2.5 million pounds of manure on the streets each and every day (Simon & Cannon, 2001). ■

It is difficult for most people today to imagine how different life was a century ago. Not only was life much harder back then, but it was also much shorter. Statistical records show that 100 years ago, life expectancy was just forty-six years for men and forty-eight years for women, compared to seventy-five and eighty years today.

Over the course of the past century, much has changed for the better. Yet as this chapter explains, social change is not all positive. On the contrary, change has negative consequences, too, creating unexpected new problems. Indeed, as

 **MEDIA** Learn about the lives of men and women, black and white, living in New York City a century ago at http://www.albany.edu/mumford/1920/groups.html

we shall see, early sociologists were mixed in their assessment of *modernity*, changes brought about by the Industrial Revolution. Likewise, today's sociologists point to both good and bad aspects of *postmodernity*, the recent transformations of society caused by the Information Revolution and the postindustrial economy. The one thing that is clear is that—for better and worse—the rate of change has never been faster than it is now.

## What Is Social Change?

In earlier chapters, we examined relatively fixed or *static* social patterns, including status and role, social stratification, and social institutions. We also looked at the *dynamic* forces that have shaped our way of life, ranging from innovations in technology to the growth of bureaucracy and the expansion of cities. These are all dimensions of **social change,** *the transformation of culture and social institutions over time.* The process of social change has four major characteristics:

1.  **Social change happens all the time.** "Nothing is constant except death and taxes" goes the old saying. Yet even our thoughts about death have changed dramatically as life expectancy in the United States has doubled over the course of a century. Back in 1900, the Streichers and almost all other people in the United States paid little or no taxes on their earnings; taxes increased dramatically over the course of the twentieth century, along with the size and scope of government. In short, just about everything is subject to the twists and turns of change.

    Still, some societies change faster than others. As Chapter 4 ("Society") explained, hunting and gathering societies change quite slowly; members of today's high-income societies, by contrast, experience significant change within a single lifetime.

**YOUR TURN**

What are the three most important changes that have occurred during your lifetime? Explain your answer.

It is also true that in a given society, some cultural elements change faster than others. William Ogburn's (1964) theory of *cultural lag* (see Chapter 3, "Culture") states that material culture (that is, things) usually changes faster than nonmaterial culture (ideas and attitudes). For example, the genetic technology that allows scientists to alter and perhaps even to create life has developed more rapidly than our ethical standards for deciding when and how to use it.

2.  **Social change is sometimes intentional but often unplanned.** Industrial societies actively promote many kinds of change. For example, scientists seek more efficient forms of energy, and advertisers try to convince us that life is incomplete without this or that new gadget. Yet rarely can anyone envision all the consequences of the changes that are set in motion.

    Back in 1900, when the country still relied on horses for transportation, many people looked ahead to motorized vehicles that would carry them in a single day distances that used to take weeks or months. But no one could see how much the mobility provided by automobiles would alter life in the United States, scattering family members, threatening the environment, and reshaping cities and suburbs. Nor could automotive pioneers have predicted the more than 42,000 deaths that occur in car accidents each year in the United States alone.

3.  **Social change is controversial.** The history of the automobile shows that social change brings both good and bad consequences. Capitalists welcomed the Industrial Revolution because new technology increased productivity and swelled profits. However, workers feared that machines would make their skills obsolete and resisted the push toward "progress."

    Today, as in the past, changing patterns of social interaction between black people and white people, women and men, and gays and heterosexuals are welcomed by some people and opposed by others.

4.  **Some changes matter more than others.** Some changes (such as clothing fads) have only passing significance; others (like the invention of computers) may change the entire world. Will the Information Revolution turn out to be as important as the Industrial Revolution? Like the automobile and television, the computer has both positive and negative effects, providing new kinds of jobs while eliminating old ones, isolating people in offices while linking people in global electronic networks, offering vast amounts of information while threatening personal privacy.

## Causes of Social Change

Social change has many causes. In a world linked by sophisticated communication and transportation technology, change in one place often sets off change elsewhere.

These young boys are performing in a hip-hop dance competition in Chengdu, China, in 2005. Hip-hop music, dress style, and dancing have become popular in China, a clear case of cultural diffusion. Cultural patterns move from place to place, but not always with the same understandings of what they mean. How might Chinese youth understand hip-hop differently from the young African Americans in the United States who originated it?

## CULTURE AND CHANGE

Chapter 3 ("Culture") identified three important sources of cultural change. First, *invention* produces new objects, ideas, and social patterns. Rocket propulsion research, which began in the 1940s, has produced spacecraft that reach toward the stars. Today we take such technology for granted; during this century, a significant number of people may well travel in space.

Second, *discovery* occurs when people take note of existing elements of the world. Medical advances, for example, offer a growing understanding of the human body. Beyond the direct effects on human health, medical discoveries have stretched life expectancy, setting in motion the "graying" of U.S. society (see Chapter 15, "Aging and the Elderly").

Third, *diffusion* creates change as products, people, and information spread from one society to another. Ralph Linton (1937a) recognized that many familiar elements of our culture came from other lands. For example, the cloth used to make our clothing was developed in Asia, the clocks we see all around us were invented in Europe, and the coins we carry in our pockets were first used in Turkey.

In general, material things diffuse more easily than cultural ideas. That is, new breakthroughs such as the science of cloning occur faster than our understanding of when—and even whether—they are morally desirable.

## CONFLICT AND CHANGE

Tension and conflict in a society also produce change. Karl Marx saw class conflict as the engine that drives societies from one historical era to another (see Chapter 4, "Society," and Chapter 10, "Social Stratification"). In industrial-capitalist societies, he maintained, the struggle between capitalists and workers pushes society toward a socialist system of production.

In the more than 100 years since Marx's death, this model has proved simplistic. Yet Marx correctly foresaw that social conflict arising from inequality (involving not just class but also race and gender) would force changes in every society, including our own, to improve the lives of working people.

## IDEAS AND CHANGE

Max Weber also contributed to our understanding of social change. Although Weber agreed that conflict could bring about change, he traced the roots of most social change to ideas. For example, people with charisma (Martin Luther King Jr. was one example) can carry a message that sometimes changes the world.

Weber also highlighted the importance of ideas by showing how the religious beliefs of early Protestants set the stage for the spread of industrial capitalism (see Chapter 4, "Society"). The fact that industrial capitalism developed primarily in areas of Western Europe where the Protestant work ethic was strong proved to Weber (1958, orig. 1904–05) the power of ideas to bring about change.

Ideas also direct social movements. Chapter 23 ("Collective Behavior and Social Movements") explained how change occurs when people join together in the pursuit of a common goal, such as cleaning up the environment or improving the lives of oppressed people.

## DEMOGRAPHIC CHANGE

Population patterns also play a part in social change. A century ago, as the chapter opening suggested, the typical household (4.8 people) was almost twice as large as it is today (2.6 people). Women are having fewer children, and more people are living alone. In addition, change is taking place as our population grows older. As Chapter 15 ("Aging and the Elderly") explained, 12 percent of the U.S. population was over age sixty-five in 2000, three times the proportion in 1900. By the year 2030, seniors will account for 20 percent of the total (U.S. Census Bureau, 2004). Medical research and health care services already focus extensively on

### Who Stays Put? Residential Stability across the United States

Overall, only about 9 percent of U.S. residents have not moved during the last thirty years. Counties with a higher proportion of "long-termers" typically have experienced less change over recent decades: Many neighborhoods have been in place since before World War II, and many of the same families live in them. As you look at the map, what can you say about these stable areas? Why are most of these counties rural and at some distance from the coasts?

Source: U.S. Census Bureau (1996).

the elderly, and life will change in countless additional ways as homes and household products are redesigned to meet the needs of older consumers.

Migration within and among societies is another demographic factor that promotes change. Between 1870 and 1930, tens of millions of immigrants entered the industrial cities in the United States. Millions more from rural areas joined the rush. As a result, farm communities declined, cities expanded, and for the first time, the United States became a mostly urban nation. Similarly, changes are taking place today as people move from the Snowbelt to the Sunbelt and mix with new immigrants from Latin America and Asia.

Where in the United States have demographic changes been greatest, and which areas have been least affected? National Map 24–1 provides one answer, showing counties where the largest share of people have lived in their present homes for thirty years or more.

## Modernity

A central concept in the study of social change is **modernity,** *social patterns resulting from industrialization.* In everyday usage, *modernity* (its Latin root means "lately") refers to the present in relation to the past. Sociologists include in this catchall concept all of the social patterns set in motion by the Industrial Revolution, which began in Western Europe in the 1750s. **Modernization,** then, is *the process*

*of social change begun by industrialization.* The timeline inside the front cover of the text highlights important events that mark the emergence of modernity. Table 24–1 on page 642 provides a snapshot of some of the changes that took place during the twentieth century.

### FOUR DIMENSIONS OF MODERNIZATION

Peter Berger (1977), in his influential study of social change, identified four major characteristics of modernization:

1. **The decline of small, traditional communities.** Modernity involves "the progressive weakening, if not destruction, of the . . . relatively cohesive communities in which human beings have found solidarity and meaning throughout most of history" (Berger, 1977:72). For thousands of years, in the camps of hunters and gatherers and in the rural villages of Europe and North America, people lived in small communities where social life revolved around family and neighborhood. Such traditional worlds gave each person a well-defined place that, although limiting range of choice, offered a strong sense of identity, belonging, and purpose.

   Small, isolated communities still exist in remote corners of the United States, of course, but they are home to only a small percentage of our nation's people. And their isolation is little more than geographic. Cars, telephones, television, and computers give rural

**TABLE 24–1**

## The United States: A Century of Change

| | 1900 | 2000 |
|---|---|---|
| National population | 76 million | 281 million |
| Percentage urban | 40% | 80% |
| Life expectancy | 46 years (men), 48 years (women) | 74 years (men), 79 years (women) |
| Median age | 22.9 years | 35.3 years |
| Average household income | $8,000 (in 2000 dollars) | $40,000 (in 2000 dollars) |
| Share of income spent on food | 43% | 15% |
| Share of homes with flush toilets | 10% | 98% |
| Average number of cars | 1 car for every 2,000 households | 1.3 cars for every household |
| Divorce rate | about 1 in 20 marriages | about 8 in 20 marriages |
| Average gallons of petroleum products consumed per person per year | 34 | 1,100 |

families the pulse of the larger society and connect them to the entire world.

2. **The expansion of personal choice.** Members of traditional, preindustrial societies view their lives as shaped by forces beyond human control—gods, spirits, or simply fate. As the power of tradition weakens, people come to see their lives as an unending series of options, a process Berger calls *individualization.* Many people in the United States, for example, choose a "lifestyle" (sometimes adopting one after another), showing an openness to change. Indeed, a common belief in our modern culture is that people *should* take control of their lives.

3. **Increasing social diversity.** In preindustrial societies, strong family ties and powerful religious beliefs enforce conformity and discourage diversity and change. Modernization promotes a more rational, scientific worldview as tradition loses its hold and people gain more and more individual choice. The growth of cities, the expansion of impersonal bureaucracy, and the social mix of people from various backgrounds combine to foster diverse beliefs and behavior.

4. **Orientation toward the future and a growing awareness of time.** Premodern people focus on the past, but people in modern societies think more about the future. Modern people are not only forward-looking but optimistic that new inventions and discoveries will improve their lives.

   Modern people also organize their daily routines down to the very minute. With the introduction of clocks in the late Middle Ages, Europeans began to

think not in terms of sunlight and seasons but in terms of days, hours, and minutes. Preoccupied with personal gain, modern people demand precise measurement of time and are likely to agree that "time is money." Berger points out that one good indicator of a society's degree of modernization is the share of people wearing wristwatches.

Finally, recall that modernization touched off the development of sociology itself. As Chapter 1 ("The Sociological Perspective") explained, the discipline originated in the wake of the Industrial Revolution in Western Europe, where social change was proceeding most rapidly. Early European and U.S. sociologists tried to analyze the rise of modern society and its consequences, both good and bad, for human beings.

### FERDINAND TÖNNIES: THE LOSS OF COMMUNITY

The German sociologist Ferdinand Tönnies (1855–1937) produced a lasting account of modernization in his theory of *Gemeinschaft* and *Gesellschaft* (see Chapter 22, "Population, Urbanization, and Environment"). Like Peter Berger, whose work he influenced, Tönnies (1963, orig. 1887) viewed modernization as the progressive loss of *Gemeinschaft*, or human community. As Tönnies saw it, the Industrial Revolution weakened the social fabric of family and tradition by introducing a businesslike emphasis on facts, efficiency, and money. European and North American societies gradually became rootless and impersonal as people came to associate mostly on the basis of self-interest—the state Tönnies termed *Gesellschaft.*

 For a short biography of Tönnies, visit the Gallery of Sociologists at http://www. TheSociologyPage.com

In response to the accelerating pace of change in the nineteenth century, Paul Gauguin left his native France for the South Seas where he was captivated by a simpler and seemingly timeless way of life. He romanticized this environment in his painting, *Nave Nave Moe (Sacred Spring)*.

Paul Gauguin, French (1848–1903), *Nave Nave Moe (Sacred Spring)*, 1894. Hermitage, St. Petersburg, Russia. Oil on canvas, 73 × 98 cm.
© The Bridgeman Art Library International Ltd.

Early in the twentieth century, at least some parts of the United States approximated Tönnies's concept of *Gemeinschaft*. Families that had lived for generations in small villages and towns were bound together in a hardworking, slow-moving way of life. Telephones (invented in 1876) were rare; it wasn't until 1915 that someone placed the first coast-to-coast call (see the timeline inside the front cover of this book). Living without television (introduced in 1933 and not widespread until after 1950), families entertained themselves, often gathering with friends in the evening to share stories, sorrows, or song. Without rapid transportation (Henry Ford's assembly line began in 1908, but cars became commonplace only after World War II), many people's hometown was their entire world.

Inevitable tensions and conflicts divided these communities of the past. But according to Tönnies, because of the traditional spirit of *Gemeinschaft*, people were "essentially united in spite of all separating factors" (1963:65, orig. 1887).

Modernity turns societies inside out so that, as Tönnies put it, people are "essentially separated in spite of uniting factors" (1963:65, orig. 1887). This is the world of *Gesellschaft*, where, especially in large cities, most people live among strangers and ignore the people they pass on the street. Trust is hard to come by in a mobile and anonymous society where people tend to put their personal needs ahead of group loyalty and an increasing majority of adults believe "you can't be too careful" in dealing with people (NORC, 2003:181). No wonder researchers conclude that even as we become more affluent, the social health of modern societies has declined (D. G. Myers, 2000).

**Critical review** Tönnies's theory of *Gemeinschaft* and *Gesellschaft* is the most widely cited model of modernization. The theory's strength lies in combining various dimensions of change: growing population, the rise of cities, and increasing impersonality in social interaction. But modern life, though often impersonal, still has some degree of *Gemeinschaft*. Even in a world of strangers, modern friendships can be strong and lasting. Some analysts also think that Tönnies favored—perhaps even romanticized—traditional societies while overlooking bonds of family, neighborhood, and friendship that continue to flourish in modern societies.

## EMILE DURKHEIM: THE DIVISION OF LABOR

The French sociologist Emile Durkheim, whose work is discussed in Chapter 4 ("Society"), shared Tönnies's interest in the profound social changes that resulted from the Industrial Revolution. For Durkheim (1964a, orig. 1893), modernization is defined by an increasing *division of labor,* or specialized economic activity. Every member of a traditional society performs more or less the same daily round of activities; modern societies function by having people perform highly specific roles.

Durkheim explained that preindustrial societies are held together by *mechanical solidarity,* or shared moral sentiments. In other words, members of preindustrial societies view everyone as basically alike, doing the same kind of work and belonging together. Durkheim's concept of mechanical solidarity is virtually the same as Tönnies's *Gemeinschaft*.

George Tooker's 1950 painting *The Subway* depicts a common problem of modern life: Weakening social ties and eroding traditions create a generic humanity in which everyone is alike yet each person is an anxious stranger in the midst of others.

George Tooker, *The Subway*, 1950, egg tempera on gesso panel, 18⅛ × 36⅛", Whitney Museum of American Art, New York. Purchased with funds from the Juliana Force Purchase Award, 50.23. Photograph © 2000 Whitney Museum of American Art.

With modernization, the division of labor becomes more and more pronounced. To Durkheim, this change means less mechanical solidarity but more of another kind of tie: *organic solidarity,* or mutual dependency between people engaged in specialized work. Put simply, modern societies are held together not by likeness but by difference: All of us must depend on others to meet most of our needs. Organic solidarity corresponds to Tönnies's concept of *Gesellschaft.*

Despite obvious similarities in their thinking, Durkheim and Tönnies viewed modernity somewhat differently. To Tönnies, modern *Gesellschaft* amounts to the loss of social solidarity, because modern people lose the "natural" and "organic" bonds of the rural village, leaving only the "artificial" and "mechanical" ties of the big, industrial city. Durkheim had a different view of modernity, even reversing Tönnies's language to bring home the point. Durkheim labeled modern society "organic," arguing that modern society is no less natural than any other, and he described traditional societies as "mechanical" because they are so regimented. Durkheim viewed modernization not as the *loss* of community but as a change from community based on bonds of likeness (kinship and neighborhood) to community based on economic interdependence (the division of labor). Durkheim's view of modernity is thus both more complex and more positive than Tönnies's view.

**Critical review** Durkheim's work, which resembles that of Tönnies, is a highly influential analysis of modernity. Of the two, Durkheim was more optimistic; still, he feared that modern societies might become so diverse that they would collapse into *anomie,* a condition in which norms and values are so weak and inconsistent that society provides little moral guidance to individuals. Living with weak moral norms, modern people can become egocentric, placing their own needs above those of others and finding little purpose in life.

The suicide rate—which Durkheim considered a good index of anomie—did in fact increase in the United States over the course of the twentieth century, and the vast majority of U.S. adults report that they see moral questions not in clear terms of right and wrong but in confusing "shades of gray" (NORC, 2003:359). Yet shared norms and values still seem strong enough to give most individuals some sense of meaning and purpose. Whatever the hazards of anomie, most people seem to value the personal freedom modern society gives us.

## MAX WEBER: RATIONALIZATION

For Max Weber (also discussed in Chapter 4, "Society"), modernity meant replacing a traditional worldview with a rational way of thinking. In preindustrial societies, tradition acts as a constant brake on change. To traditional people, "truth" is roughly the same as "what has always been" (1978:36, orig. 1921). To modern people, however, "truth" is the result of rational calculation. Because they value efficiency and have little reverence for the past, modern people adopt whatever social patterns allow them to achieve their goals.

Echoing Tönnies and Durkheim, who held that industrialization weakens tradition, Weber declared modern society to be "disenchanted." The unquestioned truths of an earlier time had been challenged by rational thinking. In short, modern society turns away from the gods. Throughout his life, Weber studied various modern "types"—the capitalist, the scientist, the bureaucrat—all of whom share the detached worldview that Weber believed was coming to dominate humanity.

Max Weber maintained that the distinctive character of modern society was its rational worldview. Virtually all of Weber's work on modernity centered on types of people he considered typical of their age: the scientist, the capitalist, and the bureaucrat. Each is rational to the core: The scientist is committed to the orderly discovery of truth, the capitalist to the orderly pursuit of profit, and the bureaucrat to orderly conformity to a system of rules.

**Critical review** Compared with Tönnies and especially Durkheim, Weber was critical of modern society. He knew that science could produce technological and organizational wonders but worried that science was turning us away from more basic questions about the meaning and purpose of human existence. Weber feared that rationalization, especially in bureaucracies, would erode the human spirit with endless rules and regulations.

### YOUR TURN

Looking at Weber's three "modern types" shown in the drawing, state in your own words what they have in common. What social traits would you expect all of them to lack?

Some of Weber's critics think that the alienation he attributed to bureaucracy actually stemmed from social inequality. That criticism leads us to the ideas of Karl Marx.

### KARL MARX: CAPITALISM

For Karl Marx, modern society was synonymous with capitalism; he saw the Industrial Revolution as primarily a *capitalist revolution.* Marx traced the emergence of the bourgeoisie in medieval Europe to the expansion of commerce. The bourgeoisie gradually displaced the feudal aristocracy as the Industrial Revolution gave it a powerful new productive system.

Marx agreed that modernity weakened small communities (as described by Tönnies), sharpened the division of labor (as noted by Durkheim), and fostered a rational worldview (as Weber claimed). But he saw all these simply as conditions necessary for capitalism to flourish. Capitalism, according to Marx, draws population from farms and small towns into an ever-expanding market system centered in cities; specialization is needed for efficient factories; and rationality is exemplified by the capitalists' endless pursuit of profit.

 For more on Durkheim, Weber, and Marx, visit the Gallery of Sociologists at http://www.TheSociologyPage.com

Earlier chapters have painted Marx as a spirited critic of capitalist society, but his vision of modernity also includes a good bit of optimism. Unlike Weber, who viewed modern society as an "iron cage" of bureaucracy, Marx believed that social conflict in capitalist societies would sow seeds of revolutionary change, leading to an egalitarian socialism. Such a society, as he saw it, would harness the wonders of industrial technology to enrich people's lives and also rid the world of social classes, the source of social conflict and so much suffering. Although Marx was an outspoken critic of modern society, he nevertheless imagined a future of human freedom, creativity, and community.

**Critical review** Marx's theory of modernization is a complex theory of capitalism. But he underestimated the dominance of bureaucracy in modern societies. In socialist societies in particular, the stifling effects of bureaucracy turned out to be as bad as, or even worse than, the dehumanizing aspects of capitalism. The upheavals in Eastern Europe and the former Soviet Union in the late 1980s and early 1990s reveal the depth of popular opposition to oppressive state bureaucracies.

## YOUR TURN

Of the four theorists just discussed—Tönnies, Durkheim, Weber, and Marx—who was the most optimistic about modern society? Who was the most pessimistic? Explain your responses.

# Theoretical Analysis of Modernity

The rise of modernity is a complex process involving many dimensions of change, as described in previous chapters and summarized in the Summing Up table. How can we make sense of so many changes going on all at once? Sociologists have developed two broad explanations of modern society, one guided by the structural-functional approach and one based on social-conflict theory.

## STRUCTURAL-FUNCTIONAL THEORY: MODERNITY AS MASS SOCIETY

*November 11, on Interstate 275. From the car window, we see BP and Sunoco gas stations, a Kmart and a Wal-Mart, an AmeriSuites hotel, a Bob Evans, a Chi-Chi's Mexican restaurant, and a McDonald's. This road happens to circle Cincinnati. But it could be almost anywhere in the United States.*

One broad approach—drawing on the ideas of Ferdinand Tönnies, Emile Durkheim, and Max Weber—understands modernization as the emergence of *mass society* (Kornhauser, 1959; Nisbet, 1966, 1969; Berger, Berger, & Kellner, 1974; Pearson, 1993). A **mass society** is *a society in which prosperity and bureaucracy have weakened traditional social ties.* A mass society is highly productive; on average, people have more income than ever. At the same time, it is marked by weak kinship and impersonal neighborhoods, so individuals often feel socially isolated. Although many people have material plenty, they are spiritually weak and often experience moral uncertainty about how to live.

### The Mass Scale of Modern Life

Mass-society theory argues, first, that the scale of modern life has greatly increased. Before the Industrial Revolution, Europe and North America formed a mosaic of countless rural villages and small towns. In these small communities, which inspired Tönnies's concept of *Gemeinschaft,* people lived out their lives surrounded by kin and guided by a shared heritage. Gossip was an informal yet highly effective way to ensure conformity to community standards. These small communities, with their strong moral values and their low tolerance of social diversity, exemplified the state of mechanical solidarity described by Durkheim.

For example, before 1690, English law demanded that everyone participate regularly in the Christian ritual of Holy Communion (Laslett, 1984). On the North American continent, only Rhode Island among the New England colonies tolerated religious dissent. Because social differences were repressed in favor of conformity to established norms, subcultures and countercultures were few, and change proceeded slowly.

Increasing population, the growth of cities, and specialized economic activity driven by the Industrial Revolution gradually altered this pattern. People came to know one another by their jobs (for example, as "the doctor" or "the bank clerk") rather than by their kinship group or hometown. People looked on most others simply as strangers. The face-to-face communication of the village was eventually replaced by the impersonal mass media: newspapers, radio, television, and computer networks. Large organizations steadily assumed more and more responsibility for seeing to the daily tasks that had once been carried out by family, friends, and neighbors; public education drew more and more people to schools; police, lawyers, and courts supervised a formal criminal justice system. Even charity became the work of faceless bureaucrats working for various social welfare agencies.

Geographic mobility and exposure to diverse ways of life all weaken traditional values. People become more tolerant of social diversity, defending individual rights and freedom of choice. Treating people differently because of their race, sex, or religion comes to be defined as backward and unjust. In the process, minorities at the margins of society gain greater power and broader participation in public life.

The mass media give rise to a national culture that washes over traditional differences that set off one region from another. As one analyst put it, "Even in Baton Rouge, La., the local kids don't say 'y'all' anymore; they say 'you guys' just like on TV" (Gibbs, 2000:42). In this way, mass-society theorists fear, transforming people of various backgrounds into a generic mass may end up dehumanizing everyone.

## Traditional and Modern Societies: The Big Picture

| Elements of Society | Traditional Societies | Modern Societies |
|---|---|---|
| **Cultural Patterns** | | |
| Values | Homogeneous; sacred character; few subcultures and countercultures | Heterogeneous; secular character; many subcultures and countercultures |
| Norms | Great moral significance; little tolerance of diversity | Variable moral significance; high tolerance of diversity |
| Time orientation | Present linked to past | Present linked to future |
| Technology | Preindustrial; human and animal energy | Industrial; advanced energy sources |
| **Social Structure** | | |
| Status and role | Few statuses, most ascribed; few specialized roles | Many statuses, some ascribed and some achieved; many specialized roles |
| Relationships | Typically primary; little anonymity or privacy | Typically secondary; much anonymity and privacy |
| Communication | Face to face | Face-to-face communication supplemented by mass media |
| Social control | Informal gossip | Formal police and legal system |
| Social stratification | Rigid patterns of social inequality; little mobility | Fluid patterns of social inequality; high mobility |
| Gender patterns | Pronounced patriarchy; women's lives centered on the home | Declining patriarchy; increasing number of women in the paid labor force |
| Settlement patterns | Small-scale; population typically small and widely dispersed in rural villages and small towns | Large-scale; population typically large and concentrated in cities |
| **Social Institutions** | | |
| Economy | Based on agriculture; much manufacturing in the home; little white-collar work | Based on industrial mass production; factories become centers of production; increasing white-collar work |
| State | Small-scale government; little state intervention in society | Large-scale government; much state intervention in society |
| Family | Extended family as the primary means of socialization and economic production | Nuclear family retains some socialization functions but is more a unit of consumption than of production |
| Religion | Religion guides worldview; little religious pluralism | Religion weakens with the rise of science; extensive religious pluralism |
| Education | Formal schooling limited to elites | Basic schooling becomes universal, with growing proportion receiving advanced education |
| Health | High birth and death rates; short life expectancy because of low standard of living and simple medical technology | Low birth and death rates; longer life expectancy because of higher standard of living and sophisticated medical technology |
| **Social Change** | Slow; change evident over many generations | Rapid; change evident within a single generation |

## YOUR TURN

Can you give five examples of "mass culture" that are the same throughout the United States? What elements of culture tend to be distinctive from region to region?

## The Ever-Expanding State

In the small-scale preindustrial societies of Europe, government amounted to little more than a local noble. A royal family formally reigned over an entire nation, but without efficient transportation or communication, even absolute monarchs had far less power than today's political leaders.

As technological innovation allowed government to expand, the centralized state grew in size and importance. At the time the United States gained independence from Great Britain, the federal government was a tiny organization with the main purpose of providing national defense. Since then, government has assumed responsibility for more and more areas of social life: schooling the population, regulating wages and working conditions, establishing standards for products of all sorts, and offering financial assistance to the

Social-conflict theory sees modernity not as a mass society but as a class society in which some categories of people are second-class citizens. This six-year-old boy waits for his mother to finish cooking a simple dinner outside their trailer on the Navajo Reservation near Window Rock, Arizona. The family lives without electricity or running water—a situation shared by thousands of other Navajo families.

ill and the unemployed. To pay for such programs, taxes have soared: Today's average worker labors almost four months each year to pay for the broad array of services that government provides.

In a mass society, power resides in large bureaucracies, leaving people in local communities little control over their lives. For example, state officials mandate that local schools must have a standardized educational program, local products must be government-certified, and every citizen must maintain extensive tax records. Although such regulations may protect people and advance social equality, they also force us to deal more and more with nameless officials in distant and often unresponsive bureaucracies, and they undermine the autonomy of families and local communities.

**Critical review** The growing scale of modern life certainly has positive aspects, but only at the price of losing some of our cultural heritage. Modern societies increase individual rights, tolerate greater social differences, and raise standards of living (Inglehart & Baker, 2000). But they are prone to what Weber feared most—excessive bureaucracy—as well as Tönnies's self-centeredness and Durkheim's anomie. Modern society's size, complexity, and tolerance of diversity all but doom traditional values and family patterns, leaving individuals isolated, powerless, and materialistic. As Chapter 17 ("Politics and Government") noted, voter apathy is a serious problem in the United States. But should we be surprised that individuals in vast, impersonal societies think no one person can make much of a difference?

Critics sometimes say that mass-society theory romanticizes the past. They remind us that many people in small towns were actually eager to set out for a higher standard of living in cities. Moreover, mass-society theory ignores problems of social inequality. Critics say this theory attracts conservatives who defend conventional morality and overlook the historical inequality of women and other minorities.

## SOCIAL-CONFLICT THEORY: MODERNITY AS CLASS SOCIETY

The second interpretation of modernity derives largely from the ideas of Karl Marx. From a social-conflict perspective, modernity takes the form of a **class society,** *a capitalist society with pronounced social stratification.* That is, although agreeing that modern societies have expanded to a mass scale, this approach views the heart of modernization as an expanding capitalist economy, marked by inequality (Habermas, 1970; Polenberg, 1980; Blumberg, 1981; Harrington, 1984; Buechler, 2000).

### Capitalism

Class-society theory follows Marx in claiming that the increasing scale of social life in modern society results from the growth and greed unleashed by capitalism. Because a capitalist economy pursues ever-greater profits, both production and consumption steadily increase.

According to Marx, capitalism rests on "naked self-interest" (Marx & Engels, 1972:337, orig. 1848). This self-centeredness weakens the social ties that once united small communities. Capitalism also treats people as commodities: a source of labor and a market for capitalist products.

Capitalism supports science, not just as the key to greater productivity but as an ideology that justifies the status quo. That is, modern societies encourage people to view

# SUMMING UP

## Two Interpretations of Modernity

|  | Mass Society | Class Society |
|---|---|---|
| **Process of modernization** | Industrialization; growth of bureaucracy | Rise of capitalism |
| **Effects of modernization** | Increasing scale of life; rise of the state and other formal organizations | Expansion of the capitalist economy; persistence of social inequality |

human well-being as a technical puzzle to be solved by engineers and other experts rather than through the pursuit of social justice. For example, a capitalist culture seeks to improve health through scientific medicine rather than by eliminating poverty, which is a core cause of poor health.

Business also raises the banner of scientific logic, trying to increase profits through greater efficiency. As Chapter 16 ("The Economy and Work") explains, today's capitalist corporations have reached enormous size and control unimaginable wealth as a result of "going global" as multinationals. From the class-society point of view, the expanding scale of life is less a function of *Gesellschaft* than the inevitable and destructive consequence of capitalism.

## Persistent Inequality

Modernity has gradually worn away the rigid categories that set nobles apart from commoners in preindustrial societies. But class-society theory maintains that elites persist as capitalist millionaires rather than nobles born to wealth and power. In the United States, we may have no hereditary monarchy, but the richest 5 percent of the population controls about 60 percent of all privately held property.

What of the state? Mass-society theorists argue that the state works to increase equality and combat social problems. Marx disagreed; he doubted that the state could accomplish more than minor reforms because as he saw it, the real power lies in the hands of capitalists, who control the economy. Other class-society theorists add that to the extent that working people and minorities do enjoy greater political rights and a higher standard of living today, these changes were the result of political struggle, not government goodwill. In short, they conclude, despite our pretensions of democracy, most people are powerless in the face of wealthy elites.

**Critical review**   Class-society theory dismisses Durkheim's argument that people in modern societies suffer from anomie, claiming instead that they suffer from alienation and powerlessness. Not surprisingly, then, the class-society interpretation of modernity enjoys widespread support among liberals and radicals who favor greater equality and call for extensive regulation or the abolition of the capitalist marketplace.

A basic criticism of class-society theory is that it overlooks the increasing prosperity of modern societies and the fact that discrimination based on race, ethnicity, and gender is now illegal and is widely viewed as a social problem. In addition, most people in the United States do not want an egalitarian society; they prefer a system of unequal rewards that reflects personal differences in talent and effort.

Based on socialism's failure to generate a high standard of living, few observers think that a centralized economy would cure the ills of modernity. Many other problems in the United States—from unemployment, hunger, and industrial pollution to unresponsive government—are also found in socialist nations.

The Summing Up table contrasts the two interpretations of modernity. Mass-society theory focuses on the increasing scale of life and the growth of government; class-society theory stresses the expansion of capitalism and the persistence of inequality.

## MODERNITY AND THE INDIVIDUAL

Both mass- and class-society theories look at the broad societal changes that have taken place since the Industrial Revolution. But from these macro-level approaches we can also draw micro-level insights into how modernity shapes individual lives.

### Mass Society: Problems of Identity

Modernity freed individuals from the small, tightly knit communities of the past. Most people in modern societies have the privacy and freedom to express their individuality.

However, mass-society theory suggests that so much social diversity, widespread isolation, and rapid social change make it difficult for many people to establish any coherent identity at all (Wheelis, 1958; Berger, Berger, & Kellner, 1974).

Chapter 5 ("Socialization") explained that people's personalities are largely a product of their social experiences. The small, homogeneous, and slowly changing societies of the past provided a firm, if narrow, foundation for building a personal identity. Even today, the Amish communities that flourish in the United States and Canada teach young men and women "correct" ways to think and behave. Not everyone born into an Amish community can tolerate strict demands for conformity, but most members establish a well-integrated and satisfying personal identity (see Hostetler, 1980; Kraybill & Olshan, 1994).

Mass societies are quite another story. Socially diverse and rapidly changing, they offer only shifting sands on which to build a personal identity. Left to make many life decisions on their own, many people—especially those with greater wealth—face a bewildering array of options. The freedom to choose has little value without standards to help us make good choices, and in a tolerant mass society, people may find little reason to choose one path over another. As a result, many people shuttle from one identity to another, changing their lifestyles, relationships, and even religions in search of an elusive "true self." Given the widespread "relativism" of modern societies, people without a moral compass lack the security and certainty once provided by tradition.

To David Riesman (1970, orig. 1950), modernization brings changes in **social character,** *personality patterns common to members of a particular society.* Preindustrial societies promote what Riesman calls **tradition-directedness,** *rigid conformity to time-honored ways of living.* Members of traditional societies model their lives on those of their ancestors, so that "living a good life" amounts to "doing what our people have always done."

Tradition-directedness corresponds to Tönnies's *Gemeinschaft* and Durkheim's mechanical solidarity. Culturally conservative, tradition-directed people think and act alike. Unlike the conformity sometimes found in modern societies, the uniformity of tradition-directedness is not an effort to imitate a popular celebrity or follow the latest fashions. Instead, people are alike because they all draw on the same solid cultural foundation. Amish women and men exemplify tradition-directedness; in Amish culture, tradition ties everyone to ancestors and descendants in an unbroken chain of righteous living.

Members of diverse and rapidly changing societies consider a tradition-directed personality deviant because it seems so rigid. Modern people, by and large, prize personal flexibility, the capacity to adapt, and sensitivity to others. Riesman calls this type of social character **other-directedness,** *openness to the latest trends and fashions, often expressed by imitating others.* Because their socialization occurs in societies that are continuously in flux, other-directed people develop fluid identities marked by superficiality, inconsistency, and change. They try on different "selves," almost like so many pieces of new clothing, seek out role models, and engage in varied "performances" as they move from setting to setting (Goffman, 1959). In a traditional society, such "shiftiness" makes a person untrustworthy, but in a changing, modern society, the chameleonlike ability to fit in virtually anywhere is very useful.

In societies that value the up-to-date rather than the traditional, people look to others for approval, using members of their own generation rather than elders as role models. Peer pressure can be irresistible to people without strong standards to guide them. Our society urges individuals to be true to themselves. But when social surroundings change so rapidly, how can people develop the self to which they should be true? This problem lies at the root of the identity crisis so widespread in industrial societies today. "Who am I?" is a nagging question that many of us struggle to answer. In truth, this problem is not so much us as the inherently unstable mass society in which we live.

## YOUR TURN

Would you call yourself more tradition-directed or more other-directed? Where do you turn for standards in making choices about how to live?

## Class Society: Problems of Powerlessness

Class-society theory paints a different picture of modernity's effects on individuals. This approach maintains that persistent social inequality undermines modern society's promise of individual freedom. For some people, modernity serves up great privilege, but for many, everyday life means coping with economic uncertainty and a growing sense of powerlessness (K. S. Newman, 1993; Ehrenreich, 2001).

For racial and ethnic minorities, the problem of relative disadvantage looms even larger. Similarly, although women participate more broadly in modern societies, they continue to run up against traditional barriers of sexism. This approach rejects mass-society theory's claim that people suffer from too much freedom. According to class-society theory,

Mass-society theory relates feelings of anxiety and lack of meaning in the modern world to rapid social change that washes away tradition. This notion of modern emptiness is captured in the photo at the left. Class-society theory, by contrast, ties such feelings to social inequality, by which some categories of people are made into second-class citizens (or not made citizens at all), an idea expressed in the photo at the right.

our society still denies a majority of people full participation in social life.

As Chapter 12 ("Global Stratification") explained, the expanding scope of world capitalism has placed more of Earth's population under the influence of multinational corporations. As a result, about three-fourths of the world's income is concentrated in the high-income nations, where only 18 percent of its people live. Is it any wonder, class-society theorists ask, that people in poor nations seek greater power to shape their own lives?

The problem of widespread powerlessness led Herbert Marcuse (1964) to challenge Max Weber's statement that modern society is rational. Marcuse condemned modern society as irrational for failing to meet the needs of so many people. Although modern capitalist societies produce unparalleled wealth, poverty remains the daily plight of more than 1 billion people. Marcuse adds that technological advances further reduce people's control over their own lives. High technology gives a great deal of power to a small core of specialists—not the majority of people—who now dominate the discussion of issues such as computing, energy production, and medical care. Countering the common view that technology *solves* the world's problems, Marcuse believed that science *causes* them. In sum, class-society theory asserts that people suffer because modern, scientific

societies concentrate both wealth and power in the hands of a privileged few.

## MODERNITY AND PROGRESS

In modern societies, most people expect, and applaud, social change. We link modernity to the idea of *progress* (from Latin, meaning "moving forward"), a state of continual improvement. By contrast, we see stability as stagnation.

Given our bias in favor of change, our society tends to regard traditional cultures as backward. But change, particularly toward material affluence, is a mixed blessing. As the Thinking Globally box on pages 652–53 shows, social change is too complex simply to equate with progress.

Even getting rich has both advantages and disadvantages, as the cases of the Kaiapo and the Gullah show. Historically, among people in the United States, a rising standard of living has made lives longer and materially more comfortable. At the same time, many people wonder if today's routines are too stressful, with families often having little time to relax or simply spend time together. Perhaps this is why, in most high-income countries, measures of happiness show a decline over the course of recent decades (D. G. Myers, 2000).

Science, too, has its pluses and minuses. People in the United States are more confident than people in other

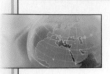
# Does "Modernity" Mean "Progress"?
# Brazil's Kaiapo and Georgia's Gullah Community

The firelight flickers in the gathering darkness. Chief Kanhonk sits, as he has done at the end of the day for many years, ready to begin an evening of animated storytelling (Simons, 2007). This is the hour when the Kaiapo, a small society in Brazil's lush Amazon region, celebrate their heritage. Because the Kaiapo are a traditional people with no written language, the elders rely on evenings by the fire to pass along their culture to their children and grandchildren. In the past, evenings like this have been filled with tales of brave Kaiapo warriors fighting off Portuguese traders who were in pursuit of slaves and gold.

But as the minutes pass, only a few older villagers assemble for the evening ritual. "It is the Big Ghost," one man grumbles, explaining the poor turnout. The "Big Ghost" has indeed descended on them; its bluish glow spills from windows throughout the village.

The Kaiapo children—and many adults as well—are watching sitcoms on television. The installation of a satellite dish in the village several years ago has had consequences far greater than anyone imagined. In the end, what their enemies failed to do with guns, the Kaiapo may well do to themselves with prime-time programming.

The Kaiapo are among the 230,000 native peoples who inhabit Brazil. They stand out because of their striking body paint and ornate ceremonial dress. During the 1980s, they

became rich from gold mining and harvesting mahogany trees. Now they must decide whether their newfound fortune is a blessing or a curse.

To some, affluence means the opportunity to learn about the outside world through travel and television.

 To see pictures of Brazil's Kaiapo, go to http://www.ddbstock.com/largeimage/amindns.html

Others, like Chief Kanhonk, are not so sure. Sitting by the fire, he thinks aloud, "I have been saying that people must buy useful things like knives and fishing hooks. Television does not fill the stomach. It only shows our children and grandchildren white people's things." Bebtopup, the oldest priest, nods in agreement: "The night is the time the old people teach the young people. Television has stolen the night" (Simons, 2007).

Far to the north, in the United States, half an hour by ferry from the coast of Georgia,

nations that science improves our lives (Inglehart et al., 2000). But surveys also show that many adults in the United States feel that science "makes our way of life change too fast" (NORC, 2003:346).

New technology has always sparked controversy. A century ago, the introduction of automobiles and telephones allowed more rapid transportation and more efficient communication. But at the same time, such technology weakened traditional attachments to hometowns and even to families. Today, people might well wonder whether computer technology will do the same thing, giving us access to people around the world but shielding us

from the community right outside our doors; providing more information than ever before but in the process threatening personal privacy. In short, we all realize that social change comes faster all the time, but we may disagree about whether a particular change is good or bad for society.

## MODERNITY: GLOBAL VARIATION

*October 1, Kobe, Japan.* Riding the computer-controlled monorail high above the streets of Kobe or the 200-mile-per-hour

lies the swampy island community of Hog Hammock. The seventy African American residents of the island today trace their ancestry back to the first slaves who settled there in 1802.

Walking past the colorful houses nestled among pine trees draped with Spanish moss, visitors feel transported back in time. The local people, known as Gullahs (or, in some places, Geechees) speak a mixture of English and West African languages. They fish, living much as they have for hundreds of years.

But the future of this way of life is now in doubt. Few young people who are raised in Hog Hammock can find work beyond fishing and making traditional crafts. "We have been here nine generations and we are still here," says one local. Then, referring to the island's nineteen children, she adds, "It's not that they don't want to be here, it's that there's nothing here for them—they need to have jobs" (Curry, 2001:41).

Just as important, with people on the mainland looking for waterside homes for vacations or year-round living, the island is now becoming prime real estate. Not long ago, one of the

Learn more about Gullah culture at http://www.knowitall.org/gullahnet

larger houses went up for sale, and the community was shocked to learn that its asking price was more than $1 million. The locals know only too well that higher property values will mean high taxes that few can afford to pay. In short, Hog Hammock is likely to become another Hilton Head, once a Gullah community on the South Carolina coast that is now home to well-to-do people from the mainland.

The odds are that the people of Hog Hammock will be selling their homes and moving inland. But few people are happy at the thought of

selling out, even for a good price. On the contrary, moving away will mean the end of their cultural heritage.

The stories of both the Kaiapo and the people of Hog Hammock show us that change is not a simple path toward "progress." These people may be moving toward modernity, but this process will have both positive and negative consequences. In the end, both groups of people may enjoy a higher standard of living with better shelter, more clothing, and new technology. On the other hand, their new affluence will come at the price of their traditions. The drama of these people is now being played out around the world as more and more traditional cultures are being lured away from their heritage by the affluence and materialism of rich societies.

WHAT DO YOU THINK?

1. Why is social change both a winning and a losing proposition for traditional peoples?
2. Do the changes described here improve the lives of the Kaiapo? What about the Gullah community?
3. Do traditional people have any choice about becoming modern? Explain your answer.

*bullet train to Tokyo, we see Japan as the society of the future; its people are in love with high technology. Yet the Japanese remain strikingly traditional in other respects: Few corporate executives and almost no senior politicians are women, young people still show seniors great respect, and public orderliness contrasts with the chaos of many U.S. cities.*

Japan is a nation at once traditional and modern. This contradiction reminds us that although it is useful to contrast traditional and modern societies, the old and the new often coexist in unexpected ways. In the People's Republic of China, ancient Confucian principles are mixed with contemporary socialist thinking. In Saudi Arabia and Qatar, the embrace of modern technology is mixed with respect for the ancient principles of Islam. Likewise, in Mexico and much of Latin America, people observe centuries-old Christian rituals even as they struggle to move ahead economically. In short, combinations of traditional and modern are far from unusual; rather, they are found throughout the world. "In the *Times*" on pages 654–55 describes patterns of change coming to a traditional village in Tibet.

November 25, 2004

# Modernity Tips Balance in a Remote Corner of Kashmir

**By AMY WALDMAN**

LEH, Kashmir—The young man wore Western clothes, but he paused as he passed the prayer wheel. Then, without self-consciousness, he mounted the steps and spun, circumambulating the wheel in search of good fortune.

"I feel great because I'm doing something for my God," he said afterward.

The young man, Tsewang Tamchos, 16, is a product of Ladakh, a remote repository of Tibetan Buddhism on a high-altitude Himalayan plateau in the northern areas of Kashmir, a disputed state. But he is a product of a wider world, too: his school in Delhi, the music of Eminem, the ambitions of an upwardly mobile family whose material fortunes improve with each generation.

As in many cultures, the people of Ladakh, a sparsely populated region, live in the fold between tradition and modernity. But few places have provided as concentrated a laboratory for how modernization is tipping that balance.

In less than four decades, Ladakh has gone from being closed to the outside world to reflecting it. With each generation, the ties to the land, to the past, weaken, as options and opportunities widen. The culture and economy have moved from community-oriented to competitive, from living off the land to working for cash and spending it.

For generations, Ladakh, a barren, moonlike landscape punctuated by monasteries, was almost cut off from the outside world. . . . It took 16 days to get to Srinagar, the state's summer capital, across passes that soar above 13,000 feet. Its people developed a way of life attuned to the land, and in tune with one another. Nothing was wasted. . . . Human waste fertilized fields; worn-out clothes patched irrigation channels. . . .

In 1974, Ladakh opened to foreign tourists for the first time, and they quickly became a pillar of the economy. . . .

The influence of outsiders has gradually leached into Ladakh's way of life. Before [as one long-time resident noted], the economy was not based on money. Rich and poor alike needed each other for the harvest. Now rich men can hire laborers from Nepal or poorer Indian states, and many do. "There is a lot of competition now," he said. "Everyone is trying to have a car."

The notion, and the novelty, of competition surfaces in conversations in the car-choked streets of Leh or nearby villages.

At 35, Tashi Palzes is old enough to remember a time with no competition in her village, Phyang Puluhu, which sits on several steep terraces in the valley behind the Phyang monastery.

Today, she, like everyone, is racing against her neighbors, and sees herself as winning. She has not one, but two

# Postmodernity

If modernity was the product of the Industrial Revolution, is the Information Revolution creating a postmodern era? A number of scholars think so, and they use the term **postmodernity** to refer to *social patterns characteristic of postindustrial societies.*

Precisely what postmodernism is remains a matter of debate. The term has been used for decades in literary, philosophical, and even architectural circles. It moved into sociology on a wave of social criticism that has been building since the spread of left-leaning politics in the 1960s. Although there are many variants of postmodern thinking, all share the following five themes (Hall & Neitz, 1993; Inglehart, 1997; Rudel & Gerson, 1999):

1. **In important respects, modernity has failed.** The promise of modernity was a life free from want. As postmodernist critics see it, however, the twentieth century was unsuccessful in solving social problems like poverty because many people still lack financial security.

2. **The bright light of "progress" is fading.** Modern people look to the future, expecting that their lives will improve in significant ways. Members (and even leaders) of postmodern societies, however, are less confident about what the future holds. The strong optimism that carried society into the modern era more than a century ago has given way to stark pessimism; most U.S. adults believe that life is getting worse (NORC, 2003:208).

3. **Science no longer holds the answers.** The defining trait of the modern era was a scientific outlook and a confident belief that technology would make life

televisions—the second one in color—and a satellite dish on her roof. She wears not the handspun traditional dress of a Ladakhi woman but a secondhand Gap sweatshirt, bought at the Leh bazaar.

Earlier, she said, villagers did not have much and did not need much. Now they have more needs—better clothes, better education, more televisions—and thus more work. Life is simultaneously more comfortable and more difficult. . . .

In the Leh home of Tsewang Tamchos, too, each generation brings substantial change. His grandparents live in the Nubra Valley, about 75 miles away.

They do not read or write; they farm. They grew up drinking unlimited quantities of butter tea, the salty staple of Ladakhi life.

His father, Tsering Tundup, 44, is a government forester. He says butter tea is bad for his blood pressure, and limits his intake to two cups a day. The house he has built his family in Leh has elements of tradition—the Buddhist prayer room, the wooden ceiling in the kitchen—but in most respects is modern.

His children study out of the state, Tsewang in Delhi and his 19-year-old sister, Tsering, in Chandigarh.

Tsewang's parents want him to be an engineer, and he does as well, but Ladakh has few opportunities for engineers. He would like to live here, but does not know if he will.

He does plan to marry a Ladakhi woman. "I don't want to change my culture," he said. "That's the only thing I have."

Adapted from the original article by Amy Waldman published in *The New York Times* on November 25, 2004. Copyright © 2004 by The New York Times Company. Reprinted with permission.

## WHAT DO YOU THINK?

1. List five examples of cultural diffusion in the article, and explain how they are causing changes to this traditional society.

2. Do you think the only way societies can remain traditional is to remain isolated from the rest of the world? What advantages and disadvantages do you see in doing so?

3. In what specific ways does modern life differ from traditional life in Ladakh?

better. But postmodern critics argue that science has not solved many old problems (such as poor health) and has even created new problems (such as pollution and declining natural resources).

Postmodernist thinkers discredit science, claiming that it implies a singular truth. On the contrary, they maintain, there is no one truth. This means that objective reality does not exist; rather, many realities result from social construction.

4. **Cultural debates are intensifying.** Now that more people have all the material things they really need, ideas are taking on more importance. In this sense, postmodernity is also a postmaterialist era, in which more careers involve working with symbols and in which issues such as social justice, the environment, and animal rights command more and more public attention.

5. **Social institutions are changing.** Just as industrialization brought a sweeping transformation to social institutions, the rise of a postindustrial society is remaking society all over again. For example, the postmodern family no longer conforms to any single pattern; on the contrary, individuals are choosing among many new family forms.

**Critical review** Analysts who claim that the United States and other high-income societies are entering a postmodern era criticize modernity for failing to meet human needs. In defense of modernity, there have been marked increases in longevity and living standards over the course of the past century. Even if we accept postmodernist views that science is bankrupt and progress is a sham, what are the alternatives?

## Tracking Change: Is Life in the United States Getting Better or Worse?

We began this chapter with a look at what life was like in a large U.S. city in 1900, more than a century ago. It is easy to see that in many ways, life is far better for us than it was for our grandparents and great-grandparents. In recent decades, however, not all indicators have been good. Here is a look at some trends shaping the United States since 1970 (Miringoff & Miringoff, 1999; D. G. Myers, 2000).

First, the good news: By some measures, shown in the first set of figures, life in this country is clearly improving. Infant mortality has fallen steadily; that is, fewer and fewer children die soon after birth. In addition, an increasing share of people are reaching old age, and after reaching sixty-five, they are living longer than ever. More good news: The poverty rate among the elderly is well below what it was in 1970. Schooling is another area of improvement: The share of people dropping out of high school is down, and the share completing college is up.

Second, some "no news" results: A number of indicators show that life is about the same as it was in the 1970s.

**The good news . . .**

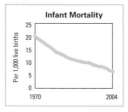
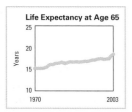
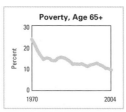
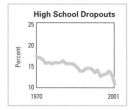
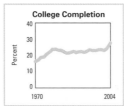

**No news . . .**

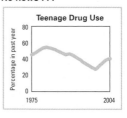
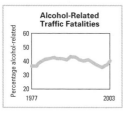
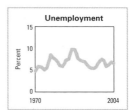
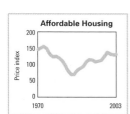

The Applying Sociology box offers evidence suggesting that life in the United States is getting better in some ways but not in others.

## Looking Ahead: Modernization and Our Global Future

Back in Chapter 1 (see page 8), we imagined the entire world reduced to a village of 1,000 people. About 180 residents of this "global village" come from high-income countries. Another 180 people are so poor that their lives are at risk.

The tragic plight of the world's poor shows that the world is in desperate need of change. Chapter 12 ("Global Stratification") presented two competing views of why 1 billion people around the world are poor. *Modernization theory* claims that in the past the entire world was poor and that technological change, especially the Industrial Revolution, enhanced human productivity and raised living standards in many nations. From this point of view, the solution to global poverty is to promote technological development around the world.

For reasons suggested earlier, however, global modernization may be difficult. Recall that David Riesman portrayed preindustrial people as *tradition-directed* and likely to resist change. So modernization theorists advocate

**The bad news . . .**

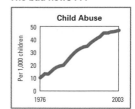

Child Abuse
Per 1,000 children
50 40 30 20 10 0
1976 — 2003

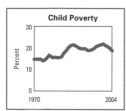

Child Poverty
Percent
30 20 10 0
1970 — 2004

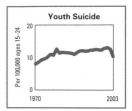

Youth Suicide
Per 100,000 ages 15–24
20 10 0
1970 — 2003

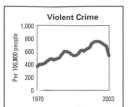

Violent Crime
Per 100,000 people
1,000 800 600 400 200 0
1970 — 2003

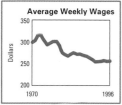

Average Weekly Wages
Dollars
350 300 250 200
1970 — 1996

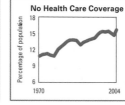

No Health Care Coverage
Percentage of population
18 15 12 9 6
1970 — 2004

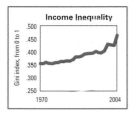

Income Inequality
Gini index, from 0 to 1
.500 .450 .400 .350 .300 .250
1970 — 2004

For example, teenage drug use was about the same in 2004 as it was a generation ago. Likewise, alcohol-related traffic deaths number about the same. Unemployment has had its ups and downs, but the overall level has stayed about the same. Finally, there was about the same amount of affordable housing in the United States in 2003 as in 1970.

Third, the bad news: By some measures, several having to do with children, the quality of life in the United States has actually fallen. The official rate of child abuse is up, as is the level of child poverty and the rate of

suicide among young people. Although the level of violent crime fell through most of the 1990s, it remains above the 1970 level. Average hourly wages, one measure of economic security, show a downward trend, meaning that more families have to rely on two or more earners to maintain family income. The number of people without health insurance is also on the rise. Finally, economic inequality in this country has been increasing.

Overall, the evidence does not support any simple ideas about "progress over time." Social change has been—and probably will continue to be—a

complex process that reflects the kinds of priorities we set for this nation as well as our will to achieve them.

WHAT DO YOU THINK?

1. Some analysts claim that U.S. society embodies a paradox: Over decades, we see increasing economic health but declining social health. Based on the data here, do you agree? Why or why not?
2. Which of the trends do you find most important? Why?
3. On balance, do you think the quality of life in the United States is improving? Why or why not?

that the world's rich societies help poor countries grow economically. Industrial nations can speed development by exporting technology to poor regions, welcoming students from these countries, and providing foreign aid to stimulate economic growth.

The review of modernization theory in Chapter 12 points to some success with policies in Latin America and to greater success in the small Asian countries of Taiwan, South Korea, Singapore, and Hong Kong (now part of the People's Republic of China). But jump-starting development in the poorest countries of the world poses greater challenges. And even where dramatic change has occurred, modernization involves a trade-off. Traditional people, such as Brazil's Kaiapo, may gain wealth through economic

development, but they lose their cultural identity and values as they are drawn into a global "McCulture," which is based on Western materialism, pop music, trendy clothes, and fast food. One Brazilian anthropologist expressed hope about the future of the Kaiapo: "At least they quickly understood the consequences of watching television. . . . Now [they] can make a choice" (Simons, 2007).

But not everyone thinks that modernization is really an option. According to a second approach to global stratification, *dependency theory,* today's poor societies have little ability to modernize, even if they want to. From this point of view, the major barrier to economic development is not traditionalism but the global domination of rich capitalist societies.

## THINKING IT THROUGH

# Personal Freedom and Social Responsibility: Can We Have It Both Ways?

Shortly after midnight on a crisp March evening in 1964, a car pulled to a stop in the parking lot of a New York apartment complex. Kitty Genovese had just finished her shift as a manager at a nearby bar. She turned off the headlights, locked the doors of her vehicle, and headed across the blacktop toward the entrance to her building. Seconds later, a man wielding a knife lunged at her, and as she screamed in terror, he stabbed her repeatedly. Windows opened above as curious neighbors looked down to see what was going on. But the attack continued—for more than thirty minutes—until Genovese lay dead in the doorway. The police never identified her killer, and their investigation revealed the stunning fact that *not one of dozens of neighbors who witnessed the attack on Kitty Genovese went to her aid or even called the police.*

Decades after this tragic event, we still confront the question of what we owe others. As members of modern societies, we prize our individual rights and personal privacy, but we sometimes withdraw from public responsibility and turn a cold shoulder to people in need. When a cry for help is met with indifference, have we pushed our modern idea of personal freedom too far? In a cultural climate of expanding individual rights, can we keep a sense of human community?

These questions highlight the tension between traditional and modern social systems, which we can see in the writings of all the sociologists discussed in this chapter. Tönnies, Durkheim, and others concluded that in some respects, traditional community and modern individualism don't mix. That is, society can unite its members in a moral community, but only by limiting their range of personal choices about how to live. In short, although we value both community and autonomy, we can't have it both ways.

The sociologist Amitai Etzioni (1993, 1996, 2003) has tried to strike a middle ground. The *communitarian movement* rests on the simple idea that with rights must come responsibilities. Put another way, our pursuit of self-interest must be balanced by a commitment to the larger community.

Etzioni claims that modern people have become too concerned about individual rights. We expect the system to work for us, but we are reluctant to support the system. For example, we believe that people accused of a crime have the right to their day in court, but fewer and fewer of us are willing to perform jury duty; similarly, we are quick to accept government services but reluctant to support these services with our taxes.

The communitarians advance four proposals to balance individual rights and public responsibilities. First, our society should halt the expanding "culture of rights" by which we put our own interests ahead of social responsibility; the Constitution, which is quoted so often when discussing individual rights,

---

Dependency theory asserts that rich nations achieved their modernization at the expense of poor ones, plundering poor nations' natural resources and exploiting their human labor. Even today, the world's poorest countries remain locked in a disadvantageous economic relationship with rich nations, dependent on wealthy countries to buy their raw materials and in return provide them with whatever manufactured products they can afford. According to this view, continuing ties with rich societies only perpetuates current patterns of global inequality.

Whichever approach you find more convincing, keep in mind that change in the United States is no longer separate from change in the rest of the world. At the beginning of the twentieth century, most people in today's high-income countries lived in relatively small settlements with limited awareness of the larger world. Today, a century later, the entire world has become one huge village because the lives of all people are increasingly linked.

The last century witnessed unprecedented human achievement. Yet solutions to many problems of human existence—including finding meaning in life, resolving conflicts between nations, and eliminating poverty—have eluded us. The Thinking It Through box examines one dilemma: balancing individual freedom and personal responsibility. To this list of pressing matters new concerns have been added, such as controlling population growth and establishing an environmentally sustainable society. In the next hundred years, we must be prepared to tackle such problems with imagination, compassion, and determination. Our growing understanding of human society gives us reason to be hopeful that we can get the job done.

does not provide us with the right to do whatever we want. Second, we must remember that all rights involve responsibilities; we cannot simply take from society without giving something back. Third, the well-being of everyone may require limiting our individual rights; for example, pilots and bus drivers who are responsible for public safety may be asked to take a drug test. Fourth, no one can ignore key responsibilities such as upholding the law and responding to a cry for help from someone like Kitty Genovese.

The communitarian movement appeals to many people who believe in both personal freedom and social responsibility. But Etzioni's proposals have drawn criticism from both sides of the political spectrum. To those on the left, serious problems ranging from voter apathy and street crime to disappearing pensions and millions of workers without medical care cannot be solved with some vague notion of "social responsibility." As they see it, what we need is expanded government programs to protect people and lessen inequality.

Conservatives, on the political right, see different problems in Etzioni's proposals (Pearson, 1995). As they see it, the communitarian movement favors liberal goals, such as confronting prejudice and protecting the environment, but ignores conservative goals such as strengthening religious belief and supporting traditional families.

Etzioni responds that the criticism coming from both sides suggests he has found a moderate, sensible answer to a serious problem. But the debate may also indicate that in a society as diverse as the United States, people who are so quick to assert their rights are not so quick to agree on their responsibilities.

In today's world, people can find new ways to express age-old virtues such as concern for their neighbors and extending a hand to those in need. Habitat for Humanity, an organization with chapters in cities and towns across the United States, is made up of people who want to help local families realize their dream of owning a home.

WHAT DO YOU THINK?

1. Have you ever failed to come to the aid of someone in need or danger? Why?
2. Nearly half a century ago, President Kennedy stated, "Ask not what your country can do for you—ask what you can do for your country." Do you think people today support this idea? Why or why not?
3. Do you agree with Etzioni's call for balance between individual rights and social responsibilities? Explain your answer.

# MAKING THE GRADE

The following learning tools will help you see what you know, identify what you still need to learn, and expand your understanding beyond the text. You can also visit the text's Companion Website™ at http://www.prenhall.com/macionis to find additional practice tests.

## KEY POINTS

### What Is Social Change?

Every society changes all the time, sometimes faster, sometimes slower. Social change often generates controversy.

### Causes of Social Change

Social change takes many forms. Invention produces new objects and ideas; discovery gives us a fresh awareness of things in the world; diffusion spreads objects or ideas from one place to another. Causes of social change include social conflict (Marx) and ideas (Weber), as well as migration and other demographic factors.

### Modernity

Modernity refers to the social consequences of industrialization, which include the erosion of traditional communities, expanding personal choice, increasingly diverse beliefs, and a focus on the future.

Ferdinand Tönnies described modernization as the transition from *Gemeinschaft* to *Gesellschaft*, with the decline of traditional community and the rise of individualism.

Emile Durkheim saw modernization as a society's expanding division of labor. Mechanical solidarity, based on shared activities and beliefs, is gradually replaced by organic solidarity, in which specialization makes people interdependent.

Max Weber saw modernity as the decline of tradition and rise of rationality. Weber feared the dehumanizing effects of rational organization.

Karl Marx saw modernity as the triumph of capitalism over feudalism. Capitalism creates social conflict, which Marx claimed would bring about revolutionary change toward an egalitarian socialist society.

## Theoretical Analysis of Modernity

According to mass-society theory, modernity increases the scale of life, enlarging the role of government and other formal organizations in carrying out tasks previously performed by families in local communities. Cultural diversity and rapid social change make it difficult for people in modern societies to develop stable identities and to find meaning in their lives.

According to class-society theory, modernity involves the rise of capitalism. By concentrating wealth in the hands of a few, modern capitalist societies generate widespread feelings of powerlessness.

Social change is too complex and controversial simply to be equated with social progress.

## Postmodernity

Postmodernity refers to the cultural traits of postindustrial societies. Postmodern criticism of society centers on the failure of modernity, and specifically science, to fulfill its promise of prosperity and well-being.

## Looking Ahead:
## Modernization and Our Global Future

Modernization theory links global poverty to the power of tradition. Rich nations can help poor countries develop their economies.

Dependency theory explains global poverty as the product of the world economic system. The operation of multinational corporations makes poor nations economically dependent on rich nations.

## KEY CONCEPTS

**social change** (p. 639)  the transformation of culture and social institutions over time

**modernity** (p. 641)  social patterns resulting from industrialization

**modernization** (p. 641)  the process of social change begun by industrialization

**mass society** (p. 646)  a society in which prosperity and bureaucracy have weakened traditional social ties

**class society** (p. 648)  a capitalist society with pronounced social stratification

**social character** (p. 650)  personality patterns common to members of a particular society

**tradition-directedness** (p. 650)  rigid conformity to time-honored ways of living

**other-directedness** (p. 650)  openness to the latest trends and fashions, often expressed by imitating others

**postmodernity** (p. 654)  social patterns characteristic of postindustrial societies

## SAMPLE TEST QUESTIONS

These questions are similar to those found in the test bank that accompanies this textbook.

### Multiple-Choice Questions

1. Sociologists use the term "modernity" to refer to social patterns that emerged
   a. with the first human civilizations.
   b. with the fall of Rome.
   c. after the Industrial Revolution.
   d. along with the Information Revolution.

2. Which of the following are common causes of social change?
   a. invention of new ideas and things
   b. diffusion from one cultural system to another
   c. discovery of existing things
   d. all of the above

3. Karl Marx highlighted the importance of _____ in the process of social change.
   a. immigration and demographic factors
   b. ideas
   c. social conflict
   d. cultural diffusion

4. Max Weber's analysis of how Calvinism helped create the spirit of capitalism highlighted the importance of _____ in the process of social change.
   - a. invention
   - b. ideas
   - c. social conflict
   - d. cultural diffusion

5. Which term was used by Ferdinand Tönnies to describe a traditional society?
   - a. *Gemeinschaft*
   - b. *Gesellschaft*
   - c. mechanical solidarity
   - d. organic solidarity

6. According to Emile Durkheim, modern societies have
   - a. respect for established tradition.
   - b. widespread alienation.
   - c. common values and beliefs.
   - d. an increasing division of labor.

7. For Max Weber, modernity meant the rise of _____; for Karl Marx, modernity meant_____.
   - a. capitalism, anomie
   - b. rationality, capitalism
   - c. tradition, self-interest
   - d. specialization, *Gesellschaft*

8. Which of the following statements about modernity as a mass society is *not* correct?
   - a. There is more poverty today than in past centuries.
   - b. Kinship ties have become weaker.

   - c. Bureaucracy, including government, has increased in size.
   - d. People experience moral uncertainty about how to live.

9. Sociologists who describe modernity in terms of class society focus on which of the following?
   - a. rationality as a way of thinking about the world
   - b. mutual interdependency
   - c. the rise of capitalism
   - d. the high risk of anomie

10. David Riesman described the other-directed social character typical of modern people as
    - a. rigid conformity to tradition.
    - b. eagerness to follow the latest fashions and fads.
    - c. highly individualistic.
    - d. all of the above.

ANSWERS: 1(c); 2(d); 3(c); 4(b); 5(a); 6(d); 7(b); 8(a); 9(c); 10(b).

## Essay Questions

1. Discuss how Tönnies, Durkheim, Weber, and Marx described modern society. What are similarities and differences in their understandings of modernity?

2. What traits lead some analysts to call the United States a "mass society"? Why do other analysts describe the United States as a "class society"?

## APPLICATIONS & EXERCISES

1. Ask an elderly relative or friend to name the most important social changes during his or her lifetime. Do you think your world will change as much during your lifetime?

2. Ask people in your class or friendship group to make five predictions about U.S. society in the year 2050, when today's twenty-year-olds will be senior citizens. Compare notes. On what issues is there agreement?

3. Do you think the rate of social change has been increasing? Do some research about modes of travel—including walking, riding animals, trains, cars, airplanes, and rockets—throughout history, and see what pattern emerges. How many of these modes of travel were available even 300 years ago?

## INVESTIGATE *with* Research Navigator

Research Navigator.com
RESOURCES FOR COLLEGE RESEARCH ASSIGNMENTS

Follow the instructions on page 27 of this text to access the features of **Research Navigator**™. Once at the Web site, enter your Login Name and Password. Then, to use the **ContentSelect**™ database, enter keywords such as "social change," "modernization," and "postmodernity," and the search engine will supply relevant and recent scholarly and popular press publications. Use the *New York Times* **Search-by-Subject Archive** to find recent news articles related to sociology and the **Link Library** feature to find relevant Web links organized by the key terms associated with this chapter.

# GLOSSARY

**abortion**   the deliberate termination of a pregnancy

**absolute poverty**   a deprivation of resources that is life-threatening

**achieved status**   a social position a person takes on voluntarily that reflects personal ability and effort

**activity theory**   the idea that a high level of activity increases personal satisfaction in old age

**Afrocentrism**   emphasizing and promoting African cultural patterns

**ageism**   prejudice and discrimination against older people

**age-sex pyramid**   a graphic representation of the age and sex of a population

**age stratification**   the unequal distribution of wealth, power, and privilege among people at different stages of the life course

**agriculture**   large-scale cultivation using plows harnessed to animals or more powerful energy sources

**alienation**   the experience of isolation and misery resulting from powerlessness

**animism**   the belief that elements of the natural world are conscious life forms that affect humanity

**anomie**   Durkheim's term for a condition in which society provides too little moral guidance to individuals

**anticipatory socialization**   learning that helps a person achieve a desired position

**ascribed status**   a social position a person receives at birth or takes on involuntarily later in life

**asexuality**   a lack of sexual attraction to people of either sex

**assimilation**   the process by which minorities gradually adopt patterns of the dominant culture

**authoritarianism**   a political system that denies the people participation in government

**authority**   power that people perceive as legitimate rather than coercive

**beliefs**   specific statements that people hold to be true

**bilateral descent**   a system tracing kinship through both men and women

**bisexuality**   sexual attraction to people of both sexes

**blue-collar occupations**   lower-prestige jobs that involve mostly manual labor

**bureaucracy**   an organizational model rationally designed to perform tasks efficiently

**bureaucratic inertia**   the tendency of bureaucratic organizations to perpetuate themselves

**bureaucratic ritualism**   a focus on rules and regulations to the point of undermining an organization's goals

**capitalism**   an economic system in which natural resources and the means of producing goods and services are privately owned

**capitalists**   people who own and operate factories and other businesses in pursuit of profits

**caregiving**   informal and unpaid care provided to a dependent person by family members, other relatives, or friends

**caste system**   social stratification based on ascription, or birth

**cause and effect**   a relationship in which change in one variable (the independent variable) causes change in another (the dependent variable)

**charisma**   extraordinary personal qualities that can infuse people with emotion and turn them into followers

**charismatic authority**   power legitimized by extraordinary personal abilities that inspire devotion and obedience

**church**   a type of religious organization that is well integrated into the larger society

**civil religion**   a quasi-religious loyalty binding individuals in a basically secular society

**claims making**   the process of trying to convince the public and public officials of the importance of joining a social movement to address a particular issue

**class conflict**   conflict between entire classes over the distribution of a society's wealth and power

**class consciousness**   Marx's term for workers' recognition of themselves as a class unified in opposition to capitalists and ultimately to capitalism itself

**class society**   a capitalist society with pronounced social stratification

**class system**   social stratification based on both birth and individual achievement

**cohabitation**   the sharing of a household by an unmarried couple

**cohort**   a category of people with something in common, usually their age

**collective behavior**   activity involving a large number of people that is unplanned, often controversial, and sometimes dangerous

**collectivity**   a large number of people whose minimal interaction occurs in the absence of well-defined and conventional norms

**colonialism**   the process by which some nations enrich themselves through political and economic control of other nations

**communism**   a hypothetical economic and political system in which all members of a society are socially equal

**community-based corrections**   correctional programs operating within society at large rather than behind prison walls

**concept**   a mental construct that represents some part of the world in a simplified form

**concrete operational stage**   Piaget's term for the level of human development at which individuals first see causal connections in their surroundings

**conglomerate**   a giant corporation composed of many smaller corporations

**conspicuous consumption**   buying and using products because of the "statement" they make about social position

**control**   holding constant all variables except one in order to see clearly the effect of that variable

**corporate crime**   the illegal actions of a corporation or people acting on its behalf

**corporation**   an organization with a legal existence, including rights and liabilities, separate from that of its members

**correlation**   a relationship in which two (or more) variables change together

**counterculture**   cultural patterns that strongly oppose those widely accepted within a society

**crime**   the violation of a society's formally enacted criminal law

**crimes against the person**   crimes that direct violence or the threat of violence against others; also known as *violent crimes*

**crimes against property**   crimes that involve theft of property belonging to others; also known as *property crimes*

**criminal justice system**   a formal response by police, courts, and prison officials to alleged violations of the law

**criminal recidivism**   later offenses committed by people previously convicted of crimes

**critical sociology**   the study of society that focuses on the need for social change

**crowd** a temporary gathering of people who share a common focus of attention and who influence one another

**crude birth rate** the number of live births in a given year for every 1,000 people in a population

**crude death rate** the number of deaths in a given year for every 1,000 people in a population

**cult** a religious organization that is largely outside a society's cultural traditions

**cultural integration** the close relationships among various elements of a cultural system

**cultural lag** the fact that some cultural elements change more quickly than others, disrupting a cultural system

**cultural relativism** the practice of judging a culture by its own standards

**cultural transmission** the process by which one generation passes culture to the next

**cultural universals** traits that are part of every known culture

**culture** the values, beliefs, behavior, and material objects that together form a people's way of life

**culture shock** personal disorientation when experiencing an unfamiliar way of life

**Davis-Moore thesis** the assertion that social stratification is a universal pattern because it has beneficial consequences for the operation of a society

**deductive logical thought** reasoning that transforms general theory into specific hypotheses suitable for testing

**democracy** a political system that gives power to the people as a whole

**demographic transition theory** the thesis that population patterns reflect a society's level of technological development

**demography** the study of human population

**denomination** a church, independent of the state, that recognizes religious pluralism

**dependency theory** a model of economic and social development that explains global inequality in terms of the historical exploitation of poor nations by rich ones

**dependent variable** a variable that is changed by another (independent) variable

**descent** the system by which members of a society trace kinship over generations

**deterrence** the attempt to discourage criminality through the use of punishment

**deviance** the recognized violation of cultural norms

**direct-fee system** a medical care system in which patients pay directly for the services of physicians and hospitals

**disaster** an event, generally unexpected, that causes extensive harm to people and damage to property

**discrimination** unequal treatment of various categories of people

**disengagement theory** the idea that society functions in an orderly way by disengaging people from positions of responsibility as they reach old age

**division of labor** specialized economic activity

**dramaturgical analysis** Erving Goffman's term for the study of social interaction in terms of theatrical performance

**dyad** a social group with two members

**eating disorder** an intense form of dieting or other unhealthy method of weight control driven by the desire to be very thin

**ecologically sustainable culture** a way of life that meets the needs of the present generation without threatening the environmental legacy of future generations

**ecology** the study of the interaction of living organisms and the natural environment

**economy** the social institution that organizes a society's production, distribution, and consumption of goods and services

**ecosystem** a system composed of the interaction of all living organisms and their natural environment

**education** the social institution through which society provides its members with important knowledge, including basic facts, job skills, and cultural norms and values

**ego** Freud's term for a person's conscious efforts to balance innate pleasure-seeking drives with the demands of society

**empirical evidence** information we can verify with our senses

**endogamy** marriage between people of the same social category

**environmental deficit** profound long-term harm to the natural environment caused by humanity's focus on short-term material affluence

**environmental racism** the pattern by which environmental hazards are greatest for poor people, especially minorities

**ethnicity** a shared cultural heritage

**ethnocentrism** the practice of judging another culture by the standards of one's own culture

**ethnomethodology** Harold Garfinkel's term for the study of the way people make sense of their everyday surroundings

**Eurocentrism** the dominance of European (especially English) cultural patterns

**euthanasia** assisting in the death of a person suffering from an incurable disease; also known as *mercy killing*

**exogamy** marriage between people of different social categories

**experiment** a research method for investigating cause and effect under highly controlled conditions

**expressive leadership** group leadership that focuses on the group's well-being

**extended family** a family consisting of parents and children as well as other kin; also known as a *consanguine family*

**fad** an unconventional social pattern that people embrace briefly but enthusiastically

**faith** belief based on conviction rather than scientific evidence

**false consciousness** Marx's term for explanations of social problems as the shortcomings of individuals rather than as the flaws of society

**family** a social institution found in all societies that unites people in cooperative groups to care for one another, including any children

**family violence** emotional, physical, or sexual abuse of one family member by another

**fashion** a social pattern favored by a large number of people

**feminism** the advocacy of social equality for women and men, in opposition to patriarchy and sexism

**feminization of poverty** the trend of women making up an increasing proportion of the poor

**fertility** the incidence of childbearing in a country's population

**folkways** norms for routine or casual interaction

**formal operational stage** Piaget's term for the level of human development at which individuals think abstractly and critically

**formal organization** a large secondary group organized to achieve its goals efficiently

**functional illiteracy**  a lack of the reading and writing skills needed for everyday living

**fundamentalism**  a conservative religious doctrine that opposes intellectualism and worldly accommodation in favor of restoring traditional, otherworldly religion

*Gemeinschaft*  a type of social organization in which people are closely tied by kinship and tradition

**gender**  the personal traits and social positions that members of a society attach to being female or male

**gender-conflict approach**  a point of view that focuses on inequality and conflict between women and men

**gender roles (sex roles)**  attitudes and activities that a society links to each sex

**gender stratification**  the unequal distribution of wealth, power, and privilege between men and women

**generalized other**  George Herbert Mead's term for widespread cultural norms and values we use as a reference in evaluating ourselves

**genocide**  the systematic killing of one category of people by another

**gerontocracy**  a form of social organization in which the elderly have the most wealth, power, and prestige

**gerontology**  the study of aging and the elderly

*Gesellschaft*  a type of social organization in which people come together only on the basis of individual self-interest

**global economy**  expanding economic activity that crosses national borders

**global perspective**  the study of the larger world and our society's place in it

**global stratification**  patterns of social inequality in the world as a whole

**global warming**  a rise in Earth's average temperature due to an increasing concentration of carbon dioxide in the atmosphere

**gossip**  rumor about people's personal affairs

**government**  a formal organization that directs the political life of a society

**groupthink**  the tendency of group members to conform, resulting in a narrow view of some issue

**hate crime**  a criminal act against a person or a person's property by an offender motivated by racial or other bias

**Hawthorne effect**  a change in a subject's behavior caused simply by the awareness of being studied

**health**  a state of complete physical, mental, and social well-being

**health maintenance organization (HMO)**  an organization that provides comprehensive medical care to subscribers for a fixed fee

**heterosexism**  a view that labels anyone who is not heterosexual as "queer"

**heterosexuality**  sexual attraction to someone of the other sex

**high culture**  cultural patterns that distinguish a society's elite

**high-income countries**  nations with the highest overall standards of living

**holistic medicine**  an approach to health care that emphasizes the prevention of illness and takes into account a person's entire physical and social environment

**homogamy**  marriage between people with the same social characteristics

**homophobia**  discomfort over close personal interaction with people thought to be gay, lesbian, or bisexual

**homosexuality**  sexual attraction to someone of the same sex

**horticulture**  the use of hand tools to raise crops

**hunting and gathering**  the use of simple tools to hunt animals and gather vegetation for food

**hypothesis**  a statement of a possible relationship between two (or more) variables

**id**  Freud's term for the human being's basic drives

**ideal type**  an abstract statement of the essential characteristics of any social phenomenon

**ideology**  cultural beliefs that justify particular social arrangements, including patterns of inequality

**incest taboo**  a norm forbidding sexual relations or marriage between certain relatives

**income**  earnings from work or investments

**independent variable**  a variable that causes change in another (dependent) variable

**inductive logical thought**  reasoning that transforms specific observations into general theory

**industrialism**  the production of goods using advanced sources of energy to drive large machinery

**infant mortality rate**  the number of deaths among infants under one year of age for each 1,000 live births in a given year

**infidelity**  sexual activity outside marriage

**in-group**  a social group toward which a member feels respect and loyalty

**institutional prejudice and discrimination**  bias built into the operation of society's institutions

**instrumental leadership**  group leadership that focuses on the completion of tasks

**intergenerational social mobility**  upward or downward social mobility of children in relation to their parents

**interpretive sociology**  the study of society that focuses on the meanings people attach to their social world

**intersection theory**  the interplay of race, class, and gender, often resulting in multiple dimensions of disadvantage

**intersexual people**  people whose bodies (including genitals) have both female and male characteristics

**interview**  a series of questions a researcher asks respondents in person

**intragenerational social mobility**  a change in social position occurring during a person's lifetime

**kinship**  a social bond based on common ancestry, marriage, or adoption

**labeling theory**  the idea that deviance and conformity result not so much from what people do as from how others respond to those actions

**labor unions**  organizations of workers that seek to improve wages and working conditions through various strategies, including negotiations and strikes

**language**  a system of symbols that allows people to communicate with one another

**latent functions**  the unrecognized and unintended consequences of any social pattern

**liberation theology**  the combination of Christian principles with political activism, often Marxist in character

**life expectancy**  the average life span of a country's population

**looking-glass self** Cooley's term for a self-image based on how we think others see us

**low-income countries** nations with a low standard of living in which most people are poor

**macro-level orientation** a broad focus on social structures that shape society as a whole

**mainstreaming** integrating students with disabilities or special needs into the overall educational program

**manifest functions** the recognized and intended consequences of any social pattern

**marriage** a legal relationship, usually involving economic cooperation, sexual activity, and childbearing

**Marxist political-economy model** an analysis that explains politics in terms of the operation of a society's economic system

**mass behavior** collective behavior among people spread over a wide geographic area

**mass hysteria (moral panic)** a form of dispersed collective behavior in which people react to a real or imagined event with irrational and even frantic fear

**mass media** the means for delivering impersonal communications to a vast audience

**mass society** a society in which prosperity and bureaucracy have weakened traditional social ties

**master status** a status that has special importance for social identity, often shaping a person's entire life

**material culture** the physical things created by members of a society

**matriarchy** a form of social organization in which females dominate males

**matrilineal descent** a system tracing kinship through women

**matrilocality** a residential pattern in which a married couple lives with or near the wife's family

**measurement** a procedure for determining the value of a variable in a specific case

**mechanical solidarity** Durkheim's term for social bonds, based on common sentiments and shared moral values, that are strong among members of preindustrial societies

**medicalization of deviance** the transformation of moral and legal deviance into a medical condition

**medicine** the social institution that focuses on fighting disease and improving health

**megalopolis** a vast urban region containing a number of cities and their surrounding suburbs

**meritocracy** social stratification based on personal merit

**metropolis** a large city that socially and economically dominates an urban area

**micro-level orientation** a close-up focus on social interaction in specific situations

**middle-income countries** nations with a standard of living about average for the world as a whole

**migration** the movement of people into and out of a specified territory

**military-industrial complex** the close association of the federal government, the military, and defense industries

**minority** any category of people distinguished by physical or cultural difference that a society sets apart and subordinates

**miscegenation** biological reproduction by partners of different racial categories

**mob** a highly emotional crowd that pursues a violent or destructive goal

**modernity** social patterns resulting from industrialization

**modernization** the process of social change begun by industrialization

**modernization theory** a model of economic and social development that explains global inequality in terms of technological and cultural differences between nations

**monarchy** a political system in which a single family rules from generation to generation

**monogamy** marriage that unites two partners

**monopoly** the domination of a market by a single producer

**monotheism** belief in a single divine power

**mores** norms that are widely observed and have great moral significance

**mortality** the incidence of death in a country's population

**multiculturalism** an educational program recognizing the cultural diversity of the United States and promoting the equality of all cultural traditions

**multinational corporation** a large business that operates in many countries

**natural environment** Earth's surface and atmosphere, including living organisms, air, water, soil, and other resources necessary to sustain life

**neocolonialism** a new form of global power relationships that involves not direct political control but economic exploitation by multinational corporations

**neolocality** a residential pattern in which a married couple lives apart from both sets of parents

**network** a web of weak social ties

**nonmaterial culture** the ideas created by members of a society

**nonverbal communication** communication using body movements, gestures, and facial expressions rather than speech

**norms** rules and expectations by which a society guides the behavior of its members

**nuclear family** a family composed of one or two parents and their children; also known as a *conjugal family*

**nuclear proliferation** the acquisition of nuclear weapons technology by more and more nations

**objectivity** personal neutrality in conducting research

**oligarchy** the rule of the many by the few

**oligopoly** the domination of a market by a few producers

**operationalize a variable** specifying exactly what is to be measured before assigning a value to a variable

**organic solidarity** Durkheim's term for social bonds, based on specialization and interdependence, that are strong among members of industrial societies

**organizational environment** factors outside an organization that affect its operation

**organized crime** a business supplying illegal goods or services

**other-directedness** openness to the latest trends and fashions, often expressed by imitating others

**out-group** a social group toward which a person feels a sense of competition or opposition

**panic** a form of localized collective behavior in which people in one place react to a threat or other stimulus with irrational, frantic, and often self-destructive behavior

**participant observation**  a research method in which investigators systematically observe people while joining them in their routine activities

**pastoralism**  the domestication of animals

**patriarchy**  a form of social organization in which males dominate females

**patrilineal descent**  a system tracing kinship through men

**patrilocality**  a residential pattern in which a married couple lives with or near the husband's family

**peer group**  a social group whose members have interests, social position, and age in common

**personality**  a person's fairly consistent patterns of acting, thinking, and feeling

**personal space**  the surrounding area over which a person makes some claim to privacy

**plea bargaining**  a legal negotiation in which a prosecutor reduces a charge in exchange for a defendant's guilty plea

**pluralism**  a state in which people of all races and ethnicities are distinct but have equal social standing

**pluralist model**  an analysis of politics that sees power as spread among many competing interest groups

**political action committee (PAC)**  an organization formed by a special-interest group, independent of political parties, to raise and spend money in support of political goals

**political revolution**  the overthrow of one political system in order to establish another

**politics**  the social institution that distributes power, sets a society's goals, and makes decisions

**polyandry**  marriage that unites one woman and two or more men

**polygamy**  marriage that unites a person with two or more spouses

**polygyny**  marriage that unites one man and two or more women

**polytheism**  belief in many gods

**popular culture**  cultural patterns that are widespread among a society's population

**population**  the people who are the focus of research

**pornography**  sexually explicit material intended to cause sexual arousal

**positivism**  a way of understanding based on science

**postindustrial economy**  a productive system based on service work and high technology

**postindustrialism**  technology that supports an information-based economy

**postmodernity**  social patterns characteristic of postindustrial societies

**power**  the ability to achieve desired ends despite resistance from others

**power-elite model**  an analysis of politics that sees power as concentrated among the rich

**prejudice**  a rigid and unfair generalization about an entire category of people

**preoperational stage**  Piaget's term for the level of human development at which individuals first use language and other symbols

**presentation of self**  Erving Goffman's term for a person's efforts to create specific impressions in the minds of others

**primary group**  a small social group whose members share personal and lasting relationships

**primary labor market**  jobs that provide extensive benefits to workers

**primary sector**  the part of the economy that draws raw materials from the natural environment

**primary sex characteristics**  the genitals, organs used for reproduction

**profane**  an ordinary element of everyday life

**profession**  a prestigious white-collar occupation that requires extensive formal education

**proletarians**  people who sell their labor for wages

**propaganda**  information presented with the intention of shaping public opinion

**prostitution**  the selling of sexual services

**public opinion**  widespread attitudes about controversial issues

**queer theory**  a growing body of research findings that challenges the heterosexual bias in U.S. society

**questionnaire**  a series of written questions a researcher presents to subjects

**race**  a socially constructed category of people who share biologically transmitted traits that members of a society consider important

**race-conflict approach**  a point of view that focuses on inequality and conflict between people of different racial and ethnic categories

**racism**  the belief that one racial category is innately superior or inferior to another

**rain forests**  regions of dense forestation, most of which circle the globe close to the equator

**rationality**  a way of thinking that emphasizes deliberate, matter-of-fact calculation of the most efficient way to accomplish a particular task

**rationalization of society**  Weber's term for the historical change from tradition to rationality as the main mode of human thought

**rational-legal authority**  power legitimized by legally enacted rules and regulations; also known as *bureaucratic authority*

**reference group**  a social group that serves as a point of reference in making evaluations and decisions

**rehabilitation**  a program for reforming the offender to prevent later offenses

**relative deprivation**  a perceived disadvantage arising from some specific comparison

**relative poverty**  the deprivation of some people in relation to those who have more

**reliability**  consistency in measurement

**religion**  a social institution involving beliefs and practices based on recognizing the sacred

**religiosity**  the importance of religion in a person's life

**replication**  repetition of research by other investigators

**research method**  a systematic plan for doing research

**resocialization**  efforts to radically change an inmate's personality by carefully controlling the environment

**retribution**  an act of moral vengeance by which society makes the offender suffer as much as the suffering caused by the crime

**riot**  a social eruption that is highly emotional, violent, and undirected

**ritual**  formal, ceremonial behavior

**role**  behavior expected of someone who holds a particular status

**role conflict**  conflict among the roles connected to two or more statuses

**role set**  a number of roles attached to a single status

**role strain**  tension among the roles connected to a single status

**routinization of charisma**  the transformation of charismatic authority into some combination of traditional and bureaucratic authority

**rumor**  unconfirmed information that people spread informally, often by word of mouth

**sacred** set apart as extraordinary, inspiring awe and reverence

**sample** a part of a population that represents the whole

**Sapir-Whorf thesis** the idea that people see and understand the world through the cultural lens of language

**scapegoat** a person or category of people, typically with little power, whom people unfairly blame for their own troubles

**schooling** formal instruction under the direction of specially trained teachers

**science** a logical system that bases knowledge on direct, systematic observation

**scientific management** Frederick Taylor's term for the application of scientific principles to the operation of a business or other large organization

**scientific sociology** the study of society based on systematic observation of social behavior

**secondary group** a large and impersonal social group whose members pursue a specific goal or activity

**secondary labor market** jobs that provide minimal benefits to workers

**secondary sector** the part of the economy that transforms raw materials into manufactured goods

**secondary sex characteristics** bodily development, apart from the genitals, that distinguishes biologically mature females and males

**sect** a type of religious organization that stands apart from the larger society

**secularization** the historical decline in the importance of the supernatural and the sacred

**segregation** the physical and social separation of categories of people

**self** George Herbert Mead's term for the part of an individual's personality composed of self-awareness and self-image

**sensorimotor stage** Piaget's term for the level of human development at which individuals experience the world only through their senses

**sex** the biological distinction between females and males

**sexism** the belief that one sex is innately superior to the other

**sex ratio** the number of males for every 100 females in a nation's population

**sexual harassment** comments, gestures, or physical contact of a sexual nature that are deliberate, repeated, and unwelcome

**sexual orientation** a person's romantic and emotional attraction to another person

**sick role** patterns of behavior defined as appropriate for people who are ill

**significant others** people, such as parents, who have special importance for socialization

**social change** the transformation of culture and social institutions over time

**social character** personality patterns common to members of a particular society

**social conflict** the struggle between segments of society over valued resources

**social-conflict approach** a framework for building theory that sees society as an arena of inequality that generates conflict and change

**social construction of reality** the process by which people creatively shape reality through social interaction

**social control** attempts by society to regulate people's thoughts and behavior

**social dysfunction** any social pattern that may disrupt the operation of society

**social epidemiology** the study of how health and disease are distributed throughout a society's population

**social functions** the consequences of any social pattern for the operation of society as a whole

**social group** two or more people who identify and interact with one another

**social institutions** the major spheres of social life, or societal subsystems, organized to meet human needs

**social interaction** the process by which people act and react in relation to others

**socialism** an economic system in which natural resources and the means of producing goods and services are collectively owned

**socialization** the lifelong social experience by which people develop their human potential and learn culture

**socialized medicine** a medical care system in which the government owns and operates most medical facilities and employs most physicians

**social mobility** a change in position within the social hierarchy

**social movement** an organized activity that encourages or discourages social change

**social stratification** a system by which a society ranks categories of people in a hierarchy

**social structure** any relatively stable pattern of social behavior

**societal protection** rendering an offender incapable of further offenses temporarily through imprisonment or permanently by execution

**society** people who interact in a defined territory and share a culture

**sociobiology** a theoretical approach that explores ways in which human biology affects how we create culture

**sociocultural evolution** Lenski's term for the changes that occur as a society gains new technology

**socioeconomic status (SES)** a composite ranking based on various dimensions of social inequality

**sociological perspective** the special point of view of sociology that sees general patterns of society in the lives of particular people

**sociology** the systematic study of human society

**special-interest group** people organized to address some economic or social issue

**spurious correlation** an apparent but false relationship between two (or more) variables that is caused by some other variable

**state capitalism** an economic and political system in which companies are privately owned but cooperate closely with the government

**state church** a church formally allied with the state

**status** a social position that a person holds

**status consistency** the degree of consistency in a person's social standing across various dimensions of social inequality

**status set** all the statuses a person holds at a given time

**stereotype** an exaggerated description applied to every person in some category

**stigma** a powerfully negative label that greatly changes a person's self-concept and social identity

**structural-functional approach** a framework for building theory that sees society as a complex system whose parts work together to promote solidarity and stability

**structural social mobility** a shift in the social position of large numbers of people due more to changes in society itself than to individual efforts

**subculture** cultural patterns that set apart some segment of a society's population

**suburbs** urban areas beyond the political boundaries of a city

**superego** Freud's term for the cultural values and norms internalized by an individual

**survey** a research method in which subjects respond to a series of statements or questions in a questionnaire or an interview

**symbol** anything that carries a particular meaning recognized by people who share a culture

**symbolic-interaction approach** a framework for building theory that sees society as the product of the everyday interactions of individuals

**technology** knowledge that people use to make a way of life in their surroundings

**terrorism** acts of violence or the threat of violence used as a political strategy by an individual or a group

**tertiary sector** the part of the economy that involves services rather than goods

**theoretical approach** a basic image of society that guides thinking and research

**theory** a statement of how and why specific facts are related

**Thomas theorem** W. I. Thomas's statement that situations that are defined as real are real in their consequences

**total institution** a setting in which people are isolated from the rest of society and manipulated by an administrative staff

**totalitarianism** a highly centralized political system that extensively regulates people's lives

**totem** an object in the natural world collectively defined as sacred

**tracking** assigning students to different types of educational programs

**tradition** values and beliefs passed from generation to generation

**traditional authority** power legitimized by respect for long-established cultural patterns

**tradition-directedness** rigid conformity to time-honored ways of living

**transsexuals** people who feel they are one sex even though biologically they are the other

**triad** a social group with three members

**underground economy** economic activity involving income not reported to the government as required by law

**urban ecology** the study of the link between the physical and social dimensions of cities

**urbanization** the concentration of population into cities

**validity** actually measuring exactly what you intend to measure

**values** culturally defined standards that people use to decide what is desireable, good, and beautiful, and that serve as broad guidelines for social living

**variable** a concept whose value changes from case to case

**victimless crimes** violations of law in which there are no obvious victims

**war** organized, armed conflict among the people of two or more nations, directed by their governments

**wealth** the total value of money and other assets, minus outstanding debts

**welfare capitalism** an economic and political system that combines a mostly market-based economy with extensive social welfare programs

**welfare state** government agencies and programs that provide benefits to the population

**white-collar crime** crime committed by people of high social position in the course of their occupations

**white-collar occupations** higher-prestige jobs that involve mostly mental activity

**zero population growth** the level of reproduction that maintains population in a steady state

# REFERENCES

ABBOTT, ANDREW. *The System of Professions: An Essay on the Division of Expert Labor.* Chicago: University of Chicago Press, 1988.

ABERLE, DAVID F. *The Peyote Religion among the Navaho.* Chicago: Aldine, 1966.

ADLER, JERRY. "When Harry Called Sally . . ." *Newsweek* (October 1, 1990):74.

ADORNO, T. W., et al. *The Authoritarian Personality.* New York: Harper & Brothers, 1950.

AGUIRRE, BENIGNO E., and E. L. QUARANTELLI. "Methodological, Ideological, and Conceptual-Theoretical Criticisms of Collective Behavior: A Critical Evaluation and Implications for Future Study." *Sociological Focus.* Vol. 16, No. 3 (August 1983):195–216.

AGUIRRE, BENIGNO E., E. L. QUARANTELLI, and JORGE L. MENDOZA. "The Collective Behavior of Fads: Characteristics, Effects, and Career of Streaking." *American Sociological Review.* Vol. 53, No. 4 (August 1988):569–84.

AIZCORBE, ANA M., ARTHUR B. KENNICKELL, and KEVIN B. MOORE. "Recent Changes in U.S. Family Finances: Evidence from the 1998 and 2001 Survey of Consumer Finances." *Federal Reserve Bulletin.* Vol. 89, No. 1 (January 2003):1–32. [Online] Available September 25, 2003, at http://www.federalreserve.gov/pubs/bulletin/2003/0103lead.pdf

AKERS, RONALD L., MARVIN D. KROHN, LONN LANZA-KADUCE, and MARCIA RADOSEVICH. "Social Learning and Deviant Behavior." *American Sociological Review.* Vol. 44, No. 4 (August 1979):636–55.

ALAN GUTTMACHER INSTITUTE. "Can More Progress Be Made? Teenage Sexual and Reproductive Behavior in Developed Countries." 2001. [Online] Available May 30, 2005, at http://www.guttmacher.org/pubs/summaries/euroteens_summ.pdf

———. "Teen Pregnancy: Trends and Lessons Learned." *Issues in Brief.* 2002 Series, No. 1. 2002. [Online] Available May 30, 2005, at http://www.agi-usa.org/pubs/ib_1-02.pdf

———. "U.S. Teenage Pregnancy Statistics: Overall Trends, Trends by Race and Ethnicity and State-by-State Information." Updated February 19, 2004. [Online] Available May 30, 2005, at http://www.agi-usa.org/pubs/state_pregnancy_trends.pdf

ALBON, JOAN. "Retention of Cultural Values and Differential Urban Adaptation: Samoans and American Indians in a West Coast City." *Social Forces.* Vol. 49, No. 3 (March 1971):385–93.

ALLAN, EMILIE ANDERSEN, and DARRELL J. STEFFENSMEIER. "Youth, Underemployment, and Property Crime: Differential Effects of Job Availability and Job Quality on Juvenile and Young Adult Arrest Rates." *American Sociological Review.* Vol. 54, No. 1 (February 1989):107–23.

ALLEN, THOMAS B., and CHARLES O. HYMAN. *We Americans: Celebrating a Nation, Its People, and Its Past.* Washington, D.C.: National Geographic, 1999.

ALLEN, WALTER R. "African American Family Life in Social Context: Crisis and Hope." *Sociological Forum.* Vol. 10, No. 4 (December 1995):569–92.

ALSTER, NORM. "When Gray Heads Roll, Is Age Bias at Work?" *New York Times* (January 30, 2005). [Online] Available April 15, 2005, at http://www.researchnavigator.com

ALTER, JONATHAN. "The Death Penalty on Trial." *Newsweek* (June 12, 2000):24–34.

ALTONJI, JOSEPH G., ULRICH DORASZELSKI, and LEWIS SEGAL. "Black/White Differences in Wealth." *Economic Perspectives.* Vol. 24, No. 1 (First Quarter 2000):38–50.

AMATO, PAUL R. "What Children Learn from Divorce." *Population Today.* Vol. 29, No. 1 (January 2001):1, 4.

AMATO, PAUL R., and JULIANA M. SOBOLEWSKI. "The Effects of Divorce and Marital Discord on Adult Children's Psychological Well-Being." *American Sociological Review.* Vol. 66, No. 6 (December 2001):900–21.

AMBLER, JOHN S., and JODY NEATHERY. "Education Policy and Equality: Some Evidence from Europe." *Social Science Quarterly.* Vol. 80, No. 3 (September 1999):437–56.

AMERICAN BAR ASSOCIATION. "First-Year Enrollment in ABA-Approved Law Schools, 1947–2004 (Percentage of Women)." [Online] Available October 17, 2005, at http://www.abanet.org/legaled/statistics/femstats.html

AMERICAN CATHOLIC. "John Jay Study Reveals Extent of Abuse Problem." [Online] Available September 13, 2005, at http://www.americancatholic.org/news/clergysexabuse/johnjaycns.asp

*AMERICAN DEMOGRAPHICS.* "Zandi Group Survey." Vol. 20 (March 3, 1998):38.

———. (April 2002):6.

AMERICAN PSYCHOLOGICAL ASSOCIATION. *Violence and Youth: Psychology's Response.* Washington, D.C.: American Psychological Association, 1993.

AMERICAN SOCIOLOGICAL ASSOCIATION. "Code of Ethics." Washington, D.C.: American Sociological Association, 1997.

———. *Careers in Sociology.* 6th ed. Washington, D.C.: American Sociological Association, 2002.

———. *The Importance of Collecting Data and Doing Social Scientific Research on Race.* Washington, D.C.: American Sociological Association, 2003.

AMNESTY INTERNATIONAL. "Abolitionist and Retentionist Countries." [Online] Available June 4, 2005a, at http://web.amnesty.org/pages/deathpenalty-countries-eng

———. "Facts and Figures on the Death Penalty." [Online] Available June 4, 2005b, at http://web.amnesty.org/pages/deathpenalty-facts-eng

ANDERSON, ELIJAH. "The Code of the Streets." *Atlantic Monthly.* Vol. 273 (May 1994):81–94.

———. "The Ideologically Driven Critique." *American Journal of Sociology.* Vol. 197, No. 6 (May 2002):1533–50.

ANDERSON, JOHN WARD. "Early to Wed: The Child Brides of India." *Washington Post* (May 24, 1995):A27, A30.

ANDERSON, ROBERT N., and BETTY L. SMITH. "Deaths: Leading Causes for 2002." *National Vital Statistics Reports.* Vol. 53, No. 17 (March 7, 2005). Hyattsville, Md.: National Center for Health Statistics.

ANNAN, KOFI. "Astonishing Facts." *New York Times* (September 27, 1998):16.

APPLEBOME, PETER. "70 Years after Scopes Trial, Creation Debate Lives." *New York Times* (March 10, 1996):1, 10.

APUZZO, ALAN. "R.I. Official: Club Owners Not Helpful." [Online] Available February 24, 2003, at http://news.yahoo.com

ARENDT, HANNAH. *Between Past and Future: Six Exercises in Political Thought.* Cleveland, Ohio: Meridian Books, 1963.

ARIAS, ELIZABETH. "United States Life Tables, 2001." *National Vital Statistics Report.* Vol. 52, No. 14 (February 18, 2004). Hyattsville, Md.: National Center for Health Statistics.

———. "United States Life Tables, 2002." *National Vital Statistics Reports.* Vol. 53, No. 6 (November 10, 2004). Hyattsville, Md.: National Center for Health Statistics.

ARIÈS, PHILIPPE. *Centuries of Childhood: A Social History of Family Life.* New York: Vintage Books, 1965.

———. *Western Attitudes toward Death: From the Middle Ages to the Present.* Baltimore: Johns Hopkins University Press, 1974.

ARMSTRONG, ELISABETH. *The Retreat from Organization: U.S. Feminism Reconceptualized.* Albany: State University of New York Press, 2002.

ARONOWITZ, STANLEY. *The Politics of Identity: Class, Culture, and Social Movements.* New York: Routledge, 1992.

ARROW, KENNETH, SAMUEL BOWLES, and STEVEN DURLAUF. *Meritocracy and Economic Inequality.* Princeton, N.J.: Princeton University Press, 2000.

ASANTE, MOLEFI KETE. *Afrocentricity.* Trenton, N.J.: Africa World Press, 1988.

ASCH, SOLOMON. *Social Psychology.* Englewood Cliffs, N.J.: Prentice Hall, 1952.

ASHFORD, LORI S. "New Perspectives on Population: Lessons from Cairo." *Population Bulletin.* Vol. 50, No. 1 (March 1995):2–44.

———. "Young Women in Sub-Saharan Africa Face a High Risk of HIV Infection." *Population Today.* Vol. 30, No. 2 (February/March 2002):3, 6.

ASTIN, ALEXANDER W., LETICIA OSEGUERA, LINDA J. SAX, and WILLIAM S. KORN. *The American Freshman: Thirty-Five Year Trends.* Los Angeles: UCLA Higher Education Research Institute, 2002.

ATCHLEY, ROBERT C. *Aging: Continuity and Change.* Belmont, Calif.: Wadsworth, 1983.

AUSTER, CAROL J., and MINDY MACRONE. "The Classroom as a Negotiated Social Setting: An Empirical Study of the Effects of Faculty Members' Behavior on Students' Participation." *Teaching Sociology.* Vol. 22, No. 4 (October 1994):289–300.

AXINN, WILLIAM G., and JENNIFER S. BARBER. "Mass Education and Fertility Transition." *American Sociological Review.* Vol. 66, No. 4 (August 2001):481–505.

BAINBRIDGE, JAY, MARCIA K. MEYERS, and JANE WALDFOGEL. "Childcare Reform and the Employment of Single Mothers." *Social Science Quarterly.* Vol. 84, No. 4 (December 2003):771–91.

BAKALAR, NICHOLAS. "Reactions: Go On, Laugh Your Heart Out." *New York Times* (March 8, 2005). [Online] Available March 11, 2005, at http://www.nytimes.com/2005/03/08/health/08reac.html

BAKER, MARY ANNE, et al. *Women Today: A Multidisciplinary Approach to Women's Studies.* Monterey, Calif.: Brooks/Cole, 1980.

BAKER, PATRICIA S., WILLIAM C. YOELS, JEFFREY M. CLAIR, and RICHARD M. ALLMAN. "Laughter in the Triadic Geriatric Encounters: A Transcript-Based Analysis." In REBECCA J. ERIKSON and BEVERLY CUTHBERTSON-JOHNSON, eds., *Social Perspectives on Emotion.* Vol. 4. Greenwich, Conn.: JAI Press, 1997:179–207.

BAKER, ROSS. "Business as Usual." *American Demographics*. Vol. 19, No. 4 (April 1997):28.

BALTES, PAUL B., and K. WARNER SCHAIE. "The Myth of the Twilight Years." *Psychology Today*. Vol. 7, No. 10 (March 1974):35–39.

BALTZELL, E. DIGBY. *The Protestant Establishment: Aristocracy and Caste in America*. New York: Vintage Books, 1964.

———. "Introduction to the 1967 Edition." In W.E.B. DU BOIS, *The Philadelphia Negro: A Social Study*. New York: Schocken Books, 1967; orig. 1899.

———. *Philadelphia Gentlemen: The Making of a National Upper Class*. Philadelphia: University of Pennsylvania Press, 1979a; orig. 1958.

———. *Puritan Boston and Quaker Philadelphia*. New York: Free Press, 1979b.

———. *Sporting Gentlemen: From the Age of Honor to the Cult of the Superstar*. New York: Free Press, 1995.

BANFIELD, EDWARD C. *The Unheavenly City Revisited*. Boston: Little, Brown, 1974.

BARASH, DAVID. *The Whisperings Within*. New York: Penguin Books, 1981.

BARNES, JULIAN E. "Wanted: Readers." *U.S. News & World Report* (September 9, 2002a):44–45.

———. "War Profiteering." *U.S. News & World Report* (May 13, 2002b):20–24.

———. "Unequal Education." *U.S. News & World Report* (March 22, 2004):66–75.

BARON, JAMES N., MICHAEL T. HANNAN, and M. DIANE BURTON. "Building the Iron Cage: Determinants of Managerial Intensity in the Early Years of Organizations." *American Sociological Review*. Vol. 64, No. 4 (August 1999):527–47.

BARONE, MICHAEL. "Lessons of History." *U.S. News & World Report* (May 20, 2002):24.

BAROVICK, HARRIET. "Tongues That Go Out of Style." *Time* (June 10, 2002):22.

BARR, ROBERT. "Archbishop of Canterbury Is Enthroned." [Online] Available February 27, 2003, at http://news.yahoo.com

BARSTOW, DAVID, and C. J. CHIVERS. "A Volatile Mixture Exploded into Rampage in Central Park." *New York Times* (June 17, 2000):A1, B7.

BARTLETT, DONALD L., and JAMES B. STEELE. "Corporate Welfare." *Time* (November 9, 1998):36–54.

———. "How the Little Guy Gets Crunched." *Time* (February 7, 2000):38–41.

———. "Wheel of Misfortune." *Time* (December 16, 2002):44–58.

BASSUK, ELLEN J. "The Homelessness Problem." *Scientific American*. Vol. 251, No. 1 (July 1984):40–45.

BAUER, P. T. *Equality, the Third World, and Economic Delusion*. Cambridge, Mass.: Harvard University Press, 1981.

BAUMGARTNER, M. P. "Introduction: The Moral Voice of the Community." *Sociological Focus*. Vol. 31, No. 2 (May 1998):105–17.

BAYDAR, NAZLI, and JEANNE BROOKS-GUNN. "Effect of Maternal Employment and Child-Care Arrangements on Preschoolers' Cognitive and Behavioral Outcomes: Evidence from Children from the National Longitudinal Survey of Youth." *Developmental Psychology*. Vol. 27, No. 6 (November 1991):932–35.

BEARAK, BARRY. "Lives Held Cheap in Bangladesh Sweatshops." *New York Times* (April 15, 2001):A1, A12.

BECKER, ANNE. Paper presented at the annual meeting of the American Psychiatric Association, Washington, D.C., May 19, 1999. Reported in "Eating Disorders Jump When Fiji Gets Television." *Toledo Blade* (May 20, 1999):12.

BECKER, HOWARD S. *Outside: Studies in the Sociology of Deviance*. New York: Free Press, 1966.

BEDARD, PAUL. "Washington Whispers." *U.S. News & World Report* (March 25, 2002):2.

BEEGHLEY, LEONARD. *The Structure of Social Stratification in the United States*. Needham Heights, Mass.: Allyn & Bacon, 1989.

BEGLEY, SHARON. "Gray Matters." *Newsweek* (March 7, 1995):48–54.

———. "How to Beat the Heat." *Newsweek* (December 8, 1997):34–38.

BEINS, BARNEY, cited in "Examples of Spuriousness." *Teaching Methods*. No. 2 (Fall 1993):3.

BELL, DANIEL. *The Coming of Post-Industrial Society: A Venture in Social Forecasting*. New York: Basic Books, 1973.

BELLAH, ROBERT N. *The Broken Covenant*. New York: Seabury Press, 1975.

BELLAH, ROBERT N., RICHARD MADSEN, WILLIAM M. SULLIVAN, ANN SWIDLER, and STEVEN M. TIPTON. *Habits of the Heart: Individualism and Commitment in American Life*. New York: Harper & Row, 1985.

BELLANDI, DEANNA. "Study Finds Meal Portion Sizes Growing." [Online] Available January 3, 2003, at http://news.yahoo.com

BELLUCK, PAM. "Black Youths' Rate of Suicide Rising Sharply." *New York Times* (March 20, 1998):A1, A18.

BEM, SANDRA LIPSITZ. *The Lenses of Gender: Transforming the Debate on Sexual Inequality*. New Haven, Conn.: Yale University Press, 1993.

BENEDICT, RUTH. "Continuities and Discontinuities in Cultural Conditioning." *Psychiatry*. Vol. 1, No. 2 (May 1938):161–67.

BENJAMIN, LOIS. *The Black Elite: Facing the Color Line in the Twilight of the Twentieth Century*. Chicago: Nelson-Hall, 1991.

BENJAMIN, MATTHEW. "Suite Deals." *U.S. News & World Report* (April 29, 2002): 32–34.

BENNETT, WILLIAM J. "School Reform: What Remains to Be Done." *Wall Street Journal* (September 2, 1997):A18.

BENOKRAITIS, NIJOLE, and JOE R. FEAGIN. *Modern Sexism: Blatant, Subtle, and Overt Discrimination*. 2nd ed. Englewood Cliffs, N.J.: Prentice Hall, 1995.

BERGAMO, MONICA, and GERSON CAMAROTTI. "Brazil's Landless Millions." *World Press Review*. Vol. 43, No. 7 (July 1996):46–47.

BERGEN, RAQUEL KENNEDY. "Interviewing Survivors of Marital Rape: Doing Feminist Research on Sensitive Topics." In CLAIRE M. RENZETTI and RAYMOND M. LEE, eds., *Researching Sensitive Topics*. Thousand Oaks, Calif.: Sage, 1993.

BERGER, PETER L. *Invitation to Sociology*. New York: Anchor Books, 1963.

———. *The Sacred Canopy: Elements of a Sociological Theory of Religion*. Garden City, N.Y.: Doubleday, 1967.

———. *Facing Up to Modernity: Excursions in Society, Politics, and Religion*. New York: Basic Books, 1977.

———. *The Capitalist Revolution: Fifty Propositions about Prosperity, Equality, and Liberty*. New York: Basic Books, 1986.

———. "Sociology: A Disinvitation?" *Society*. Vol. 30, No. 1 (November/ December 1992):12–18.

BERGER, PETER L., BRIGITTE BERGER, and HANSFRIED KELLNER. *The Homeless Mind: Modernization and Consciousness*. New York: Vintage Books, 1974.

BERGESEN, ALBERT, ed. *Crises in the World-System*. Beverly Hills, Calif.: Sage, 1983.

BERK, RICHARD A. *Collective Behavior*. Dubuque, Iowa: Brown, 1974.

BERNARD, JESSIE. *The Female World*. New York: Free Press, 1981.

———. *The Future of Marriage*. 2nd ed. New Haven, Conn.: Yale University Press, 1982.

BERRILL, KEVIN T. "Anti-Gay Violence and Victimization in the United States: An Overview." In GREGORY M. HEREK and KEVIN T. BERRILL, *Hate Crimes: Confronting Violence against Lesbians and Gay Men*. Newbury Park, Calif.: Sage, 1992:19–45.

BERRY, BRIAN L., and PHILIP H. REES. "The Factorial Ecology of Calcutta." *American Journal of Sociology*. Vol. 74, No. 5 (March 1969):445–91.

BERSCHEID, ELLEN, and ELAINE HATFIELD. *Interpersonal Attraction*. 2nd ed. Reading, Mass.: Addison-Wesley, 1983.

BERTEAU, CELESTE. "Disconnected Intimacy: AOL Instant Messenger Use among Kenyon College Students." Senior thesis. Kenyon College, 2005.

BESHAROV, DOUGLAS J., and PETER GERMANIS. "Welfare Reform: Four Years Later." *Public Interest*. No. 140 (Summer 2000):17–35.

BESHAROV, DOUGLAS J., and LISA A. LAUMANN. "Child Abuse Reporting." *Society*. Vol. 34, No. 4 (May/June 1996):40–46.

BEST, JOEL. "Victimization and the Victim Industry." *Society*. Vol. 34, No. 2 (May/June 1997):9–17.

BEST, RAPHAELA. *We've All Got Scars: What Boys and Girls Learn in Elementary School*. Bloomington: Indiana University Press, 1983.

BIAN, YANJIE. "Chinese Social Stratification and Social Mobility." *Annual Review of Sociology*. Vol. 28 (2002):91–116.

BIANCHI, SUZANNE M., and LYNNE M. CASPER. "American Families." *Population Bulletin*. Vol. 55, No. 4 (December 2000):3–43.

BIANCHI, SUZANNE M., and DAPHNE SPAIN. "Women, Work, and Family in America." *Population Bulletin*. Vol. 51, No. 3 (December 1996):2–48.

BLACKWOOD, EVELYN, and SASKIA WIERINGA, eds. *Female Desires: Same-Sex Relations and Transgender Practices across Cultures*. New York: Columbia University Press, 1999.

BLANK, JONAH. "The Muslim Mainstream." *U.S. News & World Report* (July 20, 1998):22–25.

BLANKENHORN, DAVID. *Fatherless America: Confronting Our Most Urgent Social Problem*. New York: HarperCollins, 1995.

BLAU, JUDITH R., and PETER M. BLAU. "The Cost of Inequality: Metropolitan Structure and Violent Crime." *American Sociological Review*. Vol. 47, No. 1 (February 1982):114–29.

BLAU, PETER M. *Exchange and Power in Social Life*. New York: Wiley, 1964.

———. *Inequality and Heterogeneity: A Primitive Theory of Social Structure*. New York: Free Press, 1977.

BLAU, PETER M., TERRY C. BLUM, and JOSEPH E. SCHWARTZ. "Heterogeneity and Intermarriage." *American Sociological Review*. Vol. 47, No. 1 (February 1982):45–62.

BLAU, PETER M., and OTIS DUDLEY DUNCAN. *The American Occupational Structure*. New York: Wiley, 1967.

BLAUSTEIN, ALBERT P., and ROBERT L. ZANGRANDO. *Civil Rights and the Black American*. New York: Washington Square Press, 1968.

BLUMBERG, PAUL. *Inequality in an Age of Decline*. New York: Oxford University Press, 1981.

BLUMER, HERBERT G. "Collective Behavior." In ALFRED MCCLUNG LEE, ed., *Principles of Sociology*. 3rd ed. New York: Barnes & Noble Books, 1969: 65–121.

BLUMSTEIN, PHILIP, and PEPPER SCHWARTZ. *American Couples*. New York: Morrow, 1983.

BOBO, LAWRENCE, and VINCENT L. HUTCHINGS. "Perceptions of Racial Group Competition: Extending Blumer's Theory of Group Position to a Multiracial Social Context." *American Sociological Review*. Vol. 61, No. 6 (December 1996):951–72.

BOERNER, CHRISTOPHER, and THOMAS LAMBERT. "Environmental Injustice." *Public Interest*. No. 124 (Winter 1995):61–82.

BOGARDUS, EMORY S. "Social Distance and Its Origins." *Sociology and Social Research*. Vol. 9 (July/August 1925):216–25.

———. *A Forty-Year Racial Distance Study*. Los Angeles: University of Southern California Press, 1967.

BOHANNAN, CECIL. "The Economic Correlates of Homelessness in Sixty Cities." *Social Science Quarterly*. Vol. 72, No. 4 (December 1991):817–25.

BOHLEN, CELESTINE. "Facing Oblivion, Rust-Belt Giants Top Russian List of Vexing Crises." *New York Times* (November 8, 1998):1, 6.

BOHON, STEPHANIE A., and CRAIG R. HUMPHREY. "Courting LULUs: Characteristics of Suitor and Objector Communities." *Rural Sociology*. Vol. 65, No. 3 (September 2000):376–95.

BONANNO, ALESSANDRO, DOUGLAS H. CONSTANCE, and HEATHER LORENZ. "Powers and Limits of Transnational Corporations: The Case of ADM." *Rural Sociology*. Vol. 65, No. 3 (September 2000):440–60.

BONNER, JANE. Research presented in the Public Broadcast System telecast *The Brain #6: The Two Brains*. Videocassette VHS 339. Newark, N.J.: WNET-13 Films, 1984.

BOOTH, ALAN, and ANN C. CROUTER, eds. *Just Living Together: Implications of Cohabitation on Families, Children, and Policy*. Mahwah, N.J.: Erlbaum, 2002.

BOOTH, ALAN, and JAMES DABBS. "Male Hormone Is Linked to Marital Problems." *Wall Street Journal* (August 19, 1992):B1.

BOOTH, WILLIAM. "By the Sweat of Their Brows: A New Economy." *Washington Post* (July 13, 1998):A1, A10–A11.

BORGMANN, ALBERT. *Crossing the Postmodern Divide*. Chicago: University of Chicago Press, 1992.

BORMANN, F. HERBERT. "The Global Environmental Deficit." *BioScience*. Vol. 40, No. 2 (1990):74.

BOSWELL, TERRY E. "A Split Labor Market Analysis of Discrimination against Chinese Immigrants, 1850–1882." *American Sociological Review*. Vol. 51, No. 3 (June 1986):352–71.

BOSWELL, TERRY E., and WILLIAM J. DIXON. "Marx's Theory of Rebellion: A Cross-National Analysis of Class Exploitation, Economic Development, and Violent Revolt." *American Sociological Review*. Vol. 58, No. 5 (October 1993):681–702.

BOTT, ELIZABETH. *Family and Social Network*. New York: Free Press, 1971; orig. 1957.

BOULDING, ELISE. *The Underside of History*. Boulder, Colo.: Westview Press, 1976.

BOWEN, WILLIAM G., and DEREK K. BOK. *The Shape of the River: Long-Term Consequences of Considering Race in College and University Admissions*. Princeton, N.J.: Princeton University Press, 1999.

BOWLES, SAMUEL, and HERBERT GINTIS. *Schooling in Capitalist America: Educational Reform and the Contradictions of Economic Life*. New York: Basic Books, 1976.

BOYER, DEBRA. "Male Prostitution and Homosexual Identity." *Journal of Homosexuality*. Vol. 17, Nos. 1–2 (1989):151–84.

BOYLE, ELIZABETH HEGER, FORTUNATA SONGORA, and GAIL FOSS. "International Discourse and Local Politics: Anti-Female-Genital-Cutting Laws in Egypt, Tanzania, and the United States." *Social Problems*. Vol. 48, No. 4 (November 2001):524–44.

BRECHIN, STEVEN R., and WILLETT KEMPTON. "Global Environmentalism: A Challenge to the Postmaterialism Thesis." *Social Science Quarterly*. Vol. 75, No. 2 (June 1994):245–69.

BRIANS, CRAIG LEONARD, and BERNARD GROFMAN. "Election Day Registration's Effect on U.S. Voter Turnout." *Social Science Quarterly*. Vol. 82, No. 1 (March 2001):170–83.

BRIGGS, TRACEY WONG. "Two Years, Changed Lives." *USA Today* (April 22, 2002): D1–D2.

BRINES, JULIE, and KARA JOYNER. "The Ties That Bind: Principles of Cohesion in Cohabitation and Marriage." *American Sociological Review*. Vol. 64, No. 3 (June 1999):333–55.

BRINK, SUSAN. "Living on the Edge." *U.S. News & World Report* (October 14, 2002):58–64.

BRINTON, MARY C. "The Social-Institutional Bases of Gender Stratification: Japan as an Illustrative Case." *American Journal of Sociology*. Vol. 94, No. 2 (September 1988):300–34.

BROCKERHOFF, MARTIN P. "An Urbanizing World." *Population Bulletin*. Vol. 55, No. 3 (September 2000):1–44.

BRODER, DAVID S. "Stock Options Belong in the Line of Fire." *Columbus Dispatch* (April 21, 2002):G3.

BRODKIN, KAREN. "How Jews Became White Folks." In PAULA S. ROTHENBERG, ed., *White Privilege*. New York: Worth, 2001.

BROOKS, DAVID. *Bobos in Paradise: The New Upper Class and How They Got There*. New York: Simon & Schuster, 2000.

BROWN, LESTER R. "Reassessing the Earth's Population." *Society*. Vol. 32, No. 4 (May/June 1995):7–10.

BROWN, LESTER R., et al., eds. *State of the World 1993: A Worldwatch Institute Report on Progress toward a Sustainable Society*. New York: Norton, 1993.

BROWNING, CHRISTOPHER R., and EDWARD O. LAUMANN. "Sexual Contact between Children and Adults: A Life Course Perspective." *American Sociological Review*. Vol. 62, No. 5 (August 1997):540–60.

BUCKLEY, STEPHEN. "A Spare and Separate Way of Life." *Washington Post* (December 18, 1996):A1, A32–A33.

BUECHLER, STEVEN M. *Social Movements in Advanced Capitalism: The Political Economy and Cultural Construction of Social Activism*. New York: Oxford University Press, 2000.

BULLETIN OF THE ATOMIC SCIENTISTS. "Current Time." [Online] Available October 19, 2005, at http://www.thebulletin.org/doomsday_clock/

BURAWOY, MICHAEL. "Review Essay: The Soviet Descent into Capitalism." *American Journal of Sociology*. Vol. 102, No. 5 (March 1997):1430–44.

BUREAU OF ALCOHOL, TOBACCO, FIREARMS, AND EXPLOSIVES. *Firearms Commerce in the United States 2001/2002*. Washington, D.C.: The Bureau, 2002.

BURKETT, ELINOR. "God Created Me to Be a Slave." *New York Times Magazine* (October 12, 1997):56–60.

BUTLER, ROBERT N. *Why Survive? Being Old in America*. New York: Harper & Row, 1975.

CALLAHAN, DANIEL. *Setting Limits: Medical Goals in an Aging Society*. New York: Simon & Schuster, 1987.

CAMARA, EVANDRO. Personal communication, 2000.

CAMERON, WILLIAM BRUCE. *Modern Social Movements: A Sociological Outline*. New York: Random House, 1966.

CAMPOLO, ANTHONY. *Partly Right: Learning from the Critics of Christianity*. Dallas: Word, 1985.

CAPEK, STELLA A. "The 'Environmental Justice' Frame: A Conceptual Discussion and an Application." *Social Problems*. Vol. 40, No. 1 (February 1993):5–24.

CAPLOW, THEODORE, HOWARD M. BAHR, JOHN MODELL, and BRUCE A. CHADWICK. *Recent Social Trends in the United States, 1960–1990*. Montreal: McGill-Queen's University Press, 1991.

CARLSON, NORMAN A. "Corrections in the United States Today: A Balance Has Been Struck." *American Criminal Law Review*. Vol. 13, No. 4 (Spring 1976):615–47.

CARMICHAEL, STOKELY, and CHARLES V. HAMILTON. *Black Power: The Politics of Liberation in America*. New York: Vintage Books, 1967.

CARMONA, RICHARD H. "The Obesity Crisis in America." Testimony before the Subcommittee on Education Reform, Committee on Education and the Workforce, United States House of Representatives. July 16, 2003. [Online] Available September 25, 2005, at http://www.surgeongeneral.gov/news/testimony/obesity07162003.htm

CARROLL, JAMES R. "Congress Is Told of Coal-Dust Fraud UMW; Senator from Minnesota Rebukes Industry." *Louisville Courier Journal* (May 27, 1999):1A.

CARUSO, DAVID B. "42 Philadelphia Schools Privatized." [Online] Available April 18, 2002, at http://news.yahoo.com

CARYL, CHRISTIAN. "Iraqi Vice." *Newsweek* (December 22, 2003):38–39.

CASTELLS, MANUEL. *The Urban Question*. Cambridge, Mass.: MIT Press, 1977.

———. *The City and the Grass Roots.* Berkeley: University of California Press, 1983.

CATALYST. *Women in Business: A Snapshot.* 2004 Factsheet. [Online] Available June 23, 2005a, at http://www.catalystwomen.org/bookstore/files/fact/ Snapshot%202004.pdf

———. *Women in the Fortune 500.* Press release. February 10, 2005. [Online] Available June 23, 2005b, at http://www.catalystwomen.org/pressroom/ releases.shtml

CENTER FOR AMERICAN WOMEN AND POLITICS. "Women in State Legislatures, 2005." Eagleton Institute of Politics, Rutgers University. June 2005. [Online] Available June 23, 2005, at http://www.cawp.rutgers.edu/Facts/ Officeholders/stleg.pdf

CENTER ON EDUCATION POLICY. "The Good News about American Education." Reported in BRIGETTE GREENBERG, "Report Finds America's Public Schools Showing Improvement." *Naples* (Fla.) *Daily News* (January 8, 2000):4a.

CENTER FOR RESPONSIVE POLITICS. 2004 Election Overview: Stats at a Glance. [Online] Available October 19, 2005, at http://www.opensecrets.org/ overview/stats.asp?cycle=2004

———. 2004 Election Overview: Totals by Sector. [Online] Available October 19, 2005, at http://www.opensecrets.org/overview/sectors.asp?cycle=2004

CENTERS FOR DISEASE CONTROL AND PREVENTION. "Trends in Cigarette Smoking among High School Students—United States, 1991–2001." *Morbidity and Mortality Weekly Report.* Vol. 51, No. 19 (May 17, 2002):409–12.

——— *HIV/AIDS Surveillance Report 2003.* Vol. 15. Atlanta, Ga.: U.S. Department of Health and Human Services, 2004. [Online] Available September 25, 2005, at http://www.cdc.gov/hiv/stats/2003SurveillanceReport.htm

———. *Sexually Transmitted Disease Surveillance, 2003.* Atlanta, Ga.: U.S. Department of Health and Human Services, September 2004. [Online] Available September 25, 2005, at http://www.cdc.gov/std/stats/toc2003.htm

———. "Annual Smoking-Attributable Mortality, Years." *Morbidity and Mortality Weekly Report.* Vol. 54, No. 25 (July 1, 2005):625–28.

———. "Cigarette Smoking among Adults—United States, 2003." *Morbidity and Mortality Weekly Report.* Vol. 54, No. 20 (May 27, 2005):509–13.

CERE, DANIEL. "Courtship Today: The View from Academia." *Public Interest.* No. 143 (Spring 2001):53–71.

CHAGNON, NAPOLEON A. *Yąnomamö: The Fierce People.* 4th ed. Austin, Tex.: Holt, Rinehart and Winston, 1992.

CHANDLER, TERTIUS, and GERALD FOX. *3000 Years of Urban History.* New York: Academic Press, 1974.

CHAVES, MARK. *Ordaining Women: Culture and Conflict in Religious Organizations.* Cambridge, Mass.: Harvard University Press, 1997.

CHAVEZ, LINDA. "Promoting Racial Harmony." In GEORGE E. CURRY, ed., *The Affirmative Action Debate.* Reading, Mass.: Addison-Wesley, 1996.

CHERLIN, ANDREW J., LINDA M. BURTON, TERA R. HART, and DIANE M. PURVIN. "The Influence of Physical and Sexual Abuse on Marriage and Cohabitation." *American Sociological Review.* Vol. 69, No. 6 (December 2004):768–89.

"China Faces Water Shortage." *Popline* (December 2001):1–4.

CHIRICOS, TED, RANEE MCENTIRE, and MARC GERTZ. "Perceived Racial and Ethnic Composition of Neighborhood and Perceived Risk of Crime." *Social Problems.* Vol. 48, No. 3 (August 2001):322–40.

CHOLDIN, HARVEY M. "Show Sampling Will Help Defeat the Undercount." *Society.* Vol. 34, No. 3 (March/April 1997):27–30.

CHRONICLE OF HIGHER EDUCATION. *Almanac 2005–06.* 2005.[Online] Available September 19, 2005, at http://chronicle.com/free/almanac/2005

CHUA-EOAN, HOWARD. "Profiles in Outrage." *Time* (September 25, 2000):38–39.

CIMINO, RICHARD, and DON LATTIN. "Choosing My Religion." *American Demographics.* Vol. 21, No. 4 (April 1999):60–65.

CLARK, J. R., and DWIGHT R. LEE. "Sentencing Laffer Curves, Political Myopia, and Prison Space." *Social Science Quarterly.* Vol. 77, No. 2 (June 1996):245–72.

CLARK, KIM. "Bankrupt Lives." *U.S. News & World Report* (September 16, 2002):52–54.

CLARK, MARGARET S., ed. *Prosocial Behavior.* Newbury Park, Calif.: Sage, 1991.

CLAWSON, DAN, and MARY ANN CLAWSON. "What Has Happened to the U.S. Labor Movement? Union Decline and Renewal." *Annual Review of Sociology.* Vol. 25 (1999):95–119.

CLEMETSON, LYNETTE. "Grandma Knows Best." *Newsweek* (June 12, 2000):60–61.

CLOUD, JOHN. "What Can the Schools Do?" *Time* (May 3, 1999):38–40.

CLOUD, JOHN, and JODIE MORSE. "Home Sweet School." *Time* (August 27, 2001):46–54.

CLOWARD, RICHARD A., and LLOYD E. OHLIN. *Delinquency and Opportunity: A Theory of Delinquent Gangs.* New York: Free Press, 1966.

COHEN, ADAM. "Test-Tube Tug-of-War." *Time* (April 6, 1998):65.

———. "A First Report Card on Vouchers." *Time* (April 26, 1999):36–38.

COHEN, ALBERT K. *Delinquent Boys: The Culture of the Gang.* New York: Free Press, 1971; orig. 1955.

COHEN, ELIAS. "The Complex Nature of Ageism: What Is It? Who Does It? Who Perceives It?" *Gerontologist.* Vol. 41, No. 5 (October 2001):576–78.

COHEN, PHILIP N., and MATT L. HUFFMAN. "Individuals, Jobs, and Labor Markets: The Devaluation of Women's Work." *American Sociological Review.* Vol. 68, No. 3 (June 2003):443–63.

COLE, GEORGE F., and CHRISTOPHER E. SMITH. *Criminal Justice in America.* 3rd ed. Belmont, Calif.: Wadsworth, 2002.

COLEMAN, JAMES S. "The Design of Organizations and the Right to Act." *Sociological Forum.* Vol. 8, No. 4 (December 1993):527–46.

COLEMAN, JAMES S., et al. *Equality of Educational Opportunity.* Washington, D.C.: U.S. Government Printing Office, 1966.

COLEMAN, JAMES S., and THOMAS HOFFER. *Public and Private High Schools: The Impact of Communities.* New York: Basic Books, 1987.

COLEMAN, JAMES S., THOMAS HOFFER, and SALLY KILGORE. *Public and Private Schools: An Analysis of Public Schools and Beyond.* Washington, D.C.: National Center for Education Statistics, 1981.

COLEMAN, RICHARD P., and BERNICE L. NEUGARTEN. *Social Status in the City.* San Francisco: Jossey-Bass, 1971.

COLLEGE BOARD. *2005 College-Bound Seniors Total Group Profile Report.* [Online] Available October 19, 2005, at http://www.collegeboard.com/prod_downloads/ about/news_info/cbsenior/yr2005/2005-college-bound-seniors. pdf

COLLINS, RANDALL. *The Credential Society: A Historical Sociology of Education and Stratification.* New York: Academic Press, 1979.

COLLYMORE, YVETTE. "Migrant Street Children on the Rise in Central America." *Population Today.* Vol. 30, No. 2 (February/March 2002):1, 4.

COLTON, HELEN. *The Gift of Touch: How Physical Contact Improves Communication, Pleasure, and Health.* New York: Seaview/Putnam, 1983.

COMMISSION FOR RACIAL JUSTICE. *CRJ Reporter.* New York: United Church of Christ, 1994.

COMTE, AUGUSTE. *Auguste Comte and Positivism: The Essential Writings.* GERTRUD LENZER, ed. New York: Harper Torchbooks, 1975; orig. 1851–54.

CONNETT, PAUL H. "The Disposable Society." In F. HERBERT BORMANN and STEPHEN R. KELLERT, eds., *Ecology, Economics, and Ethics: The Broken Circle.* New Haven, Conn.: Yale University Press, 1991:99–122.

COOK, RHODES. "House Republicans Scored a Quiet Victory in '92." *Congressional Quarterly Weekly Report.* Vol. 51, No. 16 (April 17, 1993):965–68.

COOLEY, CHARLES HORTON. *Social Organization.* New York: Schocken Books, 1962; orig. 1909.

———. *Human Nature and the Social Order.* New York: Schocken Books, 1964; orig. 1902.

CORCORAN, MARY, SANDRA K. DANZIGER, ARIEL KALIL, and KRISTIN S. SEEFELDT. "How Welfare Reform Is Affecting Women's Work." *Annual Review of Sociology.* Vol. 26 (2000):241–69.

CORNELL, BARBARA. "Pulling the Plug on TV." *Time* (October 16, 2000):F16.

CORRELL, SHELLEY J. "Gender and the Career Choice Process: The Role of Biased Self-Assessment." *American Journal of Sociology.* Vol. 106, No. 6 (May 2001):1691–1730.

CORTESE, ANTHONY J. *Provocateur: Images of Women and Minorities in Advertising.* Lanham, Md.: Rowman & Littlefield, 1999.

COSER, LEWIS. *The Functions of Social Conflict.* New York: Free Press, 1956.

———. *Masters of Sociological Thought: Ideas in Historical and Social Context.* 2nd ed. New York: Harcourt Brace Jovanovich, 1977.

COURTWRIGHT, DAVID T. *Violent Land: Single Men and Social Disorder from the Frontier to the Inner City.* Cambridge, Mass.: Harvard University Press, 1996.

"Cousin Couples." [Online] Available May 29, 2005, at http://www. CousinCouples.com

COWLEY, GEOFFREY. "The Prescription That Kills." *Newsweek* (July 17, 1995):54.

COX, HARVEY. *The Secular City.* Rev. ed. New York: Macmillan, 1971.

COYOTE (Call Off Your Old Tired Ethics). "What Is COYOTE?" 2004. [Online] Available October 11, 2005, at http://www.coyotela/what-is.html

CRANE, DIANA. *Fashion and Its Social Agenda: Class, Gender, and Identity in Clothing.* Chicago: University of Chicago Press, 2000.

CRISPELL, DIANE. "Lucky to Be Alive." *American Demographics.* Vol. 19, No. 4 (April 1997):25.

CROSSETTE, BARBARA. "Female Genital Mutilation by Immigrants Is Becoming Cause for Concern in the U.S." *New York Times International* (December 10, 1995):11.

CROUSE, JAMES, and DALE TRUSHEIM. *The Case against the SAT.* Chicago: University of Chicago Press, 1988.

CRUTSINGER, MARTIN. "Trade Deficit Hits $665.9 Billion in 2004." [Online] Available March 16, 2005, at http://news.yahoo.com

CULLEN, LISA TAKEUCHI. "Will Manage for Food." *Time* (October 14, 2002):52–56.

———. "A New Battle of the Bulge." *Time* (February 24, 2003):14.

CUMMING, ELAINE, and WILLIAM E. HENRY. *Growing Old: The Process of Disengagement.* New York: Basic Books, 1961.

CUMMINGS, SCOTT, and THOMAS LAMBERT. "Anti-Hispanic and Anti-Asian Sentiments among African Americans." *Social Science Quarterly.* Vol. 78, No. 2 (June 1997):338–53.

CURRIE, ELLIOTT. *Confronting Crime: An American Challenge.* New York: Pantheon Books, 1985.

CURRY, ANDREW. "The Gullahs' Last Stand?" *U.S. News & World Report* (June 18, 2001):40–41.

CURTIS, JAMES E., DOUGLAS E. BAER, and EDWARD G. GRABB. "Nations of Joiners: Explaining Voluntary Association Membership in Democratic Societies." *American Sociological Review.* Vol. 66, No. 6 (December 2001):783–805.

CURTISS, SUSAN. *Genie: A Psycholinguistic Study of a Modern-Day "Wild Child."* New York: Academic Press, 1977.

CUTCLIFFE, JOHN R. "Hope, Counseling, and Complicated Bereavement Reactions." *Journal of Advanced Nursing.* Vol. 28, No. 4 (October 1998):754–62.

DAHL, ROBERT A. *Who Governs?* New Haven, Conn.: Yale University Press, 1961.

———. *Dilemmas of Pluralist Democracy: Autonomy vs. Control.* New Haven, Conn.: Yale University Press, 1982.

DAHRENDORF, RALF. *Class and Class Conflict in Industrial Society.* Stanford, Calif.: Stanford University Press, 1959.

DANFORTH, MARION M., and J. CONRAD GLASS JR. "Listen to My Words, Give Meaning to My Sorrow: A Study in Cognitive Constructs in Middle-Aged Bereaved Widows." *Death Studies.* Vol. 25, No. 6 (September 2001):413–30.

DARROCH, JACQUELINE E., et al. "Teenage Sexual and Reproductive Behavior in Developed Countries: Can More Progress Be Made?" 2001. [Online] Available May 30, 2005, at http://www.guttmacher.org/pubs/eurosynth_rpt.pdf

DAVIDSON, JAMES D., RALPH E. PYLE, and DAVID V. REYES. "Persistence and Change in the Protestant Establishment, 1930–1992." *Social Forces.* Vol. 74, No. 1 (September 1995):157–75.

DAVIDSON, JULIA O'CONNELL. *Prostitution, Power, and Freedom.* Ann Arbor: University of Michigan Press, 1998.

DAVIES, CHRISTIE. *Ethnic Humor around the World: A Comparative Analysis.* Bloomington: Indiana University Press, 1990.

DAVIES, MARK, and DENISE B. KANDEL. "Parental and Peer Influences on Adolescents' Educational Plans: Some Further Evidence." *American Journal of Sociology.* Vol. 87, No. 2 (September 1981):363–87.

DAVIS, BYRON BRADLEY. "Sports World." *Christian Science Monitor* (September 9, 1997):11.

DAVIS, DONALD M., cited in "TV Is a Blonde, Blonde World." *American Demographics,* special issue: *Women Change Places.* 1993.

DAVIS, KINGSLEY. "Extreme Social Isolation of a Child." *American Journal of Sociology.* Vol. 45, No. 4 (January 1940):554–65.

———. "Final Note on a Case of Extreme Isolation." *American Journal of Sociology.* Vol. 52, No. 5 (March 1947):432–37.

———. "The Myth of Functional Analysis as a Special Method in Sociology and Anthropology." *American Sociological Review.* Vol. 24, No. 1 (February 1959):75ff.

———. "Sexual Behavior." In ROBERT K. MERTON and ROBERT NISBET, eds., *Contemporary Social Problems.* 3rd ed. New York: Harcourt Brace Jovanovich, 1971:313–60.

DAVIS, KINGSLEY, and WILBERT MOORE. "Some Principles of Stratification." *American Sociological Review.* Vol. 10, No. 2 (April 1945):242–49.

DEDRICK, DENNIS K., and RICHARD E. YINGER. "MAD, SDI, and the Nuclear Arms Race." Unpublished manuscript. Georgetown, Ky.: Georgetown College, 1990.

DEFINA, ROBERT H., and THOMAS M. ARVANITES. "The Weak Effect of Imprisonment on Crime, 1971–1998." *Social Science Quarterly.* Vol. 83, No. 3 (September 2002):635–53.

DEFRANCIS, MARC. "A Spiraling Shortage of Nurses." *Population Today.* Vol. 30, No. 2 (February/March 2002a):8–9.

———. "U.S. Elder Care Is in a Fragile State." *Population Today.* Vol. 30, No. 1 (January 2002b):1–3.

DELACROIX, JACQUES, and CHARLES C. RAGIN. "Structural Blockage: A Cross-National Study of Economic Dependency, State Efficacy, and Underdevelopment." *American Journal of Sociology.* Vol. 86, No. 6 (May 1981):1311–47.

DELLA CAVA, MARCO R. "For Dutch, It's as Easy as Asking a Doctor." *USA Today* (January 7, 1997):4A.

DE MENTE, BOYE. *Japanese Etiquette and Ethics in Business.* 5th ed. Lincolnwood, Ill.: NTC Business Books, 1987.

DEMUTH, STEPHEN, and DARRELL STEFFENSMEIER. "The Impact of Gender and Race-Ethnicity in the Pretrial Release Process." *Social Problems.* Vol. 51, No. 2 (May 2004):222–42.

DENT, DAVID J. "African-Americans Turning to Christian Academies." *New York Times,* Education Life supplement (August 4, 1996):26–29.

DERBER, CHARLES. *The Wilding of America: Money, Mayhem, and the New American Dream.* 3rd ed. New York: Worth, 2004.

DERSHOWITZ, ALAN. *The Vanishing American Jew.* Boston: Little, Brown, 1997.

DERVARICS, CHARLES. "The Coming Age of Older Women." *Population Today.* Vol. 27, No. 2 (February 1999):2–3.

DEUTSCHER, IRWIN. *Making a Difference: The Practice of Sociology.* New Brunswick, N.J.: Transaction, 1999.

DICKINSON, AMY. "When Dating Is Dangerous." *Time* (August 27, 2001):76.

DIXON, WILLIAM J., and TERRY BOSWELL. "Dependency, Disarticulation, and Denominator Effects: Another Look at Foreign Capital Penetration." *American Journal of Sociology.* Vol. 102, No. 2 (September 1996):543–62.

DOBYNS, HENRY F. "An Appraisal of Techniques with a New Hemispheric Estimate." *Current Anthropology.* Vol. 7, No. 4 (October 1966):395–446.

DOLLARD, JOHN, et al. *Frustration and Aggression.* New Haven, Conn.: Yale University Press, 1939.

DOMHOFF, G. WILLIAM. *Who Rules America Now? A View of the '80s.* Englewood Cliffs, N.J.: Prentice Hall, 1983.

DONAHUE, JOHN J., III, and STEVEN D. LEAVITT. Research cited in "New Study Claims Abortion Is Behind Decrease in Crime." *Population Today.* Vol. 28, No. 1 (January 2000):1, 4.

DONNELLY, PATRICK G., and THEO J. MAJKA. "Residents' Efforts at Neighborhood Stabilization: Facing the Challenges of Inner-City Neighborhoods." *Sociological Forum.* Vol. 13, No. 2 (June 1998):189–213.

DONOVAN, VIRGINIA K., and RONNIE LITTENBERG. "Psychology of Women: Feminist Therapy." In BARBARA HABER, ed., *The Women's Annual, 1981: The Year in Review.* Boston: Hall, 1982:211–35.

DOWNEY, DOUGLAS B., PAUL T. von HIPPEL, and BECKETT A. BROH. "Are Schools the Great Equalizer? Cognitive Inequality during the Summer Months and School Year." *American Sociological Review.* Vol. 69, No. 5 (October 2004):613–35.

DOYLE, JAMES A. *The Male Experience.* Dubuque, Iowa: Brown, 1983.

D'SOUZA, DINESH. "The Billionaire Next Door." *Forbes* (October 11, 1999): 50–62.

DU BOIS, W.E.B. *The Philadelphia Negro: A Social Study.* New York: Schocken Books, 1967; orig. 1899.

DUBOS, RENÉ. *Man Adapting.* Enlarged ed. New Haven, Conn.: Yale University Press, 1980.

DUDLEY, KATHRYN MARIE. *Debt and Dispossession: Farm Loss in America's Heartland.* Chicago: University of Chicago Press, 2000.

DUNBAR, LESLIE. *The Common Interest: How Our Social Welfare Policies Don't Work and What We Can Do about Them.* New York: Pantheon, 1988.

DUNCAN, CYNTHIA M. *Worlds Apart: Why Poverty Persists in Rural America.* New Haven, Conn.: Yale University Press, 1999.

DUNCAN, GREG J., W. JEAN YEUNG, JEANNE BROOKS-GUNN, and JUDITH R. SMITH. "How Much Does Childhood Poverty Affect the Life Chances of Children?" *American Sociological Review.* Vol. 63, No. 3 (June 1998):406–23.

DUNN, LUCIA F. "Is Combat Pay Effective? Evidence from Operation Desert Storm." *Social Science Quarterly.* Vol. 84, No. 2 (June 2003):344–58.

DUREX GLOBAL SEX SURVEY. Reported in *Time* (October 30, 2000):31.

DURKHEIM, EMILE. *The Division of Labor in Society.* New York: Free Press, 1964a; orig. 1893.

———. *The Rules of Sociological Method.* New York: Free Press, 1964b; orig. 1895.

———. *The Elementary Forms of Religious Life.* New York: Free Press, 1965; orig. 1915.

———. *Suicide.* New York: Free Press, 1966; orig. 1897.

———. *Sociology and Philosophy.* New York: Free Press, 1974; orig. 1924.

DWORKIN, ANDREA. *Intercourse.* New York: Free Press, 1987.

DWORKIN, RONALD W. "Where Have All the Nurses Gone?" *Public Interest.* No. 148 (Summer 2002):23–36.

EBAUGH, HELEN ROSE FUCHS. *Becoming an Ex: The Process of Role Exit.* Chicago: University of Chicago Press, 1988.

EBOH, CAMILLUS. "Nigerian Woman Loses Appeal against Stoning Death." [Online] Available August 19, 2002, at http://news.yahoo.com

ECK, DIANA L. *A New Religious America: How a "Christian Country" Has Become the World's Most Religiously Diverse Nation.* San Francisco: HarperSan Francisco, 2001.

EDWARDS, TAMALA M. "Flying Solo." *Time* (August 28, 2000):47–55.

EHRENREICH, BARBARA. *The Hearts of Men: American Dreams and the Flight from Commitment.* Garden City, N.Y.: Anchor Books, 1983.

———. "The Real Truth about the Female Body." *Time* (March 15, 1999):56–65.

———. *Nickel and Dimed: On (Not) Getting By in America.* New York: Henry Holt, 2001.

EICHLER, MARGRIT. *Nonsexist Research Methods: A Practical Guide.* Winchester, Mass.: Unwin Hyman, 1988.

EISEN, ARNOLD M. *The Chosen People in America: A Study of Jewish Religious Ideology.* Bloomington: Indiana University Press, 1983.

EISENBERG, DANIEL. "Paying to Keep Your Job." *Time* (October 15, 2001): 80–83.

EISENSTADT, JILL. "The Maid's Tale." *New York Times* (July 25, 2004). [Online] Available March 22, 2005, at http://www.researchnavigator.com

EISLER, BENITA. *The Lowell Offering: Writings by New England Mill Women, 1840–1845.* Philadelphia: Lippincott, 1977.

EKMAN, PAUL. "Biological and Cultural Contributions to Body and Facial Movements in the Expression of Emotions." In A. RORTY, ed., *Explaining Emotions.* Berkeley: University of California Press, 1980a:73–101.

———. *Face of Man: Universal Expression in a New Guinea Village.* New York: Garland Press, 1980b.

———. *Telling Lies: Clues to Deceit in the Marketplace, Politics, and Marriage.* New York: Norton, 1985.

EL-ATTAR, MOHAMED. Personal communication, 1991.

ELIAS, ROBERT. *The Politics of Victimization: Victims, Victimology, and Human Rights.* New York: Oxford University Press, 1986.

ELLIOT, DELBERT S., and SUZANNE S. AGETON. "Reconciling Race and Class Differences in Self-Reported and Official Estimates of Delinquency." *American Sociological Review.* Vol. 45, No. 1 (February 1980):95–110.

ELLISON, CHRISTOPHER G., JOHN P. BARTKOWSKI, and MICHELLE L. SEGAL. "Do Conservative Protestant Parents Spank More Often? Further Evidence from the National Survey of Families and Households." *Social Science Quarterly.* Vol. 77, No. 3 (September 1996):663–73.

ELLWOOD, ROBERT S. "East Asian Religions in Today's America." In JACOB NEUSNER, ed. *World Religions in America: An Introduction.* Louisville, Ky.: Westminster John Knox Press, 2000:154–71.

ELMER-DEWITT, PHILIP. "Now for the Truth about Americans and Sex." *Time* (October 17, 1994):62–70.

EMBER, MELVIN, and CAROL R. EMBER. "The Conditions Favoring Matrilocal versus Patrilocal Residence." *American Anthropologist.* Vol. 73, No. 3 (June 1971):571–94.

———. *Anthropology.* 6th ed. Englewood Cliffs, N.J.: Prentice Hall, 1991.

EMERSON, JOAN P. "Behavior in Private Places: Sustaining Definitions of Reality in Gynecological Examinations." In H. P. DREITZEL, ed., *Recent Sociology.* Vol. 2. New York: Collier, 1970:74–97.

EMERSON, MICHAEL O., GEORGE YANCEY, and KAREN J. CHAI. "Does Race Matter in Residential Segregation? Exploring the Preferences of White Americans." *American Sociological Review.* Vol. 66, No. 6 (December 2001):922–35.

ENDICOTT, KAREN. "Fathering in an Egalitarian Society." In Barry S. Hewlett, ed., *Father-Child Relations: Cultural and Bio-Social Contexts.* New York: Aldine, 1992:281–96.

ENGELS, FRIEDRICH. *The Origin of the Family.* Chicago: Kerr, 1902; orig. 1884.

ENGLAND, PAULA. "Three Reviews on Marriage." *Contemporary Sociology.* Vol. 30, No. 6 (November 2001):564–65.

ENGLAND, PAULA, JOAN M. HERMSEN, and DAVID A. COTTER. "The Devaluation of Women's Work: A Comment on Tam." *American Journal of Sociology.* Vol. 105, No. 6 (May 2000):1741–60.

ERIKSON, ERIK H. *Childhood and Society.* New York: Norton, 1963; orig. 1950.

———. *Identity and the Life Cycle.* New York: Norton, 1980.

ERIKSON, KAI T. *Everything in Its Path: Destruction of Community in the Buffalo Creek Flood.* New York: Simon & Schuster, 1976.

———. *A New Species of Trouble: Explorations in Disaster, Trauma, and Community.* New York: Norton, 1994.

———. Lecture delivered at Kenyon College, Gambier, Ohio, February 7, 2005a.

———. *Wayward Puritans: A Study in the Sociology of Deviance.* New York: Wiley, 2005b; orig. 1966.

ERIKSON, ROBERT S., NORMAN R. LUTTBEG, and KENT L. TEDIN. *American Public Opinion: Its Origins, Content, and Impact.* 2nd ed. New York: Wiley, 1980.

ESTES, RICHARD J. "The Commercial Sexual Exploitation of Children in the U.S., Canada, and Mexico." Reported in "Study Explores Sexual Exploitation." [Online] Available September 10, 2001, at http://news.yahoo.com

ETZIONI, AMITAI. *A Comparative Analysis of Complex Organization: On Power, Involvement, and Their Correlates.* Revised and enlarged ed. New York: Free Press, 1975.

———. "Too Many Rights, Too Few Responsibilities." *Society.* Vol. 28, No. 2 (January/February 1991):41–48.

———. "How to Make Marriage Matter." *Time* (September 6, 1993):76.

———. "The Responsive Community: A Communitarian Perspective." *American Sociological Review.* Vol. 61, No. 1 (February 1996):1–11.

———. *My Brother's Keeper: A Memoir and a Message.* Lanham, Md.: Rowman & Littlefield, 2003.

EVELYN, JAMILAH. "Community Colleges Play Too Small a Role in Teacher Education, Report Concludes." *Chronicle of Higher Education Online.* [Online] Available October 24, 2002, at http://chronicle.com/daily/2002/10/2002102403n.htm

FAGAN, JEFFREY, FRANKLIN E. ZIMRING, and JUNE KIM. "Declining Homicide in New York City: A Tale of Two Trends." *National Institute of Justice Journal.* No. 237 (October 1998):12–13.

FALK, GERHARD. Personal communication, 1987.

FALLON, A. E., and P. ROZIN. "Sex Differences in Perception of Desirable Body Shape." *Journal of Abnormal Psychology.* Vol. 94, No. 1 (1985):100–105.

FARLEY, CHRISTOPHER JOHN. "Winning the Right to Fly." *Time* (August 28, 1995):62–64.

FATTAH, HASSAN. "A More Diverse Community." *American Demographics.* Vol. 24, No. 7 (July/August 2002):39–43.

FEAGIN, JOE R. *The Urban Real Estate Game.* Englewood Cliffs, N.J.: Prentice Hall, 1983.

———. "Death by Discrimination?" *Newsletter of the Society for the Study of Social Problems.* Vol. 28, No. 1 (Winter 1997):15–16.

FEAGIN, JOE R., and VERA HERNÁN. *Liberation Sociology.* Boulder, Colo.: Westview Press, 2001.

FEATHERMAN, DAVID L., and ROBERT M. HAUSER. *Opportunity and Change.* New York: Academic Press, 1978.

FEATHERSTONE, MIKE, ed. *Global Culture: Nationalism, Globalization, and Modernity.* Newbury Park, Calif.: Sage, 1990.

FEDARKO, KEVIN. "Land Mines: Cheap, Deadly, and Cruel." *Time* (May 13, 1996): 54–55.

FEDERAL BUREAU OF INVESTIGATION. *Crime in the United States, 2003.* Washington, D.C.: Federal Bureau of Investigation, 2004. [Online] Available September 13, 2005, at http://www.fbi.gov

FEDERAL ELECTION COMMISSION. "PAC Activity Increases for 2004 Elections." Washington, D.C.: The Commission, 2005. [Online] Available July 29, 2005, at http://www.fec.gov/press/press2005/20050412pac/PACFinal2004.html

FELLMAN, BRUCE. "Taking the Measure of Children's TV." *Yale Alumni Magazine* (April 1995):46–51.

"Female Opinion and Defense since September 11th." *Society.* Vol. 39, No. 3 (March/April 2002):2.

FENYVESI, CHARLES. "Walled Streets." *U.S. News & World Report* (March 25, 2002):57.

FERNANDEZ, ROBERTO M., and NANCY WEINBERG. "Sifting and Sorting: Personal Contacts and Hiring in a Retail Bank." *American Sociological Review.* Vol. 62, No. 6 (December 1997):883–902.

FERRARO, KENNETH F., and JESSICA A. KELLEY-MOORE. "Cumulative Disadvantage and Health: Long-Term Consequences of Obesity?" *American Sociological Review.* Vol. 68, No. 5 (October 2003):707–29.

FERREE, MYRA MARX, and BETH B. HESS. *Controversy and Coalition: The New Feminist Movement across Four Decades of Change.* 3rd ed. New York: Routledge, 1995.

FETTO, JOHN. "Lean on Me." *American Demographics.* Vol. 22, No. 12 (December 2000):16–17.

———. "Gay Friendly?" *American Demographics.* Vol. 24, No. 5 (May 2002a):16.

———. "Roomier Rentals." *American Demographics.* Vol. 24, No. 5 (May 2002b):17.

———. "A View from the Top?" *American Demographics.* Vol. 24, No. 7 (July/August 2002c):14.

———. "Drug Money." *American Demographics*. Vol. 25, No. 2 (March 2003a):48.

———. "Me Gusta TV." *American Demographics*. Vol. 24, No. 11 (January 2003b):14–15.

FINE, GARY ALAN. "Nature and the Taming of the Wild: The Problem of 'Overpick' in the Culture of Mushroomers." *Social Problems*. Vol. 44, No. 1 (February 1997):68–88.

FINKELSTEIN, NEAL W., and RON HASKINS. "Kindergarten Children Prefer Same-Color Peers." *Child Development*. Vol. 54, No. 2 (April 1983):502–08.

FINN, CHESTER E., JR., and HERBERT J. WALBERG. "The World's Least Efficient Schools." *Wall Street Journal* (June 22, 1998):A22.

FIREBAUGH, GLENN. "Growth Effects of Foreign and Domestic Investment." *American Journal of Sociology*. Vol. 98, No. 1 (July 1992):105–30.

———. "Does Foreign Capital Harm Poor Nations? New Estimates Based on Dixon and Boswell's Measures of Capital Penetration." *American Journal of Sociology*. Vol. 102, No. 2 (September 1996):563–75.

———. "Empirics of World Income Inequality." *American Journal of Sociology*. Vol. 104, No. 6 (May 1999):1597–1630.

———. "The Trend in Between-Nation Income Inequality." *Annual Review of Sociology*. Vol. 26 (2000):323–39.

FIREBAUGH, GLENN, and FRANK D. BECK. "Does Economic Growth Benefit the Masses? Growth, Dependence, and Welfare in the Third World." *American Sociological Review*. Vol. 59, No. 5 (October 1994):631–53.

FIREBAUGH, GLENN, and KENNETH E. DAVIS. "Trends in Antiblack Prejudice, 1972–1984: Region and Cohort Effects." *American Journal of Sociology*. Vol. 94, No. 2 (September 1988):251–72.

FIREBAUGH, GLENN, and DUMITRU SANDU. "Who Supports Marketization and Democratization in Post-Communist Romania?" *Sociological Forum*. Vol. 13, No. 3 (September 1998):521–41.

FISCHER, CLAUDE W. *The Urban Experience*. 2nd ed. New York: Harcourt Brace Jovanovich, 1984.

FISHER, ELIZABETH. *Woman's Creation: Sexual Evolution and the Shaping of Society*. Garden City, N.Y.: Anchor/Doubleday, 1979.

FISHER, ROGER, and WILLIAM URY. "Getting to Yes." In WILLIAM M. EVAN and STEPHEN HILGARTNER, eds., *The Arms Race and Nuclear War*. Englewood Cliffs, N.J.: Prentice Hall, 1988:261–68.

FISKE, ALAN PAIGE. "The Cultural Relativity of Selfish Individualism: Anthropological Evidence That Humans Are Inherently Sociable." In MARGARET S. CLARK, ed., *Prosocial Behavior*. Newbury Park, Calif.: Sage, 1991:176–214.

FITZGERALD, JIM. "Martha Stewart Enjoys Comforts of Home." [Online] Available March 6, 2005, at http://news.yahoo.com

FITZGERALD, JOAN, and LOUISE SIMMONS. "From Consumption to Production: Labor Participation in Grass-Roots Movements in Pittsburgh and Hartford." *Urban Affairs Quarterly*. Vol. 26, No. 4 (June 1991):512–31.

FITZPATRICK, MARY ANNE. *Between Husbands and Wives: Communication in Marriage*. Newbury Park, Calif.: Sage, 1988.

FLAHERTY, MICHAEL G. "A Formal Approach to the Study of Amusement in Social Interaction." *Studies in Symbolic Interaction*. Vol. 5. New York: JAI Press, 1984:71–82.

———. "Two Conceptions of the Social Situation: Some Implications of Humor." *Sociological Quarterly*. Vol. 31, No. 1 (Spring 1990).

FOBES, RICHARD. "Creative Problem Solving." *Futurist*. Vol. 30, No. 1 (January/February 1996):19–22.

FOLIART, DONNE E., and MARGARET CLAUSEN. "Bereavement Practices among California Hospices: Results of a Statewide Survey." *Death Studies*. Vol. 25, No. 5 (July 2001):461–68.

FONDA, DAREN. "The Male Minority." *Time* (December 11, 2000):58–60.

———. "Selling in Tongues." *Time*, Global Business ed. (November 2001):B12–B16.

FORD, CLELLAN S., and FRANK A. BEACH. *Patterns of Sexual Behavior*. New York: Harper Bros., 1951.

FORLITI, AMY. "R.I. Nightclub Fire Kills at Least 39." [Online] Available February 21, 2003, at http://news.yahoo.com

FOUCAULT, MICHEL. *The History of Sexuality: An Introduction*. Vol. 1. ROBERT HURLEY, trans. New York: Vintage, 1990; orig. 1978.

FRANK, ANDRÉ GUNDER. *On Capitalist Underdevelopment*. Bombay: Oxford University Press, 1975.

———. *Crisis: In the World Economy*. New York: Holmes & Meier, 1980.

———. *Reflections on the World Economic Crisis*. New York: Monthly Review Press, 1981.

FRANKLIN, JOHN HOPE. *From Slavery to Freedom: A History of Negro Americans*. 3rd ed. New York: Vintage Books, 1967.

FRAZIER, E. FRANKLIN. *Black Bourgeoisie: The Rise of a New Middle Class*. New York: Free Press, 1965.

FREDRICKSON, GEORGE M. *White Supremacy: A Comparative Study in American and South African History*. New York: Oxford University Press, 1981.

FREEDMAN, ESTELLE B. *No Turning Back: The History of Feminism and the Future of Women*. New York: Ballantine Books, 2002.

FREEDOM HOUSE. *Freedom in the World 2005*. [Online] Available July 11, 2005, at http://www.freedomhouse.org

FRENCH, HOWARD W. "Teaching Japan's Salarymen to Be Their Own Men." *New York Times* (November 27, 2002):A4.

FRENCH, MARILYN. *Beyond Power: On Women, Men, and Morals*. New York: Summit Books, 1985.

FRIEDAN, BETTY. *The Fountain of Age*. New York: Simon & Schuster, 1993.

FRIEDMAN, MEYER, and RAY H. ROSENMAN. *Type A Behavior and Your Heart*. New York: Fawcett Crest, 1974.

FRIEDMAN, MILTON, and ROSE FRIEDMAN. *Free to Choose: A Personal Statement*. New York: Harcourt Brace Jovanovich, 1980.

FUGITA, STEPHEN S., and DAVID J. O'BRIEN. "Structural Assimilation, Ethnic Group Membership, and Political Participation among Japanese Americans: A Research Note." *Social Forces*. Vol. 63, No. 4 (June 1985):986–95.

FULLER, REX, and RICHARD SCHOENBERGER. "The Gender Salary Gap: Do Academic Achievement, Intern Experience, and College Major Make a Difference?" *Social Science Quarterly*. Vol. 72, No. 4 (December 1991):715–26.

FUREDI, FRANK. "New Britain: A Nation of Victims." *Society*. Vol. 35, No. 3 (April 1998):80–84.

FURSTENBERG, FRANK F., JR., and ANDREW J. CHERLIN. *Divided Families: What Happens to Children When Parents Part*. Cambridge, Mass.: Harvard University Press, 1991.

———. "Children's Adjustment to Divorce." In BONNIE J. FOX, ed., *Family Patterns, Gender Relations*. 2nd ed. New York: Oxford University Press, 2001.

GAGNÉ, PATRICIA, and RICHARD TEWKSBURY. "Conformity Pressures and Gender Resistance among Transgendered Individuals." *Social Problems*. Vol. 45, No. 1 (February 1998):81–101.

GAGNÉ, PATRICIA, RICHARD TEWKSBURY, and DEANNA McGAUGHEY. "Coming Out and Crossing Over: Identity Formation and Proclamation in a Transgender Community." *Gender and Society*. Vol. 11, No. 4 (August 1997):478–508.

GALLAGHER, CHARLES A. "Miscounting Race: Explaining Whites' Misperceptions of Racial Group Size." *Sociological Perspectives*. Vol. 46, No. 3 (2003):381–96.

GALLAGHER, MAGGIE. "Does Bradley Know What Poverty Is?" *New York Post* (October 28, 1999):37.

GALLUP ORGANIZATION. Data reported in "Americans and Homosexual Civil Unions." *Society*. Vol. 40, No. 1 (December 2002):2.

GALSTER, GEORGE. "Black Suburbanization: Has It Changed the Relative Location of Races?" *Urban Affairs Quarterly*. Vol. 26, No. 4 (June 1991):621–28.

GAMBLE, ANDREW, STEVE LUDLAM, and DAVID BAKER. "Britain's Ruling Class." *Economist*. Vol. 326, No. 7795 (January 23, 1993):10.

GAMSON, WILLIAM A. "Beyond the Science-versus-Advocacy Distinction." *Contemporary Sociology*. Vol. 28, No. 1 (January 1999):23–26.

GANLEY, ELAINE. "Among Islamic Countries, Women's Roles Vary Greatly." *Washington Times* (April 15, 1998):A13.

GANS, HERBERT J. *People and Plans: Essays on Urban Problems and Solutions*. New York: Basic Books, 1968.

GARDNER, MARILYN. "At-Home Dads Give Their New Career High Marks." *Christian Science Monitor* (May 30, 1996):1, 12.

GARDYN, REBECCA. "Retirement Redefined." *American Demographics*. Vol. 22, No. 11 (November 2000):52–57.

———. "The Mating Game." *American Demographics*. Vol. 24, No. 7 (July/August 2002):33–37.

GARFINKEL, HAROLD. "Conditions of Successful Degradation Ceremonies." *American Journal of Sociology*. Vol. 61, No. 5 (March 1956):420–24.

———. *Studies in Ethnomethodology*. Cambridge, Mass.: Polity Press, 1967.

GARREAU, JOEL. *Edge City*. New York: Doubleday, 1991.

GEERTZ, CLIFFORD. "Common Sense as a Cultural System." *Antioch Review*. Vol. 33, No. 1 (Spring 1975):5–26.

GELLES, RICHARD J., and CLAIRE PEDRICK CORNELL. *Intimate Violence in Families*. 2nd ed. Newbury Park, Calif.: Sage, 1990.

GEOHIVE. "Agglomerations." [Online] Available October 3, 2005, at http://www.geohive.com/charts/city_million.php

GERBER, THEODORE P., and MICHAEL HOUT. "More Shock than Therapy: Market Transition, Employment, and Income in Russia, 1991–1995." *American Journal of Sociology.* Vol. 104, No. 1 (July 1998):1–50.

GERGEN, DAVID. "King of the World." *U.S. News & World Report* (February 25, 2002):84.

GERLACH, MICHAEL L. *The Social Organization of Japanese Business.* Berkeley: University of California Press, 1992.

GERTH, H. H., and C. WRIGHT MILLS, eds. *From Max Weber: Essays in Sociology.* New York: Oxford University Press, 1946.

GESCHWENDER, JAMES A. *Racial Stratification in America.* Dubuque, Iowa: Brown, 1978.

GEWERTZ, DEBORAH. "A Historical Reconsideration of Female Dominance among the Chambri of Papua New Guinea." *American Ethnologist.* Vol. 8, No. 1 (1981):94–106.

GIBBS, NANCY. "The Pulse of America along the River." *Time* (July 10, 2000):42–46.

———. "What Kids (Really) Need." *Time* (April 30, 2001):48–49.

GIDDENS, ANTHONY. *The Transformation of Intimacy.* Cambridge: Polity Press, 1992.

GILBERTSON, GRETA A., and DOUGLAS T. GURAK. "Broadening the Enclave Debate: The Dual Labor Market Experiences of Dominican and Colombian Men in New York City." *Sociological Forum.* Vol. 8, No. 2 (June 1993):205–20.

GILL, RICHARD T. "What Happened to the American Way of Death?" *Public Interest.* No. 127 (Spring 1996):105–17.

GILLIGAN, CAROL. *In a Different Voice: Psychological Theory and Women's Development.* Cambridge, Mass.: Harvard University Press, 1982.

———. *Making Connections: The Relational Worlds of Adolescent Girls at Emma Willard School.* Cambridge, Mass.: Harvard University Press, 1990.

GILLON, RAANAN. "Euthanasia in the Netherlands: Down the Slippery Slope?" *Journal of Medical Ethics.* Vol. 25, No. 1 (February 1999):3–4.

GIOVANNINI, MAUREEN. "Female Anthropologist and Male Informant: Gender Conflict in a Sicilian Town." In JOHN J. MACIONIS and NIJOLE V. BENOKRAITIS, eds., *Seeing Ourselves: Classic, Contemporary, and Cross-Cultural Readings in Sociology.* 2nd ed. Englewood Cliffs, N.J.: Prentice Hall, 1992:27–32.

GLEICK, ELIZABETH. "The Marker We've Been Waiting For." *Time* (April 7, 1997):28–42.

GLENMARY RESEARCH CENTER. "Major Religious Families by Counties of the United States, 2000" (map). Nashville, Tenn.: Glenmary Research Center, 2002.

GLENN, NORVAL D., and BETH ANN SHELTON. "Regional Differences in Divorce in the United States." *Journal of Marriage and the Family.* Vol. 47, No. 3 (August 1985):641–52.

GLUECK, SHELDON, and ELEANOR GLUECK. *Unraveling Juvenile Delinquency.* New York: Commonwealth Fund, 1950.

GOESLING, BRIAN. "Changing Income Inequalities within and between Nations: New Evidence." *American Sociological Review.* Vol. 66, No. 5 (October 2001):745–61.

GOETTING, ANN. *Getting Out: Life Stories of Women Who Left Abusive Men.* New York: Columbia University Press, 1999.

GOFFMAN, ERVING. *The Presentation of Self in Everyday Life.* Garden City, N.Y.: Anchor Books, 1959.

———. *Asylums: Essays on the Social Situation of Mental Patients and Other Inmates.* Garden City, N.Y.: Anchor Books, 1961.

———. *Stigma: Notes on the Management of Spoiled Identity.* Englewood Cliffs, N.J.: Prentice Hall, 1963.

———. *Interactional Ritual: Essays on Face to Face Behavior.* Garden City, N.Y.: Anchor Books, 1967.

———. *Gender Advertisements.* New York: Harper Colophon, 1979.

GOLDBERG, BERNARD. *Bias: A CBS Insider Exposes How the Media Distort the News.* Washington, D.C.: Regnery, 2002.

GOLDBERG, STEVEN. *The Inevitability of Patriarchy.* New York: Morrow, 1974.

GOLDBERGER, PAUL. Lecture delivered at Kenyon College, Gambier, Ohio, September 22, 2002.

GOLDEN, DANIEL. "Some Community Colleges Fudge the Facts to Attract Foreign Students." *Wall Street Journal* (April 2, 2002):B1, B4.

GOLDEN, FREDERIC. "Lying Faces Unmasked." *Time* (April 5, 1999):52.

GOLDEN, FREDERIC, and MICHAEL D. LEMONICK. "The Race Is Over." *Time* (July 3, 2000):18–23.

GOLDFIELD, MICHAEL. "Rebounding Unions Target Service Sector." *Population Today.* Vol. 28, No. 7 (October 2000):3, 10.

GOLDSMITH, H. H. "Genetic Influences on Personality from Infancy." *Child Development.* Vol. 54, No. 2 (April 1983):331–35.

GOLDSTEIN, JOSHUA R., and CATHERINE T. KENNEY. "Marriage Delayed or Marriage Forgone? New Cohort Forecasts of First Marriage for U.S. Women." *American Sociological Review.* Vol. 66, No. 4 (August 2001):506–19.

GOODE, ERICH. "No Need to Panic? A Bumper Crop of Books on Moral Panics." *Sociological Forum.* Vol. 15, No. 3 (September 2000):543–52.

GOODE, WILLIAM J. "The Theoretical Importance of Love." *American Sociological Review.* Vol. 24, No. 1 (February 1959):38–47.

———. "Encroachment, Charlatanism, and the Emerging Profession: Psychology, Sociology, and Medicine." *American Sociological Review.* Vol. 25, No. 6 (December 1960):902–14.

GORDON, JAMES S. "The Paradigm of Holistic Medicine." In ARTHUR C. HASTINGS et al., eds., *Health for the Whole Person: The Complete Guide to Holistic Medicine.* Boulder, Colo.: Westview Press, 1980:3–27.

GORMAN, CHRISTINE. "Stressed-Out Kids." *Time* (December 25, 2000):168.

GORSKI, PHILIP S. "Historicizing the Secularization Debate: Church, State, and Society in Late Medieval and Early Modern Europe, ca. 1300 to 1700." *American Sociological Review.* Vol. 65, No. 1 (February 2000):138–67.

GOTHAM, KEVIN FOX. "Race, Mortgage Lending, and Loan Rejections in a U.S. City." *Sociological Focus.* Vol. 31, No. 4 (October 1998):391–405.

GOTTFREDSON, MICHAEL R., and TRAVIS HIRSCHI. "National Crime Control Policies." *Society.* Vol. 32, No. 2 (January/February 1995):30–36.

GOTTMANN, JEAN. *Megalopolis.* New York: Twentieth Century Fund, 1961.

GOUGH, KATHLEEN. "The Origin of the Family." In JOHN J. MACIONIS and NIJOLE V. BENOKRAITIS, eds., *Seeing Ourselves: Classic, Contemporary, and Cross-Cultural Readings in Sociology.* Englewood Cliffs, N.J.: Prentice Hall, 1989.

GOULD, STEPHEN J. "Evolution as Fact and Theory." *Discover* (May 1981):35–37.

GOULDNER, ALVIN. *The Coming Crisis of Western Sociology.* New York: Avon Books, 1970.

GRANT, DON SHERMAN II, and MICHAEL WALLACE. "Why Do Strikes Turn Violent?" *American Journal of Sociology.* Vol. 96, No. 5 (March 1991):1117–50.

GRANT, DONALD L. *The Anti-Lynching Movement.* San Francisco: R&E Research Associates, 1975.

GRATTET, RYKEN. "Hate Crimes: Better Data or Increasing Frequency?" *Population Today.* Vol. 28, No. 5 (July 2000):1, 4.

GREELEY, ANDREW M. *Religious Change in America.* Cambridge, Mass.: Harvard University Press, 1989.

———. "Religious Revival in Eastern Europe." *Society.* Vol. 39, No. 2 (January/February 2002):76–77.

GREEN, GARY PAUL, LEANN M. TIGGES, and DANIEL DIAZ. "Racial and Ethnic Differences in Job-Search Strategies in Atlanta, Boston, and Los Angeles." *Social Science Quarterly.* Vol. 80, No. 2 (June 1999):263–90.

GREENBERG, DAVID F. *The Construction of Homosexuality.* Chicago: University of Chicago Press, 1988.

GREENE, BOB. "Empty House on the Prairie." *New York Times* (March 2, 2005). [Online] Available May 24, 2005, at http://www.researchnavigator.com

GREENFIELD, LAWRENCE A. *Child Victimizers: Violent Offenders and Their Victims.* Washington, D.C.: U.S. Bureau of Justice Statistics, 1996.

GREENHOUSE, STEVEN. "Despite Defeat on China Bill, Labor Is on the Rise." *New York Times* (May 20, 2000): A1, A18.

GREENSPAN, STANLEY I. *The Four-Thirds Solution: Solving the Child-Care Crisis in America.* Cambridge, Mass.: Perseus, 2001.

GURAK, DOUGLAS T., and JOSEPH P. FITZPATRICK. "Intermarriage among Hispanic Ethnic Groups in New York City." *American Journal of Sociology.* Vol. 87, No. 4 (January 1982):921–34.

GURNETT, KATE. "On the Forefront of Feminism." *Albany Times Union* (July 5, 1998):G-1, G-6.

GWYNNE, S. C., and JOHN F. DICKERSON. "Lost in the E-Mail." *Time* (April 21, 1997):88–90.

HABERMAS, JÜRGEN. *Toward a Rational Society: Student Protest, Science, and Politics.* JEREMY J. SHAPIRO, trans. Boston: Beacon Press, 1970.

HADAWAY, C. KIRK, PENNY LONG MARLER, and MARK CHAVES. "What the Polls Don't Show: A Closer Look at U.S. Church Attendance." *American Sociological Review.* Vol. 58, No. 6 (December 1993):741–52.

HADDEN, JEFFREY K., and CHARLES E. SWAIN. *Prime-Time Preachers: The Rising Power of Televangelism.* Reading, Mass.: Addison-Wesley, 1981.

HAFNER, KATIE. "Making Sense of the Internet." *Newsweek* (October 24, 1994): 46–48.

HAGAN, JACQUELINE MARIA. "Social Networks, Gender, and Immigrant Incorporation: Resources and Restraints." *American Sociological Review.* Vol. 63, No. 1 (February 1998):55–67.

HAIG, ROBIN ANDREW. *The Anatomy of Humor: Biopsychosocial and Therapeutic Perspectives.* Springfield, Ill.: Thomas, 1988.

HALBERSTAM, DAVID. *The Reckoning.* New York: Avon Books, 1986.

HALBFINGER, DAVID M., and STEVEN A. HOLMES. "Military Mirrors Working-Class America." *New York Times* (March 20, 2003). [Online] Available April 28, 2005, at http://www.researchnavigator.com

HALEDJIAN, DEAN. "How to Tell a Businessman from a Businesswoman." Annandale: Northern Virginia Community College, 1997.

HALL, JOHN R., and MARY JO NEITZ. *Culture: Sociological Perspectives.* Englewood Cliffs, N.J.: Prentice Hall, 1993.

HALL, KELLEY J., and BETSY LUCAL. "Tapping in Parallel Universes: Using Superhero Comic Books in Sociology Courses." *Teaching Sociology.* Vol. 27, No. 1 (January 1999):60–66.

HALLINAN, MAUREEN T. "The Sociological Study of Social Change." *American Sociological Review.* Vol. 62, No. 1 (February 1997):1–11.

HAMER, DEAN, and PETER COPELAND. *The Science of Desire: The Search for the Gay Gene and the Biology of Behavior.* New York: Simon & Schuster, 1994.

HAMILTON, ANITA. "Speeders, Say Cheese." *Time* (September 17, 2001):32.

HAMILTON, RICHARD F. "*The Communist Manifesto* at 150." *Society.* Vol. 38, No. 2 (January/February 2001):75–80.

HAMRICK, MICHAEL H., DAVID J. ANSPAUGH, and GENE EZELL. *Health.* Columbus, Ohio: Merrill, 1986.

HAN, WENJUI, and JANE WALDFOGEL. "Child Care Costs and Women's Employment: A Comparison of Single and Married Mothers with Preschool-Aged Children." *Social Science Quarterly.* Vol. 83, No. 5 (September 2001):552–68.

HANDLIN, OSCAR. *Boston's Immigrants, 1790–1865: A Study in Acculturation.* Cambridge, Mass.: Harvard University Press, 1941.

HANEY, CRAIG, W. CURTIS BANKS, and PHILIP G. ZIMBARDO. "Interpersonal Dynamics in a Simulated Prison." *International Journal of Criminology and Penology.* Vol. 1 (1973):69–97.

HANEY, LYNNE. "After the Fall: East European Women since the Collapse of State Socialism." *Contexts.* Vol. 1, No. 3 (Fall 2002):27–36.

HARKNETT, KRISTEN, and SARA S. McLANAHAN. "Racial and Ethnic Differences in Marriage after the Birth of a Child." *American Sociological Review.* Vol. 69, No. 6 (December 2004):790–811.

HARLOW, HARRY F., and MARGARET KUENNE HARLOW. "Social Deprivation in Monkeys." *Scientific American* (November 1962):137–46.

HARPSTER, PAULA, and ELIZABETH MONK-TURNER. "Why Men Do Housework: A Test of Gender Production and the Relative Resources Model." *Sociological Focus.* Vol. 31, No. 1 (February 1998):45–59.

HARRIES, KEITH D. *Serious Violence: Patterns of Homicide and Assault in America.* Springfield, Ill.: Thomas, 1990.

HARRINGTON, MICHAEL. *The New American Poverty.* New York: Penguin Books, 1984.

HARRIS, CHAUNCY D., and EDWARD L. ULLMAN. "The Nature of Cities." *Annals of the American Academy of Political and Social Sciences.* Vol. 242, No. 1 (November 1945):7–17.

HARRIS, DAVID R., and JEREMIAH JOSEPH SIM. "Who Is Multiracial? Assessing the Complexity of Lived Race." Vol. 67, No. 4 (August 2002):614–27.

HARRIS, MARVIN. *Cultural Anthropology.* 2nd ed. New York: Harper & Row, 1987.

HARRISON, C. KEITH. "Black Athletes at the Millennium." *Society.* Vol. 37, No. 3 (March/April 2000):35–39.

HAUB, CARL. "How Many People Have Ever Lived on Earth?" *Population Today.* Vol. 30, No. 8 (November/December 2002):3–4.

HAWTHORNE, PETER. "South Africa's Makeover." *Time* (July 12, 1999).

HAYDEN, THOMAS. "Losing Our Voices." *U.S. News & World Report* (May 26, 2003):42.

HAYWARD, MARK D., EILEEN M. CRIMMINS, TONI P. MILES, and YU YANG. "The Significance of Socioeconomic Status in Explaining the Racial Gap in Chronic Health Conditions." *American Sociological Review.* Vol. 65, No. 6 (December 2000):910–30.

HEATH, JULIA A., and W. DAVID BOURNE. "Husbands and Housework: Parity or Parody?" *Social Science Quarterly.* Vol. 76, No. 1 (March 1995):195–202.

HELGESEN, SALLY. *The Female Advantage: Women's Ways of Leadership.* New York: Doubleday, 1990.

HELIN, DAVID W. "When Slogans Go Wrong." *American Demographics.* Vol. 14, No. 2 (February 1992):14.

HELLMICH, NANCI. "Environment, Economics Partly to Blame." *USA Today* (October 9, 2002):9D.

HENLEY, NANCY, MYKOL HAMILTON, and BARRIE THORNE. "Womanspeak and Manspeak: Sex Differences in Communication, Verbal and Nonverbal." In JOHN J. MACIONIS and NIJOLE V. BENOKRAITIS, eds., *Seeing Ourselves: Classic,*

*Contemporary, and Cross-Cultural Readings in Sociology.* 2nd ed. Englewood Cliffs, N.J.: Prentice Hall, 1992:10–15.

HERDA-RAPP, ANN. "The Power of Informal Leadership: Women Leaders in the Civil Rights Movement." *Sociological Focus.* Vol. 31, No. 4 (October 1998): 341–55.

HEREK, GREGORY M. "Myths about Sexual Orientation: A Lawyer's Guide to Social Science Research." *Law and Sexuality.* No. 1 (1991):133–72.

HERMAN, DIANNE. "The Rape Culture." In JOHN J. MACIONIS and NIJOLE V. BENOKRAITIS, eds., *Seeing Ourselves: Classic, Contemporary, and Cross-Cultural Readings in Sociology.* 5th ed. Upper Saddle River, N.J.: Prentice Hall, 2001.

HERPERTZ, SABINE C., and HENNING SASS. "Emotional Deficiency and Psychopathy." *Behavioral Sciences and the Law.* Vol. 18, No. 5 (September/October 2000):567–80.

HERRING, HUBERT B. "An Aging Nation Is Choosing Younger Bosses." *New York Times* (February 20, 2005). [Online] Available April 12, 2005, at http://www.researchnavigator.com

HERRNSTEIN, RICHARD J., and CHARLES MURRAY. *The Bell Curve: Intelligence and Class Structure in American Life.* New York: Free Press, 1994.

HERZOG, BRAD. "A Man of His Words." *Cornell Alumni Magazine.* Vol. 106, No. 4 (January/February 2004):58–63.

HESS, BETH B. "Breaking and Entering the Establishment: Committing Social Change and Confronting the Backlash." *Social Problems.* Vol. 46, No. 1 (February 1999):1–12.

HEWLETT, BARRY S. "Husband-Wife Reciprocity and the Father-Infant Relationship among Aka Pygmies." In BARRY S. HEWLETT, ed., *Father-Child Relations: Cultural and Bio-Social Contexts.* New York: Aldine, 1992:153–76.

HEYMANN, PHILIP B. "Civil Liberties and Human Rights in the Aftermath of September 11." *Harvard Journal of Law and Public Policy.* Vol. 25, No. 2 (Spring 2002):441–57.

HIGHTOWER, JIM. *Eat Your Heart Out: Food Profiteering in America.* New York: Crown, 1975.

HILL, MARK E. "Race of the Interviewer and Perception of Skin Color: Evidence from the Multi-City Study of Urban Inequality." *American Sociological Review.* Vol. 67, No. 1 (February 2002):99–108.

HIMES, CHRISTINE L. "Elderly Americans." *Population Bulletin.* Vol. 56, No. 4 (December 2001):3–40.

HIRSCHI, TRAVIS. *Causes of Delinquency.* Berkeley: University of California Press, 1969.

HOBERMAN, JOHN. *Darwin's Athletes: How Sport Has Damaged Black America and Preserved the Myth of Race.* Boston: Houghton Mifflin, 1997.

——— "Response to Three Reviews of *Darwin's Athletes.*" *Social Science Quarterly.* Vol. 79, No. 4 (December 1998):898–903.

HOBSON, KATHERINE. "Kissing Cousins." *U.S. News & World Report* (April 15, 2002):77.

HOCHSCHILD, ARLIE RUSSELL. "Emotion Work, Feeling Rules, and Social Structure." *American Journal of Sociology.* Vol. 85, No. 3 (November 1979): 551–75.

———. *The Managed Heart.* Berkeley: University of California Press, 1983.

HOFFERTH, SANDRA. "Did Welfare Reform Work? Implications for 2002 and Beyond." *Contexts.* Vol. 1, No. 1 (Spring 2002):45–51.

HOGAN, RICHARD, and CAROLYN C. PERRUCCI. "Producing and Reproducing the Class and Status Differences: Racial and Gender Gaps in U.S. Employment and Retirement Income." *Social Problems.* Vol. 45, No. 4 (November 1998): 528–49.

HOLMES, THOMAS H., and RICHARD H. RAHE. "The Social Readjustment Rating Scale." *Journal of Psychosomatic Research.* Vol. 11 (1967):213-18.

HOLMSTROM, DAVID. "Abuse of Elderly, Even by Adult Children, Gets More Attention and Official Concern." *Christian Science Monitor* (July 28, 1994):1.

HONEYWELL, ROY J. *The Educational Work of Thomas Jefferson.* Cambridge, Mass.: Harvard University Press, 1931.

HOPE, TRINA L., HAROLD G. GRASMICK, and LAURA J. POINTON. "The Family in Gottfredson and Hrischi's General Theory of Crime: Structure, Parenting, and Self-Control." *Sociological Focus.* Vol. 36, No. 4 (November 2003): 291–311.

HORN, WADE F., and DOUGLAS TYNAN. "Revamping Special Education." *Public Interest.* No. 144 (Summer 2001):36–53.

HOROWITZ, IRVING LOUIS. *The Decomposition of Sociology.* New York: Oxford University Press, 1993.

HORTON, HAYWARD DERRICK. "Critical Demography: The Paradigm of the Future?" *Sociological Forum.* Vol. 14, No. 3 (September 1999):363–67.

HOSTETLER, JOHN A. *Amish Society.* 3rd ed. Baltimore: Johns Hopkins University Press, 1980.

HOUT, MICHAEL. "More Universalism, Less Structural Mobility: The American Occupational Structure in the 1980s." *American Journal of Sociology.* Vol. 95, No. 6 (May 1998):1358–1400.

HOUT, MICHAEL, CLEM BROOKS, and JEFF MANZA. "The Persistence of Classes in Post-Industrial Societies." *International Sociology.* Vol. 8, No. 3 (September 1993):259–77.

HOUT, MICHAEL, and CLAUDE S. FISHER. "Why More Americans Have No Religious Preference: Politics and Generations." *American Sociological Review.* Vol. 67, No. 2 (April 2002):165–90.

HOUT, MICHAEL, ANDREW M. GREELEY, and MELISSA J. WILDE. "The Demographic Imperative in Religious Change in the United States." *American Journal of Sociology.* Vol. 107, No. 2 (September 2001):468–500.

HOYERT, DONNA L., HSIANG-CHING KUNG, and BETTY L. SMITH. "Deaths: Preliminary Data for 2003." *National Vital Statistics Report.* Vol. 53, No. 15 (February 28, 2005).

HOYT, HOMER. *The Structure and Growth of Residential Neighborhoods in American Cities.* Washington, D.C.: Federal Housing Administration, 1939.

HSU, FRANCIS L. K. *The Challenge of the American Dream: The Chinese in the United States.* Belmont, Calif.: Wadsworth, 1971.

HUCHINGSON, JAMES E. "Science and Religion." *Miami* (Fla.) *Herald* (December 25, 1994):1M, 6M.

HUFFMAN, KAREN. *Psychology in Action.* New York: Wiley, 2000.

HUGHES, MICHAEL, and MELVIN E. THOMAS. "The Continuing Significance of Race Revisited: A Study of Race, Class, and Quality of Life in America, 1972 to 1996." *American Sociological Review.* Vol. 63, No. 6 (December 1998): 785–95.

HUMAN RIGHTS WATCH. "Children's Rights: Child Labor." 2004. [Online] Available August 29, 2005, at http://www.hrw.org/children/labor.htm

HUMMER, ROBERT A., RICHARD G. ROGERS, CHARLES B. NAM, and FELICIA B. LE CLERE. "Race/Ethnicity, Nativity, and U.S. Adult Mortality." *Social Science Quarterly.* Vol. 80, No. 1 (March 1999):136–53.

HUNTER, JAMES DAVISON. *American Evangelicalism: Conservative Religion and the Quandary of Modernity.* New Brunswick, N.J.: Rutgers University Press, 1983.

———. "Conservative Protestantism." In PHILIP E. HAMMOND, ed., *The Sacred in a Secular Age.* Berkeley: University of California Press, 1985:50–66.

———. *Evangelicalism: The Coming Generation.* Chicago: University of Chicago Press, 1987.

HYMOWITZ, CAROL. "World's Poorest Women Advance by Entrepreneurship." *Wall Street Journal* (September 9, 1995):B1.

HYMOWITZ, KAY S. "Kids Today Are Growing Up Way Too Fast." *Wall Street Journal* (October 28, 1998):A22.

———. "What to Tell the Kids about Sex." *Public Interest.* No. 153 (Fall 2003): 3–18.

IANNACCONE, LAURENCE R. "Why Strict Churches Are Strong." *American Journal of Sociology.* Vol. 99, No. 5 (March 1994):1180–1211.

IDE, THOMAS R., and ARTHUR J. CORDELL. "Automating Work." *Society.* Vol. 31, No. 6 (September/October 1994):65–71.

INCIARDI, JAMES A. *Elements of Criminal Justice.* 2nd ed. New York: Oxford University Press, 2000.

INCIARDI, JAMES A., HILARY L. SURRATT, and PAULO R. TELLES. *Sex, Drugs, and HIV/AIDS in Brazil.* Boulder, Colo.: Westview Press, 2000.

INGLEHART, RONALD. *Modernization and Postmodernization: Cultural, Economic, and Political Change in 43 Societies.* Princeton, N.J.: Princeton University Press, 1997.

INGLEHART, RONALD, et al. *World Values Surveys and European Values Surveys, 1981–1984, 1990–1993, and 1995–1997.* Computer file. Ann Arbor, Mich.: Interuniversity Consortium for Political and Social Research, 2000.

INGLEHART, RONALD, and WAYNE E. BAKER. "Modernization, Cultural Change, and the Persistence of Traditional Values." *American Sociological Review.* Vol. 65, No. 1 (February 2000):19–51.

INTERNAL REVENUE SERVICE. "Personal Wealth, 1998." *Statistics of Income Bulletin* (April 2003):88.

———. "Corporation Income Tax Returns, 2001." *Statistics of Income Bulletin* (September 2004). [Online] Available November 3, 2004, at http://www.irs.gov/pub/irs-soi/01corart.pdf

INTERNATIONAL LABOUR ORGANISATION. *World Labour Report, 1997–98.* "Table 1.2. Trade Union Density." Rev. November 1, 2002. [Online] Available October 9, 2004, at http://www.ilo.org/public/english/dialogue/ifpdial/publ/wlr97/annex/tab12.htm

INTERNATIONAL MONETARY FUND. *World Economic Outlook.* April 2000. [Online] Available http://www.imf.org/external/pubs/ft/weo/2000/01/index.htm

INTERNATIONAL TELECOMMUNICATION UNION. *World Telecommunication Development Report.* Data cited in WORLD BANK, *2005 World Development Indicators.* Washington, D.C.: World Bank, 2005.

INTER-PARLIAMENTARY UNION. "Women in National Parliaments." 2005. [Online] Available June 25, 2005, at http://www.ipu.org/wmn-e/classif.htm and http://www.ipu.org/wmn-e/world.htm

ISRAEL, GLENN D., LIONEL J. BEAULIEU, and GLEN HARTLESS. "The Influence of Family and Community Social Capital on Educational Achievement." *Rural Sociology.* Vol. 66, No. 1 (March 2001):43–68.

ISRAELY, JEFF. "Something in the Air." *Time* (December 9, 2002):16.

JACOBS, DAVID, and JASON T. CARMICHAEL. "The Political Sociology of the Death Penalty: A Pooled Time-Series Analysis." *American Sociological Review.* Vol. 67, No. 1 (February 2002):109–31.

JACOBS, DAVID, and RONALD E. HELMS. "Toward a Political Model of Incarceration: A Time-Series Examination of Multiple Explanations for Prison Admission Rates." *American Journal of Sociology.* Vol. 102, No. 2 (September 1996):323–57.

JACOBSON, JENNIFER. "Professors Are Finding Better Pay and More Freedom at Community Colleges." *Chronicle of Higher Education Online.* 2003. [Online] Available March 7, 2003, at http://chronicle.com

JACOBY, RUSSELL, and NAOMI GLAUBERMAN, eds. *The Bell Curve Debate.* New York: Random House, 1995.

JACQUET, CONSTANT H., and ALICE M. JONES. *Yearbook of American and Canadian Churches, 1991.* Nashville, Tenn.: Abingdon Press, 1991.

JAMES, DAVID R. "City Limits on Racial Equality: The Effects of City-Suburb Boundaries on Public School Desegregation, 1968–1976." *American Sociological Review.* Vol. 54, No. 6 (December 1989):963–85.

JANIS, IRVING L. *Victims of Groupthink.* Boston: Houghton Mifflin, 1972.

———. *Crucial Decisions: Leadership in Policymaking and Crisis Management.* New York: Free Press, 1989.

JAPANESE MINISTRY OF HEALTH, LABOUR, AND WELFARE. STATISTICS AND INFORMATION DEPARTMENT. *International Comparisons of Divorce Rates.* [Online] Available July 18, 2005, at http://web-jpn.org/stat/stats/02VIT33.html

JASPER, JAMES M. "The Emotions of Protest: Affective and Reactive Emotions in and around Social Movements." *Sociological Forum.* Vol. 13, No. 3 (September 1998):397–424.

JENKINS, J. CRAIG. *Images of Terror: What We Can and Can't Know about Terrorism.* Hawthorne, N.Y.: Aldine de Gruyter, 2003.

JENKINS, J. CRAIG, DAVID JACOBS, and JON AGONE. "Political Opportunities and African-American Protest, 1948–1997." *American Journal of Sociology.* Vol. 109, No. 2 (September 2003):277–303.

JENKINS, J. CRAIG, and CHARLES PERROW. "Insurgency of the Powerless: Farm Worker Movements, 1946–1972." *American Sociological Review.* Vol. 42, No. 2 (April 1977):249–68.

JENKINS, J. CRAIG, and MICHAEL WALLACE. "The Generalized Action Potential of Protest Movements: The New Class, Social Trends, and Political Exclusion Explanations." *Sociological Forum.* Vol. 11, No. 2 (June 1996):183–207.

JENNESS, VALERIE, and RYKEN GRATTET. *Making a Hate Crime: From Movement to Law Enforcement.* New York: Russell Sage Foundation, 2001.

JOHNSON, CATHRYN. "Gender, Legitimate Authority, and Leader-Subordinate Conversations." *American Sociological Review.* Vol. 59, No. 1 (February 1994):122–35.

JOHNSON, DIRK. "Death of a Small Town." *Newsweek* (September 10, 2001): 30–31.

JOHNSON, KENNETH M. "The Rural Rebound." *Population Reference Bureau Reports on America.* Vol. 1, No. 3 (September 1999). [Online] Available October 9, 2004, at http://www.prb.org/Content/NavigationMenu/PRB/About PRB/Reports_on_America/ReportonAmericaRuralRebound.pdf

JOHNSON, KENNETH M., and GLENN V. FUGUITT. "Continuity and Change in Rural Migration Patterns, 1950–1995." *Rural Sociology.* Vol. 65, No. 1 (March 2000):27–49.

JOHNSON, PAUL. "The Seven Deadly Sins of Terrorism." In BENJAMIN NETANYAHU, ed., *International Terrorism.* New Brunswick, N.J.: Transaction Books, 1981:12–22.

JOHNSTON, DAVID CAY. "Voting, America's Not Keen On. Coffee Is Another Matter." *New York Times* (November 10, 1996):sec. 4, p. 2.

JOHNSTON, R. J. "Residential Area Characteristics." In D. T. HERBERT and R. J. JOHNSTON, eds., *Social Areas in Cities. Vol. 1: Spatial Processes and Form.* New York: Wiley, 1976:193–235.

JONES, ANDREW E. G., and DAVID WILSON. *The Urban Growth Machine: Critical Perspectives.* Albany: State University of New York Press, 1999.

JONES, D. GARETH. "Brain Death." *Journal of Medical Ethics.* Vol. 24, No. 4 (August 1998):237–43.

JONES, JUDY. "More Miners Will Be Offered Free X-Rays; Federal Agency Wants to Monitor Black-Lung Cases." *Louisville Courier Journal* (May 13, 1999):1A.

JONES, KATHARINE W. *Accent on Privilege: English Identities and Anglophilia in the U.S.* Philadelphia: Temple University Press, 2001.

JORDAN, ELLEN, and ANGELA COWAN. "Warrior Narratives in the Kindergarten Classroom: Renegotiating the Social Contract?" *Gender and Society.* Vol. 9, No. 6 (December 1995):727–43.

JORDAN, MARY. "New Factors Sustain Age-Old Ritual." *Washington Post* (March 31, 1998):A12.

JOSEPHY, ALVIN M., JR. *Now That the Buffalo's Gone: A Study of Today's American Indians.* New York: Knopf, 1982.

JOYNSON, ROBERT B. "Fallible Judgments." *Society.* Vol. 31, No. 3 (March/April 1994):45–52.

KADLEC, DANIEL. "Everyone, Back in the (Labor) Pool." *Time* (July 29, 2002):22–31.

KAIN, EDWARD L. "A Note on the Integration of AIDS into the Sociology of Human Sexuality." *Teaching Sociology.* Vol. 15, No. 4 (July 1987):320–23.

———. *The Myth of Family Decline: Understanding Families in a World of Rapid Social Change.* Lexington, Mass.: Lexington Books, 1990.

KALLEBERG, ARNE L., BARBARA F. RESKIN, and KEN HUDSON. "Bad Jobs in America: Standard and Nonstandard Employment Relations and Job Quality in the United States." *American Sociological Review.* Vol. 65, No 2 (April 2000): 256–78.

KALLEBERG, ARNE L., and MARK E. VAN BUREN. "Is Bigger Better? Explaining the Relationship between Organization Size and Job Rewards." *American Sociological Review.* Vol. 61, No. 1 (February 1996):47–66.

KAMINER, WENDY. "Volunteers: Who Knows What's in It for Them?" *Ms.* (December 1984):93–96, 126–28.

———. "Demasculinizing the Army." *New York Times Review of Books* (June 15, 1997):7.

KANE, EMILY W. "Racial and Ethnic Variations in Gender-Related Attitudes." *Annual Review of Sociology.* Vol. 26 (2000):419–39.

KANTER, ROSABETH MOSS. *Men and Women of the Corporation.* New York: Basic Books, 1977.

KANTER, ROSABETH MOSS, and BARRY A. STEIN. "The Gender Pioneers: Women in an Industrial Sales Force." In ROSABETH MOSS KANTER and BARRY A. STEIN, eds., *Life in Organizations.* New York: Basic Books, 1979:134–60.

KANTROWITZ, BARBARA, and PAT WINGERT. "Unmarried with Children." *Newsweek* (May 28, 2001):46–52.

———. "What's at Stake." *Newsweek* (January 27, 2003):30 37.

KAO, GRACE. "Group Images and Possible Selves among Adolescents: Linking Stereotypes to Expectations by Race and Ethnicity." *Sociological Forum.* Vol. 15, No. 3 (September 2000):407–30.

KAPFERER, JEAN-NOEL. "How Rumors Are Born." *Society.* Vol. 29, No. 5 (July/August 1992):53–60.

KAPLAN, DAVID E., and MICHAEL SCHAFFER. "Losing the Psywar." *U.S. News & World Report* (October 8, 2001):46.

KAPTCHUK, TED. "The Holistic Logic of Chinese Medicine." In BERKELEY HOLISTIC HEALTH CENTER, *The New Holistic Health Handbook: Living Well in a New Age.* SHEPARD BLISS et al., eds. Lexington, Mass.: Steven Greene Press, 1985:41.

KARATNYCKY, ADRIAN. "The 2001–2002 Freedom House Survey of Freedom: The Democracy Gap." In *Freedom in the World: The Annual Survey of Political Rights and Civil Liberties, 2001–2002.* New York: Freedom House, 2002: 7–18.

KARP, DAVID A., and WILLIAM C. YOELS. "The College Classroom: Some Observations on the Meaning of Student Participation." *Sociology and Social Research.* Vol. 60, No. 4 (July 1976):421–39.

KARRFALT, WAYNE. "A Multicultural Mecca." *American Demographics.* Vol. 25, No. 4 (May 2003):54–55.

KATES, ROBERT W. "Ending Hunger: Current Status and Future Prospects." *Consequences.* Vol. 2, No. 2 (Summer 1996):3–11.

KAUFMAN, LESLIE. "Surge in Homeless Families Sets Off Debate on Cause." *New York Times* (July 29, 2004). [Online] Available March 24, 2005, at http://www.researchnavigator.com

KAUFMAN, MICHAEL T. "Face It: Your Looks Are Revealing." *New York Times* (2002).

KAUFMAN, ROBERT L. "Assessing Alternative Perspectives on Race and Sex Employment Segregation." *American Sociological Review.* Vol. 67, No. 4 (August 2002):547–72.

KAUFMAN, WALTER. *Religions in Four Dimensions: Existential, Aesthetic, Historical, and Comparative.* New York: Reader's Digest Press, 1976.

KAY, PAUL, and WILLETT KEMPTON. "What Is the Sapir-Whorf Hypothesis?" *American Anthropologist.* Vol. 86, No. 1 (March 1984):65–79.

KEISTER, LISA A. *Wealth in America: Trends in Wealth Inequality.* Cambridge: Cambridge University Press, 2000.

———. "Religion and Wealth: The Role of Religious Affiliation and Participation in Early Adult Asset Accumulation." *Social Forces.* Vol. 82, No. 1 (September 2003):175–207.

KEISTER, LISA A., and STEPHANIE MOLLER. "Wealth Inequality in the United States." *Annual Review of Sociology.* Vol. 26 (2000):63–81.

KELLER, HELEN. *The Story of My Life.* New York: Doubleday Page, 1903.

KELLERT, STEPHEN R., and F. HERBERT BORMANN. "Closing the Circle: Weaving Strands among Ecology, Economics, and Ethics." In F. HERBERT BORMANN and STEPHEN R. KELLERT, eds., *Ecology, Economics, and Ethics: The Broken Circle.* New Haven, Conn.: Yale University Press, 1991:205–10.

KENT, MARY M., and MARK MATHER. "What Drives U.S. Population Growth?" *Population Bulletin.* Vol. 57, No. 4 (December 2002):3–40.

KENTOR, JEFFREY. "The Long-Term Effects of Foreign Investment Dependence on Economic Growth, 1940–1990." *American Journal of Sociology.* Vol. 103, No. 4 (January 1998):1024–46.

———. "The Long-Term Effects of Globalization on Income Inequality, Population Growth, and Economic Development." *Social Problems.* Vol. 48, No. 4 (November 2001):435–55.

KERCKHOFF, ALAN C., RICHARD T. CAMPBELL, and IDEE WINFIELD-LAIRD. "Social Mobility in Great Britain and the United States." *American Journal of Sociology.* Vol. 91, No. 2 (September 1985):281–308.

KERR, RICHARD A. "Climate Models Heat Up." *Science Now* (January 26, 2005):1–3.

KEYS, JENNIFER. "Feeling Rules That Script the Abortion Experience." Paper presented at the annual meeting of the American Sociological Association, Chicago, August 2002.

KIDRON, MICHAEL, and RONALD SEGAL. *The New State of the World Atlas.* New York: Simon & Schuster, 1991.

KILBOURNE, BROCK K. "The Conway and Siegelman Claims against Religious Cults: An Assessment of Their Data." *Journal for the Scientific Study of Religion.* Vol. 22, No. 4 (December 1983):380–85.

KILGORE, SALLY B. "The Organizational Context of Tracking in Schools." *American Sociological Review.* Vol. 56, No. 2 (April 1991):189–203.

KING, KATHLEEN PIKER, and DENNIS E. CLAYSON. "The Differential Perceptions of Male and Female Deviants." *Sociological Focus.* Vol. 21, No. 2 (April 1988): 153–64.

KINKEAD, GWEN. *Chinatown: A Portrait of a Closed Society.* New York: Harper-Collins, 1992.

KINSEY, ALFRED, WARDELL BAXTER POMEROY, and CLYDE E. MARTIN. *Sexual Behavior in the Human Male.* Philadelphia: Saunders, 1948.

KINSEY, ALFRED, WARDELL BAXTER POMEROY, CLYDE E. MARTIN, and PAUL H. GEBHARD. *Sexual Behavior in the Human Female.* Philadelphia: Saunders, 1953.

KITTRIE, NICHOLAS N. *The Right to Be Different: Deviance and Enforced Therapy.* Baltimore: Johns Hopkins University Press, 1971.

KLEIN, DANIEL B., and CHARLOTTA STERN. "How Politically Diverse Are the Social Sciences and Humanities? Survey Evidence from Six Fields." National Association of Scholars. 2004. [Online] Available January 13, 2005, at http://www.nas.org/aa/klein_launch.htm

KLUCKHOHN, CLYDE. "As an Anthropologist Views It." In ALBERT DEUTH, ed., *Sex Habits of American Men.* New York: Prentice Hall, 1948.

KNOX, NOELLE. "European Gay Union Trends Influence U.S. Debate." *USA Today* (July 14, 2004):5A.

KOCHANEK, KENNETH D., et al. "Deaths: Final Data for 2002." *National Vital Statistics Report.* Vol. 53, No. 5 (October 12, 2004). Hyattsville, Md.: National Center for Health Statistics.

KOELLN, KENNETH, ROSE M. RUBIN, and MARION SMITH PICARD. "Vulnerable Elderly Households: Expenditures on Necessities by Older Americans." *Social Science Quarterly.* Vol. 76, No. 3 (September 1995):619–33.

KOHLBERG, LAWRENCE. *The Psychology of Moral Development: The Nature and Validity of Moral Stages.* New York: Harper & Row, 1981.

KOHLBERG, LAWRENCE, and CAROL GILLIGAN. "The Adolescent as Philosopher: The Discovery of Self in a Postconventional World." *Daedalus.* No. 100 (Fall 1971):1051–86.

KOHN, MELVIN L. *Class and Conformity: A Study in Values.* 2nd ed. Homewood, Ill.: Dorsey Press, 1977.

———. "The 'Bell Curve' from the Perspective of Research on Social Structure and Personality." *Sociological Forum.* Vol. 11, No. 2 (1996):395.

KOLATA, GINA. "When Grandmother Is the Mother, Until Birth." *New York Times* (August 5, 1991):1, 11.

KONO, CLIFFORD, DONALD PALMER, ROGER FRIEDLAND, and MATTHEW ZAFONTE. "Lost in Space: The Geography of Corporate Interlocking Directorates." *American Journal of Sociology.* Vol. 103, No. 4 (January 1998):863–911.

KOONTZ, STEPHANIE. *The Way We Never Were: American Families and the Nostalgia Trap.* New York: Basic Books, 1992.

KORNHAUSER, WILLIAM. *The Politics of Mass Society.* New York: Free Press, 1959.

KORZENIEWICZ, ROBERTO P., and KIMBERLY AWBREY. "Democratic Transitions and the Semiperiphery of the World Economy." *Sociological Forum.* Vol. 7, No. 4 (December 1992):609–40.

KOSTERS, MARVIN. "Looking for Jobs in All the Wrong Places." *Public Interest.* No. 125 (Fall 1996):125–31.

KOZOL, JONATHAN. *Rachel and Her Children: Homeless Families in America.* New York: Crown, 1988.

———. *Savage Inequalities: Children in America's Schools.* New York: Harper Perennial, 1992.

KRAL, BRIGITTA. "The Eyes of Jane Elliott." *Horizon Magazine.* 2000. [Online] Available June 8, 2005, at http://www.horizonmag.com/4/jane-elliott.asp

KRAYBILL, DONALD B. *The Riddle of Amish Culture.* Baltimore: Johns Hopkins University Press, 1989.

———. "The Amish Encounter with Modernity." In DONALD B. KRAYBILL and MARC A. OLSHAN, eds., *The Amish Struggle with Modernity.* Hanover, N.H.: University Press of New England, 1994:21–33.

KRAYBILL, DONALD B., and MARC A. OLSHAN, eds. *The Amish Struggle with Modernity.* Hanover, N.H.: University Press of New England, 1994.

KRUEGER, PATRICK M., RICHARD G. ROGERS, ROBERT A. HUMMER, FELICIA B. LECLERE, and STEPHANIE A. BOND HUIE. "Socioeconomic Status and Age: The Effect of Income Sources and Portfolios on U.S. Adult Maturity." *Sociological Forum.* Vol. 18, No. 3 (September 2003):465–82.

KRUGMAN, PAUL. "For Richer: How the Permissive Capitalism of the Boom Destroyed American Equality." *New York Times Magazine* (September 20, 2002):62–67, 76–77, 141–42.

KRUKS, GABRIEL N. "Gay and Lesbian Homeless/Street Youth: Special Issues and Concerns." *Journal of Adolescent Health.* Special Issue. No. 12 (1991): 515–18.

KRYSAN, MARIA. "Community Undesirability in Black and White: Examining Racial Residential Preferences through Community Perceptions." *Social Problems.* Vol. 49, No. 4 (November 2002):521–43.

KÜBLER-ROSS, ELISABETH. *On Death and Dying.* New York: Macmillan, 1969.

KUTTNER, ROBERT. "Targeting Cheats." *American Prospect Online* (March 26, 2004). [Online] Available April 23, 2005, at http://www.prospect.org/webfeatures/2004

KUUMBA, M. BAHATI. "A Cross-Cultural Race/Class/Gender Critique of Contemporary Population Policy: The Impact of Globalization." *Sociological Forum.* Vol. 14, No. 3 (March 1999):447–63.

KUZNETS, SIMON. "Economic Growth and Income Inequality." *American Economic Review.* Vol. 14, No. 1 (March 1955):1–28.

———. *Modern Economic Growth: Rate, Structure, and Spread.* New Haven, Conn.: Yale University Press, 1966.

LACAYO, RICHARD. "The Brawl over Sprawl." *Time* (March 22, 1999):44–48.

———. "Blood at the Root." *Time* (April 10, 2000):122–23.

LACH, JENNIFER. "The Color of Money." *American Demographics.* Vol. 21, No. 2 (February 1999):59–60.

LADD, JOHN. "The Definition of Death and the Right to Die." In JOHN LADD, ed., *Ethical Issues Relating to Life and Death.* New York: Oxford University Press, 1979:118–45.

LAI, H. M. "Chinese." In *Harvard Encyclopedia of American Ethnic Groups.* Cambridge, Mass.: Harvard University Press, 1980:217–33.

LANDSBERG, MITCHELL. "Health Disaster Brings Early Death in Russia." *Washington Times* (March 15, 1998):A8.

LANGBEIN, LAURA I., and ROSEANA BESS. "Sports in School: Source of Amity or Antipathy?" *Social Science Quarterly.* Vol. 83, No. 2 (June 2002):436–54.

LAPCHICK, RICHARD. *The 2004 Racial and Gender Report Cards.* Institute for Diversity and Ethics in Sport, University of Central Florida. 2005. [Online] Available July 6, 2005, at http://www.bus.ucf.edu/sport/cgi-bin/site/sitew.cgi?page=/news/index.htx

LAPPÉ, FRANCES MOORE, and JOSEPH COLLINS. *World Hunger: Twelve Myths.* New York: Grove Press/Food First Books, 1986.

LAPPÉ, FRANCES MOORE, JOSEPH COLLINS, and PETER ROSSET. *World Hunger: Twelve Myths.* 2nd ed. New York: Grove Press, 1998.

LAREAU, ANNETTE. "Invisible Inequality: Social Class and Childrearing in Black Families and White Familes." *American Sociological Review.* Vol. 67, No. 5 (October 2002):747–76.

LAROSSA, RALPH, and DONALD C. REITZES. "Two? Two and One-Half? Thirty Months? Chronometrical Childhood in Early Twentieth-Century America." *Sociological Forum.* Vol. 166, No. 3 (September 2001):385–407.

LARSON, GERALD JAMES. "Hinduism in India and in America." In JACOB NEUSNER, ed., *World Religions in America: An Introduction.* Louisville, Ky.: Westminster John Knox Press, 2000:124–41.

LASLETT, BARBARA. "Family Membership, Past and Present." *Social Problems.* Vol. 25, No. 5 (June 1978):476–90.

LASLETT, PETER. *The World We Have Lost: England before the Industrial Age.* 3rd ed. New York: Scribner, 1984.

LASSWELL, MARK. "A Tribe at War: Not the Yanomami, the Anthropologists." *Wall Street Journal* (November 17, 2000):A17.

LAUMANN, EDWARD O., JOHN H. GAGNON, ROBERT T. MICHAEL, and STUART MICHAELS. *The Social Organization of Sexuality: Sexual Practices in the United States.* Chicago: University of Chicago Press, 1994.

LAVELLE, MARIANNE. "Payback Time." *U.S. News & World Report* (March 11, 2002):36–40.

LAVIN, DANIELLE, and DOUGLAS W. MAYNARD. "Standardization vs. Rapport: Respondent Laughter and Interviewer Reaction during Telephone Surveys." *American Sociological Review.* Vol. 66, No. 3 (June 2001):453–79.

LEACH, COLIN WAYNE. "Democracy's Dilemma: Explaining Racial Inequality in Egalitarian Societies." *Sociological Forum.* Vol. 17, No. 4 (December 2002): 681–96.

LEACOCK, ELEANOR. "Women's Status in Egalitarian Societies: Implications for Social Evolution." *Current Anthropology.* Vol. 19, No. 2 (June 1978):247–75.

LEAVITT, JUDITH WALZER. "Women and Health in America: An Overview." In JUDITH WALZER LEAVITT, ed., *Women and Health in America.* Madison: University of Wisconsin Press, 1984:3–7.

LE BON, GUSTAVE. *The Crowd: A Study of the Popular Mind.* New York: Viking Press, 1960; orig. 1895.

LEE, FELICIA R. "Long Buried, Death Goes Public Again." *New York Times* (2002). [Online] Available November 2, 2002, at http://www.researchnavigator.com

LEE, SHARON M., and BARRY EDMONSTON. "New Marriages, New Families: U.S. Racial and Hispanic Intermarriage." *Population Bulletin.* Vol. 60, No. 2 (June 2005):3–36

LEFEBVRE, HENRI. *The Production of Space.* Oxford: Blackwell, 1991.

LELAND, JOHN. "Bisexuality." *Newsweek* (July 17, 1995):44–49.

LEMERT, EDWIN M. *Social Pathology.* New York: McGraw-Hill, 1951.

———. *Human Deviance, Social Problems, and Social Control.* 2nd ed. Englewood Cliffs, N.J.: Prentice Hall, 1972.

LEMONICK, MICHAEL D. "The Search for a Murder Gene." *Time* (January 20, 2003):100.

LENGERMANN, PATRICIA MADOO, and JILL NIEBRUGGE-BRANTLEY. *The Women Founders: Sociology and Social Theory, 1830–1930.* New York: McGraw-Hill, 1998.

LENGERMANN, PATRICIA MADOO, and RUTH A. WALLACE. *Gender in America: Social Control and Social Change.* Englewood Cliffs, N.J.: Prentice Hall, 1985.

LENSKI, GERHARD E. *Power and Privilege: A Theory of Social Stratification.* New York: McGraw-Hill, 1966.

LENSKI, GERHARD E., PATRICK NOLAN, and JEAN LENSKI. *Human Societies: An Introduction to Macrosociology.* 7th ed. New York: McGraw-Hill, 1995.

LEONARD, EILEEN B. *Women, Crime, and Society: A Critique of Theoretical Criminology.* White Plains, N.Y.: Longman, 1982.

LETHBRIDGE-CEJKU, MARGARET, and JACKLINE VICKERIE. *Summary Health Statistics for U.S. Adults: National Health Interview Survey, 2003.* Vital and Health Statistics, Series 10, No. 225. Hyattsville, Md.: National Center for Health Statistics, 2005.

LETSCHER, MARTIN. "Tell Fads from Trends." *American Demographics.* Vol. 16, No. 12 (December 1994):38–45.

LEVAY, SIMON. *The Sexual Brain.* Cambridge, Mass.: MIT Press, 1993.

LEVER, JANET. "Sex Differences in the Complexity of Children's Play and Games." *American Sociological Review.* Vol. 43, No. 4 (August 1978):471–83.

LEVIN, JACK, and ARNOLD ARLUKE. *Gossip: The Inside Scoop.* New York: Plenum, 1987.

———. *Student Eating Disorders: Anorexia Nervosa and Bulimia.* Washington, D.C.: National Educational Association, 1987.

LEVINE, MICHAEL P. "Reducing Hostility Can Prevent Heart Disease." *Mount Vernon* (Ohio) *News* (August 7, 1990):4A.

LEVINE, SAMANTHA. "The Price of Child Abuse." *U.S. News & World Report* (April 9, 2001):58.

————. "Playing God in Illinois." *U.S. News & World Report* (January 13, 2003):13.

LEWIS, OSCAR. *The Children of Sanchez.* New York: Random House, 1961.

LIAZOS, ALEXANDER. "The Poverty of the Sociology of Deviance: Nuts, Sluts, and Preverts." *Social Problems.* Vol. 20, No. 1 (Summer 1972):103–20.

————. *People First: An Introduction to Social Problems.* Needham Heights, Mass.: Allyn & Bacon, 1982.

LICHTER, DANIEL T., and MARTHA L. CROWLEY. "Poverty in America: Beyond Welfare Reform." *Population Bulletin.* Vol. 57, No. 2 (June 2002):3–34.

LICHTER, DANIEL T., and RUKMALIE JAYAKODY. "Welfare Reform: How Do We Measure Success?" *Annual Review of Sociology.* Vol. 28 (2002):117–41.

LICHTER, S. ROBERT, and DANIEL R. AMUNDSON. "Distorted Reality: Hispanic Characters in TV Entertainment." In CLARA E. RODRIGUEZ, ed., *Latin Looks: Images of Latinas and Latinos in the U.S. Media.* Boulder, Colo.: Westview Press, 1997:57–79.

LICHTER, S. ROBERT, STANLEY ROTHMAN, and LINDA S. LICHTER. *The Media Elite: America's New Powerbrokers.* New York: Hastings House, 1990.

LIN, GE, and PETER ROGERSON. Research reported in DIANE CRISPELL, "Sons and Daughters Who Keep in Touch." *American Demographics.* Vol. 16, No. 8 (August 1994):15–16.

LIN, NAN, KAREN COOK, and RONALD S. BURT, eds. *Social Capital: Theory and Research.* Hawthorne, N.Y.: Aldine de Gruyter, 2001.

LIN, NAN, and WEN XIE. "Occupational Prestige in Urban China." *American Journal of Sociology.* Vol. 93, No. 4 (January 1988):793–832.

LINDAUER, DAVID L., and AKILA WEERAPANA. "Relief for Poor Nations." *Society.* Vol. 39, No. 3 (March/April 2002):54–58.

LINDLAW, SCOTT. "President Signs Education Bill." 2002. [Online] Available January 8, 2002, at http://news.yahoo.com

LINDSTROM, BONNIE. "Chicago's Post-Industrial Suburbs." *Sociological Focus.* Vol. 28, No. 4 (October 1995):399–412.

LING, PYAU. "Causes of Chinese Emigration." In AMY TACHIKI et al., eds., *Roots: An Asian American Reader.* Los Angeles: UCLA Asian American Studies Center, 1971:134–38.

LINN, MICHAEL. "Class Notes 1970." *Cornell Alumni News.* Vol. 99, No. 2 (September 1996):25.

LINO, MARK. *Expenditures on Children by Families, 2004.* U.S. Department of Agriculture, Center for Nutrition Policy and Promotion. Miscellaneous Publication No. 1528–2004. Washington, D.C.: U.S. Government Printing Office, 2005.

LINTON, RALPH. "One Hundred Percent American." *American Mercury.* Vol. 40, No. 160 (April 1937a):427–29.

————. *The Study of Man.* New York: Appleton-Century, 1937b.

LIPSET, SEYMOUR MARTIN. *Political Man: The Social Bases of Politics.* Garden City, N.Y.: Anchor/Doubleday, 1963.

————. "Canada and the United States." CHARLES F. DONAN and JOHN H. SIGLER, eds. Englewood Cliffs, N.J.: Prentice Hall, 1985.

LISKA, ALLEN E., and BARBARA D. WARNER. "Functions of Crime: A Paradoxical Process." *American Journal of Sociology.* Vol. 96, No. 6 (May 1991):1441–63.

LITTLE, CRAIG, and ANDREA RANKIN. "Why Do They Start It? Explaining Reported Early-Teen Sexual Activity." *Sociological Forum.* Vol. 16, No. 4 (December 2001):703–29.

LIVINGSTON, KEN. "Politics and Mental Illness." *Public Interest.* No. 143 (Winter, 1999):105–9.

LOBO, SUSAN. "Census-Taking and the Invisibility of Urban American Indians." *Population Today.* Vol. 30, No. 4 (May/June 2002):3–4.

LOFLAND, LYN. *A World of Strangers.* New York: Basic Books, 1973.

LOGAN, JOHN R., RICHARD D. ALBA, and WENQUAN ZHANG. "Immigrant Enclaves and Ethnic Communities in New York and Los Angeles." *American Sociological Review.* Vol. 67, No. 2 (April 2002):299–322.

LONGINO, CHARLES F., JR. "Myths of an Aging America." *American Demographics.* Vol. 16, No. 8 (August 1994):36–42.

LORD, MARY. "Good Teachers the Newest Imports." *U.S. News & World Report* (April 9, 2001):54.

————. "A Battle for Children's Futures." *U.S. News & World Report* (March 4, 2002):35–36.

LORD, WALTER. *A Night to Remember.* Rev. ed. New York: Holt, Rinehart and Winston, 1976.

LORENZ, FREDERICK O., and BRENT T. BRUTON. "Experiments in Surveys: Linking Mass Class Questionnaires to Introductory Research Methods." *Teaching Sociology.* Vol. 24, No. 3 (July 1996):264–71.

LOVEMAN, MARA. "Is 'Race' Essential?" *American Sociological Review.* Vol. 64, No. 6 (December 1999):890–98.

LOVGREN, STEFEN. "Will All the Blue Men End Up in Timbuktu?" *U.S. News & World Report* (December 7, 1998):40.

LUND, DALE A. "Conclusions about Bereavement in Later Life and Implications for Interventions and Future Research." In DALE A. LUND, ed., *Older Bereaved Spouses: Research with Practical Applications.* London: Taylor-Francis-Hemisphere, 1989:217–31.

————. "Caregiving." *Encyclopedia of Adult Development.* Phoenix, Ariz.: Oryx Press, 1993:57–63.

LUND, DALE A., MICHAEL S. CASERTA, and MARGARET F. DIMOND. "Gender Differences through Two Years of Bereavement among the Elderly." *Gerontologist.* Vol. 26, No. 3 (1986):314–20.

LUNDMAN, RICHARD L. Personal communication, 1999.

LYNCH, MICHAEL, and DAVID BOGEN. "Sociology's Asociological 'Core': An Examination of Textbook Sociology in Light of the Sociology of Scientific Knowledge." *American Sociological Review.* Vol. 62, No. 3 (June 1997):481–93.

LYND, ROBERT S., and HELEN MERRELL LYND. *Middletown in Transition.* New York: Harcourt, Brace & World, 1937.

LYNOTT, PATRICIA PASSUTH, and BARBARA J. LOGUE. "The 'Hurried Child': The Myth of Lost Childhood on Contemporary American Society." *Sociological Forum.* Vol. 8, No. 3 (September 1993):471–91.

MABRY, MARCUS, and TOM MASLAND. "The Man after Mandela." *Newsweek* (June 7, 1999):54–55.

MACCOBY, ELEANOR EMMONS, and CAROL NAGY JACKLIN. *The Psychology of Sex Differences.* Stanford, Calif.: Stanford University Press, 1974.

MACE, DAVID, and VERA MACE. *Marriage East and West.* Garden City, N.Y.: Doubleday/Dolphin, 1960.

MACIONIS, JOHN J. "Intimacy: Structure and Process in Interpersonal Relationships." *Alternative Lifestyles.* Vol. 1, No. 1 (February 1978):113–30.

————. "A Sociological Analysis of Humor." Presentation to the Texas Junior College Teachers Association, Houston, 1987.

————. *Social Problems.* 2nd ed. Upper Saddle River, N.J.: Prentice Hall, 2005.

MACIONIS, JOHN J., and LINDA GERBER. *Sociology* (5th Canadian ed.). Scarborough, Ontario: Prentice Hall Allyn & Bacon Canada, 2005.

MACIONIS, JOHN J., and VINCENT R. PARRILLO. *Cities and Urban Life.* 3rd ed. Upper Saddle River, N.J.: Prentice Hall, 2004.

MACKAY, JUDITH. *The Penguin Atlas of Human Sexual Behavior.* New York: Penguin, 2000.

MACPHERSON, KAREN. "Children Have a Full-Time Media Habit, Study Says." *Toledo Blade* (November 18, 1999):3.

MADDOX, SETMA. "Organizational Culture and Leadership Style: Factors Affecting Self-Managed Work Team Performance." Paper presented at the annual meeting of the Southwest Social Science Association, Dallas, February 1994.

MALTHUS, THOMAS ROBERT. *First Essay on Population 1798.* London: Macmillan, 1926; orig. 1798.

MANZA, JEFF, and CLEM BROOKS. "The Religious Factor in U.S. Presidential Elections, 1960–1992." *American Journal of Sociology.* Vol. 103, No. 1 (July 1997):38–81.

MARATHONGUIDE. "Marathon Records." 2005. [Online] Available June 22, 2005, at http://www.marathonguide.com/#Records

MARCUSE, HERBERT. *One-Dimensional Man.* Boston: Beacon Press, 1964.

MARÍN, GERARDO, and BARBARA VAN OSS MARÍN. *Research with Hispanic Populations.* Newbury Park, Calif.: Sage, 1991.

MARKLEIN, MARY BETH. "Optimism Rises as SAT Math Scores Hit 30-Year High." *USA Today* (August 30, 2000):1A.

MARKOFF, JOHN. "Remember Big Brother? Now He's a Company Man." *New York Times* (March 31, 1991):7.

MARKS, ALEXANDRA. "U.S. Shelters Swell—with Families." *Christian Science Monitor* (2001). [Online] Available December 4, 2001, at http://www.csmonitor.com

MARQUAND, ROBERT. "Worship Shift: Americans Seek Feeling of 'Awe.'" *Christian Science Monitor* (May 28, 1997):1, 8.

MARQUAND, ROBERT, and DANIEL B. WOOD. "Rise in Cults as Millennium Approaches." *Christian Science Monitor* (March 28, 1997):1, 18.

MARQUARDT, ELIZABETH, and NORVAL GLENN. *Hooking Up, Hanging Out, and Hoping for Mr. Right.* New York: Institute for American Values, 2001.

MARSHALL, SUSAN E. "Ladies against Women: Mobilization Dilemmas of Antifeminist Movements." *Social Problems.* Vol. 32, No. 4 (April 1985):348–62.

MARTIN, CAROL LYNN, and RICHARD A. FABES. Research cited in MARIANNE SZEGEDY-MASZAK, "The Power of Gender." *U.S. News & World Report* (June 4, 2001):52.

MARTIN, JOHN M., and ANNE T. ROMANO. *Multinational Crime: Terrorism, Espionage, Drug and Arms Trafficking.* Newbury Park, Calif.: Sage, 1992.

MARTIN, JOYCE A., et al. "Births: Final Data for 2003." *National Vital Statistics Report.* Vol. 54, No. 2 (September 8, 2005). Hyattsville, Md.: National Center for Health Statistics.

MARTINEZ, RAMIRO, JR. "Latinos and Lethal Violence: The Impact of Poverty and Inequality." *Social Problems.* Vol. 43, No. 2 (May 1996):131–46.

MARULLO, SAM. "The Functions and Dysfunctions of Preparations for Fighting Nuclear War." *Sociological Focus.* Vol. 20, No. 2 (April 1987):135–53.

MARX, KARL. Excerpt from "A Contribution to the Critique of Political Economy." In KARL MARX and FRIEDRICH ENGELS, *Marx and Engels: Basic Writings on Politics and Philosophy.* LEWIS S. FEURER, ed. Garden City, N.Y.: Anchor Books, 1959:42–46.

———. *Karl Marx: Early Writings.* T. B. BOTTOMORE, ed. New York: McGraw-Hill, 1964.

———. *Capital.* FRIEDRICH ENGELS, ed. New York: International Publishers, 1967; orig. 1867.

MARX, KARL, and FRIEDRICH ENGELS. "Manifesto of the Communist Party." In ROBERT C. TUCKER, ed., *The Marx-Engels Reader.* New York: Norton, 1972:331–62; orig. 1848.

———. *The Marx-Engels Reader.* 2nd ed. ROBERT C. TUCKER, ed. New York: Norton, 1978; orig. 1859.

MARX, LEO. "The Environment and the 'Two Cultures' Divide." In JAMES RODGER FLEMING and HENRY A. GEMERY, eds., *Science, Technology, and the Environment: Multidisciplinary Perspectives.* Akron, Ohio: University of Akron Press, 1994:3–21.

MASSEY, DOUGLAS S. "Housing Discrimination 101." *Population Today.* Vol. 28, No. 6 (August/September 2000):1, 4.

MASSEY, DOUGLAS S., and NANCY A. DENTON. "Hypersegregation in U.S. Metropolitan Areas: Black and Hispanic Segregation along Five Dimensions." *Demography.* Vol. 26, No. 3 (August 1989):373–91.

MATHEWS, T. J., and BRADY E. HAMILTON. "Trend Analysis of the Sex Ratio at Birth in the United States." *National Vital Statistics Reports.* Vol. 53, No. 20 (June 14, 2005). Hyattsville, Md.: National Center for Health Statistics.

MATLOFF, JUDITH. "Nomadic 'Blue Men' of the Desert Try to Go Roam Again." *Christian Science Monitor* (September 9, 1997):7.

MATTHIESSEN, PETER. *Indian Country.* New York: Viking Press, 1984.

MAUER, MARC. *The Crisis of the Young African American Male and the Criminal Justice System.* Report prepared for U.S. Commission on Civil Rights. Washington, D.C., April 15–16, 1999. [Online] Available June 5, 2005, at http://www.sentencingproject.org/pdfs/5022.pdf

MAURO, TONY. "Ruling Likely Will Add Fuel to Already Divisive Debate." *USA Today* (January 7, 1997):1A, 2A.

MAUSS, ARMAND L. *Social Problems of Social Movements.* Philadelphia: Lippincott, 1975.

MAYO, KATHERINE. *Mother India.* New York: Harcourt, Brace, 1927.

MCADAM, DOUG. *Political Process and the Development of Black Insurgency, 1930–1970.* Chicago: University of Chicago Press, 1982.

———. "Tactical Innovation and the Pace of Insurgency." *American Sociological Review.* Vol. 48, No. 6 (December 1983):735–54.

———. *Freedom Summer.* New York: Oxford University Press, 1988.

———. "The Biographical Consequences of Activism." *American Sociological Review.* Vol. 54, No. 5 (October 1989):744–60.

———. "Gender as a Mediator of the Activist Experience: The Case of Freedom Summer." *American Journal of Sociology.* Vol. 97, No. 5 (March 1992):1211–40.

MCADAM, DOUG, JOHN D. MCCARTHY, and MAYER N. ZALD. "Social Movements." In NEIL J. SMELSER, ed., *Handbook of Sociology.* Newbury Park, Calif.: Sage, 1988: 695–737.

———, eds. *Comparative Perspectives on Social Movements: Political Opportunities, Mobilizing Structures, and Cultural Framings.* New York: Cambridge University Press, 1996.

MCBROOM, WILLIAM H., and FRED W. REED. "Recent Trends in Conservatism: Evidence of Non-Unitary Patterns." *Sociological Focus.* Vol. 23, No. 4 (October 1990):355–65.

MCCAFFREY, DAWN, and JENNIFER KEYS. "Competitive Framing Processes in the Abortion Debate: Polarization-Vilification, Frame Saving, and Frame Debunking." *Sociological Quarterly.* Vol. 41, No. 1 (Winter 2000):41–61.

MCCALL, WILLIAM. "Oregon Suicides More than Double." [Online] Available March 4, 2003, at http://news.yahoo.com

MCCARTHY, JOHN D., and MAYER N. ZALD. "Resource Mobilization and Social Movements: A Partial Theory." *American Journal of Sociology.* Vol. 82, No. 6 (May 1977):1212–41.

MCCARTNEY, SCOTT. "U.S. Mulls Raising Pilot Retirement Age." *Baltimore Sun* (February 28, 2005). [Online] Available April 16, 2005, at http://www.Baltimoresun.com

MCCOLM, R. BRUCE, et al. *Freedom in the World: Political Rights and Civil Liberties, 1990–1991.* New York: Freedom House, 1991.

MCDONALD, KIM A. "Debate over How to Gauge Global Warming Heats Up Meeting of Climatologists." *Chronicle of Higher Education.* Vol. 45, No. 22 (February 5, 1999):A17.

MCDONALD, PETER. "Low Fertility Not Politically Sustainable." *Population Today.* Vol. 29, No. 6 (August/September 2001):3, 8.

MCGUIRE, MEREDITH B. *Religion: The Social Context.* 2nd ed. Belmont, Calif.: Wadsworth, 1987.

MCGURN, WILLIAM. "Philadelphia Dims Edison's Light." *Wall Street Journal* (March 20, 2002):A22.

MCKEE, VICTORIA. "Blue Blood and the Color of Money." *New York Times* (June 9, 1996):49–50.

MCLANAHAN, SARA. "Life without Father: What Happens to the Children?" *Contexts.* Vol. 1, No. 1 (Spring 2002):35–44.

MCLEOD, JANE D., and MICHAEL J. SHANAHAN. "Poverty, Parenting, and Children's Mental Health." *American Sociological Review.* Vol. 58, No. 3 (June 1993):351–66.

MCLEOD, JAY. *Ain't No Makin' It: Aspirations and Attainment in a Low-Income Neighborhood.* Boulder, Colo.: Westview Press, 1995.

MCPHAIL, CLARK. *The Myth of the Maddening Crowd.* New York: Aldine, 1991.

MCPHAIL, CLARK, and RONALD T. WOHLSTEIN. "Individual and Collective Behaviors within Gatherings, Demonstrations, and Riots." *Annual Review of Sociology.* Vol. 9. Palo Alto, Calif.: Annual Reviews, 1983:579–600.

MEAD, GEORGE HERBERT. *Mind, Self, and Society.* CHARLES W. MORRIS, ed. Chicago: University of Chicago Press, 1962; orig. 1934.

MEAD, MARGARET. *Sex and Temperament in Three Primitive Societies.* New York: Morrow, 1963; orig. 1935.

MEADOWS, DONELLA H., DENNIS L. MEADOWS, JORGAN RANDERS, and WILLIAM W. BEHRENS III. *The Limits to Growth: A Report on the Club of Rome's Project on the Predicament of Mankind.* New York: Universe, 1972.

MELTZER, BERNARD N. "Mead's Social Psychology." In JEROME G. MANIS and BERNARD N. MELTZER, eds., *Symbolic Interaction: A Reader in Social Psychology.* 3rd ed. Needham Heights, Mass.: Allyn & Bacon, 1978.

MELUCCI, ALBERTO. *Nomads of the Present: Social Movements and Individual Needs in Contemporary Society.* Philadelphia: Temple University Press, 1989.

MENJIVAR, CECILIA. "Immigrant Kinship Networks and the Impact of the Receiving Context: Salvadorans in San Francisco in the Early 1990s." *Social Problems.* Vol. 44, No. 1 (February 1997):104–23.

MERTON, ROBERT K. "Social Structure and Anomie." *American Sociological Review.* Vol. 3, No. 6 (October 1938):672–82.

———. *Social Theory and Social Structure.* New York: Free Press, 1968.

METZ, MICHAEL E., and MICHAEL H. MINER. "Psychosexual and Psychosocial Aspects of Male Aging and Sexual Health." *Canadian Journal of Human Sexuality.* Vol. 7, No. 3 (Summer 1998):245–60.

METZGER, KURT. Data presented in "Cities and Race." *Society.* Vol. 39, No. 1 (December 2001):2.

MICHELS, ROBERT. *Political Parties.* Glencoe, Ill.: Free Press, 1949; orig. 1911.

MILBRATH, LESTER W. *Envisioning a Sustainable Society: Learning Our Way Out.* Albany: State University of New York Press, 1989.

MILGRAM, STANLEY. "Behavioral Study of Obedience." *Journal of Abnormal and Social Psychology.* Vol. 67, No. 4 (1963):371–78.

———. "Group Pressure and Action against a Person." *Journal of Abnormal and Social Psychology.* Vol. 69, No. 2 (August 1964):137–43.

———. "Some Conditions of Obedience and Disobedience to Authority." *Human Relations.* Vol. 18, No. 1 (February 1965):57–76.

———. "The Small World Problem." *Psychology Today* (May 1967):60–67.

MILLER, ALAN S., and RODNEY STARK. "Gender and Religiousness: Can Socialization Explanations Be Saved?" *American Journal of Sociology.* Vol. 107, No. 6 (May 2002):1399–1423.

MILLER, ARTHUR G. *The Obedience Experiments: A Case of Controversy in Social Science.* New York: Praeger, 1986.

MILLER, DAVID L. *Introduction to Collective Behavior.* Belmont, Calif.: Wadsworth, 1985.

MILLER, FREDERICK D. "The End of SDS and the Emergence of Weatherman: Demise through Success." In JO FREEMAN, ed., *Social Movements of the Sixties and Seventies.* White Plains, N.Y.: Longman, 1983:279–97.

MILLER, G. TYLER JR. *Living in the Environment: An Introduction to Environmental Science.* Belmont, Calif.: Wadsworth, 1992.

MILLER, MATTHEW, and PETER NEWCOMB, eds. "The Forbes 400." *Forbes* (Special issue, October 10, 2005).

MILLER, WALTER B. "Lower-Class Culture as a Generating Milieu of Gang Delinquency." In MARVIN E. WOLFGANG, LEONARD SAVITZ, and NORMAN JOHNSTON, eds., *The Sociology of Crime and Delinquency*. 2nd ed. New York: Wiley, 1970:351–63.

MILLER, WILLIAM J., and RICK A. MATTHEWS. "Youth Employment, Differential Association, and Juvenile Delinquency." *Sociological Focus*. Vol. 34, No. 3 (August 2001):251–68.

MILLS, C. WRIGHT. *The Power Elite*. New York: Oxford University Press, 1956.

———. *The Sociological Imagination*. New York: Oxford University Press, 1959.

MIRACLE, TINA S., ANDREW W. MIRACLE, and ROY F. BAUMEISTER. *Human Sexuality: Meeting Your Basic Needs*. Upper Saddle River, N.J.: Prentice Hall, 2003.

MIRINGOFF, MARC, and MARQUE-LUISA MIRINGOFF. "The Social Health of the Nation." *Economist*. Vol. 352, No. 8128 (July 17, 1999):suppl. 6–7.

MITCHELL, ALISON. "Give Me a Home Where the Buffalo Roam Less." *New York Times* (January 20, 2002):sec. 4, p. 5.

MOEN, PHYLLIS, DONNA DEMPSTER-MCCLAIN, and ROBIN M. WILLIAMS. "Successful Aging: A Life-Course Perspective on Women's Multiple Roles and Health." *American Journal of Sociology*. Vol. 97, No. 6 (May 1992):1612–38.

MOLOTCH, HARVEY. "The City as a Growth Machine." *American Journal of Sociology*. Vol. 82, No. 2 (September 1976):309–33.

MONTAIGNE, FEN. "Russia Rising." *National Geographic*. Vol. 200, No. 5 (September 2001):2–31.

MOORE, GWEN, et al. "Elite Interlocks in Three U.S. Sectors: Nonprofit, Corporate, and Government." *Social Science Quarterly*. Vol. 83, No. 3 (September 2002):726–44.

MOORE, WILBERT E. "Modernization as Rationalization: Processes and Restraints." In MANNING NASH, ed., *Essays on Economic Development and Cultural Change in Honor of Bert F. Hoselitz*. Chicago: University of Chicago Press, 1977:29–42.

———. *World Modernization: The Limits of Convergence*. New York: Elsevier, 1979.

MORRIS, ALDON. "Black Southern Sit-In Movement: An Analysis of Internal Organization." *American Sociological Review*. Vol. 46, No. 6 (December 1981):744–67.

MORRISON, DENTON E. "Some Notes toward Theory on Relative Deprivation, Social Movements, and Social Change." In LOUIS E. GENEVIE, ed., *Collective Behavior and Social Movements*. Itasca, Ill.: Peacock, 1978:202–9.

MORSE, JODIE. "A Victory for Vouchers." *Time* (July 8, 2002):32–34.

MOUW, TED. "Job Relocation and the Racial Gap in Unemployment in Detroit and Chicago, 1980 to 1990." *American Sociological Review*. Vol. 65, No. 5 (October 2000):730–53.

MUMFORD, LEWIS. *The City in History: Its Origins, Its Transformations, and Its Prospects*. New York: Harcourt, Brace & World, 1961.

MUNSON, MARTHA L., and PAUL D. SUTTON. "Births, Marriages, Divorces, and Deaths: Provisional Data for 2004." *National Vital Statistics Report*. Vol. 53, No. 21 (June 28, 2005). Hyattsville, Md.: National Center for Health Statistics.

MURDOCK, GEORGE PETER. "Comparative Data on the Division of Labor by Sex." *Social Forces*. Vol. 15, No. 4 (May 1937):551–53.

———. "The Common Denominator of Cultures." In RALPH LINTON, ed., *The Science of Man in World Crisis*. New York: Columbia University Press, 1945:123–42.

———. *Social Structure*. New York: Free Press, 1965; orig. 1949.

MURPHY, SHERRY L. "Deaths: Final Data for 1998." *National Vital Statistics Report*. Vol. 48, No. 11 (November 2000):1–105. Hyattsville, Md.: National Center for Health Statistics.

MURRAY, STEPHEN O., and WILL ROSCOE, eds. *Boy-Wives and Female-Husbands: Studies of African Homosexualities*. New York: St. Martin's Press, 1998.

MYERS, DAVID G. *The American Paradox: Spiritual Hunger in an Age of Plenty*. New Haven, Conn.: Yale University Press, 2000.

MYERS, NORMAN. "Humanity's Growth." In SIR EDMUND HILLARY, ed., *Ecology 2000: The Changing Face of the Earth*. New York: Beaufort Books, 1984a: 16–35.

———. "The Mega-Extinction of Animals and Plants." In SIR EDMUND HILLARY, ed., *Ecology 2000: The Changing Face of the Earth*. New York: Beaufort Books, 1984b:82–107.

———. "Biological Diversity and Global Security." In F. HERBERT BORMANN and STEPHEN R. KELLERT, eds., *Ecology, Economics, and Ethics: The Broken Circle*. New Haven, Conn.: Yale University Press, 1991:11–25.

MYERS, SHEILA, and HAROLD G. GRASMICK. "The Social Rights and Responsibilities of Pregnant Women: An Application of Parsons' Sick Role Model."

Paper presented to the Southwestern Sociological Association, Little Rock, Ark., March 1989.

MYRDAL, GUNNAR. *An American Dilemma: The Negro Problem and Modern Democracy*. New York: Harper Bros., 1944.

NATIONAL ASSESSMENT OF EDUCATIONAL PROGRESS. "Achievement-Level Trends in Mathematics 1990–2005." *The Nation's Report Card*. [Online] Available October 21, 2005, at http://nces.ed.gov/nationsreportcard

NATIONAL CENTER FOR EDUCATION STATISTICS. *Digest of Education Statistics, 2003*. Washington, D.C.: U.S. Government Printing Office, 2004.

———. *Dropout Rates in the United States, 2001*. Washington, D.C.: U.S. Government Printing Office, 2004. [Online] Available November 6, 2004, at http://www.nces.ed.gov/pubs2005/2005046.pdf

NATIONAL CENTER ON ELDER ABUSE. *Elder Abuse Prevalence and Incidence*. Washington, D.C.: U.S. Government Printing Office, 2005. [Online] Available July 24, 2005, at http://www.elderabusecenter.org/pdf/publication/FinalStatistics050331.pdf

NATIONAL CLEARINGHOUSE ON CHILD ABUSE AND NEGLECT INFORMATION. "*Child Maltreatment, 2003*: Summary of Key Findings." 2005. [Online] Available July 18, 2005, at http://nccanch.acf.hhs.gov/pubs/factsheets/canstats.pdf

NATIONAL COMMISSION ON EXCELLENCE IN EDUCATION. *A Nation at Risk*. Washington, D.C.: U.S. Government Printing Office, 1983.

NAVARRO, MIREYA. "Puerto Rican Presence Wanes in New York." *New York Times* (February 28, 2000):A1, A20.

———. "For Younger Latinas, a Shift to Smaller Families." *New York Times* (December 5, 2004). [Online] Available April 30, 2005, at http://www.researchnavigator.com

NELSON, AMY L. "The Effect of Economic Restructuring on Family Poverty in the Industrial Heartland, 1970–1990." *Sociological Focus*. Vol. 31, No. 2 (May 1998):201–16.

NELSON, JOEL I. "Work and Benefits: The Multiple Problems of Service Sector Employment." *Social Problems*. Vol. 42, No. 2 (May 1994):240–55.

NESBITT, PAULA D. *Feminization of the Clergy in America: Occupational and Organizational Perspectives*. New York: Oxford University Press, 1997.

NESSMAN, RAVI. "Stampede at Soccer Match Kills 47." [Online]. Available April 11, 2001, at http://news.yahoo.com

NEUGARTEN, BERNICE L. "Grow Old with Me. The Best Is Yet to Be." *Psychology Today* (December 1971):45–48, 79, 81.

———. "Personality and Aging." In JAMES E. BIRREN and K. WARNER SCHAIE, eds., *Handbook of the Psychology of Aging*. New York: Van Nostrand Reinhold, 1977:626–49.

NEUHOUSER, KEVIN. "The Radicalization of the Brazilian Catholic Church in Comparative Perspective." *American Sociological Review*. Vol. 54, No. 2 (April 1989):233–44.

NEUMAN, W. LAURENCE. *Social Research Methods: Qualitative and Quantitative Approaches*. 4th ed. Boston: Allyn & Bacon, 2000.

NEWMAN, KATHERINE S. *Declining Fortunes: The Withering of the American Dream*. New York: Basic Books, 1993.

NEWMAN, WILLIAM M. *American Pluralism: A Study of Minority Groups and Social Theory*. New York: Harper & Row, 1973.

NICHOLSON, NIGEL. "Evolved to Chat: The New Word on Gossip." *Psychology Today* (May/June 2001):41–45.

NIELSEN, FRANCOIS, and ARTHUR S. ALDERSON. "The Kuznets Curve: The Great U-Turn: Income Inequality in U.S. Counties, 1970 to 1990." *American Sociological Review*. Vol. 62, No. 1 (February 1997):12–33.

NISBET, ROBERT A. *The Sociological Tradition*. New York: Basic Books, 1966.

———. *The Quest for Community*. New York: Oxford University Press, 1969.

NOCK, STEVEN L., JAMES D. WRIGHT, and LAURA SANCHEZ. "America's Divorce Problem." *Society*. Vol. 36, No. 4 (May/June 1999):43–52.

NOLAN, PATRICK, and GERHARD LENSKI. *Human Societies: An Introduction to Macrosociology*. 8th ed. New York: McGraw-Hill, 1999.

———. *Human Societies: An Introduction to Macrosociology*. 9th ed. Boulder, Colo.: Paradigm, 2004.

NORBECK, EDWARD. "Class Structure." In *Kodansha Encyclopedia of Japan*. Tokyo: Kodansha, 1983:322–25.

NORC. *General Social Surveys, 1972–1991: Cumulative Codebook*. Chicago: National Opinion Research Center, 1991.

———. *General Social Surveys, 1972–2002: Cumulative Codebook*. Chicago: National Opinion Research Center, 2003.

NORD, MARK. "Does It Cost Less to Live in Rural Areas? Evidence from New Data on Food Scarcity and Hunger." *Rural Sociology*. Vol. 65, No. 1 (March 2000):104–25.

NOVAK, VIVECA. "The Cost of Poor Advice." *Time* (July 5, 1999):38.

NULAND, SHERWIN B. "The Hazards of Hospitalization." *Wall Street Journal* (December 2, 1999):A22.

OAKES, JEANNIE. "Classroom Social Relationships: Exploring the Bowles and Gintis Hypothesis." *Sociology of Education.* Vol. 55, No. 4 (October 1982):197–212.

———. *Keeping Track: How High Schools Structure Inequality.* New Haven, Conn.: Yale University Press, 1985.

OBERSCHALL, ANTHONY. *Social Conflict and Social Movements.* Englewood Cliffs, N.J.: Prentice Hall, 1973.

O'CONNOR, RORY J. "Internet Declared Protected Speech." *Glens Falls* (N.Y.) *Post-Star* (June 27, 1997):A1–A2.

OGAWA, NAOHIRO, and ROBERT D. RETHERFORD. "Shifting Costs of Caring for the Elderly Back to Families in Japan: Will It Work?" *Population and Development Review.* Vol. 23, No. 1 (March 1997):59–95.

OGBURN, WILLIAM F. *On Culture and Social Change.* Chicago: University of Chicago Press, 1964.

OGDEN, RUSSEL D. "Nonphysician-Assisted Suicide: The Technological Imperative of the Deathing Counterculture." *Death Studies.* Vol. 25, No. 5 (July 2001):387–402.

O'HARE, WILLIAM P. "The Rise of Hispanic Affluence." *American Demographics.* Vol. 12, No. 8 (August 1990):40–43.

———. "Tracking the Trends in Low-Income Working Families." *Population Today.* Vol. 30, No. 6 (August/September 2002):1–3.

O'HARE, WILLIAM P., WILLIAM H. FREY, and DAN FOST. "Asians in the Suburbs." *American Demographics.* Vol. 16, No. 9 (May 1994):32–38.

O'HARROW, ROBERT, JR. "ID Theft Scam Hits D.C. Area Residents." [Online] Available February 21, 2005, at http://news.yahoo.com

OLSEN, GREGG M. "Remodeling Sweden: The Rise and Demise of the Compromise in a Global Economy." *Social Problems.* Vol. 43, No. 1 (February 1996):1–20.

OLZAK, SUSAN. "Labor Unrest, Immigration, and Ethnic Conflict in Urban America, 1880–1914." *American Journal of Sociology.* Vol. 94, No. 6 (May 1989):1303–33.

OLZAK, SUSAN, and ELIZABETH WEST. "Ethnic Conflict and the Rise and Fall of Ethnic Newspapers." *American Sociological Review.* Vol. 56, No. 4 (August 1991):458–74.

OMESTAD, THOMAS. "A Balance of Terror." *U.S. News & World Report* (February 3, 2003):33–35.

O'NEILL, BRIAN, and DEBORAH BALK. "World Population Futures." *Population Bulletin.* Vol. 56, No. 3 (September 2001):3–40.

"Online Privacy: It's Time for Rules in Wonderland." *Business Week* (March 20, 2000):82–96.

ORECKLIN, MICHELLE. "Earnings Report: J.K. and Judy." *Time* (January 13, 2003):72.

ORHANT, MELANIE. "Human Trafficking Exposed." *Population Today.* Vol. 30, No. 1 (January 2002):1, 4.

ORLANSKY, MICHAEL D., and WILLIAM L. HEWARD. *Voices: Interviews with Handicapped People.* Columbus, Ohio: Merrill, 1981.

ORWIN, CLIFFORD. "All Quiet on the Western Front?" *Public Interest.* No. 123 (Spring 1996):3–9.

OSTRANDER, SUSAN A. "Upper-Class Women: The Feminine Side of Privilege." *Qualitative Sociology.* Vol. 3, No. 1 (Spring 1980):23–44.

———. *Women of the Upper Class.* Philadelphia: Temple University Press, 1984.

OUCHI, WILLIAM. *Theory Z: How American Business Can Meet the Japanese Challenge.* Reading, Mass.: Addison-Wesley, 1981.

"Our Cheating Hearts." Editorial. *U.S. News & World Report* (May 6, 2002):4.

OVADIA, SETH. "Race, Class, and Gender Differences in High School Seniors' Values: Applying Intersection Theory in Empirical Analysis." *Social Science Quarterly.* Vol. 82, No. 2 (June 2001):341–56.

OWEN, CAROLYN A., HOWARD C. ELSNER, and THOMAS R. McFAUL. "A Half-Century of Social Distance Research: National Replication of the Bogardus Studies." *Sociology and Social Research.* Vol. 66, No. 1 (1977):80–98.

PACKARD, MARK. Personal communication, 2002.

PACKER, GEORGE. "Smart-Mobbing the War." *New York Times Magazine* (March 9, 2003):46–49.

PAGER, DEVAH. "The Mark of a Criminal Record." *American Journal of Sociology.* Vol. 108, No. 5 (March 2003):937–75.

PAKULSKI, JAN. "Mass Social Movements and Social Class." *International Sociology.* Vol. 8, No. 2 (June 1993):131–58.

PALMORE, ERDMAN. "Predictors of Successful Aging." *Gerontologist.* Vol. 19, No. 5 (October 1979):427–31.

PARINI, JAY. "The Meaning of Emeritus." *Dartmouth Alumni Magazine* (July/August 2001):40–43.

PARIS, PETER J. "The Religious World of African Americans." In JACOB NEUSNER, ed., *World Religions in America: An Introduction.* Revised and expanded ed. Louisville, Ky.: Westminster John Knox Press, 2000:48–65.

PARK, ROBERT E. *Race and Culture.* Glencoe, Ill.: Free Press, 1950.

PARRILLO, VINCENT N. "Diversity in America: A Sociohistorical Analysis." *Sociological Forum.* Vol. 9, No. 4 (December 1994):42–45.

———. *Strangers to These Shores.* 7th ed. Boston: Allyn & Bacon, 2003a.

———. "Updating the Bogardus Social Distance Studies: A New National Survey." Revised version of a paper presented at the annual meeting of the American Sociological Association (August 17, 2002). Provided by the author, 2003b.

PARSONS, TALCOTT. "Age and Sex in the Social Structure of the United States." *American Sociological Review.* Vol. 7, No. 4 (August 1942):604–16.

———. *Essays in Sociological Theory.* New York: Free Press, 1954.

———. *The Social System.* New York: Free Press, 1964; orig. 1951.

———. *Societies: Evolutionary and Comparative Perspectives.* Englewood Cliffs, N.J.: Prentice Hall, 1966.

PARSONS, TALCOTT, and ROBERT F. BALES, eds. *Family, Socialization, and Interaction Process.* New York: Free Press, 1955.

PASSY, FLORENCE, and MARCO GIUGNI. "Social Networks and Individual Perceptions: Explaining Differential Participation in Social Movements." *Sociological Forum.* Vol. 16, No. 1 (March 2001):123–53.

PATTERSON, ELISSA F. "The Philosophy and Physics of Holistic Health Care: Spiritual Healing as a Workable Interpretation." *Journal of Advanced Nursing.* Vol. 27, No. 2 (February 1998):287–93.

PATTILLO-McCOY, MARY. "Church Culture as a Strategy of Action in the Black Community." *American Sociological Review.* Vol. 63, No. 6 (December 1998): 767–84.

PAUL, PAMELA. "News, Noticias, Nouvelles." *American Demographics.* Vol. 23, No. 11 (November, 2001):26–31.

PEAR, ROBERT, and ERIK ECKHOLM. "When Healers Are Entrepreneurs: A Debate over Costs and Ethics." *New York Times* (June 2, 1991):1, 17.

PEARSON, DAVID E. "Post-Mass Culture." *Society.* Vol. 30, No. 5 (July/August 1993):17–22.

———. "Community and Sociology." *Society.* Vol. 32, No. 5 (July/August 1995): 44–50.

PEASE, JOHN, and LEE MARTIN. "Want Ads and Jobs for the Poor: A Glaring Mismatch." *Sociological Forum.* Vol. 12, No. 4 (December 1997):545–64.

PEDERSON, DANIEL, VERN E. SMITH, and JERRY ADLER. "Sprawling, Sprawling . . ." *Newsweek* (July 19, 1999):23–27.

PERLMUTTER, PHILIP. "Minority Group Prejudice." *Society.* Vol. 39, No. 3 (March/April 2002):59–65.

PERRUCCI, ROBERT. "Inventing Social Justice: SSSP and the Twenty-First Century." *Social Problems.* Vol. 48, No. 2 (May 2001):159–67.

PESSEN, EDWARD. *Riches, Class, and Power: America before the Civil War.* New Brunswick, N.J.: Transaction, 1990.

*Peters Atlas of the World.* New York: Harper & Row, 1990.

PETERSEN, TROND, ISHAK SAPORTA, and MARC-DAVID L. SEIDEL. "Offering a Job: Meritocracy and Social Networks." *American Journal of Sociology.* Vol. 106, No. 3 (November 2000):763–816.

PETERSILIA, JOAN. "Probation in the United States: Practices and Challenges." *National Institute of Justice Journal.* No. 233 (September 1997):4.

PETERSON, SCOTT. "Women Live on Own Terms behind the Veil." *Christian Science Monitor* (July 31, 1996):1, 10.

PHILADELPHIA, DESA. "Rookie Teacher, Age 50." *Time* (April 9, 2001):66–68.

———. "Tastier, Plusher—and Fast." *Time* (September 30, 2002):57.

PHILLIPS, MELANIE. "What about the Overclass?" *Public Interest.* No. 145 (Fall 2001):38–43.

PICHARDO, NELSON A. "The Power Elite and Elite-Driven Countermovements: The Associated Farmers of California during the 1930s." *Sociological Forum.* Vol. 10, No. 1 (March 1995):21–49.

PINCHOT, GIFFORD, and ELIZABETH PINCHOT. *The End of Bureaucracy and the Rise of the Intelligent Organization.* San Francisco: Berrett-Koehler, 1993.

PINHEY, THOMAS K., DONALD H. RUBINSTEIN, and RICHARD S. COLFAX. "Overweight and Happiness: The Reflected Self-Appraisal Hypothesis Reconsidered." *Social Science Quarterly.* Vol. 78, No. 3 (September 1997): 747–55.

PINKER, STEVEN. *The Language Instinct.* New York: Morrow, 1994.

———. "Are Your Genes to Blame?" *Time* (January 20, 2003):98–100.

PIRANDELLO, LUIGI. "The Pleasure of Honesty" (1917). In *To Clothe the Naked and Two Other Plays*. New York: Dutton, 1962:143–98.

PITTS, LEONARD, JR. "When a Win Sparks a Riot." *Philadelphia Inquirer* (June 26, 2000):A11.

PIVEN, FRANCES FOX, and RICHARD A. CLOWARD. *Poor People's Movements: Why They Succeed, How They Fail*. New York: Pantheon Books, 1977.

PODOLNY, JOEL M., and JAMES N. BARON. "Resources and Relationships: Social Networks and Mobility in the Workplace." *American Sociological Review*. Vol. 62, No. 5 (October 1997):673–93.

POLENBERG, RICHARD. *One Nation Divisible: Class, Race, and Ethnicity in the United States since 1938*. New York: Pelican, 1980.

POLLARD, KEVIN. "Play Ball! Demographics and Major League Baseball." *Population Today*. Vol. 24, No. 4 (April 1996):3.

POLSBY, NELSON W. "Three Problems in the Analysis of Community Power." *American Sociological Review*. Vol. 24, No. 6 (December 1959):796–803.

POMER, MARSHALL I. "Labor Market Structure, Intragenerational Mobility, and Discrimination: Black Male Advancement out of Low-Paying Occupations, 1962–1973." *American Sociological Review*. Vol. 51, No. 5 (October 1986): 650–59.

POPENOE, DAVID. "Family Decline in the Swedish Welfare State." *Public Interest*. No. 102 (Winter 1991):65–77.

———. "American Family Decline, 1960–1990: A Review and Appraisal." *Journal of Marriage and the Family*. Vol. 55, No. 3 (August 1993a):527–55.

———. "Parental Androgyny." *Society*. Vol. 30, No. 6 (September/October 1993b):5–11.

———. "Scandinavian Welfare." *Society*. Vol. 31, No. 6 (September/October, 1994):78–81.

———. "Can the Nuclear Family Be Revived?" *Society*. Vol. 36, No. 5 (July/August 1999):28–30.

POPENOE, DAVID, and BARBARA DAFOE WHITEHEAD. *Should We Live Together? What Young Adults Need to Know about Cohabitation before Marriage*. New Brunswick, N.J.: National Marriage Project, 1999.

POPULATION ACTION INTERNATIONAL. *People in the Balance: Population and Resources at the Turn of the Millennium*. Washington, D.C.: Population Action International, 2000.

POPULATION REFERENCE BUREAU. *1999 World Population Data Sheet*. Washington, D.C.: Population Reference Bureau, 1999.

———. *2003 World Population Data Sheet*. Washington, D.C.: Population Reference Bureau, 2003.

———. *2005 World Population Data Sheet*. Washington, D.C.: Population Reference Bureau, 2005.

*Population Today*. "Majority of Children in Poverty Live with Parents Who Work." Vol. 23, No. 4 (April 1995):6.

PORTER, EDUARDO. "Even 126 Sizes Do Not Fit All." *Wall Street Journal* (March 2, 2001):B1.

———. "Old, in the Way, and Hard at Work." *New York Times* (August 29, 2004). [Online] Available April 15, 2005, at http://www.researchnavigator.com

PORTES, ALEJANDRO, and LEIF JENSEN. "The Enclave and the Entrants: Patterns of Ethnic Enterprise in Miami before and after Mariel." *American Sociological Review*. Vol. 54, No. 6 (December 1989):929–49.

POSTEL, SANDRA. "Facing Water Scarcity." In LESTER R. BROWN et al., eds., *State of the World, 1993: A Worldwatch Institute Report on Progress toward a Sustainable Society*. New York: Norton, 1993:22–41.

POWELL, CHRIS, and GEORGE E. C. PATON, eds. *Humor in Society: Resistance and Control*. New York: St. Martin's Press, 1988.

PRIMEGGIA, SALVATORE, and JOSEPH A. VARACALLI. "Southern Italian Comedy: Old to New World." In JOSEPH V. SCELSA, SALVATORE J. LA GUMINA, and LYDIO TOMASI, eds., *Italian Americans in Transition*. New York: American Italian Historical Association, 1990:241–52.

PUTKA, GARY. "SAT to Become a Better Gauge." *Wall Street Journal* (November 1, 1990):B1.

PYLE, RALPH E., and JEROME R. KOCH. "The Religious Affiliation of American Elites, 1930s to 1990s: A Note on the Pace of Disestablishment." *Sociological Focus*. Vol. 34, No. 2 (May 2001):125–37.

QUILLIAN, LINCOLN, and DEVAH PAGER. "Black Neighbors, Higher Crime? The Role of Racial Stereotypes in Evaluations of Neighborhood Crime." *American Journal of Sociology*. Vol. 107, No. 3 (November 2001):717–67.

QUINNEY, RICHARD. *Class, State and Crime: On the Theory and Practice of Criminal Justice*. New York: McKay, 1977.

RABKIN, JEREMY. "The Supreme Court in the Culture Wars." *Public Interest*. No. 125 (Fall 1996):3–26.

RANK, MARK R., and THOMAS A. HIRSCHL. "Rags or Riches? Estimating the Probabilities of Poverty and Affluence across the Adult American Life Span." *Social Science Quarterly*. Vol. 82, No. 4 (December 2001):651–69.

RAPHAEL, RAY. *The Men from the Boys: Rites of Passage in Male America*. Lincoln: University of Nebraska Press, 1988.

RATNESAR, ROMESH. "Not Gone, but Forgotten?" *Time* (February 8, 1998): 30–31.

RAYMOND, JOAN. "The Multicultural Report." *American Demographics*. Vol. 23, No. 11 (November 2001):S1–S6.

RECKLESS, WALTER C., and SIMON DINITZ. "Pioneering with Self-Concept as a Vulnerability Factor in Delinquency." *Journal of Criminal Law, Criminology, and Police Science*. Vol. 58, No. 4 (December 1967):515–23.

RECTOR, ROBERT. "America Has the World's Richest Poor People." *Wall Street Journal* (September 24, 1998):A18.

REMOFF, HEATHER TREXLER. *Sexual Choice: A Woman's Decision*. New York: Dutton/ Lewis, 1984.

RESKIN, BARBARA F., and DEBRA BRANCH McBRIER. "Why Not Ascription? Organizations' Employment of Male and Female Managers." *American Sociological Review*. Vol. 65, No. 2 (April 2000):210–33.

REVKIN, ANDREW C. "Can Global Warming Be Studied Too Much?" *New York Times* (December 3, 2002):D1, D4.

RHODES, STEVE. "The Luck of the Draw." *Newsweek* (April 26, 1999):41.

RIDDLE, JOHN M., J. WORTH ESTES, and JOSIAH C. RUSSELL. "Ever since Eve: Birth Control in the Ancient World." *Archaeology*. Vol. 47, No. 2 (March/April 1994):29–35.

RIDGEWAY, CECILIA L. *The Dynamics of Small Groups*. New York: St. Martin's Press, 1983.

RIESMAN, DAVID. *The Lonely Crowd: A Study of the Changing American Character*. New Haven, Conn.: Yale University Press, 1970; orig. 1950.

RIMER, SARA. "Blacks Carry Load of Care for Their Elderly." *New York Times* (March 15, 1998):1, 22.

RISMAN, BARBARA, and PEPPER SCHWARTZ. "After the Sexual Revolution: Gender Politics in Teen Dating." *Contexts*. Vol. 1, No. 1 (Spring 2002):16–24.

RITZER, GEORGE. *The McDonaldization of Society: An Investigation into the Changing Character of Contemporary Social Life*. Thousand Oaks, Calif.: Pine Forge Press, 1993.

———. *The McDonaldization of Society*. Rev. ed. Thousand Oaks, Calif.: Sage, 1996.

———. *The McDonaldization Thesis: Explorations and Extensions*. Thousand Oaks, Calif.: Sage, 1998.

———. "The Globalization of McDonaldization." *Spark* (February 2000): 8–9.

RITZER, GEORGE, and DAVID WALCZAK. *Working: Conflict and Change*. 4th ed. Englewood Cliffs, N.J.: Prentice Hall, 1990.

ROBERTS, J. DEOTIS. *Roots of a Black Future: Family and Church*. Philadelphia: Westminster Press, 1980.

ROBINSON, LINDA. "A Timeworn Terrorism List." *U.S. News & World Report* (May 20, 2002):18, 21.

ROBINSON, THOMAS N., et al. "Effects of Reducing Children's Television and Video Game Use on Aggressive Behavior." *Archives of Pediatrics and Adolescent Medicine*. Vol. 155, No. 1 (January 2001):17–23.

ROESCH, ROBERTA. "Violent Families." *Parents*. Vol. 59, No. 9 (September 1984): 74–76, 150–52.

ROETHLISBERGER, F. J., and WILLIAM J. DICKSON. *Management and the Worker*. Cambridge, Mass.: Harvard University Press, 1939.

ROGERS, RICHARD G., REBECCA ROSENBLATT, ROBERT A. HUMMER, and PATRICK M. KRUEGER. "Black-White Differentials in Adult Homicide Mortality in the United States." *Social Science Quarterly*. Vol. 82, No. 3 (September 2001): 435–52.

ROGERS-DILLON, ROBIN H. "What Do We Really Know about Welfare Reform?" *Society*. Vol. 38, No. 2 (January/February 2001):7–15.

ROMERO, FRANCINE SANDERS, and ADRIAN LISERIO. "Saving Open Spaces: Determinants of 1998 and 1999 'Antisprawl' Ballot Measures." *Social Science Quarterly*. Vol. 83, No. 1 (March 2002):341–52.

ROSE, FRED. "Toward a Class-Cultural Theory of Social Movements: Reinterpreting New Social Movements." *Sociological Forum*. Vol. 12, No. 3 (September 1997):461–94.

ROSE, JERRY D. *Outbreaks*. New York: Free Press, 1982.

ROSE, LOWELL C., and ALEC M. GALLUP. *The 37th Annual Phi Delta Kappa/Gallup Poll of the Public's Attitudes toward the Public Schools*. 2005. [Online] Available September 27, 2005, at http://www.pdkintl.org/kappan/k0509pol.pdf

ROSEN, ELLEN ISRAEL. *Bitter Choices: Blue-Collar Women in and out of Work.* Chicago: University of Chicago Press, 1987.

ROSENBAUM, DAVID E. "Americans Want a Right to Die. Or So They Think." *New York Times* (June 8, 1997):E3.

ROSENBAUM, MARC. "Americans' Views on Taxes." Report of an NPR/Kaiser Family Foundation/Kennedy School of Government poll. Lecture delivered at Kenyon College, Gambier, Ohio, April 23, 2003.

ROSENDAHL, MONA. *Inside the Revolution: Everyday Life in Socialist Cuba.* Ithaca, N.Y.: Cornell University Press, 1997.

ROSENFELD, RICHARD. "Crime Decline in Context." *Contexts.* Vol. 1, No. 1 (Spring 2002):20–34.

ROSENTHAL, ELIZABETH. "Canada's National Health Plan Gives Care to All, with Limits." *New York Times* (April 30, 1991):A1, A16.

ROSNOW, RALPH L., and GARY ALAN FINE. *Rumor and Gossip: The Social Psychology of Hearsay.* New York: Elsevier, 1976.

ROSS, JOHN. "To Die in the Street: Mexico City's Homeless Population Boom as Economic Crisis Shakes Social Protections." *SSSP Newsletter.* Vol. 27, No. 2 (Summer 1996):14–15.

ROSSI, ALICE S. "Gender and Parenthood." In ALICE S. ROSSI, ed., *Gender and the Life Course.* New York: Aldine, 1985:161–91.

ROSTOW, WALT W. *The Stages of Economic Growth: A Non-Communist Manifesto.* Cambridge: Cambridge University Press, 1960.

———. *The World Economy: History and Prospect.* Austin: University of Texas Press, 1978.

ROTHMAN, BARBARA KATZ. "Of Maps and Imaginations: Sociology Confronts the Genome." *Social Problems.* Vol. 42, No. 1 (February 1995):1–10.

ROTHMAN, STANLEY, and AMY E. BLACK. "Who Rules Now? American Elites in the 1990s." *Society.* Vol. 35, No. 6 (September/October 1998):17–20.

ROTHMAN, STANLEY, STEPHEN POWERS, and DAVID ROTHMAN. "Feminism in Films." *Society.* Vol. 30, No. 3 (March/April 1993):66–72.

ROUSSEAU, CARYN. "Unions Rally at Wal-Mart Stores." [Online] Available November 22, 2002, at http://news.yahoo.com

ROZELL, MARK J., CLYDE WILCOX, and JOHN C. GREEN. "Religious Constituencies and Support for the Christian Right in the 1990s." *Social Science Quarterly.* Vol. 79, No. 4 (December 1998):815–27.

RUBENSTEIN, ELI A. "The Not So Golden Years." *Newsweek* (October 7, 1991):13.

RUBIN, JOEL. "E-Mail Too Formal? Try a Text Message." Columbia News Service, March 7, 2003. [Online] Available April 25, 2005, at http://www.jrn.columbia.edu/studentwork/cns/2003-03-07/85.asp

RUBIN, LILLIAN BRESLOW. *Worlds of Pain: Life in the Working-Class Family.* New York: Basic Books, 1976.

RUDEL, THOMAS K., and JUDITH M. GERSON. "Postmodernism, Institutional Change, and Academic Workers: A Sociology of Knowledge." *Social Science Quarterly.* Vol. 80, No. 2 (June 1999):213–28.

RUDOLPH, ELLEN. "Women's Talk: Japanese Women." *New York Times Magazine* (September 1, 1991).

RULE, JAMES, and PETER BRANTLEY. "Computerized Surveillance in the Workplace: Forms and Delusions." *Sociological Forum.* Vol. 7, No. 3 (September 1992):405–23.

RUSSELL, CHERYL. "Are We in the Dumps?" *American Demographics.* Vol. 17, No. 1 (January 1995a):6.

———. "True Crime." *American Demographics.* Vol. 17, No. 8 (August 1995b):22–31.

RUSSELL, CHERYL, and MARCIA MOGELONSKY. "Riding High on the Market." *American Demographics.* Vol. 22, No. 4 (April 2000):44–54.

RUTHERFORD, MEGAN. "Women Run the World." *Time* (June 28, 1999):72.

RYAN, PATRICK J. "The Roots of Muslim Anger." *America* (November 26, 2001):8–16.

RYMER, RUSS. *Genie.* New York: HarperPerennial, 1994.

SACHS, JEFFREY. "The Real Causes of Famine." *Time* (October 26, 1998):69.

SAINT JEAN, YANICK, and JOE R. FEAGIN. *Double Burden: Black Women and Everyday Racism.* Armonk, N.Y.: Sharpe, 1998.

SALA-I-MARTIN, XAVIER. "The World Distribution of Income." Working Paper No. 8933. Cambridge, Mass.: National Bureau of Economic Research, 2002.

SALE, KIRKPATRICK. *The Conquest of Paradise: Christopher Columbus and the Columbian Legacy.* New York: Knopf, 1990.

SAMPSON, ANTHONY. *The Changing Anatomy of Britain.* New York: Random House, 1982.

SAMUELSON, ROBERT J. "The Rich and Everyone Else." *Newsweek* (January 27, 2003):57.

SANSOM, WILLIAM. *A Contest of Ladies.* London: Hogarth, 1956.

SAPIR, EDWARD. "The Status of Linguistics as a Science." *Language.* Vol. 5, No. 4 (1929):207–14.

———. *Selected Writings of Edward Sapir in Language, Culture, and Personality.* DAVID G. MANDELBAUM, ed. Berkeley: University of California Press, 1949.

SAPORITO, BILL. "Can Wal-Mart Get Any Bigger?" *Time* (January 13, 2003): 38–43.

SAVISHINSKY, JOEL S. *Breaking the Watch: The Meanings of Retirement in America.* Ithaca, N.Y.: Cornell University Press, 2000.

SAX, LINDA J., et al. *The American Freshman: National Norms for Fall 2003.* Los Angeles: UCLA Higher Education Research Institute, 2003.

———. *The American Freshman: National Norms for Fall 2004.* Los Angeles: UCLA Higher Education Research Institute, 2004.

SCANLON, STEPHAN J. "Food Availability and Access in Less Industrialized Societies: A Test and Interpretation of Neo-Malthusian and Technoecological Theories." *Sociological Forum.* Vol. 16, No. 2 (June 2001):231–62.

SCHAFFER, MICHAEL. "American Dreamers." *U.S. News & World Report* (August 26, 2002):12–16.

SCHAUB, DIANA. "From Boys to Men." *Public Interest.* No. 127 (Spring 1997): 108–14.

SCHEFF, THOMAS J. *Being Mentally Ill: A Sociological Theory.* 2nd ed. New York: Aldine, 1984.

SCHLESINGER, ARTHUR. "The City in American Civilization." In A. B. CALLOW JR., ed., *American Urban History.* New York: Oxford University Press, 1969:25–41.

SCHLESINGER, ARTHUR, JR. "The Cult of Ethnicity: Good and Bad." *Time* (July 8, 1991):21.

SCHLESINGER, JACOB M. "Finally, U.S. Median Income Approaches Old Heights." *Wall Street Journal* (September 25, 1998):B1.

SCHLOSSER, ERIC. *Fast-Food Nation: The Dark Side of the All-American Meal.* New York: Perennial, 2002.

SCHMIDT, ROGER. *Exploring Religion.* Belmont, Calif.: Wadsworth, 1980.

SCHMITT, ERIC. "Whites in Minority in Largest Cities, the Census Shows." *New York Times* (April 30, 2001):A1, A12.

SCHNAIBERG, ALLAN, and KENNETH ALAN GOULD. *Environment and Society: The Enduring Conflict.* New York: St. Martin's Press, 1994.

SCHNEIDER, MARK, MELISSA MARSCHALL, PAUL TESKE, and CHRISTINE ROCH. "School Choice and Culture Wars in the Classroom: What Different Parents Seek from Education." *Social Science Quarterly.* Vol. 79, No. 3 (September 1998):489–501.

SCHOFER, EVAN, and MARION FOURCADE-GOURINCHAS. "The Structural Contexts of Civil Engagement: Voluntary Association Membership in Comparative Perspective." *American Sociological Review.* Vol. 66, No. 6 (December 2001): 806–28.

SCHULTZ, T. PAUL. "Inequality in the Distribution of Personal Income in the World: How It Is Changing and Why." *Journal of Population Economics.* Vol. 11, No. 2 (1998):307–44.

SCHUMAN, HOWARD, and MARIA KRYSAN. "A Historical Note on Whites' Beliefs about Racial Inequality." *American Sociological Review.* Vol. 64, No. 6 (December 1999):847–55.

SCHUR, LISA A., and DOUGLAS L. KRUSE. "What Determines Voter Turnout? Lessons from Citizens with Disabilities." *Social Science Quarterly.* Vol. 81, No. 2 (June 2000):571–87.

SCHWARTZ, BARRY. "Memory as a Cultural System: Abraham Lincoln in World War II." *American Sociological Review.* Vol. 61, No. 5 (October 1996): 908–27.

SCHWARTZ, FELICE N. "Management, Women, and the New Facts of Life." *Harvard Business Review.* Vol. 89, No. 1 (January/February 1989):65–76.

SCOMMEGNA, PAOLA. "Increased Cohabitation Changing Children's Family Settings." *Population Today.* Vol. 30, No. 7 (July 2002):3, 6.

SEAGER, JONI. *The Penguin Atlas of Women in the World.* 3rd ed. New York: Penguin Putnam, 2003.

SEARS, DAVID O., and JOHN B. MCCONAHAY. *The Politics of Violence: The New Urban Blacks and the Watts Riot.* Boston: Houghton Mifflin, 1973.

SEGAL, MADY WECHSLER, and AMANDA FAITH HANSEN. "Value Rationales in Policy Debates on Women in the Military: A Content Analysis of Congressional Testimony, 1941–1985." *Social Science Quarterly.* Vol. 73, No. 2 (June 1992): 296–309.

SEIDMAN, STEVEN, ed. *Queer Theory/Sociology.* Cambridge, Mass.: Blackwell, 1996.

SEKULIC, DUSKO, GARTH MASSEY, and RANDY HODSON. "Who Were the Yugoslavs? Failed Sources of Common Identity in the Former Yugoslavia." *American Sociological Review.* Vol. 59, No. 1 (February 1994):83–97.

SENNETT, RICHARD. *The Corrosion of Character: The Personal Consequences of Work in the New Capitalism.* New York: Norton, 1998.

SENNETT, RICHARD, and JONATHAN COBB. *The Hidden Injuries of Class.* New York: Vintage Books, 1973.

SENTENCING PROJECT. "Facts about Prisons and Prisoners." May 2005. [Online] Available June 5, 2005, at http://www.sentencingproject.org/pdfs/1035.pdf

SHAPIRO, JOSEPH P. "Back to Work, on Mission." *U.S. News & World Report* (June 4, 2001).

SHARPE, ANITA. "The Rich Aren't So Different After All." *Wall Street Journal* (November 12, 1996):B1, B10.

SHAWCROSS, WILLIAM. *Sideshow: Kissinger, Nixon and the Destruction of Cambodia.* New York: Pocket Books, 1979.

SHEA, RACHEL HARTIGAN. "The New Insecurity." *U.S. News & World Report* (March 25, 2002):40.

SHEEHAN, TOM. "Senior Esteem as a Factor in Socioeconomic Complexity." *Gerontologist.* Vol. 16, No. 5 (October 1976):433–40.

SHELDON, WILLIAM H., EMIL M. HARTL, and EUGENE MCDERMOTT. *Varieties of Delinquent Youth.* New York: Harper Bros., 1949.

SHELER, JEFFREY L. "Faith in America." *U.S. News & World Report* (May 6, 2002): 40–44.

SHERKAT, DARREN E., and CHRISTOPHER G. ELLISON. "Recent Developments and Current Controversies in the Sociology of Religion." *Annual Review of Sociology.* Vol. 25 (1999):363–94.

SHERMAN, LAWRENCE W., and DOUGLAS A. SMITH. "Crime, Punishment, and Stake in Conformity: Legal and Informal Control of Domestic Violence." *American Sociological Review.* Vol. 57, No. 5 (October 1992):680–90.

SHEVKY, ESHREF, and WENDELL BELL. *Social Area Analysis.* Stanford, Calif.: Stanford University Press, 1955.

SHIPLEY, JOSEPH T. *Dictionary of Word Origins.* Totowa, N.J.: Roman & Allanheld, 1985.

SHIVELY, JOELLEN. "Cowboys and Indians: Perceptions of Western Films among American Indians and Anglos." *American Sociological Review.* Vol. 57, No. 6 (December 1992):725–34.

SHUPE, ANSON. *In the Name of All That's Holy: A Theory of Clergy Malfeasance.* Westport, Conn.: Praeger, 1995.

SHUPE, ANSON, WILLIAM A. STACEY, and LONNIE R. HAZLEWOOD. *Violent Men, Violent Couples: The Dynamics of Domestic Violence.* Lexington, Mass.: Lexington Books, 1987.

SIMMEL, GEORG. *The Sociology of Georg Simmel.* KURT WOLFF, ed. New York: Free Press, 1950:118–69; orig. 1902.

———. "Fashion." In DONALD N. LEVINE, ed., *Georg Simmel: On Individuality and Social Forms.* Chicago: University of Chicago Press, 1971; orig. 1904.

SIMON, JULIAN. *The Ultimate Resource.* Princeton, N.J.: Princeton University Press, 1981.

———. "More People, Greater Wealth, More Resources, Healthier Environment." In THEODORE D. GOLDFARB, ed., *Taking Sides: Clashing Views on Controversial Environmental Issues.* 6th ed. Guilford, Conn.: Dushkin, 1995.

SIMON, ROGER, and ANGIE CANNON. "An Amazing Journey." *U.S. News & World Report* (August 6, 2001):10–19.

SIMONS, MARLISE. "The Price of Modernization: The Case of Brazil's Kaiapo Indians." In JOHN J. MACIONIS and NIJOLE V. BENOKRAITIS, eds., *Seeing Ourselves: Classic, Contemporary, and Cross-Cultural Readings in Sociology.* 7th ed. Upper Saddle River, N.J.: Prentice Hall, 2007.

SIMPSON, GEORGE EATON, and J. MILTON YINGER. *Racial and Cultural Minorities: An Analysis of Prejudice and Discrimination.* 4th ed. New York: Harper & Row, 1972.

SIPES, RICHARD G. "War, Sports, and Aggression: An Empirical Test of Two Rival Theories." *American Anthropologist.* Vol. 75, No. 1 (January 1973):64–86.

SIVARD, RUTH LEGER. *World Military and Social Expenditures, 1987–88.* 12th ed. Washington, D.C.: World Priorities, 1988.

———. *World Military and Social Expenditures, 1992–93.* 17th ed. Washington, D.C.: World Priorities, 1993.

SIZER, THEODORE R. *Horace's Compromise: The Dilemma of the American High School.* Boston: Houghton Mifflin, 1984.

SKOCPOL, THEDA. *States and Social Revolutions: A Comparative Analysis of France, Russia, and China.* Cambridge: Cambridge University Press, 1979.

SMAIL, J. KENNETH. "Let's *Reduce* Global Population!" In JOHN J. MACIONIS and NIJOLE V. BENOKRAITIS, eds., *Seeing Ourselves: Classic, Contemporary, and Cross-Cultural Readings in Sociology.* 7th ed. Upper Saddle River, N.J.: Prentice Hall, 2007.

SMART, TIM. "Not Acting Their Age." *U.S. News & World Report* (June 4, 2001): 54–60.

SMELSER, NEIL J. *Theory of Collective Behavior.* New York: Free Press, 1962.

SMITH, ADAM. *An Inquiry into the Nature and Causes of the Wealth of Nations.* New York: Modern Library, 1937; orig. 1776.

SMITH, CRAIG S. "Authorities Took Victim's Organs, His Brother Says." *Columbus* (Ohio) *Dispatch* (March 11, 2001):A3.

SMITH, DOUGLAS A. "Police Response to Interpersonal Violence: Defining the Parameters of Legal Control." *Social Forces.* Vol. 65, No. 3 (March 1987):767–82.

SMITH, DOUGLAS A., and PATRICK R. GARTIN. "Specifying Specific Deterrence: The Influence of Arrest on Future Criminal Activity." *American Sociological Review.* Vol. 54, No. 1 (February 1989):94–105.

SMITH, DOUGLAS A., and CHRISTY A. VISHER. "Street-Level Justice: Situational Determinants of Police Arrest Decisions." *Social Problems.* Vol. 29, No. 2 (December 1981):167–77.

SMITH, RYAN A. "Race, Gender, and Authority in the Workplace: Theory and Research." *Annual Review of Sociology.* Vol. 28 (2002):509–42.

SMITH, TOM W. "Anti-Semitism Decreases but Persists." *Society.* Vol. 33, No. 3 (March/April 1996):2.

———. "Are We Grown Up Yet? U.S. Study Says Not 'til 26." [Online] Available May 23, 2003, at http://news.yahoo.com

SMITH-LOVIN, LYNN, and CHARLES BRODY. "Interruptions in Group Discussions: The Effects of Gender and Group Composition." *American Journal of Sociology.* Vol. 54, No. 3 (June 1989):424–35.

SMOLOWE, JILL. "When Violence Hits Home." *Time* (July 4, 1994):18–25.

SNELL, MARILYN BERLIN. "The Purge of Nurture." *New Perspectives Quarterly.* Vol. 7, No. 1 (Winter 1990):1–2.

SOBEL, RACHEL K. "Herpes Tests Give Answers You Might Need to Know." *U.S. News & World Report* (June 18, 2001):53.

*Society.* "Female Opinion and Defense since September 11th." Vol. 39, No. 3 (March/April 2002):2.

SOUTH, SCOTT J., and KIM L. LLOYD. "Spousal Alternatives and Marital Dissolution." *American Sociological Review.* Vol. 60, No. 1 (February 1995):21–35.

SOUTH, SCOTT J., and STEVEN F. MESSNER. "Structural Determinants of Intergroup Association: Interracial Marriage and Crime." *American Journal of Sociology.* Vol. 91, No. 6 (May 1986):1409–30.

SOWELL, THOMAS. *Ethnic America.* New York: Basic Books, 1981.

———. *Compassion versus Guilt, and Other Essays.* New York: Morrow, 1987.

———. *Race and Culture.* New York: Basic Books, 1994.

———. "Ethnicity and IQ." In STEVEN FRASER, ed., *The Bell Curve Wars: Race, Intelligence, and the Future of America.* New York: Basic Books, 1995: 70–79.

SPECTER, MICHAEL. "Plunging Life Expectancy Puzzles Russia." *New York Times* (August 2, 1995):A1, A2.

———. "Yogurt? Caucasus Centenarians 'Never Eat It.'" *New York Times* (March 14, 1998):A1, A4.

SPEIER, HANS. "Wit and Politics: An Essay on Laughter and Power." ROBERT JACKALL, ed. and trans. *American Journal of Sociology.* Vol. 103, No. 5 (March 1998):1352–1401.

SPITZER, STEVEN. "Toward a Marxian Theory of Deviance." In DELOS H. KELLY, ed., *Criminal Behavior: Readings in Criminology.* New York: St. Martin's Press, 1980:175–91.

STACEY, JUDITH. *Patriarchy and Socialist Revolution in China.* Berkeley: University of California Press, 1983.

———. *Brave New Families: Stories of Domestic Upheaval in Late Twentieth-Century America.* New York: Basic Books, 1990.

———. "Good Riddance to 'The Family': A Response to David Popenoe." *Journal of Marriage and the Family.* Vol. 55, No. 3 (August 1993):545–47.

STACK, CAROL B. *All Our Kin: Strategies for Survival in a Black Community.* New York: Harper & Row, 1975.

STACK, STEVEN. "Occupation and Suicide." *Social Science Quarterly.* Vol. 82, No. 2 (June 2001):384–96.

STACK, STEVEN, IRA WASSERMAN, and ROGER KERN. "Adult Social Bonds and the Use of Internet Pornography." *Social Science Quarterly.* Vol. 85, No. 1 (March 2004):75–88.

STAHURA, JOHN M. "Suburban Development, Black Suburbanization, and the Black Civil Rights Movement since World War II." *American Sociological Review.* Vol. 51, No. 1 (February 1986):131–44.

STAPINSKI, HELENE. "Let's Talk Dirty." *American Demographics.* Vol. 20, No. 11 (November 1998):50–56.

STARK, RODNEY. *Sociology.* Belmont, Calif.: Wadsworth, 1985.

STARK, RODNEY, and WILLIAM SIMS BAINBRIDGE. "Of Churches, Sects, and Cults: Preliminary Concepts for a Theory of Religious Movements." *Journal for the Scientific Study of Religion.* Vol. 18, No. 2 (June 1979):117–31.

———. "Secularization and Cult Formation in the Jazz Age." *Journal for the Scientific Study of Religion.* Vol. 20, No. 4 (December 1981):360–73.

STARK, RODNEY, and ROGER FINKE. *Acts of Faith: Explaining the Human Side of Religion.* Berkeley: University of California Press, 2000.

STARR, PAUL. *The Social Transformation of American Medicine.* New York: Basic Books, 1982.

STEELE, RANDY. "Awful but Lawful." *Boating* (June 2000):36.

STEELE, SHELBY. *The Content of Our Character: A New Vision of Race in America.* New York: St. Martin's Press, 1990.

STEINBERG, LAURENCE. "Failure outside the Classroom." *Wall Street Journal* (July 11, 1996):A14.

STEPHENS, JOHN D. *The Transition from Capitalism to Socialism.* Urbana: University of Illinois Press, 1986.

STERKE, CLAIRE E. *Tricking and Tripping: Prostitution in the Era of AIDS.* Putnam Valley, N.Y.: Social Change Press, 2000.

STEVENS, GILLIAN, and GRAY SWICEGOOD. "The Linguistic Context of Ethnic Endogamy." *American Sociological Review.* Vol. 52, No. 1 (February 1987):73–82.

STIER, HAYA. "Continuity and Change in Women's Occupations following First Childbirth." *Social Science Quarterly.* Vol. 77, No. 1 (March 1996):60–75.

STOFFERAHN, CURTIS W. "Underemployment: Social Fact or Socially Constructed Reality?" *Rural Sociology.* Vol. 65, No. 2 (June 2000):311–30.

STONE, LAWRENCE. *The Family, Sex, and Marriage in England, 1500–1800.* New York: Harper & Row, 1977.

STONE, PAMELA. "Ghettoized and Marginalized: The Coverage of Racial and Ethnic Groups in Introductory Sociology Texts." *Teaching Sociology.* Vol. 24, No. 4 (October 1996):356–63.

STORMS, MICHAEL D. "Theories of Sexual Orientation." *Journal of Personality and Social Psychology.* Vol. 38, No. 5 (May 1980):783–92.

STOUFFER, SAMUEL A., et al. *The American Soldier: Adjustment during Army Life.* Princeton, N.J.: Princeton University Press, 1949.

STOUT, DAVID. "Supreme Court Splits on Diversity Efforts at University of Michigan." [Online] Available June 23, 2003, at http://news.yahoo.com.

STRATTON, LESLIE S. "Why Does More Housework Lower Women's Wages? Testing Hypotheses Involving Job Effort and Hours Flexibility." *Social Sciences Quarterly.* Vol. 82, No. 1 (March 2001):67–76.

STREIB, GORDON F. "Are the Aged a Minority Group?" In BERNICE L. NEUGARTEN, ed., *Middle Age and Aging: A Reader in Social Psychology.* Chicago: University of Chicago Press, 1968:35–46.

STROSS, RANDALL E. "The McPeace Dividend." *U.S. News & World Report* (April 1, 2002):36.

SULLIVAN, ANDREW. Lecture delivered at Kenyon College, Gambier, Ohio, April 4, 2002.

SULLIVAN, BARBARA. "McDonald's Sees India as Golden Opportunity." *Chicago Tribune* (April 5, 1995):B1.

SUMNER, WILLIAM GRAHAM. *Folkways.* New York: Dover, 1959; orig. 1906.

SUN, LENA H. "WWII's Forgotten Internees Await Apology." *Washington Post* (March 9, 1998):A1, A5, A6.

SUTHERLAND, EDWIN H. "White Collar Criminality." *American Sociological Review.* Vol. 5, No. 1 (February 1940):1–12.

SWARTZ, STEVE. "Why Michael Milken Stands to Qualify for Guinness Book." *Wall Street Journal* (March 31, 1989):1, 4.

SZASZ, THOMAS S. "Idleness and Lawlessness in the Therapeutic State." *Society.* Vol. 32, No. 4 (May/June 1995):30–35.

———. "Cleansing the Modern Heart." *Society.* Vol. 40, No. 4 (May/June 2003):52–59.

———. "Protecting Patients against Psychiatric Intervention." *Society.* Vol. 41, No. 3 (March/April 2004):7–10.

TAJFEL, HENRI. "Social Psychology of Intergroup Relations." *Annual Review of Psychology.* Palo Alto, Calif.: Annual Reviews, 1982:1–39.

TAKAKI, RONALD. *Strangers from a Different Shore.* Boston: Back Bay Books, 1998.

TALLICHET, SUZANNE E. "Barriers to Women's Advancement in Underground Coal Mining." *Rural Sociology.* Vol. 65, No. 2 (June 2000):234–52.

TANNEN, DEBORAH. *You Just Don't Understand: Women and Men in Conversation.* New York: Morrow, 1990.

———. *Talking from 9 to 5: How Women's and Men's Conversational Styles Affect Who Gets Heard, Who Gets Credit, and What Gets Done at Work.* New York: Morrow, 1994.

TAX FOUNDATION. *America Celebrates Tax Freedom Day.* Special report. No. 134 (April 2005). [Online] Available October 19, 2005, at http://www.taxfoundation.org/publications/showtype/27.html

TAVRIS, CAROL, and CAROL WADE. *Psychology in Perspective.* 3rd ed. Upper Saddle River, N.J.: Prentice Hall, 2001.

TAYLOR, FREDERICK WINSLOW. *The Principles of Scientific Management.* New York: Harper Bros., 1911.

TERKEL, STUDS. *Working.* New York: Pantheon Books, 1974.

"Terrorist Attacks Spur Unseen Human Toll." *Popline* (December 2001):1–2.

TERRY, DON. "In Crackdown on Bias, a New Tool." *New York Times* (June 12, 1993):8.

TEWKSBURY, RICHARD, and PATRICIA GAGNÉ. "Transgenderists: Products of Non-normative Intersections of Sex, Gender, and Sexuality." *Journal of Men's Studies.* Vol. 5, No. 2 (November 1996):105–29.

THERNSTROM, ABIGAIL, and STEPHAN THERNSTROM. "American Apartheid? Don't Believe It." *Wall Street Journal* (March 2, 1998):A18.

THOMAS, EDWARD J. *The Life of Buddha as Legend and History.* London: Routledge & Kegan Paul, 1975.

THOMAS, PAULETTE. "Success at a Huge Personal Cost." *Wall Street Journal* (July 26, 1995):B1, B6.

THOMAS, PIRI. *Down These Mean Streets.* New York: Signet, 1967.

THOMAS, W. I. "The Relation of Research to the Social Process." In MORRIS JANOWITZ, ed., *W. I. Thomas on Social Organization and Social Personality.* Chicago: University of Chicago Press, 1966:289–305; orig. 1931.

THOMMA, STEVEN. "Christian Coalition Demands Action from GOP." *Philadelphia Inquirer* (September 14, 1997):A2.

THOMPSON, DICK. "Gene Maverick." *Time* (January 11, 1999):54–55.

THOMPSON, MARK. "Fatal Neglect." *Time* (October 27, 1997):34–38.

———. "Shining a Light on Abuse." *Time* (August 3, 1998):42–43.

THOMPSON, MARK, and DOUGLAS WALLER. "Shield of Dreams." *Time* (May 8, 2001):45–47.

THORLINDSSON, THOROLFUR, and THORODDUR BJARNASON. "Modeling Durkheim on the Micro Level: A Study of Youth Suicidality." *American Sociological Review.* Vol. 63, No. 1 (February 1998):94–110.

THORNBERRY, TERRANCE, and MARGARET FARNSWORTH. "Social Correlates of Criminal Involvement: Further Evidence on the Relationship between Social Status and Criminal Behavior." *American Sociological Review.* Vol. 47, No. 4 (August 1982):505–18.

THORNE, BARRIE, CHERIS KRAMARAE, and NANCY HENLEY, eds. *Language, Gender, and Society.* Rowley, Mass.: Newbury House, 1983.

TILLY, CHARLES. *From Mobilization to Revolution.* Reading, Mass.: Addison-Wesley, 1978.

———. "Does Modernization Breed Revolution?" In JACK A. GOLDSTONE, ed., *Revolutions: Theoretical, Comparative, and Historical Studies.* New York: Harcourt Brace Jovanovich, 1986:47–57.

TIRYAKIAN, EDWARD A. "Revisiting Sociology's First Classic: The Division of Labor in Society and Its Actuality." *Sociological Forum.* Vol. 9, No. 1 (March 1994):3–16.

TITTLE, CHARLES R., WAYNE J. VILLEMEZ, and DOUGLAS A. SMITH. "The Myth of Social Class and Criminality: An Empirical Assessment of the Empirical Evidence." *American Sociological Review.* Vol. 43, No. 5 (October 1978):643–56.

TOCQUEVILLE, ALEXIS DE. *The Old Regime and the French Revolution.* STUART GILBERT, trans. Garden City, N.Y.: Anchor/Doubleday, 1955; orig. 1856.

TOLSON, JAY. "The Trouble with Elites." *Wilson Quarterly.* Vol. 19, No. 1 (Winter 1995):6–8.

TÖNNIES, FERDINAND. *Community and Society (Gemeinschaft und Gesellschaft).* New York: Harper & Row, 1963; orig. 1887.

TOOSSI, MITRA. "Labor Force Projections to 2012: The Graying of the U.S. Workforce." *Monthly Labor Review.* Vol. 127, No. 2 (February 2004):37–57. [Online] Available July 30, 2004, at http://www.bls.gov/opub/mlr/2004/02/art3full.pdf

TOPPO, GREG, and ANTHONY DE BARROS. "Reality Weighs Down Dreams of College." *USA Today* (February 2, 2005):A1.

TORRES, LISA, and MATT L. HUFFMAN. "Social Networks and Job Search Outcomes among Male and Female Professional, Technical, and Managerial Workers." *Sociological Focus.* Vol. 35, No. 1 (February 2002):25–42.

TREAS, JUDITH. "Older Americans in the 1990s and Beyond." *Population Bulletin.* Vol. 50, No. 2 (May 1995):2–46.

TRENT, KATHERINE. "Family Context and Adolescents' Expectations about Marriage, Fertility, and Nonmarital Childbearing." *Social Science Quarterly.* Vol. 75, No. 2 (June 1994):319–39.

TROELTSCH, ERNST. *The Social Teaching of the Christian Churches.* New York: Macmillan, 1931.

TUCKER, JAMES. "New Age Religion and the Cult of the Self." *Society.* Vol. 39, No. 2 (February 2002):46–51.

TUMIN, MELVIN M. "Some Principles of Stratification: A Critical Analysis." *American Sociological Review.* Vol. 18, No. 4 (August 1953):387–94.

———. *Social Stratification: The Forms and Functions of Inequality.* 2nd ed. Englewood Cliffs, N.J.: Prentice Hall, 1985.

TURNER, JONATHAN. *On the Origins of Human Emotions: A Sociological Inquiry into the Evolution of Human Emotions.* Stanford, Calif.: Stanford University Press, 2000.

TURNER, RALPH H., and LEWIS M. KILLIAN. *Collective Behavior.* 3rd ed. Englewood Cliffs, N.J.: Prentice Hall, 1987

———. *Collective Behavior.* 4th ed. Englewood Cliffs, N.J.: Prentice Hall, 1993.

TYLER, S. LYMAN. *A History of Indian Policy.* Washington, D.C.: U.S. Department of the Interior, Bureau of Indian Affairs, 1973.

UDRY, J. RICHARD. "Biological Limitations of Gender Construction." *American Sociological Review.* Vol. 65, No. 3 (June 2000):443–57.

UGGEN, CHRISTOPHER. "Ex-Offenders and the Conformist Alternative: A Job-Quality Model of Work and Crime." *Social Problems.* Vol. 46, No. 1 (February 1999):127–51.

UGGEN, CHRISTOPHER, and JEFF MANZA. "Democratic Contraction? Political Consequences of Felon Disenfranchisement in the United States." *American Sociological Review.* Vol. 67, No. 6 (December 2002):777–803.

UNESCO. Data reported in "Tower of Babel Is Tumbling Down—Slowly." *U.S. News & World Report* (July 2, 2001):9.

UNITED NATIONS. *The World's Women, 2000: Trends and Statistics.* New York: United Nations, 2000.

UNITED NATIONS. "Executive Summary." *World Population Ageing 1950–2050.* New York: United Nations, 2002. [Online] Available October 20, 2005, at http://www.un.org/esa/population/publications/worldageing19502050/index.htm

UNITED NATIONS. *AIDS Epidemic Update.* December 2004. [Online] Available September 28, 2005, at http://www.unaids.org/

UNITED NATIONS DEVELOPMENT PROGRAMME. *Human Development Report 1990.* New York: Oxford University Press, 1990.

———. *Human Development Report 1995.* New York: Oxford University Press, 1995.

———. *Human Development Report 1996.* New York: Oxford University Press, 1996.

———. *Human Development Report 2000.* New York: Oxford University Press, 2000.

———. *Human Development Report 2001.* New York: Oxford University Press, 2001.

———. *Human Development Report 2004.* New York: Oxford University Press, 2004.

———. *Human Development Report 2005.* New York: Oxford University Press, 2005.

UPTHEGROVE, TAYNA R., VINCENT J. ROSCIGNO, and CAMILLE ZUBRINSKY CHARLES. "Big Money Collegiate Sports: Racial Concentration, Contradictory Pressures, and Academic Performance." *Social Science Quarterly.* Vol. 80, No. 4 (December 1999):718–37.

URBAN INSTITUTE. "Nearly 3 out of 4 Young Children with Employed Mothers Are Regularly in Child Care." *Fast Facts on Welfare Policy.* April 28, 2004. [Online] Available July 18, 2005, at http://www.urban.org/UploadedPDF/900706.pdf

U.S. BUREAU OF ECONOMIC ANALYSIS. "Foreign Direct Investment in the United States: Selected Items by Detailed Country." [Online] Available October 18, 2005, at http://www.bea.doc.gov/bea/di/fdilongcty.htm

U.S. BUREAU OF JUSTICE STATISTICS. *Capital Punishment, 2003.* Washington, D.C.: U.S. Government Printing Office, 2004. [Online] Available June 5, 2005, at http://www.ojp.usdoj.gov/bjs/pub/pdf/cp03.pdf

———. *Criminal Victimization, 2003.* Washington, D.C.: U.S. Government Printing Office, 2004. [Online] Available October 14, 2005, at http://www.ojp.usdoj.gov/bjs/pub/pdf/cv03.pdf

———. *Criminal Victimization, 2004.* Washington, D.C.: U.S. Government Printing Office, 2005. [Online] Available October 13, 2005, at http://www.ojp.usdoj.gov/bjs/pub/pdf/cv04.pdf

———. "Family Violence Statistics: Including Statistics on Strangers and Acquaintances." Washington, D.C.: U.S. Government Printing Office, 2005.

———. *Prison and Jail Inmates at Midyear 2004.* April 2005. [Online] Available October 14, 2005, at http://www.ojp.usdoj.gov/bjs/pub/pdf/pjim04.pdf

———. *Sourcebook of Criminal Justice Statistics Online.* [Online] Available September 13, 2005, at http://www.albany.edu/sourcebook/

U.S. CENSUS BUREAU. *65+ in the United States.* Washington, D.C.: U.S. Government Printing Office, 1996.

———. "Census Bureau Counts 170,000 at Homeless Shelters." News release, October 31, 2000.

———. *Educational Attainment in the United States: March 2000* (Update). Current Population Reports, P20–536. Washington, D.C.: U.S. Government Printing Office, 2000.

———. *America's Families and Living Arrangements: 2000.* Current Population Reports, P20-537. Washington, D.C.: U.S. Government Printing Office, 2001. [Online] Available October 28, 2005, at http://www.census.gov/population/www/socdemo/hh-fam.htm/

———. *The Black Population: 2000.* Census 2000 Brief, C2KBR/01–5. Washington, D.C.: U.S. Government Printing Office, 2001. [Online] Available October 24, 2002, at http://www.census.gov/population/www/cen2000/briefs.html

———. *The Hispanic Population: 2000.* Census 2000 Brief, C2KBR/01–3. Washington, D.C.: U.S. Government Printing Office, 2001. [Online] Available October 24, 2002, at http://www.census.gov/population/www/cen2000/briefs.html

———. *Mapping Census 2000: The Geography of U.S. Diversity.* Census Special Reports, Series CENSR/01–1. Washington, D.C.: U.S. Government Printing Office, 2001.

———. *Money Income in the United States: 2000.* Current Population Reports, P60–213. Washington, D.C.: U.S. Government Printing Office, 2001.

———. *The Native Hawaiian and Other Pacific Islander Population: 2000.* Census 2000 Brief, C2KBR/01–14. Washington, D.C.: U.S. Government Printing Office, 2001. [Online] Available October 24, 2002, at http://www.census.gov/population/www/cen2000/briefs.html

———. *Overview of Race and Hispanic Origin: 2000.* Census 2000 Brief, C2KBR/01–1. Washington, D.C.: U.S. Government Printing Office, 2001. [Online] Available October 24, 2002, at http://www.census.gov/population/www/cen2000/briefs.html

———. *Population Change and Distribution: 1990 to 2000.* Census 2000 Brief, C2KBR/01–2. [Online] Available April 2001 at http://www.census.gov/population/www/cen2000/briefs.html

———. *Poverty in the United States: 2000.* Current Population Reports, P60-214. Washington, D.C.: U.S. Government Printing Office, 2001.

———. *The 65 Years and Over Population: 2000.* Census 2000 Brief, C2KBR/01–10. Washington, D.C.: U.S. Government Printing Office, 2001. [Online] Available October 24, 2002, at http://www.census.gov/population/www/cen2000/briefs.html

———. *The Two or More Races Population: 2000.* Census 2000 Brief, C2KBR/01–6. Washington, D.C.: U.S. Government Printing Office, 2001. [Online] Available October 24, 2002, at http://www.census.gov/population/www/cen2000/briefs.html

———. *The White Population: 2000.* Census 2000 Brief, C2KBR/01–4. Washington, D.C.: U.S. Government Printing Office, 2001. [Online] Available October 24, 2002, at http://www.census.gov/population/www/cen2000/briefs.html

———. *The American Indian and Alaska Native Population: 2000.* Census 2000 Brief, C2KBR/01–15. Washington, D.C.: U.S. Government Printing Office, 2002. [Online] Available October 24, 2002, at http://www.census.gov/population/www/cen2000/briefs.html

———. *The Asian Population: 2000.* Census 2000 Brief, C2KBR/01–16. Washington, D.C.: U.S. Government Printing Office, 2002. [Online] Available October 24, 2002, at http://www.census.gov/population/www/cen2000/briefs.html

———. *Historical Income Tables—People.* Tables P-10, P-36. [Online] Available September 26, 2002, at http://www.census.gov/hhes/income/histinc/histinctb.html

———. *Custodial Mothers and Fathers and Their Child Support: 2001.* Current Population Reports, P60-225. October, 2003. [Online] Available October 28, 2005, at http://www.census.gov/hhes/www/childsupport/childsupport.html

———. *Fertility of American Women: June 2002.* Current Population Reports, P20-548. Washington, D.C.: U.S. Government Printing Office, 2003.

———. *Grandparents Living with Grandchildren: 2000.* Census 2000 Brief, C2KBR-31. Washington, D.C.: U.S. Government Printing Office, 2003.

———. *The Hispanic Population in the United States: March 2002.* Current Population Reports (P20–545). Washington, D.C.: U.S. Government Printing Office, 2003.

———. *Language Use and English-Speaking Ability: 2000.* Census 2000 Brief, C2KBR-29. Washington, D.C.: U.S. Government Printing Office, 2003.

———. *Married-Couple and Unmarried-Partner Households: 2000.* Washington, D.C.: U.S. Government Printing Office, 2003.

———. *America's Families and Living Arrangements: 2003.* Current Population Survey (P20-553). Washington, D.C.: U.S. Government Printing Office, 2004.

———. Census 2000 American Indian and Alaska Native Summary File (AIANSF). "(Table) DP-3. Profile of Selected Economic Characteristics, 2000." [Online] Available October 8, 2004, at http://factfinder.census.gov/

———. Census 2000 Summary File 3. "(Table) QT-P13. Ancestry, 2000." [Online] Available October 7, 2004, at http://factfinder.census.gov/

———. *Income, Poverty, and Health Insurance Coverage in the United States, 2003.* Current Population Reports (P60-226). Washington, D.C.: U.S. Government Printing Office, 2004.

———. *School Enrollment—Social and Economic Characteristics of Students: October 2002.* "(Table) 15." Rev. January 8, 2004. [Online] Available August 16, 2004, at http://www.census.gov/population/socdemo/school/cps2002.html

———. *Statistical Abstract of the United States: 2004–2005.* Washington, D.C.: U.S. Government Printing Office, 2004.

———. "(Table) 2a. Projected Population of the United States, by Age and Sex: 2000 to 2050." Rev. March 18, 2004. [Online] Available July 24, 2005, at http://www.census.gov/ipc/www/usinterimproj/natprojtab02a.pdf

———. "About Metropolitan and Micropolitan Statistical Areas." Rev. June 7, 2005. [Online] Available October 23, 2005, at http://www.census.gov/population/www/estimates/aboutmetro.html

———. *America's Families and Living Arrangements: 2004.* Detailed tables. Rev. June 29, 2005. [Online] Available October 21, 2005, at http://www.census.gov/population/www/socdemo/hh-fam/cps2004.html

———. Current Population Survey, 2005 Annual Social and Economic Supplement. "(Tables) FINC-01, FINC-02." Rev. June 24, 2005. [Online] Available October 14, 2005, at http://pubdb3.census.gov/macro/032005/faminc/toc.htm

———. Current Population Survey, 2005 Annual Social and Economic Supplement. "(Table) H101." Rev. July 19, 2005. [Online] Available October 23, 2005, at http://pubdb3.census.gov/macro/032005/health/toc.htm

———. Current Population Survey, 2005 Annual Social and Economic Supplement. "(Tables) PINC-01, PINC-03, PINC-05." Rev. May 5, 2005. [Online] Available September 13, 2005, at http://pubdb3.census.gov/macro/032005/perinc/toc.htm

———. Current Population Survey, 2005 Annual Social and Economic Supplement. "(Tables) POV01, POV06, POV14." Rev. June 10, 2005. [Online] Available September 15, 2005, at http://pubdb3.census.gov/macro/032005/pov/toc.htm

———. *Educational Attainment in the United States: 2004.* Detailed tables. Rev. March 27, 2005. [Online] Available October 21, 2005, at http://www.census.gov/population/www/socdemo/education/cps2004.html

———. Historical Income Tables—Families. "(Tables) F-1, F-2, F-3, F-6, F-23." Rev. June 22, 2005. [Online] Available September 14, 2005, at http://www.census.gov/hhes/www/income/histinc/incfamdet.html

———. Historical Income Tables—People. "(Tables) P-10, P-54." Rev. May 18, 2005. [Online] Available October 14, 2005, at http://www.census.gov/hhes/www/income/histinc/incpertoc.html

———. Historical Poverty Tables—Families. "(Table) 4." Rev. August 30, 2005. [Online] Available October 14, 2005, at http://www.census.gov/hhes/www/poverty/histpov/famindex.html

———. Historical Tables—Educational Attainment. "(Table) A-2." March 2005. [Online] Available October 27, 2005, at http://www.census.gov/population/socdemo/educ-attn.html

———. *Housing Vacancies and Homeownership.* (CPS/HVS). Annual Statistics: 2004. Table 20. Homeownership Rates by Race and Ethnicity of Householder: 1994 to 2004. Washington, D.C.: U.S. Government Printing Office, 2005.

———. *Income, Poverty, and Health Insurance Coverage in the United States: 2004.* Current Population Reports (P60-229). Washington, D.C.: U.S. Government Printing Office, 2005.

———. International Database. IDB Population Pyramids. April 26, 2005. [Online] Available October 23, 2005, at http://www.census.gov/ipc/www/idbpyr.html

———. National Population Estimates tables. Rev. January 28, 2005. [Online] Available October 27, 2005 at http://www.census.gov/popest/estimates.php,

http://www.census.gov/popest/national/asrh, and http://www.census.gov/popest/national/index.html

———. "Port St. Lucie, Florida, Is Fastest-Growing City, Census Bureau Says." Press release, June 30, 2005. [Online] Available October 23, 2005, at http://www.census.gov/Press-Release/www/releases/archives/population/005268.html

———. Voting and Registration in the Election of November 2004. "(Tables) 1, 2, 8." Rev. May 25, 2005. [Online] Available October 19, 2005, at http://www.census.gov/population/socdemo/voting/cps2004.html

U.S. CHARTER SCHOOLS. "About the Charter School Movement." [Online] Available October 21, 2005, at http://www.uscharterschools.org/pub/uscs_docs/o/movement.htm

U.S. CITIZENSHIP AND IMMIGRATION SERVICES. *2003 Yearbook of Immigration Statistics.* September 2004. [Online] Available October 19, 2005, at http://uscis.gov/graphics/shared/statistics/yearbook/2003/2003Yearbook.pdf

U.S. DEPARTMENT OF EDUCATION. *Evaluation of the Public Charter Schools Program: Final Report. 2004.* [Online] Available October 21, 2005, at http://www.ed.gov/rschstat/eval/choice/pcsp-final/finalreport.pdf

U.S. DEPARTMENT OF HEALTH AND HUMAN SERVICES. *Administration for Children and Families. Temporary Assistance for Needy Families (TANF) Program; Third Annual Report to Congress, August 2000.* Washington, D.C.: The Administration, 2000.

U.S. DEPARTMENT OF HOMELAND SECURITY. *2004 Yearbook of Immigration Statistics.* Rev. June 24, 2005. [Online] Available July 23, 2005, at http://uscis.gov/graphics/shared/statistics/yearbook/YrBk04Im.htm

U.S. DEPARTMENT OF HOUSING AND URBAN DEVELOPMENT. "The Forgotten Americans: Homelessness—Programs and the People They Serve." December 1999. [Online] Available October 4, 2004, at http://www.huduser.org/publications/homeless/homelessness/contents.html

U.S. DEPARTMENT OF JUSTICE. *The Sexual Victimization of College Women.* December 2000. [Online] Available October 17, 2005, at http://www.ncjrs.org/pdffiles1/nij/182369.pdf

U.S. DEPARTMENT OF LABOR. Bureau of Labor Statistics. *Employment and Earnings.* Vol. 52, No. 1 (January 2005). [Online] Available October 17, 2005, at http://www.bls.gov/cps

———. Bureau of Labor Statistics. *Women in the Labor Force: A Databook.* Report 985. Washington, D.C.: U.S. Government Printing Office, 2005.

U.S. DEPARTMENT OF STATE. "Remarks on Release of 'Country Reports on Terrorism' for 2004." Washington, D.C. (April 27, 2005). [Online] Available September 26, 2005, at http://www.state.gov/s/ct/rls/rm/45279.htm

U.S. ENVIRONMENTAL PROTECTION AGENCY. "Municipal Solid Waste." May 17, 2005. [Online] Available October 3, 2005, at http://www.epa.gov/msw/facts.htm

U.S. EQUAL EMPLOYMENT OPPORTUNITY COMMISSION. "Occupational Employment in Private Industry by Race/Ethnic Group/Sex, and by Industry, United States, 2003." Rev. May 9, 2005. [Online] Available July 7, 2005, at http://www.eeoc.gov/stats/jobpat/2003/national.html

U.S. FEDERAL INTERAGENCY FORUM ON AGING-RELATED STATISTICS. *Older Americans 2004: Key Indicators of Well Being.* Rev. July 13, 2005. [Online] Available October 1, 2005, at http://www.agingstats.gov/chartbook2004/healthstatus.html

U.S. SMALL BUSINESS ADMINISTRATION. *Minorities in Business, 2001.* 2001. [Online] Available October 28, 2005, at http://www.sba.gov/advo/research/minority.html

———. *Women in Business, 2001.* October 2001. [Online] Available October 28, 2005, at http://www.sba.gov/advo/research/women.html

VALDEZ, A. "In the Hood: Street Gangs Discover White-Collar Crime." *Police.* Vol. 21, No. 5 (May 1997):49–50, 56.

VALLAS, STEPHEN P., and JOHN P. BECK. "The Transformation of Work Revisited: The Limits of Flexibility in American Manufacturing." *Social Problems.* Vol. 43, No. 3 (August 1996):339–61.

VALOCCHI, STEVE. "The Emergence of the Integrationist Ideology in the Civil Rights Movement." *Social Problems.* Vol. 43, No. 1 (February 1996):116–30.

VAN BIEMA, DAVID. "Buddhism in America." *Time* (October 13, 1997):71–81.

———. "Spiriting Prayer into School." *Time* (April 27, 1998):38–41.

———. "A Surge of Teen Spirit." *Time* (May 31, 1999):58–59.

VANDIVERE, SHARON, et al. *Unsupervised Time: Factors Associated with Self-Care.* Washington, D.C.: Urban Institute, 2003. [Online] Available July 18, 2005, at http://www.urban.org/UploadedPDF/310894_OP71.pdf

VAN DYKE, NELLA, and SARAH A. SOULE. "Structural Social Change and the Mobilizing Effect of Threat: Explaining Levels of Patriot and Militia Organizing in the United States." *Social Problems*. Vol. 49, No. 4 (November 2002):497–520.

VEBLEN, THORSTEIN. *The Theory of the Leisure Class*. New York: New American Library, 1953; orig. 1899.

VEDDER, RICHARD, and LOWELL GALLAWAY. "Declining Black Employment." *Society*. Vol. 30, No. 5 (July/August 1993):56–63.

VINOVSKIS, MARIS A. "Have Social Historians Lost the Civil War? Some Preliminary Demographic Speculations." *Journal of American History*. Vol. 76, No. 1 (June 1989):34–58.

VOGEL, EZRA F. *The Four Little Dragons: The Spread of Industrialization in East Asia*. Cambridge, Mass.: Harvard University Press, 1991.

VOGEL, LISE. *Marxism and the Oppression of Women: Toward a Unitary Theory*. New Brunswick, N.J.: Rutgers University Press, 1983.

VOLD, GEORGE B., and THOMAS J. BERNARD. *Theoretical Criminology*. 3rd ed. New York: Oxford University Press, 1986.

VONNEGUT, KURT, JR. "Harrison Bergeron." In *Welcome to the Monkey House*. New York: Delacorte Press, 1968:7–13.

WAHL, JENNY B. "From Riches to Riches: Intergenerational Transfers and the Evidence from Estate Tax Returns." *Social Science Quarterly*. Vol. 84, No. 2 (June 2003):278–96.

WALDER, ANDREW G. "Career Mobility and the Communist Political Order." *American Sociological Review*. Vol. 60, No. 3 (June 1995):309–28.

WALDFOGEL, JANE. "The Effect of Children on Women's Wages." *American Sociological Review*. Vol. 62, No. 2 (April 1997):209–17.

WALDROP, JUDITH. "Live Long and Prosper." *American Demographics*. Vol. 14, No. 10 (October 1992):40–45.

WALKER, KAREN. "'Always There for Me': Friendship Patterns and Expectations among Middle- and Working-Class Men and Women." *Sociological Forum*. Vol. 10, No. 2 (June 1995):273–96.

WALL, THOMAS F. *Medical Ethics: Basic Moral Issues*. Washington, D.C.: University Press of America, 1980.

WALLERSTEIN, IMMANUEL. *The Modern World-System: Capitalist Agriculture and the Origins of the European World-Economy in the Sixteenth Century*. New York: Academic Press, 1974.

———. *The Capitalist World-Economy*. New York: Cambridge University Press, 1979.

———. "Crises: The World Economy, the Movements, and the Ideologies." In ALBERT BERGESEN, ed., *Crises in the World-System*. Beverly Hills, Calif.: Sage, 1983:21–36.

———. *The Politics of the World Economy: The States, the Movements, and the Civilizations*. Cambridge: Cambridge University Press, 1984.

WALLERSTEIN, JUDITH S., and SANDRA BLAKESLEE. *Second Chances: Men, Women, and Children a Decade after Divorce*. New York: Ticknor & Fields, 1989.

WALSH, MARY WILLIAMS. "No Time to Put Your Feet Up as Retirement Comes in Stages." *New York Times* (April 15, 2001):1, 18.

WALTON, JOHN, and CHARLES RAGIN. "Global and National Sources of Political Protest: Third World Responses to the Debt Crisis." *American Sociological Review*. Vol. 55, No. 6 (December 1990):876–90.

WARNER, W. LLOYD, and PAUL S. LUNT. *The Social Life of a Modern Community*. New Haven, Conn.: Yale University Press, 1941.

WARR, MARK, and CHRISTOPHER G. ELLISON. "Rethinking Social Reactions to Crime: Personal and Altruistic Fear in Family Households." *American Journal of Sociology*. Vol. 106, No. 3 (November 2000):551–78.

WATERS, MELISSA S., WILL CARRINGTON HEATH, and JOHN KEITH WATSON. "A Positive Model of the Determination of Religious Affiliation." *Social Science Quarterly*. Vol. 76, No. 1 (March 1995):105–23.

WATTS, DUNCAN J. "Networks, Dynamics, and the Small-World Phenomenon." *American Journal of Sociology*. Vol. 105, No. 2 (September 1999):493–527.

WEBER, ADNA FERRIN. *The Growth of Cities*. New York: Columbia University Press, 1963; orig. 1899.

WEBER, MAX. *The Protestant Ethic and the Spirit of Capitalism*. New York: Scribner, 1958; orig. 1904–05.

———. *Economy and Society: An Outline of Interpretive Sociology*. GUENTHER ROTH and CLAUS WITTICH, eds. Berkeley: University of California Press, 1978; orig. 1921.

WEBSTER, ANDREW. *Introduction to the Sociology of Development*. London: Macmillan, 1984.

WEEKS, JOHN R. "The Demography of Islamic Nations." *Population Bulletin*. Vol. 43, No. 4 (December 1988).

WEIDENBAUM, MURRAY. "The Evolving Corporate Board." *Society*. Vol. 32, No. 3 (March/April 1995):9–20.

WEINBERG, GEORGE. *Society and the Healthy Homosexual*. Garden City, N.Y.: Anchor Books, 1973.

WEISBERG, D. KELLY. *Children of the Night: A Study of Adolescent Prostitution*. Lexington, Mass.: Heath, 1985.

WEITZMAN, LENORE J. *The Divorce Revolution: The Unexpected Social and Economic Consequences for Women and Children in America*. New York: Free Press, 1985.

———. "The Economic Consequences of Divorce Are Still Unequal: Comment on Peterson." *American Sociological Review*. Vol. 61, No. 3 (June 1996):537–38.

WELLER, JACK M., and E. L. QUARANTELLI. "Neglected Characteristics of Collective Behavior." *American Journal of Sociology*. Vol. 79, No. 3 (November 1973):665–85.

WELLNER, ALISON STEIN. "Discovering Native America." *American Demographics*. Vol. 23, No. 8 (August 2001):21.

———. "The Power of the Purse." *American Demographics*. Vol. 24, No. 7 (January/February 2002):S3–S10.

WERTHEIMER, BARBARA MAYER. "The Factory Bell." In LINDA K. KERBER and JANE DE HART MATHEWS, eds., *Women's America: Refocusing the Past*. New York: Oxford University Press, 1982:130–40.

WESSELMAN, HANK. *Visionseeker: Shared Wisdom from the Place of Refuge*. Carlsbad, Calif.: Hay House, 2001.

WESTERN, BRUCE. "The Impact of Incarceration on Wage Mobility and Inequality." *American Sociological Review*. Vol. 67, No. 4 (August 2002):526–46.

WHALEN, JACK, and RICHARD FLACKS. *Beyond the Barricades: The Sixties Generation Grows Up*. Philadelphia: Temple University Press, 1989.

WHEELIS, ALLEN. *The Quest for Identity*. New York: Norton, 1958.

WHITAKER, MARK. "Ten Ways to Fight Terrorism." *Newsweek* (July 1, 1985): 26–29.

WHITE, JACK E. "I'm Just Who I Am." *Time* (May 5, 1997):32–36.

WHITE, RALPH, and RONALD LIPPITT. "Leader Behavior and Member Reaction in Three 'Social Climates.'" In DORWIN CARTWRIGHT and ALVIN ZANDER, eds., *Group Dynamics*. Evanston, Ill.: Row & Peterson, 1953:586–611.

WHITE, WALTER. *Rope and Faggot*. New York: Arno Press/New York Times, 1969; orig. 1929.

WHITMAN, DAVID. "Shattering Myths about the Homeless." *U.S. News & World Report* (March 20, 1989):26, 28.

WHORF, BENJAMIN LEE. "The Relation of Habitual Thought and Behavior to Language." In *Language, Thought, and Reality*. Cambridge, Mass.: Technology Press of MIT; New York: Wiley, 1956:134–59; orig. 1941.

WHYTE, WILLIAM FOOTE. *Street Corner Society*. 3rd ed. Chicago: University of Chicago Press, 1981; orig. 1943.

WICKHAM, DEWAYNE. "Homeless Receive Little Attention from Candidates." [Online] Accessed October 24, 2000, at http://www.usatoday.com/usatonline

WILCOX, CLYDE. "Race, Gender, and Support for Women in the Military." *Social Science Quarterly*. Vol. 73, No. 2 (June 1992):310–23.

WILDAVSKY, BEN. "Small World, Isn't It?" *U.S. News & World Report* (April 1, 2002):68.

WILES, P. J. D. *Economic Institutions Compared*. New York: Halsted Press, 1977.

WILKINSON, DORIS. "Transforming the Social Order: The Role of the University in Social Change." *Sociological Forum*. Vol. 9, No. 3 (September 1994): 325–41.

WILLIAMS, JOHNNY E. "Linking Beliefs to Collective Action: Politicized Religious Beliefs and the Civil Rights Movement." *Sociological Forum*. Vol. 17, No. 2 (June 2002):203–22.

WILLIAMS, PETER W. *America's Religions: From Their Origins to the Twenty-First Century*. Urbana: University of Illinois Press, 2002.

WILLIAMS, RHYS H., and N. J. DEMERATH III. "Religion and Political Process in an American City." *American Sociological Review*. Vol. 56, No. 4 (August 1991):417–31.

WILLIAMS, ROBIN M., JR. *American Society: A Sociological Interpretation*. 3rd ed. New York: Knopf, 1970.

WILLIAMSON, JEFFREY G., and PETER H. LINDERT. *American Inequality: A Macroeconomic History*. New York: Academic Press, 1980.

WILSON, BARBARA. "National Television Violence Study." Reported in JULIA DUIN, "Study Finds Cartoon Heroes Initiate Too Much Violence." *Washington Times* (April 17, 1998):A4.

WILSON, EDWARD O. "Biodiversity, Prosperity, and Value." In F. HERBERT BORMANN and STEPHEN R. KELLERT, eds., *Ecology, Economics, and Ethics: The Broken Circle*. New Haven, Conn.: Yale University Press, 1991:3–10.

WILSON, JAMES Q. "Crime, Race, and Values." *Society*. Vol. 30, No. 1 (November/December 1992):90–93.

WILSON, THOMAS C. "Urbanism and Tolerance: A Test of Some Hypotheses Drawn from Wirth and Stouffer." *American Sociological Review*. Vol. 50, No. 1 (February 1985):117–23.

———. "Urbanism and Unconventionality: The Case of Sexual Behavior." *Social Science Quarterly*. Vol. 76, No. 2 (June 1995):346–63.

WILSON, WILLIAM JULIUS. *The Declining Significance of Race*. Chicago: University of Chicago Press, 1978.

———. *When Work Disappears: The World of the New Urban Poor*. New York: Knopf, 1996a.

———. "Work." *New York Times Magazine* (August 18, 1996b):26 ff.

WINES, MICHAEL. "Democracy Has to Start Somewhere." *New York Times* (February 6, 2005). [Online] Available April 24, 2005, at http://www.research navigator.com

WINNICK, LOUIS. "America's 'Model Minority'." *Commentary*. Vol. 90, No. 2 (August 1990):22–29.

WINSHIP, CHRISTOPHER, and JENNY BERRIEN. "Boston Cops and Black Churches." *Public Interest*. No. 136 (Summer 1999):52–68.

WINTER, GREG. "Wider Gap Found between Wealthy and Poor Schools." *New York Times* (October 6, 2004). [Online] Available June 8, 2005, at http://www.researchnavigator.com

WINTERS, REBECCA. "Trouble for School Inc." *Time* (May 27, 2002):53.

WIRTH, LOUIS. "Urbanism as a Way of Life." *American Journal of Sociology*. Vol. 44, No. 1 (July 1938):1–24.

WITKIN, GORDON. "The Crime Bust." *U.S. News & World Report* (May 25, 1998):28–40.

WITT, G. EVANS. "Say What You Mean." *American Demographics*. Vol. 21, No. 2 (February 1999):23.

WITT, LOUISE. "Why We're Losing the War against Obesity." *American Demographics*. Vol. 25, No. 10 (January 2004):27–31.

WOLF, NAOMI. *The Beauty Myth: How Images of Beauty Are Used against Women*. New York: Morrow, 1990.

WOLFE, DAVID B. "Targeting the Mature Mind." *American Demographics*. Vol. 16, No. 3 (March 1994):32–36.

WOLFGANG, MARVIN E., ROBERT M. FIGLIO, and THORSTEN SELLIN. *Delinquency in a Birth Cohort*. Chicago: University of Chicago Press, 1972.

WOLFGANG, MARVIN E., TERRENCE P. THORNBERRY, and ROBERT M. FIGLIO. *From Boy to Man, from Delinquency to Crime*. Chicago: University of Chicago Press, 1987.

WONDERS, NANCY A., and RAYMOND MICHALOWSKI. "Bodies, Borders, and Sex Tourism in a Globalized World: A Tale of Two Cities—Amsterdam and Havana." *Social Problems*. Vol. 48, No. 4 (November 2001):545–71.

WONG, BUCK. "Need for Awareness: An Essay on Chinatown, San Francisco." In AMY TACHIKI et al., eds., *Roots: An Asian American Reader*. Los Angeles: UCLA Asian American Studies Center, 1971:265–73.

WOODWARD, KENNETH L. "Feminism and the Churches." *Newsweek* (February 13, 1989):58–61.

———. "Talking to God." *Newsweek* (January 6, 1992a):38–44.

———. "The Elite, and How to Avoid It." *Newsweek* (July 20, 1992b):55.

WORLD BANK. *World Development Report 1993*. New York: Oxford University Press, 1993.

———. *Entering the 21st Century: World Development Report 1999/2000*. New York: Oxford University Press, 2000.

———. *World Development Report 2000/2001*. Washington, D.C.: World Bank, 2001.

———. *2004 World Development Indicators*. Washington, D.C.: World Bank, 2004.

———. *2005 World Development Indicators*. Washington, D.C.: World Bank, 2005.

"WORLD DIVORCE RATES." [Online] Available October 21, 2005, at http://www.divorcereform.org/gul.html

WORLD VALUES SURVEY. "Latest Publications: Predict 2005—FIGURE." 2004. [Online] Available April 25, 2005, at http://www.worldvaluessurvey.com/library/index.html

WORSLEY, PETER. "Models of the World System." In MIKE FEATHERSTONE, ed., *Global Culture: Nationalism, Globalization, and Modernity*. Newbury Park, Calif.: Sage, 1990:83–95.

WREN, CHRISTOPHER S. "In Soweto-by-the-Sea, Misery Lives on as Apartheid Fades." *New York Times* (June 9, 1991):1, 7.

WRIGHT, JAMES D. "Address Unknown: Homelessness in Contemporary America." *Society*. Vol. 26, No. 6 (September/October 1989):45–53.

———. "Ten Essential Observations on Guns in America." *Society*. Vol. 32, No. 3 (March/April 1995):63–68.

WRIGHT, QUINCY. "Causes of War in the Atomic Age." In WILLIAM M. EVAN and STEPHEN HILGARTNER, eds., *The Arms Race and Nuclear War*. Englewood Cliffs, N.J.: Prentice Hall, 1987:7–10.

WRIGHT, RICHARD A. *In Defense of Prisons*. Westport, Conn.: Greenwood Press, 1994.

WRIGHT, ROBERT. "Sin in the Global Village." *Time* (October 19, 1998):130.

WRIGHT, STUART A., and ELIZABETH S. PIPER. "Families and Cults: Familial Factors Related to Youth Leaving or Remaining in Deviant Religious Groups." *Journal of Marriage and the Family*. Vol. 48, No. 1 (February 1986):15–25.

WU, LAWRENCE L. "Effects of Family Instability, Income, and Income Instability on the Risk of a Premarital Birth." *American Sociological Review*. Vol. 61, No. 3 (June 1996):386–406.

YANG, FENGGANG, and HELEN ROSE FUCHS EBAUGH. "Transformations in New Immigrant Religions and Their Global Implications." *American Sociological Review*. Vol. 66, No. 2 (April 2001):269–88.

YANKELOVICH, DANIEL. "How Changes in the Economy Are Reshaping American Values." In HENRY J. AARON, THOMAS E. MANN, and TIMOTHY TAYLOR, eds., *Values and Public Policy*. Washington, D.C.: Brookings Institution, 1994:20.

YATES, RONALD E. "Growing Old in Japan: They Ask Gods for a Way Out." *Philadelphia Inquirer* (August 14, 1986):3A.

YEATTS, DALE E. "Creating the High Performance Self-Managed Work Team: A Review of Theoretical Perspectives." Paper presented at the annual meeting of the Southwest Social Science Association, Dallas, February 1994.

YIN, SANDRA. "Wanted: One Million Nurses." *American Demographics*. Vol. 24, No. 8 (September 2002):63–65.

YOELS, WILLIAM C., and JEFFREY MICHAEL CLAIR. "Laughter in the Clinic: Humor in Social Organization." *Symbolic Interaction*. Vol. 18, No. 1 (1995):39–58.

YORK, RICHARD, EUGENE A. ROSA, and THOMAS DEITZ. "Bridging Environmental Science with Environmental Policy: Plasticity of Population, Affluence, and Technology." *Social Science Quarterly*. Vol. 83, No. 1 (March 2002):18–34.

YUDELMAN, MONTAGUE, and LAURA J. M. KEALY. "The Graying of Farmers." *Population Today*. Vol. 28, No. 4 (May/June, 2000):6.

ZAKARIA, FAREED. "How to Wage the Peace." *Newsweek* (April 21, 2003):38, 48.

ZALMAN, MARVIN, and STEVEN STACK. "The Relationship between Euthanasia and Suicide in the Netherlands: A Time-Series Analysis, 1950–1990." *Social Science Quarterly*. Vol. 77, No. 3 (September 1996):576–93.

ZHAO, DINGXIN. "Ecologies of Social Movements: Student Mobilization during the 1989 Prodemocracy Movement in Beijing." *American Journal of Sociology*. Vol. 103, No. 6 (May 1998):1493–1529.

ZHOU, XUEGUANG, and LIREN HOU. "Children of the Cultural Revolution: The State and the Life Course in the People's Republic of China." *American Sociological Review*. Vol. 64, No. 1 (February 1999):12–36.

ZICKLIN, G. "Rebiologizing Sexual Orientation: A Critique." Paper presented at the annual meeting of the Society for the Study of Social Problems, Pittsburgh, 1992.

ZIMBARDO, PHILIP G. "Pathology of Imprisonment." *Society*. Vol. 9, No. 1 (April 1972):4–8.

ZIPP, JOHN F. "The Impact of Social Structure on Mate Selection: An Empirical Evaluation of an Active-Learning Exercise." *Teaching Sociology*. Vol. 30, No. 2 (April 2002):174–84.

ZOGBY INTERNATIONAL. Poll reported in SANDRA YIN, "Race and Politics." *American Demographics*. Vol. 23, No. 8 (August 2001):11–13.

ZURCHER, LOUIS A., and DAVID A. SNOW. "Collective Behavior and Social Movements." In MORRIS ROSENBERG and RALPH H. TURNER, eds., *Social Psychology: Sociological Perspectives*. New York: Basic Books, 1981:447–82.

# PHOTO CREDITS

Bettmann, 321 (left); Robert van der Hilst/Corbis/Bettmann, 321 (center); Wolfgang Kaehler/Corbis/Bettmann, 321 (right); Marilyn Humphries/The Image Works, 322; Mark Edwards/Still Pictures/Peter Arnold, Inc., 325.

**CHAPTER 13:** Bob Daemmrich/The Image Works; 332 (left); Corbis Royalty Free, 332 (center); Joe Bator/Corbis/Bettmann, 332 (right); Gideon Mendel/Corbis/Bettmann, 333; Corbis/Bettmann, 334; Nancy Richmond/The Image Works, 336; Angela Fisher/Carol Beckwith/Robert Estall Photo Agency, 337; CBS TV/Picture Desk, Inc./Kobal Collection, 340; Topham/The Image Works, 341; AP Wide World Photos, 344; David Grossman/The Image Works, 347; Kuenzig/laif/Aurora Photos, 349; Willinger/Hulton Archive/ Getty Images Inc.—Hulton Archive Photos, 351; HBO/Picture Desk, Inc./ Kobal Collection, 352.

**CHAPTER 14:** Marcia Keegan, Corbis/Bettmann, 360 (left); Carole Bellaiche/Corbis/Sygma 360 (center); Kevin Fleming/Corbis/Bettmann, 360 (right); David R. Frazier Photolibrary, Inc., 361; Bryant Mason, College Relations, Bronx Community College, 362; Joel Gordon/Joel Gordon Photography, 363 (top left); Leong Ka Tai, 363 (top center); Owen Franken/Corbis/ Bettmann, 363 (top right); Charles O'Rear/Corbis/Bettmann, 363 (bottom left); Paul W. Liebhardt, 363 (bottom center); Lisi Dennis/Lisl Dennis, 363 (bottom right); AP Wide World Photos, 364; Bob Daemmrich Photography, Inc., 367; Paul Conklin/PhotoEdit, 369; Western History Collections, University of Oklahoma Libraries, 373; Corbis/Bettmann, 378 (left); Culver Pictures, Inc., 378 (left center); Photographs and Prints Division, Schomburg Center for Research in Black Culture/The New York Public Library/Astor, Lenox and Tilden Foundations, 378 (right center); UPI/Corbis/Bettmann, 378 (right); A. Ramey/Woodfin Camp & Associates, 380; Warner Bros. TV/Amblin TV/ Picture Desk, Inc./Kobal Collection, 382; M. Lee Fatherree/Carmen Lomas Garza, 383; Carl D. Walsh/Aurora & Quanta Productions Inc., 386.

**CHAPTER 15:** Karen Kasmauski/Corbis/Bettmann, 392 (left); UN/DPI, 392 (center); AP Wide World Photos, 392 (right); Ariel Skelley/Corbis/ Bettmann, 393; David Young-Wolff/PhotoEdit, 394; Tom Wagner/Corbis/ SABA Press Photos, Inc., 396; Michael Newman/PhotoEdit, 398 (left); © John Garrett/Corbis, 398 (right); Laima Druskis/Pearson Education/PH College, 407; Chris Rainier/Corbis/Bettmann, 409; Spencer Grant/Stock Boston, 411; Merie W. Wallace/Warner Bros/Bureau L.A. Collections/Corbis/ Bettmann, 412.

**CHAPTER 16:** Jonathan Blair/Corbis/Bettmann, 416 (left); Beawiharta/ Reuters/Corbis/Bettmann, 416 (center); Jim Pickerell/The Stock Connection, 416 (right); Mark Wilson/Getty Images, Inc.—Liaison, 417; AP Wide World Photos, 418, AP Wide World Photos, 419; Underwood & Underwood/Library of Congress, 420; Sven-Olof Lindblad/Photo Researchers, Inc., 422; Bellavia/ REA/Corbis/SABA Press Photos, Inc., 425 (left); John Bryson/Corbis/Sygma, 425 (right); Alamy Images, 426; Gamma Press USA, Inc., 427; Chien-Chi Chang/Magnum Photos, Inc., 431; Matthew Borkoski/Index Stock Imagery, Inc., 433.

**CHAPTER 17:** Paul Fusco/Magnum Photos, Inc, 442 (left); Toby Talbot/AP Wide World Photos, 442 (center); Jason Reed/Reuters/Corbis/Reuters America LLC, 442 (right); William Thomas/Getty Images, 443; AP Wide World Photos, 444; Durand/SIPA Press, 446; David Ball/Index Stock Imagery, Inc., 449; Ramin Talaie/Corbis/Bettmann, 451 (left); Joel Gordon Photography, 451 (right); AP Wide World Photos, 457; AP Wide World Photos, 459; Joe McNally, Life Magazine © TimePix.

**CHAPTER 18:** Corbis Royalty Free, 468 (left, center); Owen Franken/ Corbis/Bettmann, 468 (right); © David Turnley/Corbis, 469; Michael Newman/PhotoEdit, 470; Getty Images, 471 (left); AP Wide World Photos, 471 (right); John Terence Turner/Getty Images, Inc.—Taxi, 472; The Bridgeman Art Library International, 475; Paul Marcus/Studio SPM, Inc., 476; AP Wide World Photos, 478; The Cartoon Bank, 479; Mark J. Barrett/Creative Eye/MIRA.com, 486; Bill Bachmann/The Image Works, 488.

**CHAPTER 19:** Bojan Brecelj/Corbis/Bettmann, 496 (left); Mashkov Yuri/ITAR-TASS/Corbis/Bettmann, 496 (center) Friedrich Stark/Das Fotoarchiv/Peter Arnold, Inc., 496 (right); Jason Reed/Reuters/Corbis/ Reuters America LLC, 497; Getty Images, Inc., 498; Michael Newman/PhotoEdit, 499; Galen Rowell/ Peter Arnold, Inc., 500; © David Rubinger/Bettmann/CORBIS All Rights Reserved, 502; © Doranne Jacobson/International Images, 504; Ian Berry/Magnum Photos, Inc., 505; Annie Griffiths Belt/NGS Image Collection, 508; AP Wide World Photos, 511; ©

Bettmann/CORBIS All rights reserved, 516; Philip North-Coombes/Getty Images Inc.—Stone Allstock, 517; © Gary Braasch/Bettmann/CORBIS All rights reserved, 521.

**CHAPTER 20:** Lynsey Addario/Corbis/Bettmann, 524 (left); UN/DPI, 524 (center); Louise Gubb/Corbis/SABA Press Photos, Inc., 524 (right); Paul Barton/Corbis/Bettmann, 525; © Andrew Holbrooke/Bettmann/CORBIS All rights reserved, 526; AP Wide World Photos, 527; Bob Daemmrich Photography, Inc., 531; Michael Newman/PhotoEdit, 532 (left); Getty Images, Inc., 532 (right); Lawrence Migdale/Pix, 539; AP Wide World Photos, 543; Bob Daemmrich Photography, Inc., 544; Kevin Virobik-Adams, Progressive Photo, 546.

**CHAPTER 21:** Gregory Primo Gottman, 550 (left); Richard T. Nowitz/Corbis/Bettmann (550 (center); Gideon Mendel/Corbis/Bettmann, 550 (right); AP Wide World Photos, 551; Martin Parr/Magnum Photos, Inc., 552; Steve Prezant/Corbis/Stock Market, 555; © Lucy Nicholson/Bettmann/CORBIS All Rights Reserved, 557; George Mulala/Peter Arnold, Inc., 560; Adalbert Franz Seligmann, *Allgemeines Krankenhaus* (General Hospital), 19th Century Painting, canvas. *Professor Theodor Billroth lectures at the General Hospital, Vienna. 1880.* Erich Lessing/Art Resource, NY, 563; Galen Rowell/Mountain Light Photography, Inc., 566; John Cancalosi/Stock Boston, 567; Billy E. Barnes/ PhotoEdit, 569; Al Diaz, 572; Steve Murez/Black Star, 574.

**CHAPTER 22:** Dinodia/The Image Works, 578 (left); Lester Lefkowitz/ Corbis/Bettmann, 578 (center); David Austen/Woodfin Camp & Associates, 578 (right); Wilfried Krecichwost/Zefa/Corbis Zefa Collection, 579; © Annie Griffiths/Bettmann/CORBIS All Rights Reserved, 580; AP Wide World Photos, 585; David and Peter Turnley/Corbis/Bettmann, 587; Lauren Goodsmith/ The Image Works, 588; Mario Tursi /Miramax /Dimension Films /The Kobal Collection, 590; Steve C. Wilson/Online USA, Inc./Getty Images Inc.— Hulton Archive Photos, 592; Christie's Images Inc., 593 (left); SuperStock, Inc., 593 (right); James King-Holmes/Science Photo Library/Photo Researchers, Inc., 597; Culver Pictures, Inc., 600; Dave Amit/Reuters/Landov LLC, 601; Eric Pasquier/Corbis/Sygma, 604.

**CHAPTER 23:** Bobby Yip/Reuters/Corbis/Reuters America LLC, 610 (left); A. Ramey/PhotoEdit, 610 (center); Fabrizio Bensch/Reuters/Corbis/Reuters America LLC, 610 (right); AP Wide World Photos, 611, 612, 613; © David Butow/Corbis SABA, 615; Sabina Dowell, 617; © Joel Gordon 2005—All rights reserved, 619; Rick Wilking/Reuters/Corbis/Bettmann, 620 (left); Al Grillo/Peter Arnold, Inc., 620 (center); AP Wide World Photos, 620 (right); CORBIS–NY, 621; AP Wide World Photos, 625; Corbis/Bettmann, 627 (left); Huynh Cong "Nick" Ut/AP Wide World Photos, 627 (right).

**CHAPTER 24:** Joe McDonald/Coribs/Bettmann, 636 (left); Ed Kashi/Corbis/ Bettmann, 636 (center); B.S.P.I./Corbis/Bettmann, 636 (right); Robert Essel NYC/Corbis/Bettmann, 637; Culver Pictures, Inc., 638; China Images/Getty Images, Inc., 640; The Bridgeman Art Library International, 643; Whitney Museum of American Art, 644; Eric Draper/AP Wide World Photos, 648; Ed Pritchard/Getty Images Inc.—Stone Allstock, 651 (left); Mark Richards/PhotoEdit, 651 (right); Mauri Rautkari/WWF UK (World Wide Fund For Nature), 652; Kelly-Mooney Photography/Corbis/Bettmann, 653; Paul Howell/Getty Images, Inc.—Liaison, 658.

Timeline: 1807: Getty Images Inc.—Hulton Archive Photos; 1829: Association of American Railroads; 1848: North Carolina Museum of History; 1876: Property of AT&T Archives, reprinted with permission of AT&T; 1886 (top): Irene Springer/Pearson Education/PH College; 1886 (bottom): "Coca-Cola" is a registered trademark of The Coca-Cola Company and is reproduced with kind permission from The Coca-Cola Company; 1893: Library of Congress; 1910: Tim Ridley © Dorling Kindersley; 1912: Wilton, Chris Alan/Getty Images Inc.—Image Bank; 1913: Library of Congress; 1921: Getty Images Inc.—Hulton Archive Photos; 1927: Corbis/Bettmann; 1931: Texas State Library and Archives Commission; 1945: U.S. Air Force; 1946: Photo courtesy of Unisys Corporation; 1947: © CORBIS/Bettmann; 1950: Corbis/Bettmann; 1952: © Dorling Kindersley; 1955: AP Wide World Photos; 1964: Getty Images Inc.—Hulton Archive Photos; 1969 (top): AP Wide World Photos; 1969 (bottom): NASA/Johnson Space Center; 1970: Jason Laure/Woodfin Camp & Associates; 1980: Laima Druskis/Pearson Education/PH College; 1981: Jan Butchofsky-Houser/AP Wide World Photos; 1987: John Serafin; 1990s: Gerald Lopez © Dorling Kindersley; 2000: Brady/Pearson Education/PH College.

# NAME INDEX

# SUBJECT INDEX

beauty and, 73, 195
child labor and, 80
communication and, 64
crime and, 240–41
deviance and, 224
emotions, showing, 158
homosexuality and, 203
humor and, 161–62
intelligence and, 370
languages and, 66
male circumcision, 213
modesty and, 197
nonverbal communication and, 155, 157
personal space and, 155
sexual expression and, 196–97
sexuality and, 213
sexual practices and, 196–97, 213
symbols and, 66
U.S. and Canada compared, 86
Cultural integration, 79
Cultural lag, 79, 639
Cultural relativism, 81
Cultural transmission, 66
Cultural universals, 82
Culture
change, 79–81
conflict and, 76–77
counter-, 78–79
defined, 60–62, 64
diversity in, 74–75
elements of, 64–73
emotions and influence of, 158
evolution and, 83–85
freedom and, 85
functions of, 82–83
gender and, 335–36
global, 81–82
high versus popular, 75
ideal versus real, 73
inequality and, 83
information technology and, 74
intelligence and, 62–64
language and, 64, 66–68
material, 60–61, 73–74
modernization theory, 320–21
multiculturalism, 76–78
nonmaterial, 60
norms, 71–72
poverty and, 296, 319
reality building and, 151
shock, 61–62, 63, 65–66
social change and, 640
social-conflict analysis, 83, 85
sociobiology approach, 83–85
structural-functional analysis, 82–83, 85
sub-, 75–76
technology and, 73–74
theoretical analysis of, 82–85
theory, 627–28, 629
theory and racism, 371
transmission of, 66
values and beliefs, 68–71
of victimization, 70–71
Cyber symbols, 64, 65
Czechoslovakia, socialism, decline of, 427
Czech Republic, market reforms, 427

Darwin, Charles, 83–84, 118–119, 264, 521
Data, using existing research, 49–51
Date rape, 210
Dating, 476, 477–78

Davis-Moore thesis, 264–65
Death with Dignity Act (1997), 410–11
Death and dying (see also Mortality rates)
bereavement, 411–12
defining, 409, 562
ethical issues, 409–11, 413, 562–63
euthanasia, 410–11, 413, 562–63
historical patterns, 408–9
hospice movement, 412, 413
leading causes of, in U.S., 553
penalty, 241, 246
right-to-die debate, 410–11, 562
of a spouse, 480
as a stage of life, 135–37
stages of, 136, 411
Death instinct, 121
Death rates, crude, 581
Debt bondage, 317
Deception, spotting, 154
Declaration of Independence, 13, 378
Decline, social movements and, 630–31
Deductive logical thought/reasoning, 52, 53
De facto segregation, 373
Degradation ceremony, 229
De jure segregation, 373
Demeanor, social interaction and, 155
Democracy
bureaucracy and, 446, 448
capitalist versus socialist approaches, 448
defined, 446
economic inequality and, 448
freedom and, 448, 464
gap, 464
political freedom, map of, 447
U.S. value, 69
Democratic leadership, 171
Democratic party, 452
Democratic Republic of the Congo
gross domestic product, 313
as a low-income country, 309, 311, 313
quality of life, 313
Demographic transition theory, 586
Demography (see also Population/population growth)
defined, 580
fertility, 580–81
migration, 582
mortality, 581–82
social change and, 640–41
Denmark, homosexual marriages, 489
Denominations, 503–4
Dependency theory
capitalist world economy, 324–25
colonialism and, 323–24
compared to modernization theory, 326
defined, 323
evaluation of, 326–27
high-income countries and, 325–26
historical, 323
Dependent variables, 35
Deprivation theory, 624–25, 629
Descent patterns, 473
Desegregation, 372
Deterrence
of criminals, 244, 246
of war, 461
Development, human (see Human development)
Deviance (see also Crime)

biological context, 223
capitalism and, 232
control theory, 231
cultural differences, 224
defined, 222–23
differential association theory, 230–31
Durkheim's work, 224–25
functions of, 225
gender differences and, 235–36
Hirschi's control theory, 231
labeling theory, 228–29
medicalization of, 229–30
Merton's strain theory, 226
personality factors, 223–24
power and, 232
primary, 229
Puritans, example of, 225–26
secondary, 229
social-conflict analysis, 232–34
social control, 222–23
social foundations of, 224
strain theory, 226
structural-functional analysis, 224–27, 234
subcultures, 226–28
Sutherland's differential association theory, 230–31
symbolic-interaction analysis, 228–31, 234
Deviant career, 229
Dharma, 320, 509
Differential association theory, 230–31
Diffusion
culture, 80
social change and, 640
Diplomacy, peace and, 461–62
Direct-fee system, 568
Disabilities, physical, 146
Disabled
changes in attitudes toward, 151, 152–53
education for, 544–45
Disarmament, peace and, 461–62
Disasters
defined, 619
impact of, 620, 621
intentional, 619–20
natural, 619
technological, 619
Discipline problems, school, 538
Discoveries
cultural change and, 79–80
social change and, 640
Discrimination (see also Racial discrimination)
age, 394, 406
defined, 372
institutional, 372
prejudice and, 372
women and, 344
workplace, 182–83
Disengagement theory, 407
Diversity (see also Social diversity)
biodiversity, declining, 604–5
language, in the U.S., 78
racial, in the U.S., 128
religious, across U.S., 514
workplace, 431, 432
Divine right, 446
Division of labor, 111, 643–44
Divorce
causes of, 485–86
children and, 486–87
child support, 487

rates for U.S., 485
reproductive technology and effects on, 492
Doe v. Bolton, 216
Domestication of animals, 94–95
Domestic violence, 487–88
Double standards, 40
sexual behavior and, 84, 200, 201
Down These Mean Streets (Thomas), 149–50
Downward social mobility, 289
Dramaturgical analysis
defined, 151
elements of, 21
embarrassment, 156–57
idealization, 156
nonverbal communication, 153–56
performances, 151–52
Dred Scott case, 378–79
Dropout, school, 539–41
Drug abuse
deviance and medicalization of, 230
HIV/AIDS and sharing of needles, 560
Drug trade
crime and, 240, 248
decline in, 248
Due process, 242
Durkheim, work of
on deviance, 224–25
division of labor, 643–44
on mechanical and organic solidarity, 593–94
on religion, 498, 499
on society, 92, 108–11
Dyad, 173–74

Earnings (see Economy; Global economy; Income)
Eastern Europe (See Europe, eastern)
Eating disorders, 557, 558
Ecologically sustainable culture, 605
Ecology, 597
Economic equality, capitalism versus socialism and, 426
Economic inequality (see Income inequality)
Economic productivity, capitalism versus socialism and, 426
Economic systems
capitalism, 424
socialism, 424–27
state capitalism, 426
welfare capitalism, 425–26
Economy (see also Global economy; Income)
agricultural revolution, 418–19
capitalism, 424
capitalism, state, 426
capitalism, welfare, 425–26
in China, 263
command, 424
corporations, 433–37
crime rates and, 248
defined, 418
education and role of, 526–27
European, 266–67
future issues, 437
historical overview, 418–22
Industrial Revolution, 419–20
Information Revolution, 421, 432–33
laissez-faire, 424
map, agricultural employment 423
map, service sector work, 423

perestroika, in Soviet Union, 262, 626
political-economy model/theory, 456, 628, 629
politics and, 451–52
postindustrial, 421
postindustrial society and, 421, 427–37
sectors of, 421–22
socialism, 424–25, 426–27
underground, 431
urban political, 596
Ecosystem, 597
Ecuador
beauty in, 195
as a middle-income country, 309, 310
Edge cities, 592
Education (*see also* Colleges; Schools)
academic standards, 540–42
adult, 545
affirmative action, 386–87
of African Americans, 372, 373, 379, 535
of Asian Americans, 381
in Britain, 529
*Brown v. Board of Education of Topeka*, 372
busing, 534–35
defined, 526
disabled students, 544–45
drop outs, 539–41
economic development and, 526–27
functions of, 530–31
future for, 545–46
gender differences, 284, 335, 339, 344
GI Bill, 536
grade inflation, 542
of Hispanic Americans, 385, 535
home schooling, 544
illiteracy map, 528
in India, 527
in Japan, 527–29
of Japanese Americans, 381
mainstreaming, 545
mandatory, 529
of Native Americans, 375
prayer in schools, 515, 516
problems in, 537–42
progressive, 530
school choice, 542–44
segregation, 372, 534–35
sex, 213
shortages of teachers/instructors, 545
social class and, 282
social-conflict analysis, 538
social inequality and, 532–36
social interaction and, 531
structural-functional analysis, 538
student passivity, 538–39
symbolic-interaction analysis, 538
terrorism and effects on, 530
in the U.S., 529–30
violence and, 538
Efficiency
McDonaldization concept, 187–88
U.S. value, 69
Ego, 121
Egypt
female genital mutilation, 349
population growth and control, 588, 596
Pyramids of Giza, 95, 96

sibling marriages in ancient, 197, 475
water supply problems, 581, 601
Elderly (*see also* Aging)
abuse of, 406
ageism, 406
biological changes, 397–98
care giving, 405–6, 480
children caring for, 480
cultural differences, 398–99
death and dying, 135–37, 408–12, 413
discrimination, 394, 406
gender differences, 397, 401–2, 405
graying of the U.S., 394–97
health issues, 397–98
in hunting and gathering societies, 399
in industrial and postindustrial societies, 399–400
living arrangements, 401–3
as minorities, 406–7
in pastoral, horticultural, and agrarian societies, 399
poverty and, 294, 404–5
psychological changes, 398
retirement, 402–4
sex and, 202
social isolation and, 401–2
socialization and, 135
transitions and challenges of, 401–6
younger versus older, 397
Elections (*see* Voting)
Electronic church, 520
Electronic mail (*see* E-mail)
El Salvador, as a middle-income country, 309, 310
E-mail
organizational structure and effects of, 179
privacy issues, 186
surveys using, 44
symbols used in, 65
Embarrassment, social interaction and, 156–57
Emergence, social movements and, 629–30
Emergent-norm theory, 616
Emigration, 582
Emotions
biological side of, 157
cultural side of, 158
expressing, 157, 158
managing, 158, 159
social interaction and, 157–58
Empirical evidence, 31
Employment (*see* Labor; Work/workplace)
Empty nest syndrome, 480
Enclosure movement, 12
Endogamy, 256, 471
Energy, industrialization and, 419
England (*see* Britain)
English language, 67
Enron Corp., 179, 233, 431
Entrepreneurs, women as, 342
Environment
acid rain, 601–2
air pollution, 602–3
biodiversity, declining, 604–5
deficit, 598
definition of natural, 597
future for, 605–6
global, 597
global warming, 604
growth problems and effects on, 598–99

organizational, 178
rain forests, 603
recycling, 600
solid waste issues, 599–600
technology, effects on, 597–98
water pollution, 601–2
water supply, 601
Environmental Protection Agency (EPA), 599–600
Environmental racism, 605
Episcopalians, social class and, 512
Equal opportunity
affirmative action, 386–87
U.S. value, 69
Equal Rights Amendment (ERA), 353, 354
Erikson's developmental stages, 126–27
Eros (life instinct), 121
Estate system, 258–59
Estonia, market reforms, 427
Ethics
death and dying and, 409–11, 562–63
euthanasia, 410–11, 413, 562–63
genetic research, 574
informed consent, 41
research, 40–41
right-to-die debate, 410–11, 562
Ethiopia
female genital mutilation, 348, 349
gross domestic product, 313
as a low-income country, 313
quality of life, 313
Ethnicity (*see also under* Race)
assimilation, 373
categories, 365
crime and, 239–40
defined, 364
genocide, 374
group dynamics and, 174
hate crimes, 235
income inequality and, 283–84, 285
majority/minority patterns of interaction, 372–74
pluralism, 372–73
poverty and, 294–95
prejudice, 366–69
religion and, 513
social class and, 283–84
U.S. Census Bureau definition of, 33
workplace discrimination, 183
Ethnic villages/enclaves, 373, 388
Ethnocentrism, 80–81
Ethnographies, 47
Ethnomethodology, 150
Eurocentrism, 77
Europe
early cities in, 589
high-income countries in, 308, 309
union membership, decline in, 429
Europe, eastern
middle-income countries in, 309, 310, 313
socialism, decline of, 427
European Union, economy, 266–67
Euthanasia, 410–11, 413, 562–63
Evolution
culture and, 83–85
human development and, 118–19, 521
Exogamy, 471
Experimental groups, 41
Experiments
defined, 41
example of, 43

hypothesis testing, 41–43
Expressions, social interaction and facial, 153, 154, 155, 157
Expressive leadership, 170
Extended family, 471
Extramarital sex, 201, 202–3
Eye contact, social interaction and, 153–54, 155–56

Facial expressions, social interaction and, 153, 154, 155, 157
Factories
Industrial Revolution and, 419
loss of jobs in U.S., 422
women in, 420
Fads, 618–19
Faith, defined, 499
False consciousness, 101
Family
of affinity, 471
African American, 483–84
authority patterns, 473
basic concepts, 470
blended, 487
child rearing, 479–80, 481
cohabitation, 489
cousin marriage laws in U.S., first-, 197
cultural capital and, 128
defined, 470
descent patterns, 473
divorce and, 485–87
extended, 471
female-headed, 483, 484
forms, alternative, 488–91
future of, 492
gender socialization and, 339
global variations, 471–73
Hispanic American, 483
homosexual couples, 489–90
in hunting and gathering societies, 93–94
incest taboo, 475
in industrial societies, 98
marriage patterns, 471, 473
mixed marriages, effects of, 484–85
Native American, 482
nuclear, 471
one-parent, 488–89
poverty, 484
remarriage and, 487
reproductive technology and impact on, 492
residential patterns, 473
single (one)-parent, 488–89, 491
size, 4, 480
social class and, 289, 481
social-conflict analysis, 476, 477
social-exchange analysis, 476–77
socialization and, 127–28, 474
stages of, 477–80
structural-functional analysis, 474–75, 477
symbolic-interaction analysis, 476, 477
Temporary Assistance for Needy Families (TANF), 299
traditional, 490–91
violence, 487–88
women, as head of households, 483, 484
Family and Medical Leave Act (1993), 480
Fashion, 618–19
FBI, crime statistics, 236, 237, 238
Fecundity, 580

Greece
  early cities in, 589
  homosexuality and ancient, 203
Greenhouse effect, 604
Greenpeace, 450
Green Revolution, 322, 325
Gross domestic product (GDP)
  defined, 313
  economic productivity and, 426
  in high-, low-, and middle-income
    countries, 309n, 313
Groups (see Social groups)
Groupthink, 172
Guilt
  Erikson's stage, 126
  superego, 121
Guinea
  gross domestic product, 313
  as a low-income country, 313
  quality of life, 313
  women, social status of, 337, 338
Gullah community, 651, 652–53
Gun(s)
  control, 240, 453
  ownership statistics, 240
Gynocentricity, 39
Gypsies, 366

Habitat for Humanity, 659
Haiti
  gross domestic product, 313
  as a low-income country, 313
  quality of life, 313, 323
  shantytowns in, 325
Hand gestures, social interaction and,
  154, 155
Hate crimes, 234–35
Hawthorne effect, 41–43
Health and health issues
  AIDs/HIV, 559–62
  college students and, 571
  defined, 552–53
  eating disorders, 557, 558
  elderly and, 397–98
  future for, 573–74
  gender differences, 555–56, 558
  in high-income countries, 554
  historical, 553
  insurance, 568–69
  in low-income countries,
    553–54
  marriage and, 485
  obesity, 557–58, 559
  poverty and effects on, 315
  racial differences, 556
  sexually transmitted diseases,
    559–62
  social inequality and, 553
  smoking, 556–57
  social class and, 288, 556
  social-conflict analysis, 572–73
  structural-functional analysis, 570,
    573
  symbolic-interaction analysis,
    570–71, 573
  in the U.S., 554–62
Health insurance, U.S., 568–69
Health maintenance organizations
  (HMOs), 569
Heaven's Gate cult, 505
Hermaphrodites, 196
Herpes, genital, 559
Heterosexism, 214–15
Heterosexuality, defined, 203
High culture, 75

Higher education (see Colleges;
  Education)
High-income countries (see also name
  of country)
  age at death, global median, 314,
    315
  childbearing, map on, 4
  countries considered, 7, 308, 309
  defined, 7, 307
  dependency theory, 325–26
  economic sectors, 421
  family size, 480
  gross domestic product (GDP),
    309n, 313
  health in, 554
  income inequality, 272, 273
  map of, 309
  modernization theory, 322–23
  per capita income, 308
  population growth, 587
  productivity of, 308, 309
  prostitution in, 208
  quality of life index, 313
  television ownership, 131
  values in, 71, 72
Hinduism, 509, 510
Hispanic Americans/Latinos (see also
  Race; Racial discrimination;
  Racial segregation; Racism)
  affluent, 285
  conducting research with, 42
  Cuban Americans, 387–88
  demographics map, 384
  education and, 385, 535
  ethnic villages, 373
  family life, 483
  family size, 480n
  feminism and, 355
  HIV/AIDS and, 560
  income inequality and, 284, 291,
    346
  income of, 385, 483
  las colonias, 311
  machismo, 483
  Mexican Americans, 385
  parenting, single, 484, 488
  political party identification and,
    452
  poverty and, 294, 385, 405
  Puerto Ricans, 385–86
  sexually transmitted diseases and,
    559
  social class and, 284
  social standing of, 385
  statistics on, 383–85
  stereotypes, 366
  voting participation and, 454
  women, as head of household, 483,
    484
  women, working, 427, 432
  work and, 427, 432
Hispanic American women (see
  Women, Hispanic American)
Hispanics, personal space and, 42
Historical research, use of existing
  sources, 49–51
HIV/AIDS
  claims making, 624
  death from, statistics on, 559–60
  globally, 560, 561
  symptoms, 560
  transmission of, 560, 562
  treatment of, 562
HMOs (health maintenance
  organizations), 569
Holistic medicine, 564–65

Holocaust, 374, 509
Homelessness, 298, 300–301
Home schooling, 544
Homogamy, 479
Homophobia, 206
Homosexuality (homosexuals)
  attitudes toward, 204, 205–6
  cultural differences, 203
  defined, 203
  gay rights movements, 205–6
  genetics and, 204
  hate crimes, 234–35
  HIV/AIDS and, 560
  marriages, 489–90
  parenting, 490
  prostitution and, 209
  queer theory, 214–15
  statistics on, 204, 205
Hong Kong
  description of, 588
  as a high-income country, 308, 309
  modernization theory, 323
Hooking up, 211
Horizontal social mobility, 290
Horticultural societies, 94–95
  elderly in, 399
  social stratification and, 271
Hospice movement, 412, 413
Houses of correction, 245
Housework, 147, 148, 342, 343
Hull House, 18
Human development
  cognitive development, 122–23
  moral development, 123–24
  nature versus nurture, 118–19
  personality development, 121–22
  self, development of, 124–26
  social isolation and, 119–20
  socialization and, 121–27
  stages of, 126–27
Human Genome Project, 574
Human immunodeficiency virus
  (HIV) (see HIV/AIDS)
Human trafficking, 318
Humor
  conflict and, 163
  cultural differences, 161–62
  dynamics of, 161
  function of, 162–63
  social interaction and, 161–63
  topics of, 161–62
Hungary, socialism, decline of, 427
Hunting and gathering societies,
  93–94
  elderly in, 399
  gender differences/roles, 336
  health in, 553
  religion and, 94, 95, 505
  social stratification and, 271
Hutus, 374
Hydrologic cycle, 600
Hypersegregation, 374
Hypothesis
  defined, 41
  testing, 41–43

"I," Mead's self, 125
Id, 121
Ideal culture, 73
Idealism, 82, 104–8
Idealization, 156
Ideology
  defined, 263
  historical patterns, 264
  Marx, views of, 263

Plato's views, 263
  social stratification and, 263–64
Ideal type, 104
Identity
  Erikson's developmental stages,
    126–27
  modernity/mass society and,
    649–50
Illiteracy
  functional, 541
  global, 527, 528
Imagination, sociological, 6, 7
Imitation, 125
Immigrants
  social change and, 641
  work for, 367
Immigration
  cities, growth of, 12, 588–91
  defined, 582
  Hull House/settlement houses, 18
  multiculturalism, 76–78
  statistics on, 388
Impression management, 151
Incarceration (see Correction systems;
  Prisons)
Incest taboo, 197, 212, 475
Income
  African Americans and, 379,
    483–84
  Asian Americans and, 381
  defined, 280–81
  distribution of, in the U.S., 280, 281,
    282
  distribution of world, 307
  elderly and, 404–5
  Hispanic Americans and, 284, 291,
    346, 385, 483
  mean annual, U.S., 290, 291, 292
  Native Americans and, 375
  social mobility and, 290, 291
Income inequality
  African Americans and, 379,
    483–84
  democracy and, 448
  gender differences, 291, 340–44,
    536, 537
  global, 262, 272, 273
  Hispanic Americans and, 284, 291,
    346, 385, 483
  income of, 385
  Kuznets curve, 271–72
  race and, 283–84, 285, 290–91
  in the U.S., 280–81
Independent variables, 35
India
  Buddhism, 509–10
  caste system, 256
  child labor in, 527
  child weddings in, 478
  crime in, 240
  education in, 527
  female genital mutilation, 348
  Hinduism, 509, 510
  marriage in, 471, 478
  as a middle-income country, 309,
    310
  poverty, 319, 320
  servile forms of marriage, 317
  water supply problems, 601
Indians (see also Native Americans)
  use of term, 375
Individualism
  divorce and, 485
  modernization theory, 321, 642,
    649–50
  U.S., 450–51

Low-income countries (*see also* name of country)
age at death, global median, 314, 315
childbearing, map on, 4
countries considered, 8, 309, 311
defined, 8, 307
dependency theory, 323–27
economic sectors, 421
education, 526–27
family size, 480
gross domestic product (GDP), 309n, 313
health in, 553–54
HIV/AIDS in, 560, 561
map of, 309
modernization theory, 320–23
population density, 311
population growth, 587
poverty in, 553–54
productivity in, 312
prostitution and, 209
quality of life index, 313
urbanization in, 596
values in, 70–71, 72
Lummi Indians, 482–83
Lutherans, 512
social class and, 513
Lynching, 379, 614

Machismo, 483
Macro-level orientation, 20
Magnet schools, 543
Mainstreaming, 545
Malaysia
Batek, 93
gross domestic product, 313
as a middle-income country, 309, 310, 313
quality of life, 313
Semai, 61, 93, 459
women forbidden to wear tight-fitting jeans, 224
Male traits (*see* Men)
Mali
Tuareg of, 92, 94, 105
women, social status of, 337, 338
Malthusian theory, 585–86
Management, scientific, 182
Manifest functions, 15, 16
*Manifesto of the Communist Party* (Marx and Engels), 102
Manila
crime in, 240
description of, 312
Manufacturing (*see also* Work/workplace)
factories, 419, 420
Industrial Revolution and, 419
social change and, 12
Maoris (New Zealand), 196
Maps
adolescent pregnancy in U.S., 207
age at death, median, 314
agricultural employment, 423
birth control, 202
Buddhism, 510
capital punishment, 241
on childbearing, 4
Christianity, 507
demographics of African Americans, Asian Americans, and Hispanic Americans, 384
economic development, globally, 309
elderly population in the U.S., 397

family size, 4
female genital mutilation, 348
gender power, 338
government positions, women in, 345, 346
health patterns across the U.S., 554
Hinduism, 510
HIV/AIDS, 560, 561
housework performed by women, 148
illiteracy, 528
income inequality, 272, 273
Internet users map, 176
Islam, 507
job projections to 2010, 437
land controlled by Native Americans, 374
language diversity in the U.S., 78
on languages, 67, 78
life expectancy, 400
marital forms, 474
marriage laws in U.S., first-cousin, 197
minorities across the U.S., 366
obesity in U.S., 559
per capita income in U.S., 288
political freedom, 447
population change across U.S., 582
population growth, global, 584
poverty across U.S., 296
presidential election of 2004, popular vote, 454
prostitution, 208
racial diversity in the U.S., 128
religious affiliation across U.S., 514
religious diversity across U.S., 514
residential stability across U.S., 641
service-sector employment, 423
on suicide rates, 14
teachers' salaries across U.S., 533
on technology, high, 106
violent crimes in U.S., 237
water consumption, global, 581
Marginality, 6
Marital rape, 487–88
Market economy, capitalism and, 424
Marriage
arranged, 256, 477–78
child weddings, 477–78
courtship, 477–78
death of spouse, 480
defined, 470
descent patterns, 473
divorce, 485–87
endogamy, 256, 471
exogamy, 471
extramarital sex, 201, 202–3
global map, 474
health and, 485
homogamy, 479
homosexual, 489–90
incest taboo, 197
infidelity, 479
interracial, 484–85
laws in U.S., first-cousin, 197
love, romantic, 478–79
mate selection, 477–78
monogamy, 471
patterns, 471, 473
polyandry, 473
polygamy, 471, 473
polygyny, 473
remarriage, 487
residential patterns, 473
same-sex, 1, 206
servile forms of, 317

sexual satisfaction in, 479
sibling, 197, 475
social structure and, 1
violence in, 487–88
working class, 289
Marxism
capitalism, 101, 102–3, 645–46, 648–49
class conflict, 102–3, 265–66, 640
class-society theory, 648–49
communism, 102
criticism of, 266–67
ideology and, 263
materialism, 101
modernity and, 645–46
political-economy model, 456, 628
religion and, 500–501
social change and, 640
social conflict, 101, 648–49
socialism, 103–4, 425
social movements and, 628
social stratification and, 263
society, views on, 100–104
suffering and law of nature, 586
Marxist revolution, 645
Masai, 65
Masculine traits (*see* Men)
Massage parlors, 209
Mass behavior (*see also* Collective behavior; Social movements)
defined, 616
disasters, 619–20
fads, 618–19
fashion, 618
gossip, 616–17
mass hysteria/moral panic, 619
panic, 619
propaganda, 618
public opinion, 618
rumors, 616, 617
Mass hysteria, 619
Mass media (*see* Media)
Mass production, 419
Mass society
class society versus, 649
defined, 646
Mass-society theory, 625–26, 629
Master status, 145–46, 365
Material culture, 60–61, 73–74
Materialism
culture and, 73–74, 83
Marx and views on, 101
U.S. value, 69
Matriarchy, 337
Matrilineal descent, 473
Matrilocality, 473
Matrimony (*see* Marriage)
Mauritania, slavery in, 317, 318
McDonaldization concept, 186–88
McDonald's, use of computers and outsourcing at, 434–35
"Me," Mead's self, 125
Mead's social self theory, 124–26
Mean, 34
Meaning, importance of, 38
Measurements
defined, 33
reliability and validity, 33–34
statistical, 34
Mechanical solidarity, 110, 593–94, 643
Media
advertising, 340, 341
definition of mass, 130
gender differences, 340
gender socialization and, 340

socialization and, 130–33
television, 131–33
war and role of, 461
Median, 34
Medicaid, 569
Medicalization of deviance, 229–30
Medicare, 569
Medicine and medical care
access to, 572
in Britain, 567
in Canada, 567, 568
in capitalist countries, 566–68
in China, 566
defined, 563
future for, 573–74
genetic research, 574
holistic, 564–65
insurance companies, 568–69
in Japan, 568
new reproductive technology, 492
nursing shortage, 569–70
oral contraceptives, 200
paying for, 565–69
physicians, role of, 563–64, 570
politics and, 572–73
in Russia, 566, 567
scientific, 563–64
social-conflict analysis, 572–73
in socialist countries, 566, 567
socialized, 566–68
structural-functional analysis, 570, 573
in Sweden, 566
symbolic-interaction analysis, 570–71, 573
in the U.S., 568–70
Megalopolis, 592
Melanesians, sexuality and, 213
Melting pot, 373
Men (*see also* Gender differences; Gender inequality)
advertising, portrayed in, 356–57
aggressiveness in, 338
child support, 486, 487
circumcision, 213
extramarital sex, 203
feminism and, 354
homosexual, 204, 205
machismo, 483
masculine traits a health threat, 555
patriarchy, 336–38
patrilineal descent, 473
patrilocality, 473
political party identification and, 452
premarital sex, 201
rape of, 210
social mobility and, 290
Type A personality, 337, 555
violence against, 347, 487
*Mens rea,* 236
Mental illness, seen as deviant, 229
Mercy killing (euthanasia), 410–11, 413, 562–63
Meritocracy
in Britain, 258–60
defined, 258
Metaphysical stage, 14
Methodists, 506, 512
social class and, 513
Metropolis, defined, 590
Mexican Americans
education and, 385
income of, 385
poverty and, 385
social standing of, 385

in hunting and gathering societies, 93
matrilineal descent, 473
in the military, 345–36
as minorities, 346
political party identification and, 452
politics and, 344–45
population growth and role of, 588
poverty and, 295, 316
premarital sex, 201
prostitution, 207–9
religion and, 502–3
sexual revolution, 199–200
single-parenthood, 483, 484, 488–89, 491
as slaves, 317–18
social mobility and, 291
social movements and, 629
status of, globally, 336, 337
upper-upper class, 286
Women, African American
as head of household, 484
as leaders, 378
life expectancy and, 556
parenting and role of grandmothers, 480
work and, 346, 427, 432
Women, Asian American
as head of household, 484
work and, 261, 383, 427, 432
Women, Hispanic American/Latinos
as head of household, 483, 484
work and, 346, 427, 432
Women, Islamic
constraints put on, 235–36
female genital mutilation, 213
modesty, 197
Qur'an and portrayal of, 502
social standing of, 508
wearing of makeup banned, 224

Women, violence against
assaults, 347
date rape, 210
domestic violence, 487–88
elder abuse, 406
female genital mutilation, 213, 347, 348, 349
pornography as a cause, 207, 350
prostitution and, 209
rape, 209–10
rape, marital, 487–88
sexual harassment, 348, 350
Women, in the workplace
African American, 346, 427, 432
Asian American, 427, 432
discrimination, 183
earnings gap, 291
as entrepreneurs, 342
female advantage, 183
Filipino Americans, 383
gender inequality, 340–43
glass ceiling, 342
Hispanic American, 346, 427, 432
income inequality, 291, 342–44
Japanese, 261
in managerial positions, 183
mills, 420
occupations, 340–41
pink-collar jobs, 341
racial differences, 427
in secondary labor market, 428
self-employed, 430
statistics on, 340
whites, 427, 432
Women's movement, feminism, 353–55
Work/workplace (see also Women, in the workplace)
blue-collar, 267
changes in the nature of, 184–85, 427–28

child labor, 80, 132, 133, 321, 527
computers, effects of, 433, 434–35
debt bondage, 317
discrimination, 182–83, 291
diversity, 431, 432
division of labor, 111, 643–44
elderly and, 399
ethic, Protestant, 377
expressing emotions at, 158
factories, 419, 422
garment industry, in Bangladesh, 306
gender differences, 340–44, 431, 432, 427, 432
global economy and effects on U.S., 292–94
housework and, 147, 148, 342, 343
immigrants and, 367
income inequality, 291, 342–44
Industrial Revolution, 419–20
in industrial societies, 97–98
Information Revolution and, 432–33
Japanese, 183–84
job projections to 2010, 437
jobs with the highest concentrations of women, 342
lack of, and poverty, 296, 297
legal protections, 268
managerial positions in the U.S., 183
mills, 420
pink-collar jobs, 341
in postindustrial economy, 421, 427–37
professions, 429–30
projections of, to 2010, map of, 437
prostitution as, 208–9
Protestant work ethic, 377
racial differences, 427, 432
scientific management, 182

self-employment, 430
service, 428
social class and, 282, 283
teams, 185
technology and, 432–33
unemployment, 430
unions, 268, 428
U.S. value, 69
white-collar, 267
Workforce
capitalism and alienation of, 103
diversity, 431, 432
Working class
blue-collar, 267
defined, 287
marriages, 289
Working poor, 287, 296, 298
WorldCom, 431
World economy, Wallerstein's capitalist, 324–25
World Trade Center (see September 11, 2001 attacks)
World War II
Japanese American internment, 382
reference group study, 172

Xenophobia, 388

Yanomamö, 61, 63, 73, 74, 459
Yugoslavia
cultural conflict in, 75–76
genocide, 620

Zambia, economic inequality, 262
Zero population growth, 587
Zimbabwe, education in, 527

# Expanded Author-Written Test Item File

The Macionis, *Sociology*, 11/E, Test Item File is the only test bank in the market written by the textbook author. John Macionis has provided a test bank that you can rely on to be consistent with the material presented in the text and one that contains only high-quality, class-tested questions.

In this new edition, we have expanded the Test Item File to include assessment questions for key supplements including the *ABC News* videos, TIME: Sociology, Special Edition '06, and the Kauzlarich *Sociological Classics: A Prentice Hall Pocket Reader* to help you better integrate these learning resources into your course. We also have added a new Total Assessment Guide that categorizes test questions as "Conceptual," "Factual," or "Applied," and as "Multiple Choice," "True/False," or "Essay" questions to help save you time in test preparation.

# Expanded Instructor's Manual

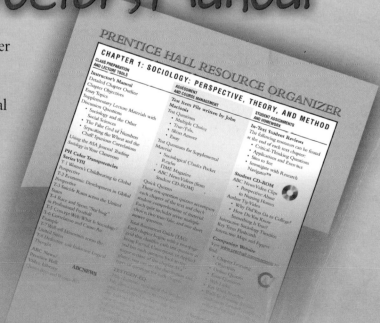

The Instructor's Manual includes detailed chapter outlines and discussion questions, statistical information, research findings, and supplemental lecture information. In this eleventh edition, we have added the new Resource Organizer, which correlates every text chapter with the instructor and student supplements that accompany the Macionis, *Sociology*, 11/E, textbook and helps you save valuable time!

NEW

# Tools for Success!

## "Making the Grade"
## End-of- Chapter Review

The end-of-chapter material has been completely redesigned to help students make the best use of their textbook as a study tool and be more successful in the course. Students can easily focus on important concepts from the chapter and are given actual practice with sample test questions and applications and exercises written by John Macionis to help them test their knowledge.

# Student Study Guide

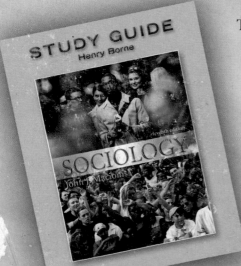

This valuable learning resource helps students study smarter! The study guide includes chapter overviews, summaries of key topics and concepts, application exercises, and end-of-chapter tests with answers provided. To order *Sociology*, 11/e, packaged with the Student Study Guide, please give this ISBN to your bookstore: **0-13-195134-3.**